CHIEF
MODERN POETS
OF
ENGLAND AND AMERICA

CHIEF
MODERN POETS
OF
ENGLAND & AMERICA

FOURTH EDITION

Selected and Edited by

GERALD DEWITT SANDERS

JOHN HERBERT NELSON

M. L. ROSENTHAL

New York
The Macmillan Company

Sixth Printing, 1966
Library of Congress catalog card number: 62–7528

The Macmillan Company, New York
Collier-Macmillan Canada, Ltd., Toronto, Ontario

Printed in the United States of America

CREDITS AND ACKNOWLEDGMENTS

The Clarendon Press, Oxford, for "Low Barometer" from *The New Verse of Robert Bridges* and "Johannes Milton, Senex" and "I Never Shall Love the Snow Again" from *The Shorter Poems of Robert Bridges.*

"Forests," "Lucy," and "A Robin," from *The Fleeting,* copyright, 1933, by Walter de la Mare, are used by arrangement with the author and with the consent of the publisher, Alfred A. Knopf, Inc., N. Y.

Doubleday & Company, Inc., for the poems by Robert Graves from *Collected Poems,* by Robert Graves. Copyright 1955 by Robert Graves. Reprinted by permission of Doubleday & Company, Inc., and Cassell & Co., Ltd.

E. P. Dutton & Co., Inc.: The selections from *The Old Huntsman, Counter-Attack,* and *Picture-Show* by Siegfried Sassoon are used by permission of E. P. Dutton and Co., Inc.

Grove Press, Inc., for the poems by Edward Muir from *Collected Poems 1921–1951,* copyright, 1957, and *One Foot in Eden,* copyright, 1956.

Harcourt, Brace & World, Inc., for the poems by William Empson from *Collected Poems,* copyright, 1935, 1940, 1949, by William Empson. Reprinted by permission of Harcourt, Brace & World, Inc.

Harper & Brothers, for "The Committee" and "Almost Human" from *Pegasus and Other Poems,* copyright, © 1957, by Cecil Day Lewis, reprinted by permission of Harper & Brothers; and for selections from *The Heart's Journey* by Siegfried Sassoon.

Holt, Rinehart and Winston, Inc., for selections from *Last Poems* from *Complete Poems* by A. E. Housman, copyright 1922, © 1959 by Holt, Rinehart and Winston, Inc. Copyright, 1950, by Barclay's Bank, Ltd.; and for selections from *Collected Poems, Down-adown-Derry, Memory and Other Poems, Motley and Other Poems, The Veil and Other Poems, Peacock Pie,* and *Poems for Children* by Walter de la Mare.

Houghton Mifflin Company: The selections from John Betjeman's *Collected Poems*, copyright, 1959, are reprinted by permission of and arrangement with Houghton Mifflin Company, the authorized publishers.

"For My Funeral" by A. E. Housman is used by permission of the estate of the late A. E. Housman.

Alfred A. Knopf, Inc., for selections from *October and Other Poems* by Robert Bridges; from *The Fleeting* by Walter de la Mare; and from *More Poems* by A. E. Housman.

D. H. Lawrence: "When I Went to the Circus," "Swan," "Willy Wet-Leg" and "When the Ripe Fruit Falls" from *Pansies*, published by Alfred A. Knopf, Inc., are reprinted by permission of the author's estate, copyright 1929 by Frieda Lawrence Ravagli.

The Macmillan Company: For selections from *Wessex Poems* (copyright 1898), *Poems of the Past and Present* (copyright 1902), *Time's Laughingstocks* (copyright 1909), *Satires of Circumstance* (copyright 1914), *Moments of Vision* (copyright 1917), *Late Lyrics and Earlier* (copyright 1922), *Human Shows—Far Phantasies* (copyright 1925), and *Winter Words in Various Moods and Metres* (copyright 1928 by Florence E. Hardy and Sydney E. Cockerell) by Thomas Hardy;

from *Salt Water Ballads* (copyright 1902), *The Story of a Roundhouse and Other Poems* (copyright 1912), *Dauber* (copyright 1913), *Reynard the Fox* (copyright 1919), *Enslaved and Other Poems* (copyright 1920), and *Collected Poems* (copyright 1912, 1913, and 1914 by The Macmillan Company, and 1916, 1919, 1920, 1921, 1922, 1923, and 1925 by John Masefield) by John Masefield;

from *Insurrections* (copyright 1909), *The Hill of Vision* (copyright 1912), *The Rocky Road to Dublin* (copyright 1915), *Songs from the Clay* (copyright 1915), *Reincarnations* (copyright 1918), and *Collected Poems* (copyright 1909, 1912, 1915, 1918, 1925, 1926) by James Stephens;

from *In the Seven Woods* (copyright 1903), *The Green Helmet and Other Poems* (copyright 1912), *Responsibilities and Other Poems* (copyright 1916), *Lyric Poems* (copyright 1916), *The Wild Swans at Coole* (copyright 1917), *Later Poems* (copyright 1922), *Early Poems and Stories* (copyright 1925), *The Tower* (copyright 1928), *The Winding Stair and Other Poems* (copyright 1933), *Collected Poems* (copyright 1933), and *Last Poems and Plays* (copyright 1940) by W.B. Yeats;

"The Unborn," "Channel Firing," "Wessex Heights," "The Walk," "I Found Her Out There," "The Voice," "After a Journey," "The Phantom Horsewoman," "At a Watering-Place," "Near Lanivet," "The Five Students," "During Wind and Rain," "Afterwards," "And There Was A Great Calm," and "A Drizzling Easter Morning" from *Collected Poems* by Thomas Hardy. Copyright 1925 by The Macmillan Company, and used with their permission.

From *The Dynasts* by Thomas Hardy. Copyright 1904 by The Macmillan Company, renewed 1931 by Florence E. Hardy. Used with permission of The Macmillan Company.

"The Stolen Child," "Who Goes with Fergus," "The Man Who Dreamed," from *Collected Poems* by W. B. Yeats. Copyright 1906 by The Macmillan Company, renewed 1934 by W. B. Yeats. Used with permission of The Macmillan Company.

"Adam's Curse," and "The Old Men Admiring," from *Collected Poems* by W. B. Yeats. Copyright 1912 by The Macmillan Company, renewed 1940 by Bertha Georgie Yeats. Used with permission of The Macmillan Company.

"When Helen Lived," "The Three Hermits," "Beggar to Beggar Cried," "The Magi," "The Dolls," "The Coat," from *Collected Poems* by W. B. Yeats. Copyright 1916 by The Macmillan Company, and renewed 1944 by Bertha Georgie Yeats. Used with permission of The Macmillan Company.

"Solomon to Sheba," "The Scholars," "On Woman," "The Fisherman," "A Deep-Sworn Vow," "The Cat and the Moon," "Two Songs of a Fool," from *Collected Poems* by W. B. Yeats. Copyright 1919 by The Macmillan Company, renewed 1946 by Bertha Georgie Yeats. Used with permission of The Macmillan Company.

"Easter," "The Second Coming," from *Collected Poems* by W. B. Yeats. Copyright 1924 by The Macmillan Company, renewed 1952 by Bertha Georgie Yeats. Used with permission of The Macmillan Company.

"Two Songs from a Play" and "Leda and the Swan," from *Collected Poems* by W. B. Yeats. Copyright 1928 by The Macmillan Company, renewed 1956 by Bertha Georgie Yeats. Used with permission of The Macmillan Company.

"A Dialogue of Self and Soul," "Three Movements," "For Anne Gregory," "The Choice," "Swift's Epitaph," "Byzantium," "Words for Music Perhaps," "A Woman Young and Old," and "Church and State," from *Collected Poems* by W. B. Yeats. Copyright 1933 by The Macmillan Company, and used with their permission.

"Lapis Lazuli," "An Acre of Grass," "The Wild Old Wicked Men," "The Great Day," "Parnell," "A Model for the Laureate," "Those Images," "News for the Delphic Oracle," "John Kinsella's Lament," "The Statesman's Holiday," "The Long-Legged Fly," "The Apparitions," "Crazy Jane on the Mountain," "Cuchulain Comforted," and "Under Ben Bulben," from *Collected Poems* by W. B. Yeats. Copyright 1940 by Bertha Georgie Yeats. Used with permission of The Macmillan Company.

"Purgatory," from *Last Poems and Plays* by W. B. Yeats. Copyright 1940 by Bertha Georgie Yeats, and used with permission of The Macmillan Company.

"A Glass of Beer," from *Collected Poems* by James Stephens. Copyright 1918 by The Macmillan Company, renewed 1946 by James Stephens. Used with permission of The Macmillan Company.

The Marvell Press: "Places, Loved Ones," "Dry-Point," "Going," "Church Going," "Age," "Myxomatosis," "Toads," "Poetry of Departures," and "Deceptions," by Philip Larkin, are reprinted from *The Less Deceived* by permission of The Marvell Press, Hessle, Yorkshire, England.

Harold Matson Co.: "Now I Have Come to Reason," "Do Not Expect Again a Phoenix Hour," and "Sing We the Two Lieutenants," by C. Day Lewis, copyright 1940 by C. Day Lewis, are reprinted by permission of Harold Matson Company.

John Murray, London: For selections from *Poetical Works* by Robert Bridges.

New Directions: "Arms and the Boy," "Greater Love," "Insensibility," "Dulce et Decorum," "Mental Cases," "Futility," "Disabled," "Anthem for Doomed Youth," and "Strange Meeting" from *Poems of Wilfred Owen*. All rights reserved. Reprinted by permission of New Directions.

"The Force That Through the Green Fuse," "Light Breaks Where No Sun Shines," "And Death Shall Have No Dominion," "After the Funeral," "Twenty-four Years," "A Refusal to Mourn the Death," "A Winter's Tale," "In My Craft or Sullen Art," "Ceremony after a Fire Raid," "Fern Hill," and "Altarwise by Owl Light," from *The Collected Poems of Dylan Thomas*. Copyright 1952, 1953 by Dylan Thomas. Reprinted by permission of New Directions.

Ivan Obolensky, Inc.: "Distinctions," "Paring the Apple," "Poem," "Farewell to Van Gogh," "On the Hall at Stowey," and "Antecedents: a Homage and Valediction," from *Seeing is Believing*, copyright, 1958, are used by permission of Ivan Obolensky, Inc.

Oxford University Press, Inc.: "The Summer Malison," "The Wreck of the *Deutschland*," "Hurrahing in Harvest," "To R. B.," "As Kingfishers Catch Fire," and "Not, I'll Not, Carrion Comfort," from *Poems* of Gerard Manley Hopkins. Third edition edited by W. H. Gardner. Copyright 1948 by Oxford University Press, Inc. Reprinted by permission. Other selections from Hopkins from *Poems*, copyright 1919, are used by permission of The Oxford University Press, Inc.

Random House, Inc.: "Doom is dark and deeper," "Petition" "1929," "Taller today, we remember similar evenings," "O Where are you going?" and "Watch any day his nonchalant pauses" (POEMS) W. H. Auden. Copyright 1934 by The Modern Library, Inc. Reprinted from *The Collected Poetry of W. H. Auden* by permission of Random House, Inc.,

"Law Like Love," "September 1, 1939," "In Memory of W. B. Yeats," "Musee des Beaux Arts," and "The Capital" (ANOTHER TIME) W. H. Auden. Copyright 1940 by W. H. Auden. Reprinted from *The Collected Poetry of W. H. Auden* by permission of Random House, Inc.

"The Presumptuous," "The Useful," and "Vocation" (DOUBLE MAN) W. H. Auden. Copyright 1941 by W. H. Auden. Reprinted from *The Collected Poetry of W. H. Auden* by permission of Random House, Inc.

"Oh what is that sound," "Now the leaves are falling fast," and "Fish in the unruffled lakes," (ON THIS ISLAND) W. H. Auden. Copyright 1937 by Wystan Hugh Auden. Reprinted from *The Collected Poetry of W. H. Auden* by Random House, Inc.

Edith Sitwell. "Dirge for the New Sunrise," Copyright, 1948, 1954, by Edith Sitwell.

The Viking Press, Inc.: "Gloire de Dijon," "River Roses," "Song of a Man Who Has Come Through," "New Heaven and Earth," "Hymn to Priapus," "Spring Morning," "Lightning," "Brooding Grief," "Piano," "Snake," "Humming Bird," "Tortoise Gallantry," "Baby Tortoise," "Tortoise Shell," "Love on the Farm," "Release," "Passing Visit to Helen," and "Sorrow," from *Collected Poems* by D. H. Lawrence. Copyright 1929 by Jonathan Cape and Harrison Smith, Inc., 1957 by Frieda Lawrence Ravagli. Reprinted by permission of The Viking Press, Inc.

"Bavarian Gentians," "Trees in the Garden," "The Gods! The Gods!", "The Ship of Death," and "Whales Weep Not" from *Last Poems* by D. H. Lawrence. Copyright 1933 by Frieda Lawrence. Reprinted by permission of The Viking Press, Inc.

"On Reading the War Diary of a Defunct Ambassador" and "An Old World Effect" from *Satirical Poems* (copyright 1926) and "It Was the Love of Life," "December Stillness," and "Vigils" from *Vigils* (copyright 1936) by Siegfried Sassoon. Reprinted by permission of The Viking Press, Inc.

Appleton-Century-Crofts, Inc.: "The Apple-Barrel of Johnny Appleseed" from *Going-to-the-Sun* by Vachel Lindsay, Copyright, 1923, D. Appleton & Company; and "The Flower-Fed Buffaloes," from *Going-to-the-Stars* by Vachel Lindsay, Copyright, 1926, D. Appleton & Company, are reprinted by permission of the publishers Appleton-Century-Crofts, Inc.

"The Comet of Going-to-the-Sun" from *Going-to-the-Sun,* by Vachel Lindsay, Copyright, 1923, D. Appleton & Company; and "Rain" and "Nancy Hanks, Mother of Abraham Lincoln" from *Going-to-the-Stars* by Vachel Lindsay, Copyright, 1926, D. Appleton & Company, are reprinted by permission of D. Appleton & Company.

Brandt & Brandt: "The Window," Copyright, 1946, by Conrad Aiken. Reprinted by permission of Brandt & Brandt.

Duell, Sloan & Pearce, Inc.: Sonnets I and XV from *And in the Human Heart* by Conrad Aiken are reprinted by permission of Duell, Sloan & Pearce, Inc.

Mrs. Norma Millay Ellis: "Passer Mortuus," "Elegy," "Wild Swans," "Pity Me Not because the Light of Day," "Dirge Without Music," "Not That It Matters, Not That My Heart's Cry," "Sonnet to Gath," "Women Have Loved Before as I Love Now," "Hearing Your Words, and Not a Word among Them," "Now by the Path I Climbed," "O Sleep Forever in the Latmian Cave," "See Where Capella with Her Golden Kids," "The Broken Dike, the Levee Washed Away," and "The Strawberry Shrub," by Edna St. Vincent Millay, are reprinted by permission of Mrs. Norma Millay Ellis.

Farrar, Straus & Cudahy, Inc.: "Words for Hart Crane" and "Skunk Hour" from *Life Studies* by Robert Lowell, copyright 1959 by Robert Lowell, are used by permission of the publishers, Farrar, Straus and Cudahy, Inc.

The Four Seas Company: "Morning Song of Senlin" from *The Charnel Rose,* Copyright, 1918, is reprinted by permission of The Four Seas Company.

Grove Press, Inc.: "Oread," "Orchard," "Pear Tree," "The Helmsman," "Heat," and "Erige Cor Tuum ad Me in Caelum," by Hilda Doolittle are reprinted by permission of Grove Press, Inc.

Harcourt, Brace & World, Inc.: "Red-Headed Restaurant Cashier," "The Hangman at Home," "Death Snips Proud Men," "Losers," "Sandhill People," "Mist Forms," "Four Preludes on Playthings of the Wind," "The Lawyers Know Too Much," "Ossawatomie," "Threes," "A. E. F.," and "Balloon Faces" from *Smoke and Steel* by Carl Sandburg, copyright, 1920, by Harcourt, Brace & World, Inc. Reprinted by permission of the publishers.

"Washington Monument by Night" from *Slabs of the Sunburnt West* by Carl Sandburg, copyright, 1922, by Harcourt, Brace & World, Inc.; copyright, 1950, by Carl Sandburg. Reprinted by permission of the publishers.

Section I from *The People, Yes* by Carl Sandburg, copyright, 1936, by Harcourt, Brace & World, Inc. Reprinted by permission of the publishers.

"The Love Song of J. Alfred Prufrock," "Gerontion," "Whispers of Immortality," "Sweeney among the Nightingales," "Marina," "The Waste Land," and "Rhapsody on a Windy Night" from *Collected Poems 1909–1935* by T. S. Eliot, copyright, 1936, by Harcourt, Brace & World, Inc.; and "Burnt Norton" from *Four Quartets*, copyright, 1943, by T. S. Eliot are reprinted by permission of Harcourt, Brace & World, Inc.

"All in green went my love riding," "the hours rise up putting off stars," "when god lets my body be," "Who's most afraid of death?", "Nobody loses all the time," "Ponder, darling, these busted statues," "It is so long since my heart," "If I have made, my lady," "If you can't eat," "A pretty a day," "As freedom is a breakfastfood," "Anyone lived in a pretty how town," "My father moved through dooms of love," "I am so glad," and "Love is the every only god," copyright, 1923, 1925, 1940, 1951, 1953, 1954, by E. E. Cummings; copyright, 1926, by Horace Liveright. Reprinted from *Poems 1923–1954* by E. E. Cummings by permission of Harcourt, Brace & World, Inc.

"Longface Mahoney Discusses Heaven," "No Cock Crows at Morning," "O Mors Aeterna," "Homage to Columbus," "Emerson: Last Days at Concord," "Salvos for Randolph Bourne," Sections I and XIV from "Chorus for Survival" and Sections I and V from "Monologues from the Passion of M'Phail" from *Poems 1930–1940*, copyright, 1930, 1933, 1935, 1941, by Horace Gregory. Reprinted by permission of Harcourt, Brace & World, Inc.

"A Camp in the Prussian Forest" and "The Marchen" from *Losses* by Randall Jarrell, copyright, 1948, by Harcourt, Brace & World, Inc.; and "The Orient Express," "A Soul," and "The Black Swan" from *The Seven-League Crutches*, copyright, 1951, by Randall Jarrell are reprinted by permission of Harcourt, Brace & World, Inc.

"The Quaker Graveyard in Nantucket," "Children of Light," "The Drunken Fisherman," "As a Plane Tree by the Water," "Mr. Edwards and the Spider," and "The Dead in Europe" from *Lord Weary's Castle*, copyright, 1944, 1946, by Robert Lowell are reprinted by permission of Harcourt, Brace & World, Inc.

"Tywater," "A Simplification," "The Beautiful Changes" from *The Beautiful Changes and Other Poems*, copyright, 1947, by Richard Wilbur;

"Part of a Letter," "Museum Piece," "Juggler," "Still, Citizen Sparrow," "The Death of a Toad" from *Ceremony and Other Poems,* copyright, 1948, 1949, 1950, by Richard Wilbur; "Altitudes," "Love Calls Us to Things of This World," "Mind," "Marginalia," and "Speech for the Repeal of the McCarran Act" from *Things of This World* © 1956 by Richard Wilbur; and "Merlin Enthralled" by Richard Wilbur, copyright, 1953, by *The New Yorker Magazine,* Inc., reprinted from *Things of This World,* are reprinted by permission of Harcourt, Brace & World, Inc.

Harper & Brothers: "The Committee" and "Almost Human" from *Pegasus and Other Poems.* Copyright © 1957 by Cecil Day Lewis, reprinted by permission of Harper & Brothers.

"What Is Paradise" and " 'Twas Like a Maelstrom" by Emily Dickinson from *Bolts of Melody* edited by Mabel Loomis Todd and Millicent Todd Bingham. Copyright 1945 by Millicent Todd Bingham, reprinted by permission of Harper & Brothers.

"God's World," and "Thou Art Not Lovelier Than Lilacs" from *Renascence and Other Poems,* published by Harper & Brothers (copyright 1917 by Edna St. Vincent Millay), "The Philosopher" and "Oh, Think Not I am Faithful to a Vow" from *A Few Figs from Thistles,* published by Harper & Brothers (copyright 1922 by Edna St. Vincent Millay), "Elegy Before Death" and "Song of a Second April" from *Second April,* published by Harper & Brothers (copyright 1921 by Edna St. Vincent Millay), "I Know I Am but Summer to Your Heart" and "Euclid Alone Has Looked on Beauty Bare" from *The Harp Weaver and Other Poems,* published by Harper & Brothers (copyright 1920, 1921, 1922, 1923 by Edna St. Vincent Millay), "On the Wide Heath" from *Wine from These Grapes,* published by Harper & Brothers (copyright 1934 by Edna St. Vincent Millay), and Sonnets XI and XXX from *Fatal Interview,* published by Harper & Brothers (copyright 1931 by Edna St. Vincent Millay), by Edna St. Vincent Millay, are reprinted by permission of Harper & Brothers and of the author.

Harvard University Press: Poems by Emily Dickinson included in this volume are reprinted by permission of the President and Fellows of Harvard College and the Trustees of Amherst College from *The Poems of Emily Dickinson,* edited by Thomas H. Johnson, The Belknap Press of Harvard University Press, Cambridge, Mass., copyright, 1951 and 1955, by the President and Fellows of Harvard College.

Holt, Rinehart and Winston, Inc.: The selections in this volume from *Complete Poems of Robert Frost.* Copyright, 1923, 1928, 1930, 1949, by Holt, Rinehart and Winston, Inc. Copyright, 1936, 1942, 1951, 1956, by Robert Frost. By permission of Holt, Rinehart and Winston, Inc.

Selections from *Chicago Poems* and *Cornhuskers* by Carl Sandburg are reprinted by permission of Henry Holt and Company.

Houghton Mifflin Company: The selections from *Poems 1924–1933,* copyright, 1925, 1926, 1928, 1932, 1933, by Archilbald MacLeish are reprinted by permission of and arrangement with Houghton Mifflin Company, the authorized publishers.

"2nd Air Force" and "The Death of the Ball Turret Gunner" from *Little*

"When Doris Danced," "The Fury of Aerial Bombardment," and "The Horse Chestnut" from *Collected Poems 1930–1960*, © Richard Eberhart 1960, are reprinted by permission of Oxford University Press, Inc.

"The Pool" by H. D. is reprinted by permission of Norman Holmes Pearson.

Random House: The selections from *Collected Poems of Kenneth Fearing* are reprinted by permission of Random House, Inc., and of the author.

"Nova," "The Answer," and "The Purse-Seine" (SUCH COUNSELS YOU GAVE TO ME and Other Poems) Robinson Jeffers. Copyright 1937 by Random House, Inc. Reprinted from *SUCH COUNSELS YOU GAVE TO ME and Other Poems*, by Robinson Jeffers, by permission.

"Gray Weather," "Life from the Lifeless" (SOLSTICE and Other Poems) Robinson Jeffers. Copyright 1935 by The Modern Library, Inc. Reprinted from *THE SELECTED POETRY OF ROBINSON JEFFERS* by permission of Random House, Inc.

"The Bloody Sire," "Watch the Lights Fade" (BE ANGRY AT THE SUN and Other Poems) Robinson Jeffers. Copyright 1941 by Robinson Jeffers. Reprinted from *BE ANGRY AT THE SUN and Other Poems*, by Robinson Jeffers, by permission of Random House, Inc.

"Hurt Hawks," "Meditation on Saviors" (CAWDOR and Other Poems) Robinson Jeffers. Copyright 1928 and renewed 1956 by Robinson Jeffers. Reprinted from *THE SELECTED POETRY OF ROBINSON JEFFERS*, by permission of Random House, Inc.

"Shine, Perishing Republic," "Joy" (ROAN STALLION, TAMAR, and Other Poems) Robinson Jeffers. Copyright 1925 and renewed 1953 by Robinson Jeffers. Reprinted from *The Selected Poetry of Robinson Jeffers* by permission of Random House, Inc.

"Margrave," "Fire on the Hills" (THURSO'S LANDING, DEAR JUDAS and Other Poems) Robinson Jeffers. Copyright 1932 and renewed 1959 by Robinson Jeffers. Reprinted from *The Selected Poetry of Robinson Jeffers* by permission of Random House, Inc.

"Crumbs or the Loaf," "Still the Mind Smiles" (GIVE YOUR HEART TO THE HAWKS and Other Poems) Robinson Jeffers. Copyright 1933 and renewed 1960 by Robinson Jeffers. Reprinted from *The Selected Poetry of Robinson Jeffers* by permission of Random House, Inc.

"Gale in April" (ROAN STALLION, TAMAR and Other Poems) Robinson Jeffers. Copyright 1925 and renewed 1953 by Robinson Jeffers. Reprinted from *Roan Stallion, Tamar and Other Poems*, by Robinson Jeffers, by permission of Random House, Inc.

"Auto Wreck," "Buick," "The Dome of Sunday," "Drug Store" (PERSON, PLACE AND THING) Karl Shapiro. Copyright 1941 by Karl Shapiro. Reprinted from *Poems 1940–1953*, by Karl Shapiro, by permission of Random House, Inc.

"Nostalgia," "Poet," No. 1 from "Six Religious Lyrics" (PERSON, PLACE AND THING) Karl Shapiro. Copyright 1942 by Karl Jay Shapiro. Reprinted from *Poems 1940–1953*, by Karl Shapiro, by permission of Random House, Inc.

"The Intellectual" (V-LETTER and Other Poems) Karl Shapiro. Copyright 1944 by Karl Shapiro. Reprinted from *Poems 1940–1953*, by Karl Shapiro, by permission of Random House, Inc.

"The Phenomenon" (POEMS 1940–1953) Karl Shapiro. Copyright 1953 by Karl Shapiro. Reprinted from *Poems 1940–1953*, by Karl Shapiro, by permission of Random House, Inc. Originally published in *The New Yorker*.

Charles Scribner's Sons: The selections from *Selected Poems* and *Preludes for Memnon* by Conrad Aiken; and from *The Children of the Night* and *The Town Down the River* by E. A. Robinson are reprinted by permission of Charles Scribner's Sons.

PREFACE TO THE FOURTH EDITION

British and American poetry of this century no longer needs defending. The age of Yeats has produced work equal in beauty and brilliance to that of any of the other great literary periods of our language. Rich in experimentation, this age has also been rich in the revitalization of poetic traditions. Moreover, throughout its tumultuous history there has run a quiet, pure stream of lyricism undefiled that has its source in the early beginnings of English poetry.

This anthology, intended for students, aims to give a balanced view of the many-sided modern achievement. The superb daring of a Pound or Eliot on the one hand, and the more conventionally contained power of a Frost or Stevens or Muir on the other, are, with many other contrasting values, essential to our poetic scene. Since its first, pioneering edition in 1929, *Chief Modern Poets of England and America* has sought to represent this scene in some depth by selecting a reasonable number of outstanding poets and giving enough of the best work of each to provide a meaningful context for any one poem. The advantages for study and appreciation over the usual anthology practice of providing a few feasts and a vast number of passing nibbles should, we hope, be clear.

In our selection of poets and poems, the primary standard has been excellence, with some attention to current informed opinion and to various further considerations useful to intelligent study. Thus the inclusion of Emily Dickinson and Gerard Manley Hopkins, though it violates the principle of representing only poets whose main achievement is of this century, seems necessary because they came into their own only in our age. They "lived before their time"—their poetry is more truly ours than that of many writers still living. Again, with a poet like Yeats it is especially valuable to gain a ground sense of his development over a long career during which his whole method and way of thinking changed dynamically. Lawrence is significant not only in his own right, but also because of his great influence on later poets, while it is historically important to see Auden as a spokesman of several moods of the 1930's and 1940's. Other poets, like Housman and Miss Millay and Betjeman, are figures of the age whose enormous popular appeal—we are speaking of work far about the level of *merely* popular verse—is one sort of real imperative. Our greatest regret is that, although we provide a *sampling* of poets who have most recently come to the fore, our overall purpose and limitations of space do not allow representation of some whose work is comparable with that we include.

As in earlier editions, British and American writers are arranged separately. In each part we print the poets in order of their birth and their poems in order of book publication, the date of which is noted at the end of each poem.* The only exceptions to this arrangement are Hopkins and Dickinson; because of problems relating to the publication of these two poets, the order of composition seems preferable and has been followed. Where there are two dates, the first is that of composition, the second that of original book publication. For a poem untitled by its author, we use the first line as the title, but place it in square brackets. When the author himself uses a first line as his title, we follow his example in the matter of quotation marks. In general the text is that of the latest edition of a poet's work, although in one or two cases an earlier version seems superior and has been retained. Contrariwise, poets have sometimes told us of further revisions, and we have changed the text accordingly. A brief critical introduction precedes the British section of the book, and another precedes the American section. In each instance we intend it neither as a definitive statement for the student nor as an obstruction to the teacher, but merely as a series of suggestions toward greater rapport with the poets.

The other editors wish here to acknowledge their indebtedness to John Herbert Nelson, whose taste and intelligence were largely instrumental in the choice of poems and in the basic design, still retained, of the earlier editions. As other duties have prevented Dean Nelson's participation in this edition, all slings and arrows should be directed at the undersigned.

G.D.S.
M.L.R.

* To avoid confusing students, however, we have followed Yeats's own dating, given in the several editions of *The Collected Poems,* rather than that of the *Variorum Edition* and Allan Wade's *Bibliography* (both listed on p. I-467).

CONTENTS

Modern British Authors

Modern American Authors

CHIEF
MODERN POETS
OF
ENGLAND AND AMERICA

Modern British Poetry

Modern poetry in English has been strongly influenced by the French Symbolists of the last century and their predecessors. It shares with Mallarmé and Verlaine their interest in a psychologically evocative method and manner. It has been deeply affected by Rimbaud's way of thinking through images rather than through overt exposition. It is saturated with the ironies, the despair at modern civilization, and the personal alienation of Baudelaire, Laforgue, and others. It distrusts windiness and didacticism of every kind.

British poetry began in the 1890's to show the strong impress of the great French writers, though the work of that decade seems to us now somewhat affected and less than full-bodied in its preoccupation with "evil" and "Beauty" and the "Religion of Art." It was the age of Walter Pater, Oscar Wilde, and Arthur Symons, names we often associate with a pose of world-weary decadence. But the poets of the nineties were far more than mere poseurs. There was something very durable in their insights and preoccupations. William Butler Yeats, in his youth an outstanding poet of that period, stood until his death, in 1939, as a living link between its idiom and that of our century. He became, indeed, our most powerful single poetic voice. One of the chief reasons (and one of the most useful starting-points for an understanding of his accomplishment) lay in his extension of the creed of the nineties that exalted aesthetic values over religious and moral ones. He used this creed to encompass the great philosophical, political, and doctrinal questions of the times, rather than to reject them and assert his own superiority as an artist to them.

Even without the French, the nineties had ample native precedent for their special kind of aestheticism. They had their own models in the lyricism, the spontaneity, the "magic" of Elizabethan poetry. They had also its rapid dramatic complexities, its cultivation of the conceit and other verbal pyrotechnics, and its brooding depths to study and imitate—though they left this task, largely, to a later generation, including the mature Yeats, to pursue. Again, they had behind them the pursuit of mystery, the imaginative flights, and the tragic sense of the gap between reality and the ideal of Blake and the great Romantics; and the music of Tennyson, Swinburne, and the pre-Raphaelites was very much a part of their own apprenticeship. The classical economy and concentration of Housman and Bridges, whose poems are nevertheless highly melodic, the beautiful strangeness of de la Mare, and the "songs" of Auden are a few instances of the continuation into modern times of well-established traditions. In general, our best contemporary poets have never lost touch with these traditions, however much they may have experimented with them in their several fashions.

The most drastic experimentation has been done by Americans, by and large, rather than by British writers. Think of the revolution in modern verse and it will be Eliot's *The Waste Land* or Pound's *Cantos* or the explosions of Cummings or Williams that first come to mind. The student may ponder this fact and come to many possible explanations. One of them, perhaps, is that the transition to the modern was a more gradual process in England; English poetry has grown naturally through several phases since the Renaissance, while American poetry had to discover its own motives, language, and materials after a long subservience to English culture. Even the innovations of Gerard Manley Hopkins, who lived entirely within the last century yet seems indisputably modern, have their acknowledged antecedents in Anglo-Saxon and Middle English poetry and in the versification of Milton's *Samson Agonistes*.

Hopkins was a doubly "alienated" personality in that he was a Jesuit priest in a predominantly Protestant country and, at the same time, a man intensely responsive to sensory-stimuli despite his ascetic vocation. When he became a candidate for priesthood, he renounced poetry for a number of years, until requested by his superiors to write about the tragic incident described in "The Wreck of the *Deutschland*." Always especially intrigued by the paradoxes implicit in nature (see his early "Winter with the Gulf Stream"), he devoted this long elegy to the mystery of Christian faith as well as to the heroism and pathos of the nuns aboard the

Deutschland. The internal struggle between the artist's bent and his spiritual discipline may well have entered this poem of multiple conflict, as it entered the sonnet "The Windhover," in which the poet is amazed at himself for allowing the physical beauty and power of a mere bird to stir him so, and as it entered the "terrible sonnets" he wrote toward the end of his life. "The Wreck of the *Deutschland*" argues that one must "stress" one's affirmation; the inner self must reach out toward Christ as the tall nun of the poem does, eager to be put to the test of faith on which salvation depends. The argument is clearly related to Hopkins's "sprung rhythm" technique, whose primary characteristic is the arrangement of stressed syllables in such a way that a special rhetorical emphasis is superimposed on the "normal" rhythm of a poem. It is easy, after reading Hopkins and Bridges side by side, to see why the latter poet, though for a long time Hopkins's faithful correspondent and the first editor of Hopkins's *Poems* (1918), felt constrained to temper his admiration with some harsh criticism of their "faults of taste" and "artistic wantonness."

Whatever the extravagances of Hopkins, however, they pointed the way to the future in all their essential aspects far more than the quieter perfectionism of Bridges. Though Yeats and Hardy were not directly influenced by "sprung rhythm," both developed ways of bringing the movement of common speech and impassioned argument into a supposedly conventional verse-form. They thus, in effect, substituted that movement for the conventional one as the dominant element in their rhythm, while preserving the enormous advantages of the patterned structure of traditional verse. Hardy's close interest in and talent for catching the tones and data of ordinary life are as important to his poetry as to his fiction, and his ironic sense of human fate works with equal poignancy in both modes. He had a ready command of language and sound, if not a poetically rich one, and needed the ready-made molds of stanzaic form he employed to discipline his endlessly active contemplation of the surface of life. The driving artistic instinct that led Hopkins to allow himself to express his sensuousness and to try to justify it by finding all nature a proliferation of manifestations of the indwelling Divine Spirit forced him into some crucial formal inventions. Hardy has little to parallel this side of Hopkins. His is essentially a poetry of common sense, of a good man who hopes for the best but expects the worst. When he invents, it is by straining words to fit a set pattern amidst an active flow of ideas. Beyond that he cannot go very far. Thus, in *The Dynasts* all he can do is improvise a host of spirits who look down on the history of Napoleon's defeat by England and discuss it endlessly: a trite allegorical device whereby the Spirit of the Pities, the Spirit of the Years, the Spirit Ironical, and so on make Hardyesque speeches on the meaning of Fate and the possibilities of man.

Hardy cannot be discounted. His great strength lay in his eye and ear for reality. He was a superb gossip in his poetry, which is full of the most vividly dramatic and revealing sketches. Moreover, he wrote some beautiful lyric poems and possessed a happy wit. But we are rarely free from his heavy-handed and gloomy pondering of the meaning of what he presents, as in Hopkins we are rarely free of the poet's doctrinal pressures. Yeats tips the balance the other way. He is almost always more interested in the poetic possibilities of a theme or problem than in its literal meaning or solution, even when he is writing about Ireland's conflicts or dealing with his mystical conceptions of history and of personality. The difference may seem slight—after all, Yeats does present genuine issues and does advocate certain attitudes. But his method proved tremendously liberating. In a curious way the symbols of his poetry become at once more important than what they symbolize.

In, for instance, "Leda and the Swan," "The Cat and the Moon," and "Crazy Jane Talks with the Bishop," these poems can be accurately described as having to do, in the first, with the relationship between the human and the divine; in the second, between living, individual beings and the abstract cyclical process behind all existence; in the third, between the sacredness of the sexual principle and the assumptions of official religion. And they are very simple in their details, bold and clear in their statement, and compelling in their living, singing idiom. Even when Yeats gives us difficult and ambiguous ideas, there is usually a brilliantly lucid surface. But the symbols in these poems also have many further connotations, particularly in the light they throw on one another when placed in opposition. In Yeats's poetry we are taken again and again beyond the limits of the situation or picture he originally presents (Zeus ravishing Leda, a cat "dancing" in moonlight, a woman replying to a priest's reproaches) to a level of awareness with enormous emotional authority. His aim was to reach through to universal realizations rooted in the subconscious mind. There seems little doubt that Yeats's constant attempts to achieve this kind of awareness while keeping his writing vigorously immediate had a great deal to do with the steady increase of power that his later work shows.

The name of Yeats so overshadows the poetry of modern Britain that it is impossible to think of other poets as comparably "great." One must go to Auden, forty-two years his junior, and to Thomas, a dozen years younger still, to find names in any sense rivaling his. Of the figures born before century's end, however, a number have written poetry of originality and relevance whose impact remains as effective as ever. John Masefield, it is true, cannot command the kind of recognition his *The Everlasting Mercy* once brought him, though his gift for story-telling and description in a swift, dramatic verse style should not be forgotten. And James Stephens, despite his fine ear for Irish folk-speech and his charm and immediacy and imagination, seems to have receded with that Celtic revival of which he was so much a part. But the war poems of Siegfried Sassoon and Wilfrid Owen remain in all their clear, bold pathos, and the "Georgian" countryside poetry of the former writer still retains its nostalgic realism that links his work with that of Robert Frost in the United States and of a number of Sassoon's fellow-Englishmen who once comprised a notable literary movement. Most important, the work of Edwin Muir, Dame Edith Sitwell, Robert Graves, and D. H. Lawrence retains its intrinsic interest. (We should add the name of Hugh MacDiarmid, but because his best writing is in Scots we have not included him in this volume.)

Dame Edith's poetry is especially attractive in its early period, when she experimented so joyously with synaesthesia (the mingling of sense effects, as in "the morning light creaks down again") or with a kind of half-whimsical, half-impressionistic incantatory verse not unlike that of Vachel Lindsay on occasion. Her success comes largely from her ability to compress into a single image a visual and an aural perception, and also from her sprightly pacing of rhythmic movement. Robert Graves at his best is not nearly so "stylized" as Dame Edith at hers, and by the same token he does not run her constant risk of affectation and preciosity. His work is an excellent example of poetry of the middle ground, at which in general the British are far more successful than the Americans. Without rising to great impassioned heights, without any dazzling explorations either of technique or sensibility, he gives us the idiom of a well-educated, humorous, forthright, nonconforming adult mind. Graves is not insensitive to the subtleties of intense emotion, and he has a highly developed sense of awe and mystery. We must recall that he is the author of *The White Goddess,* and that his poetry has many Romantic overtones as well as sardonic ones to reflect this fact. He is extremely versatile—tender and delicate at one moment, bawdy at another—but mainly he is a richly gifted talker, full of anecdotes and specialized lore, who knows how to intrigue, amuse, and shock a listener.

Edwin Muir is perhaps the one modern British poet closest in mood to the Continent. A heavy fatalism pervades his writing—an ironic sense of the inability to break out of the trap of time that is close to Kafka and to Existentialism. Muir, with his slow yet compulsive rhythms, caught the terror of our age of totalitarianism and mass-refugeeism with a terrible pathos. He felt in this age the defeat of Western humanism; history had become a nightmare in which the goals of man receded forever, and in which "the road" or "the journey" became more inescapably important than its destination. In Muir too we find some of the most poignant expression of a common modern theme, the betrayal of innocence by time and history. Muir's poetry provides a bitter contrast to that of D. H. Lawrence, who believed that the trap of the times could be broken by a kind of mystical shedding of the false self created by modern civilization. Lawrence, so alive to life's primal values, felt that they could be regained through the right kind of attunement with the physical universe. The key to this attunement was the realization of the true, unconscious self in the sexual relationship, but its object was not mere self-gratification but the discovery of the uniqueness of oneself and of other individual beings—in contrast to the blurring of all such distinctions by an impersonal civilization. Lawrence's empathy with birds, flowers, and other people made this conception a painfully real one to him, not an abstract proposition. Like Whitman, whose parallelism and general verse technique he obviously follows, he felt himself a prophet and a healer in his poems.

This motif of "rebirth" through attunement with the universe of nature, with its idealization of the life-force and of the sexual principle and its implied program of a cultural revolution against the premises of the modern state, has influenced many younger writers. Kathleen Raine's poetry, almost purely incantatory and "primitive," may well be a special feminine, and quite idiosyncratically personal, distillation of this motif. The early work of Auden, too, is permeated with the spirit of Lawrence, albeit in a strange amalgam with Marxian and Freudian attitudes. "Rebirth" can mean social as well as personal rebirth, and it is interesting to see how Auden combines these ideas with each other and with the Christian idea of resurrection as well. He follows out another implication of Lawrence's also in his early work. If the self is unknown to us in a world like ours, one of the great sources of confusion and tragic error must be the ambiguity of our sense of identity. The theme is developed with great skill and compassion in "The Decoys." Another youthful influence was Hopkins, whose crowding of images and unusual employment of grammatical and syntactical elements to compress and give tension to his presentation can also be seen in the Auden of the early thirties. One reason for the influence would seem to be the attempt by both poets to reconcile purely private with larger, doctrinal perspectives. Another may be suggested by the word "doctrinal"—the need to assert a doctrine in the face of a world insisting on its denial is common to the Catholic English poet of the 1870's and 1880's and the English Leftist poet of the 1930's. The analogy is easy to push too far. After the Spanish Civil War Auden moved away from his earlier position to a more skeptically liberal politics strongly affected by a heavier religious emphasis and an existential mood, not unlike that of Muir, foreshadowed in the words that end his "Spain 1937":

> History to the defeated
> May say Alas but cannot help or pardon.

Auden, like Graves and Betjeman, has the ease and virtuosity of an accomplished man of letters, but he is also—more than they—capable of more extreme commitment and feeling than this characterization implies. He must be compared with Dryden and with Byron for his range and sudden depths. The names usually linked with his in the thirties are those of Stephen Spender, C. Day Lewis, and Louis MacNeice. These writers shared with him a sense of the historical moment that was sometimes as violent as a physical sensation. None has his bright, volatile, daring intelligence; but Spender, though he does not escape sentimentality, has values of exaltation and melody Auden never touches, and an open, almost naive freedom of emotional statement he rarely allows himself. MacNeice has an easy, sometimes racy colloquialism and a zest for little details of experience and for talking about ideas that is engaging in itself. Day Lewis has a severity of form, and a surprisingly moving body of love poetry that shows a Metaphysical influence and yet is not at all derivative. All four poets shared a certain manner for a while, rather discursive, allusive and pointed at the same time—the manner of Day Lewis's "Overtures to Death" with its allegorical use of family relationships and addresses to Death in a kind of Freudian-Marxian *mélange* of hints and nudges. This is the aspect of their writing in the thirties which has become most dated. The originality and significance of their several efforts to show "private faces in public places," as Auden once put it, remains.

The one poet of great power to emerge in England since the thirties was Dylan Thomas, who first gained recognition in that decade but came into his greatest popularity after World War II. Thomas's poetry was, with a few exceptions, thoroughly nonpolitical. In a sense it was nonintellectual, too, quite the opposite of the ideology-conscious Auden and of the almost completely cerebral William Empson, whose poetry puts his readers to work like students in a course on logic. (Actually, Empson is not at all devoid of feeling and sense perception: he has them, if not exactly in abundance, but unlike Thomas he gives little clue to his meanings until we have fathomed his literal thought.) Thomas is also very much the antithesis of John Betjeman, in recent years the most widely read modern English poet. Betjeman is extremely topical, very much concerned about what has happened to his country under the Welfare State and given to nostalgia for certain phases of her immediate past. He is an extraordinary writer of light verse and of a rather wry, usually charming, and occasionally very serious and touching verse of personal reminiscence. And occasionally he strikes a very dark note and displays unexpected depths. But British poetry has not broken through the barriers of basically conventional virtuosity since Thomas stormed onto and off the contemporary scene.

Thomas can be compared more easily with the Americans Hart Crane and Robert Lowell than with any other British poet except Yeats at his most excited. His theme is essentially unvarying throughout his career—the terror of the nature of life, and his refusal to accept that terror. A thought that occurs to every sensitive child, that our birth is the beginning of our death, is the main theme with which Thomas struggles continually. The Crucifixion is thus the symbol of every life; we are all sacrificed to the mechanical and vital processes of nature, and we share our predicament with the lower orders of being, though we are unable to communicate the fact to them. To counter this tragic awareness which is inseparable from human consciousness, Thomas repeatedly asserts his refusal to submit to it. "And death shall have no dominion," he shouts in one poem, and in another speaks of a communion of being, the "synagogue of the ear of corn" and the "round Zion of the waterbead," into which we enter joyously after death. He is strangely close to Lawrence in his identification of the sexual principle both as that which must be affirmed and as that which crucifies man. Yet there is none of the haranguing of Lawrence, nothing of his propagandism and prophecy, but simply the realization of the elementary conditions of life and his shouting that he will not allow it to be so. The wild proliferation of images, the endless inventiveness of a profusion of felicitous and suggestive phrasing, the sustained swelling of the music of the poems took audiences in England and America without a struggle.

Philip Larkin and Charles Tomlinson are exemplars of the more promising recent developments in British verse. They have little of Thomas's exuberance, but their experiments with compressed, image-centered, evocative statement show a desire to reopen the Symbolist tradition and to draw new energies from the directions of modern American poetry. Tomlinson's work particularly (see, for example, his "Antecedents: A Homage and a Valediction," which calls explicit attention to these relationships) gives evidence that a new stocktaking may now be in progress.

Thomas Hardy

HAP

If but some vengeful god would call to me
From up the sky, and laugh: "Thou suffering thing,
Know that thy sorrow is my ecstasy,
That thy love's loss is my hate's profiting!"
Then would I bear it, clench myself, and die,
Steeled by the sense of ire unmerited;
Half-eased in that a Powerfuller than I
Had willed and meted me the tears I shed.

But not so. How arrives it joy lies slain,
And why unblooms the best hope ever sown?
—Crass Casualty obstructs the sun and rain,
And dicing Time for gladness casts a moan. . . .
These purblind Doomsters had as readily strown
Blisses about my pilgrimage as pain.   *1866, 1898*

NEUTRAL TONES

We stood by a pond that winter day,
And the sun was white, as though chidden of God,
And a few leaves lay on the starving sod;
      —They had fallen from an ash, and were gray.

Your eyes on me were as eyes that rove
Over tedious riddles of years ago;
And some words played between us to and fro
      On which lost the more by our love.

The smile on your mouth was the deadest thing
Alive enough to have strength to die;
And a grin of bitterness swept thereby
      Like an ominous bird a-wing. . . .

Since then, keen lessons that love deceives,
And wrings with wrong, have shaped to me
Your face, and the God-curst sun, and a tree,
　　And a pond edged with grayish leaves.

　　　　　　　　　　　　　1867, 1898

THE SOULS OF THE SLAIN

The thick lids of Night closed upon me
　　Alone at the Bill
　　Of the Isle by the Race[1]—
Many-caverned, bald, wrinkled of face—
And with darkness and silence the spirit was on me
　　To brood and be still.

No wind fanned the flats of the ocean,
　　Or promontory sides,
　　Or the ooze by the strand,
Or the bent-bearded slope of the land,
Whose base took its rest amid everlong motion
　　Of criss-crossing tides.

Soon from out of the Southward seemed nearing
　　A whirr, as of wings
　　Waved by mighty-vanned flies,
Or by night-moths of measureless size,
And in softness and smoothness well-nigh beyond hearing
　　Of corporal things.

And they bore to the bluff, and alighted—
　　A dim-discerned train
　　Of sprites without mould,
Frameless souls none might touch or might hold—
On the ledge by the turreted lantern, far-sighted
　　By men of the main.

And I heard them say "Home!" and I knew them
　　For souls of the felled
　　On the earth's nether bord
Under Capricorn, whither they'd warred,

---

[1] The "Race" is the turbulent sea-area off the Bill of Portland, where contrary tides meet.—*Author's note.*

And I neared in my awe, and gave heedfulness to them
   With breathings inheld.

Then, it seemed, there approached from the northward
   A senior soul-flame
   Of the like filmy hue:
   And he met them and spake: "Is it you,
O my men?" Said they, "Aye! We bear homeward and hearthward
   To feast on our fame!"

  "I've flown there before you," he said then:
   "Your households are well;
   But—your kin linger less
  On your glory and war-mightiness
Than on dearer things."—"Dearer?" cried these from the dead then,
   "Of what do they tell?"

  "Some mothers muse sadly, and murmur
   Your doings as boys—
   Recall the quaint ways
  Of your babyhood's innocent days.
Some pray that, ere dying, your faith had grown firmer,
   And higher your joys.

  "A father broods: 'Would I had set him
   To some humble trade,
   And so slacked his high fire,
  And his passionate martial desire;
And told him no stories to woo him and whet him
   To this dire crusade!'

  "And, General, how hold out our sweethearts,
   Sworn loyal as doves?"
   —"Many mourn; many think
  It is not unattractive to prink
Them in sables for heroes. Some fickle and fleet hearts
   Have found them new loves."

  "And our wives?" quoth another resignedly,
   "Dwell they on our deeds?"
   —"Deeds of home; that live yet
  Fresh as new—deeds of fondness or fret;
Ancient words that were kindly expressed or unkindly,
   These, these have their heeds."

—"Alas! then it seems that our glory
　　Weighs less in their thought
　　Than our old homely acts,
　And the long-ago commonplace facts
Of our lives—held by us as scarce part of our story,
　　And rated as nought!"

Then bitterly some: "Was it wise now
　　To raise the tomb-door
　　For such knowledge? Away!"
But the rest: "Fame we prized till to-day;
Yet that hearts keep us green for old kindness we prize now
　　A thousand times more!"

Thus speaking, the trooped apparitions
　　Began to disband
　　And resolve them in two:
Those whose record was lovely and true
Bore to northward for home: those of bitter traditions
　　Again left the land,

And, towering to seaward in legions,
　　They paused at a spot
　　Overbending the Race—
That engulphing, ghast, sinister place—
Whither headlong they plunged, to the fathomless regions
　　Of myriads forgot.

And the spirits of those who were homing
　　Passed on, rushingly,
　　Like the Pentecost Wind;
And the whirr of their wayfaring thinned
And surceased on the sky, and but left in the gloaming
　　Sea-mutterings and me.   *December 1899, 1902*

THE LACKING SENSE

SCENE.—*A sad-coloured landscape, Waddon Vale*

"O Time, whence comes the Mother's moody look amid her labours,
As of one who all unwittingly has wounded where she loves?
　Why weaves she not her world-webs to according lutes and tabors,
With nevermore this too remorseful air upon her face,
　　As of angel fallen from grace?"

—"Her look is but her story: construe not its symbols keenly:
    In her wonderworks yea surely has she wounded where she loves.
The sense of ills misdealt for blisses blanks the mien most queenly,
    Self-smitings kill self-joys; and everywhere beneath the sun
        Such deeds her hands have done."

—"And how explains thy Ancient Mind her crimes upon her creatures,
    These fallings from her fair beginnings, woundings where she loves,
Into her would-be perfect motions, modes, effects, and features
    Admitting cramps, black humours, wan decay, and baleful blights,
        Distress into delights?"

—"Ah! knowest thou not her secret yet, her vainly veiled deficience,
    Whence it comes that all unwittingly she wounds the lives she loves?
That sightless are those orbs of hers?—which bar to her omniscience
    Brings those fearful unfulfilments, that red ravage through her zones
        Whereat all creation groans.

"She whispers it in each pathetic strenuous slow endeavour,
    When in mothering she unwittingly sets wounds on what she loves;
Yet her primal doom pursues her, faultful, fatal is she ever;
    Though so deft and nigh to vision is her facile finger-touch
        That the seers marvel much.

"Deal, then, her groping skill no scorn, no note of malediction;
    Not long on thee will press the hand that hurts the lives it loves;
And while she plods dead-reckoning on, in darkness of affliction,
    Assist her where thy creaturely dependence can or may,
        For thou art of her clay."   1902

THE SUBALTERNS

"Poor wanderer," said the leaden sky,
    "I fain would lighten thee,
But there are laws in force on high
    Which say it must not be."

—"I would not freeze thee, shorn one," cried
    The North, "knew I but how
To warm my breath, to slack my stride;
    But I am ruled as thou."

—"Tomorrow I attack thee, wight,"
    Said Sickness. "Yet I swear

I bear thy little ark no spite,
    But am bid enter there."

—"Come hither, Son," I heard Death say;
    "I did not will a grave
Should end thy pilgrimage today,
    But I, too, am a slave!"

We smiled upon each other then,
    And life to me had less
Of that fell look it wore ere when
    They owned their passiveness.   *1902*

MUTE OPINION

I traversed a dominion
Whose spokesmen spake out strong
Their purpose and opinion
Through pulpit, press, and song.
I scarce had means to note there
A large-eyed few, and dumb,
Who thought not as those thought there
That stirred the heat and hum.

When, grown a Shade, beholding
That land in lifetime trode,
To learn if its unfolding
Fulfilled its clamored code,
I saw, in web unbroken,
Its history outwrought
Not as the loud had spoken,
But as the mute had thought.   *1902*

HIS IMMORTALITY

I saw a dead man's finer part
Shining within each faithful heart
Of those bereft. Then said I: "This must be
    His immortality."

I looked there as the seasons wore,
And still his soul continuously bore
A life in theirs. But less its shine excelled
    Than when I first beheld.

His fellow-yearsmen passed, and then
In later hearts I looked for him again;
And found him—shrunk, alas! into a thin
  And spectral mannikin.

Lastly I ask—now old and chill—
If aught of him remain unperished still;
And find, in me alone, a feeble spark,
  Dying amid the dark.   *1899, 1902*

THE LAST CHRYSANTHEMUM

Why should this flower delay so long
  To show its tremulous plumes?
Now is the time of plaintive robin-song
  When flowers are in their tombs.

Through the slow summer, when the sun
  Called to each frond and whorl
That all he could for flowers was being done,
  Why did it not uncurl?

It must have felt that fervid call
  Although it took no heed,
Waking but now, when leaves like corpses fall,
  And saps all retrocede.

Too late its beauty, lonely thing,
  The season's shine is spent,
Nothing remains for it but shivering
  In tempests turbulent.

Had it a reason for delay,
  Dreaming in witlessness
That for a bloom so delicately gay
  Winter would stay its stress?

—I talk as if the thing were born
  With sense to work its mind;
Yet it is but one mask of many worn
  By the Great Face behind.   *1902*

THE DARKLING THRUSH

I leant upon a coppice gate
    When Frost was spectre-gray,
And Winter's dregs made desolate
    The weakening eye of day.
The tangled bine-stems scored the sky
    Like strings of broken lyres,
And all mankind that haunted nigh
    Had sought their household fires.

The land's sharp features seemed to be
    The Century's corpse outleant,
His crypt the cloudy canopy,
    The wind his death-lament.
The ancient pulse of germ and birth
    Was shrunken hard and dry,
And every spirit upon earth
    Seemed fervorless as I.

At once a voice arose among
    The bleak twigs overhead
In a full-hearted evensong
    Of joy illimited;
An aged thrush, frail, gaunt, and small,
    In blast-beruffled plume,
Had chosen thus to fling his soul
    Upon the growing gloom.

So little cause for carolings
    Of such ecstatic sound
Was written on terrestrial things
    Afar or nigh around,
That I could think there trembled through
    His happy good-night air
Some blessed Hope, whereof he knew
    And I was unaware.
        December 1900, 1902

THE COMET AT YELL'HAM

It bends far over Yell'ham Plain,
    And we, from Yell'ham Height,

Stand and regard its fiery train,
So soon to swim from sight.

It will return long years hence, when
As now its strange swift shine
Will fall on Yell'ham; but not then
On that sweet form of thine.   *1902*

THE RUINED MAID

"O 'Melia, my dear, this does everything crown!
Who could have supposed I should meet you in Town?
And whence such fair garments, such prosperi-ty?"—
"O didn't you know I'd been ruined?" said she.

—"You left us in tatters, without shoes or socks,
Tired of digging potatoes, and spudding up docks;
And now you've gay bracelets and bright feathers three!"—
"Yes: that's how we dress when we're ruined," said she.

—"At home in the barton you said 'thee' and 'thou,'
And 'thik oon,' and 'theäs oon,' and 't'other'; but now
Your talking quite fits 'ee for high compa-ny!"—
"Some polish is gained with one's ruin," said she.

—"Your hands were like paws then, your face blue and bleak,
But now I'm bewitched by your delicate cheek,
And your little gloves fit as on any la-dy!"—
"We never do work when we're ruined," said she.

—"You used to call home-life a hag-ridden dream,
And you'd sigh, and you'd sock; but at present you seem
To know not of megrims or melancho-ly!"—
"True. One's pretty lively when ruined," said she.

—"I wish I had feathers, a fine sweeping gown,
And a delicate face, and could strut about Town!"—
"My dear—a raw country girl, such as you be,
Cannot quite expect that. You ain't ruined," said she.

1866; 1902

THE RESPECTABLE BURGHER

ON "THE HIGHER CRITICISM"

Since Reverend Doctors now declare
That clerks and people must prepare
To doubt if Adam ever were;
To hold the flood a local scare;
To argue, though the stolid stare,
That everything had happened ere
The prophets to its happening sware;
That David was no giant-slayer,
Nor one to call a God-obeyer
In certain details we could spare,
But rather was a debonair
Shrewd bandit, skilled as banjo-player:
That Solomon sang the fleshly Fair,
And gave the Church no thought whate'er,
That Esther with her royal wear,
And Mordecai, the son of Jair,
And Joshua's triumphs, Job's despair,
And Balaam's ass's bitter blare;
Nebuchadnezzar's furnace-flare,
And Daniel and the den affair,
And other stories rich and rare,
Were writ to make old doctrine wear
Something of a romantic air:
That the Nain widow's only heir,
And Lazarus with cadaverous glare
(As done in oils by Piombo's care)
Did not return from Sheol's lair:
That Jael set a fiendish snare,
That Pontius Pilate acted square,
That never a sword cut Malchus' ear;
And (but for shame I must forbear)
That —— —— did not reappear! . . .
—Since thus they hint, nor turn a hair,
All churchgoing will I forswear,
And sit on Sundays in my chair,
And read that moderate man Voltaire.

                                        1902

IN TENEBRIS: II

Considerabam ad dexteram, et videbam; et non erat qui cognosceret me. . . .
Non est qui requirat animam meam.—Psalm cxlii.

When the clouds' swoln bosoms echo back the shouts of the many and
strong
That things are all as they best may be, save a few to be right ere long,
And my eyes have not the vision in them to discern what to these is so
clear,
The blot seems straightway in me alone; one better he were not here.

The stout upstanders say, All's well with us; ruers have nought to rue!
And what the potent say so oft, can it fail to be somewhat true?
Breezily go they, breezily come; their dust smokes around their career,
Till I think I am one born out of due time, who has no calling here.

Their dawns bring lusty joys, it seems; their evenings all that is sweet;
Our times are blessed times, they cry: Life shapes it as is most meet,
And nothing is much the matter; there are many smiles to a tear;
Then what is the matter is I, I say. Why should such an one be
here? . . .

Let him in whose ears the low-voiced Best is killed by the clash of the
First,
Who holds that if way to the Better there be, it exacts a full look at
the Worst,
Who feels that delight is a delicate growth cramped by crookedness,
custom, and fear,
Get him up and be gone as one shaped awry; he disturbs the order here.

                                            1895–96, 1902

From THE DYNASTS:

THE FIELD OF TALAVERA

Talavera town, on the river Tagus, is at the extreme right of the foreground; a mountain range on the extreme left.
    The allied army under SIR ARTHUR WELLESLEY stretches between—the
English on the left, the Spanish on the right—part holding a hill to the
left-centre of the scene, divided from the mountains by a valley, and part
holding a redoubt to the right-centre. This army of more than fifty thousand
all told, of which twenty-two thousand only are English, has its back to the
spectator.

Beyond, in a wood of olive, oak, and cork, are the fifty to sixty thousand French, facing the spectator and the allies. Their right includes a strong battery upon a hill which fronts the one on the English left.

Behind all, the heights of Salinas close the prospect, the small river Alberche flowing at their foot from left to right into the Tagus, which advances in foreshortened perspective to the town at the right front corner of the scene as aforesaid. . . .

The hot and dusty July afternoon having turned to twilight, shady masses of men start into motion from the French position, come towards the foreground, silently ascend the hill on the left of the English, and assail the latter in a violent outburst of fire and lead. They nearly gain possession of the hill assailed.

CHORUS OF RUMOURS (aerial music)

Ten of the night is Talavera tolling:
Now do Ruffin's ranks come surging upward,
Backed by bold Vilatte's. Lapisse from the vale, too,
    Darkly upswells there!——

Downhill from the crest the English fling them,
And with their bayonets roll the enemy backward:
So the first fierce charge of the ardent Frenchmen
    England repels there!

Having fallen back into the darkness the French presently reascend in yet larger masses. The high square knapsack which every English foot-soldier carries, and his shako, and its tuft, outline themselves against the dim light as the ranks stand awaiting the shock.

CHORUS OF RUMOURS

Pushing they spread, and shout as they reach the summit,
Strength and stir new-primed in their plump battalions:
Puffs of flame blown forth on the lines opposing
    Higher and higher.

There those hold them mute, though at speaking distance—
Mute, while the clicking flints, and the crash of the volley
Throw on the weighted gloom an immense distraction
    Pending their fire.

Fronting visages each ranksman reads there,
Epaulettes, and cheeks, and shining eyeballs,
(Called from the dark a trice by the fleeting panflash)
    Pressing them nigher!

The French again fall back in disorder into the hollow, and LAPISSE draws off on the right. As the sinking sound of the muskets tells what has happened the English raise a shout.

CHORUS OF PITIES

Thus the dim nocturnal voice of the conflict
Closes with the receding roar of the gun-fire.
Harness loosened then, and their day-long strenuous
    Strain unbending,

Worn-out lines lie down where they late stood staunchly—
Cloaks around them rolled—by the bivouac embers:
There to pursue at dawn the dynasts' death-game
    Unto the ending!

The morning breaks. There is another murderous attempt to dislodge the English from the hill, the assault being pressed with a determination that excites the admiration of the English themselves.

The French are seen descending into the valley, crossing it, and climbing it on the other side under the fire of HILL's whole division, all to no purpose. In their retreat they leave behind them on the slopes nearly two thousand lying.

The day advances to noon, and the air trembles in the intense heat. The combat flags, and is suspended.

SPIRIT OF THE PITIES

What do I see but thirsty, throbbing bands
From these inimic hosts defiling down
In homely need towards the little stream
That parts their enmities, and drinking there!
They get to grasping hands across the rill,
Sealing their sameness as earth's sojourners.—
What more could plead the wryness of the times
Than such unstudied piteous pantomimes!

SPIRIT IRONIC

It is only that Life's queer mechanics chance to work out in this grotesque shape just now. The groping tentativeness of an Immanent Will . . . cannot be asked to learn logic at this time of day! The spectacle of Its instruments, set to riddle one another through, and then to drink together in peace and concord, is where the humour comes in, and makes the play worth seeing!

SPIRIT SINISTER

Come, Sprite, don't carry your ironies too far, or you may wake up
the Unconscious Itself, and tempt It to let all the clockwork of the show
run down to spite us! Where will be our theatre then, and where my
enjoyment?

The drums roll, and the men of the two nations part from their comrade
ship at the Alberche brook, the dark masses of the French army assembling,
anew. SIR ARTHUR WELLESLEY has seated himself on a mound that commands a full view of the contested hill, and remains there motionless a long
time. When the French form for battle he is seen to have come to a conclusion. He mounts, gives his orders, and the aides ride off.

The French advance steadily through the sultry atmosphere, the skir-
mishers in front, and the columns after, moving, yet seemingly motionless.
Their eighty cannon peal out and their shots mow every space in the line
of them. Up the great valley and the terraces of the hill whose fame is at
that moment being woven, comes VILATTE, boring his way with foot and
horse, and RUFFIN's men following behind.

According to the order given, the Twenty-third Light Dragoons and the
German Hussars advance at a chosen moment against the head of these
columns. On the way they disappear.

SPIRIT OF THE PITIES

Why this bedevilment? What can have chanced?

SPIRIT OF RUMOUR

It so befalls that as their chargers near
The inimical wall of flesh with its iron frise,
A treacherous chasm uptrips them: zealous men
And docile horses roll to dismal death
And horrid mutilation.

SPIRIT OF THE PITIES

Those who live
Even now advance! I'll see no more. Relate.

SPIRIT OF RUMOUR

Yes, those pant on. Then further Frenchmen cross,
And Polish Lancers, and Westphalian Horse,
Who ring around these luckless Islanders,
And sweep them down like reeds by the river-brink
In scouring floods; till scarce a man remains.

Meanwhile on the British right SEBASTIANI's corps has precipitated itself in column against GENERAL CAMPBELL's division, the division of LAPISSE against the centre, and at the same time the hill on the English left is again assaulted. The English are pressed sorely here, the bellowing battery tearing lanes through their masses.

SPIRIT OF RUMOUR (continuing)

The French reserves of foot and horse now on,
Smiting the Islanders in breast and brain
Till their mid-lines are shattered. . . . Now there ticks
The moment of the crisis; now the next,
Which brings the turning stroke.

SIR ARTHUR WELLESLEY sends down the Forty-eighth regiment under COLONEL DONELLAN to support the wasting troops. It advances amid those retreating, opening to let them pass.

SPIRIT OF RUMOUR (continuing)

     Then pales, enerved,
The hitherto unflinching enemy!
Lapisse is pierced to death; the flagging French
Decline into the hollows whence they came.
The too exhausted English and reduced
Lack strength to follow.—Now the western sun,
Conning with unmoved face both quick and dead,
Gilds horsemen slackening, and footmen stilled,
Till all around breathes drowsed hostility.
  Last, the swealed herbage lifts a leering light,
And flames traverse the field; and hurt and slain,
Opposed, opposers, in a common plight
Are scorched together on the dusk champaign.

The fire dies down, and darkness enwraps the scene.

1908

From THE DYNASTS, III, VI, viii

CHORUS OF THE YEARS

Yea, the coneys are scared by the thud of hoofs,
And their white scuts flash at their vanishing heels,
And swallows abandon the hamlet-roofs.

The mole's tunnelled chambers are crushed by wheels,
The lark's eggs scattered, their owners fled,
And the hare's hid litter the sapper unseals.

The snail draws in at the terrible tread,
But in vain; he is crushed by the felloe-rim;
The worm asks what can be overhead,

And wriggles deep from a scene so grim,
And guesses him safe; for he does not know
What a foul red flood will soak down to him!

Beaten about by the heel and the toe
Are butterflies, sick of the day's long rheum,
To die of a worse than the weather-foe.

Trodden and bruised to a miry tomb
Are ears that have greened but will never be gold,
And flowers in the bud that will never bloom.   *1908*

SHUT OUT THAT MOON

Close up the casement, draw the blind,
   Shut out that stealing moon,
She wears too much the guise she wore
   Before our lutes were strewn
With years-deep dust, and names we read
   On a white stone were hewn.

Step not out on the dew-dashed lawn
   To view the Lady's Chair,
Immense Orion's glittering form,
   The Less and Greater Bear:
Stay in; to such sights we were drawn
   When faded ones were fair.

Brush not the bough for midnight scents
   That come forth lingeringly,
And wake the same sweet sentiments
   They breathed to you and me
When living seemed a laugh, and love
   All it was said to be.

Within the common lamp-lit room
  Prison my eyes and thought;
Let dingy details crudely loom,
  Mechanic speech be wrought:
Too fragrant was Life's early bloom,
  Too tart the fruit it brought!

1904, 1909

AFTER THE FAIR

The singers are gone from the Cornmarket-place
  With their broadsheets of rhymes,
The street rings no longer in treble and bass
  With their skits on the times,
And the Cross, lately thronged, is a dim naked space
  That but echoes the stammering chimes.

From Clock-corner steps, as each quarter ding-dongs,
  Away the folk roam
By the "Hart" and Grey's Bridge into byways and "drongs,"
  Or across the ridged loam;
The younger ones shrilling the lately heard songs,
  The old saying, "Would we were home."

The shy-seeming maiden so mute in the fair
  Now rattles and talks,
And that one who looked the most swaggering there
  Grows sad as she walks,
And she who seemed eaten by cankering care
  In statuesque sturdiness stalks.

And midnight clears High Street of all but the ghosts
  Of its buried burghees,
From the latest far back to those old Roman hosts
  Whose remains one yet sees,
Who loved, laughed, and fought, hailed their friends, drank their toasts
  At their meeting-times here, just as these!   *1902, 1909*

THE REMINDER

While I watch the Christmas blaze
Paint the room with ruddy rays,

Something makes my vision glide
To the frosty scene outside.

There, to reach a rotting berry,
Toils a thrush,—constrained to very
Dregs of food by sharp distress,
Taking such with thankfulness.

Why, O starving bird, when I
One day's joy would justify,
And put misery out of view,
Do you make me notice you!   *1909*

THE UNBORN

I rose at night, and visited
    The Cave of the Unborn:
And crowding shapes surrounded me
For tidings of the life to be,
Who long had prayed the silent Head
    To haste its advent morn.

Their eyes were lit with artless trust,
    Hope thrilled their every tone;
"A scene the loveliest, is it not?
A pure delight, a beauty-spot
Where all is gentle, true and just,
    And darkness is unknown?"

My heart was anguished for their sake,
    I could not frame a word;
And they descried my sunken face,
And seemed to read therein, and trace
The news that pity would not break,
    Nor truth leave unaverred.

And as I silently retired
    I turned and watched them still,
And they came helter-skelter out,
Driven forward like a rabble rout
Into the world they had so desired,
    By the all-immanent Will.
            1905, 1909

THE MAN HE KILLED

"Had he and I but met
    By some old ancient inn,
We should have sat us down to wet
    Right many a nipperkin!

"But ranged as infantry,
    And staring face to face,
I shot at him as he at me,
    And killed him in his place.

"I shot him dead because—
    Because he was my foe,
Just so: my foe of course he was;
    That's clear enough; although

"He thought he'd 'list, perhaps,
    Off-hand like—just as I—
Was out of work—had sold his traps—
    No other reason why.

"Yes; quaint and curious war is!
    You shoot a fellow down
You'd treat if met where any bar is,
    Or help to half-a-crown."

                1902, 1909

CHANNEL FIRING

That night your great guns, unawares,
Shook all our coffins as we lay,
And broke the chancel window-squares,
We thought it was the Judgment-day

And sat upright. While drearisome
Arose the howl of wakened hounds:
The mouse let fall the altar-crumb,
The worms drew back into the mounds,

The glebe cow drooled. Till God called, "No;
It's gunnery practice out at sea

Just as before you went below;
The world is as it used to be:

"All nations striving strong to make
Red war yet redder. Mad as hatters
They do no more for Christés sake
Than you who are helpless in such matters.

"That this is not the judgment-hour
For some of them's a blessed thing,
For if it were they'd have to scour
Hell's floor for so much threatening. . . .

"Ha, ha. It will be warmer when
I blow the trumpet (if indeed
I ever do; for you are men,
And rest eternal sorely need)."

So down we lay again. "I wonder,
Will the world ever saner be,"
Said one, "than when He sent us under
In our indifferent century!"

And many a skeleton shook his head.
"Instead of preaching forty year,"
My neighbour Parson Thirdly said,
"I wish I had stuck to pipes and beer."

Again the guns disturbed the hour,
Roaring their readiness to avenge,
As far inland as Stourton Tower,
And Camelot, and starlit Stonehenge.

April 1914, 1914

WESSEX HEIGHTS

There are some heights in Wessex, shaped as if by a kindly hand
For thinking, dreaming, dying on, and at crises when I stand,
Say, on Ingpen Beacon eastward, or on Wylls-Neck westwardly,
I seem where I was before my birth, and after death may be.

In the lowlands I have no comrade, not even the lone man's friend—
Her who suffereth long and is kind; accepts what he is too weak to
    mend:

Down there they are dubious and askance; there nobody thinks as I,
But mind-chains do not clank where one's next neighbour is the sky.

In the towns I am tracked by phantoms having weird detective ways—
Shadows of beings who fellowed with myself of earlier days:
They hang about at places, and they say harsh heavy things—
Men with a wintry sneer, and women with tart disparagings.

Down there I seem to be false to myself, my simple self that was,
And is not now, and I see him watching, wondering what crass cause
Can have merged him into such a strange continuator as this,
Who yet has something in common with himself, my chrysalis.

I cannot go to the great grey Plain; there's a figure against the moon,
Nobody sees it but I, and it makes my breast beat out of tune;
I cannot go to the tall-spired town, being barred by the forms now passed
For everybody but me, in whose long vision they stand there fast.

There's a ghost at Yell'ham Bottom chiding loud at the fall of the night,
There's a ghost in Froom-side Vale, thin lipped and vague, in a shroud
    of white,
There is one in the railway train whenever I do not want it near,
I see its profile against the pane, saying what I would not hear.

As for one rare fair woman, I am now but a thought of hers,
I enter her mind and another thought succeeds me that she prefers;
Yet my love for her in its fulness she herself even did not know;
Well, time cures hearts of tenderness, and now I can let her go.

So I am found on Ingpen Beacon, or on Wylls-Neck to the west,
Or else on homely Bulbarrow, or little Pilsdon Crest,
Where men have never cared to haunt, nor women have walked with
    me,
And ghosts then keep their distance; and I know some liberty.

                                                    1896, 1914

THE YEAR'S AWAKENING

How do you know that the pilgrim track
Along the belting zodiac
Swept by the sun in his seeming rounds
Is traced by now to the Fishes' bounds
And into the Ram, when weeks of cloud

Have wrapt the sky in a clammy shroud,
And never as yet a tinct of spring
Has shown in the Earth's apparelling;
    O vespering bird, how do you know,
        How do you know?

How do you know, deep underground,
Hid in your bed from sight and sound,
Without a turn in temperature,
With weather life can scarce endure,
That light has won a fraction's strength,
And day put on some moments' length,
Whereof in merest rote will come,
Weeks hence, mild airs that do not numb,
    O crocus root, how do you know,
        How do you know?   *1910, 1914*

AT A WATERING-PLACE

They sit and smoke on the esplanade,
The man and his friend, and regard the bay
Where the far chalk cliffs, to the left displayed,
Smile sallowly in the decline of day.
And saunterers pass with laugh and jest—
A handsome couple among the rest.

"That smart proud pair," says the man to his friend,
"Are to marry next week. . . . How little he thinks
That dozens of days and nights on end
I have stroked her neck, unhooked the links
Of her sleeve to get at her upper arm. . . .
Well, bliss is in ignorance: what's the harm!"
        April 1911, 1914

THE WALK

    You did not walk with me
    Of late to the hill-top tree
        By the gated ways,
        As in earlier days;
        You were weak and lame,
        So you never came,
And I went alone, and I did not mind,
Not thinking of you as left behind.

I walked up there to-day
Just in the former way;
　　Surveyed around
　　The familiar ground
　　By myself again:
　　What difference, then?
Only that underlying sense
Of the look of a room on returning thence.

1914

"I FOUND HER OUT THERE"

I found her out there
On a slope few see,
That falls westwardly
To the salt-edged air,
Where the ocean breaks
On the purple strand,
And the hurricane shakes
The solid land.

I brought her here,
And have laid her to rest
In a noiseless nest
No sea beats near.
She will never be stirred
In her loamy cell
By the waves long heard
And loved so well.

So she does not sleep
By those haunted heights
The Atlantic smites
And the blind gales sweep,
Whence she often would gaze
At Dundagel's famed head,
While the dipping blaze
Dyed her face fire-red;

And would sigh at the tale
Of sunk Lyonnesse,
As a wind-tugged tress
Flapped her cheek like a flail;

Or listen at whiles
With a thought-bound brow
To the murmuring miles
She is far from now.

Yet her shade, maybe,
Will creep underground
Till it catch the sound
Of that western sea
As it swells and sobs
Where she once domiciled,
And joy in its throbs
With the heart of a child.

1914

THE VOICE

Woman much missed, how you call to me, call to me,
Saying that now you are not as you were
When you had changed from the one who was all to me,
But as at first, when our day was fair.

Can it be you that I hear? Let me view you, then,
Standing as when I drew near to the town
Where you would wait for me: yes, as I knew you then,
Even to the original air-blue gown!

Or is it only the breeze, in its listlessness
Travelling across the wet mead to me here,
You being ever dissolved to wan wistlessness,
Heard no more again far or near?

Thus I; faltering forward,
Leaves around me falling,
Wind oozing thin through the thorn from norward,
And the woman calling.   *December 1912, 1914*

AFTER A JOURNEY

Hereto I come to view a voiceless ghost;
  Whither, O whither will its whim now draw me?
Up the cliff, down, till I'm lonely, lost,
  And the unseen waters' ejaculations awe me.

Where you will next be there's no knowing,
　　Facing round about me everywhere,
　　　　With your nut-coloured hair,
And gray eyes, and rose-flush coming and going.

Yes: I have re-entered your olden haunts at last;
　　Through the years, through the dead scenes I have tracked you;
What have you now found to say of our past—
　　Scanned across the dark space wherein I have lacked you?
Summer gave us sweets, but autumn wrought division?
　　Things were not lastly as firstly well
　　　　With us twain, you tell?
But all's closed now, despite Time's derision.

I see what you are doing: you are leading me on
　　To the spots we knew when we haunted here together,
The waterfall, above which the mist-bow shone
　　At the then fair hour in the then fair weather,
And the cave just under, with a voice still so hollow
　　That it seems to call out to me from forty years ago,
　　　　When you were all aglow,
And not the thin ghost that I now fraily follow!

Ignorant of what there is flitting here to see,
　　The waked birds preen and the seals flop lazily,
Soon you will have, Dear, to vanish from me,
　　For the stars close their shutters and the dawn whitens hazily.
Trust me, I mind not, though Life lours,
　　The bringing me here; nay, bring me here again!
　　　　I am just the same as when
Our days were a joy, and our paths through flowers.

1914

THE PHANTOM HORSEWOMAN

　　　　Queer are the ways of a man I know:
　　　　　　He comes and stands
　　　　　　In a careworn craze,
　　　　　　And looks at the sands
　　　　　　And the seaward haze
　　　　　　With moveless hands
　　　　　　And face and gaze,
　　　　　　Then turns to go . . .
　　　　And what does he see when he gazes so?

They say he sees as an instant thing
    More clear than to-day,
    A sweet soft scene
    That once was in play
    By that briny green;
    Yes, notes alway
    Warm, real, and keen,
    What his back years bring—
A phantom of his own figuring.

Of this vision of his they might say more:
    Not only there
    Does he see this sight,
    But everywhere
    In his brain—day, night,
    As if on the air
    It were drawn rose bright—
    Yea, far from that shore
Does he carry this vision of heretofore:

A ghost-girl-rider. And though, toil-tried,
    He withers daily,
    Time touches her not,
    But she still rides gaily
    In his rapt thought
    On that shagged and shaly
    Atlantic spot,
    And as when first eyed
Draws rein and sings to the swing of the tide.

1913, 1914

NEAR LANIVET, 1872

There was a stunted handpost just on the crest,
    Only a few feet high:
She was tired, and we stopped in the twilight-time for her rest,
    At the crossways close thereby.

She leant back, being so weary, against its stem,
    And laid her arms on its own,
Each open palm stretched out to each end of them,
    Her sad face sideways thrown.

Her white-clothed form at this dim-lit cease of day
    Made her look as one crucified
In my gaze at her from the midst of the dusty way,
    And hurriedly "Don't," I cried.

I do not think she heard. Loosing thence she said,
    As she stepped forth ready to go,
"I am rested now.—Something strange came into my head;
    I wish I had not leant so!"

And wordless we moved onward down from the hill
    In the west cloud's murked obscure,
And looking back we could see the handpost still
    In the solitude of the moor.

"It struck her too," I thought, for as if afraid
    She heavily breathed as we trailed;
Till she said, "I did not think how 'twould look in the shade,
    When I leant there like one nailed."

I, lightly: "There's nothing in it. For *you*, anyhow!"
    —"O I know there is not," said she . . .
"Yet I wonder . . . If no one is bodily crucified now,
    In spirit one may be!"

And we dragged on and on, while we seemed to see
    In the running of Time's far glass
Her crucified, as she had wondered if she might be
    Some day.—Alas, alas!

                                 1917

THE BLINDED BIRD

So zestfully canst thou sing?
And all this indignity,
With God's consent, on thee!
Blinded ere yet a-wing
By the red-hot needle thou,
I stand and wonder how
So zestfully thou canst sing!

Resenting not such wrong,
Thy grievous pain forgot,
Eternal dark thy lot,

Groping thy whole life long,
After that stab of fire,
Enjailed in pitiless wire;
Resenting not such wrong!

Who hath charity? This bird.
Who suffereth long and is kind,
Is not provoked, though blind
And alive ensepulchred?
Who hopeth, endureth all things?
Who thinketh no evil, but sings?
Who is divine? This bird.   *1917*

THE OXEN

Christmas Eve, and twelve of the clock.
  "Now they are all on their knees,"
An elder said as we sat in a flock
  By the embers in hearthside ease.

We pictured the meek mild creatures where
  They dwelt in their strawy pen,
Nor did it occur to one of us there
  To doubt they were kneeling then.

So fair a fancy few would weave
  In these years! Yet, I feel,
If someone said on Christmas Eve,
  "Come; see the oxen kneel,

"In the lonely barton by yonder coomb
  Our childhood used to know,"
I should go with him in the gloom,
  Hoping it might be so.   *1915, 1917*

THE FIVE STUDENTS

The sparrow dips in his wheel-rut bath,
  The sun grows passionate-eyed,
And boils the dew to smoke by the paddock-path;
  As strenuously we stride,—
Five of us; dark He, fair He, dark She, fair She, I,
  All beating by.

The air is shaken, the high-road hot,
　　Shadowless swoons the day,
The greens are sobered and cattle at rest; but not
　　We on our urgent way,—
Four of us; fair She, dark She, fair He, I, are there,
　　But one—elsewhere.

Autumn moulds the hard fruit mellow,
　　And forward still we press
Through moors, briar-meshed plantations, clay-pits yellow,
　　As in the spring hours—yes,
Three of us: fair He, fair She, I, as heretofore,
　　But—fallen one more.

The leaf drops: earthworms draw it in
　　At night-time noiselessly,
The fingers of birch and beech are skeleton-thin,
　　And yet on the beat are we,—
Two of us; fair She, I. But no more left to go
　　The track we know.

Icicles tag the church-aisle leads,
　　The flag-rope gibbers hoarse,
The home-bound foot-folk wrap their snow-flaked heads,
　　Yet I still stalk the course—
One of us. . . . Dark and fair He, dark and fair She, gone.
　　The rest—anon.　　　　　　*1917*

DURING WIND AND RAIN

They sing their dearest songs—
　　He, she, all of them—yea,
Treble and tenor and bass,
　　And one to play;
With the candles mooning each face. . . .
　　Ah, no; the years O!
How the sick leaves reel down in throngs!

They clear the creeping moss—
　　Elders and juniors—aye,
Making the pathways neat
　　And the garden gay;

And they build a shady seat. . . .
    Ah, no; the years, the years;
See, the white storm-birds wing across!

    They are blithely breakfasting all—
    Men and maidens—yea,
    Under the summer tree,
      With a glimpse of the bay,
    While pet fowl come to the knee. . . .
    Ah, no; the years O!
And the rotten rose is ript from the wall.

    They change to a high new house,
    He, she, all of them—aye,
    Clocks and carpets and chairs
      On the lawn all day,
    And brightest things that are theirs. . . .
    Ah, no; the years, the years;
Down their carved names the rain-drop ploughs.

1917

"FOR LIFE I HAD NEVER CARED GREATLY"

For Life I had never cared greatly,
    As worth a man's while;
    Peradventures unsought,
    Peradventures that finished in nought,
Had kept me from youth and through manhood till lately
    Unwon by its style.

In earliest years—why I know not—
    I viewed it askance;
    Conditions of doubt,
    Conditions that leaked slowly out,
May haply have bent me to stand and to show not
    Much zest for its dance.

With symphonies soft and sweet colour
    It courted me then,
    Till evasions seemed wrong,
    Till evasions gave in to its song,
And I warmed, until living aloofly loomed duller
    Than life among men.

Anew I found nought to set eyes on,
　　When, lifting its hand,
　　It uncloaked a star,
Uncloaked it from fog-damps afar,
And showed its beams burning from pole to horizon
　　As bright as a brand.

And so, the rough highway forgetting,
　　I pace hill and dale
　　Regarding the sky,
　　Regarding the vision on high,
And thus re-illumed have no humour for letting
　　My pilgrimage fail.　　　　　　　　*1917*

THE PITY OF IT

I walked in loamy Wessex lanes, afar
From rail-track and from highway, and I heard
In field and farmstead many an ancient word
Of local lineage like "Thu bist," "Er war,"
"Ich woll," "Er sholl," and by-talk similar,
Nigh as they speak who in this month's moon gird
At England's very loins, thereunto spurred
By gangs whose glory threats and slaughters are.

Then seemed a Heart crying: "Whosoever they be
At root and bottom of this, who flung this flame
Between kin folk kin tongued even as are we,

"Sinister, ugly, lurid, be their fame;
May their familiars grow to shun their name,
And their brood perish everlastingly."
　　　　　　　　　　　　April 1915, 1917

IN TIME OF "THE BREAKING OF NATIONS"

(JEREMIAH li, 20)

Only a man harrowing clods
　　In a slow silent walk
With an old horse that stumbles and nods
　　Half asleep as they stalk.

Only thin smoke without flame
From the heaps of couch-grass;
Yet this will go onward the same
Though Dynasties pass.

Yonder a maid and her wight
Come whispering by:
War's annals will fade into night
Ere their story die.   *1915, 1917*

AFTERWARDS

When the Present has latched its postern behind my tremulous stay,
And the May month flaps its glad green leaves like wings,
Delicate-filmed as new-spun silk, will the neighbours say,
"He was a man who used to notice such things"?

If it be in the dusk when, like an eyelid's soundless blink,
The dewfall-hawk comes crossing the shades to alight
Upon the wind-warped upland thorn, a gazer may think,
"To him this must have been a familiar sight."

If I pass during some nocturnal blackness, mothy and warm,
When the hedgehog travels furtively over the lawn,
One may say, "He strove that such innocent creatures should come to
no harm,
But he could do little for them; and now he is gone."

If, when hearing that I have been stilled at last, they stand at the door,
Watching the full-starred heavens that winter sees,
Will this thought rise on those who will meet my face no more,
"He was one who had an eye for such mysteries"?

And will any say when my bell of quittance is heard in the gloom,
And a crossing breeze cuts a pause in its outrollings,
Till they rise again, as they were a new bell's boom,
"He hears it not now, but used to notice such things"?   *1917*

"THE CURTAINS NOW ARE DRAWN"

(SONG)

The curtains now are drawn,
And the spindrift strikes the glass,

Blown up the jaggèd pass
By the surly salt sou'-west,
And the sneering glare is gone
Behind the yonder crest,
    While she sings to me:
"O the dream that thou art my Love, be it thine,
And the dream that I am thy Love, be it mine,
And death may come, but loving is divine."

I stand here in the rain,
With its smite upon her stone,
And the grasses that have grown
Over women, children, men,
And their texts that "Life is vain";
But I hear the notes as when
    Once she sang to me:
"O the dream that thou art my Love, be it thine,
And the dream that I am thy Love, be it mine,
And death may come, but loving is divine."

                                        1913, 1922

"ACCORDING TO THE MIGHTY WORKING"

When moiling seems at cease
    In the vague void of night-time,
    And heaven's wide roomage stormless
    Between the dusk and light-time,
    And fear at last is formless,
We call the allurement Peace.

Peace, this hid riot, Change,
    This revel of quick-cued mumming,
    This never truly being,
    This evermore becoming,
    This spinner's wheel onfleeing
Outside perception's range.   *1917, 1922*

GOING AND STAYING

The moving sun-shapes on the spray,
The sparkles where the brook was flowing,
Pink faces, plightings, moonlit May,
These were the things we wished would stay;
    But they were going.

Seasons of blankness as of snow,
The silent bleed of a world decaying,
The moan of multitudes in woe,
These were the things we wished would go;
     But they were staying.

Then we looked closelier at Time,
And saw his ghostly arms revolving
To sweep off woeful things with prime,
Things sinister with things sublime
     Alike dissolving.   1922

THE CONTRETEMPS

A forward rush by the lamp in the gloom,
    And we clasped, and almost kissed;
But she was not the woman whom
I had promised to meet in the thawing brume
On that harbour-bridge; nor was I he of her tryst.

So loosening from me swift she said:
    "O why, why feign to be
The one I had meant!—to whom I have sped
To fly with, being so sorrily wed!"
—'Twas thus and thus that she upbraided me.

My assignation had struck upon
    Some others' like it, I found.
And her lover rose on the night anon;
And then her husband entered on
The lamplit, snowflaked, sloppiness around.

"Take her and welcome, man!" he cried:
    "I wash my hands of her.
I'll find me twice as good a bride!"
—All this to me, whom he had eyed,
Plainly, as his wife's planned deliverer.

And next the lover: "Little I knew,
    Madam, you had a third!
Kissing here in my very view!"
—Husband and lover then withdrew.
I let them; and I told them not they erred.

Why not? Well, there faced she and I—
    Two strangers who'd kissed, or near,
Chancewise. To see stand weeping by
A woman once embraced, will try
The tension of a man the most austere.

So it began; and I was young,
    She pretty, by the lamp,
As flakes came waltzing down among
    The waves of her clinging hair, that hung
Heavily on her temples, dark and damp.

And there alone still stood we two;
    She one cast off for me,
Or so it seemed: while night ondrew,
    Forcing a parley what should do
We twain hearts caught in one catastrophe.

In stranded souls a common strait
    Wakes latencies unknown,
Whose impulse may precipitate
    A life-long leap. The hour was late,
And there was the Jersey boat with its funnel agroan.

"Is wary walking worth much pother?"
    It grunted, as still it stayed.
"One pairing is as good as another
    Where all is venture! Take each other,
And scrap the oaths that you have aforetime made." . . .

—Of the four involved there walks but one
    On earth at this late day.
And what of the chapter so begun?
    In that odd complex what was done?
Well; happiness comes in full to none:
Let peace lie on lulled lips: I will not say.   *1922*

"AND THERE WAS A GREAT CALM"

(ON THE SIGNING OF THE ARMISTICE, NOV. 11, 1918)

There had been years of Passion—scorching, cold,
And much Despair, and Anger heaving high,

Care whitely watching, Sorrows manifold,
Among the young, among the weak and old,
And the pensive Spirit of Pity whispered, "Why?"

Men had not paused to answer. Foes distraught
Pierced the thinned peoples in a brute-like blindness,
Philosophies that sages long had taught,
And Selflessness, were as an unknown thought,
And "Hell!" and "Shell!" were yapped at Lovingkindness.

The feeble folk at home had grown full-used
To "dug-outs," "snipers," "Huns," from the war-adept
In the mornings heard, and at evetides perused;
To day-dreamt men in millions, when they mused—
To nightmare-men in millions when they slept.

Waking to wish existence timeless, null,
Sirius they watched above where armies fell;
He seemed to check his flapping when, in the lull
Of night a boom came thencewise, like the dull
Plunge of a stone dropped into some deep well.

So, when old hopes that earth was bettering slowly
Were dead and damned, there sounded "War is done!"
One morrow. Said the bereft, and meek, and lowly,
"Will men some day be given to grace? yea, wholly,
And in good sooth, as our dreams used to run?"

Breathless they paused. Out there men raised their glance
To where had stood those poplars lank and lopped,
As they had raised it through the four years' dance
Of Death in the now familiar flats of France;
And murmured, "Strange, this! How? All firing stopped?"

Aye; all was hushed. The about-to-fire fired not,
The aimed-at moved away in trance-lipped song.
One checkless regiment slung a clinching shot
And turned. The Spirit of Irony smirked out, "What?
Spoil peradventures woven of Rage and Wrong?"

Thenceforth no flying fires inflamed the gray,
No hurtlings shook the dewdrop from the thorn,
No moan perplexed the mute bird on the spray;

Worn horses mused: "We are not whipped to-day";
No weft-winged engines blurred the moon's thin horn.

Calm fell. From Heaven distilled a clemency;
There was peace on earth, and silence in the sky;
Some could, some could not, shake off misery:
The Sinister Spirit sneered: "It had to be!"
And again the Spirit of Pity whispered, "Why?"   *1922*

THE FALLOW DEER AT THE LONELY HOUSE

One without looks in to-night
    Through the curtain-chink
From the sheet of glistening white;
One without looks in to-night
    As we sit and think
    By the fender-brink.

We do not discern those eyes
    Watching in the snow;
Lit by lamps of rosy dyes
We do not discern those eyes
    Wondering, aglow,
    Fourfooted, tiptoe.   *1922*

THE SELFSAME SONG

A bird sings the selfsame song,
With never a fault in its flow,
That we listened to here those long
    Long years ago.

A pleasing marvel is how
A strain of such rapturous rote
Should have gone on thus till now
    Unchanged in a note!

—But it's not the selfsame bird.—
No: perished to dust is he. . . .
As also are those who heard
    That song with me.

1922

FIRST OR LAST

(SONG)

If grief come early
Joy comes late,
If joy come early
Grief will wait;
    Aye, my dear and tender!

Wise ones joy them early
While the cheeks are red,
Banish grief till surly
Time has dulled their dread.

    And joy being ours
    Ere youth has flown,
    The later hours
    May find us gone;
        Aye, my dear and tender!

1922

A DRIZZLING EASTER MORNING

And he is risen? Well, be it so. . . .
And still the pensive lands complain,
And dead men wait as long ago,
As if, much doubting, they would know
What they are ransomed from, before
They pass again their sheltering door.

I stand amid them in the rain,
While blusters vex the yew and vane;
And on the road the weary wain
Plods forward, laden heavily;
And toilers with their aches are fain
For endless rest—though risen is he.

1922

AN ANCIENT TO ANCIENTS

Where once we danced, where once we sang,
        Gentlemen,
The floors are sunken, cobwebs hang,
And cracks creep; worms have fed upon

The doors. Yea, sprightlier times were then
Than now, with harps and tabrets gone,
        Gentlemen!

Where once we rowed, where once we sailed,
        Gentlemen,
And damsels took the tiller, veiled
Against too strong a stare (God wot
Their fancy, then or anywhen!)
Upon that shore we are clean forgot,
        Gentlemen!

We have lost somewhat, afar and near,
        Gentlemen,
The thinning of our ranks each year
Affords a hint we are nigh undone,
That we shall not be ever again
The marked of many, loved of one,
        Gentlemen.

In dance the polka hit our wish,
        Gentlemen,
The paced quadrille, the spry schottische,
"Sir Roger."—And in opera spheres
The "Girl" (the famed "Bohemian"),
And "Trovatore," held the ears,
        Gentlemen.

This season's paintings do not please,
        Gentlemen,
Like Etty, Mulready, Maclise;
Throbbing romance has waned and wanned;
No wizard wields the witching pen
Of Bulwer, Scott, Dumas, and Sand,
        Gentlemen.

The bower we shrined to Tennyson,
        Gentlemen,
Is roof-wrecked; damps there drip upon
Sagged seats, the creeper-nails are rust,
The spider is sole denizen;
Even she who voiced those rhymes is dust,
        Gentlemen!

We who met sunrise sanguine-souled,
> Gentlemen,
Are wearing weary. We are old;
These younger press; we feel our rout
Is imminent to Aïdes' den,—
That evening shades are stretching out,
> Gentlemen!

And yet, though ours be failing frames,
> Gentlemen,
So were some others' history names,
Who trode their track light-limbed and fast
As these youth, and not alien
From enterprise, to their long last.
> Gentlemen.

Sophocles, Plato, Socrates,
> Gentlemen,
Pythagoras, Thucydides,
Herodotus, and Homer,—yea,
Clement, Augustin, Origen,
Burnt brightlier towards their setting-day,
> Gentlemen.

And ye, red-lipped and smooth-browed; list,
> Gentlemen;
Much is there waits you we have missed;
Much lore we leave you worth the knowing,
Much, much has lain outside our ken:
Nay, rush not: time serves: we are going,
> Gentlemen.   *1922*

SNOW IN THE SUBURBS

Every branch big with it,
> Bent every twig with it;
Every fork like a white web-foot;
Every street and pavement mute:
Some flakes have lost their way, and grope back upward, when
Meeting those meandering down they turn and descend again.
> The palings are glued together like a wall,
And there is no waft of wind with the fleecy fall.

A sparrow enters the tree,
    Whereon immediately
A snow-lump thrice his own slight size
Descends on him and showers his head and eyes,
        And overturns him,
        And near inurns him,
And lights on a nether twig, when its brush
Starts off a volley of other lodging lumps with a rush.

    The steps are a blanched slope,
    Up which, with feeble hope,
A black cat comes, wide-eyed and thin;
            And we take him in.   *1925*

ON THE PORTRAIT OF A WOMAN
ABOUT TO BE HANGED

Comely and capable one of our race,
Posing there in your gown of grace,
        Plain, yet becoming;
            Could subtlest breast
            Ever have guessed
What was behind that innocent face,
            Drumming, drumming!

Would that your Causer, ere knoll your knell
For this riot of passion, might deign to tell
        Why, since It made you
            Sound in the germ,
            It sent a worm
To madden Its handiwork, when It might well
        Not have assayed you,

Not have implanted, to your deep rue,
The Clytæmnestra spirit in you,
        And with purblind vision
            Sowed a tare
            In a field so fair,
And a thing of symmetry, seemly to view,
        Brought to derision!
                        January 6, 1923, 1925

Gerard Manley Hopkins

THE SUMMER MALISON

Maidens shall weep at merry morn,
And hedges break and lose the kine,
And field-flowers make the fields forlorn,
And noonday have a shallow shine,
And barley turn to weed and wild,
And seven ears crown the lodged corn,
And mother have no milk for child,
    And father be overworn.

And John shall lie, where winds are dead,
And hate the ill-visaged cursing tars,
And James shall hate his faded red,
Grown wicked in the wicked wars.
No rains shall fresh the flats of sea,
Nor close the clayfields' sharded sores,
And every heart think loathingly
    Its dearest changed to bores.

1865, 1930

WINTER WITH THE GULF STREAM

The boughs, the boughs are bare enough
But earth has never felt the snow.
Frost-furred our ivies are and rough

With bills of rime the brambles shew.
The hoarse leaves crawl on hissing ground
Because the sighing wind is low.

But if the rain-blasts be unbound
And from dank feathers wring the drops
The clogged brook runs with choking sound

Kneading the mounded mire that stops
His channel under clammy coats
Of foliage fallen in the copse.

A simple passage of weak notes
Is all the winter bird dare try.
The bugle moon by daylight floats

So glassy white about the sky,
So like a berg of hyaline,
And pencilled blue so daintily,

I never saw her so divine.
But through black branches, rarely drest
In scarves of silky shot and shine,

The webbed and the watery west
Where yonder crimson fireball sits
Looks laid for feasting and for rest.

I see long reefs of violets
In beryl-covered fens so dim,
A gold-water Pactolus frets

Its brindled wharves and yellow brim,
The waxen colours weep and run,
And slendering to his burning rim

Into the flat blue mist the sun
Drops out and all our day is done.

1871, 1918

THE WRECK OF THE DEUTSCHLAND

*To the happy memory of five Franciscan Nuns, exiles by the Falk Laws,
drowned between midnight and morning of Dec. 7th, 1875.*

PART THE FIRST

Thou mastering me
God! giver of breath and bread;
World's strand, sway of the sea;
Lord of living and dead;
Thou hast bound bones and veins in me, fastened me flesh,

And after it almost unmade, what with dread,
　　Thy doing: and dost thou touch me afresh?
Over again I feel thy finger and find thee.

　　　　　I did say yes
　　　　O at lightning and lashed rod;
　　Thou heardst me truer than tongue confess
　　　　Thy terror, O Christ, O God;
　　Thou knowest the walls, altar and hour and night:
　　The swoon of a heart that the sweep and the hurl of thee trod
　　　　Hard down with a horror of height:
And the midriff astrain with leaning of, laced with fire of stress.

　　　　The frown of his face
　　　　Before me, the hurtle of hell
　　Behind, where, where was a, where was a place?
　　　　I whirled out wings that spell
　　And fled with a fling of the heart to the heart of the Host.
　　My heart, but you were dovewinged, I can tell,
　　　　Carrier-witted, I am bold to boast,
To flash from the flame to the flame then, tower from the grace to the
　　grace.

　　　　I am soft sift
　　　　In an hourglass—at the wall
　　Fast, but mined with a motion, a drift,
　　　　And it crowds and it combs to the fall;
　　I steady as a water in a well, to a poise, to a pane,
　　But roped with, always, all the way down from the tall
　　　　Fells or flanks of the voel, a vein
Of the gospel proffer, a pressure, a principle, Christ's gift.

　　　　I kiss my hand
　　　　To the stars, lovely-asunder
　　Starlight, wafting him out of it; and
　　　　Glow, glory in thunder;
　　Kiss my hand to the dappled-with-damson west:
　　Since, tho' he is under the world's splendour and wonder,
　　　　His mystery must be instressed, stressed;
For I greet him the days I meet him, and bless when I understand.

　　　　Not out of his bliss
　　　　Springs the stress felt

Nor first from heaven (and few know this)
    Swings the stroke dealt—
Stroke and a stress that stars and storms deliver,
    That guilt is hushed by, hearts are flushed by and melt—
      But it rides time like riding a river
(And here the faithful waver, the faithless fable and miss).

      It dates from day
    Of his going in Galilee;
   Warm-laid grave of a womb-life grey;
      Manger, maiden's knee;
The dense and the driven Passion, and frightful sweat;
   Thence the discharge of it, there its swelling to be,
      Though felt before, though in high flood yet—
What none would have known of it, only the heart, being hard at bay,

      Is out with it! Oh,
    We lash with the best or worst
  Word last! How a lush-kept plush-capped sloe
      Will, mouthed to flesh-burst,
Gush!—flush the man, the being with it, sour or sweet,
  Brim, in a flash, full!—Hither then, last or first,
      To hero of Calvary, Christ, 's feet—
Never ask if meaning it, wanting it, warned of it—men go.

      Be adored among men,
    God, three-numberèd form;
  Wring thy rebel, dogged in den,
      Man's malice, with wrecking and storm.
Beyond saying sweet, past telling of tongue,
  Thou art lightning and love, I found it, a winter and warm;
      Father and fondler of heart thou hast wrung:
Hast thy dark descending and most art merciful then.

      With an anvil-ding
    And with fire in him forge thy will
  Or rather, rather then, stealing as Spring
      Through him, melt him but master him still:
Whether at once, as once at a crash Paul,
  Or as Austin, a lingering-out swéet skíll,
      Make mercy in all of us, out of us all
Mastery, but be adored, but be adored King.

PART THE SECOND

"Some find me a sword; some
    The flange and the rail; flame,
Fang, or flood" goes Death on drum,
    And storms bugle his fame.
But wé dream we are rooted in earth—Dust!
Flesh falls within sight of us, we, though our flower the same,
    Wave with the meadow, forget that there must
The sour scythe cringe, and the blear share come.

On Saturday sailed from Bremen,
    American-outward-bound,
Take settler and seamen, tell men with women,
    Two hundred souls in the round—
O Father, not under thy feathers nor ever as guessing
The goal was a shoal, of a fourth the doom to be drowned;
    Yet did the dark side of the bay of thy blessing
Not vault them, the millions of rounds of thy mercy not reeve even
    them in?

Into the snows she sweeps,
    Hurling the haven behind,
The Deutschland, on Sunday; and so the sky keeps,
    For the infinite air is unkind,
And the sea flint-flake, black-backed in the regular blow,
Sitting Eastnortheast, in cursed quarter, the wind;
    Wiry and white-fiery and whirlwind-swivellèd snow
Spins to the widow-making unchilding unfathering deeps.

She drove in the dark to leeward,
    She struck—not a reef or a rock
But the combs of a smother of sand: night drew her
    Dead to the Kentish Knock;
And she beat the bank down with her bows and the ride of her
    keel:
The breakers rolled on her beam with ruinous shock;
    And canvas and compass, the whorl and the wheel
Idle for ever to waft her or wind her with, these she endured.

Hope had grown grey hairs,
    Hope had mourning on,
Trenched with tears, carved with cares,

Hope was twelve hours gone;
And frightful a nightfall folded rueful a day
Nor rescue, only rocket and lightship, shone,
And lives at last were washing away:
To the shrouds they took,—they shook in the hurling and horrible airs

One stirred from the rigging to save
The wild woman-kind below,
With a rope's end round the man, handy and brave—
He was pitched to his death at a blow,
For all his dreadnought breast and braids of thew:
They could tell him for hours, dandled the to and fro
Through the cobbled foam-fleece, what could he do
With the burl of the fountains of air, buck and the flood of the wave?

They fought with God's cold—
And they could not and fell to the deck
(Crushed them) or water (and drowned them) or rolled
With the sea-romp over the wreck.
Night roared, with the heart-break hearing a heart-broke rabble,
The woman's wailing, the crying of child without check—
Till a lioness arose breasting the babble,
A prophetess towered in the tumult, a virginal tongue told.

Ah, touched in your bower of bone
Are you! turned for an exquisite smart,
Have you! make words break from me here all alone,
Do you!—mother of being in me, heart.
O unteachably after evil, but uttering truth,
Why, tears! is it? tears; such a melting, a madrigal start!
Never-eldering revel and river of youth,
What can it be, this glee? the good you have there of your own?

Sister, a sister calling
A master, her master and mine!—
And the inboard seas run swirling and hawling;
The rash smart sloggering brine
Blinds her; but she that weather sees one thing, one;
Has one fetch in her: she rears herself to divine
Ears, and the call of the tall nun
To the men in the tops and the tackle rode over the storm's brawling.

She was first of a five and came
Of a coifèd sisterhood.

(O Deutschland, double a desperate name!
O world wide of its good!
But Gertrude, lily, and Luther, are two of a town,
Christ's lily and beast of the waste wood:
From life's dawn it is drawn down,
Abel is Cain's brother and breasts they have sucked the same.)

Loathed for a love men knew in them,
Banned by the land of their birth,
Rhine refused them. Thames would ruin them;
Surf, snow, river and earth
Gnashed: but thou art above, thou Orion of light;
Thy unchancelling poising palms were weighing the worth,
Thou martyr-master: in thy sight
Storm flakes were scroll-leaved flowers, lily showers—sweet heaven was
astrew in them.

Five! The finding and sake
And cipher of suffering Christ.
Mark, the mark is of man's make
And the word of it Sacrificed.
But he scores it in scarlet himself on his own bespoken,
Before-time-taken, dearest prizèd and priced—
Stigma, signal, cinquefoil token
For lettering of the lamb's fleece, ruddying of the rose-flake.

Joy fall to thee, father Francis,
Drawn to the Life that died;
With the gnarls of the nails in thee, niche of the lance, his
Lovescape crucified
And seal of his seraph-arrival! and these thy daughters
And five-livèd and leavèd favour and pride,
Are sisterly sealed in wild waters,
To bathe in his fall-gold mercies, to breathe in his all-fire glances.

Away in the loveable west,
On a pastoral forehead of Wales,
I was under a roof here, I was at rest,
And they the prey of the gales;
She to the black-about air, to the breaker, the thickly
Falling flakes, to the throng that catches and quails
Was calling "O Christ, Christ, come quickly":
The cross to her she calls Christ to her, christens her wild-worst Best.

The majesty! what did she mean?
Breathe, arch and original Breath.
Is it love in her of the being as her lover had been?
Breathe, body of lovely Death.
They were else-minded then, altogether, the men
Woke thee with a *we are perishing* in the weather of Gennesareth.
Or is it that she cried for the crown then,
The keener to come at the comfort for feeling the combating keen?

For how to the heart's cheering
The down-dugged ground-hugged grey
Hovers off, the jay-blue heavens appearing
Of pied and peeled May!
Blue-beating and hoary-glow height; or night, still higher,
With belled fire and the moth-soft Milky Way,
What by your measure is the heaven of desire,
The treasure never eyesight got, nor was ever guessed what for the
hearing?

No, but it was not these.
The jading and jar of the cart,
Time's tasking, it is fathers that asking for ease
Of the sodden-with-its-sorrowing heart,
Not danger, electrical horror; then further it finds
The appealing of the Passion is tenderer in prayer apart:
Other, I gather, in measure her mind's
Burden, in wind's burly and beat of endragonèd seas.

But how shall I . . . make me room there:
Reach me a . . . Fancy, come faster—
Strike you the sight of it? look at it loom there,
Thing that she . . . there then! the Master,
Ipse, the only one, Christ, King, Head:
He was to cure the extremity where he had cast her;
Do, deal, lord it with living and dead;
Let him ride, her pride, in his triumph, despatch and have done with
his doom there.

Ah! there was a heart right
There was single eye!
Read the unshapeable shock night
And knew the who and the why;
Wording it how but by him that present and past,

Heaven and earth are word of, worded by?—
　　The Simon Peter of a soul! to the blast
Tarpeian-fast, but a blown beacon of light.

　　　　Jesu, heart's light,
　　　　Jesu, maid's son,
　　What was the feast followed the night
　　　　Thou hadst glory of this nun?—
Feast of the one woman without stain.
For so conceivèd, so to conceive thee is done;
　　But here was heart-throe, birth of a brain,
Word, that heard and kept thee and uttered thee outright.

　　　　Well, she has thee for the pain, for the
　　　　Patience; but pity of the rest of them!
　　Heart, go and bleed at a bitterer vein for the
　　　　Comfortless unconfessed of them—
No not uncomforted: lovely-felicitous Providence
Finger of a tender of, O of a feathery delicacy, the breast of the
　　　　Maiden could obey so, be a bell to, ring of it, and
Startle the poor sheep back! is the shipwrack then a harvest, does tem-
　　pest carry the grain for thee?

　　　　I admire thee, master of the tides,
　　　　Of the Yore-flood, of the year's fall;
　　The recurb and the recovery of the gulf's sides,
　　　　The girth of it and the wharf of it and the wall;
Stanching, quenching ocean of a motionable mind;
Ground of being, and granite of it: past all
　　　　Grasp God, throned behind
Death with a sovereignty that heeds but hides, bodes but abides;

　　　　With a mercy that outrides
　　　　The all of water, an ark
　　For the listener; for the lingerer with a love glides
　　　　Lower than death and the dark;
A vein for the visiting of the past-prayer, pent in prison,
The-last-breath penitent spirits—the uttermost mark
　　　　Our passion-plungèd giant risen,
The Christ of the Father compassionate, fetched in the storm of his
　　strides.

　　　　Now burn, new born to the world,
　　　　Doubled-naturèd name,

The heaven-flung, heart-fleshed, maiden-furled
    Miracle-in-Mary-of-flame,
Mid-numbered He in three of the thunder-throne!
Not a dooms-day dazzle in his coming nor dark as he came;
    Kind, but royally reclaiming his own;
A released shower, let flash to the shire, not a lightning of fire hard-
    hurled.

    Dame, at our door
    Drowned, and among our shoals,
Remember us in the roads, the heaven-haven of the Reward:
    Our King back, oh, upon English souls!
Let him easter in us, be a dayspring to the dimness of us, be a
    crimson-cresseted east,
More brightening her, rare-dear Britain, as his reign rolls,
    Pride, rose, prince, hero of us, high-priest,
Our hearts' charity's hearth's fire, our thoughts' chivalry's throng's Lord.
                                      1875, 1918

GOD'S GRANDEUR

The world is charged with the grandeur of God.
    It will flame out, like shining from shook foil;
    It gathers to a greatness, like the ooze of oil
Crushed. Why do men then now not reck his rod?
Generations have trod, have trod, have trod;
    And all is seared with trade; bleared, smeared with toil;
    And wears man's smudge and shares man's smell: the soil
Is bare now, nor can foot feel, being shod.

And for all this, nature is never spent;
    There lives the dearest freshness deep down things;
And though the last lights off the black West went
    Oh, morning, at the brown brink eastward, springs—
Because the Holy Ghost over the bent
    World broods with warm breast and with ah! bright wings.
                                        1877, 1918

THE LANTERN OUT OF DOORS

Sometimes a lantern moves along the night,
    That interests our eyes. And who goes there?
    I think; where from and bound, I wonder, where,
With, all down darkness wide, his wading light?

Men go by me whom either beauty bright
  In mould or mind or what not else makes rare:
  They rain against our much-thick and marsh air
Rich beams, till death or distance buys them quite.

Death or distance soon consumes them: wind
  What most I may eye after, be in at the end
I cannot, and out of sight is out of mind.

Christ minds; Christ's interest, what to avow or amend
  There, éyes them, heart wánts, care haúnts, foot fóllows kínd,
  Their ránsom, théir rescue, ánd first, fást, last friénd. 1877, 1918

THE WINDHOVER:

TO CHRIST OUR LORD

I caught this morning morning's minion, king-
  dom of daylight's dauphin, dapple-dawn-drawn Falcon, in his riding
  Of the rolling level underneath him steady air, and striding
High there, how he rung upon the rein of a wimpling wing
In his ecstasy! then off, off forth on swing,
  As a skate's heel sweeps smooth on a bow-bend: the hurl and gliding
  Rebuffed the big wind. My heart in hiding
Stirred for a bird,—the achieve of, the mastery of the thing!

Brute beauty and valor and act, oh, air, pride, plume, here
  Buckle! AND the fire that breaks from thee then, a billion
Times told lovelier, more dangerous, O my chevalier!

No wonder of it: shéer plód makes plough down sillion
Shine, and blue-bleak embers, ah my dear,
  Fall, gall themselves, and gash gold-vermilion. 1877, 1918

PIED BEAUTY

Glory be to God for dappled things—
  For skies of couple-colour as a brinded cow;
    For rose-moles all in stipple upon trout that swim;
Fresh-firecoal chestnut-falls; finches' wings;
  Landscape plotted and pieced—fold, fallow, and plough;
    And áll trádes, their gear and tackle and trim.

All things counter, original, spare, strange;
  Whatever is fickle, freckled (who knows how?)
  With swift, slow; sweet, sour; adazzle, dim;
He fathers-forth whose beauty is past change:
          Praise him.   *1877, 1918*

HURRAHING IN HARVEST

Summer ends now; now, barbarous in beauty, the stooks arise
  Around; up above, what wind-walks! what lovely behaviour
  Of silk-sack clouds! has wilder, wilful-wavier
Meal-drift moulded ever and melted across skies?

I walk, I lift up, I lift up heart, eyes,
  Down all that glory in the heavens to glean our Saviour;
  And, éyes, heárt, what looks, what lips yet gave you a
Rapturous love's greeting of realer, of rounder replies?

And the azurous hung hills are his world-wielding shoulder
  Majestic—as a stallion stalwart, very-violet-sweet!—
These things, these things were here and but the beholder
  Wanting; which two when they once meet,
The heart rears wings bold and bolder
  And hurls for him, O half hurls earth for him off under his feet.
          1877, 1918

THE CAGED SKYLARK

As a dare-gale skylark scanted in a dull cage
  Man's mounting spirit in his bone-house, mean house, dwells—
  That bird beyond the remembering his free fells;
This in drudgery, day-labouring-out life's age.

Though aloft on turf or perch or poor low stage,
  Both sing sometímes the sweetest, sweetest spells,
  Yet both droop deadly sómetimes in their cells
Or wring their barriers in bursts of fear or rage.

Not that the sweet-fowl, song-fowl, needs no rest—
Why, hear him, hear him babble and drop down to his nest,
  But his own nest, wild nest, no prison.

Man's spirit will be flesh-bound when found at best,
But uncumbered: meadow-down is not distressed
  For a rainbow footing it nor he for his bónes rísen.   *1877, 1918*

SPRING AND FALL: to a young child

Márgarét, are you gríeving
Over Goldengrove unleaving?
Léaves, líke the things of man, you
With your fresh thoughts care for, can you?
Áh! ás the heart grows older
It will come to such sights colder
By and by, nor spare a sigh
Though worlds of wanwood leafmeal lie;
And yet you wíll weep and know why.
Now no matter, child, the name:
Sórrow's spríngs áre the same.
Nor mouth had, no nor mind, expressed
What heart heard of, ghost guessed:
It is the blight man was born for,
It is Margaret you mourn for.   *1880, 1918*

SPELT FROM SIBYL'S LEAVES

Earnest, earthless, equal attuneable, ǀ vaulty, voluminous, . . stupendous
Evening strains to be tíme's vást, ǀ womb-of-all, home-of-all, hearse-of-
all night.
Her fond yellow hornlight wound to the west, ǀ her wild hollow hoar-
light hung to the height
Waste; her earliest stars, earl-stars, ǀ stárs principal, overbend us,
Fíre-féaturing heaven. For earth ǀ her being has unbound, her dapple
is at an end, as-
tray or aswarm, all throughther, in throngs; ǀ self ín self steepèd and
páshed—qúite
Disremembering, dísmémbering ǀ áll now. Heart, you round me right
With: Óur évening is over us; óur night ǀ whélms, whélms, ánd will
end us.
Only the beak-leaved boughs dragonish ǀ damask the tool-smooth bleak
light; black,
Ever so black on it. Óur tale, O óur oracle! ǀ Lét life, wáned, ah lét life
wind
Off hér once skéined stained véined varíety ǀ upon, áll on twó spools;
párt, pen, páck
Now her áll in twó flocks, twó folds--black, white; ǀ right, wrong;
reckon but, reck but, mind
But thése two; wáre of a wórld where bút these ǀ twó tell, each off the
óther; of a rack

Where, selfwrung selfstrung, sheathe-andshelterless | thóughts agaínst
    thoughts ín groans grínd.   *1918*

INVERSNAID

This darksome burn, horseback brown,
His rollrock highroad roaring down,
In coop and in comb the fleece of his foam
Flutes and low to the lake falls home.

A windpuff-bonnet of fáwn-fróth
Turns and twindles over the broth
Of a pool so pitchblack, féll-frówning,
It rounds and rounds Despair to drowning.

Degged with dew, dappled with dew
Are the groins of the braes that the brook treads through,
Wiry heathpacks, flitches of fern,
And the beadbonny ash that sits over the burn.

What would the world be, once bereft
Of wet and of wildness? Let them be left,
O let them be left, wildness and wet;
Long live the weeds and the wilderness yet.   *1881, 1918*

[AS KINGFISHERS CATCH FIRE]

As kingfishers catch fire, dragonflies dráw fláme;
As tumbled over rim in roundy wells
Stones ring; like each tucked string tells, each hung bell's
Bow swung finds tongue to fling out broad its name;
Each mortal thing does one thing and the same:
Deals out that being indoors each one dwells;
Selves—goes itself; *myself* it speaks and spells;
Crying *Whát I dó is me: for that I came.*

Í say móre: the just man justices;
Kéeps gráce: thát keeps all his goings graces;
Acts in God's eye what in God's eye he is—
Chríst—for Christ plays in ten thousand places,
Lovely in limbs, and lovely in eyes not his
To the Father through the features of men's faces.

                                              1882, 1918

THE LEADEN ECHO AND THE GOLDEN ECHO

(MAIDENS' SONG FROM ST. WINEFRED'S WELL)

THE LEADEN ECHO

How to kéep—is there ány any, is there none such, nowhere known
   some, bow or brooch or braid or brace, láce, latch or catch or key
   to keep
Back beauty, keep it, beauty, beauty, beauty, . . . from vanishing
   away?
Ó is there no frowning of these wrinkles, rankèd wrinkles deep,
Dówn? no waving off of these most mournful messengers, still mes-
   sengers, sad and stealing messengers of grey?
No there's none, there's none, O no there's none,
Nor can you long be, what you now are, called fair,
Do what you may do, what, do what you may,
And wisdom is early to despair:
Be beginning; since, no, nothing can be done
To keep at bay
Age and age's evils, hoar hair,
Ruck and wrinkle, drooping, dying, death's worst, winding sheets,
   tombs and worms and tumbling to decay;
So be beginning, be beginning to despair.
O there's none; no no no there's none:
Be beginning to despair, to despair,
Despair, despair, despair, despair.

THE GOLDEN ECHO

     Spare!
There ís one, yes I have one (Hush there!);
Only not within seeing of the sun,
Not within the singeing of the strong sun,
  Tall sun's tingeing, or treacherous the tainting of the earth's air,
Somewhere elsewhere there is ah well where! one,
Óne. Yes I cán tell such a key, I dó know such a place,
Where whatever's prized and passes of us, everything that's fresh and
   fast flying of us, seems to us sweet of us and swiftly away with,
   done away with, undone,
Úndone, done with, soon done with, and yet dearly and dangerously
   sweet
Of us, the wimpled-water-dimpled, not-by-morning-matchèd face,
  The flower of beauty, fleece of beauty, too too apt to, ah! to fleet,

Never fleets móre, fastened with the tenderest truth
To its own best being and its loveliness of youth: it is an everlastingness
    of, O it is an all youth!
Come then, your ways and airs and looks, locks, maiden gear, gallantry
    and gaiety and grace,
Winning ways, airs innocent, maiden manners, sweet looks, loose locks,
    long locks, lovelocks, gaygear, going gallant, girlgrace—
Resign them, sign them, seal them, send them, motion them with breath,
And with sighs soaring, soaring síghs deliver
Them; beauty-in-the-ghost, deliver it, early now, long before death
Give beauty back, beauty, beauty, beauty, back to God, beauty's self
    and beauty's giver.
See; not a hair is, not an eyelash, not the least lash lost; every hair
Is, hair of the head, numbered.
Nay, what we had lighthanded left in surly the mere mould
Will have waked and have waxed and have walked with the wind what
    while we slept,
This side, that side hurling a heavyheaded hundredfold
What while we, while we slumbered.
O then, weary then whý should we tread? O why are we so haggard at
    the heart, so care-coiled, care-killed, so fagged, so fashed, so cogged,
    so cumbered,
When the thing we freely fórfeit is kept with fonder a care,
Fonder a care kept than we could have kept it, kept
Far with fonder a care (and we, we should have lost it) finer, fonder
A care kept.—Where kept? Do but tell us where kept, where.—
Yonder.—What high as that! We follow, now we follow.—Yonder, yes
    yonder, yonder,
Yonder.   *1882, 1918*

[NO WORST, THERE IS NONE]

No worst, there is none. Pitched past pitch of grief,
More pangs will, schooled at forepangs, wilder wring.
Comforter, where, where is your comforting?
Mary, mother of us, where is your relief?
My cries heave, herds-long; huddle in a main, a chief
Woe, world-sorrow; on an age-old anvil wince and sing—
Then lull, then leave off. Fury had shrieked "No ling-
ering! Let me be fell: force I must be brief."

        O the mind, mind has mountains; cliffs of fall
Frightful, sheer, no-man-fathomed. Hold them cheap

May who ne'er hung there. Nor does long our small
Durance deal with that steep or deep. Here! creep,
Wretch, under a comfort serves in a whirlwind: all
Life death does end and each day dies with sleep.   *1918*

[NOT, I'LL NOT, CARRION COMFORT]

Not, I'll not, carrion comfort, Despair, not feast on thee;
Not untwist—slack they may be—these last strands of man
In me ór, most weary, cry *I can no more.* I can;
Can something, hope, wish day come, not choose not to be.
But ah, but O thou terrible, why wouldst thou rude on me
Thy wring-world right foot rock? lay a lionlimb against me? scan
With darksome devouring eyes my bruisèd bones? and fan,
O in turns of tempest, me heaped there; me frantic to avoid thee and
    flee?

Why? That my chaff might fly; my grain lie, sheer and clear.
Nay in all that toil, that coil, since (seems) I kissed the rod,
Hand rather, my heart lo! lapped strength, stole joy, would laugh, chéer.
Cheer whom though? the hero whose heaven-handling flung me, fóot
    tród
Me? or me that fought him? O which one? is it each one? That night,
    that year
Of now done darkness I wretch lay wrestling with (my God!) my God.
                                                    1885–87, 1918

[I WAKE AND FEEL THE FELL OF DARK]

I wake and feel the fell of dark, not day.
What hours, O what black hoürs we have spent
This night! what sights you, heart, saw; ways you went!
And more must, in yet longer light's delay.
    With witness I speak this. But where I say
Hours I mean years, mean life. And my lament
Is cries countless, cries like dead letters sent
To dearest him that lives alas! away.

    I am gall, I am heartburn. God's most deep decree
Bitter would have me taste: my taste was me;
Bones built in me, flesh filled, blood brimmed the curse.
    Selfyeast of spirit a dull dough sours. I see

The lost are like this, and their scourge to be
As I am mine, their sweating selves; but worse.

c. 1885, 1918

[THOU ART INDEED JUST, LORD]

*Justus quidem tu es, Domine, si disputem tecum: verumtamen justa loquar
ad te: Quare via impiorum prosperatur? &c.*

Thou are indeed just, Lord, if I contend
With thee; but, sir, so what I plead is just.
Why do sinners' ways prosper? and why must
Disappointment all I endeavor end?
    Wert thou my enemy, O thou my friend,
How wouldst thou worse, I wonder, than thou dost
Defeat, thwart me? Oh, the sots and thralls of lust
Do in spare hours more thrive than I that spend,
Sir, life upon thy cause. See, banks and brakes
Now, leavèd how thick! lacèd they are again
With fretty chervil, look, and fresh wind shakes
Them; birds build—but not I build; no, but strain,
Time's eunuch, and not breed one work that wakes.
Mine, O thou lord of life, send my roots rain.

1889, 1918

TO R. B.

The fine delight that fathers thought; the strong
Spur, live and lancing like the blowpipe flame,
Breathes once and, quenchèd faster than it came,
Leaves yet the mind a mother of immortal song.
Nine months she then, nay years, nine years she long
Within her wears, bears, cares and combs the same:
The widow of an insight lost she lives, with aim
Now known and hand at work now never wrong.
    Sweet fire the sire of muse, my soul needs this;
I want the one rapture of an inspiration.
O then if in my lagging lines you miss
The roll, the rise, the carol, the creation,
My winter world, that scarcely breathes that bliss
Now, yields you, with some sighs, our explanation.

1889, 1918

Robert Bridges

ELEGY

The wood is bare: a river-mist is steeping
   The trees that winter's chill of life bereaves:
Only their stiffened boughs break silence, weeping
      Over their fallen leaves;

That lie upon the dank earth brown and rotten,
   Miry and matted in the soaking wet:
Forgotten with the spring, that is forgotten
      By them that can forget.

Yet it was here we walked when ferns were springing,
   And through the mossy bank shot bud and blade:—
Here found in summer, when the birds were singing,
      A green and pleasant shade.

'Twas here we loved in sunnier days and greener;
   And now, in this disconsolate decay,
I come to see her where I most have seen her,
      And touch the happier day.

For on this path, at every turn and corner,
   The fancy of her figure on me falls:
Yet walks she with the slow step of a mourner,
      Nor hears my voice that calls.

So through my heart there winds a track of feeling,
   A path of memory, that is all her own:
Whereto her phantom beauty ever stealing
      Haunts the sad spot alone.

About her steps the trunks are bare, the branches
   Drip heavy tears upon her downcast head;
And bleed from unseen wounds that no sun stanches,
      For the year's sun is dead.

And dead leaves wrap the fruits that summer planted:
And birds that love the South have taken wing.
The wanderer, loitering o'er the scene enchanted,
    Weeps, and despairs of spring.   *1873*

[I WILL NOT LET THEE GO]

I will not let thee go.
Ends all our month-long love in this?
   Can it be summed up so,
   Quit in a single kiss?
I will not let thee go.

I will not let thee go.
If thy words' breath could scare thy deeds,
   As the soft south can blow
   And toss the feathered seeds,
Then might I let thee go.

I will not let thee go.
Had not the great sun seen, I might;
   Or were he reckoned slow
   To bring the false to light,
Then might I let thee go.

I will not let thee go.
The stars that crowd the summer skies
   Have watched us so below
   With all their million eyes,
I dare not let thee go.

I will not let thee go.
Have we not chid the changeful moon,
   Now rising late, and now
   Because she set too soon,
And shall I let thee go?

I will not let thee go.
Have not the young flowers been content,
   Plucked ere their buds could blow,
   To seal our sacrament?
I cannot let thee go.

I will not let thee go.
I hold thee by too many bands:
Thou sayest farewell, and lo!
I have thee by the hands,
And will not let thee go.   *1873*

[O WEARY PILGRIMS, CHANTING OF YOUR WOE]

O weary pilgrims, chanting of your woe,
That turn your eyes to all the peaks that shine,
Hailing in each the citadel divine
The which ye thought to have enter'd long ago;
Until at length your feeble steps and slow
Falter upon the threshold of the shrine,
And your hearts overburden'd doubt in fine
Whether it be Jerusalem or no:

Disheartened pilgrims, I am one of you;
For, having worshipp'd many a barren face,
I scarce now greet the goal I journeyed to:
I stand a pagan in the holy place;
Beneath the lamp of truth I am found untrue,
And question with the God that I embrace.
          1876

A PASSER-BY

Whither, O splendid ship, thy white sails crowding,
    Leaning across the bosom of the urgent West,
That fearest nor sea rising, nor sky clouding,
    Whither away, fair rover, and what thy quest?
    Ah! soon, when Winter has all our vales opprest,
When skies are cold and misty, and hail is hurling,
    Wilt thou glide on the blue Pacific, or rest
In a summer haven asleep, thy white sails furling.

I there before thee, in the country that well thou knowest,
    Already arrived am inhaling the odorous air:
I watch thee enter unerringly where thou goest,
    And anchor queen of the strange shipping there,
    Thy sails for awnings spread, thy masts bare;
Nor is aught from the foaming reef to the snow-capped, grandest
    Peak, that is over the feathery palms more fair
Than thou, so upright, so stately, and still thou standest.

And yet, O splendid ship, unhailed and nameless,
    I know not if, aiming a fancy, I rightly divine
That thou has a purpose joyful, a courage blameless,
    Thy port assured in a happier land than mine.
    But for all I have given thee, beauty enough is thine,
As thou, aslant with trim tackle and shrouding,
    From the proud nostril curve of a prow's line
In the offing scatterest foam, thy white sails crowding.   *1879*

LONDON SNOW

When men were all asleep the snow came flying,
In large white flakes falling on the city brown,
Stealthily and perpetually settling and loosely lying,
    Hushing the latest traffic of the drowsy town;
Deadening, muffling, stifling its murmurs failing;
Lazily and incessantly floating down and down:
    Silently sifting and veiling road, roof and railing;
Hiding difference, making unevenness even,
Into angles and crevices softly drifting and sailing.
    All night it fell, and when full inches seven
It lay in the depth of its uncompacted lightness,
The clouds blew off from a high and frosty heaven;
    And all woke earlier for the unaccustomed brightness
Of the winter dawning, the strange unheavenly glare:
The eye marvelled—marvelled at the dazzling whiteness;
    The ear hearkened to the stillness of the solemn air;
No sound of wheel rumbling nor of foot falling,
And the busy morning cries came thin and spare.
    Then boys I heard, as they went to school, calling,
They gathered up the crystal manna to freeze
Their tongues with tasting, their hands with snowballing;
    Or rioted in a drift, plunging up to the knees;
Or peering up from under the white-mossed wonder,
"O look at the trees!" they cried, "O look at the trees!"
    With lessened load a few carts creak and blunder,
Following along the white deserted way,
A country company long dispersed asunder:
    When now already the sun, in pale display
Standing by Paul's high dome, spread forth below
His sparkling beams, and awoke the stir of the day.
    For now doors open, and war is waged with the snow;
And trains of somber men, past tale of number

Tread long brown paths, as toward their toil they go:
  But even for them awhile no cares encumber
Their minds diverted; the daily word is unspoken,
The daily thoughts of labour and sorrow slumber
At the sight of the beauty that greets them, for the charm they have
    broken.   *1880*

ON A DEAD CHILD

Perfect little body, without fault or stain on thee,
  With promise of strength and manhood full and fair!
        Though cold and stark and bare,
The bloom and the charm of life doth awhile remain on thee.

Thy mother's treasure wert thou; alas! no longer
  To visit her heart with wondrous joy; to be
        Thy father's pride;—ah, he
Must gather his faith together, and his strength make stronger.

To me, as I move thee now in the last duty,
  Dost thou with a turn or gesture anon respond;
        Startling my fancy fond
With a chance attitude of the head, a freak of beauty.

Thy hand clasps, as 'twas wont, my finger, and holds it:
  But the grasp is the clasp of Death, heartbreaking and stiff;
        Yet feels to my hand as if
'Twas still thy will, thy pleasure and trust that enfolds it.

So I lay thee there, thy sunken eyelids closing,—
  Go lie thou there in thy coffin, thy last little bed!—
        Propping thy wise, sad head,
Thy firm, pale hands across thy chest disposing.

So quiet! doth the change content thee?—Death, whither hath he taken
    thee?
  To a world, do I think, that rights the disaster of this?
        The vision of which I miss,
Who weep for the body, and wish but to warm thee and awaken thee?

Ah! little at best can all our hopes avail us
  To lift this sorrow, or cheer us, when in the dark,
        Unwilling, alone we embark,
And the things we have seen and have known and have heard of,
    fail us.   *1880*

[THE VERY NAMES OF THINGS BELOVED]

The very names of things belov'd are dear,
And sounds will gather beauty from their sense,
As many a face thro' love's long residence
Groweth to fair instead of plain and sere:
But when I say thy name it hath no peer,
And I suppose fortune determined thence
Her dower, that such beauty's excellence
Should have a perfect title for the ear.

Thus may I think the adopting Muses chose
Their sons by name, knowing none would be heard
Or writ so oft in all the world as those,—
Dan Chaucer, mighty Shakespeare, then for third
The classic Milton, and to us arose
Shelley with liquid music in the word.   1889

[THE WORLD COMES NOT TO AN END]

The world comes not to an end: her city-hives
Swarm with the tokens of a changeless trade,
With rolling wheel, driver and flagging jade,
Rich men and beggars, children, priests, and wives.
New homes on old are set, as lives on lives;
Invention with invention overlaid:
But still or tool or toy or book or blade
Shaped for the hand, that holds and toils and strives.

The men to-day toil as their fathers taught,
With little better'd means; for works depend
On works and overlap, and thought on thought:
And thro' all change the smiles of hope amend
The weariest face, the same love changed in nought:
In this thing too the world comes not to an end.   1889

THE PHILOSOPHER TO HIS MISTRESS

Because thou canst not see,
Because thou canst not know
The black and hopeless woe
That hath encompassed me:

Because, should I confess
The thought of my despair,
My words would wound thee less
Than swords can hurt the air:

Because with thee I seem
As one invited near
To taste the faery cheer
Of spirits in a dream;
Of whom he knoweth nought
Save that they vie to make
All motion, voice and thought
A pleasure for his sake:

Therefore more sweet and strange
Has been the mystery
Of thy long love to me,
That doth not quit, nor change,
Nor tax my solemn heart,
That kisseth in a gloom,
Knowing not who thou art
That givest, nor to whom.

Therefore the tender touch
Is more; more dear the smile:
And thy light words beguile
My wisdom overmuch:
And O with swiftness fly
The fancies of my song
To happy worlds, where I
Still in thy love belong.   *1890*

[THE EVENING DARKENS OVER]

The evening darkens over
After a day so bright
The windcapt waves discover
That wild will be the night.
There's sound of distant thunder.

The latest sea-birds hover
Along the cliff's sheer height;
As in the memory wander

Last flutterings of delight,
White wings lost on the white.

There's not a ship in sight;
And as the sun goes under
Thick clouds conspire to cover
The moon that should rise yonder.
Thou art alone, fond lover.   *1890*

[I LOVE ALL BEAUTEOUS THINGS]

I love all beauteous things,
    I seek and adore them;
God hath no better praise,
And man in his hasty days
    Is honoured for them.

I too will something make
    And joy in the making;
Although to-morrow it seem
Like the empty words of a dream
    Remembered on waking.
                                1890

[I NEVER SHALL LOVE THE SNOW AGAIN]

I never shall love the snow again
    Since Maurice died:
With corniced drift it blocked the lane
And sheeted in a desolate plain
    The country side.

The trees with silvery rime bedight
    Their branches bare.
By day no sun appeared; by night
The hidden moon shed thievish light
    In the misty air.

We fed the birds that flew around
    In flocks to be fed:
No shelter in holly or brake they found.
The speckled thrush on the frozen ground
    Lay frozen and dead.

We skated on stream and pond; we cut
　　The crinching snow
To Doric temple or Arctic hut;
We laughed and sang at nightfall, shut
　　By the fireside glow.

Yet grudged we our keen delights before
　　Maurice should come.
We said, In-door or out-of-door
We shall love life for a month or more,
　　When he is home.

They brought him home; 'twas two days late
　　For Christmas day:
Wrapped in white, in solemn state,
A flower in his hand, all still and straight
　　Our Maurice lay.

And two days ere the year outgave
　　We laid him low.
The best of us truly were not brave,
When we laid Maurice down in his grave
　　Under the snow.　　1893

NIGHTINGALES

Beautiful must be the mountains whence ye come,
And bright in the fruitful valleys the streams, wherefrom
　　Ye learn your song:
Where are those starry woods? O might I wander there,
　　Among the flowers, which in that heavenly air
　　Bloom the year long!

Nay, barren are those mountains and spent the streams:
Our song is the voice of desire, that haunts our dreams,
　　A throe of the heart,
Whose pining visions dim, forbidden hopes profound,
　　No dying cadence nor long sigh can sound,
　　For all our art.

Alone, aloud in the raptured ear of men
We pour our dark nocturnal secret; and then,
　　As night is withdrawn

From these sweet-springing meads and bursting boughs of May,
  Dream, while the innumerable choir of day
    Welcome the dawn.   *1893*

[WHO HAS NOT WALKED UPON THE SHORE]

Who has not walked upon the shore,
And who does not the morning know,
The day the angry gale is o'er,
The hour the wind has ceased to blow?

The horses of the strong southwest
Are pastured round his tropic tent,
Careless how long the ocean's breast
Sob on and sigh for passion spent.

The frightened birds, that fled inland
To house in rock and tower and tree
Are gathering on the peaceful strand
To tempt again the sunny sea;

Whereon the timid ships steal out
And laugh to find their foe asleep,
That lately scattered them about,
And drave them to the fold like sheep.

The snow-white clouds he northward chased
Break into phalanx, line, and band;
All one way to the south they haste,
The south, their pleasant fatherland.

From distant hills their shadows creep,
Arrive in turn and mount the lea,
And flit across the downs, and leap
Sheer off the cliff upon the sea;

And sail and sail far out of sight.
But still I watch their fleecy trains,
That piling all the south with light,
Dapple in France the fertile plains.

                         1873, 1894

[MY DELIGHT AND THY DELIGHT]

My delight and thy delight
Walking, like two angels white,
In the gardens of the night:

My desire and thy desire
Twining to a tongue of fire,
Leaping live, and laughing higher;
Thro' the everlasting strife
In the mystery of life.

Love, from whom the world begun,
Hath the secret of the sun.

Love can tell, and love alone,
Whence the million stars were strewn,
Why each atom knows its own,
How, in spite of woe and death,
Gay is life, and sweet is breath:

This he taught us, this we knew,
Happy in his science true,
Hand in hand as we stood
Neath the shadows of the wood,
Heart to heart as we lay
In the dawning of the day.   *1899*

PATER FILIO

Sense with keenest edge unusèd,
    Yet unsteel'd by scathing fire;
Lovely feet as yet unbruisèd
    On the ways of dark desire;
Sweetest hope that lookest smiling
O'er the wilderness defiling!

Why such beauty, to be blighted
    By the swarm of foul destruction?
Why such innocence delighted,
    When sin stalks to thy seduction?
All the litanies e'er chaunted
Shall not keep thy faith undaunted.

I have pray'd the sainted Morning
    To unclasp her hands to hold thee;
From resignful Eve's adorning
    Stol'n a robe of peace to enfold thee;
With all charms of man's contriving
Arm'd thee for thy lonely striving.

Me too once unthinking Nature
    —Whence Love's timeless mockery took me,—
Fashion'd so divine a creature,
    Yea, and like a beast forsook me.
I forgave, but tell the measure
Of her crime in thee, my treasure.   *1899*

EROS

Why hast thou nothing in thy face?
Thou idol of the human race,
Thou tyrant of the human heart,
The flower of lovely youth that art;
Yea, and that standest in thy youth
An image of eternal Truth,
With thy exuberant flesh so fair,
That only Pheidias might compare,
Ere from his chaste marmoreal form
Time had decayed the colours warm;
Like to his gods in thy proud dress,
Thy starry sheen of nakedness.

Surely thy body is thy mind,
For in thy face is nought to find,
Only thy soft unchristen'd smile,
That shadows neither love nor guile,
But shameless will and power immense,
In secret sensuous innocence.

O king of joy, what is thy thought?
I dream thou knowest it is nought,
And wouldst in darkness come, but thou
Makest the light where'er thou go.
Ah yet no victim of thy grace,
None who e'er long'd for thy embrace,
Hath cared to look upon thy face.   *1899*

MELANCHOLIA

The sickness of desire, that in dark days
Looks on the imagination of despair,
Forgetteth man, and stinteth God his praise;
Nor but in sleep findeth a cure for care.
Incertainty that once gave scope to dream
Of laughing enterprise and glory untold,
Is now a blackness that no stars redeem,
A wall of terror in a night of cold.

Fool! thou that hast impossibly desired
And now impatiently despairest, see
How nought is changed: Joy's wisdom is attired
Splendid for others' eyes if not for thee:
Not love or beauty or youth from earth is fled:
If they delight thee not, 'tis thou art dead.   *1905*

JOHANNES MILTON, SENEX

Scazons

Since I believe in God the Father Almighty,
Man's Maker and Judge, Overruler of Fortune,
'Twere strange should I praise anything and refuse Him praise,
Should love the creature forgetting the Creator,
Nor unto Him in suff'ring and sorrow turn me:
Nay how could I withdraw me from His embracing?

But since that I have seen not, and cannot know Him,
Nor in my earthly temple apprehend rightly
His wisdom and the heav'nly purpose eternal;
Therefore will I be bound to no studied system
Nor argument, nor with delusion enslave me,
Nor seek to please Him in any foolish invention,
Which my spirit within me, that loveth beauty
And hateth evil, hath reprov'd as unworthy:

But I cherish my freedom in loving service,
Gratefully adoring for delight beyond asking
Or thinking, and in hours of anguish and darkness
Confiding always on His excellent greatness.   *1914*

LOW BAROMETER

The south-wind strengthens to a gale,
Across the moon the clouds fly fast,
The house is smitten as with a flail,
The chimney shudders to the blast.

On such a night, when Air has loosed
Its guardian grasp on blood and brain,
Old terrors then of god or ghost
Creep from their caves to life again;

And Reason kens he herits in
A haunted house. Tenants unknown
Assert their squalid lease of sin
With earlier title than his own.

Unbodied presences, the pack'd
Pollution and remorse of Time,
Slipp'd from oblivion reënact
The horrors of unhouseld crime.

Some men would quell the thing with prayer
Whose sightless footsteps pad the floor,
Whose fearful trespass mounts the stair
Or bursts the lock'd forbidden door.

Some have seen corpses long interr'd
Escape from hallowing control,
Pale charnel forms—nay ev'n have heard
The shrilling of a troubled soul,

That wanders till the dawn hath cross'd
The dolorous dark, or Earth hath wound
Closer her storm-spredd cloke, and thrust
The baleful phantoms underground.   *1925*

A. E. Housman

[INTO MY HEART AN AIR THAT KILLS]

Into my heart an air that kills
From yon far country blows:
What are those blue remembered hills,
What spires, what farms are those?

That is the land of lost content,
I see it shining plain,
The happy highways where I went
And cannot come again.
c. 1890, 1896

[WITH RUE MY HEART IS LADEN]

With rue my heart is laden
For golden friends I had,
For many a rose-lipt maiden
And many a lightfoot lad.

By brooks too broad for leaping
The lightfoot boys are laid;
The rose-lipt girls are sleeping
In fields where roses fade.
Aug. 1893, 1896

[FROM FAR, FROM EVE AND MORNING]

From far, from eve and morning
And yon twelve-winded sky,
The stuff of life to knit me
Blew hither; here am I.

Now—for a breath I tarry
Nor yet disperse apart—
Take my hand quick and tell me
What have you in your heart.

I·83

Speak now, and I will answer;
How shall I help you, say;
Ere to the wind's twelve quarters
I take my endless way.

c. 1893, 1896

[WHITE IN THE MOON THE LONG ROAD LIES]

White in the moon the long road lies,
The moon stands blank above;
White in the moon the long road lies
That leads me from my love.

Still hangs the hedge without a gust,
Still, still the shadows stay:
My feet upon the moonlit dust
Pursue the ceaseless way.

The world is round, so travellers tell,
And straight though reach the track,
Trudge on, trudge on, 'twill all be well,
The way will guide one back.

But ere the circle homeward hies
Far, far must it remove:
White in the moon the long road lies
That leads me from my love.

1894, 1896

[FAREWELL TO BARN AND STACK AND TREE]

"Farewell to barn and stack and tree,
Farewell to Severn shore.
Terence, look your last at me,
For I come home no more.

"The sun burns on the half-mown hill,
By now the blood is dried;
And Maurice amongst the hay lies still
And my knife is in his side.

"My mother thinks us long away;
'Tis time the field were mown.

She had two sons at rising day,
  To-night she'll be alone.

"And here's a bloody hand to shake,
  And oh, man, here's good-bye;
We'll sweat no more on scythe and rake,
  My bloody hands and I.

"I wish you strength to bring you pride,
  And a love to keep you clean,
And I wish you luck, come Lammastide,
  At racing on the green.

"Long for me the rick will wait,
  And long will wait the fold,
And long will stand the empty plate,
  And dinner will be cold."

                  Aug. 1894, 1896

[WHEN I WAS ONE-AND-TWENTY]

When I was one-and-twenty
  I heard a wise man say,
"Give crowns and pounds and guineas
  But not your heart away;
Give pearls away and rubies
  But keep your fancy free."
But I was one-and-twenty,
  No use to talk to me.

When I was one-and-twenty
  I heard him say again,
"The heart out of the bosom
  Was never given in vain;
'Tis paid with sighs a plenty
  And sold for endless rue."
And I am two-and-twenty,
  And oh, 'tis true, 'tis true.

                  Jan. 1895, 1896

REVEILLE

Wake: the silver dusk returning
  Up the beach of darkness brims,

And the ship of sunrise burning
    Strands upon the eastern rims.

Wake: the vaulted shadow shatters,
    Trampled to the floor it spanned,
And the tent of night in tatters
    Straws the sky-pavilioned land.

Up, lad, up, 'tis late for lying:
    Hear the drums of morning play;
Hark, the empty highways crying
    "Who'll beyond the hills away?"

Towns and countries woo together,
    Forelands beacon, belfries call;
Never lad that trod on leather
    Lived to feast his heart with all.

Up, lad: thews that lie and cumber
    Sunlit pallets never thrive;
Morns abed and daylight slumber
    Were not meant for man alive.

Clay lies still, but blood's a rover;
    Breath's a ware that will not keep.
Up, lad: when the journey's over
    There'll be time enough to sleep.
                    Jan. 1895, 1896

[ON MOONLIT HEATH AND LONESOME BANK]

On moonlit heath and lonesome bank
    The sheep beside me graze;
And yon the gallows used to clank
    Fast by the four cross ways.

A careless shepherd once would keep
    The flocks by moonlight there,
And high amongst the glimmering sheep
    The dead man stood on air.

They hang us now in Shrewsbury jail:
    The whistles blow forlorn,

And trains all night groan on the rail
  To men that die at morn.

There sleeps in Shrewsbury jail to-night,
  Or wakes, as may betide,
A better lad, if things went right,
  Than most that sleep outside.

And naked to the hangman's noose
  The morning clocks will ring
A neck God made for other use
  Than strangling in a string.

And sharp the link of life will snap,
  And dead on air will stand
Heels that held up as straight a chap
  As treads upon the land.

So here I'll watch the night and wait
  To see the morning shine,
When he will hear the stroke of eight
  And not the stroke of nine;

And wish my friend as sound a sleep
  As lads' I did not know,
That shepherded the moonlit sheep
  A hundred years ago.
                    Feb. 1895, 1896

[WHEN I WATCH THE LIVING MEET]

When I watch the living meet,
  And the moving pageant file
Warm and breathing through the street
  Where I lodge a little while,

If the heats of hate and lust
  In the house of flesh are strong
Let me mind the house of dust
  Where my sojourn shall be long.

In the nation that is not
  Nothing stands that stood before;
There revenges are forgot,
  And the hater hates no more;

Lovers lying two and two
Ask not whom they sleep beside,
And the bridegroom all night through
Never turns him to the bride.

c. Feb. 1895, 1896

[OTHERS, I AM NOT THE FIRST]

Others, I am not the first,
Have willed more mischief than they durst;
If in the breathless night I too
Shiver now, 'tis nothing new.

More than I, if truth were told,
Have stood and sweated hot and cold,
And through their reins in ice and fire
Fear contended with desire.

Agued once like me were they,
But I like them shall win my way
Lastly to the bed of mold
Where there's neither heat nor cold.

But from my grave across my brow
Plays no wind of healing now,
And fire and ice within me fight
Beneath the suffocating night.   *1896*

TO AN ATHLETE DYING YOUNG

The time you won your town the race
We chaired you through the market-place;
Man and boy stood cheering by,
And home we brought you shoulder-high.

To-day, the road all runners come,
Shoulder-high we bring you home,
And set you at your threshold down,
Townsman of a stiller town.

Smart lad, to slip betimes away
From fields where glory does not stay,
And early though the laurel grows
It withers quicker than the rose.

Eyes the shady night has shut
Cannot see the record cut,
And silence sounds no worse than cheers
After earth has stopped the ears.

Now you will not swell the rout
Of lads that wore their honours out,
Runners whom renown outran
And the name died before the man.

So set, before its echoes fade,
The fleet foot on the sill of shade,
And hold to the low lintel up
The still-defended challenge-cup.

And round that early-laurelled head
Will flock to gaze the strengthless dead,
And find unwithered on its curls
The garland briefer than a girl's.
c. March 1895, 1896

[LOVELIEST OF TREES]

Loveliest of trees, the cherry now
Is hung with bloom along the bough
And stands about the woodland ride,
Wearing white for Eastertide.

Now, of my threescore years and ten,
Twenty will not come again,
And take from seventy springs a score,
It only leaves me fifty more.

And since to look at things in bloom
Fifty springs are little room,
About the woodlands I will go
To see the cherry hung with snow.
c. May 1895, 1896

[IS MY TEAM PLOUGHING]

"Is my team ploughing,
　　That I was used to drive
And hear the harness jingle
　　When I was a man alive?"

Ay, the horses trample,
  The harness jingles now;
No change though you lie under
  The land you used to plough.

"Is football playing
  Along the river shore,
With lads to chase the leather,
  Now I stand up no more?"

Ay, the ball is flying,
  The lads play heart and soul;
The goal stands up, the keeper
  Stands up to keep the goal.

"Is my girl happy,
  That I thought hard to leave,
And has she tired of weeping
  As she lies down at eve?"

Ay, she lies down lightly,
  She lies not down to weep:
Your girl is well contented.
  Be still, my lad, and sleep.

"Is my friend hearty,
  Now I am thin and pine,
And has he found to sleep in
  A better bed than mine?"

Yes, lad, I lie easy,
  I lie as lads would choose;
I cheer a dead man's sweetheart—
  Never ask me whose.
          May–autumn 1895, 1896

[THINK NO MORE, LAD]

Think no more, lad; laugh, be jolly:
  Why should men make haste to die?
Empty heads and tongues a-talking
Make the rough road easy walking,
And the feather pate of folly
  Bears the falling sky.

Oh, 'tis jesting, dancing, drinking
  Spins the heavy world around.
If young hearts were not so clever,
Oh, they would be young for ever:
Think no more; 'tis only thinking
  Lays lads underground.
                              c. Sept. 1895, 1896

[TERENCE, THIS IS STUPID STUFF]

  "Terence, this is stupid stuff:
You eat your victuals fast enough;
There can't be much amiss, 'tis clear,
To see the rate you drink your beer.
But oh, good Lord, the verse you make,
It gives a chap the belly-ache.
The cow, the old cow, she is dead;
It sleeps well, the hornèd head:
We poor lads, 'tis our turn now
To hear such tunes as killed the cow.
Pretty friendship 'tis to rhyme
Your friends to death before their time
Moping melancholy mad:
Come, pipe a tune to dance to, lad."

  Why, if 'tis dancing you would be,
There's brisker pipes than poetry.
Say, for what were hop-yards meant,
Or why was Burton built on Trent?
Oh, many a peer of England brews
Livelier liquor than the Muse,
And malt does more than Milton can
To justify God's ways to man.
Ale, man, ale's the stuff to drink
For fellows whom it hurts to think:
Look into the pewter pot
To see the world as the world's not.
And faith, 'tis pleasant till 'tis past:
The mischief is that 'twill not last.
Oh, I have been to Ludlow fair
And left my necktie God knows where,
And carried half-way home, or near,
Pints and quarts of Ludlow beer:

Then the world seemed none so bad,
And I myself a sterling lad;
And down in lovely muck I've lain,
Happy till I woke again.
Then I saw the morning sky:
Heigho, the tale was all a lie;
The world, it was the old world yet,
I was I, my things were wet,
And nothing now remained to do
But begin the game anew.

Therefore, since the world has still
Much good, but much less good than ill,
And while the sun and moon endure
Luck's a chance, but trouble's sure,
I'd face it as a wise man would,
And train for ill and not for good.
'Tis true, the stuff I bring for sale
Is not so brisk a brew as ale:
Out of a stem that scored the hand
I wrung it in a weary land.
But take it: if the smack is sour,
The better for the embittered hour;
It should do good to heart and head
When your soul is in my soul's stead;
And I will friend you, if I may,
In the dark and cloudy day.

There was a king reigned in the East:
There, when kings will sit to feast,
They get their fill before they think
With poisoned meat and poisoned drink.
He gathered all that springs to birth
From the many-venomed earth;
First a little, thence to more,
He sampled all her killing store;
And easy, smiling, seasoned sound,
Sate the king when healths went round.
They put arsenic in his meat
And stared aghast to watch him eat;
They poured strychnine in his cup
And shook to see him drink it up:
They shook, they stared as white's their shirt:

Them it was their poison hurt.
—I tell the tale that I heard told.
Mithridates, he died old.

c. Sept. 1895, 1896

[YONDER SEE THE MORNING BLINK]

Yonder see the morning blink:
  The sun is up, and up must I,
To wash and dress and eat and drink
And look at things and talk and think
  And work, and God knows why.

Oh, often have I washed and dressed
  And what's to show for all my pain?
Let me lie abed and rest:
Ten thousand times I've done my best
  And all's to do again.

Dec. 1895, 1922

[THE CHESTNUT CASTS HIS FLAMBEAUX]

The chestnut casts his flambeaux, and the flowers
  Stream from the hawthorn on the wind away,
The doors clap to, the pane is blind with showers.
  Pass me the can, lad; there's an end of May.

There's one spoilt spring to scant our mortal lot,
  One season ruined of our little store.
May will be fine next year as like as not:
  Oh ay, but then we shall be twenty-four.

We for a certainty are not the first
  Have sat in taverns while the tempest hurled
Their hopeful plans to emptiness, and cursed
  Whatever brute and blackguard made the world.

It is in truth iniquity on high
  To cheat our sentenced souls of aught they crave,
And mar the merriment as you and I
  Fare on our long fool's-errand to the grave.

Iniquity it is; but pass the can.
  My lad, no pair of kings our mothers bore;

Our only portion is the estate of man:
    We want the moon, but we shall get no more.

If here to-day the cloud of thunder lours
    To-morrow it will hie on far behests;
The flesh will grieve on other bones than ours
    Soon, and the soul will mourn in other breasts.

The troubles of our proud and angry dust
    Are from eternity, and shall not fail.
Bear them we can, and if we can we must.
    Shoulder the sky, my lad, and drink your ale.

                      1896–1922, 1922

[NOW DREARY DAWNS THE EASTERN LIGHT]

Now dreary dawns the eastern light,
    And fall of eve is drear,
And cold the poor man lies at night,
    And so goes out the year.

Little is the luck I've had,
    And oh, 'tis comfort small
To think that many another lad
    Has had no luck at all.

                      1896–1922, 1922

[AS I GIRD ON FOR FIGHTING]

As I gird on for fighting
    My sword upon my thigh,
I think on old ill fortunes
    Of better men than I.

Think I, the round world over,
    What golden lads are low
With hurts not mine to mourn for
    And shames I shall not know.

What evil luck soever
    For me remains in store,
'Tis sure much finer fellows
    Have fared much worse before.

So here are things to think on
  That ought to make me brave,
As I strap on for fighting
  My sword that will not save.

    c. 1900, 1922

[THE RAIN, IT STREAMS ON STONE]

The rain, it streams on stone and hillock,
  The boot clings to the clay.
Since all is done that's due and right
Let's home; and now, my lad, good-night,
  For I must turn away.

Good-night, my lad, for nought's eternal;
  No league of ours, for sure.
To-morrow I shall miss you less,
And ache of heart and heaviness
  Are things that time should cure.

Over the hill the highway marches
  And what's beyond is wide:
Oh, soon enough will pine to nought
Remembrance and the faithful thought
  That sits the grave beside.

The skies, they are not always raining
  Nor grey the twelvemonth through;
And I shall meet good days and mirth,
And range the lovely lands of earth
  With friends no worse than you.

But oh, my man, the house is fallen
  That none can build again;
My man, how full of joy and woe
Your mother bore you years ago
  To-night to lie in the rain.

    1902–22, 1922

EIGHT O'CLOCK

He stood, and heard the steeple
  Sprinkle the quarters on the morning town.

One, two, three, four, to market-place and people
It tossed them down.

Strapped, noosed, nighing his hour,
   He stood and counted them and cursed his luck;
And then the clock collected in the tower
   Its strength, and struck.   *1922*

[WAKE NOT FOR THE WORLD-HEARD THUNDER]

Wake not for the world-heard thunder
   Nor the chime that earthquakes toll.
Star may plot in heaven with planet,
Lightning rive the rock of granite,
Tempest tread the oakwood under:
   Fear not you for flesh nor soul.
Marching, fighting, victory past,
Stretch your limbs in peace at last.

Stir not for the soldiers drilling
   Nor the fever nothing cures:
Throb of drum and timbal's rattle
Call but man alive to battle,
And the fife with death-notes filling
   Screams for blood but not for yours.
Times enough you bled your best;
Sleep on now, and take your rest.

Sleep, my lad; the French are landed,
   London's burning, Windsor's down;
Clasp your cloak of earth about you,
We must man the ditch without you,
March unled and fight short-handed,
   Charge to fall and swim to drown.
Duty, friendship, bravery o'er,
Sleep away, lad; wake no more.
     March 1922, 1922

EPITAPH ON AN ARMY OF MERCENARIES

These, in the day when heaven was falling,
   The hour when earth's foundations fled,
Followed their mercenary calling
   And took their wages and are dead.

Their shoulders held the sky suspended;
  They stood, and earth's foundations stay;
What God abandoned, these defended,
  And saved the sum of things for pay.

           March 1922, 1922

[THE NIGHT IS FREEZING FAST]

The night is freezing fast,
  To-morrow comes December;
    And winterfalls of old
Are with me from the past;
  And chiefly I remember
    How Dick would hate the cold.

Fall, winter, fall; for he,
  Prompt hand and headpiece clever,
    Has woven a winter robe,
And made of earth and sea
  His overcoat for ever,
    And wears the turning globe.

           April 1922, 1922

FOR MY FUNERAL

O thou that from thy mansion
  Through time and place to roam,
Dost send abroad thy children,
  And then dost call them home,

That men and tribes and nations
  And all thy hand hath made
May shelter them from sunshine
  In thine eternal shade:

We now to peace and darkness
  And earth and thee restore
Thy creature that thou madest
  And wilt cast forth no more.

           1925, 1936

W. B. Yeats

THE STOLEN CHILD

Where dips the rocky highland
Of Sleuth Wood in the lake,
There lies a leafy island
Where flapping herons wake
The drowsy water-rats;
There we've hid our faery vats,
Full of berries
And of reddest stolen cherries.
Come away, O human child!
To the waters and the wild
With a faery, hand in hand,
For the world's more full of weeping than you can understand.

Where the wave of moonlight glosses
The dim grey sands with light,
Far off by furthest Rosses
We foot it all the night,
Weaving olden dances,
Mingling hands and mingling glances
Till the moon has taken flight;
To and fro we leap
And chase the frothy bubbles,
While the world is full of troubles
And is anxious in its sleep.
Come away, O human child!
To the waters and the wild
With a faery, hand in hand,
For the world's more full of weeping than you can understand.

Where the wandering water gushes
From the hills above Glen-Car,
In pools among the rushes
That scarce could bathe a star,
We seek for slumbering trout

And whispering in their ears
Give them unquiet dreams;
Leaning softly out
From ferns that drop their tears
Over the young streams.
Come away, O human child!
To the waters and the wild
With a faery, hand in hand,
For the world's more full of weeping than you can understand.

Away with us he's going,
The solemn-eyed:
He'll hear no more the lowing
Of the calves on the warm hillside
Or the kettle on the hob
Sing peace into his breast,
Or see the brown mice bob
Round and round the oatmeal-chest.
For he comes, the human child,
To the waters and the wild
With a faery, hand in hand,
From a world more full of weeping than he can understand.

1889

DOWN BY THE SALLEY GARDENS

Down by the salley gardens my love and I did meet;
She passed the salley gardens with little snow-white feet.
She bid me take love easy, as the leaves grow on the tree;
But I, being young and foolish, with her would not agree.

In a field by the river my love and I did stand,
And on my leaning shoulder she laid her snow-white hand.
She bid me take life easy, as the grass grows on the weirs;
But I was young and foolish, and now am full of tears.   *1889*

THE ROSE OF THE WORLD

Who dreamed that beauty passes like a dream?
For these red lips, with all their mournful pride,
Mournful that no new wonder may betide,
Troy passed away in one high funeral gleam,
And Usna's children died.

We and the labouring world are passing by:
Amid men's souls, that waver and give place,
Like the pale waters in their wintry race,
Under the passing stars, foam of the sky,
Lives on this lonely face.

Bow down, archangels, in your dim abode:
Before you were, or any hearts to beat,
Weary and kind, one lingered by His seat;
He made the world to be a grassy road
Before her wandering feet.   *1893*

THE LAKE ISLE OF INNISFREE

I will arise and go now, and go to Innisfree,
And a small cabin build there, of clay and wattles made:
Nine bean-rows will I have there, a hive for the honey bee,
And live alone in the bee-loud glade.

And I shall have some peace there, for peace comes dropping slow,
Dropping from the veils of the morning to where the cricket sings;
There midnight's all a glimmer, and noon a purple glow,
And evening full of the linnet's wings.

I will arise and go now, for always night and day
I hear lake water lapping with low sounds by the shore;
While I stand on the roadway, or on the pavements grey,
I hear it in the deep heart's core.   *1893*

THE PITY OF LOVE

A pity beyond all telling
Is hid in the heart of love:
The folk who are buying and selling,
The clouds on their journey above,
The cold wet winds ever blowing,
And the shadowy hazel grove
Where mouse-grey waters are flowing,
Threaten the head that I love.   *1893*

WHEN YOU ARE OLD

When you are old and grey and full of sleep,
And nodding by the fire, take down this book,
And slowly read, and dream of the soft look
Your eyes had once, and of their shadows deep;

How many loved your moments of glad grace,
And loved your beauty with love false or true;
But one man loved the pilgrim soul in you,
And loved the sorrows of your changing face;

And bending down beside the glowing bars,
Murmur, a little sadly, how Love fled
And paced upon the mountains overhead
And hid his face amid a crowd of stars.   *1893*

WHO GOES WITH FERGUS?

Who will go drive with Fergus now,
And pierce the deep wood's woven shade,
And dance upon the level shore?
Young man, lift up your russet brow,
And lift your tender eyelids, maid,
And brood on hopes and fear no more.

And no more turn aside and brood
Upon love's bitter mystery;
For Fergus rules the brazen cars,
And rules the shadows of the wood,
And the white breast of the dim sea
And all dishevelled wandering stars.   *1893*

THE MAN WHO DREAMED OF FAERYLAND

He stood among a crowd at Dromahair;
His heart hung all upon a silken dress,
And he had known at last some tenderness,
Before earth took him to her stony care;
But when a man poured fish into a pile,
It seemed they raised their little silver heads,
And sang what gold morning or evening sheds
Upon a woven world-forgotten isle
Where people love beside the ravelled seas;
That Time can never mar a lover's vows
Under that woven changeless roof of boughs:
The singing shook him out of his new ease.

He wandered by the sands of Lissadell;
His mind ran all on money cares and fears,

And he had known at last some prudent years
Before they heaped his grave under the hill;
But while he passed before a plashy place,
A lug-worm with its grey and muddy mouth
Sang that somewhere to north or west or south
There dwelt a gay, exulting, gentle race
Under the golden or the silver skies;
That if a dancer stayed his hungry foot
It seemed the sun and moon were in the fruit:
And at that singing he was no more wise.

He mused beside the well of Scanavin,
He mused upon his mockers: without fail
His sudden vengeance were a country tale,
When earthy night had drunk his body in;
But one small knot-grass growing by the pool
Sang where—unnecessary cruel voice—
Old silence bids its chosen race rejoice,
Whatever ravelled waters rise and fall
Or stormy silver fret the gold of day,
And midnight there enfold them like a fleece
And lover there by lover be at peace.
The tale drove his fine angry mood away.

He slept under the hill of Lugnagall;
And might have known at last unhaunted sleep
Under that cold and vapour-turbaned steep,
Now that the earth had taken man and all:
Did not the worms that spired about his bones
Proclaim with that unwearied, reedy cry
That God has laid His fingers on the sky,
That from those fingers glittering summer runs
Upon the dancer by the dreamless wave.
Why should those lovers that no lovers miss
Dream, until God burn Nature with a kiss?
The man has found no comfort in the grave.

1893

RED HANRAHAN'S SONG ABOUT IRELAND

The old brown thorn-trees break in two high over Cummen Strand,
Under a bitter black wind that blows from the left hand;
Our courage breaks like an old tree in a black wind and dies,

But we have hidden in our hearts the flame out of the eyes
Of Cathleen, the daughter of Houlihan.

The wind has bundled up the clouds high over Knocknarea,
And thrown the thunder on the stones for all that Maeve can say.
Angers that are like noisy clouds have set our hearts abeat;
But we have all bent low and low and kissed the quiet feet
Of Cathleen, the daughter of Houlihan.

The yellow pool has overflowed high up on Clooth-na-Bare,
For the wet winds are blowing out of the clinging air;
Like heavy flooded waters our bodies and our blood:
But purer than a tall candle before the Holy Rood
Is Cathleen, the daughter of Houlihan.   1897

THE LOVER TELLS OF THE ROSE IN HIS HEART

All things uncomely and broken, all things worn out and old,
The cry of a child by the roadway, the creak of a lumbering cart,
The heavy steps of the ploughman, splashing the wintry mould,
Are wronging your image that blossoms a rose in the deeps of my heart.

The wrong of unshapely things is a wrong too great to be told;
I hunger to build them anew and sit on a green knoll apart,
With the earth and the sky and the water, remade, like a casket of gold
For my dreams of your image that blossoms a rose in the deeps of my
        heart.   1899

THE SONG OF WANDERING AENGUS

I went out to the hazel wood,
Because a fire was in my head,
And cut and peeled a hazel wand,
And hooked a berry to a thread;
And when white moths were on the wing,
And moth-like stars were flickering out,
I dropped the berry in a stream
And caught a little silver trout.

When I had laid it on the floor
I went to blow the fire aflame,
But something rustled on the floor,
And some one called me by my name:

It had become a glimmering girl
With apple blossom in her hair
Who called me by my name and ran
And faded through the brightening air.

Though I am old with wandering
Through hollow lands and hilly lands,
I will find out where she has gone,
And kiss her lips and take her hands;
And walk among long dappled grass,
And pluck till time and times are done
The silver apples of the moon,
The golden apples of the sun.   *1899*

HE WISHES FOR THE CLOTHS OF HEAVEN

Had I the heavens' embroidered cloths,
Enwrought with golden and silver light,
The blue and the dim and the dark cloths
Of night and light and the half-light,
I would spread the cloths under your feet:
But I, being poor, have only my dreams;
I have spread my dreams under your feet;
Tread softly because you tread on my dreams.
   1899

IN THE SEVEN WOODS

I have heard the pigeons of the Seven Woods
Make their faint thunder, and the garden bees
Hum in the lime-tree flowers; and put away
The unavailing outcries and the old bitterness
That empty the heart. I have forgot awhile
Tara uprooted, and new commonness
Upon the throne and crying about the streets
And hanging its paper flowers from post to post,
Because it is alone of all things happy.
I am contented, for I know that Quiet
Wanders laughing and eating her wild heart
Among pigeons and bees, while that Great Archer,
Who but awaits His hour to shoot, still hangs
A cloudy quiver over Pairc-na-lee.
   August 1902, 1904

NEVER GIVE ALL THE HEART

Never give all the heart, for love
Will hardly seem worth thinking of
To passionate women if it seem
Certain, and they never dream
That it fades out from kiss to kiss;
For everything that's lovely is
But a brief, dreamy, kind delight.
O never give the heart outright,
For they, for all smooth lips can say,
Have given their hearts up to the play.
And who could play it well enough
If deaf and dumb and blind with love?
He that made this knows all the cost,
For he gave all his heart and lost.

                                   1904

ADAM'S CURSE

We sat together at one summer's end,
That beautiful mild woman, your close friend,
And you and I, and talked of poetry.
I said: "A line will take us hours maybe;
Yet if it does not seem a moment's thought,
Our stitching and unstitching has been naught.
Better go down upon your marrow-bones
And scrub a kitchen pavement, or break stones
Like an old pauper, in all kinds of weather;
For to articulate sweet sounds together
Is to work harder than all these, and yet
Be thought an idler by the noisy set
Of bankers, schoolmasters, and clergymen
The martyrs call the world."

                              And thereupon
That beautiful mild woman for whose sake
There's many a one shall find out all heartache
On finding that her voice is sweet and low
Replied: "To be born woman is to know—
Although they do not talk of it at school—
That we must labour to be beautiful."

I said: "It's certain there is no fine thing
Since Adam's fall but needs much labouring.
There have been lovers who thought love should be
So much compounded of high courtesy
That they would sigh and quote with learned looks
Precedents out of beautiful old books;
Yet now it seems an idle trade enough."

We sat grown quiet at the name of love;
We saw the last embers of daylight die,
And in the trembling blue-green of the sky
A moon, worn as if it had been a shell
Washed by time's waters as they rose and fell
About the stars and broke in days and years.

I had a thought for no one's but your ears:
That you were beautiful, and that I strove
To love you in the old high way of love;
That it had all seemed happy, and yet we'd grown
As weary-hearted as that hollow moon.   *1904*

THE OLD MEN ADMIRING THEMSELVES IN THE WATER

I heard the old, old men say,
"Everything alters,
And one by one we drop away."
They had hands like claws, and their knees
Were twisted like the old thorn-trees
By the waters.
I heard the old, old men say,
"All that's beautiful drifts away
Like the waters."   *1904*

NO SECOND TROY

Why should I blame her that she filled my days
With misery, or that she would of late
Have taught to ignorant men most violent ways,
Or hurled the little streets upon the great,
Had they but courage equal to desire?
What could have made her peaceful with a mind
That nobleness made simple as a fire,

With beauty like a tightened bow, a kind
That is not natural in an age like this,
Being high and solitary and most stern?
Why, what could she have done, being what she is?
Was there another Troy for her to burn?   *1910*

UPON A HOUSE SHAKEN BY THE LAND AGITATION

How should the world be luckier if this house,
Where passion and precision have been one
Time out of mind, became too ruinous
To breed the lidless eye that loves the sun?
And the sweet laughing eagle thoughts that grow
Where wings have memory of wings, and all
That comes of the best knit to the best? Although
Mean roof-trees were the sturdier for its fall,
How should their luck run high enough to reach
The gifts that govern men, and after these
To gradual Time's last gift, a written speech
Wrought of high laughter, loveliness and ease?

1910

ALL THINGS CAN TEMPT ME

All things can tempt me from this craft of verse:
One time it was a woman's face, or worse—
The seeming needs of my fool-driven land;
Now nothing but comes readier to the hand
Than this accustomed toil. When I was young,
I had not given a penny for a song
Did not the poet sing it with such airs
That one believed he had a sword upstairs;
Yet would be now, could I but have my wish,
Colder and dumber and deafer than a fish.   *1910*

BROWN PENNY

I whispered, "I am too young."
And then, "I am old enough";
Wherefore I threw a penny
To find out if I might love.
"Go and love, go and love, young man,
If the lady be young and fair."

Ah, penny, brown penny, brown penny,
I am looped in the loops of her hair.

O love is the crooked thing,
There is nobody wise enough
To find out all that is in it,
For he would be thinking of love
Till the stars had run away
And the shadows eaten the moon.
Ah, penny, brown penny, brown penny,
One cannot begin it too soon.   *1910*

SEPTEMBER *1913*

What need you, being come to sense,
But fumble in a greasy till
And add the halfpence to the pence
And prayer to shivering prayer, until
You have dried the marrow from the bone?
For men were born to pray and save:
Romantic Ireland's dead and gone,
It's with O'Leary in the grave.

Yet they were of a different kind,
The names that stilled your childish play,
They have gone about the world like wind,
But little time had they to pray
For whom the hangman's rope was spun,
And what, God help us, could they save?
Romantic Ireland's dead and gone,
It's with O'Leary in the grave.

Was it for this the wild geese spread
The grey wing upon every tide;
For this that all that blood was shed,
For this Edward Fitzgerald died,
And Robert Emmet and Wolfe Tone,
All that delirium of the brave?
Romantic Ireland's dead and gone,
It's with O'Leary in the grave.

Yet could we turn the years again,
And call those exiles as they were

In all their loneliness and pain,
You'd cry, "Some woman's yellow hair
Has maddened every mother's son":
They weighed so lightly what they gave.
But let them be, they're dead and gone,
They're with O'Leary in the grave.   *1914*

WHEN HELEN LIVED

We have cried in our despair
That men desert,
For some trivial affair
Or noisy, insolent sport,
Beauty that we have won
From bitterest hours;
Yet we, had we walked within
Those topless towers
Where Helen walked with her boy,
Had given but as the rest
Of the men and women of Troy,
A word and a jest.   *1914*

THE THREE HERMITS

Three old hermits took the air
By a cold and desolate sea,
First was muttering a prayer,
Second rummaged for a flea;
On a windy stone, the third,
Giddy with his hundredth year,
Sang unnoticed like a bird:
"Though the Door of Death is near
And what waits behind the door,
Three times in a single day
I, though upright on the shore,
Fall asleep when I should pray."
So the first, but now the second:
"We're but given what we have earned
When all thoughts and deeds are reckoned,
So it's plain to be discerned
That the shades of holy men
Who have failed, being weak of will,

Pass the Door of Birth again,
And are plagued by crowds, until
They've the passion to escape."
Moaned the other, "They are thrown
Into some most fearful shape."
But the second mocked his moan:
"They are not changed to anything,
Having loved God once, but maybe
To a poet or a king
Or a witty lovely lady."
While he'd rummaged rags and hair,
Caught and cracked his flea, the third,
Giddy with his hundredth year,
Sang unnoticed like a bird.   *1914*

BEGGAR TO BEGGAR CRIED

"Time to put off the world and go somewhere
And find my health again in the sea air,"
Beggar to beggar cried, being frenzy-struck,
"And make my soul before my pate is bare."

"And get a comfortable wife and house
To rid me of the devil in my shoes,"
Beggar to beggar cried, being frenzy-struck,
"And the worse devil that is between my thighs."

"And though I'd marry with a comely lass,
She need not be too comely—let it pass,"
Beggar to beggar cried, being frenzy-struck,
"But there's a devil in a looking-glass."

"Nor should she be too rich, because the rich
Are driven by wealth as beggars by the itch,"
Beggar to beggar cried, being frenzy-struck,
"And cannot have a humorous happy speech."

"And there I'll grow respected at my ease,
And hear amid the garden's nightly peace,"
Beggar to beggar cried, being frenzy-struck,
"The wind-blown clamour of the barnacle-geese."

1914

THE MAGI

Now as at all times I can see in the mind's eye,
In their stiff, painted clothes, the pale unsatisfied ones
Appear and disappear in the blue depth of the sky
With all their ancient faces like rain-beaten stones,
And all their helms of silver hovering side by side,
And all their eyes still fixed, hoping to find once more,
Being by Calvary's turbulence unsatisfied,
The uncontrollable mystery on the bestial floor.   *1914*

THE DOLLS

A doll in the doll-maker's house
Looks at the cradle and bawls:
"That is an insult to us."
But the oldest of all the dolls,
Who had seen, being kept for show,
Generations of his sort,
Out-screams the whole shelf: "Although
There's not a man can report
Evil of this place,
The man and the woman bring
Hither, to our disgrace,
A noisy and filthy thing."
Hearing him groan and stretch
The doll-maker's wife is aware
Her husband has heard the wretch,
And crouched by the arm of his chair,
She murmurs into his ear,
Head upon shoulder leant:
"My dear, my dear, O dear,
It was an accident."   *1914*

A COAT

I made my song a coat
Covered with embroideries
Out of old mythologies
From heel to throat;
But the fools caught it,

Wore it in the world's eyes
As though they'd wrought it.
Song, let them take it,
For there's more enterprise
In walking naked.   *1914*

THE WILD SWANS AT COOLE

The trees are in their autumn beauty,
The woodland paths are dry,
Under the October twilight the water
Mirrors a still sky;
Upon the brimming water among the stones
Are nine-and-fifty swans.

The nineteenth autumn has come upon me
Since I first made my count;
I saw, before I had well finished,
All suddenly mount
And scatter wheeling in great broken rings
Upon their clamorous wings.

I have looked upon those brilliant creatures,
And now my heart is sore.
All's changed since I, hearing at twilight,
The first time on this shore,
The bell-beat of their wings above my head,
Trod with a lighter tread.

Unwearied still, lover by lover,
They paddle in the cold
Companionable streams or climb the air;
Their hearts have not grown old;
Passion or conquest, wander where they will,
Attend upon them still.

But now they drift on the still water
Mysterious, beautiful;
Among what rushes will they build,
By what lake's edge or pool
Delight men's eyes when I awake some day
To find they have flown away?   *1919*

SOLOMON TO SHEBA

Sang Solomon to Sheba,
And kissed her dusky face,
"All day long from mid-day
We have talked in the one place,
All day long from shadowless noon
We have gone round and round
In the narrow theme of love
Like an old horse in a pound."

To Solomon sang Sheba,
Planted on his knees,
"If you had broached a matter
That might the learned please,
You had before the sun had thrown
Our shadows on the ground
Discovered that my thoughts, not it,
Are but a narrow pound."

Sang Solomon to Sheba,
And kissed her Arab eyes,
"There's not a man or woman
Born under the skies
Dare match in learning with us two,
And all day long we have found
There's not a thing but love can make
The world a narrow pound."   *1919*

TO A YOUNG BEAUTY

Dear fellow-artist, why so free
With every sort of company,
With every Jack and Jill?
Choose your companions from the best;
Who draws a bucket with the rest
Soon topples down the hill.

You may, that mirror for a school,
Be passionate, not bountiful
As common beauties may,
Who were not born to keep in trim

With old Ezekiel's cherubim
But those of Beauvarlet.

I know what wages beauty gives,
How hard a life her servant lives,
Yet praise the winters gone:
There is not a fool can call me friend,
And I may dine at journey's end
With Landor and with Donne.   *1919*

THE SCHOLARS

Bald heads forgetful of their sins,
Old, learned, respectable bald heads
Edit and annotate the lines
That young men, tossing on their beds,
Rhymed out in love's despair
To flatter beauty's ignorant ear.

All shuffle there; all cough in ink;
All wear the carpet with their shoes;
All think what other people think;
All know the man their neighbour knows.
Lord, what would they say
Did their Catullus walk that way?   *1919*

TOM O'ROUGHLEY

"Though logic-choppers rule the town,
And every man and maid and boy
Has marked a distant object down,
An aimless joy is a pure joy,"
Or so did Tom O'Roughley say
That saw the surges running by,
"And wisdom is a butterfly
And not a gloomy bird of prey.

"If little planned is little sinned
But little need the grave distress.
What's dying but a second wind?
How but in zig-zag wantonness
Could trumpeter Michael be so brave?"
Or something of that sort he said,

"And if my dearest friend were dead
I'd dance a measure on his grave."

1919

ON WOMAN

May God be praised for woman
That gives up all her mind,
A man may find in no man
A friendship of her kind
That covers all he has brought
As with her flesh and bone,
Nor quarrels with a thought
Because it is not her own.

Though pedantry denies,
It's plain the Bible means
That Solomon grew wise
While talking with his queens,
Yet never could, although
They say he counted grass,
Count all the praises due
When Sheba was his lass,
When she the iron wrought, or
When from the smithy fire
It shuddered in the water:
Harshness of their desire
That made them stretch and yawn,
Pleasure that comes with sleep,
Shudder that made them one.
What else He give or keep
God grant me—no, not here,
For I am not so bold
To hope a thing so dear
Now I am growing old,
But when, if the tale's true,
The Pestle of the moon
That pounds up all anew
Brings me to birth again—
To find what once I had
And know what once I have known,
Until I am driven mad,
Sleep driven from my bed,

By tenderness and care,
Pity, an aching head,
Gnashing of teeth, despair;
And all because of some one
Perverse creature of chance,
And live like Solomon
That Sheba led a dance.　　*1919*

THE FISHERMAN

Although I can see him still,
The freckled man who goes
To a grey place on a hill
In grey Connemara clothes
At dawn to cast his flies,
It's long since I began
To call up to the eyes
This wise and simple man.
All day I'd looked in the face
What I had hoped 'twould be
To write for my own race
And the reality;
The living men that I hate,
The dead man that I loved,
The craven man in his seat,
The insolent unreproved,
And no knave brought to book
Who has won a drunken cheer,
The witty man and his joke
Aimed at the commonest ear,
The clever man who cries
The catch-cries of the clown,
The beating down of the wise
And great Art beaten down.

Maybe a twelvemonth since
Suddenly I began,
In scorn of this audience,
Imagining a man,
And his sun-freckled face,
And grey Connemara cloth,
Climbing up to a place

Where stone is dark under froth,
And the down-turn of his wrist
When the flies drop in the stream;
A man who does not exist,
A man who is but a dream;
And cried, "Before I am old
I shall have written him one
Poem maybe as cold
And passionate as the dawn."

1919

THE PEOPLE

"What have I earned for all that work," I said,
"For all that I have done at my own charge?
The daily spite of this unmannerly town,
Where who has served the most is most defamed,
The reputation of his lifetime lost
Between the night and morning. I might have lived,
And you know well how great the longing has been,
Where every day my footfall should have lit
In the green shadow of Ferrara wall;
Or climbed among the images of the past—
The unperturbed and courtly images—
Evening and morning, the steep street of Urbino
To where the duchess and her people talked
The stately midnight through until they stood
In their great window looking at the dawn;
I might have had no friend that could not mix
Courtesy and passion into one like those
That saw the wicks grow yellow in the dawn;
I might have used the one substantial right
My trade allows: chosen my company,
And chosen what scenery had pleased me best."
Thereon my phoenix answered in reproof,
"The drunkards, pilferers of public funds,
All the dishonest crowd I had driven away,
When my luck changed and they dared meet my face,
Crawled from obscurity, and set upon me
Those I had served and some that I had fed;
Yet never have I, now nor any time,
Complained of the people."

All I could reply
Was: "You, that have not lived in thought but deed,
Can have the purity of a natural force,
But I, whose virtues are the definitions
Of the analytic mind, can neither close
The eye of the mind nor keep my tongue from speech."
And yet, because my heart leaped at her words,
I was abashed, and now they come to mind
After nine years, I sink my head abashed.   *1919*

A DEEP-SWORN VOW

Others because you did not keep
That deep-sworn vow have been friends of mine;
Yet always when I look death in the face,
When I clamber to the heights of sleep,
Or when I grow excited with wine,
Suddenly I meet your face.   *1919*

EGO DOMINUS TUUS

Hic. On the grey sand beside the shallow stream
    Under your old wind-beaten tower, where still
    A lamp burns on beside the open book
    That Michael Robartes left, you walk in the moon,
    And, though you have passed the best of life, still trace,
    Enthralled by the unconquerable delusion,
    Magical shapes.

Ille.   By the help of an image
    I call to my own opposite, summon all
    That I have handled least, least looked upon.

Hic. And I would find myself and not an image.

Ille. That is our modern hope, and by its light
    We have lit upon the gentle, sensitive mind,
    And lost the old nonchalance of the hand;
    Whether we have chosen chisel, pen or brush,
    We are but critics, or but half create,
    Timid, entangled, empty and abashed,
    Lacking the countenance of our friends.

Hic.   And yet
The chief imagination of Christendom,
Dante Alighieri, so utterly found himself
That he has made that hollow face of his
More plain to the mind's eye than any face
But that of Christ.

Ille.   And did he find himself,
Or was the hunger that had made it hollow
A hunger for the apple on the bough
Most out of reach? and is that spectral image
The man that Lapo and that Guido knew?
I think he fashioned from his opposite
An image that might have been a stony face
Staring upon a Bedouin's horse-hair roof
From doored and windowed cliff, or half upturned
Among the coarse grass and the camel-dung.
He set his chisel to the hardest stone.
Being mocked by Guido for his lecherous life,
Derided and deriding, driven out
To climb that stair and eat that bitter bread,
He found the unpersuadable justice, he found
The most exalted lady loved by a man.

Hic. Yet surely there are men who have made their art
Out of no tragic war, lovers of life,
Impulsive men that look for happiness
And sing when they have found it.

Ille.   No, not sing,
For those that love the world serve it in action,
Grow rich, popular and full of influence,
And should they paint or write still it is action:
The struggle of the fly in marmalade.
The rhetorician would deceive his neighbors,
The sentimentalist himself; while art
Is but a vision of reality.
What portion in the world can the artist have
Who has awakened from the common dream
But dissipation and despair?

Hic.   And yet
No one denies to Keats love of the world;
Remember his deliberate happiness.

Ille. His art is happy, but who knows his mind?
I see a schoolboy when I think of him,
With face and nose pressed to a sweet-shop window,
For certainly he sank into his grave
His senses and his heart unsatisfied,
And made—being poor, ailing and ignorant,
Shut out from all the luxury of the world,
The coarse-bred son of a livery-stable keeper—
Luxuriant song.

Hic.   Why should you leave the lamp
Burning alone beside an open book,
And trace these characters upon the sands?
A style is found by sedentary toil
And by the imitation of great masters.

Ille. Because I seek an image, not a book.
Those men that in their writings are most wise
Own nothing but their blind, stupefied hearts.
I call to the mysterious one who yet
Shall walk the wet sands by the edge of the stream
And look most like me, being indeed my double,
And prove of all imaginable things
The most unlike, being my anti-self,
And standing by these characters disclose
All that I seek; and whisper it as though
He were afraid the birds, who cry aloud
Their momentary cries before it is dawn,
Would carry it away to blasphemous men.   *1919*

THE CAT AND THE MOON

The cat went here and there
And the moon spun round like a top,
And the nearest kin of the moon,
The creeping cat, looked up.
Black Minnaloushe stared at the moon,
For, wander and wail as he would,
The pure cold light in the sky
Troubled his animal blood.
Minnaloushe runs in the grass
Lifting his delicate feet.
Do you dance, Minnaloushe, do you dance?

When two close kindred meet,
What better than call a dance?
Maybe the moon may learn,
Tired of that courtly fashion,
A new dance turn.
Minnaloushe creeps through the grass
From moonlit place to place,
The sacred moon overhead
Has taken a new phase.
Does Minnaloushe know that his pupils
Will pass from change to change,
And that from round to crescent,
From crescent to round they range?
Minnaloushe creeps through the grass
Alone, important and wise,
And lifts to the changing moon
                    His changing eyes.   *1919*

TWO SONGS OF A FOOL

I

A speckled cat and a tame hare
Eat at my hearthstone
And sleep there;
And both look up to me alone
For learning and defence
As I look up to Providence.

I start out of my sleep to think
Some day I may forget
Their food and drink;
Or, the house door left unshut,
The hare may run till it's found
The horn's sweet note and the tooth of the hound.

I bear a burden that might well try
Men that do all by rule,
And what can I
That am a wandering-witted fool
But pray to God that He ease
My great responsibilities?

II

I slept on my three-legged stool by the fire,
The speckled cat slept on my knee;
We never thought to enquire
Where the brown hare might be,
And whether the door were shut.
Who knows how she drank the wind
Stretched up on two legs from the mat,
Before she had settled her mind
To drum with her heel and to leap?
Had I but awakened from sleep
And called her name, she had heard,
It may be, and had not stirred,
That now, it may be, has found
The horn's sweet note and the tooth of the hound.

1919

EASTER *1916*

I have met them at close of day
Coming with vivid faces
From counter or desk among grey
Eighteenth-century houses.
I have passed with a nod of the head
Or polite meaningless words,
Or have lingered awhile and said
Polite meaningless words,
And thought before I had done
Of a mocking tale or a gibe
To please a companion
Around the fire at the club,
Being certain that they and I
But lived where motley is worn:
All changed, changed utterly:
A terrible beauty is born.

That woman's days were spent
In ignorant good-will,
Her nights in argument
Until her voice grew shrill.

What voice more sweet than hers
When, young and beautiful,
She rode to harriers?
This man had kept a school
And rode our wingèd horse;
This other his helper and friend
Was coming into his force;
He might have won fame in the end,
So sensitive his nature seemed,
So daring and sweet his thought.
This other man I had dreamed
A drunken, vainglorious lout.
He had done most bitter wrong
To some who are near my heart,
Yet I number him in the song;
He, too, has resigned his part
In the casual comedy;
He, too, has been changed in his turn,
Transformed utterly:
A terrible beauty is born.

Hearts with one purpose alone
Through summer and winter seem
Enchanted to a stone
To trouble the living stream.
The horse that comes from the road,
The rider, the birds that range
From cloud to tumbling cloud,
Minute by minute they change;
A shadow of cloud on the stream
Changes minute by minute;
A horse-hoof slides on the brim,
And a horse plashes within it;
The long-legged moor-hens dive,
And hens to moor-cocks call;
Minute by minute they live:
The stone's in the midst of all.

Too long a sacrifice
Can make a stone of the heart.
O when may it suffice?
That is Heaven's part, our part
To murmur name upon name,

As a mother names her child
When sleep at last has come
On limbs that had run wild.
What is it but nightfall?
No, no, not night but death;
Was it needless death after all?
For England may keep faith
For all that is done and said.
We know their dream; enough
To know they dreamed and are dead;
And what if excess of love
Bewildered them till they died?
I write it out in a verse—
MacDonagh and MacBride
And Connolly and Pearse
Now and in time to be,
Wherever green is worn,
Are changed, changed utterly:
A terrible beauty is born.

September 25, 1916; 1921

THE ROSE TREE

"O words are lightly spoken,"
Said Pearse to Connolly,
"Maybe a breath of politic words
Has withered our Rose Tree;
Or maybe but a wind that blows
Across the bitter sea."

"It needs to be but watered,"
James Connolly replied,
"To make the green come out again
And spread on every side,
And shake the blossom from the bud
To be the garden's pride."

"But where can we draw water,"
Said Pearse to Connolly,
"When all the wells are parched away?
O plain as plain can be
There's nothing but our own red blood
Can make a right Rose Tree." *1921*

THE SECOND COMING

Turning and turning in the widening gyre
The falcon cannot hear the falconer;
Things fall apart; the centre cannot hold;
Mere anarchy is loosed upon the world,
The blood-dimmed tide is loosed, and everywhere
The ceremony of innocence is drowned;
The best lack all conviction, while the worst
Are full of passionate intensity.

Surely some revelation is at hand;
Surely the Second Coming is at hand.
The Second Coming! Hardly are those words out
When a vast image out of *Spiritus Mundi*
Troubles my sight: somewhere in sands of the desert
A shape with lion body and the head of a man,
A gaze blank and pitiless as the sun,
Is moving its slow thighs, while all about it
Reel shadows of the indignant desert birds.
The darkness drops again; but now I know
That twenty centuries of stony sleep
Were vexed to nightmare by a rocking cradle,
And what rough beast, its hour come round at last,
Slouches towards Bethlehem to be born?   *1921*

A PRAYER FOR MY DAUGHTER

Once more the storm is howling, and half hid
Under this cradle-hood and coverlid
My child sleeps on. There is no obstacle
But Gregory's wood and one bare hill
Whereby the haystack- and roof-levelling wind,
Bred on the Atlantic, can be stayed;
And for an hour I have walked and prayed
Because of the great gloom that is in my mind.

I have walked and prayed for this young child an hour
And heard the sea-wind scream upon the tower,
And under the arches of the bridge, and scream
In the elms above the flooded stream;
Imagining in excited reverie
That the future years had come,

Dancing to a frenzied drum,
Out of the murderous innocence of the sea.

May she be granted beauty and yet not
Beauty to make a stranger's eye distraught,
Or hers before a looking-glass, for such,
Being made beautiful overmuch,
Consider beauty a sufficient end,
Lose natural kindness and maybe
The heart-revealing intimacy
That chooses right, and never find a friend.

Helen being chosen found life flat and dull
And later had much trouble from a fool,
While that great Queen, that rose out of the spray,
Being fatherless could have her way
Yet chose a bandy-leggèd smith for man.
It's certain that fine women eat
A crazy salad with their meat,
Whereby the Horn of Plenty is undone.

In courtesy I'd have her chiefly learned;
Hearts are not had as a gift but hearts are earned
By those that are not entirely beautiful;
Yet many, that have played the fool
For beauty's very self, has charm made wise,
And many a poor man that has roved,
Loved and thought himself beloved,
From a glad kindness cannot take his eyes.

May she become a flourishing hidden tree
That all her thoughts may like the linnet be,
And have no business but dispensing round
Their magnanimities of sound,
Nor but in merriment begin a chase,
Nor but in merriment a quarrel.
Oh, may she live like some green laurel
Rooted in one dear perpetual place.

My mind, because the minds that I have loved,
The sort of beauty that I have approved,
Prosper but little, has dried up of late,
Yet knows that to be choked with hate

May well be of all evil chances chief.
If there's no hatred in a mind
Assault and battery of the wind
Can never tear the linnet from the leaf.

An intellectual hatred is the worst,
So let her think opinions are accursed.
Have I not seen the loveliest woman born
Out of the mouth of Plenty's horn,
Because of her opinionated mind
Barter that horn and every good
By quiet natures understood
For an old bellows full of angry wind?

Considering that, all hatred driven hence,
The soul recovers radical innocence
And learns at last that it is self-delighting,
Self-appeasing, self-affrighting,
And that its own sweet will is Heaven's will;
She can, though every face should scowl
And every windy quarter howl
Or every bellows burst, be happy still.

And may her bridegroom bring her to a house
Where all's accustomed, ceremonious;
For arrogance and hatred are the wares
Peddled in the thoroughfares.
How but in custom and in ceremony
Are innocence and beauty born?
Ceremony's a name for the rich horn,
And custom for the spreading laurel tree.

June 1919, 1921

SAILING TO BYZANTIUM

That is no country for old men. The young
In one another's arms, birds in the trees
—Those dying generations—at their song,
The salmon-falls, the mackerel-crowded seas,
Fish, flesh, or fowl, commend all summer long
Whatever is begotten, born, and dies.
Caught in that sensual music all neglect
Monuments of unaging intellect.

An aged man is but a paltry thing,
A tattered coat upon a stick, unless
Soul clap its hands and sing, and louder sing
For every tatter in its mortal dress,
Nor is there singing school but studying
Monuments of its own magnificence;
And therefore I have sailed the seas and come
To the holy city of Byzantium.

O sages standing in God's holy fire
As in the gold mosaic of a wall,
Come from the holy fire, perne in a gyre,
And be the singing-masters of my soul.
Consume my heart away; sick with desire
And fastened to a dying animal
It knows not what it is; and gather me
Into the artifice of eternity.

Once out of nature I shall never take
My bodily form from any natural thing,
But such a form as Grecian goldsmiths make
Of hammered gold and gold enamelling
To keep a drowsy emperor awake;
Or set upon a golden bough to sing
To lords and ladies of Byzantium
Of what is past, or passing, or to come.   *1928*

THE TOWER

I

What shall I do with this absurdity—
O heart, O troubled heart—this caricature,
Decrepit age that has been tied to me
As to a dog's tail?
                    Never had I more
Excited, passionate, fantastical
Imagination, nor an ear and eye
That more expected the impossible—
No, not in boyhood when with rod and fly,
Or the humbler worm, I climbed Ben Bulben's back
And had the livelong summer day to spend.
It seems that I must bid the Muse go pack,

Choose Plato and Plotinus for a friend
Until imagination, ear and eye,
Can be content with argument and deal
In abstract things; or be derided by
A sort of battered kettle at the heel.

II

I pace upon the battlements and stare
On the foundations of a house, or where
Tree, like a sooty finger, starts from the earth;
And send imagination forth
Under the day's declining beam, and call
Images and memories
From ruin or from ancient trees,
For I would ask a question of them all.

Beyond that ridge lived Mrs. French, and once
When every silver candlestick or sconce
Lit up the dark mahogany and the wine,
A serving-man, that could divine
That most respected lady's every wish,
Ran and with the garden shears
Clipped an insolent farmer's ears
And brought them in a little covered dish.

Some few remembered still when I was young,
A peasant girl commended by a song,
Who'd lived somewhere upon that rocky place,
And praised the color of her face,
And had the greater joy in praising her,
Remembering that, if walked she there,
Farmers jostled at the fair
So great a glory did the song confer.

And certain men, being maddened by those rhymes,
Or else by toasting her a score of times,
Rose from the table and declared it right
To test their fancy by their sight;
But they mistook the brightness of the moon
For the prosaic light of day—
Music had driven their wits astray—
And one was drowned in the great bog of Cloone.

Strange, but the man who made the song was blind,
Yet, now I have considered it, I find
That nothing strange; the tragedy began
With Homer that was a blind man,
And Helen has all living hearts betrayed.
O may the moon and sunlight seem
One inextricable beam,
For if I triumph I must make men mad.

And I myself created Hanrahan
And drove him drunk or sober through the dawn
From somewhere in the neighbouring cottages.
Caught by an old man's juggleries
He stumbled, tumbled, fumbled to and fro
And had but broken knees for hire
And horrible splendor of desire;
I thought it all out twenty years ago:

Good fellows shuffled cards in an old bawn;
And when that ancient ruffian's turn was on
He so bewitched the cards under his thumb
That all, but the one card, became
A pack of hounds and not a pack of cards,
And that he changed into a hare.
Hanrahan rose in frenzy there
And followed up those baying creatures towards—

O towards I have forgotten what—enough!
I must recall a man that neither love
Nor music nor an enemy's clipped ear
Could, he was so harried, cheer;
A figure that has grown so fabulous
There's not a neighbor left to say
When he finished his dog's day:
An ancient bankrupt master of this house.

Before that ruin came, for centuries,
Rough men-at-arms, cross-gartered to the knees
Or shod in iron, climbed the narrow stairs,
And certain men-at-arms there were
Whose images, in the Great Memory stored,
Come with loud cry and panting breast
To break upon a sleeper's rest
While their great wooden dice beat on the board.

As I would question all, come all who can;
Come old, necessitous, half-mounted man;
And bring beauty's blind rambling celebrant;
The red man the juggler sent
Through God-forsaken meadows; Mrs. French,
Gifted with so fine an ear;
The man drowned in a bog's mire,
When mocking muses chose the country wench.

Did all old men and women, rich and poor,
Who trod upon these rocks or passed this door,
Whether in public or in secret rage
As I do now against old age?
But I have found an answer in those eyes
That are impatient to be gone;
Go therefore; but leave Hanrahan,
For I need all his mighty memories.

Old lecher with a love on every wind,
Bring up out of that deep considering mind
All that you have discovered in the grave,
For it is certain that you have
Reckoned up every unforeknown, unseeing
Plunge, lured by a softening eye,
Or by a touch or a sigh,
Into the labyrinth of another's being;

Does the imagination dwell the most
Upon a woman won or a woman lost?
If on the lost, admit you turned aside
From a great labyrinth out of pride,
Cowardice, some silly over-subtle thought
Or anything called conscience once;
And that if memory recur, the sun's
Under eclipse and the day blotted out.

III

It is time that I wrote my will;
I choose upstanding men,
That climb the streams until
The fountain leap, and at dawn
Drop their cast at the side

Of dripping stone; I declare
They shall inherit my pride,
The pride of people that were
Bound neither to Cause nor to State,
Neither to slaves that were spat on,
Nor to the tyrants that spat,
The people of Burke and of Grattan
That gave, though free to refuse—
Pride, like that of the morn,
When the headlong light is loose,
Or that of the fabulous horn,
Or that of the sudden shower
When all streams are dry,
Or that of the hour
When the swan must fix his eye
Upon a fading gleam,
Float out upon a long
Last reach of glittering stream
And there sing his last song.
And I declare my faith:
I mock Plotinus' thought
And cry in Plato's teeth,
Death and life were not
Till man made up the whole,
Made lock, stock and barrel
Out of his bitter soul,
Aye, sun and moon and star, all,
And further add to that
That, being dead, we rise,
Dream and so create
Translunar Paradise.
I have prepared my peace
With learned Italian things
And the proud stones of Greece,
Poet's imaginings
And memories of love,
Memories of the words of women,
All those things whereof
Man makes a superhuman,
Mirror-resembling dream.

As at the loophole there,
The daws chatter and scream,

And drop twigs layer upon layer.
When they have mounted up,
The mother bird will rest
On their hollow top,
And so warm her wild nest.

I leave both faith and pride
To young upstanding men
Climbing the mountain-side,
That under bursting dawn
They may drop a fly;
Being of that metal made
Till it was broken by
This sedentary trade.

Now shall I make my soul,
Compelling it to study
In a learned school
Till the wreck of body,
Slow decay of blood,
Testy delirium
Or dull decrepitude,
Or what worse evil come—
The death of friends, or death
Of every brilliant eye
That made a catch in the breath—
Seem but the clouds of the sky
When the horizon fades;
Or a bird's sleepy cry
Among the deepening shades.   *1926, 1928*

TWO SONGS FROM A PLAY

I

I saw a staring virgin stand
Where holy Dionysus died,
And tear the heart out of his side,
And lay the heart upon her hand
And bear that beating heart away;
And then did all the Muses sing
Of Magnus Annus at the spring,
As though God's death were but a play.

Another Troy must rise and set,
Another lineage feed the crow,
Another Argo's painted prow
Drive to a flashier bauble yet.
The Roman Empire stood appalled:
It dropped the reigns of peace and war
When that fierce virgin and her Star
Out of the fabulous darkness called.

II

In pity for man's darkening thought
He walked that room and issued thence
In Galilean turbulence;
The Babylonian starlight brought
A fabulous, formless darkness in;
Odour of blood when Christ was slain
Made all Platonic tolerance vain
And vain all Doric discipline.

Everything that man esteems
Endures a moment or a day.
Love's pleasure drives his love away,
The painter's brush consumes his dreams;
The herald's cry, the soldier's tread
Exhaust his glory and his might:
Whatever flames upon the night
Man's own resinous heart has fed.   *1928*

LEDA AND THE SWAN

A sudden blow: the great wings beating still
Above the staggering girl, her thighs caressed
By the dark webs, her nape caught in his bill,
He holds her helpless breast upon his breast.

How can those terrified vague fingers push
The feathered glory from her loosening thighs?
And how can body, laid in that white rush,
But feel the strange heart beating where it lies?

A shudder in the loins engenders there
The broken wall, the burning roof and tower
And Agamemnon dead.

Being so caught up,
So mastered by the brute blood of the air,
Did she put on his knowledge with his power
Before the indifferent beak could let her drop?

1923, 1928

AMONG SCHOOL CHILDREN

I walk through the long schoolroom questioning;
A kind old nun in a white hood replies;
The children learn to cipher and to sing,
To study reading-books and history,
To cut and sew, be neat in everything
In the best modern way—the children's eyes
In momentary wonder stare upon
A sixty-year-old smiling public man.

I dream of a Ledæan body, bent
Above a sinking fire, a tale that she
Told of a harsh reproof, or trivial event
That changed some childish day to tragedy—
Told, and it seemed that our two natures blent
Into a sphere from youthful sympathy,
Or else, to alter Plato's parable,
Into the yolk and white of the one shell.

And thinking of that fit of grief or rage
I look upon one child or t'other there
And wonder if she stood so at that age—
For even daughters of the swan can share
Something of every paddler's heritage—
And had that color upon cheek or hair;
And thereupon my heart is driven wild:
She stands before me as a living child.

Her present image floats into the mind—
Did Quattrocento finger fashion it
Hollow of cheek as though it drank the wind
And took a mess of shadows for its meat?
And I though never of Ledæan kind
Had pretty plumage once—enough of that,
Better to smile on all that smile, and show
There is a comfortable kind of old scarecrow.

What youthful mother, a shape upon her lap
Honey of generation had betrayed,
And that must sleep, shriek, struggle to escape
As recollection or the drug decide,
Would think her son, did she but see that shape
With sixty or more winters on its head,
A compensation for the pang of his birth,
Or the uncertainty of his setting forth?

Plato thought nature but a spume that plays
Upon a ghostly paradigm of things;
Solider Aristotle played the taws
Upon the bottom of a king of kings;
World-famous golden-thighed Pythagoras
Fingered upon a fiddle stick or strings
What a star sang and careless Muses heard:
Old clothes upon old sticks to scare a bird.

Both nuns and mothers worship images,
But those the candles light are not as those
That animate a mother's reveries,
But keep a marble or a bronze repose.
And yet they too break hearts—O Presences
That passion, piety or affection knows,
And that all heavenly glory symbolize—
O self-born mockers of man's enterprise;

Labour is blossoming or dancing where
The body is not bruised to pleasure soul,
Nor beauty born out of its own despair,
Nor blear-eyed wisdom out of midnight oil.
O chestnut-tree, great-rooted blossomer,
Are you the leaf, the blossom or the bole?
O body swayed to music, O brightening glance,
How can we know the dancer from the dance?

1928

A DIALOGUE OF SELF AND SOUL

I

My Soul. I summon to the winding ancient stair;
Set all your mind upon the steep ascent,

Upon the broken, crumbling battlement,
Upon the breathless starlit air,
Upon the star that marks the hidden pole;
Fix every wandering thought upon
That quarter where all thought is done:
Who can distinguish darkness from the soul?

My Self. The consecrated blade upon my knees
Is Sato's ancient blade, still as it was,
Still razor-keen, still like a looking-glass
Unspotted by the centuries;
That flowering, silken, old embroidery, torn
From some court-lady's dress and round
The wooden scabbard bound and wound,
Can, tattered, still protect, faded adorn.

My Soul. Why should the imagination of a man
Long past his prime remember things that are
Emblematical of love and war?
Think of ancestral night that can,
If but imagination scorn the earth
And intellect its wandering
To this and that and t'other thing,
Deliver from the crime of death and birth.

My Self. Montashigi, third of his family, fashioned it
Five hundred years ago, about it lie
Flowers from I know not what embroidery—
Heart's purple—and all these I set
For emblems of the day against the tower
Emblematical of the night,
And claim as by a soldier's right
A charter to commit the crime once more.

My Soul. Such fullness in that quarter overflows
And falls into the basin of the mind
That man is stricken deaf and dumb and blind,
For intellect no longer knows
Is from the *Ought,* or *Knower* from the *Known—*
That is to say, ascends to Heaven;
Only the dead can be forgiven;
But when I think of that my tongue's a stone.

II

My Self. A living man is blind and drinks his drop.
What matter if the ditches are impure?
What matter if I live it all once more?
Endure that toil of growing up;
The ignominy of boyhood; the distress
Of boyhood changing into man;
The unfinished man and his pain
Brought face to face with his own clumsiness;

The finished man among his enemies?—
How in the name of Heaven can he escape
That defiling and disfigured shape
The mirror of malicious eyes
Casts upon his eyes until at last
He thinks that shape must be his shape?
And what's the good of an escape
If honour find him in the wintry blast?

I am content to live it all again
And yet again, if it be life to pitch
Into the frog-spawn of a blind man's ditch,
A blind man battering blind men;
Or into that most fecund ditch of all,
The folly that man does
Or must suffer, if he woos
A proud woman not kindred of his soul.

I am content to follow to its source
Every event in action or in thought;
Measure the lot; forgive myself the lot!
When such as I cast out remorse
So great a sweetness flows into the breast
We must laugh and we must sing,
We are blest by everything,
Everything we look upon is blest.   *1933*

THREE MOVEMENTS

Shakespearean fish swam the sea, far away from land;
Romantic fish swam in nets coming to the hand;
What are all those fish that lie gasping on the strand?
                                        1933

COOLE PARK AND BALLYLEE, 1931

Under my window-ledge the waters race,
Otters below and moor-hens on the top,
Run for a mile undimmed in Heaven's face
Then darkening through "dark" Raftery's "cellar" drop,
Run underground, rise in a rocky place
In Coole demesne, and there to finish up
Spread to a lake and drop into a hole.
What's water but the generated soul?

Upon the border of that lake's a wood
Now all dry sticks under a wintry sun,
And in a copse of beeches there I stood,
For Nature's pulled her tragic buskin on
And all the rant's a mirror of my mood:
At sudden thunder of the mounting swan
I turned about and looked where branches break
The glittering reaches of the flooded lake.

Another emblem there! That stormy white
But seems a concentration of the sky;
And, like the soul, it sails into the sight
And in the morning's gone, no man knows why;
And is so lovely that it sets to right
What knowledge or its lack had set awry,
So arrogantly pure, a child might think
It can be murdered with a spot of ink.

Sound of a stick upon the floor, a sound
From somebody that toils from chair to chair;
Beloved books that famous hands have bound,
Old marble heads, old pictures everywhere;
Great rooms where travelled men and children found
Content or joy; a last inheritor
Where none has reigned that lacked a name and fame
Or out of folly into folly came.

A spot whereon the founders lived and died
Seemed once more dear than life; ancestral trees,
Or gardens rich in memory glorified
Marriages, alliances, and families,

And every bride's ambition satisfied.
Where fashion or mere fantasy decrees
We shift about—all that great glory spent—
Like some poor Arab tribesman and his tent.

We were the last romantics—chose for theme
Traditional sanctity and loveliness;
Whatever's written in what poets name
The book of the people; whatever most can bless
The mind of man or elevate a rhyme;
But all is changed, that high horse riderless,
Though mounted in that saddle Homer rode
Where the swan drifts upon a darkening flood.   *1933*

FOR ANNE GREGORY

"Never shall a young man,
Thrown into despair
By those great honey-coloured
Ramparts at your ear,
Love you for yourself alone
And not your yellow hair."

"But I can get a hair-dye
And set such colour there,
Brown, or black, or carrot,
That young men in despair
May love me for myself alone
And not my yellow hair."

"I heard an old religious man
But yesternight declare
That he had found a text to prove
That only God, my dear,
Could love you for yourself alone
And not your yellow hair."   *1933*

SWIFT'S EPITAPH

Swift had sailed into his rest;
Savage indignation there
Cannot lacerate his breast.
Imitate him if you dare,

World-besotted traveller; he
Served human liberty.
                    1933

THE CHOICE

The intellect of man is forced to choose
Perfection of the life, or of the work,
And if it take the second must refuse
A heavenly mansion, raging in the dark.
When all that story's finished, what's the news?
In luck or out the toil has left its mark:
That old perplexity an empty purse,
Or the day's vanity, the night's remorse.   1933

BYZANTIUM

The unpurged images of day recede;
The Emperor's drunken soldiery are abed;
Night resonance recedes, night-walkers' song
After great cathedral gong;
A starlit or a moonlit dome disdains
All that man is,
All mere complexities,
The fury and the mire of human veins.

Before me floats an image, man or shade,
Shade more than man, more image than a shade;
For Hades' bobbin bound in mummy-cloth
May unwind the winding path;
A mouth that has no moisture and no breath
Breathless mouths may summon;
I hail the superhuman;
I call it death-in-life and life-in-death.

Miracle, bird or golden handiwork,
More miracle than bird or handiwork,
Planted on the star-lit golden bough,
Can like the cocks of Hades crow,
Or, by the moon embittered, scorn aloud
In glory of changeless metal
Common bird or petal
And all complexities of mire or blood.

At midnight on the Emperor's pavement flit
Flames that no faggot feeds, nor steel has lit,
Nor storm disturbs, flames begotten of flame,
Where blood-begotten spirits come
And all complexities of fury leave,
Dying into a dance,
An agony of trance,
An agony of flame that cannot singe a sleeve.

Astraddle on the dolphin's mire and blood,
Spirit after spirit! The smithies break the flood,
The golden smithies of the Emperor!
Marbles of the dancing floor
Break bitter furies of complexity,
Those images that yet
Fresh images beget,
That dolphin-torn, that gong-tormented sea.

1930, 1933

From WORDS FOR MUSIC PERHAPS

I

CRAZY JANE AND THE BISHOP

Bring me to the blasted oak
That I, midnight upon the stroke,
(*All find safety in the tomb.*)
May call down curses on his head
Because of my dear Jack that's dead.
Coxcomb was the least he said:
The solid man and the coxcomb.

Nor was he Bishop when his ban
Banished Jack the Journeyman,
(*All find safety in the tomb.*)
Nor so much as parish priest,
Yet he, an old book in his fist,
Cried that we lived like beast and beast:
The solid man and the coxcomb.

The Bishop has a skin, God knows,
Wrinkled like the foot of a goose,
(*All find safety in the tomb.*)

Nor can he hide in holy black
The heron's hunch upon his back,
But a birch-tree stood my Jack:
The solid man and the coxcomb.

Jack had my virginity,
And bids me to the oak, for he
(*All find safety in the tomb.*)
Wanders out into the night
And there is shelter under it,
But should that other come, I spit:
The solid man and the coxcomb.

II

CRAZY JANE REPROVED

I care not what the sailors say:
All those dreadful thunder-stones,
All that storm that blots the day
Can but show that Heaven yawns;
Great Europa played the fool
That changed a lover for a bull.
Fol de rol, fol de rol.

To round that shell's elaborate whorl,
Adorning every secret track
With the delicate mother-of-pearl,
Made the joints of Heaven crack:
So never hang your heart upon
A roaring, ranting journeyman.
Fol de rol, fol de rol.

III

CRAZY JANE ON THE DAY OF JUDGMENT

"Love is all
Unsatisfied
That cannot take the whole
Body and soul";
And that is what Jane said.

"Take the sour
If you take me,
I can scoff and lour

And scold for an hour."
"That's certainly the case," said he.

"Naked I lay,
The grass my bed;
Naked and hidden away,
That black day";
And that is what Jane said.

"What can be shown?
What true love be?
All could be known or shown
If Time were but gone."
"That's certainly the case," said he.

IV

CRAZY JANE AND JACK THE JOURNEYMAN

I know, although when looks meet
I tremble to the bone,
The more I leave the door unlatched
The sooner love is gone,
For love is but a skein unwound
Between the dark and dawn.

A lonely ghost the ghost is
That to God shall come;
I—love's skein upon the ground,
My body in the tomb—
Shall leap into the light lost
In my mother's womb.

But were I left to lie alone
In an empty bed,
The skein so bound us ghost to ghost
When he turned his head
Passing on the road that night,
Mine must walk when dead.

V

CRAZY JANE ON GOD

That lover of a night
Came when he would,

Went in the dawning light
Whether I would or no;
Men come, men go,
All things remain in God.

Banners choke the sky;
Men-at-arms tread;
Armoured horses neigh
Where the great battle was
In the narrow pass:
All things remain in God.

Before their eyes a house
That from childhood stood
Uninhabited, ruinous,
Suddenly lit up
From door to top:
All things remain in God.

I had wild Jack for a lover;
Though like a road
That men pass over
My body makes no moan
But sings on;
All things remain in God.

VI

CRAZY JANE TALKS WITH THE BISHOP

I met the Bishop on the road
And much said he and I.
"Those breasts are flat and fallen now,
Those veins must soon be dry;
Live in a heavenly mansion,
Not in some foul sty."

"Fair and foul are near of kin,
And fair needs foul," I cried.
"My friends are gone, but that's a truth
Nor grave nor bed denied,
Learned in bodily lowliness
And in the heart's pride.

"A woman can be proud and stiff
When on love intent;
But Love has pitched his mansion in
The place of excrement;
For nothing can be sole or whole
That has not been rent."

VII

CRAZY JANE GROWN OLD LOOKS AT THE DANCERS

I found that ivory image there
Dancing with her chosen youth,
But when he wound her coal-black hair
As though to strangle her, no scream
Or bodily movement did I dare,
Eyes under eyelids did so gleam;
Love is like the lion's tooth.

When she, and though some said she played
I said that she had danced heart's truth,
Drew a knife to strike him dead,
I could but leave him to his fate;
For no matter what is said
They had all that had their hate;
Love is like the lion's tooth.

Did he die or did she die?
Seemed to die or died they both?
God be with the times when I
Cared not a thraneen for what chanced
So that I had the limbs to try
Such a dance as there was danced—
Love is like the lion's tooth.

XVII

AFTER LONG SILENCE

Speech after long silence; it is right,
All other lovers being estranged or dead,
Unfriendly lamplight hid under its shade,
The curtains drawn upon unfriendly night,
That we descant and yet again descant

Upon the supreme theme of Art and Song:
Bodily decrepitude is wisdom; young
We loved each other and were ignorant.

XX

"I AM OF IRELAND"

"I am of Ireland,
And the Holy Land of Ireland,
And time runs on," cried she.
"Come out of charity,
Come dance with me in Ireland."

One man, one man alone
In that outlandish gear,
One solitary man
Of all that rambled there
Had turned his stately head.
"That is a long way off,
And time runs on," he said,
"And the night grows rough."

"I am of Ireland,
And the Holy Land of Ireland,
And time runs on," cried she.
"Come out of charity,
And dance with me in Ireland."

"The fiddlers are all thumbs,
Or the fiddle-string accursed,
The drums and the kettledrums
And the trumpets all are burst,
And the trombone," cried he,
"The trumpet and trombone,"
And cocked a malicious eye,
"But time runs on, runs on."

"I am of Ireland,
And the Holy Land of Ireland,
And time runs on," cried she.
"Come out of charity,
And dance with me in Ireland."
                August 19, 1931, 1933

From A WOMAN YOUNG AND OLD

VI. CHOSEN

The lot of love is chosen. I learnt that much
Struggling for an image on the track
Of the whirling Zodiac.
Scarce did he my body touch,
Scarce sank he from the west
Or found a subterranean rest
On the maternal midnight of my breast
Before I had marked him on his northern way,
And seemed to stand although in bed I lay.

I struggled with the horror of daybreak,
I chose it for my lot! If questioned on
My utmost pleasure with a man
By some new-married bride, I take
That stillness for a theme
Where his heart my heart did seem
And both adrift on the miraculous stream
Where—wrote a learned astrologer—
The Zodiac is changed into a sphere.

IX. A LAST CONFESSION

What lively lad most pleasured me
Of all that with me lay?
I answer that I gave my soul
And loved in misery,
But had great pleasure with a lad
That I loved bodily.

Flinging from his arms I laughed
To think his passion such
He fancied that I gave a soul
Did but our bodies touch,
And laughed upon his breast to think
Beast gave beast as much.

I gave what other women gave
That stepped out of their clothes,
But when this soul, its body off,

Naked to naked goes,
He it has found shall find therein
What none other knows,

And give his own and take his own
And rule in his own right;
And though it loved in misery
Close and cling so tight,
There's not a bird of day that dare
Extinguish that delight.   *1933*

CHURCH AND STATE

Here is fresh matter, poet,
Matter for old age meet;
Might of the Church and the State,
Their mobs put under their feet.
O but heart's wine shall run pure,
Mind's bread grow sweet.

That were a cowardly song,
Wander in dreams no more;
What if the Church and the State
Are the mob that howls at the door!
Wine shall run thick to the end,
Bread taste sour.

August 1934, 1935

LAPIS LAZULI

I have heard that hysterical women say
They are sick of the palette and fiddle-bow,
Of poets that are always gay,
For everybody knows or else should know
That if nothing drastic is done
Aeroplane and Zeppelin will come out,
Pitch like King Billy bomb-balls in
Until the town lie beaten flat.

All perform their tragic play,
There struts Hamlet, there is Lear,
That's Ophelia, that Cordelia;

Yet they, should the last scene be there,
The great stage curtain about to drop,
If worthy their prominent part in the play,
Do not break up their lines to weep.
They know that Hamlet and Lear are gay;
Gaiety transfiguring all that dread.
All men have aimed at, found and lost;
Black out; Heaven blazing into the head:
Tragedy wrought to its uttermost.
Though Hamlet rambles and Lear rages,
And all the drop-scenes drop at once
Upon a hundred thousand stages,
It cannot grow by an inch or an ounce.

On their own feet they came, or on shipboard,
Camel-back, horse-back, ass-back, mule-back,
Old civilisations put to the sword.
Then they and their wisdom went to rack:
No handiwork of Callimachus,
Who handled marble as if it were bronze,
Made draperies that seemed to rise
When sea-wind swept the corner, stands;
His long lamp-chimney shaped like the stem
Of a slender palm, stood but a day;
All things fall and are built again,
And those that build them again are gay.

Two Chinamen, behind them a third,
Are carved in lapis lazuli,
Over them flies a long-legged bird,
A symbol of longevity;
The third, doubtless a serving-man,
Carries a musical instrument.

Every discoloration of the stone,
Every accidental crack or dent,
Seems a water-course or an avalanche,
Or lofty slope where it still snows
Though doubtless plum or cherry-branch
Sweetens the little half-way house
Those Chinamen climb towards, and I
Delight to imagine them seated there;
There, on the mountain and the sky,

On all the tragic scene they stare.
One asks for mournful melodies;
Accomplished fingers begin to play.
Their eyes mid many wrinkles, their eyes,
Their ancient, glittering eyes, are gay.   *1938*

AN ACRE OF GRASS

Picture and book remain,
An acre of green grass
For air and exercise,
Now strength of body goes;
Midnight, an old house
Where nothing stirs but a mouse.

My temptation is quiet.
Here at life's end
Neither loose imagination,
Nor the mill of the mind
Consuming its rag and bone,
Can make the truth known.

Grant me an old man's frenzy,
Myself must I remake
Till I am Timon and Lear
Or that William Blake
Who beat upon the wall
Till Truth obeyed his call;

A mind Michael Angelo knew
That can pierce the clouds,
Or inspired by frenzy
Shake the dead in their shrouds;
Forgotten else by mankind,
An old man's eagle mind.   *1938*

WHAT THEN?

His chosen comrades thought at school
He must grow a famous man;
He thought the same and lived by rule,
All his twenties crammed with toil;
"What then?" sang Plato's ghost. "What then?"

Everything he wrote was read,
After certain years he won
Sufficient money for his need,
Friends that have been friends indeed;
"What then?" sang Plato's ghost. "What then?"

All his happier dreams came true—
A small old house, wife, daughter, son,
Grounds where plum and cabbage grew,
Poets and Wits about him drew;
"What then?" sang Plato's ghost. "What then?"

"The work is done," grown old he thought,
"According to my boyish plan;
Let the fools rage, I swerved in naught,
Something to perfection brought;"
But louder sang that ghost, "What then?"   1938

THE WILD OLD WICKED MAN

"Because I am mad about women
I am mad about the hills,"
Said that wild old wicked man
Who travels where God wills.
"Not to die on the straw at home,
Those hands to close these eyes,
That is all I ask, my dear,
From the old man in the skies.
                    Daybreak and a candle-end.

"Kind are all your words, my dear,
Do not the rest withhold.
Who can know the year, my dear,
When an old man's blood grows cold?
I have what no young man can have
Because he loves too much.
Words I have that can pierce the heart,
But what can he do but touch?"
                    Daybreak and a candle-end.

Then said she to that wild old man,
His stout stick under his hand,
"Love to give or to withhold

Is not at my command.
I gave it all to an older man:
That old man in the skies.
Hands that are busy with His beads
Can never close those eyes."
                    Daybreak and a candle-end.

"Go your ways, O go your ways,
I choose another mark,
Girls down on the seashore
Who understand the dark;
Bawdy talk for the fishermen;
A dance for the fisher-lads;
When dark hangs upon the water
They turn down their beds.
                    Daybreak and a candle-end.

"A young man in the dark am I,
But a wild old man in the light,
That can make a cat laugh, or
Can touch by mother wit
Things hid in their marrow-bones
From time long passed away,
Hid from all those warty lads
That by their bodies lay.
                    Daybreak and a candle-end.

"All men live in suffering,
I know as few can know,
Whether they take the upper road
Or stay content on the low,
Rower bent in his row-boat
Or weaver bent at his loom,
Horseman erect upon horseback
Or child hid in the womb.
                    Daybreak and a candle-end.

"That some stream of lightning
From the old man in the skies
Can burn out that suffering
No right-taught man denies.
But a coarse old man am I,
I choose the second-best.

I forget it all awhile
Upon a woman's breast."
Daybreak and a candle-end.
1938

THE GREAT DAY

Hurrah for revolution and more cannon-shot!
A beggar upon horseback lashes a beggar on foot.
Hurrah for revolution and cannon come again!
The beggars have changed places, but the lash goes on.
1938

PARNELL

Parnell came down the road, he said to a cheering man:
"Ireland shall get her freedom and you still break stone."
1938

A MODEL FOR THE LAUREATE

On thrones from China to Peru
All sorts of kings have sat
That men and women of all sorts
Proclaimed both good and great;
And what's the odds if such as these
For reason of the State
Should keep their lovers waiting,
        Keep their lovers waiting?

Some boast of beggar-kings and kings
Of rascals black and white
That rule because a strong right arm
Puts all men in a fright,
And drunk or sober live at ease
Where none gainsay their right,
And keep their lovers waiting,
        Keep their lovers waiting.

The Muse is mute when public men
Applaud a modern throne:
Those cheers that can be bought or sold,
That office fools have run,
That waxen seal, that signature,

For things like these what decent man
Would keep his lover waiting,
    Keep his lover waiting?   *1938*

THOSE IMAGES

What if I bade you leave
The cavern of the mind?
There's better exercise
In the sunlight and wind.

I never bade you go
To Moscow or to Rome.
Renounce that drudgery,
Call the Muses home.

Seek those images
That constitute the wild,
The lion and the virgin,
The harlot and the child.

Find in middle air
An eagle on the wing,
Recognise the five
That make the Muses sing.
          1938

NEWS FOR THE DELPHIC ORACLE

I

There all the golden codgers lay,
There the silver dew,
And the great water sighed for love,
And the wind sighed too.
Man-picker Niamh leant and sighed
By Oisin on the grass;
There sighed amid his choir of love
Tall Pythagoras.
Plotinus came and looked about,
The salt-flakes on his breast,
And having stretched and yawned awhile
Lay sighing like the rest.

II

Straddling each a dolphin's back
And steadied by a fin,
Those Innocents re-live their death,
Their wounds open again.
The ecstatic waters laugh because
Their cries are sweet and strange,
Through their ancestral patterns dance,
And the brute dolphins plunge
Until, in some cliff-sheltered bay
Where wades the choir of love
Proffering its sacred laurel crowns,
They pitch their burdens off.

III

Slim adolescence that a nymph has stripped,
Peleus on Thetis stares.
Her limbs are delicate as an eyelid,
Love has blinded him with tears;
But Thetis' belly listens.
Down the mountain walls
From where Pan's cavern is
Intolerable music falls.
Foul goat-head, brutal arm appear,
Belly, shoulder, bum,
Flash fishlike; nymphs and satyrs
Copulate in the foam.   *1940*

LONG-LEGGED FLY

That civilisation may not sink,
Its great battle lost,
Quiet the dog, tether the pony
To a distant post;
Our master Caesar is in the tent
Where the maps are spread,
His eyes fixed upon nothing,
A hand under his head.
Like a long-legged fly upon the stream
His mind moves upon silence.

That the topless towers be burnt
And men recall that face,
Move most gently if move you must
In this lonely place.
She thinks, part woman, three parts a child,
That nobody looks; her feet
Practise a tinker shuffle
Picked up on a street.
Like a long-legged fly upon the stream
Her mind moves upon silence.

That girls at puberty may find
The first Adam in their thought,
Shut the door of the Pope's chapel,
Keep those children out.
There on that scaffolding reclines
Michael Angelo.
With no more sound than the mice make
His hand moves to and fro.
Like a long-legged fly upon the stream
His mind moves upon silence.   1940

JOHN KINSELLA'S LAMENT FOR MRS. MARY MOORE

A bloody and a sudden end,
    Gunshot or a noose,
For Death who takes what man would keep,
    Leaves what man would lose.
He might have had my sister,
    My cousins by the score,
But nothing satisfied the fool
    But my dear Mary Moore,
None other knows what pleasures man
    At table or in bed.
What shall I do for pretty girls
    Now my old bawd is dead?

Though stiff to strike a bargain,
    Like an old Jew man,
Her bargain struck we laughed and talked
    And emptied many a can;
And O! but she had stories,
    Though not for the priest's ear,

To keep the soul of man alive,
    Banish age and care,
And being old she put a skin
    On everything she said.
What shall I do for pretty girls
    Now my old bawd is dead?

The priests have got a book that says
    But for Adam's sin
Eden's Garden would be there
    And I there within.
No expectation fails there,
    No pleasing habit ends,
No man grows old, no girl grows cold,
    But friends walk by friends.
Who quarrels over halfpennies
    That plucks the trees for bread?
What shall I do for pretty girls
    Now my old bawd is dead?   1940

THE APPARITIONS

Because there is safety in derision
I talked about an apparition,
I took no trouble to convince,
Or seem plausible to a man of sense,
Distrustful of that popular eye
Whether it be bold or sly.
Fifteen apparitions have I seen;
The worst a coat upon a coat-hanger.

I have found nothing half so good
As my long-planned half solitude,
Where I can sit up half the night
With some friend that has the wit
Not to allow his looks to tell
When I am unintelligible.
Fifteen apparitions have I seen;
The worst a coat upon a coat-hanger.

When a man grows old his joy
Grows more deep day after day,
His empty heart is full at length,

But he has need of all that strength
Because of the increasing Night
That opens her mystery and fright.
Fifteen apparitions have I seen;
The worst a coat upon a coat-hanger.

                                        1940

THE STATESMAN'S HOLIDAY

I lived among great houses,
Riches drove out rank,
Base drove out the better blood,
And mind and body shrank.
No Oscar ruled the table,
But I'd a troop of friends
That knowing better talk had gone
Talked of odds and ends.
Some knew what ailed the world
But never said a thing,
So I have picked a better trade
And night and morning sing:
Tall dames go walking in grass-green Avalon.

Am I a great Lord Chancellor
That slept upon the Sack?
Commanding officer that tore
The khaki from his back?
Or am I de Valéra,
Or the King of Greece,
Or the man that made the motors?
Ach, call me what you please!
Here's a Montenegrin lute,
And its old sole string
Makes me sweet music
And I delight to sing:
Tall dames go walking in grass-green Avalon.

With boys and girls about him,
With any sort of clothes,
With a hat out of fashion,
With old patched shoes,
With a ragged bandit cloak,
With an eye like a hawk,

With a stiff straight back,
With a strutting turkey walk,
With a bag full of pennies,
With a monkey on a chain,
With a great cock's feather,
With an old foul tune.
Tall dames go walking in grass-green Avalon.

1940

CRAZY JANE ON THE MOUNTAIN

I am tired of cursing the Bishop,
(Said Crazy Jane)
Nine books or nine hats
Would not make him a man.
I have found something worse
To meditate on.
A King had some beautiful cousins,
But where are they gone?
Battered to death in a cellar,
And he stuck to his throne.
Last night I lay on the mountain,
(Said Crazy Jane)
There in a two-horsed carriage
That on two wheels ran
Great-bladdered Emer sat,
Her violent man
Cuchulain sat at her side;
Thereupon,
Propped upon my two knees,
I kissed a stone;
I lay stretched out in the dirt
And I cried tears down.   1940

THE CIRCUS ANIMALS' DESERTION

I

I sought a theme and sought for it in vain,
I sought it daily for six weeks or so.
Maybe at last, being but a broken man,
I must be satisfied with my heart, although

Winter and summer till old age began
My circus animals were all on show,
Those stilted boys, that burnished chariot,
Lion and woman and the Lord knows what.

II

What can I but enumerate old themes?
First that sea-rider Oisin led by the nose
Through three enchanted islands, allegorical dreams,
Vain gaiety, vain battle, vain repose,
Themes of the embittered heart, or so it seems,
That might adorn old songs or courtly shows;
But what cared I that set him on to ride,
I, starved for the bosom of his faery bride?

And then a counter-truth filled out its play,
The Countess Cathleen was the name I gave it;
She, pity-crazed, had given her soul away,
But masterful Heaven had intervened to save it.
I thought my dear must her own soul destroy,
So did fanaticism and hate enslave it,
And this brought forth a dream and soon enough
This dream itself had all my thought and love.

And when the Fool and Blind Man stole the bread
Cuchulain fought the ungovernable sea;
Heart-mysteries there, and yet when all is said
It was the dream itself enchanted me:
Character isolated by a deed
To engross the present and dominate memory.
Players and painted stage took all my love,
And not those things that they were emblems of.

III

Those masterful images because complete
Grew in pure mind, but out of what began?
A mound of refuse or the sweepings of a street,
Old kettles, old bottles, and a broken can,
Old iron, old bones, old rags, that raving slut
Who keeps the till. Now that my ladder's gone,
I must lie down where all the ladders start,
In the foul rag-and-bone shop of the heart.   *1940*

POLITICS

"In our time the destiny of man presents its meaning in political terms."
—Thomas Mann

How can I, that girl standing there,
My attention fix
On Roman or on Russian
Or on Spanish politics?
Yet here's a travelled man that knows
What he talks about,
And there's a politician
That has read and thought,
And maybe what they say is true
Of war and war's alarms,
But O that I were young again
And held her in my arms!   *1940*

CUCHULAIN COMFORTED

A man that had six mortal wounds, a man
Violent and famous, strode among the dead;
Eyes stared out of the branches and were gone.

Then certain Shrouds that muttered head to head
Came and were gone. He leant upon a tree
As though to meditate on wounds and blood.

A Shroud that seemed to have authority
Among those bird-like things came, and let fall
A bundle of linen. Shrouds by two and three

Came creeping up because the man was still.
And thereupon that linen-carrier said:
"Your life can grow much sweeter if you will

"Obey our ancient rule and make a shroud;
Mainly because of what we only know
The rattle of those arms makes us afraid.

"We thread the needles' eyes, and all we do
All must together do." That done, the man
Took up the nearest and began to sew.

"Now must we sing and sing the best we can,
But first you must be told our character:
Convicted cowards all, by kindred slain

"Or driven from home and left to die in fear."
They sang, but had nor human tunes nor words,
Though all was done in common as before;

They had changed their throats and had the throats of birds.
January 13, 1939, 1940

THE BLACK TOWER

Say that the men of the old black tower,
Though they but feed as the goatherd feeds,
Their money spent, their wine gone sour,
Lack nothing that a soldier needs,
That all are oath-bound men:
Those banners come not in.

There in the tomb stand the dead upright,
But winds come up from the shore:
They shake when the winds roar,
Old bones upon the mountain shake.

Those banners come to bribe or threaten,
Or whisper that a man's a fool
Who, when his own right king's forgotten,
Cares what king sets up his rule.
If he died long ago
Why do you dread us so?

There in the tomb drops the faint moonlight,
But wind comes up from the shore:
They shake when the winds roar,
Old bones upon the mountain shake.

The tower's old cook that must climb and clamber
Catching small birds in the dew of the morn
When we hale men lie stretched in slumber
Swears that he hears the king's great horn.
But he's a lying hound:
Stand we on guard oath-bound!

There in the tomb the dark grows blacker,
But wind comes up from the shore:

They shake when the winds roar,
Old bones upon the mountain shake.

January 21, 1939, 1940

UNDER BEN BULBEN

I

Swear by what the sages spoke
Round the Mareotic Lake
That the Witch of Atlas knew,
Spoke and set the cocks a-crow.

Swear by those horsemen, by those women
Complexion and form prove superhuman,
That pale, long-visaged company
That air in immortality
Completeness of their passions won;
Now they ride the wintry dawn
Where Ben Bulben sets the scene.

Here's the gist of what they mean.

II

Many times man lives and dies
Between his two eternities,
That of race and that of soul,
And ancient Ireland knew it all.
Whether man die in his bed
Or the rifle knocks him dead,
A brief parting from those dear
Is the worst man has to fear.
Though grave-diggers' toil is long,
Sharp their spades, their muscles strong,
They but thrust their buried men
Back in the human mind again.

III

You that Mitchel's prayer have heard,
"Send war in our time, O Lord!"
Know that when all words are said
And a man is fighting mad,
Something drops from eyes long blind,

He completes his partial mind,
For an instant stands at ease,
Laughs aloud, his heart at peace.
Even the wisest man grows tense
With some sort of violence
Before he can accomplish fate,
Know his work or choose his mate.

IV

Poet and sculptor, do the work,
Nor let the modish painter shirk
What his great forefathers did,
Bring the soul of man to God,
Make him fill the cradles right.

Measurement began our might:
Forms a stark Egyptian thought,
Forms that gentler Phidias wrought.
Michael Angelo left a proof
On the Sistine Chapel roof,
Where but half-awakened Adam
Can disturb globe-trotting Madam
Till her bowels are in heat,
Proof that there's a purpose set
Before the secret working mind:
Profane perfection of mankind.

Quattrocento put in paint
On backgrounds for a God or Saint
Gardens where a soul's at ease;
Where everything that meets the eye,
Flowers and grass and cloudless sky,
Resemble forms that are or seem
When sleepers wake and yet still dream,
And when it's vanished still declare,
With only bed and bedstead there,
That heavens had opened.
                          Gyres run on;
When that greater dream had gone
Calvert and Wilson, Blake and Claude,
Prepared a rest for the people of God,
Palmer's phrase, but after that
Confusion fell upon our thought.

V

Irish poets, learn your trade,
Sing whatever is well made,
Scorn the sort now growing up
All out of shape from toe to top,
Their unremembering hearts and heads
Base-born products of base beds.
Sing the peasantry, and then
Hard-riding country gentlemen,
The holiness of monks, and after
Porter-drinkers' randy laughter;
Sing the lords and ladies gay
That were beaten into the clay
Through seven heroic centuries;
Cast your mind on other days
That we in coming days may be
Still the indomitable Irishry.

VI

Under bare Ben Bulben's head
In Drumcliff churchyard Yeats is laid.
An ancestor was rector there
Long years ago, a church stands near,
By the road an ancient cross.
No marble, no conventional phrase;
On limestone quarried near the spot
By his command these words are cut:

> *Cast a cold eye*
> *On life, on death.*
> *Horseman, pass by!*

September 4, 1938, 1940

PURGATORY

PERSONS IN THE PLAY

A Boy   An Old Man

> [*Scene: a ruined house and a bare tree in the background.*

BOY. Half-door, hall door,
  Hither and thither, day and night,

Hill or hollow, shouldering this pack,
Hearing you talk.
OLD MAN. Study that house.
I think about its jokes and stories;
I try to remember what the butler
Said to a drunken gamekeeper
In mid-October, but I cannot.
If I cannot, none living can.
Where are the jokes and stories of a house,
Its threshold gone to patch a pig-sty?
BOY. So you have come this path before?
OLD MAN. The moonlight falls upon the path,
The shadow of a cloud upon the house,
And that's symbolical; study that tree,
What is it like?
BOY. A silly old man.
OLD MAN. It's like—no matter what it's like.
I saw it a year ago stripped bare as now,
So I chose a better trade.
I saw it fifty years ago
Before the thunderbolt had riven it,
Green leaves, ripe leaves, leaves thick as butter,
Fat, greasy life. Stand there and look,
Because there is somebody in that house.
                    [*The Boy puts down pack and stands*
                          in the doorway.

BOY. There's nobody here.
OLD MAN. There's somebody there.
BOY. The floor is gone, the windows gone,
And where there should be roof there's sky,
And here's a bit of an egg-shell thrown
Out of a jackdaw's nest.
OLD MAN. But there are some
That do not care what's gone, what's left:
The souls in Purgatory that come back
To habitations and familiar spots.
BOY. Your wits are out again.
OLD MAN. Re-live
Their transgressions, and that not once
But many times; they know at last
The consequence of those transgressions
Whether upon others or upon themselves;
Upon others, others may bring help,

For when the consequence is at an end
The dream must end; if upon themselves,
There is no help but in themselves
And in the mercy of God.

BOY.   I have had enough!
Talk to the jackdaws, if talk you must.

OLD MAN.   Stop! Sit there upon that stone.
That is the house where I was born.

BOY.   The big old house that was burnt down?

OLD MAN.   My mother that was your grand-dam owned it,
This scenery and this countryside,
Kennel and stable, horse and hound—
She had a horse at the Curragh, and there met
My father, a groom in a training stable,
Looked at him and married him.
Her mother never spoke to her again,
And she did right.

BOY.   What's right and wrong?
My granddad got the girl and the money.

OLD MAN.   Looked at him and married him,
And he squandered everything she had.
She never knew the worst, because
She died in giving birth to me,
But now she knows it all, being dead.
Great people lived and died in this house;
Magistrates, colonels, members of Parliament,
Captains and Governors, and long ago
Men that had fought at Aughrim and the Boyne.
Some that had gone on Government work
To London or to India came home to die,
Or came from London every spring
To look at the may-blossom in the park.
They had loved the trees that he cut down
To pay what he had lost at cards
Or spent on horses, drink and women;
Had loved the house, had loved all
The intricate passages of the house,
But he killed the house; to kill a house
Where great men grew up, married, died,
I here declare a capital offence.

BOY.   My God, but you had luck! Grand clothes,
And maybe a grand horse to ride.

OLD MAN.   That he might keep me upon his level

He never sent me to school, but some
Half-loved me for my half of her:
A gamekeeper's wife taught me to read,
A Catholic curate taught me Latin.
There were old books and books made fine
By eighteenth-century French binding, books
Modern and ancient, books by the ton.
BOY.   What education have you given me?
OLD MAN.   I gave the education that befits
A bastard that a pedlar got
Upon a tinker's daughter in a ditch.
When I had come to sixteen years old
My father burned down the house when drunk.
BOY.   But that is my age, sixteen years old,
At the Puck Fair.
OLD MAN.   And everything was burnt;
Books, library, all were burnt.
BOY.   Is what I have heard upon the road the truth,
That you killed him in the burning house?
OLD MAN.   There's nobody here but our two selves?
BOY.   Nobody, Father.
OLD MAN.   I stuck him with a knife,
That knife that cuts my dinner now,
And after that I left him in the fire.
They dragged him out, somebody saw
The knife-wound but could not be certain
Because the body was all black and charred.
Then some that were his drunken friends
Swore they would put me upon trial,
Spoke of quarrels, a threat I had made.
The gamekeeper gave me some old clothes,
I ran away, worked here and there
Till I became a pedlar on the roads,
No good trade, but good enough
Because I am my father's son,
Because of what I did or may do.
Listen to the hoof-beats! Listen, listen!
BOY.   I cannot hear a sound.
OLD MAN.   Beat! Beat!
This night is the anniversary
Of my mother's wedding night,
Or of the night wherein I was begotten.
My father is riding from the public-house,

A whiskey-bottle under his arm.

> [*A window is lit showing a young girl.*]

Look at the window; she stands there
Listening, the servants are all in bed,
She is alone, he has stayed late
Bragging and drinking in the public-house.

BOY.   There's nothing but an empty gap in the wall.
You have made it up. No, you are mad!
You are getting madder every day.

OLD MAN.   It's louder now because he rides
Upon a gravelled avenue
All grass today. The hoof-beat stops,
He has gone to the other side of the house,
Gone to the stable, put the horse up.
She has gone down to open the door.
This night she is no better than her man
And does not mind that he is half drunk,
She is mad about him. They mount the stairs,
She brings him into her own chamber.
And that is the marriage-chamber now.
The window is dimly lit again.

Do not let him touch you! It is not true
That drunken men cannot beget,
And if he touch he must beget
And you must bear his murderer.
Deaf! Both deaf! If I should throw
A stick or a stone they would not hear;
And that's a proof my wits are out.
But there's a problem: she must live
Through everything in exact detail,
Driven to it by remorse, and yet
Can she renew the sexual act
And find no pleasure in it, and if not,
If pleasure and remorse must both be there,
Which is the greater?

> I lack schooling.

Go fetch Tertullian; he and I
Will ravel all that problem out
Whilst those two lie upon the mattress
Begetting me.

> Come back! Come back!

And so you thought to slip away,

My bag of money between your fingers,
And that I could not talk and see!
You have been rummaging in the pack.

> [*The light in the window has faded
> out.*

BOY. You never gave me my right share.
OLD MAN. And had I given it, young as you are,
You would have spent it upon drink.
BOY. What if I did? I had a right
To get it and spend it as I chose.
OLD MAN. Give me that bag and no more words.
BOY. I will not.
OLD MAN.   I will break your fingers.

> [*They struggle for the bag. In the
> struggle it drops, scattering the
> money. The Old Man staggers but
> does not fall. They stand looking at
> each other. The window is lit up. A
> man is seen pouring whiskey into a
> glass.*

BOY. What if I killed you? You killed my granddad,
Because you were young and he was old.
Now I am young and you are old.
OLD MAN. [*staring at window*] Better-looking, those sixteen years—
BOY. What are you muttering?
OLD MAN.   Younger—and yet
She should have known he was not her kind.
BOY. What are you saying? Out with it! [*Old man points to window.*]
My God! The window is lit up
And somebody stands there, although
The floorboards are all burnt away.
OLD MAN. The window is lit up because my father
Has come to find a glass for his whiskey.
He leans there like some tired beast.
BOY. A dead, living, murdered man!
OLD MAN. "Then the bride-sleep fell upon Adam":
Where did I read those words?
                And yet
There's nothing leaning in the window
But the impression upon my mother's mind;
Being dead she is alone in her remorse.
BOY. A body that was a bundle of old bones
Before I was born. Horrible! Horrible! [*He covers his eyes.*]
OLD MAN. That beast there would know nothing, being nothing,

If I should kill a man under the window
He would not even turn his head. [*He stabs the* BOY.]
My father and my son on the same jack-knife!
That finishes—there—there—there—

> [*He stabs again and again. The win-*
> *dow grows dark.*

"Hush-a-bye baby, thy father's a knight,
Thy mother a lady, lovely and bright."
No, that is something that I read in a book,
And if I sing it must be to my mother,
And I lack rhyme.

> [*The stage has grown dark except*
> *where the tree stands in white light.*

Study that tree.
It stands there like a purified soul,
All cold, sweet, glistening light.
Dear mother, the window is dark again,
But you are in the light because
I finished all that consequence.
I killed that lad because had he grown up
He would have struck a woman's fancy,
Begot, and passed pollution on.
I am a wretched foul old man
And therefore harmless. When I have stuck
This old jack-knife into a sod
And pulled it out all bright again,
And picked up all the money that he dropped,
I'll to a distant place, and there
Tell my old jokes among new men.

> [*He cleans the knife and begins to*
> *pick up money.*

Hoof-beats! Dear God,
How quickly it returns—beat—beat—!

Her mind cannot hold up that dream.
Twice a murderer and all for nothing,
And she must animate that dead night
Not once but many times!
                         O God,
Release my mother's soul from its dream!
Mankind can do no more. Appease
The misery of the living and the remorse of the dead.   1939

THE END

Walter de la Mare

THE SILVER PENNY

"Sailorman, I'll give to you
   My bright silver penny,
If out to sea you'll sail me
   And my dear sister Jenny."

"Get in, young sir, I'll sail ye
   And your dear sister Jenny,
But pay she shall her golden locks
   Instead of your penny."

They sail away, they sail away,
   O fierce the winds blew!
The foam flew in clouds,
   And dark the night grew!

And all the wild sea-water
   Climbed steep into the boat;
Back to the shore again
   Sail will they not.

Drowned is the sailorman,
   Drowned is sweet Jenny,
And drowned in the deep sea
   A bright silver penny.   *1902*

THE FUNERAL

They dressed us up in black,
Susan and Tom and me;
And, walking through the fields
All beautiful to see,
With branches high in the air

I-173

And daisy and buttercup,
We heard the lark in the clouds,—
In black dressed up.

They took us to the graves,
Susan and Tom and me,
Where the long grasses grow
And the funeral tree:
We stood and watched; and the wind
Came softly out of the sky
And blew in Susan's hair,
As I stood close by.

Back through the fields we came,
Tom and Susan and me,
And we sat in the nursery together,
And had our tea.
And, looking out of the window,
I heard the thrushes sing;
But Tom fell asleep in his chair.
He was so tired, poor thing.   *1902*

REMEMBRANCE

The sky was like a waterdrop
    In shadow of a thorn,
Clear, tranquil, beautiful,
    Dark, forlorn.

Lightning along its margin ran;
    A rumour of the sea
Rose in profundity and sank
    Into infinity.

Lofty and few the elms, the stars
    In the vast boughs most bright;
I stood a dreamer in a dream
    In the unstirring night.

Not wonder, worship, not even peace
    Seemed in my heart to be:
Only the memory of one,
    Of all most dead to me.   *1906*

SHADOW

Even the beauty of the rose doth cast,
When its bright, fervid noon is past,
A still and lengthening shadow in the dust,
    Till darkness come
    And take its strange dream home.

The transient bubbles of the water paint
'Neath their frail arch a shadow faint;
The golden nimbus of the windowed saint,
    Till shine the stars,
    Casts pale and trembling bars.

The loveliest thing earth hath, a shadow hath,
A dark and livelong hint of death,
Haunting it ever till its last faint breath.
    Who, then, may tell
The beauty of heaven's shadowless asphodel?
                  1906

UNREGARDING

Put by thy days like withered flowers
    In twilight hidden away:
Memory shall upbuild thee bowers
    Sweeter than they.

Hoard not from swiftness of thy stream
    The shallowest cruse of tears:
Pool still as heaven shall lovelier dream
    In future years.

Squander thy love as she that flings
    Her soul away on night;
Lovely are love's far echoings,
    Height unto height.

O, make no compact with the sun,
    No compact with the moon!
Night falls full-cloaked, and light is gone
    Sudden and soon.   *1906*

THE THREE CHERRY TREES

There were three cherry trees once,
Grew in a garden all shady;
And there for delight of so gladsome a sight,
Walked a most beautiful lady,
Dreamed a most beautiful lady.

Birds in those branches did sing,
Blackbird and throstle and linnet,
But she walking there was by far the most fair—
Lovelier than all else within it,
Blackbird and throstle and linnet.

But blossoms to berries do come,
All hanging on stalks light and slender:
And one long summer's day charmed that lady away,
With vows sweet and merry and tender;
A lover with voice low and tender.

Moss and lichen the green branches deck;
Weeds nod in its paths green and shady;
Yet a light footstep seems there to wander in dreams,
The ghost of that beautiful lady,
That happy and beautiful lady.   *1912*

OLD SUSAN

When Susan's work was done, she would sit,
With one fat guttering candle lit,
And window opened wide to win
The sweet night air to enter in.
There, with a thumb to keep her place,
She would read, with stern and wrinkled face,
Her mild eyes gliding very slow
Across the letters to and fro,
While wagged the guttering candle flame
In the wind that through the window came.
And sometimes in the silence she
Would mumble a sentence audibly,
Or shake her head as if to say,

"You silly souls, to act this way!"
And never a sound from night I would hear,
Unless some far-off cock crowed clear;
Or her old shuffling thumb should turn
Another page; and rapt and stern,
Through her great glasses bent on me,
She would glance into reality;
And shake her round old silvery head,
With—"You!—I thought you was in bed!"—
Only to tilt her book again,
And rooted in Romance remain.   1912

MISS LOO

When thin-strewn memory I look through,
I see most clearly poor Miss Loo,
Her tabby cat, her cage of birds,
Her nose, her hair, her muffled words,
And how she would open her green eyes,
As if in some immense surprise,
Whenever as we sat at tea
She made some small remark to me.

'Tis always drowsy summer when
From out the past she comes again;
The westering sunshine in a pool
Floats in her parlour still and cool;
While the slim bird its lean wires shakes,
As into piercing song it breaks;
Till Peter's pale-green eyes ajar
Dream, wake; wake, dream, in one brief bar.
And I am sitting, dull and shy,
And she with gaze of vacancy,
And large hands folded on the tray,
Musing the afternoon away;
Her satin bosom heaving slow
With sighs that softly ebb and flow,
And her plain face in such dismay,
It seems unkind to look her way:
Until all cheerful back will come
Her gentle gleaming spirit home:
And one would think that poor Miss Loo
Asked nothing else, if she had you.   1912

THE LISTENERS

"Is there anybody there?" said the Traveller,
  Knocking on the moonlit door;
And his horse in the silence champed the grasses
  Of the forest's ferny floor:
And a bird flew up out of the turret,
  Above the Traveller's head:
And he smote upon the door again a second time;
  "Is there anybody there?" he said.
But no one descended to the Traveller;
  No head from the leaf-fringed sill
Leaned over and looked into his grey eyes,
  Where he stood perplexed and still.
But only a host of phantom listeners
  That dwelt in the lone house then
Stood listening in the quiet of the moonlight
  To that voice from the world of men:
Stood thronging the faint moonbeams on the dark stair,
  That goes down to the empty hall,
Hearkening in an air stirred and shaken
  By the lonely Traveller's call.
And he felt in his heart their strangeness,
  Their stillness answering his cry,
While his horse moved, cropping the dark turf,
  'Neath the starred and leafy sky;
For he suddenly smote on the door, even
  Louder, and lifted his head:—
"Tell them I came, and no one answered,
  That I kept my word," he said.
Never the least stir made the listeners,
  Though every word he spake
Fell echoing through the shadowiness of the still house
  From the one man left awake:
Ay, they heard his foot upon the stirrup,
  And the sound of iron on stone,
And how the silence surged softly backward,
  When the plunging hoofs were gone.   *1912*

THE TRUANTS

Ere my heart beats too coldly and faintly
  To remember sad things, yet be gay,

I would sing a brief song of the world's little children
   Magic hath stolen away.

The primroses scattered by April,
   The stars of the wide Milky Way,
Cannot outnumber the hosts of the children
   Magic hath stolen away.

The buttercup green of the meadows,
   The snow of the blossoming may,
Lovelier are not than the legions of children
   Magic hath stolen away.

The waves tossing surf in the moonbeam,
   The albatross lone on the spray,
Alone know the tears wept in vain for the children
   Magic hath stolen away.

In vain: for at hush of the evening
   When the stars twinkle into the grey,
Seems to echo the far-away calling of children
   Magic hath stolen away.   *1913*

SILVER

Slowly, silently, now the moon
Walks the night in her silver shoon;
This way, and that, she peers, and sees
Silver fruit upon silver trees;
One by one the casements catch
Her beams beneath the silvery thatch;
Crouched in his kennel, like a log,
With paws of silver sleeps the dog;
From their shadowy cote the white breasts peep
Of doves in a silver-feathered sleep;
A harvest mouse goes scampering by,
With silver claws, and silver eye;
And moveless fish in the water gleam,
By silver reeds in a silver stream.   *1913*

THE SONG OF SHADOWS

Sweep thy faint strings, Musician,
   With thy long lean hand;

Downward the starry tapers burn,
    Sinks soft the waning sand;
The old hound whimpers couched in sleep,
    The embers smolder low;
Across the walls the shadows
        Come, and go.

Sweep softly thy strings, Musician,
    The minutes mount to hours;
Frost on the windless casement weaves
    A labyrinth of flowers;
Ghosts linger in the darkening air,
    Hearken at the open door;
Music hath called them, dreaming,
        Home once more.   1913

THE GHOST

"Who knocks?" "I, who was beautiful,
    Beyond all dreams to restore,
I, from the roots of the dark thorn am hither,
    And knock on the door."

"Who speaks?" "I—once was my speech
    Sweet as the bird's on the air,
When echo lurks by the waters to heed;
    'Tis I speak thee fair."

"Dark is the hour!" "Ay, and cold."
    "Lone is my house." "Ah, but mine?"
"Sight, touch, lips, eyes yearned in vain."
    "Long dead these to thine . . ."

Silence. Still faint on the porch
    Brake the flames of the stars.
In gloom groped a hope-wearied hand
    Over keys, bolts, and bars.

A face peered. All the grey night
    In chaos of vacancy shone;
Nought but vast sorrow was there—
    The sweet cheat gone.   1918

THE DREAMER

O thou who giving helm and sword,
  Gavest the rusting rain,
And starry dark's all tender dews
  To blunt and stain:

Out of the battle I am sped,
  Unharmed yet stricken sore;
A living shape amid whispering shades
  On Lethe's shore.

No trophy in my hands I bring,
  To this sad, sighing stream,
The neighings and the trumps and cries
  Were but a dream.

Traitor to life, of life betrayed:
  O, of thy mercy deep,
A dream my all, the all I ask
  Is sleep.   *1918*

THE SCRIBE

What lovely things
  Thy hand hath made:
The smooth-plumed bird
  In its emerald shade,
The seed of the grass,
  The speck of stone
Which the wayfaring ant
  Stirs—and hastes on!

Though I should sit
  By some tarn in thy hills,
Using its ink
  As the spirit wills
To write of Earth's wonders,
  Its live, willed things,
Flit would the ages
  On soundless wings
Ere unto Z
  My pen drew nigh;

Leviathan told,
     And the honey-fly:
And still would remain
     My wit to try—
My worn reeds broken,
     The dark tarn dry,
All words forgotten—
     Thou, Lord, and I.   *1918*

THE VEIL

I think and think; yet still I fail—
Why does this lady wear a veil?
Why thus elect to mask her face
Beneath that dainty web of lace?
The tip of a small nose I see,
And two red lips, set curiously
Like twin-born cherries on one stem,
And yet she has netted even them.
Her eyes, it's plain, survey with ease
Whatever to glance upon they please.
Yet, whether hazel, grey, or blue,
Or that even lovelier lilac hue,
I cannot guess: why—why deny
Such beauty to the passer-by?
Out of a bush a nightingale
May expound his song; beneath that veil
A happy mouth no doubt can make
English sound sweeter for its sake.
But then, why muffle in, like this,
What every blossomy wind would kiss?
Why in that little night disguise
A daybreak face, those starry eyes?   *1921*

THE QUIET ENEMY

Hearken!—now the hermit bee
Drones a quiet threnody;
Greening on the stagnant pool
The criss-cross light slants silken-cool;
In the venomed yew tree wings
Preen and flit. The linnet sings.

Gradually the brave sun
Drops to a day's journey done;
In the marshy flats abide
Mists to muffle midnight-tide.
Puffed within the belfry tower
Hungry owls drowse out their hour. . . .

Walk in beauty. Vaunt thy rose.
Flaunt thy transient loveliness.
Pace for pace with thee there goes
A shape that hath not come to bless.
I thine enemy? . . . Nay, nay.
I can only watch and wait
Patient treacherous time away,
Hold ajar the wicket gate.   *1921*

THE CATECHISM

"Hast thou then nought wiser to bring
Than worn-out songs of moon and of rose?"
"Cracked my voice, and broken my wing,
            God knows."

"Tell'st thou no truth of the life that *is*;
Seek'st thou from heaven no pitying sign?"
"Ask thine own heart these mysteries,
            Not mine."

"Where then the faith thou hast brought to seed?
Where the sure hope thy soul would feign?"
"Never ebbed sweetness—even out of a weed—
            In vain."

"Fool. The night comes . . . 'Tis late. Arise.
Cold lap the waters of Jordan stream."
"Deep be their flood, and tranquil thine eyes
            With a dream."   *1921*

THE HOLLY

The sturdiest of forest trees
With acorns is inset;
Wan white blossoms the elder brings

To fruit as black as jet;
But O, in all green English woods
Is aught so fair to view
As the sleek, sharp, dark-leaved holly tree
And its berries burning through?

Towers the ash; and dazzling green
The larch her tassels wears;
Wondrous sweet are the clots of may
The tangled hawthorn bears;
But O, in heath or meadow or wold
Springs aught beneath the blue
As brisk and trim as the holly-tree bole
With its berries burning through?

When hither, thither, falls the snow,
And blazes small the frost,
Naked amid the winter stars
The elm's vast boughs are tossed;
But O, of all that summer showed
What now to winter's true
As the prickle-beribbed dark holly tree,
With berries burning through!   1930

LUCY

Strange—as I sat brooding here,
While memory plied her quiet thread,
Your once-loved face came back, my dear,
  Amid the distant dead.

That pleasant cheek, hair smooth and brown,
Clear brows, and wistful eyes—yet gay:
You stand, in your alpaca gown,
  And ghost my heart away.

I was a child then; nine years old—
And you a woman. Well, stoop close,
To heed a passion never told
  Under how faded a rose!

Do you remember? Few my pence:
I hoarded them with a miser's care,

And bought you, in passionate innocence,
   A birthday maidenhair.

I see its fronds. Again I sit,
Hunched up in bed, in the dark, alone,
Crazed with those eyes that, memory-lit,
   Now ponder on my own.

You gave me not a thought, 'tis true—
Precocious, silly child; and yet,
Perhaps of all you have loved—loved you,
   I may the last forget.

And though no single word of this
You heed—a lifetime gone—at rest;
I would that all remembrances
   As gently pierced my breast!　　　*1931*

FORESTS

Turn, now, tired mind unto your rest,
Within your secret chamber lie,
Doors shut, and windows curtained, lest
Footfall or moonbeam, stealing by,
Wake you, or night-wind sigh.

Now, Self, we are at peace—we twain;
The house is silent, except that—hark!—
Against its walls wells out again
That rapture in the empty dark;
Where, softly beaming, spark by spark,

The glow-worms stud the leaves with light;
And unseen flowers, refreshed with dew—
Jasmine, convolvulus, glimmering white,
The air with their still life endue,
And sweeten night for me and you.

Be mute all speech; and not of love
Talk we, nor call on hope, but be—
Calm as the constant stars above—
The friends of fragile memory,
Shared only now by you and me.

Thus hidden, thus silent, while the hours
From gloom to gloom their wings beat on,
Shall not a moment's peace be ours,
Till, faint with day, the east is wan,
And terrors of the dark are gone?

Nay—in the forests of the mind
Lurk beasts as fierce as those that tread
Earth's rock-strown wilds, to night resigned,
There stars of heaven no radiance shed—
Bleak-eyed Remorse, Despair becowled in lead.

With dawn these ravening shapes will go
Though One at watch will still remain:
Till knell the sunset hour, and lo!
The listening soul once more will know
Death and his pack are hot afield again. *1933*

A ROBIN

Ghost-grey the fall of night,
     Ice-bound the lane,
Lone in the dying light
     Flits he again,
Lurking where shadows steal,
Perched in his coat of blood.
Man's homestead at his heel,
     Death-still in the wood.

Where shall such creature rest?
     Where shall he hide
So wild, so strange a breast,
     What mate beside?
What bond can that bead eye—
Searching for worm or crumb—
Find with humanity
     Monstrous and mum?

Haunting the clod-bound plough,
     The rust-worn spade,
Delving beneath the bough,
     Infinite shade,
Black as the pit to see,

Winter and waste and woe—
Mate for the sexton, he
    Hops o'er the snow.

Odd restless child; it's dark;
    All wings are flown
But this one wizard's—hark!—
    Stone clapped on stone.
Changeling and solitary,
Secret and sharp and small,
Flits he from tree to tree,
    Calling on all.   1933

SOLITUDE

Ghosts there must be with me in this old house,
Deepening its midnight as the clock beats on.
Whence else upwelled—strange, sweet, yet ominous—
That moment of happiness, and then was gone?

Nimbler than air-borne music, heart may call
A speechless message to the inward ear,
As secret even as that which then befell,
Yet nought that listening could make more clear.

Delicate, subtle senses, instant, fleet!—
But oh, how near the verge at which they fail!
In vain, self hearkens for the fall of feet
Soft as its own may be, beyond the pale.   1938

THE LAST CHAPTER

I am living more alone now than I did;
This life tends inward, as the body ages;
And what is left of its strange book to read
Quickens in interest with the last few pages.

Problems abound. Its authorship? A sequel?
Its hero-villain, whose ways so little mend?
The plot? still dark. The style? a shade unequal.
And what of the denouement? And, the end?

No, no, have done! Lay the thumbed thing aside;
Forget its horrors, folly, incitements, lies;
In silence and in solitude abide,
And con what yet may bless your inward eyes.

Pace, still, for pace with you, companion goes,
Though now, through dulled and inattentive ear,
No more—as when a child's—your sick heart knows
His infinite energy and beauty near.

His, too, a World, though viewless save in glimpse;
He, too, a book of imagery bears;
And as your halting foot beside him limps,
Mark you whose badge and livery he wears.   *1938*

THE OLD SUMMERHOUSE

This blue-washed, old, thatched summerhouse—
Paint scaling, and fading from its walls—
How often from its hingeless door
I have watched—dead leaf, like the ghost of a mouse,
Rasping the worn brick floor—
The snows of the weir descending below,
And their thunderous waterfall.

Fall—fall: dark, garrulous rumor,
Until I could listen no more.
Could listen no more—for beauty with sorrow
Is a burden hard to be borne:
The evening light on the foam, and the swans, there;
That music, remote, forlorn.   *1938*

AWAY

There is no sorrow
Time heals never;
No loss, betrayal,
Beyond repair.
Balm for the soul, then,
Though grave shall sever
Lover from loved
And all they share;
See, the sweet sun shines,

The shower is over,
Flowers preen their beauty,
The day how fair!

Brood not too closely
On love, or duty;
Friends long forgotten
May wait you where
Life with death
Brings all to an issue;
None will long mourn for you,
Pray for you, miss you,
Your place left vacant,
You not there.   1938

John Masefield

SEA-FEVER

I must go down to the seas again, to the lonely sea and the sky,
And all I ask is a tall ship and a star to steer her by,
And the wheel's kick and the wind's song and the white sail's shaking,
And a grey mist on the sea's face and a grey dawn breaking.

I must go down to the seas again, for the call of the running tide
Is a wild call and a clear call that may not be denied;
And all I ask is a windy day with the white clouds flying,
And the flung spray and the blown spume, and the sea-gulls crying.

I must go down to the seas again to the vagrant gypsy life,
To the gull's way and the whale's way where the wind's like a whetted
    knife;
And all I ask is a merry yarn from a laughing fellow-rover,
And quiet sleep and a sweet dream when the long trick's over.   *1902*

"ALL YE THAT PASS BY"

On the long dusty ribbon of the long city street,
The pageant of life is passing me on multitudinous feet,
With a word here of the hills, and a song there of the sea,
And—the great movement changes—the pageant passes me.

Faces—passionate faces—of men I may not know,
They haunt me, burn me to the heart, as I turn aside to go:
The king's face and the cur's face, and the face of the stuffed swine,
They are passing, they are passing, their eyes look into mine.

I never can tire of the music of the noise of many feet,
The thrill of the blood pulsing, the tick of the heart's beat,
Of the men many as sands, of the squadrons ranked and massed
Who are passing, changing always, and never have changed or passed.
    1902

CARGOES

Quinquireme of Nineveh from distant Ophir,
Rowing home to haven in sunny Palestine,
With a cargo of ivory,
And apes and peacocks,
Sandalwood, cedarwood, and sweet white wine.

Stately Spanish galleon coming from the Isthmus,
Dipping through the Tropics by the palm-green shores,
With a cargo of diamonds,
Emeralds, amethysts,
Topazes, and cinnamon, and gold moidores.

Dirty British coaster with a salt-cake smoke stack,
Butting through the Channel in the mad March days,
With a cargo of Tyne coal,
Road-rails, pig-lead,
Firewood, iron-ware, and cheap tin trays.   *1903*

From DAUBER

(SECTION VI)

All through the windless night the clipper rolled
In a great swell with oily gradual heaves
Which rolled her down until her time-bells tolled,
Clang, and the weltering water moaned like beeves.
The thundering rattle of slatting shook the sheaves,
Startles of water made the swing ports gush,
The sea was moaning and sighing and saying "Hush!"

It was all black and starless. Peering down
Into the water, trying to pierce the gloom,
One saw a dim, smooth, oily glitter of brown
Heaving and dying away and leaving room
For yet another. Like the march of doom
Came those great powers of marching silences;
Then fog came down, dead-cold, and hid the seas.

They set the Dauber to the foghorn. There
He stood upon the poop, making to sound

Out of the pump the sailor's nasal blare,
Listening lest ice should make the note resound.
She bayed there like a solitary hound
Lost in a covert; all the watch she bayed.
The fog, come closelier down, no answer made.

Denser it grew, until the ship was lost.
The elemental hid her; she was merged
In mufflings of dark death, like a man's ghost,
New to the change of death, yet thither urged.
Then from the hidden waters something surged—
Mournful, despairing, great, greater than speech,
A noise like one slow wave on a still beach.

Mournful, and then again mournful, and still
Out of the night that mighty voice arose;
The Dauber at his foghorn felt the thrill.
Who rode that desolate sea? What forms were those?
Mournful, from things defeated, in the throes
Of memory of some conquered hunting-ground,
Out of the night of death arose the sound.

"Whales!" said the Mate. They stayed there all night long
Answering the horn. Out of the night they spoke,
Defeated creatures who had suffered wrong,
But were still noble underneath the stroke.
They filled the darkness when the Dauber woke;
The men came peering to the rail to hear,
And the sea sighed, and the fog rose up sheer.

A wall of nothing at the world's last edge,
Where no life came except defeated life.
The Dauber felt shut in within a hedge,
Behind which form was hidden and thought was rife,
And that a blinding flash, a thrust, a knife
Would sweep the hedge away and make all plain,
Brilliant beyond all words, blinding the brain.

So the night passed, but then no morning broke—
Only a something showed that night was dead.
A sea-bird, cackling like a devil, spoke,
And the fog drew away and hung like lead.
Like mighty cliffs it shaped, sullen and red;

Like glowering gods at watch it did appear,
And sometimes drew away, and then drew near.

Like islands, and like chasms, and like hell,
But always mighty and red, gloomy and ruddy,
Shutting the visible sea in like a well;
Slow heaving in vast ripples, blank and muddy,
Where the sun should have risen it streaked bloody.
The day was still-born; all the sea-fowl scattering
Splashed the still water, mewing, hovering, clattering.

Then Polar snow came down little and light,
Till all the sky was hidden by the small,
Most multitudinous drift of dirty white
Tumbling and wavering down and covering all—
Covering the sky, the sea, the clipper tall,
Furring the ropes with white, casing the mast,
Coming on no known air, but blowing past.

And all the air seemed full of gradual moan,
As though in those cloud-chasms the horns were blowing
The mort for gods cast out and overthrown,
Or for the eyeless sun plucked out and going.
Slow the low gradual moan came in the snowing;
The Dauber felt the prelude had begun.
The snowstorm fluttered by; he saw the sun

Show and pass by, gleam from one towering prison
Into another, vaster and more grim,
Which in dull crags of darkness had arisen
To muffle-to a final door on him.
The gods upon the dull crags lowered dim,
The pigeons chattered, quarrelling in the track.
In the south-west the dimness dulled to black.

Then came the cry of "Call all hands on deck!"
The Dauber knew its meaning; it was come:
Cape Horn, that tramples beauty into wreck,
And crumples steel and smites the strong man dumb.
Down clattered flying kites and staysails: some
Sang out in quick, high calls: the fair-leads skirled,
And from the south-west came the end of the world.

"Caught in her ball-dress," said the Bosun, hauling;
"Lee-ay, lee-ay!" quick, high, come the men's call;
It was all wallop of sails and startled calling.
"Let fly!" "Let go!" "Clew up!" and "Let go all!"
"Now up and make them fast!" "Here, give us a haul!"
"Now up and stow them! Quick! By God! we're done!"
The blackness crunched all memory of the sun.

"Up!" said the Mate. "Mizen top-gallants. Hurry!"
The Dauber ran, the others ran, the sails
Slatted and shook; out of the black a flurry
Whirled in fine lines, tattering the edge to trails.
Painting and art and England were old tales
Told in some other life to that pale man,
Who struggled with white fear and gulped and ran.

He struck a ringbolt in his haste and fell—
Rose, sick with pain, half-lamed in his left knee;
He reached the shrouds where clambering men pell-mell
Hustled each other up and cursed him; he
Hurried aloft with them: then from the sea
Came a cold, sudden breath that made the hair
Stiff on the neck, as though Death whispered there.

A man below him punched him in the side.
"Get up, you Dauber, or let me get past."
He saw the belly of the skysail skied,
Gulped, and clutched tight, and tried to go more fast.
Sometimes he missed his ratline and was grassed,
Scraped his shin raw against the rigid line;
The clamberers reached the futtock-shrouds' incline.

Cursing they came; one, kicking out behind,
Kicked Dauber in the mouth, and one below
Punched at his calves; the futtock-shrouds inclined;
It was a perilous path for one to go.
"Up, Dauber, up!" A curse followed a blow.
He reached the top and gasped, then on, then on.
And one voice yelled "Let go!" and one "All gone!"

Fierce clamberers, some in oilskins, some in rags,
Hustling and hurrying up, up the steep stairs.
Before the windless sails were blown to flags,

And whirled like dirty birds athwart great airs,
Ten men in all, to get this mast of theirs
Snugged to the gale in time. "Up! Damn you, run!"
The mizzen topmast head was safely won.

"Lay out!" the Bosun yelled. The Dauber laid
Out on the yard, gripping the yard and feeling
Sick at the mighty space of air displayed
Below his feet, where mewing birds were wheeling.
A giddy fear was on him; he was reeling.
He bit his lip half through, clutching the jack.
A cold sweat glued the shirt upon his back.

The yard was shaking, for a brace was loose.
He felt that he would fall; he clutched, he bent,
Clammy with natural terror to the shoes
While idiotic promptings came and went.
Snow fluttered on a wind-flaw and was spent;
He saw the water darken. Someone yelled,
"Frap it; don't stay to furl! Hold on!" He held.

Darkness came down—half darkness—in a whirl;
The sky went out, the waters disappeared.
He felt a shocking pressure of blowing hurl
The ship upon her side. The darkness speared
At her with wind; she staggered, she careered,
Then down she lay. The Dauber felt her go;
He saw his yard tilt downwards. Then the snow

Whirled all about—dense, multitudinous, cold—
Mixed with the wind's one devilish thrust and shriek,
Which whiffled out men's tears, deafened, took hold,
Flattening the flying drift against the cheek.
The yards buckled and bent, man could not speak.
The ship lay on her broadside; the wind's sound
Had devilish malice at having got her downed.

          *   *   *   *   *

How long the gale had blown he could not tell,
Only the world had changed, his life had died.
A moment now was everlasting hell.
Nature, an onslaught from the weather side,
A withering rush of death, a frost that cried,

Shrieked, till he withered at the heart; a hail
Plastered his oilskins with an icy mail.

"Cut!" yelled his mate. He looked—the sail was gone,
Blown into rags in the first furious squall;
The tatters drummed the devil's tattoo. On
The buckling yard a block thumped like a mall.
The ship lay—the sea smote her, the wind's bawl
Came, "loo, loo, loo!" The devil cried his hounds
On to the poor spent stag strayed in his bounds.

"Cut! Ease her!" yelled his mate; the Dauber heard.
His mate wormed up the tilted yard and slashed,
A rag of canvas skimmed like a darting bird.
The snow whirled, the ship bowed to it, the gear lashed,
The sea-tops were cut off and flung down smashed;
Tatters of shouts were flung, the rags of yells—
And clang, clang, clang, below beat the two bells.

"O God!" the Dauber moaned. A roaring rang,
Blasting the royals like a cannonade;
The backstays parted with a crackling clang,
The upper spars were snapped like twigs decayed—
Snapped at their heels, their jagged splinters splayed,
Like white and ghastly hairs erect with fear.
The Mate yelled, "Gone, by God, and pitched them clear!"

"Up" yelled the Bosun; "up and clear the wreck!"
The Dauber followed where he led: below
He caught one giddy glimpsing of the deck
Filled with white water, as though heaped with snow.
He saw the streamers of the rigging blow
Straight out like pennons from the splintered mast,
Then, all sense dimmed, all was an icy blast,

Roaring from nether hell and filled with ice,
Roaring and crashing on the jerking stage,
An utter bridle given to utter vice,
Limitless power mad with endless rage.
Withering the soul; a minute seemed an age.
He clutched and hacked at ropes, at rags of sail,
Thinking that comfort was a fairy-tale

Told long ago—long, long ago—long since
Heard of in other lives—imagined, dreamed—
There where the basest beggar was a prince
To him in torment where the tempest screamed.
Comfort and warmth and ease no longer seemed
Things that a man could know: soul, body, brain,
Knew nothing but the wind, the cold, the pain.

"Leave that!" the Bosun shouted; "Crojick save!"
The splitting crojick, not yet gone to rags,
Thundered below, beating till something gave,
Bellying between its buntlines into bags.
Some birds were blown past, shrieking: dark, like shags,
Their backs seemed, looking down. "Leu, leu!" they cried.
The ship lay, the seas thumped her; she had died.

They reached the crojick yard, which buckled, buckled
Like a thin whalebone to the topsail's strain.
They laid upon the yard and heaved and knuckled,
Pounding the sail, which jangled and leapt again.
It was quite hard with ice, its rope like chain,
Its strength like seven devils; it shook the mast.
They cursed and toiled and froze: a long time passed.

Two hours passed, then a dim lightening came.
Those frozen ones upon the yard could see
The mainsail and the foresail still the same,
Still battling with the hands and blowing free,
Rags tattered where the staysails used to be.
The lower topsails stood; the ship's lee deck
Seethed with four feet of water filled with wreck.

An hour more went by; the Dauber lost
All sense of hands and feet, all sense of all
But of a wind that cut him to the ghost,
And of a frozen fold he had to haul,
Of heavens that fell and never ceased to fall,
And ran in smoky snatches along the sea,
Leaping from crest to wave-crest, yelling. He

Lost sense of time; no bells went, but he felt
Ages go over him. At last, at last
They frapped the cringled crojick's icy pelt;

In frozen bulge and bunt they made it fast.
Then, scarcely live, they laid in to the mast.
The Captain's speaking trumpet gave a blare,
"Make fast the topsail, Mister, while you're there."

Some seamen cursed, but up they had to go—
Up to the topsail yard to spend an hour
Stowing a topsail in a blinding snow,
Which made the strongest man among them cower.
More men came up, the fresh hands gave them power,
They stowed the sail; then with a rattle of chain
One half the crojick burst its bonds again.

                    *   *   *   *   *

They stowed the sail, frapping it round with rope,
Leaving no surface for the wind, no fold,
Then down the weather shrouds, half dead, they grope;
That struggle with the sail had made them old.
They wondered if the crojick furl would hold.
"Lucky," said one, "it didn't spring the spar."
"Lucky!" the Bosun said, "Lucky! We are!"

She came within two shakes of turning top
Or stripping all her shroud-screws, that first quiff.
"Now fish those wash-deck buckets out of the slop.
Here's Dauber says he doesn't like Cape Stiff.
This isn't wind, man, this is only a whiff.
Hold on, all hands, hold on!" a sea, half seen,
Paused, mounted, burst, and filled the main-deck green.

The Dauber felt a mountain of water fall.
It covered him deep, deep, he felt it fill,
Over his head, the deck, the fife-rails, all,
Quieting the ship; she trembled and lay still.
Then with a rush and shatter and clanging shrill
Over she went; he saw the water cream
Over the bitts; he saw the half-deck stream.

Then in the rush he swirled, over she went;
Her lee-rail dipped, he struck, and something gave;
His legs went through a port as the roll spent;
She paused, then rolled, and back the water drave.

He drifted with it as a part of the wave,
Drowning, half-stunned, exhausted, partly frozen,
He struck the booby hatchway; then the Bosun

Leaped, seeing his chance, before the next sea burst,
And caught him as he drifted, seized him, held,
Up-ended him against the bitts, and cursed.
"This ain't the George's Swimming Baths," he yelled;
"Keep on your feet!" Another grey-back felled
The two together, and the Bose, half-blind,
Spat: "One's a joke," he cursed, "but two's unkind."

"Now, damn it, Dauber!" said the Mate. "Look out,
Or you'll be over the side!" The water freed;
Each clanging freeing-port became a spout.
The men cleared up the decks as there was need.
The Dauber's head was cut, he felt it bleed
Into his oilskins as he clutched and coiled.
Water and sky were devil's brews which boiled,

Boiled, shrieked, and glowered; but the ship was saved.
Snugged safely down, though fourteen sails were split.
Out of the dark a fiercer fury raved.
The grey-backs died and mounted, each crest lit
With a white toppling gleam that hissed from it
And slid, or leaped, or ran with whirls of cloud,
Mad with inhuman life that shrieked aloud.

The watch was called; Dauber might go below.
"Splice the main brace!" the Mate called. All laid aft
To get a gulp of momentary glow
As some reward for having saved the craft.
The steward ladled mugs, from which each quaff'd
Whisky, with water, sugar, and lime-juice, hot,
A quarter of a pint each made the tot.

Beside the lamp-room door the steward stood
Ladling it out, and each man came in turn,
Tipped his sou'-wester, drank it, grunted "Good!"
And shambled forward, letting it slowly burn:
When all were gone the Dauber lagged astern,
Torn by his frozen body's lust for heat,
The liquor's pleasant smell, so warm, so sweet,

And by a promise long since made at home
Never to taste strong liquor. Now he knew
The worth of liquor; now he wanted some.
His frozen body urged him to the brew;
Yet it seemed wrong, an evil thing to do
To break that promise. "Dauber," said the Mate,
"Drink, and turn in, man; why the hell d'ye wait?"

"Please, sir, I'm temperance." "Temperance are you, hey?
That's all the more for me! So you're for slops?
I thought you'd had enough slops for to-day.
Go to your bunk and ease her when she drops.
And—damme, steward! you brew with too much hops!
Stir up the sugar, man!—and tell your girl
How kind the Mate was teaching you to furl."

Then the Mate drank the remnants, six men's share,
And ramped into his cabin, where he stripped
And danced unclad, and was uproarious there.
In waltzes with the cabin cat he tripped,
Singing in tenor clear that he was pipped—
That "he who strove the tempest to disarm,
Must never first embrail the lee yard-arm,"

And that his name was Ginger. Dauber crept
Back to the round-house, gripping by the rail.
The wind howled by; the passionate water leapt;
The night was all one roaring with the gale.
Then at the door he stopped, uttering a wail;
His hands were perished numb and blue as veins,
He could not turn the knob for both the Spains.

A hand came shuffling aft, dodging the seas,
Singing "her nut-brown hair" between his teeth;
Taking the ocean's tumult at his ease
Even when the wash about his thighs did seethe.
His soul was happy in its happy sheath;
"What, Dauber, won't it open? Fingers cold?
You'll talk of this time, Dauber, when you're old."

He flung the door half open, and a sea
Washed them both in, over the splashboard, down;
"You silly, salt miscarriage!" sputtered he.

"Dauber, pull out the plug before we drown!
That's spoiled my laces and my velvet gown.
Where is the plug?" Groping in pitch dark water,
He sang between his teeth "The Farmer's Daughter."

It was pitch dark within there; at each roll
The chests slid to the slant; the water rushed,
Making full many a clanging tin pan bowl
Into the black below-bunks as it gushed.
The dog-tired men slept through it; they were hushed.
The water drained, and then with matches damp
The man struck heads off till he lit the lamp.

"Thank you," the Dauber said; the seaman grinned.
"This is your first foul weather?" "Yes." "I thought
Up on the yard you hadn't seen much wind.
Them's rotten sea-boots, Dauber, that you brought.
Now I must cut on deck before I'm caught."
He went; the lamp-flame smoked; he slammed the door;
A film of water loitered across the floor.

The Dauber watched it come and watched it go;
He had had revelation of the lies
Cloaking the truth men never choose to know;
He could bear witness now and cleanse their eyes.
He had beheld in suffering; he was wise;
This was the sea, this searcher of the soul—
This never-dying shriek fresh from the Pole.

He shook with cold; his hands could not undo
His oilskin buttons, so he shook and sat,
Watching his dirty fingers, dirty blue,
Hearing without the hammering tackle slat;
Within, the drops from dripping clothes went pat,
Running in little patters, gentle, sweet,
And "Ai, ai!" went the wind, and the seas beat.

His bunk was sopping wet; he clambered in,
None of his clothes were dry: his fear recurred.
Cramps bunched the muscles underneath his skin.
The great ship rolled until the lamp was blurred.
He took his Bible and tried to read a word;

Trembled at going aloft again, and then
Resolved to fight it out and show it to men.

Faces recurred, fierce memories of the yard,
The frozen sail, the savage eyes, the jests,
The oaths of one great seaman, syphilis-scarred,
The tug of leeches jammed beneath their chests,
The buntlines bellying bunts out into breasts,
The deck so desolate-grey, the sky so wild.
He fell asleep, and slept like a young child.

But not for long; the cold awoke him soon,
The hot-ache and the skin-cracks and the cramp,
The seas thundering without, the gale's wild tune,
The sopping misery of the blankets damp.
A speaking-trumpet roared; a sea-boot's stamp
Clogged at the door. A man entered to shout:
"All hands on deck! Arouse here! Tumble out!"

The caller raised the lamp; his oilskins clicked
As the thin ice upon them cracked and fell.
"Rouse out!" he said. "This lamp is frozen wick'd.
Rouse out!" His accent deepened to a yell.
"We're among ice; it's blowing up like hell.
We're going to hand both topsails. Time, I guess,
We're sheeted up. Rouse out! Don't stay to dress!"

"Is it cold on deck?" said Dauber. "Is it cold?
We're sheeted up, I tell you, inches thick!
The fo'c'sle's like a wedding-cake, I'm told.
Now tumble out, my sons; on deck here, quick!
Rouse out, away, and come and climb the stick.
I'm going to call the half-deck. Bosun! Hey!
Both topsails coming in. Heave out! Away!"

He went; the Dauber tumbled from his bunk,
Clutching the side. He heard the wind go past,
Making the great ship wallow as if drunk.
There was a shocking tumult up the mast.
"This is the end," he muttered, "come at last!
I've got to go aloft, facing this cold.
I can't. I can't. I'll never keep my hold.

"I cannot face the topsail yard again.
I never guessed what misery it would be."
The cramps and hot-ache made him sick with pain.
The ship stopped suddenly from a devilish sea,
Then, with a triumph of wash, a rush of glee,
The door burst in, and in the water rolled,
Filling the lower bunks, black, creaming, cold.

The lamp sucked out. "Wash!" went the water back,
Then in again, flooding; the Bosun swore.
"You useless thing! You Dauber! You lee slack!
Get out, you heekapoota! Shut the door!
You coo-ilyaira, what are you waiting for?
Out of my way, you thing—you useless thing!"
He slammed the door indignant, clanging the ring.

And then he lit the lamp, drowned to the waist:
"Here's a fine house! Get at the scupper-holes"—
He bent against it as the water raced—
"And pull them out to leeward when she rolls.
They say some kinds of landsmen don't have souls.
I well believe. A Port Mahon baboon
Would make more soul then you got with a spoon."

Down in the icy water Dauber groped
To find the plug; the racing water sluiced
Over his head and shoulders as she sloped.
Without, judged by the sound, all hell was loosed.
He felt cold Death about him tightly noosed.
That Death was better than the misery there
Iced on the quaking foothold high in air.

And then the thought came: "I'm a failure. All
My life has been a failure. They were right.
It will not matter if I go and fall;
I should be free then from this hell's delight.
I'll never paint. Best let it end to-night.
I'll slip over the side. I've tried and failed."
So in the ice-cold in the night he quailed.

Death would be better, death, than this long hell
Of mockery and surrender and dismay—
This long defeat of doing nothing well,

Playing the part too high for him to play.
"O Death! who hides the sorry thing away,
Take me; I've failed. I cannot play these cards."
There came a thundering from the topsail yards.

And then he bit his lips, clenching his mind,
And staggered out to muster, beating back
The coward frozen self of him that whined.
Come what cards might he meant to play the pack.
"Ai!" screamed the wind; the topsail sheet went clack;
Ice filled the air with spikes; the grey-backs burst.
"Here's Dauber," said the Mate, "on deck the first.

"Why, holy sailor, Dauber, you're a man!
I took you for a soldier. Up now, come!"
Up on the yards already they began
That battle with a gale which strikes men dumb.
The leaping topsail thundered like a drum.
The frozen snow beat in the face like shots.
The wind spun whipping wave-crests into clots.

So up upon the topsail yard again,
In the great tempest's fiercest hour, began
Probation to the Dauber's soul, of pain
Which crowds a century's torment in a span.
For the next month the ocean taught this man,
And he, in that month's torment, while she wested,
Was never warm nor dry, nor full nor rested;

But still it blew, or, if it lulled, it rose
Within the hour and blew again; and still
The water as it burst aboard her froze.
The wind blew off an ice-field, raw and chill,
Daunting man's body, tampering with his will;
But after thirty days a ghostly sun
Gave sickly promise that the storms were done.   *1912*

REVELATION

If I could come again to that dear place
Where once I came, where Beauty lived and moved,
Where, by the sea, I saw her face to face,

That soul alive by which the world has loved;
If, as I stood at gaze among the leaves,
She would appear again, as once before,
While the red herdsman gathered up his sheaves
And brimming waters trembled up the shore;
If, as I gazed, her Beauty that was dumb,
In that old time, before I learned to speak,
Would lean to me and revelation come,
Words to the lips and color to the cheek,
Joy with its searing-iron would burn me wise,
I should know all; all powers, all mysteries.   *1915*

THE END

There, on the darkened deathbed, dies the brain
That flared three several times in seventy years;
It cannot lift the silly hand again,
Nor speak, nor sing; it neither sees nor hears.
And muffled mourners put it in the ground
And then go home, and in the earth it lies,
Too dark for vision and too deep for sound,
The million cells that made a good man wise.
Yet for a few short years an influence stirs
A sense or wraith or essence of him dead,
Which makes insensate things its ministers
To those beloved, his spirit's daily bread;
Then that, too, fades; in book or deed a spark
Lingers, then that, too, fades; then all is dark.

1915

[I NEVER SEE THE RED ROSE]

I never see the red rose crown the year,
Nor feel the young grass underneath my tread,
Without the thought, "This living beauty here
Is earth's remembrance of a beauty dead.
Surely where all this glory is displayed
Love has been quick, like fire, to high ends,
Here, in this grass, an altar has been made
For some white joy, some sacrifice of friends;
Here, where I stand, some leap of human brains
Has touched immortal things and left its trace,

The earth is happy here, the gleam remains;
Beauty is here, the spirit of the place,
I touch the faith which nothing can destroy,
The earth, the living church of ancient joy."

1916

[THERE IS NO GOD, AS I WAS TAUGHT]

There is no God, as I was taught in youth,
Though each, according to his stature, builds
Some covered shrine for what he thinks the truth,
Which day by day his reddest heart-blood gilds.
There is no God; but death, the clasping sea,
In which we move like fish, deep over deep
Made of men's souls that bodies have set free,
Floods to a Justice though it seems asleep.
There is no God, but still, behind the veil,
The hurt thing works, out of its agony.
Still, like a touching of a brimming Grail,
Return the pennies given to passers-by.
There is no God, but we, who breathe the air,
Are God ourselves and touch God everywhere.

1916

From *REYNARD THE FOX*

[THE COUNTRYMEN]

Ock Gurney and old Pete were there,
Riding their bonny cobs and swearing.
Ock's wife had giv'n them both a fairing,
A horse-rosette, red, white, and blue.
Their cheeks were brown as any brew,
And every comer to the meet
Said "Hello, Ock" or "Morning, Pete;
Be you a going to a wedding?"
"Why, noa," they said, "we'm going a bedding;
Now ben't us, uncle, ben't us, Ock?"
Pete Gurney was a lusty cock
Turned sixty-three, but bright and hale,
A dairy-farmer in the vale,
Much like a robin in the face,
Much character in little space,

With little eyes like burning coal.
His mouth was like a slit or hole
In leather that was seamed and lined.
He had the russet-apple mind
That betters as the weather worsen.
He was a manly English person,
Kind to the core, brave, merry, true;
One grief he had, a grief still new,
That former Parson joined with Squire
In putting down the Playing Quire,
In church, and putting organ in.
"Ah, boys, that was a pious din
That Quire was; a pious praise
The noise was that we used to raise;
I and my serpent, George with his'n,
On Easter Day in He is Risen,
Or blessed Christmas in Venite;
And how the trombone came in mighty,
In Alleluias from the heart—
Pious, for each man played his part,
Not like 'tis now." Thus he, still sore
For changes forty years before,
When all (that could) in time and tune,
Blew trumpets to the newë moon.
He was a bachelor, from choice.
He and his nephew farmed the Boyce,
Prime pasture land for thirty cows.
Ock's wife, Selina Jane, kept house,
And jolly were the three together.

Ock had a face like summer weather,
A broad red sun, split by a smile.
He mopped his forehead all the while.
And said "By damn," and "Ben't us, Unk?"
His eyes were close and deeply sunk.
He cursed his hunter like a lover,
"Now blast your soul, my dear, give over.
Woa, now, my pretty, damn your eyes."
Like Pete he was of middle size,
Dean-oak-like, stuggy, strong in shoulder,
He stood a wrestle like a boulder,
He had a back for pitching hay.
His singing voice was like a bay.

In talk he had a sideways spit,
Each minute, to refresh his wit.
He cracked Brazil nuts with his teeth.
He challenged Cobbett of the Heath
(Weight-lifting champion) once, but lost.
Hunting was what he loved the most,
Next to his wife and Uncle Pete.
With beer to drink and cheese to eat,
And rain in May to fill the grasses,
This life was not a dream that passes
To Ock, but like the summer flower.   *1919*

ON GROWING OLD

Be with me, Beauty, for the fire is dying;
My dog and I are old, too old for roving;
Man, whose young passion sets the spindrift flying,
Is soon too lame to march, too cold for loving.
I take the book and gather to the fire,
Turning old yellow leaves; minute by minute,
The clock ticks to my heart; a withered wire
Moves a thin ghost of music in the spinet.
I cannot sail your seas, I cannot wander
Your cornland, nor your hill-land nor your valleys,
Ever again, nor share the battle yonder
Where the young knight the broken squadron rallies.
Only stay quiet while my mind remembers
The beauty of fire from the beauty of embers.

Beauty, have pity, for the strong have power,
The rich their wealth, the beautiful their grace,
Summer of man its sunlight and its flower,
Spring time of man all April in a face.
Only, as in the jostling in the Strand,
Where the mob thrusts or loiters or is loud
The beggar with the saucer in his hand
Asks only a penny from the passing crowd,
So, from this glittering world with all its fashion,
Its fire and play of men, its stir, its march,
Let me have wisdom, Beauty, wisdom and passion,
Bread to the soul, rain where the summers parch.
Give me but these, and though the darkness close
Even the night will blossom as the rose.   *1919*

THE LEMMINGS

Once in a hundred years the Lemmings come
Westward, in search of food, over the snow,
Westward, until the salt sea drowns them dumb,
Westward, till all are drowned, those Lemmings go.
Once, it is thought, there was a westward land
(Now drowned) where there was food for those starved things,
And memory of the place has burnt its brand
In the little brains of all the Lemming Kings.
Perhaps, long since, there was a land beyond
Westward from death, some city, some calm place,
Where one could taste God's quiet and be fond
With the little beauty of a human face;
But now the land is drowned, yet still we press
Westward, in search, to death, to nothingness.   1920

D. H. Lawrence

LOVE ON THE FARM

What large, dark hands are those at the window
Grasping in the golden light
Which weaves its way through the evening wind
  At my heart's delight?

Ah, only the leaves! But in the west
I see a redness suddenly come
Into the evening's anxious breast—
  'Tis the wound of love goes home!

The woodbine creeps abroad
Calling low to her lover:
  The sun-lit flirt who all the day
  Has poised above her lips in play
  And stolen kisses, shallow and gay
  Of pollen, now has gone away—
    She woos the moth with her sweet, low word;
And when above her his moth-wings hover
Then her bright breast she will uncover
And yield her honey-drop to her lover.

Into the yellow, evening glow
Saunters a man from the farm below;
Leans, and looks in at the low-built shed
Where the swallow has hung her marriage bed.
  The bird lies warm against the wall.
  She glances quick her startled eyes
  Towards him, then she turns away
  Her small head, making warm display
  Of red upon the throat. Her terrors sway
  Her out of the nest's warm, busy ball,
  Whose plaintive cry is heard as she flies

In one blue swoop from out of the sties
Into the twilight's empty hall.

Oh, water-hen, beside the rushes,
Hide your quaintly scarlet blushes,
Still your quick tail, lie still as dead,
Till the distance folds over his ominous tread!

The rabbit presses back her ears,
Turns back her liquid, anguished eyes
And crouches low; then with wild spring
Spurts from the terror of his oncoming;
To be choked back, the wire ring
Her frantic effort throttling:
    Piteous brown ball of quivering fears!
Ah, soon in his large, hard hands she dies,
And swings all loose from the swing of his walk!
Yet calm and kindly are his eyes
And ready to open in brown surprise
Should I not answer to his talk
Or should he my tears surmise.

I hear his hand on the latch, and rise from my chair
Watching the door open; he flashes bare
His strong teeth in a smile, and flashes his eyes
In a smile like triumph upon me; then careless-wise
He flings the rabbit soft on the table board
And comes toward me: he! the uplifted sword
Of his hand against my bosom and oh, the broad
Blade of his glance that asks me to applaud
His coming! With his hand he turns my face to him
And caresses me with his fingers that still smell grim
Of rabbit's fur! God, I am caught in a snare!
I know not what fine wire is round my throat;
I only know I let him finger there
My pulse of life, and let him nose like a stoat
Who sniffs with joy before he drinks the blood.

And down his mouth comes to my mouth! and down
His bright dark eyes come over me, like a hood
Upon my mind! his lips meet mine, and a flood
Of sweet fire sweeps across me, so I drown
Against him, die, and find death good.   *1913*

LIGHTNING

I felt the lurch and halt of her heart
    Next my breast, where my own heart was beating;
And I laughed to feel it plunge and bound,
And strange in my blood-swept ears was the sound
    Of the words I kept repeating,
Repeating with tightened arms, and the hot blood's blind-fold art.

Her breath flew warm against my neck,
    Warm as a flame in the close night air;
And the sense of her clinging flesh was sweet
Where her arms and my neck's blood-surge could meet.
    Holding her thus, did I care
That the black night hid her from me, blotted out every speck?

I leaned me forward to find her lips,
    And claim her utterly in a kiss,
When the lightning flew across her face,
And I saw her for the flaring space
    Of a second, afraid of the clips
Of my arms, inert with dread, wilted in fear of my kiss.

A moment, like a wavering spark,
    Her face lay there before my breast,
Pale love lost in a snow of fear,
And guarded by a glittering tear,
    And lips apart with dumb cries;
A moment, and she was taken again in the merciful dark.

I heard the thunder, and felt the rain,
    And my arm fell loose, and I was dumb.
Almost I hated her, she was so good,
Hated myself, and the place, and my blood,
    Which burned with rage, as I bade her come
Home, away home, ere the lightning floated forth again.   *1913*

RELEASE

Helen, had I known yesterday
That you could discharge the ache
    Out of the wound,
Had I known yesterday that you could take

The turgid electric ache away,
    Drink it up in the ground
Of your soft white body, as lightning
Is drunk from an agonised sky by the earth,
    I should have hated you, Helen.

But since my limbs gushed full of fire,
Since from out of my blood and bone
    Poured a heavy flame
To you, earth of my atmosphere, stone
Of my steel, lovely white flint of desire,
    You have no name,
Earth of my swaying atmosphere,
Substance of my inconstant breath,
    I cannot but cleave to you, Helen.

Since you have drunken up the drear
Death-darkened storm, and death
    Is washed from the blue
Of my eyes, I see you beautiful, and dear.
Beautiful, passive and strong, as the breath
    Of my yearning blows over you.
I see myself as the winds that hover
Half substanceless, and without grave worth.
    But you
    Are the earth I hover over.   *1916*

HYMN TO PRIAPUS

My love lies underground
With her face upturned to mine,
And her mouth unclosed in a last long kiss
That ended her life and mine.

I danced at the Christmas party
Under the mistletoe
Along with a ripe, slack country lass
Jostling to and fro.

The big, soft country lass,
Like a loose sheaf of wheat
Slipped through my arms on the threshing floor
At my feet.

The warm, soft country lass,
Sweet as an armful of wheat
At threshing-time broken, was broken
For me, and ah, it was sweet!

Now I am going home
Fulfilled and alone,
I see the great Orion standing
Looking down.

He's the star of my first beloved
Love-making.
The witness of all that bitter-sweet
Heart-aching.

Now he sees this as well,
This last commission.
Nor do I get any look
Of admonition.

He can add the reckoning up
I suppose, between now and then,
Having walked himself in the thorny, difficult
Ways of men.

He has done as I have done
No doubt:
Remembered and forgotten
Turn and about.

My love lies underground
With her face upturned to mine,
And her mouth unclosed in the last long kiss
That ended her life and mine.

She fares in the stark immortal
Fields of death;
I in these goodly, frozen
Fields beneath.

Something in me remembers
And will not forget.
The stream of my life in the darkness
Deathward set!

And something in me has forgotten,
Has ceased to care.
Desire comes up, and contentment
Is debonair.

I, who am worn and careful,
How much do I care?
How is it I grin then, and chuckle
Over despair?

Grief, grief, I suppose and sufficient
Grief makes us free
To be faithless and faithful together
As we have to be.   1917

SPRING MORNING

Ah, through the open door
Is there an almond tree
Aflame with blossom!
    —Let us fight no more.

Among the pink and blue
Of the sky and the almond flowers
A sparrow flutters.
    —We have come through,

It is really spring!—See,
When he thinks himself alone
How he bullies the flowers.
    —Ah, you and me

How happy we'll be!—See him?
He clouts the tufts of flowers
In his impudence.
    —But, did you dream

It would be so bitter? Never mind
It is finished, the spring is here.
And we're going to be summer-happy
    And summer-kind.

We have died, we have slain and been slain,
We are not our old selves any more.

I feel new and eager
   To start again.

It is gorgeous to live and forget.
And to feel quite new.
See the bird in the flowers?—he's making
   A rare to-do!

He thinks the whole blue sky
Is much less than the bit of blue egg
He's got in his nest—we'll be happy,
   You and I, I and you.

With nothing to fight any more—
In each other, at least.
See, how gorgeous the world is
   Outside the door!

San Gaudenzio, 1917

SONG OF A MAN WHO HAS COME THROUGH

Not I, not I, but the wind that blows through me!
A fine wind is blowing the new direction of Time.
If only I let it bear me, carry me, if only it carry me!
If only I am sensitive, subtle, oh, delicate, a winged gift!
If only, most lovely of all, I yield myself and am borrowed
By the fine, fine wind that takes its course through the chaos of the
   world
Like a fine, an exquisite chisel, a wedge-blade inserted;
If only I am keen and hard like the sheer tip of a wedge
Driven by invisible blows,
The rock will split, we shall come at the wonder, we shall find the
   Hesperides.

Oh, for the wonder that bubbles into my soul,
I would be a good fountain, a good well-head,
Would blur no whisper, spoil no expression.

What is the knocking?
What is the knocking at the door in the night?
It is somebody wants to do us harm.

No, no, it is the three strange angels.
Admit them, admit them.

1917

GLOIRE DE DIJON

When she rises in the morning
I linger to watch her;
Spreads the bath-cloth underneath the window
And the sunbeams catch her
Glistening white on the shoulders,
While down her sides the mellow
Golden shadow glows as
She stoops to the sponge, and the swung breasts
Sway like full-blown yellow
Gloire de Dijon roses.

She drips herself with water, and the shoulders
Glisten as silver, they crumple up
Like wet and falling roses, and I listen
For the sluicing of their rain-dishevelled petals.
In the window full of sunlight
Concentrates her golden shadow
Fold on fold, until it glows as
Mellow as the glory roses.   *Icking, 1917*

RIVER ROSES

By the Isar, in the twilight
We were wandering and singing,
By the Isar, in the evening
We climbed the huntsman's ladder and sat swinging
In the fir-tree overlooking the marshes,
While river met with river, and the ringing
Of their pale-green glacier water filled the evening.

By the Isar, in the twilight
We found the dark wild roses
Hanging red at the river; and simmering
Frogs were singing, and over the river closes
Was savour of ice and of roses; and glimmering
Fear was abroad. We whispered: "No one knows us.
Let it be as the snake disposes
Here in this simmering marsh."
          Kloster Schaeftlarn, 1917

NEW HEAVEN AND EARTH

I

And so I cross into another world
shyly and in homage linger for an invitation
from this unknown that I would trespass on.

I am very glad, and all alone in the world,
all alone, and very glad, in a new world
where I am disembarked at last.

I could cry with joy, because I am in the new world, just ventured in.
I could cry with joy, and quite freely, there is nobody to know.

And whosoever the unknown people of this unknown world may be
they will never understand my weeping for joy to be adventuring among
        them
because it will still be a gesture of the old world I am making
    which they will not understand, because it is quite, quite foreign to
        them.

II

I was so weary of the world,
I was so sick of it,
everything was tainted with myself,
skies, trees, flowers, birds, water,
people, houses, streets, vehicles, machines,
nations, armies, war, peace-talking,
work, recreation, governing, anarchy,
it was all tainted with myself, I knew it all to start with
because it was all myself.

When I gathered flowers, I knew it was myself plucking my own flow-
        ering.
When I went in a train, I knew it was myself travelling by my own
        invention.
When I heard the cannon of the war, I listened with my own ears to
        my own destruction.
When I saw the torn dead, I knew it was my own torn dead body.
It was all me, I had done it all in my own flesh.

III

I shall never forget the maniacal horror of it all in the end
when everything was me, I knew it all already, I anticipated it all in
    my soul
because I was the author and the result
I was the God and the creation at once;
creator, I looked at my creation;
created, I looked at myself, the creator:
it was a maniacal horror in the end.

I was a lover, I kissed the woman I loved,
And God of horror, I was kissing also myself.
I was a father and a begetter of children,
And oh, oh horror, I was begetting and conceiving in my own body.

IV

At last came death, sufficiency of death,
and that at last relieved me, I died.
I buried my beloved; it was good, I buried myself and was gone.
War came, and every hand raised to murder;
very good, very good, every hand raised to murder!
Very good, very good, I am a murderer!
It is good, I can murder and murder, and see them fall,
the mutilated, horror-struck youths, a multitude
one on another, and then in clusters together
smashed, all oozing with blood, and burned in heaps
going up in a foetid smoke to get rid of them,
the murdered bodies of youths and men in heaps
the heaps and heaps and horrible reeking heaps
till it is almost enough, till I am reduced perhaps;
thousands and thousands of gaping, hideous foul dead
that are youths and men and me
being burned with oil, and consumed in corrupt thick smoke, that rolls
and taints and blackens the sky, till at last it is dark, dark as night, or
    death, or hell
and I am dead, and trodden to nought in the smoke-sodden tomb;
dead and trodden to nought in the sour black earth
of the tomb; dead and trodden to nought, trodden to nought.

V

God, but it is good to have died and been trodden out,
trodden to nought in sour, dead earth,

quite to nought,
absolutely to nothing
nothing
nothing
nothing.

For when it is quite, quite nothing, then it is everything.
When I am trodden quite out, quite, quite out,
every vestige gone, then I am here
risen, and setting my foot on another world
risen, accomplishing a resurrection
risen, not born again, but risen, body the same as before,
new beyond knowledge of newness, alive beyond life,
proud beyond inkling or furthest conception of pride,
living where life was never yet dreamed of, nor hinted at,
here, in the other world, still terrestrial
myself, the same as before, yet unaccountably new.

VI

I, in the sour black tomb, trodden to absolute death
I put out my hand in the night, one night, and my hand
touched that which was verily not me,
verily it was not me.
Where I had been was a sudden blaze,
a sudden flaring blaze!
So I put my hand out further, a little further
and I felt that which was not I,
it verily was not I,
it was the unknown.

Ha, I was a blaze leaping up!
I was a tiger bursting into sunlight.
I was greedy, I was mad for the unknown.
I, new-risen, resurrected, starved from the tomb,
starved from a life of devouring always myself,
now here was I, new-awakened, with my hand stretching out
and touching the unknown, the real unknown, the unknown unknown.

My God, but I can only say
I touch, I feel the unknown!
I am the first comer!
Cortes, Pisarro, Columbus, Cabot, they are nothing, nothing!

I am the first comer!
I am the discoverer!
I have found the other world!

The unknown, the unknown!
I am thrown upon the shore.
I am covering myself with the sand.
I am filling my mouth with the earth.
I am burrowing my body into the soil.
The unknown, the new world!

VII

It was the flank of my wife
I touched with my hand, I clutched with my hand,
rising, new-awakened from the tomb!
It was the flank of my wife
whom I married years ago
at whose side I have lain for over a thousand nights
and all that previous while, she was I, she was I;
I touched her, it was I who touched and I who was touched.

Yet rising from the tomb, from the black oblivion
stretching out my hand, my hand flung like a drowned man's hand on a
      rock,
I touched her flank and knew I was carried by the current in death
over to the new world, and was climbing out on the shore,
risen, not to the old world, the old, changeless I, the old life,
wakened not to the old knowledge
but to a new earth, a new I, a new knowledge, a new world of time.

Ah no, I cannot tell you what it is, the new world.
I cannot tell you the mad, astounded rapture of its discovery.
I shall be mad with delight before I have done,
and whosoever comes after will find me in the new world
a madman in rapture.

VIII

Green streams that flow from the innermost continent of the new world,
what are they?
Green and illumined and travelling for ever
dissolved with the mystery of the innermost heart of the continent,
mystery beyond knowledge or endurance, so sumptuous
out of the well-heads of the new world.—

The other, she too has strange green eyes!
White sands and fruits unknown and perfumes that never
can blow across the dark seas to our usual world!
And land that beats with a pulse!
And valleys that draw close in love!
And strange ways where I fall into oblivion of uttermost living!—
Also she who is the other has strange-mounded breasts and strange sheer
    slopes, and white levels.

Sightless and strong oblivion in utter life takes possession of me!
The unknown, strong current of life supreme
drowns me and sweeps me away and holds me down
to the sources of mystery, in the depths,
extinguishes there my risen resurrected life
and kindles it further at the core of utter mystery.   *Greatham, 1917*

PIANO

Softly, in the dusk, a woman is singing to me;
Taking me back down the vista of years, till I see
A child sitting under the piano, in the boom of the tingling strings
And pressing the small, poised feet of a mother who smiles as she sings.

In spite of myself, the insidious mastery of song
Betrays me back, till the heart of me weeps to belong
To the old Sunday evenings at home, with winter outside
And hymns in the cozy parlour, the tinkling piano our guide.

So now it is vain for the singer to burst into clamour
With the great black piano appassionato. The glamour
Of childish days is upon me, my manhood is cast
Down in the flood of remembrance, I weep like a child for the past.
    1918

PASSING VISIT TO HELEN

Returning, I find her just the same,
At just the same old delicate game.

Still she says: "Nay, loose no flame
To lick me up and do me harm!
Be all yourself!—for oh, the charm
Of your heart of fire in which I look!
Oh, better there than in any book
Glow and enact the dramas and dreams

I love for ever!—there it seems
You are lovelier than life itself, till desire
Comes licking through the bars of your lips,
And over my face the stray fire slips,
Leaving a burn and an ugly smart
That will have the oil of illusion. Oh, heart
Of fire and beauty, loose no more
Your reptile flames of lust; ah, store
Your passion in the basket of your soul,
Be all yourself, one bonny, burning coal
That stays with steady joy of its own fire!
For in the firing all my porcelain
Of flesh does crackle and shiver and break in pain,
My ivory and marble black with stain,
My veil of sensitive mystery rent in twain,
My altars sullied, I bereft, remain
A priestess execrable, taken in vain—"

       So the refrain
Sings itself over, and so the game
Restarts itself wherein I am kept
Like a glowing brazier faintly blue of flame,
So that the delicate love-adept
Can warm her hands and invite her soul,
Sprinkling incense and salt of words
And kisses pale, and sipping the toll
Of incense-smoke that rises like birds.

Yet I've forgotten in playing this game,
Things I have known that shall have no name;
Forgetting the place from which I came
I watch her ward away the flame
Yet warm herself at the fire—then blame
Me that I flicker in the basket;
Me that I glow not with content
To have my substance so subtly spent;
Me that I interrupt her game . . .
I ought to be proud that she should ask it
Of me to be her fire-opal . . .

       It is well
Since I am here for so short a spell
Not to interrupt her?—Why should I
Break in by making any reply!   *1918*

BABY TORTOISE

You know what it is to be born alone,
Baby tortoise!

The first day to heave your feet little by little from the shell,
Not yet awake,
And remain lapsed on earth,
Not quite alive.

A tiny, fragile, half-animate bean.

To open your tiny beak-mouth, that looks as if it would never open,
Like some iron door;
To lift the upper hawk-beak from the lower base
And reach your skinny little neck
And take your first bite at some dim bit of herbage,
Alone, small insect,
Tiny bright-eye,
Slow one.

To take your first solitary bite
And move on your slow, solitary hunt.
Your bright, dark little eye,
Your eye of a dark disturbed night,
Under its slow lid, tiny baby tortoise,
So indomitable.

No one ever heard you complain.

You draw your head forward, slowly, from your little wimple
And set forward, slow-dragging, on your four-pinned toes,
Rowing slowly forward.
Whither away, small bird?

Rather like a baby working its limbs,
Except that you make slow, ageless progress
And a baby makes none.

The touch of sun excites you,
And the long ages, and the lingering chill
Make you pause to yawn,

Opening your impervious mouth,
Suddenly beak-shaped, and very wide, like some suddenly gaping
    pincers;
Soft red tongue, and thin hard gums,
Then close the wedge of your little mountain front,
Your face, baby tortoise.

Do you wonder at the world, as slowly you turn your head in its wimple
And look with laconic, black eyes?
Or is sleep coming over you again,
The non-life?

You are so hard to wake.

Are you able to wonder?
Or is it just your indomitable will and pride of the first life
Looking round
And slowly pitching itself against the inertia
Which had seemed invincible?

The vast inanimate,
And the fine brilliance of your so tiny eye,
Challenger.

Nay, tiny shell-bird,
What a huge vast inanimate it is, that you must row against,
What an incalculable inertia.

Challenger,
Little Ulysses, fore-runner,
No bigger than my thumb-nail,
Buon viaggio.

All animate creation on your shoulder,
Set forth, little Titan, under your battle-shield.

The ponderous, preponderate,
Inanimate universe;
And you are slowly moving, pioneer, you alone.

How vivid your travelling seems now, in the troubled sunshine,
Stoic, Ulyssean atom;
Suddenly hasty, reckless, on high toes.

Voiceless little bird,
Resting your head half out of your wimple
In the slow dignity of your eternal pause.
Alone, with no sense of being alone,
And hence six times more solitary;
Fulfilled of the slow passion of pitching through immemorial ages
Your little round house in the midst of chaos.

Over the garden earth,
Small bird,
Over the edge of all things.

Traveller,
With your tail tucked a little on one side
Like a gentleman in a long-skirted coat.

All life carried on your shoulder,
Invincible fore-runner.   1921

TORTOISE-SHELL

The Cross, the Cross
Goes deeper in than we know,
Deeper into life;
Right into the marrow
And through the bone.

Along the back of the baby tortoise
The scales are locked in an arch like a bridge,
Scale-lapping, like a lobster's sections
Or a bee's.

Then crossways down his sides
Tiger-stripes and wasp-bands.

Five, and five again, and five again,
And round the edges twenty-five little ones,
The sections of the baby tortoise shell.

Four, and a keystone;
Four, and a keystone;
Four, and a keystone;
Then twenty-four, and a tiny little keystone.

It needed Pythagoras to see life placing her counters on the living back
Of the baby tortoise;
Life establishing the first eternal mathematical tablet,
Not in stone, like the Judean Lord, or bronze, but in life-clouded, life-
    rosy tortoise-shell.

The first little mathematical gentleman
Stepping, wee mite, in his loose trousers
Under all the eternal dome of mathematical law.

Fives, and tens,
Threes and fours and twelves,
All the *volte face* of decimals,
The whirligig of dozens and the pinnacle of seven.

Turn him on his back,
The kicking little beetle,
And there again, on his shell-tender, earth-touching belly,
The long cleavage of division, upright of the eternal cross
And on either side count five,
On each side, two above, on each side, two below
The dark bar horizontal.

The Cross!
It goes right through him, the sprottling insect,
Through his cross-wise cloven psyche,
Through his five-fold complex-nature.

So turn him over on his toes again;
Four pin-point toes, and a problematical thumb-piece,
Four rowing limbs, and one wedge-balancing head,
Four and one makes five, which is the clue to all mathematics.

The Lord wrote it all down on the slate
Of the baby tortoise.
Outward and visible indication of the plan within,
The complex, manifold involvedness of an individual creature
Plotted out
On this small bird, this rudiment,
This little dome, this pediment
Of all creation,
This slow one.   *1921*

TORTOISE GALLANTRY

Making his advances
He does not look at her, nor sniff at her,
No, not even sniff at her, his nose is blank.

Only he senses the vulnerable folds of skin
That work beneath her while she sprawls along
In her ungainly pace,
Her folds of skin that work and row
Beneath the earth-soiled hovel in which she moves.

And so he strains beneath her housey walls
And catches her trouser-legs in his beak
Suddenly, or her skinny limb,
And strange and grimly drags at her
Like a dog,
Only agelessly silent, with a reptile's awful persistency.

Grim, gruesome gallantry, to which he is doomed.
Dragged out of an eternity of silent isolation
And doomed to partiality, partial being,
Ache, and want of being,
Want,
Self-exposure, hard humiliation, need to add himself on to her.

Born to walk alone,
Fore-runner,
Now suddenly distracted into this mazy side-track,
This awkward, harrowing pursuit,
This grim necessity from within.

Does she know
As she moves eternally slowly away?
Or is he driven against her with a bang, like a bird flying in the dark
     against a window,
All knowledgeless?

The awful concussion,
And the still more awful need to persist, to follow, follow, continue,

Driven, after aeons of pristine, fore-god-like singleness and oneness,
At the end of some mysterious, red-hot iron,

Driven away from himself into her tracks,
Forced to crash against her.

Stiff, gallant, irascible, crook-legged reptile,
Little gentleman,
Sorry plight,
We ought to look the other way.

Save that, having come with you so far,
We will go on to the end.   *1921*

SNAKE

A snake came to my water-trough
On a hot, hot day, and I in pyjamas for the heat,
To drink there.

In the deep, strange-scented shade of the great dark carob tree
I came down the steps with my pitcher
And must wait, must stand and wait, for there he was at the trough
      before me.

He reached down from a fissure in the earth-wall in the gloom
And trailed his yellow-brown slackness soft-bellied down, over the edge
      of the stone trough
And rested his throat upon the stone bottom,
And where the water had dripped from the tap, in a small clearness,
He sipped with his straight mouth,
Softly drank through his straight gums, into his slack long body,
Silently.

Someone was before me at my water-trough,
And I, like a second comer, waiting.

He lifted his head from his drinking, as cattle do,
And looked at me vaguely, as drinking cattle do,
And flickered his two-forked tongue from his lips, and mused a moment,
And stooped and drank a little more,
Being earth-brown, earth-golden from the burning bowels of the earth
On the day of Sicilian July, with Etna smoking.

The voice of my education said to me
He must be killed,
For in Sicily the black, black snakes are innocent, the gold are
      venomous.

And voices in me said, If you were a man
You would take a stick and break him now, and finish him off.

But must I confess how I liked him,
How glad I was he had come like a guest in quiet, to drink at my
    water-trough
And depart peaceful, pacified, and thankless,
Into the burning bowels of this earth?

Was it cowardice, that I dared not kill him?
Was it perversity, that I longed to talk to him?
Was it humility, to feel so honoured?
I felt so honoured.

And yet those voices:
If you were not afraid, you would kill him!

And truly I was afraid, I was most afraid,
But even so, honoured still more
That he should seek my hospitality
From out the dark door of the secret earth.

He drank enough
And lifted his head, dreamily, as one who has drunken,
And flickered his tongue like a forked night on the air, so black,
Seeming to lick his lips,
And looked around like a god, unseeing, into the air,
And slowly turned his head,
And slowly, very slowly, as if thrice adream,
Proceeded to draw his slow length curving round
And climb again the broken bank of my wall-face.

And as he put his head into that dreadful hole,
And as he slowly drew up, snake-easing his shoulders, and entered
    farther,
A sort of horror, a sort of protest against his withdrawing into that
    horrid black hole,
Deliberately going into the blackness, and slowly drawing himself after,
Overcame me now his back was turned.

I looked around, I put down my pitcher,
I picked up a clumsy log
And threw it at the water-trough with a clatter.

I think I did not hit him,
But suddenly that part of him that was left behind convulsed in undig-
    nified haste,
Writhed like lightning, and was gone
Into the black hole, the earth-lipped fissure in the wall-front,
At which, in the intense still noon, I stared with fascination.

And immediately I regretted it.
I though how paltry, how vulgar, what a mean act!
I despised myself and the voices of my accursed human education.

And I thought of the albatross,
And I wished he would come back, my snake.

For he seemed to me again like a king,
Like a king in exile, uncrowned in the underworld,
Now due to be crowned again.

And so, I missed my chance with one of the lords
Of life.
And I have something to expiate;
A pettiness.   *Taormina, 1923*

HUMMING-BIRD

I can imagine, in some otherworld
Primeval-dumb, far back
In that most awful stillness, that only gasped and hummed,
Humming-birds raced down the avenues.

Before anything had a soul,
While life was a heave of Matter, half inanimate,
This little bit chipped off in brilliance
And went whizzing through the slow, vast, succulent stems.

I believe there were no flowers then,
In the world where the humming-bird flashed ahead of creation.
I believe he pierced the slow vegetable veins with his long beak.

Probably he was big
As mosses, and little lizards, they say, were once big.
Probably he was a jabbing, terrifying monster.

We look at him through the wrong end of the telescope of Time,
Luckily for us.   *Española, 1923*

SORROW

Why does the thin grey strand
Floating up from the forgotten
Cigarette between my fingers,
Why does it trouble me?

Ah, you will understand;
When I carried my mother downstairs,
A few times only, at the beginning
Of her soft-foot malady,

I should find, for a reprimand
To my gaiety, a few long grey hairs
On the breast of my coat; and one by one
I watched them float up the dark chimney.   *1925*

BROODING GRIEF

A yellow leaf, from the darkness
Hops like a frog before me;
Why should I start and stand still?

I was watching the woman that bore me
Stretched in the brindled darkness
Of the sick-room, rigid with will
To die: and the quick leaf tore me
Back to this rainy swill
Of leaves and lamps and the city street mingled before me.

1925

MY WAY IS NOT THY WAY

My way is not thy way, and thine is not mine.
But come, before we part
Let us separately go to the Morning Star,
And meet there.

I do not point you to my road, nor yet
Call: "Oh come!"
But the Star is the same for both of us,
Winsome.

The good ghost of me goes down the distance
To the Holy Ghost.
Oh you, in the tent of the cloven flame
Meet me, you I like most.

Each man his own way forever, but towards
The hoverer between;
Who opens his flame like a tent-flap,
As we slip in unseen.

A man cannot tread like a woman,
Nor a woman step out like a man.
The ghost of each through the leaves of shadow
Moves as it can.

But the Morning Star and the Evening Star
Pitch tents of flame
Where we foregather like gypsies, none knowing
How the other came.

I ask for nothing except to slip
In the tent of the Holy Ghost
And be there in the house of the cloven flame,
Guest of the Host.

Be with me there, my woman,
Be bodily there.
Then let the flame wrap round us
Like a snare.

Be there along with me, oh men!
Reach across the hearth,
And laugh with me, while the woman rests,
For all we are worth.   1926

WHEN I WENT TO THE CIRCUS—

When I went to the circus that had pitched on the waste lot
it was full of uneasy people
frightened of the bare earth and the temporary canvas
and the smell of horses and other beasts
instead of merely the smell of man.

Monkeys rode rather grey and wizened
on curly plump piebald ponies
and the children uttered a little cry—
and dogs jumped through hoops and turned somersaults
and then the geese scuttled in in a little flock
and round the ring they went to the sound of the whip
then doubled, and back, with a funny up-flutter of wings—
and the children suddenly shouted out.

Then came the hush again, like a hush of fear.

The tight-rope lady, pink and blonde and nude-looking, with a few gold
    spangles
footed cautiously out on the rope, turned prettily, spun round
bowed, and lifted her foot in her hand, smiled, swung her parasol
to another balance, tripped round, poised, and slowly sank
her handsome thighs down, down, till she slept her splendid body on
    the rope.
When she rose, tilting her parasol, and smiled at the cautious people
they cheered, but nervously.

The trapeze man, slim and beautiful and like a fish in the air
swung great curves through the upper space, and came down like a star
—And the people applauded, with hollow, frightened applause.

The elephants, huge and grey, loomed their curved bulk through the
    dusk
and sat up, taking strange postures, showing the pink soles of their feet
and curling their precious live trunks like ammonites
and moving always with soft slow precision
as when a great ship moves to anchor.

The people watched and wondered, and seemed to resent the mystery
    that lies in beasts.

Horses, gay horses, swirling round and plaiting
in a long line, their heads laid over each other's necks;
they were happy, they enjoyed it;
all the creatures seemed to enjoy the game
in the circus, with their circus people.

But the audience, compelled to wonder
compelled to admire the bright rhythms of moving bodies

compelled to see the delicate skill of flickering human bodies
flesh flamey and a little heroic, even in a tumbling clown,
they were not really happy.
There was no gushing response, as there is at the film.

When modern people see the carnal body dauntless and flickering gay
playing among the elements neatly, beyond competition
and displaying no personality,
modern people are depressed.

Modern people feel themselves at a disadvantage.
They know they have no bodies that could play among the elements.
They have only their personalities, that are best seen flat, on the film,
flat personalities in two dimensions, imponderable and touchless.

And they grudge the circus people the swooping gay weight of limbs
that flower in mere movement,
and they grudge them the immediate, physical understanding they
      have with their circus beasts,
and they grudge them their circus-life altogether.

Yet the strange, almost frightened shout of delight that comes now and
      then from the children
shows that the children vaguely know how cheated they are of their
      birthright
in the bright wild circus flesh.   *1929*

SWAN

Far-off
at the core of space
at the quick
of time
beats
and goes still
the great swan upon the waters of all endings
the swan within vast chaos, within the electron.

For us
no longer he swims calmly
nor clacks across the forces furrowing a great gay trail
of happy energy,

nor is he nesting passive upon the atoms,
nor flying north desolative icewards
to the sleep of ice,
nor feeding in the marshes,
nor honking horn-like into the twilight.—

But he stoops, now
in the dark
upon us;
he is treading our women
and we men are put out
as the vast white bird
furrows our fatherless women
with unknown shocks
and stamps his black marsh-feet on their white and marshy flesh.

1929

WILLY WET-LEG

I can't stand Willy wet-leg,
can't stand him at any price.
He's resigned, and when you hit him
he lets you hit him twice. 1929

WHEN THE RIPE FRUIT FALLS

When the ripe fruit falls
its sweetness distils and trickles away into the veins of the earth.

When fulfilled people die
the essential oil of their experience enters
the veins of living space, and adds a glisten
to the atom, to the body of immortal chaos.

For space is alive
and it stirs like a swan
whose feathers glisten
silky with oil of distilled experience. 1929

WHALES WEEP NOT!

They say the sea is cold, but the sea contains
the hottest blood of all, and the wildest, the most urgent.

All the whales in the wider deeps, hot are they, as they urge
on and on, and dive beneath the ice-bergs.
The right whales, the sperm-whales, the hammer-heads, the killers
there they blow, there they blow, hot wild white breath out of the sea!

And they rock and they rock, through the sensual ageless ages
on the depths of the seven seas,
and through the salt they reel with drunk delight
and in the tropics tremble they with love
and roll with massive, strong desire, like gods.
Then the great bull lies up against his bride
in the blue deep of the sea
as mountain pressing on mountain, in the zest of life:
and out of the inward roaring of the inner red ocean of whale blood
the long tip reaches strong, intense, like the maelstrom-tip, and comes to
    rest
in the clasp and the soft, wild clutch of a she-whale's fathomless body.

And over the bridge of the whale's strong phallus, linking the wonder
    of whales
the burning archangels under the sea keep passing, back and forth,
keep passing archangels of bliss
from him to her, from her to him, great Cherubim
that wait on whales in mid-ocean, suspended in the waves of the sea
great heaven of whales in the waters, old hierarchies.
And enormous mother whales lie dreaming suckling their whale-tender
    young
and dreaming with strange whale eyes wide open in the waters of the
    beginning and the end.

And bull-whales gather their women and whale-calves in a ring
when danger threatens, on the surface of the ceaseless flood
and range themselves like great fierce Seraphim facing the threat
encircling their huddled monsters of love.
and all this happiness in the sea, in the salt
where God is also love, but without words:
and Aphrodite is the wife of whales
most happy, happy she!
and Venus among the fishes skips and is a she-dolphin
she is the gay, delighted porpoise sporting with love and the sea
she is the female tunny-fish, round and happy among the males
and dense with happy blood, dark rainbow bliss in the sea. *1932*

BAVARIAN GENTIANS

Not every man has gentians in his house
In soft September, at slow, sad Michaelmas.

Bavarian gentians, tall and dark, but dark
Darkening the day-time torch-like with the smoking blueness of Pluto's
    gloom
Ribbed hellish flowers erect, with their blaze of darkness spread blue
Blown into points, by the heavy white draught of the day.

Torch-flowers of the blue-smoking darkness, Pluto's dark blue blaze
Black lamps from the halls of Dio, smoking dark blue
Giving off darkness, blue darkness, upon Demeter's yellow-pale day
Reach me a gentian, give me a torch!
Let me guide myself with the blue, forked torch of a flower
Down the darker and darker stairs, where blue is darkened on blueness
Down the way Persephone goes, just now, in first-frosted September
To the sightless realm where darkness is married to dark
And Persephone herself is but a voice, as a bride
A gloom invisible enfolded in the deeper dark
Of the arms of Pluto as he ravishes her once again
And pierces her once more with his passion of the utter dark.

Among the splendour of black-blue torches, shedding fathomless dark-
    ness on the nuptials.

Give me a flower on a tall stem, and three dark flames,
For I will go to the wedding, and be wedding-guest
At the marriage of the living dark.   *1932*

THE SHIP OF DEATH

I

Now it is autumn and the falling fruit
and the long journey towards oblivion.

The apples falling like great drops of dew
to bruise themselves an exit from themselves.

And it is time to go, to bid farewell
to one's own self, and find an exit
from the fallen self.

II

Have you built your ship of death, O have you?
O build your ship of death, for you will need it.

The grim frost is at hand, when the apples will fall
thick, almost thundrous, on the hardened earth.

And death is on the air like a smell of ashes!
Ah! can't you smell it?
And in the bruised body, the frightened soul
finds itself shrinking, wincing from the cold
that blows upon it through the orifices.

III

And can a man his own quietus make
with a bare bodkin?

With daggers, bodkins, bullets, man can make
a bruise or break of exit for his life;
but is that a quietus, O tell me, is it quietus?

Surely not so! for how could murder, even self-murder
ever a quietus make?

IV

O let us talk of quiet that we know,
that we can know, the deep and lovely quiet
of a strong heart at peace!

How can we this, our own quietus, make?

V

Build then the ship of death, for you must take
the longest journey, to oblivion.

And die the death, the long and painful death
that lies between the old self and the new.

Already our bodies are fallen, bruised, badly bruised,
already our souls are oozing through the exit
of the cruel bruise.

Already the dark and endless ocean of the end
is washing in through the breaches of our wounds,
already the flood is upon us.

O build your ship of death, your little ark
and furnish it with food, with little cakes, and wine
for the dark flight down oblivion.

VI

Piecemeal the body dies, and the timid soul
has her footing washed away, as the dark flood rises.

We are dying, we are dying, we are all of us dying
and nothing will stay the death-flood rising within us
and soon it will rise on the world, on the outside world.

We are dying, we are dying, piecemeal our bodies are dying
and our strength leaves us,
and our soul cowers naked in the dark rain over the flood,
cowering in the last branches of the tree of our life.

VII

We are dying, we are dying, so all we can do
is now to be willing to die, and to build the ship
of death to carry the soul on the longest journey.

A little ship, with oars and food
and little dishes, and all accoutrements
fitting and ready for the departing soul.

Now launch the small ship, now as the body dies
and life departs, launch out, the fragile soul
in the fragile ship of courage, the ark of faith
with its store of food and little cooking pans
and change of clothes,
upon the flood's black waste
upon the waters of the end
upon the sea of death, where still we sail
darkly, for we cannot steer, and have no port.

There is no port, there is nowhere to go
only the deepening blackness darkening still

blacker upon the soundless, ungurgling flood
darkness at one with darkness, up and down
and sideways utterly dark, so there is no direction any more
and the little ship is there; yet she is gone.
She is not seen, for there is nothing to see her by.
She is gone! gone! and yet
somewhere she is there.
Nowhere!

VIII

And everything is gone, the body is gone
completely under, gone, entirely gone.
The upper darkness is heavy as the lower,
between them the little ship
is gone

It is the end, it is oblivion.

IX

And yet out of eternity a thread
separates itself on the blackness,
a horizontal thread
that fumes a little with pallor upon the dark.

Is it illusion? or does the pallor fume
a little higher?
Ah wait, wait, for there's the dawn,
the cruel dawn of coming back to life
out of oblivion.

Wait, wait, the little ship
drifting, beneath the deathly ashy grey
of a flood-dawn.

Wait, wait! even so, a flush of yellow
and strangely, O chilled wan soul, a flush of rose.

A flush of rose, and the whole thing starts again.

X

The flood subsides, and the body, like a worn sea-shell
emerges strange and lovely.

And the little ship wings home, faltering and lapsing
on the pink flood,
and the frail soul steps out, into the house again
filling the heart with peace.

Swings the heart renewed with peace
even of oblivion.

Oh build your ship of death. Oh build it!
for you will need it.
For the voyage of oblivion awaits you. 1932

TREES IN THE GARDEN

Ah in the thunder air
how still the trees are!

And the lime tree, lovely and tall, every leaf silent
hardly looses even a last breath of perfume.

And the ghostly, creamy-coloured little tree of leaves
white, ivory white among the rambling greens,
how evanescent, variegated elder, she hesitates on the green grass
as if, in another moment, she would disappear
with all her grace of foam!

And the larch that is only a column, it goes up too tall to see:
and the balsam pines that are blue with the grey-blue blueness of things
    from the sea,
and the young copper beech, its leaves red-rosy at the ends,
how still they are together, they stand so still
in the thunder air, all strangers to one another
as the green grass glows upwards, strangers in the garden. 1932

THE GODS! THE GODS!

People were bathing, and posturing themselves on the beach
and all was dreary, great robot limbs, robot breasts
robot voices, robot even the gay umbrellas.

But a woman, shy and alone, was washing herself under a tap
and the glimmer of the presence of the gods was like lilies,
and like water-lilies. 1932

James Stephens

WHAT TOMAS SAID IN A PUB

I saw God! Do you doubt it?
Do you dare to doubt it?
I saw the Almighty Man! His hand
Was resting on a mountain! And
He looked upon the World, and all about it:
I saw Him plainer than you see me now
—You mustn't doubt it!

He was not satisfied!
His look was all dissatisfied!
His beard swung on a wind, far out of sight
Behind the world's curve! And there was light
Most fearful from His forehead! And He sighed
—That star went always wrong, and from the start
I was dissatisfied!—

He lifted up His hand!
I say He heaved a dreadful hand
Over the spinning earth! Then I said,—Stay,
You must not strike it, God! I'm in the way!
And I will never move from where I stand!—
He said,—Dear child, I feared that you were dead,—
. . . And stayed His hand!   *1909*

CHILL OF THE EVE

A long green swell
Slopes soft to the sea;
And a far-off bell
Swings sweet to me;
As the grey
Chill day
Slips away
From the lea.

Spread cold and far,
Without one glow
From a mild pale star,
Is the sky's steel bow;
And the grey
Chill day
Slips away
Below.

Yon green tree grieves
To the air around;
And the whispering leaves
Have a lonely sound;
As the grey
Chill day
Slips away
From the ground.

And dark, more dark,
The shades settle down;
Far off is a spark
From the lamp-lit town;
And the grey
Chill day
Slips away
With a frown.   *1909*

THE SHELL

I

And then I pressed the shell
Close to my ear,
And listened well.

And straightway, like a bell,
Came low and clear
The slow, sad murmur of far distant seas

Whipped by an icy breeze
Upon a shore
Wind-swept and desolate.

It was a sunless strand that never bore
The footprint of a man,
Nor felt the weight

Since time began
Of any human quality or stir,
Save what the dreary winds and wave incur.

II

And in the hush of waters was the sound
Of pebbles, rolling round;
For ever rolling, with a hollow sound:

And bubbling sea-weeds, as the waters go,
Swish to and fro
Their long cold tentacles of slimy grey;

There was no day;
Nor ever came a night
Setting the stars alight

To wonder at the moon:
Was twilight only, and the frightened croon,
Smitten to whimpers, of the dreary wind

And waves that journeyed blind . . .
And then I loosed my ear.—Oh, it was sweet
To hear a cart go jolting down the street!

1909

WHY TOMAS CAM WAS GRUMPY

If I were rich what would I do?
I'd leave the horse just ready to shoe;
I'd leave the pail beside the cow;
I'd leave the furrow beneath the plough;
I'd leave the ducks, tho' they should quack:
"Our eggs will be stolen before you're back";
I'd buy a diamond brooch, a ring,
A chain of gold that I would fling
Around her neck. . . . Ah, what an itch,
If I were rich!

What would I do if I were wise?
I would not debate about the skies;
Nor would I try a book to write;
Or find the wrong in the tangled right;
I would not debate with learned men
Of how, and what, and why, and when;
—I'd train my tongue to a linnet's song,
I'd learn the words that couldn't go wrong—
And then I'd say . . . And win the prize,
If I were wise!

But I'm not that nor t'other, I bow
My back to the work that's waiting now:
I'll shoe the horse that's standing ready;
I'll milk the cow if she'll be steady;
I'll follow the plough that turns the loam;
I'll watch the ducks don't lay from home:
—And I'll curse, and curse, and curse again
Till the devil joins in with his big amen;
And none but he and I will wot
When the heart within me starts to rot;
To fester and churn its ugly brew
. . . Where's my spade! I've work to do!

1912

WHAT THE DEVIL SAID

It was night-time! God, the Father Good,
Weary of praises, on a sudden stood
From His great Throne, and leaned upon the sky:
For He had heard a sound; a little cry,
Thin as a whisper, climbing up the Steep.

And so He looked to where the Earth, asleep,
Rocked with the moon: He saw the whirling sea
Swing round the world in surgent energy,
Tangling the moonlight in its netted foam;
And, nearer, saw the white and fretted dome
Of the ice-capped pole spin back again a ray
To whistling stars, bright as a wizard's day.

But these He passed, with eyes intently wide,
Till, closer still, the mountains He espied
Squatting tremendous on the broad-backed Earth,

Each nursing twenty rivers at a birth!
And then, minutely, sought He for the cry
That had climbed the slant of space so hugely high.

He found it in a ditch outside a town:
A tattered hungry woman, crouching down
By a dead babe—So there was nought to do,
For what is done is done! And sad He drew
Back to His Heaven of ivory and gold:
And, as He sat, all suddenly there rolled,
From where the woman wept upon the sod,
Satan's deep voice—*O thou unhappy God!*   *1912*

SWEET APPLE

At the end of the bough!
At the top of the tree!
—As fragrant, as high,
And as lovely, as thou—
One sweet apple reddens,
Which all men may see,
—At the end of the bough!

Swinging full to the view!
Though the harvesters now
Overlook it, repass it,
And pass busily:
Overlook it!
Nay, pluck it!
They do not know how!

For it swings out of reach
Like a cloud! And as free
As a star; or thy beauty,
That seems too, I vow,
Remote as the sweet apple swinging
—Ah me!
At the end of the bough!   *1913*

DEIRDRE

Do not let any woman read this verse!
It is for men, and after them their sons,
And their sons' sons!

The time comes when our hearts sink utterly;
When we remember Deirdre, and her tale,
And that her lips are dust.

Once she did tread the earth: men took her hand;
They looked into her eyes and said their say,
And she replied to them.

More than two thousand years it is since she
Was beautiful: she trod the waving grass;
She saw the clouds.

Two thousand years! The grass is still the same;
The clouds as lovely as they were that time
When Deirdre was alive.

But there has been again no woman born
Who was so beautiful; not one so beautiful
Of all the women born.

Let all men go apart and mourn together!
No man can ever love her! Not a man
Can dream to be her lover!

No man can bend before her! No man say—
What could one say to her? There are no words
That one could say to her!

Now she is but a story that is told
Beside the fire! No man can ever be
The friend of that poor queen!   *1915*

THE SNARE

I hear a sudden cry of pain!
There is a rabbit in a snare:
Now I hear the cry again,
But I cannot tell from where.

But I cannot tell from where
He is calling out for aid!
Crying on the frightened air,
Making everything afraid!

Making everything afraid!
Wrinkling up his little face!
As he cries again for aid;
—And I cannot find the place!

And I cannot find the place
Where his paw is in the snare!
Little One! Oh, Little One!
I am searching everywhere!   *1915*

A GLASS OF BEER

The lanky hank of a she in the inn over there
Nearly killed me for asking the loan of a glass of beer;
May the devil grip the whey-faced slut by the hair,
And beat bad manners out of her skin for a year.

That parboiled ape, with the toughest jaw you will see
On virtue's path, and a voice that would rasp the dead,
Came roaring and raging the minute she looked at me,
And threw me out of the house on the back of my head!

If I asked her master he'd give me a cask a day;
But she, with the beer at hand, not a gill would arrange!
May she marry a ghost and bear him a kitten, and may
The High King of Glory permit her to get the mange.
                                    1918

THE WAVE OF CLIONA

My heart is withered and my health is gone,
For they, who were not easy put upon,
Masters of mirth, and of fair clemency,
Masters of wealth, and gentle charity,
They are all gone!

Mac Carthy Mor is dead!
Mac Carthy of the Lee is finishèd
Mac Carthy of Kanturk joined clay to clay,
And gat him gone, and bides as deep as they!

Their years, their gentle deeds, their flags are furled!
And deeply down, under the stiffened world,

In chests of oaken wood are princes thrust,
To crumble, day by day, into the dust
A mouth might puff at! Nor is left a trace
Of those who did of grace all that was grace!

O Wave of Cliona, cease thy bellowing!
And let mine ears forget a while to ring
At thy long, lamentable misery!
The great are dead indeed! The great are dead!
And I, in little time, will stoop my head
And put it under, and will be forgot
With them, and be with them, and, thus, be not!

Ease thee! Cease thy long keening! Cry no more!
End is! And here is end! And end is sore!
And to all lamentation be there end!

If I might come on thee, O howling friend!
Knowing that sails were drumming on the sea
Westward to Eire, and that help would be
Trampling for her upon a Spanish deck,
I'd ram thy lamentation down thy neck.   *1918*

Siegfried Sassoon

A WORKING PARTY

Three hours ago he blundered up the trench,
Sliding and poising, groping with his boots;
Sometimes he tripped and lurched against the walls
With hands that pawed the sodden bags of chalk.
He couldn't see the man who walked in front;
Only he heard the drum and rattle of feet
Stepping along the trench-boards,—often splashing
Wretchedly where the sludge was ankle-deep.

Voices would grunt, "Keep to your right,—make way!"
When squeezing past the men from the front-line:
White faces peered, puffing a point of red;
Candles and braziers glinted through the chinks
And curtain-flaps of dug-outs; then the gloom
Swallowed his sense of sight; he stooped and swore
Because a sagging wire had caught his neck.
A flare went up; the shining whiteness spread
And flickered upward, showing nimble rats,
And mounds of glimmering sand-bags, bleached with rain;
Then the slow, silver moment died in dark.
The wind came posting by with chilly gusts
And buffeting at corners, piping thin
And dreary through the crannies; rifle-shots
Would split and crack and sing along the night,
And shells came calmly through the drizzling air
To burst with hollow bang below the hill.

Three hours ago he stumbled up the trench;
Now he will never walk that road again:
He must be carried back, a jolting lump
Beyond all need of tenderness and care;
A nine-stone corpse with nothing more to do.

He was a young man with a meagre wife
And two pale children in a Midland town;
He showed the photograph to all his mates;
And they considered him a decent chap
Who did his work and hadn't much to say,
And always laughed at other people's jokes
Because he hadn't any of his own.

That night when he was busy at his job
Of piling bags along the parapet,
He thought how slow time went, stamping his feet,
And blowing on his fingers, pinched with cold.
He thought of getting back by half-past twelve,
And tot of rum to send him warm to sleep
In draughty dug-out frowsty with the fumes
Of coke, and full of snoring, weary men.

He pushed another bag along the top,
Craning his body outward; then a flare
Gave one white glimpse of No Man's Land and wire;
And as he dropped his head the instant split
His startled life with lead, and all went out.　　*1917*

"THEY"

The Bishop tells us: "When the boys come back
They will not be the same; for they'll have fought
In a just cause: they lead the last attack
On Anti-Christ; their comrade's blood has bought
New right to breed an honorable race.
They have challenged Death and dared him face to face."

"We're none of us the same!" the boys reply.
"For George lost both his legs; and Bill's stone blind;
Poor Jim's shot through the lungs and like to die;
And Bert's gone syphilitic: you'll not find
A chap who's served that hasn't found *some* change."
And the bishop said: "The ways of God are strange!"

　　　　　　　　　　　　　　　　　　　　1917

THE TROOPS

Dim, gradual thinning of the shapeless gloom
Shudders to drizzling daybreak that reveals

Disconsolate men who stamp their sodden boots
And turn dulled, sunken faces to the sky
Haggard and hopeless. They, who have beaten down
The stale despair of night, must now renew
Their desolation in the truce of dawn,
Murdering the livid hours that grope for peace.

Yet these, who cling to life with stubborn hands,
Can grin through storms of death and find a gap
In the clawed, cruel tangles of his defence.
They march from safety, and the bird-sung joy
Of grass-green thickets, to the land where all
Is ruin, and nothing blossoms but the sky
That hastens over them where they endure
Sad, smoking, flat horizons, reeking woods,
And foundered trench-lines volleying doom for doom.

O my brave brown companions, when your souls
Flock silently away, and the eyeless dead
Shame the wild beast of battle on the ridge,
Death will stand grieving in that field of war
Since your unvanquished hardihood is spent.
And through some mooned Valhalla there will pass
Battalions and battalions, scarred from hell;
The unreturning army that was youth;
The legions who have suffered and are dust. *1918*

DREAMERS

Soldiers are citizens of death's grey land,
    Drawing no dividend from time's to-morrows.
In the great hour of destiny they stand,
    Each with his feuds, and jealousies, and sorrows.
Soldiers are sworn to action; they must win
    Some flaming, fatal climax with their lives.
Soldiers are dreamers; when the guns begin
    They think of firelit homes, clean beds, and wives.

I see them in foul dug-outs, gnawed by rats,
    And in the ruined trenches, lashed with rain,
Dreaming of things they did with balls and bats,
    And mocked by hopeless longing to regain
Bank-holidays, and picture shows, and spats,
    And going to the office in the train. *1918*

PICTURE-SHOW

And still they come and go: and this is all I know—
That from the gloom I watch an endless picture-show,
Where wild or listless faces flicker on their way,
With glad or grievous hearts I'll never understand
Because Time spins so fast, and they've no time to stay
Beyond the moment's gesture of a lifted hand.

And still, between the shadow and the blinding flame,
The brave despair of men flings onward, ever the same
As in those doom-lit years that wait them, and have been . . .
And life is just the picture dancing on a screen.   *1919*

ON READING THE WAR DIARY OF A DEFUNCT AMBASSADOR

So that's your Diary—that's your private mind
Translated into shirt-sleeved History. That
Is what diplomacy has left behind
For after-ages to peruse, and find
What passed beneath your elegant silk-hat.

You were a fine old gentleman; compact
Of shrewdness, charm, refinement and finesse.
Impeccable in breeding, taste and dress,
No diplomatic quality you lacked—
No tittle of ambassadorial tact.

I can imagine you among "the guns,"
Urbanely peppering partridge, grouse, or pheasant—
Guest of those infinitely privileged ones
Whose lives are padded, petrified, and pleasant.
I visualize you feeding off gold plate
And gossiping on grave affairs of State.

Now you're defunct; your gossip's gravely printed;
The world discovers where you lunched and dined
On such and such a day; and what was hinted
By ministers and generals far behind
The all-important conflict, carnage-tinted.

The world can read the rumours that you gleaned
From various Fronts; the well-known Names you met;
Each conference you attended and convened;
And (at appropriate moments) what you ate.
Thus (if the world's acute) it can derive
Your self, exact, uncensored and alive.

The world will find no pity in your pages;
No exercise of spirit worthy of mention;
Only a public-funeral grief-convention;
And all the circumspection of the ages.
But I, for one, am grateful, overjoyed,
And unindignant that your punctual pen
Should have been so constructively employed
In manifesting to unprivileged men
The visionless officialized fatuity
That once kept Europe safe for Perpetuity.　　1926

AN OLD-WORLD EFFECT

While blue-eyed children, goggle-faced and giggling,
Stare, swollen-cheeked (bad-mannered little wretches),
Two Nature-loving ladies dip their brushes,
Glance up, gaze down; with touches broad or niggling,
Remain absorbed in half-completed sketches
Where embryonic apple-blossom flushes
Round a decrepit cottage whence they catch
The ultimate rusticity of thatch.

You ask me why these artists have selected
An unhygienic dwelling as their theme . . .
"Have they no palate for the unexpected—
No easel for a Cubist housing-scheme?"

A sapless unprolific Past they paint,
Who ramble through the guide-book toward the Quaint.
Meanwhile a blackbird pipes from the vicinity
His free fantasia against virginity.　　1926

AT THE GRAVE OF HENRY VAUGHAN

Above the voiceful windings of a river
An old green slab of simply graven stone
Shuns notice, overshadowed by a yew.

Here Vaughan lies dead, whose name flows on for ever
Through pastures of the spirit washed with dew
And starlit with eternities unknown.

Here sleeps the Silurist; the loved physician;
The face that left no portraiture behind;
The skull that housed white angels and had vision
Of daybreak through the gateways of the mind.
  Here faith and mercy, wisdom and humility
  (Whose influence shall prevail for evermore)
  Shine. And this lowly grave tells Heaven's tranquillity.
  And here stand I, a suppliant at the door.   *1927*

AT THE CENOTAPH

I saw the Prince of Darkness, with his Staff,
Standing bare-headed by the Cenotaph:
Unostentatious and respectful, there
He stood, and offered up the following prayer:
  "Make them forget, O Lord, what this Memorial
    Means; their discredited ideas revive;
  Breed new belief that War is purgatorial
    Proof of the pride and power of being alive;
  Men's biologic urge to readjust
    The Map of Europe, Lord of Hosts, increase;
  Lift up their hearts in large destructive lust;
    And crown their heads with blind vindictive Peace."
The Prince of Darkness to the Cenotaph
Bowed. As he walked away I heard him laugh.   *1933*

THE ULTIMATE ATROCITY

When the first man who wasn't quite an ape
Felt magnanimity and prayed for more,
The world's redemption stood, in human shape,
With darkness done and betterment before.
From then till now such men have multiplied;
From then till now their task has been the same,
In whom the world's redemption dreamed and died—
To whom the vision of perfection came.

I hear an aeroplane—what years ahead
Who knows?—but if from that machine should fall

The first bacterial bomb, this world might find
That all the aspirations of the dead
Had been betrayed and blotted out, and all
Their deeds denied who hoped for Humankind.

1933

[IT WAS THE LOVE OF LIFE]

It was the love of life, when I was young,
Which led me out in summer to explore
The daybreak world. A bird's first notes were sung
For childhood standing at the garden door.
That loneliness it was which made me wise
When I looked out and saw
Dark trees against the strangely brightening skies
And learnt the love of earth that is my law.

The love of life is my religion still.
Steadfast through rigorous nights, companioned only
By what I am and what I strive to be—
I seek no mystery now beyond the hill,
And wait no change but to become more lonely,
No freedom till the sleep that sets me free.   *1934*

DECEMBER STILLNESS

December stillness, teach me through your trees
That loom along the west, one with the land,
The veiled evangel of your mysteries.
  While nightfall, sad and spacious, on the down
  Deepens, and dusk imbues me where I stand,
  With grave diminishings of green and brown,
  Speak, roofless Nature, your instinctive words;
  And let me learn your secret from the sky,
  Following a flock of steadfast-journeying birds
  In lone remote migration beating by.
December stillness, crossed by twilight roads,
Teach me to travel far and bear my loads.   *1934*

VIGILS

  Lone heart, learning
  By one light burning,
  Slow discerning of worldhood's worth;

Soul, awaking
By night and taking
Roads forsaking enchanted earth:
Man, unguided
And self-divided,
Clocked by silence which tells decay;
You that keep
In a land asleep
One light burning till break of day:
You whose vigil
Is deed and sigil,
Bond and service of lives afar—
Seek, in seeing
Your own blind being,
Peace, remote in the morning star.

1934

Edith Sitwell

AUBADE

Jane, Jane,
Tall as a crane,
The morning light creaks down again.

Comb your cockscomb-ragged hair,
Jane, Jane, come down the stair.

Each dull blunt wooden stalactite
Of rain creaks, hardened by the light,

Sounding like an overtone
From some lonely world unknown.

But the creaking empty light
Will never harden into sight,

Will never penetrate your brain
With overtones like the blunt rain.

The light would show (if it could harden)
Eternities of kitchen garden,

Cockscomb flowers that none will pluck,
And wooden flowers that 'gin to cluck.

In the kitchen you must light
Flames as staring, red and white,

As carrots or as turnips, shining
Where the cold dawn light lies whining.

Cockscomb hair on the cold wind
Hangs limp, turns the milk's weak mind. . . .

Jane, Jane,
Tall as a crane,
The morning light creaks down again!

1923

DARK SONG

The fire was furry as a bear
And the flames purr. . . .
The brown bear rambles in his chain
Captive to cruel men
Through the dark and hairy wood . . .
The maid sighed, "All my blood
Is animal. They thought I sat
Like a household cat;
But through the dark woods rambled I . . .
Oh, if my blood would die!"
The fire had a bear's fur
It heard and knew. . . .
The dark earth, furry as a bear,
Grumbled too!   1923

TWO KITCHEN SONGS

I

The harsh bray and hollow
Of the pot and the pan
Seems Midas defying
The great god Apollo!
The leaves' great golden crowns
Hang on the trees;
The maids in their long gowns
Hunt me through these.
Grand'am, Grand'am,
From the pan I am
Flying . . . country gentlemen
Took flying Psyche for a hen
And aimed at her; then turned a gun
On harmless chicken-me—for fun.
The beggars' dogs howl all together,
Their tails turn to a ragged feather;
Pools, like mirrors hung in garrets,

Show each face as red as a parrot's,
Whistling hair that raises ire
In cocks and hens in the kitchen fire!
Every flame shrieks cockle-doo-doo
(With their cockscombs flaring high too);
The witch's rag-rug takes its flight
Beneath the willows' watery light:
The wells of water seem a-plume—
The old witch sweeps them with her broom—
All are chasing chicken-me. . . .
But Psyche—where, oh where, is she?   *1923*

II

Grey as a guinea-fowl is the rain
Squawking down from the boughs again.
"Anne, Anne,
Go fill the pail,"
Said the old witch who sat on the rail.
"Though there is a hole in the bucket,
Anne, Anne,
It will fill my pocket;
The water-drops when they cross my doors
Will turn to guineas and gold moidores. . . ."
The well-water hops across the floors;
Whimpering, "Anne," it cries, implores;
And the guinea-fowl-plumaged rain,
Squawking down from the boughs again,
Cried, "Anne, Anne, go fill the bucket,
There is a hole in the witch's pocket—
And the water-drops like gold moidores,
Obedient girl, will surely be yours.
So, Anne, Anne,
Go fill the pail,
Of the old witch who sits on the rail!"   *1925*

LULLABY

Though the world has slipped and gone,
Sounds my loud discordant cry
Like the steel birds' song on high:
"Still one thing is left—the Bone."
Then out danced the Babioun.

She sat in the hollow of the sea—
A socket whence the eye's put out—
She sang to the child a lullaby
(The steel birds' nest was thereabout).

"Do, do, do, do—
Thy mother's hied to the vaster race:
The Pterodactyl made its nest
And laid a steel egg in her breast—
Under the Judas-colored sun.
She'll work no more, nor dance, nor moan,
And I am come to take her place.
Do—do."

There's nothing left but earth's low bed—
(The Pterodactyl fouls its nest);
But steel wings fan thee to thy rest,
And wingless truth and larvae lie
And eyeless hope and handless fear—
All these for thee as toys are spread,
"Do—do—"

Red is the bed of Poland, Spain,
And thy mother's breast, who has grown wise
In that fouled nest. If she could rise,
Give birth again,
In wolfish pelt she'd hide thy bones
To shield thee from the world's long cold,
And down on all fours shouldst thou crawl
For thus from no height canst thou fall—
"Do—do."

She'd give no hands: there's nought to hold
And nought to make: there's dust to sift,
But no food for the hands to lift.
Do, do.

Heed my ragged lullaby,
Fear not living, fear not chance;
All is equal—blindness, sight,
There is no depth, there is no height:
Do, do.

The Judas-colored sun is gone,
And with the Ape thou art alone—
Do,
    Do.   *1940*

STREET SONG

"Love my heart for an hour, but my bone for a day—
At least the skeleton smiles, for it has a morrow:
But the hearts of the young are now the dark treasure of Death,
And summer is lonely.

"Comfort the lonely light and the sun in its sorrow,
Come like the night, for terrible is the sun
As truth, and the dying light shows only the skeleton's hunger
For peace, under the flesh like the summer rose.

"Come through the darkness of death, as once through the branches
Of youth you came, through the shade like the flowering door
That leads into Paradise, far from the street—you, the unborn
City seen by the homeless, the night of the poor.

"You walk in the city ways, where Man's threatening shadow,
Red-edged by the sun like Cain, has a changing shape—
Elegant like the Skeleton, crouched like the Tiger,
With the age-old wisdom and aptness of the Ape.

"The pulse that beats in the heart is changed to the hammer
That sounds in the Potter's Field where they build a new world
From our Bone, and the carrion-bird days' foul droppings and clamor—
But you are my night, and my peace,—

"The holy night of conception, of rest, the consoling
Darkness when all men are equal,—the wrong and the right,
And the rich and the poor are no longer separate nations,—
They are brothers in night."

This was the song I heard; but the Bone is silent!
Who knows if the sound was that of the dead light calling—
Of Caesar rolling onward his heart, that stone,
Or the burden of Atlas falling?   *1942*

TEARS

My tears were Orion's splendor with sextuple suns and the million
Flowers in the fields of the heaven, where solar systems are setting—
The rocks of great diamonds in the midst of the clear wave
By May dews and early light ripened, more diamonds begetting.
I wept for the glories of air, for the millions of dawns
And the splendors within Man's heart with the darkness warring,
I wept for the beautiful queens of the world, like a flower-bed shining,—
Now gathered, some at six, some at seven, but all in Eternity's morning.
But now my tears have shrunk and like hours are falling:
I weep for Venus whose body has changed to a metaphysical city
Whose heart-beat is now the sound of the revolutions,—for love changed
To the hospital mercy, the scientists' hope for the future,
And the darkened Man, that complex multiplicity
Of air and water, plant and animal,
Hard diamond, infinite sun.   1942

THE SWANS

In the green light of water, like the day
Under green boughs, the spray
And air-pale petals of the foam seem flowers—
Dark-leaved arbutus blooms with wax-pale bells
And their faint honey-smells,
The velvety syringa with smooth leaves,
Gloxinia with a green shade in the snow,
Jasmine and moon-clear orange-blossoms and green blooms
Of the wild strawberries from the shade of woods.
Their showers
Pelt the white women under the green trees,
Venusia, Cosmopolita, Pistillarine—
White solar statues, white rose-trees in snow
Flowering for ever, child-women, half stars
Half flowers, waves of the sea, born of a dream.

Their laughter flying through the trees like doves,
These angels come to watch their whiter ghosts
In the air-pale water, archipelagos
Of stars and young thin moons from great wings falling
As ripples widen.
These are their ghosts, their own white angels these!

O great wings spreading—
Your bones are made of amber, smooth and thin
Grown from the amber dust that was a rose
Or nymph in swan-smooth waters.
                                    But Time's winter falls
With snows as soft, as soundless. . . . Then, who knows
Rose-footed swan from snow, or girl from rose?   1942

A SONG AT MORNING

The weeping rose in her dark night of leaves
Sighed, "Dark is my heart, and dark my secret love—
Show not the fire within your heart, its light—
For to behold a rainbow in the night
Shall be the presage of your overthrow."

But morning came, and the great dews; then her philosophies
Of the heart's darkness died. And from the chrysalis of my thin sleep
That lay like light or dew upon my form
I rose and wrapped my wings about me, went
From that porphyrian darkness. Like the rose

I, too, was careless in the morning dews,
Seeing the dead and the dead hour return
To forgive the stain on our hands. I, too, at morning
Am like the rose who shouts of the red joys and redder sorrows
Fallen from young veins and heartsprings that once held
The world's incendiarism and the redness of summer,
The hope of the rose. For soon will come the morrow
When ancient Prudence and her wintery dream
Will be no more than the rose's idleness. . . .
The light of tears shall only seem the rose's light
—Nor sorrow darker than her night of leaves.   1945

DIRGE FOR THE NEW SUNRISE

(Fifteen minutes past eight o'clock, on the morning of Monday, the 6th of
August, 1945.)

Bound to my heart as Ixion to the wheel,
Nailed to my heart as the thief upon the cross,
I hang between our Christ and the gap where the world was lost

And watch the phantom Sun in Famine Street—
The ghost of the heart of Man . . . red Cain,
And the more murderous brain
Of Man, still redder Nero that conceived the death
Of his mother Earth, and tore
Her womb, to know the place where he was conceived.

But no eyes grieved—
For none were left for tears:
They were blinded as the years
Since Christ was born. Mother or Murderer, you have given or taken
    life—
Now all is one!

There was a morning when the holy Light
Was young. . . . The beautiful First Creature came
To our water-springs, and thought us without blame.

Our hearts seemed safe in our breasts and sang to the Light—
The marrow in the bone
We dreamed was safe . . . the blood in the veins, the sap in the tree
Were springs of Deity.

But I saw the little Ant-men as they ran
Carrying the world's weight of the world's filth
And the filth in the heart of Man—
Compressed till those lusts and greeds had a greater heat than that of
    the Sun.

And the ray from that heat came soundless, shook the sky
As if in search for food, and squeezed the stems
Of all that grows on the earth till they were dry—
And drank the marrow of the bone:
The eyes that saw, the lips that kissed, are gone—
Or black as thunder lie and grin at the murdered Sun.

The living blind and seeing dead together lie
As if in love. . . . There was no more hating then,
And no more love: Gone is the heart of Man.   1949

Edwin Muir

CHILDHOOD

Long time he lay upon the sunny hill,
   To his father's house below securely bound.
Far off the silent, changing sound was still,
   With the black islands lying thick around.

He saw each separate height, each vaguer hue,
   Where the massed islands rolled in mist away,
And though all ran together in his view
   He knew that unseen straits between them lay.

Often he wondered what new shores were there.
   In thought he saw the still light on the sand,
The shallow water clear in tranquil air,
   And walked through it in joy from strand to strand.

Over the sound a ship so slow would pass
   That in the black hill's gloom it seemed to lie.
The evening sound was smooth like sunken glass,
   And time seemed finished ere the ship passed by.

Grey tiny rocks slept round him where he lay,
   Moveless as they, more still as evening came,
The grasses threw straight shadows far away,
   And from the house his mother called his name.

1925

HORSES

Those lumbering horses in the steady plough,
On the bare field—I wonder why, just now,
They seemed terrible, so wild and strange,
Like magic power on the stony grange.

Perhaps some childish hour has come again,
When I watched fearful, through the blackening rain,
Their hooves like pistons in an ancient mill
Move up and down, yet seem as standing still.

Their conquering hooves which trod the stubble down
Were ritual that turned the field to brown,
And their great hulks were seraphim of gold,
Or mute ecstatic monsters on the mould.

And oh the rapture, when, one furrow done,
They marched broad-breasted to the sinking sun!
The light flowed off their bossy sides in flakes;
The furrows rolled behind like struggling snakes.

But when at dusk with steaming nostrils home
They came, they seemed gigantic in the gloam,
And warm and glowing with mysterious fire
That lit their smouldering bodies in the mire.

Their eyes as brilliant and as wide as night
Gleamed with a cruel apocalyptic light.
Their manes the leaping ire of the wind
Lifted with rage invisible and blind.

Ah, now it fades! it fades! and I must pine
Again for that dread country crystalline,
Where the blank field and the still-standing tree
Were bright and fearful presences to me.   *1925*

THE ROAD

There is a road that turning always
    Cuts off the country of Again.
Archers stand there on every side
    And as it runs time's deer is slain,
    And lies where it has lain.

That busy clock shows never an hour.
    All flies and all in flight must tarry.
The hunter shoots the empty air
    Far on before the quarry,
    Which falls through nothing 's there to parry.

The lion crouching in the centre
  With mountain head and sunset brow
Rolls down the everlasting slope
  Bones picked an age ago,
  And the bones rise up and go.

There the beginning finds the end
  Before beginning ever can be,
And the great runner never leaves
  The starting and the finishing tree,
  The budding and the fading tree.

There the ship sailing safe in harbour
  Long since in many a sea was drowned.
The treasure burning in her hold
  So near will never be found,
  Sunk past all sound.

There a man on a summer evening
  Reclines at ease upon his tomb
And is his mortal effigy.
  And there within the womb,
  The cell of doom,

The ancestral deed is thought and done,
  And in a million Edens fall
A million Adams drowned in darkness,
  For small is great and great is small,
  And a blind seed all.   1937

TROY

He all that time among the sewers of Troy
Scouring for scraps. A man so venerable
He might have been Priam's self, but Priam was dead,
Troy taken. His arms grew meagre as a boy's,
And all that flourished in that hollow famine
Was his long, white, round beard. Oh, sturdily
He swung his staff and sent the bold rats skipping
Across the scurfy hills and worm-wet valleys,
Crying: "Achilles, Ajax, turn and fight!
Stop cowards!" Till his cries, dazed and confounded,
Flew back at him with: "Coward, turn and fight!"

And the wild Greeks yelled round him.
Yet he withstood them, a brave, mad old man,
And fought the rats for Troy. The light was rat-grey,
The hills and dells, the common drain, his Simois,
Rat-grey. Mysterious shadows fell
Affrighting him whenever a cloud offended
The sun up in the other world. The rat-hordes,
Moving, were grey dust shifting in grey dust.
Proud history has such sackends. He was taken
At last by some chance robber seeking treasure
Under Troy's riven roots. Dragged to the surface.
And there he saw Troy like a burial ground
With tumbled walls for tombs, the smooth sward wrinkled
As time's last wave had long since passed that way,
The sky, the sea, Mount Ida and the islands,
No sail from edge to edge, the Greeks clean gone.
They stretched him on a rock and wrenched his limbs,
Asking: "Where is the treasure?" till he died.   1937

THE TOWN BETRAYED

Our homes are eaten out by time,
    Our lawns strewn with our listless sons,
Our harlot daughters lean and watch
    The ships crammed down with shells and guns.

Like painted prows far out they lean:
    A world behind, a world before.
The leaves are covering up our hills,
    Neptune has locked the shore.

Our yellow harvests lie forlorn
    And there we wander like the blind,
Returning from the golden field
    With famine in our mind.

Far inland now the glittering swords
    In order rise, in order fall,
In order on the dubious field
    The dubious trumpets call.

Yet here there is no word, no sign
    But quiet murder in the street.

Our leaf-light lives are spared or taken
  By men obsessed and neat.

We stand beside our windows, see
  In order dark disorder come,
And prentice killers duped by death
  Bring and not know our doom.

Our cattle wander at their will.
  To-day a horse pranced proudly by.
The dogs run wild. Vultures and kites
  Wait in the towers for us to die.

At evening on the parapet
  We sit and watch the sun go down,
Reading the landscape of the dead,
  The sea, the hills, the town.

There our ancestral ghosts are gathered.
  Fierce Agamemnon's form I see,
Watching as if his tents were time
  And Troy eternity.

We must take order, bar our gates,
  Fight off these phantoms. Inland now
Achilles, Siegfried, Lancelot
  Have sworn to bring us low.   1937

THEN

There were no men and women then at all,
But the flesh lying alone,
And angry shadows fighting on a wall
That now and then sent out a groan
Buried in lime and stone,
And sweated now and then like tortured wood
Big drops that looked yet did not look like blood.

And yet as each drop came a shadow faded
And left the wall.
There was a lull
Until another in its shadow arrayed it,
Came, fought and left a blood-mark on the wall;
And that was all; the blood was all.

If there had been women there they might have wept
For the poor blood, unowned, unwanted,
Blank as forgotten script.
The wall was haunted
By mute maternal presences whose sighing
Fluttered the fighting shadows and shook the wall
As if that fury of death itself were dying.   *1943*

THE GATE

We sat, two children, warm against the wall
Outside the towering stronghold of our fathers
That frowned its stern security down upon us.
We could not enter there. That fortress life,
Our safe protection, was too gross and strong
For our unpractised palates. Yet our guardians
Cherished our innocence with gentle hands,
(They, who had long since lost their innocence,)
And in grave play put on a childish mask
Over their tell-tale faces, as in shame
For the fine food that plumped their lusty bodies
And made them strange as gods. We sat that day
With that great parapet behind us, safe
As every day, yet outcast, safe and outcast
As castaways thrown upon an empty shore.
Before us lay our well-worn scene, a hillock
So small and smooth and green, it seemed intended
For us alone and childhood, a still pond
That opened upon no sight a quiet eye,
A little stream that tinkled down the slope.
But suddenly all seemed old
And dull and shrunken, shut within itself
In a sullen dream. We were outside, alone.
And then behind us the huge gate swung open.

                                      1943

THE RETURN

The doors flapped open in Ulysses' house,
The lolling latches gave to every hand,
Let traitor, babbler, tout and bargainer in.
The rooms and passages resounded
With ease and chaos of a public market,

The walls mere walls to lean on as you talked,
Spat on the floor, surveyed some newcomer
With an absent eye. There you could be yourself.
Dust in the nooks, weeds nodding in the yard,
The thick walls crumbling. Even the cattle came
About the doors with mild familiar stare
As if this were their place.
All round the island stretched the clean blue sea.

Sole at the house's heart Penelope
Sat at her chosen task, endless undoing
Of endless doing, endless weaving, unweaving,
In the clean chamber. Still her loom ran empty
Day after day. She thought: "Here I do nothing
Or less than nothing, making an emptiness
Amid disorder, weaving, unweaving the lie
The day demands. Ulysses, this is duty,
To do and undo, to keep a vacant gate
Where order and right and hope and peace can enter.
Oh will you ever return? Or are you dead,
And this wrought emptiness my ultimate emptiness?"

She wove and unwove and wove and did not know
That even then Ulysses on the long
And winding road of the world was on his way.   1943

THE ANNUNCIATION

The angel and the girl are met.
Earth was the only meeting place.
For the embodied never yet
Travelled beyond the shore of space.
The eternal spirits in freedom go.
See, they have come together, see,
While the destroying minutes flow,
Each reflects the other's face
Till heaven in hers and earth in his
Shine steady there. He's come to her
From far beyond the farthest star,
Feathered through time. Immediacy
Of strangest strangeness is the bliss
That from their limbs all movement takes.
Yet the increasing rapture brings

So great a wonder that it makes
Each feather tremble on his wings.

Outside the window footsteps fall
Into the ordinary day
And with the sun along the wall
Pursue their unreturning way
That was ordained in eternity.
Sound's perpetual roundabout
Rolls its numbered octaves out
And hoarsely grinds its battered tune.

But through the endless afternoon
These neither speak nor movement make,
But stare into their deepening trance
As if their gaze would never break.   *1943*

THE RETURN

The veteran Greeks came home
Sleepwandering from the war.
We saw the galleys come
Blundering over the bar.
Each soldier with his scar
In rags and tatters came home.

Reading the wall of Troy
Ten years without a change
Was such intense employ
(Just out of the arrows' range),
All the world was strange
After ten years of Troy.

Their eyes knew every stone
In the huge heartbreaking wall
Year after year grown
Till there was nothing at all
But an alley steep and small,
Tramped earth and towering stone.

Now even the hills seemed low
In the boundless sea and land,

Weakened by distance so.
How could they understand
Space empty on every hand
And the hillocks squat and low?

And when they arrived at last
They found a childish scene
Embosomed in the past,
And the war lying between—
A child's preoccupied scene
When they came home at last.

But everything trite and strange
The peace, the parcelled ground
The vinerows—never a change!
The past and the present bound
In one oblivious round
Past thinking trite and strange.

But for their grey-haired wives
And their sons grown shy and tall
They would have given their lives
To raise the battered wall
Again, if this was all
In spite of their sons and wives.

Penelope in her tower
Looked down upon the show
And saw within an hour
Each man to his wife go,
Hesitant, sure and slow:
She, alone in her tower.   *1946*

THE RIDER VICTORY

The rider Victory reins his horse
Midway across the empty bridge
As if head-tall he had met a wall.
Yet there was nothing there at all,
No bodiless barrier, ghostly ridge
To check the charger in his course
So suddenly, you'd think he'd fall.

Suspended, horse and rider stare,
Leaping on air and legendary.
In front the waiting kingdom lies,
The bridge and all the roads are free;
But halted in implacable air
Rider and horse with stony eyes
Uprear their motionless statuary.

1946

THE MYTH

My childhood all a myth
Enacted in a distant isle;
Time with his hourglass and his scythe
Stood dreaming on the dial,
And did not move the whole day long
That immobility might save
Continually the dying song,
The flower, the falling wave.
And at each corner of the wood
In which I played the ancient play,
Guarding the traditional day
The faithful watchers stood.

My youth a tragi-comedy,
Ridiculous war of dreams and shames
Waged for a Pyrrhic victory
Of reveries and names,
Which in slow-motion rout were hurled
Before sure-footed flesh and blood
That of its hunger built a world
Advancing rood by rood.
And there in practical clay compressed
The reverie played its useful part,
Fashioning a diurnal mart
Of radiant east and west.

So manhood went. Now past the prime
I see this life contrived to stay
With all its works of labouring time
By time beguiled away.
Consolidated flesh and bone

And its designs grow halt and lame;
Unshakeable arise alone
The reverie and the name.
And at each border of the land,
Like monuments a deluge leaves,
Guarding the invisible sheaves
The risen watchers stand.   *1946*

THE LABYRINTH

Since I emerged that day from the labyrinth,
Dazed with the tall and echoing passages,
The swift recoils, so many I almost feared
I'd meet myself returning at some smooth corner,
Myself or my ghost, for all there was unreal
After the straw ceased rustling and the bull
Lay dead upon the straw and I remained,
Blood-splashed, if dead or alive I could not tell
In the twilight nothingness (I might have been
A spirit seeking his body through the roads
Of intricate Hades)—ever since I came out
To the world, the still fields swift with flowers, the trees
All bright with blossom, the little green hills, the sea,
The sky and all in movement under it,
Shepherds and flocks and birds and the young and old,
(I stared in wonder at the young and the old,
For in the maze time had not been with me;
I had strayed, it seemed, past sun and season and change,
Past rest and motion, for I could not tell
At last if I moved or stayed; the maze itself
Revolved around me on its hidden axis
And swept me smoothly to its enemy,
The lovely world)—since I came out that day,
There have been times when I have heard my footsteps
Still echoing in the maze, and all the roads
That run through the noisy world, deceiving streets
That meet and part and meet, and rooms that open
Into each other—and never a final room—
Stairways and corridors and antechambers
That vacantly wait for some great audience,
The smooth sea-tracks that open and close again,
Tracks undiscoverable, indecipherable,
Paths on the earth and tunnels underground,

And bird-tracks in the air—all seemed a part
Of the great labyrinth. And then I'd stumble
In sudden blindness, hasten, almost run,
As if the maze itself were after me
And soon must catch me up. But taking thought,
I'd tell myself, "You need not hurry. This
Is the firm good earth. All roads lie free before you."
But my bad spirit would sneer, "No, do not hurry.
No need to hurry. Haste and delay are equal
In this one world, for there's no exit, none,
No place to come to, and you'll end where you are,
Deep in the centre of the endless maze."

I could not live if this were not illusion.
It is a world, perhaps; but there's another.
For once in a dream or trance I saw the gods
Each sitting on the top of his mountain-isle,
While down below the little ships sailed by,
Toy multitudes swarmed in the harbours, shepherds **drove**
Their tiny flocks to the pastures, marriage feasts
Went on below, small birthdays and holidays,
Ploughing and harvesting and life and death,
And all permissible, all acceptable,
Clear and secure as in a limpid dream.
But they, the gods, as large and bright as clouds,
Conversed across the sounds in tranquil voices
High in the sky above the untroubled sea;
And their eternal dialogue was peace
Where all these things were woven; and this our life
Was as a chord deep in that dialogue,
As easy utterance of harmonious words,
Spontaneous syllables bodying forth a world.

That was the real world; I have touched it once,
And now shall know it always. But the lie,
The maze, the wild-wood waste of falsehood, roads
That run and run and never reach an end,
Embowered in error—I'd be prisoned there
But that my soul has birdwings to fly free.

Oh these deceits are strong almost as life.
Last night I dreamt I was in the labyrinth,
And woke far on. I did not know the place. *1949*

THE COMBAT

It was not meant for human eyes,
That combat on the shabby patch
Of clods and trampled turf that lies
Somewhere beneath the sodden skies
For eye of toad or adder to catch.

And having seen it I accuse
The crested animal in his pride,
Arrayed in all the royal hues
Which hide the claws he well can use
To tear the heart out of the side.

Body of leopard, eagle's head
And whetted beak, and lion's mane,
And frost-grey hedge of feathers spread
Behind—he seemed of all things bred.
I shall not see his like again.

As for his enemy, there came in
A soft round beast as brown as clay;
All rent and patched his wretched skin;
A battered bag he might have been,
Some old used thing to throw away.

Yet he awaited face to face
The furious beast and the swift attack.
Soon over and done. That was no place
Or time for chivalry or for grace.
The fury had him on his back.

And two small paws like hands flew out
To right and left as the trees stood by.
One would have said beyond a doubt
This was the very end of the bout,
But that the creature would not die.

For ere the death-stroke he was gone,
Writhed, whirled, huddled into his den,
Safe somehow there. The fight was done,
And he had lost who had all but won.
But oh his deadly fury then.

A while the place lay blank, forlorn,
Drowsing as in relief from pain.
The cricket chirped, the grating thorn
Stirred, and a little sound was born.
The champions took their posts again.

And all began. The stealthy paw
Slashed out and in. Could nothing save
These rags and tatters from the claw?
Nothing. And yet I never saw
A beast so helpless and so brave.

And now, while the trees stand watching, still
The unequal battle rages there.
The killing beast that cannot kill
Swells and swells in his fury till
You'd almost think it was despair.   *1949*

THE INTERROGATION

We could have crossed the road but hesitated.
And then came the patrol;
The leader conscientious and intent,
The men surly, indifferent.
While we stood by and waited
The interrogation began. He says the whole
Must come out now, who, what we are,
Where we have come from, with what purpose, whose
Country or camp we plot for or betray.
Question on question.
We have stood and answered through the standing day
And watched across the road beyond the hedge
The careless lovers in pairs go by,
Hand linked in hand, wandering another star,
So near we could shout to them. We cannot choose
Answer or action here,
Though still the careless lovers saunter by
And the thoughtless field is near.
We are on the very edge,
Endurance almost done,
And still the interrogation is going on   *1949*

THE GOOD TOWN

Look at it well. This was the good town once,
Known everywhere, with streets of friendly neighbours,
Street friend to street and house to house. In summer
All day the doors stood open; lock and key
Were quaint antiquities fit for museums
With gyves and rusty chains. The ivy grew
From post to post across the prison door.
The yard behind was sweet with grass and flowers,
A place where grave philosophers loved to walk.
Old Time that promises and keeps his promise
Was our sole lord indulgent and severe,
Who gave and took away with gradual hand
That never hurried, never tarried, still
Adding, subtracting. These our houses had
Long fallen into decay but that we knew
Kindness and courage can repair time's faults,
And serving him breeds patience and courtesy
In us, light sojourners and passing subjects.
There is a virtue in tranquillity
That makes all fitting, childhood and youth and age,
Each in its place.

                          Look well. These mounds of rubble,
And shattered piers, half-windows, broken arches
And groping arms were once inwoven in walls
Covered with saints and angels, bore the roof,
Shot up the towering spire. These gaping bridges
Once spanned the quiet river which you see
Beyond that patch of raw and angry earth
Where the new concrete houses sit and stare.
Walk with me by the river. See, the poplars
Still gather quiet gazing on the stream.
The white road winds across the small green hill
And then is lost. These few things still remain.
Some of our houses too, though not what once
Lived there and drew a strength from memory.
Our people have been scattered, or have come
As strangers back to mingle with the strangers
Who occupy our rooms where none can find
The place he knew but settles where he can.

No family now sits at the evening table;
Father and son, mother and child are out,
A quaint and obsolete fashion. In our houses
Invaders speak their foreign tongues, informers
Appear and disappear, chance whores, officials
Humble or high, frightened, obsequious,
Sit carefully in corners. My old friends
(Friends ere these great disasters) are dispersed
In parties, armies, camps, conspiracies.
We avoid each other. If you see a man
Who smiles good-day or waves a lordly greeting
Be sure he's a policeman or a spy.
We know them by their free and candid air.

It was not time that brought these things upon us,
But these two wars that trampled on us twice,
Advancing and withdrawing, like a herd
Of clumsy-footed beasts on a stupid errand
Unknown to them or us. Pure chance, pure malice,
Or so it seemed. And when, the first war over,
The armies left and our own men came back
From every point by many a turning road,
Maimed, crippled, changed in body or in mind,
It was a sight to see the cripples come
Out on the fields. The land looked all awry,
The roads ran crooked and the light fell wrong.
Our fields were like a pack of cheating cards
Dealt out at random—all we had to play
In the bad game for the good stake, our life.
We played; a little shrewdness scraped us through.
Then came the second war, passed and repassed,
And now you see our town, the fine new prison,
The house-doors shut and barred, the frightened faces
Peeping round corners, secret police, informers,
And all afraid of all.

                    How did it come?
From outside, so it seemed, an endless source,
Disorder inexhaustible, strange to us,
Incomprehensible. Yet sometimes now
We ask ourselves, we the old citizens:
"Could it have come from us? Was our peace peace?
Our goodness goodness? That old life was easy

And kind and comfortable; but evil is restless
And gives no rest to the cruel or the kind.
How could our town grow wicked in a moment?
What is the answer? Perhaps no more than this,
That once the good men swayed our lives, and those
Who copied them took a while the hue of goodness.
A passing loan; while now the bad are up,
And we, poor ordinary neutral stuff,
Not good nor bad, must ape them as we can,
In sullen rage or vile obsequiousness.
Say there's a balance between good and evil
In things, and it's so mathematical,
So finely reckoned that a jot of either,
A bare preponderance will do all you need,
Make a town good, or make it what you see.
But then, you'll say, only that jot is wanting,
That grain of virtue. No: when evil comes
All things turn adverse, and we must begin
At the beginning, heave the groaning world
Back in its place again, and clamp it there.
Then all is hard and hazardous. We have seen
Good men made evil wrangling with the evil,
Straight minds grown crooked fighting crooked minds.
Our peace betrayed us; we betrayed our peace.
Look at it well. This was the good town once."

These thoughts we have, walking among our ruins.
                                        1949

THE USURPERS

And there is no answer. This our liberty
There is no answer. We do here what we will
No one has known before, nor could have borne,
For it is rooted in this deepening silence
That is our work and has become our kingdom.
If there were an answer, how could we be free?
It was not hard to still the ancestral voices:
A careless thought, less than a thought could do it.
And the old garrulous ghosts died easily,
The friendly and unfriendly, and are not missed
That once were such proud masters. In this air
Our thoughts are deeds; we dare do all we think,

Since there's no one to check us, here or elsewhere.
All round us stretches nothing; we move through nothing,
Nothing but nothing world without end. We are
Self-guided, self-impelled and self-sustained,
Archer and bow and burning arrow sped
On its wild flight through nothing to tumble down
At last on nothing, our home and cure for all.
Around us is alternate light and darkness.
We live in light and darkness. When night comes
We drop like stones plumb to its ocean ground,
While dreams stream past us upward to the place
Where light meets darkness, place of images,
Forest of ghosts, thicket of muttering voices.
We never seek that place; we are for the day
And for the night alone, at home in both.
But each has its device, and this is night's:
To hide in the very heart of night from night,
Black in its blackness.
              For these fluttering dreams,
They'd trouble us if we were credulous,
For all the ghosts that frightened frightened men
Long since were bred in that pale territory.
These we can hold in check, but not forget,
Not quite forget, they're so inconsequent.
Sometimes we've heard in sleep tongues talking so:
"I lean my face far out from eternity
For time to work its work on: time, oh time,
What have you done?" These fancies trouble us.
The day itself sometimes works spells upon us
And then the trees look unfamiliar. Yet
It is a lie that they are witnesses,
That the mountains judge us, brooks tell tales about us.
We have thought sometimes the rocks looked strangely on us.
Have fancied that the waves were angry with us,
Heard dark runes murmuring in the autumn wind,
Muttering and murmuring like old toothless women
That prophesied against us in ancient tongues.

These are imaginations. We are free.   1949

OEDIPUS

I, Oedipus, the club-foot, made to stumble,
Who long in the light have walked the world in darkness,

And once in the darkness did that which the light
Found and disowned—too well I have loved the light,
Too dearly have rued the darkness. I am one
Who as in innocent play sought out his guilt,
And now through guilt seeks other innocence,
Beset by evil thoughts, led by the gods.
There was a room, a bed of darkness, once
Known to me, now to all. Yet in that darkness,
Before the light struck, she and I who lay
There without thought of sin and knew each other
Too well, yet were to each other quite unknown
Though fastened mouth to mouth and breast to breast—
Strangers laid on one bed, as children blind,
Clear-eyed and blind as children—did we sin
Then on that bed before the light came on us,
Desiring good to each other, bringing, we thought,
Great good to each other? But neither guilt nor death.

Yet if that darkness had been darker yet,
Buried in endless dark past reach of light
Or eye of the gods, a kingdom of solid darkness
Impregnable and immortal, would we have sinned,
Or lived like the gods in deathless innocence?
For sin is born in the light; therefore we cower
Before the face of the light that none can meet
And all must seek. And when in memory now,
Woven of light and darkness, a stifling web,
I call her back, dear, dreaded, who lay with me,
I see guilt, only guilt, my nostrils choke
With the smell of guilt, and I can scarcely breathe
Here in the guiltless guilt-evoking sun.

And when young Oedipus—for it was Oedipus
And not another—on that long vanished night
Far in my night, at that predestined point
Where three paths like three fates crossed one another,
Tracing the evil figure—when I met
The stranger who menaced me, and flung the stone
That brought him death and me this that I carry,
It was not him but fear I sought to kill,
Fear that, the wise men say, is father of evil,
And was my father in flesh and blood, yet fear,
Fear only, father and fear in one dense body,

So that there was no division, no way past:
Did I sin then, by the gods admonished to sin,
By men enjoined to sin? For it is duty
Of god and man to kill the shapes of fear.

These thoughts recur, vain thoughts. The gods see all
And will what must be willed, which guards us here.
Their will in them was anger, in me was terror
Long since, but now is peace. For I am led
By them in darkness; light is all about me;
My way lies in the light; they know it; I
Am theirs to guide and hold. And I have learned,
Though blind, to see with something of their sight,
Can look into that other world and watch
King Oedipus the just, crowned and discrowned,
As one may see oneself rise in a dream,
Distant and strange. Even so I see
The meeting at the place where three roads crossed,
And who was there and why, and what was done
That had to be done and paid for. Innocent
The deed that brought the guilt of father-murder. Pure
The embrace on the bed of darkness. Innocent
And guilty. I have wrought and thought in darkness,
And stand here now, an innocent mark of shame,
That so men's guilt might be made manifest
In such a walking riddle—their guilt and mine,
For I've but acted out this fable. I have judged
Myself, obedient to the gods' high judgment,
And seen myself with their pure eyes, have learnt
That all must bear a portion of the wrong
That is driven deep into our fathomless hearts
Past sight or thought; that bearing it we may ease
The immortal burden of the gods who keep
Our natural steps and the earth and skies from harm.

1949

ONE FOOT IN EDEN

One foot in Eden still, I stand
And look across the other land.
The world's great day is growing late,
Yet strange these fields that we have planted
So long with crops of love and hate.

Time's handiworks by time are haunted,
And nothing now can separate
The corn and tares compactly grown.
The armorial weed in stillness bound
About the stalk; these are our own.
Evil and good stand thick around
In the fields of charity and sin
Where we shall lead our harvest in.

Yet still from Eden springs the root
As clean as on the starting day.
Time takes the foliage and the fruit
And burns the archetypal leaf
To shapes of terror and of grief
Scattered along the winter way.
But famished field and blackened tree
Bear flowers in Eden never known.
Blossoms of grief and charity
Bloom in these darkened fields alone.
What had Eden ever to say
Of hope and faith and pity and love
Until was buried all its day
And memory found its treasure trove?
Strange blessings never in Paradise
Fall from these beclouded skies.   *1952*

THE ANIMALS

They do not live in the world,
Are not in time and space.
From birth to death hurled
No word do they have, not one
To plant a foot upon,
Were never in any place.

For with names the world was called
Out of the empty air,
With names was built and walled,
Line and circle and square,
Dust and emerald;
Snatched from deceiving death
By the articulate breath.

But these have never trod
Twice the familiar track,
Never never turned back
Into the memoried day.
All is new and near
In the unchanging Here
Of the fifth great day of God,
That shall remain the same,
Never shall pass away.

On the sixth day we came.   *1952*

THE HORSES

Barely a twelvemonth after
The seven days war that put the world to sleep,
Late in the evening the strange horses came.
By then we had made our covenant with silence,
But in the first few days it was so still
We listened to our breathing and were afraid.
On the second day
The radios failed; we turned the knobs; no answer.
On the third day a warship passed us, heading north,
Dead bodies piled on the deck. On the sixth day
A plane plunged over us into the sea. Thereafter
Nothing. The radios dumb;
And still they stand in corners of our kitchens,
And stand, perhaps, turned on, in a million rooms
All over the world. But now if they should speak,
If on a sudden they should speak again,
If on the stroke of noon a voice should speak,
We would not listen, we would not let it bring
That old bad world that swallowed its children quick
At one great gulp. We would not have it again.
Sometimes we think of the nations lying asleep,
Curled blindly in impenetrable sorrow,
And then the thought confounds us with its strangeness.

The tractors lie about our fields; at evening
They look like dank sea-monsters couched and waiting.
We leave them where they are and let them rust:
"They'll moulder away and be like other loam."
We make our oxen drag our rusty ploughs,

Long laid aside. We have gone back
Far past our fathers' land.
                              And then, that evening
Late in the summer the strange horses came.
We heard a distant tapping on the road,
A deepening drumming; it stopped, went on again
And at the corner changed to hollow thunder.
We saw the heads
Like a wild wave charging and were afraid.
We had sold our horses in our fathers' time
To buy new tractors. Now they were strange to us
As fabulous steeds set on an ancient shield
Or illustrations in a book of knights.
We did not dare go near them. Yet they waited,
Stubborn and shy, as if they had been sent
By an old command to find our whereabouts
And that long-lost archaic companionship.
In the first moment we had never a thought
That they were creatures to be owned and used.
Among them were some half-a-dozen colts
Dropped in some wilderness of the broken world,
Yet new as if they had come from their own Eden.
Since then they have pulled our ploughs and borne our loads,
But that free servitude still can pierce our hearts.
Our life is changed; their coming our beginning.   1952

Wilfred Owen

ARMS AND THE BOY

Let the boy try along this bayonet-blade
How cold steel is, and keen with hunger of blood;
Blue with all malice, like a madman's flash;
And thinly drawn with famishing for flesh.

Lend him to stroke these blind, blunt bullet-heads
Which long to nuzzle in the hearts of lads,
Or give him cartridges of fine zinc teeth,
Sharp with the sharpness of grief and death.

For his teeth seem for laughing round an apple.
There lurk no claws behind his fingers supple;
And God will grow no talons at his heels,
Nor antlers through the thickness of his curls.

1920

GREATER LOVE

Red lips are not so red
    As the stained stones kissed by the English dead.
Kindness of wooed and wooer
Seems shame to their love pure.
O love, your eyes lose lure
    When I behold eyes blinded in my stead!

Your slender attitude
    Trembles not exquisite like limbs knife-skewed,
Rolling and rolling there
Where God seems not to care;
Till the fierce love they bear
    Cramps them in death's extreme decrepitude.

Your voice sings not so soft,—
    Though even as wind murmuring through raftered loft,—

Your dear voice is not dear,
Gentle, and evening clear,
As theirs whom none now hear
    Now earth has stopped their piteous mouths that coughed.

Heart, you were never hot,
    Nor large, nor full like hearts made great with shot;
And though your hand be pale,
Paler are all which trail
Your cross through flame and hail:
    Weep, you may weep, for you may touch them not.   *1920*

INSENSIBILITY

I

Happy are men who yet before they are killed
Can let their veins run cold.
Whom no compassion fleers
Or makes their feet
Sore on the alleys cobbled with their brothers.
The front line withers,
But they are troops who fade, not flowers
For poets' tearful fooling:
Men, gaps for filling:
Losses who might have fought
Longer; but no one bothers.

II

And some cease feeling
Even themselves or for themselves.
Dullness best solves
The tease and doubt of shelling,
And Chance's strange arithmetic
Comes simpler than the reckoning of their shilling.
They keep no check on armies' decimation.

III

Happy are these who lose imagination:
They have enough to carry with ammunition.
Their spirit drags no pack,
Their old wounds save with cold can not more ache.

Having seen all things red,
Their eyes are rid
Of the hurt of the colour of blood for ever.
And terror's first constriction over,
Their hearts remain small-drawn.
Their senses in some scorching cautery of battle
Now long since ironed,
Can laugh among the dying, unconcerned.

IV

Happy the soldier home, with not a notion
How somewhere, every dawn, some men attack,
And many sighs are drained.
Happy the lad whose mind was never trained:
His days are worth forgetting more than not.
He sings along the march
Which we march taciturn, because of dusk,
The long, forlorn, relentless trend
From larger day to huger night.

V

We wise, who with a thought besmirch
Blood over all our soul,
How should we see our task
But through his blunt and lashless eyes?
Alive, he is not vital overmuch;
Dying, not mortal overmuch;
Nor sad, nor proud,
Nor curious at all.
He cannot tell
Old men's placidity from his.

VI

But cursed are dullards whom no cannon stuns,
That they should be as stones;
Wretched are they, and mean
With paucity that never was simplicity.
By choice they made themselves immune
To pity and whatever moans in man
Before the last sea and the hapless stars;
Whatever mourns when many leave these shores;
Whatever shares
The eternal reciprocity of tears.   1920

DULCE ET DECORUM EST

Bent double, like old beggars under sacks,
Knock-kneed, coughing like hags, we cursed through sludge,
Till on the haunting flares we turned our backs,
And towards our distant rest began to trudge.
Men marched asleep. Many had lost their boots,
But limped on, blood-shod. All went lame, all blind;
Drunk with fatigue; deaf even to the hoots
Of gas-shells dropping softly behind.

Gas! Gas! Quick, boys!—An ecstasy of fumbling,
Fitting the clumsy helmets just in time,
But someone still was yelling out and stumbling
And flound'ring like a man in fire or lime.
Dim through the misty panes and thick green light,
As under a green sea, I saw him drowning.

In all my dreams before my helpless sight
He plunges at me, guttering, choking, drowning.

If in some smothering dreams, you too could pace
Behind the wagon that we flung him in,
And watch the white eyes writhing in his face,
His hanging face, like a devil's sick of sin,
If you could hear, at every jolt, the blood
Come gargling from the froth-corrupted lungs
Bitter as the cud
Of vile, incurable sores on innocent tongues,—
My friend, you would not tell with such high zest
To children ardent for some desperate glory,
The old lie: *Dulce et decorum est
Pro patria mori.*   1920

MENTAL CASES

Who are these? Why sit they here in twilight?
Wherefore rock they, purgatorial shadows,
Drooping tongues from jaws that slob their relish,
Baring teeth that leer like skulls' teeth wicked?
Stroke on stroke of pain,—but what slow panic,

Gouged these chasms round their fretted sockets?
Ever from their hair and through their hands' palms
Misery swelters. Surely we have perished
Sleeping, and walk hell; but who these hellish?

—These are men whose minds the Dead have ravished.
Memory fingers in their hair of murders,
Multitudinous murders they once witnessed.
Wading sloughs of flesh these helpless wander,
Treading blood from lungs that had loved laughter.
Always they must see these things and hear them,
Batter of guns and shatter of flying muscles,
Carnage incomparable, and human squander,
Rucked too thick for these men's extrication.

Therefore still their eyeballs shrink tormented
Back into their brains, because on their sense
Sunlight seems a blood-smear; night comes blood-black;
Dawn breaks open like a wound that bleeds afresh.
—Thus their heads wear this hilarious, hideous,
Awful falseness of set-smiling corpses.
—Thus their hands are plucking at each other;
Picking at the rope-knouts of their scourging;
Snatching after us who smote them, brother,
Pawing us who dealt them war and madness.   *1920*

FUTILITY

Move him into the sun—
Gently its touch awoke him once,
At home, whispering of fields unsown.
Always it woke him, even in France.
Until this morning and this snow.
If anything might rouse him now
The kind old sun will know.

Think how it wakes the seeds—
Woke, once, the clays of a cold star.
Are limbs, so dear-achieved, are sides
Full-nerved,—still warm,—too hard to stir?
Was it for this the clay grew tall?
—Oh, what made fatuous sunbeams toil
To break earth's sleep at all?   *1920*

DISABLED

He sat in a wheeled chair, waiting for dark,
And shivered in his ghastly suit of grey,
Legless, sewn short at elbow. Through the park
Voices of boys rang saddening like a hymn,
Voices of play and pleasures after day,
Till gathering sleep had mothered them from him.

. . . . . .

About this time Town used to swing so gay
When glow-lamps budded in the light blue trees,
And girls glanced lovelier as the air grew dim,—
In the old times, before he threw away his knees.
Now he will never feel again how slim
Girls' waists are, or how warm their subtle hands;
All of them touch him like some queer disease.

. . . . . .

There was an artist silly for his face,
For it was younger than his youth, last year.
Now, he is old; his back will never brace;
He's lost his colour very far from here,
Poured it down shell-holes till the veins ran dry,
And half his lifetime lapsed in the hot race,
And leap of purple spurted from his thigh.

. . . . . .

One time he liked a blood-smear down his leg,
After the matches, carried shoulder-high.
It was after football, when he'd drunk a peg,
He thought he'd better join.—He wonders why.
Someone had said he'd look a god in kilts,
That's why; and may be, too, to please his Meg;
Aye, that was it, to please the giddy jilts
He asked to join. He didn't have to beg;
Smiling they wrote his lie; aged nineteen years.
Germans he scarcely thought of; all their guilt,
And Austria's, did not move him. And no fears
Of Fear came yet. He thought of jewelled hilts
For daggers in plaid socks; of smart salutes;
And care of arms; and leave; and pay arrears;

Esprit de corps; and hints for young recruits.
And soon he was drafted out with drums and cheers.

. . . . . .

Some cheered him home, but not as crowds cheer Goal.
Only a solemn man who brought him fruits
Thanked him; and then inquired about his soul.

. . . . .

Now, he will spend a few sick years in Institutes,
And do what things the rules consider wise,
And take whatever pity they may dole.
To-night he noticed how the women's eyes
Passed from him to the strong men that were whole.
How cold and late it is! Why don't they come
And put him into bed? Why don't they come?   *1920*

ANTHEM FOR DOOMED YOUTH

What passing-bells for these who die as cattle?
   Only the monstrous anger of the guns.
Only the stuttering rifles' rapid rattle
   Can patter out their hasty orisons.
No mockeries for them from prayers or bells,
   Nor any voice of mourning save the choirs,—
The shrill, demented choirs of wailing shells;
   And bugles calling for them from sad shires.

What candles may be held to speed them all?
   Not in the hands of boys, but in their eyes
Shall shine the holy glimmers of good-byes.
   The pallor of girls' brows shall be their pall;
Their flowers the tenderness of silent minds,
And each slow dusk a drawing-down of blinds.
                1920

STRANGE MEETING

It seemed that out of battle I escaped
Down some profound dull tunnel, long since scooped
Through granites which titanic wars had groined.
Yet also there encumbered sleepers groaned,
Too fast in thought or death to be bestirred.

Then, as I probed them, one sprang up, and stared
With piteous recognition in fixed eyes,
Lifting distressful hands as if to bless.
And by his smile, I knew that sullen hall,
By his dead smile I knew we stood in Hell.
With a thousand pains that vision's face was grained;
Yet no blood reached there from the upper ground,
And no guns thumped, or down the flues made moan.
"Strange friend," I said, "here is no cause to mourn."
"None," said the other, "save the undone years,
The hopelessness. Whatever hope is yours,
Was my life also; I went hunting wild
After the wildest beauty in the world,
Which lies not calm in eyes, or braided hair,
But mocks the steady running of the hour,
And if it grieves, grieves richlier than here.
For by my glee might many men have laughed,
And of my weeping something had been left,
Which must die now. I mean the truth untold,
The pity of war, the pity war distilled.
Now men will go content with what we spoiled.
Or, discontent, boil bloody, and be spilled.
They will be swift with swiftness of the tigress,
None will break ranks, though nations trek from progress.
Courage was mine, and I had mystery,
Wisdom was mine, and I had mastery;
To miss the march of this retreating world
Into vain citadels that are not walled.
Then, when much blood had clogged their chariot-wheels
I would go up and wash them from sweet wells,
Even with truths that lie too deep for taint.
I would have poured my spirit without stint
But not through wounds; not on the cess of war.
Foreheads of men have bled where no wounds were.
I am the enemy you killed, my friend.
I knew you in this dark; for so you frowned
Yesterday through me as you jabbed and killed.
I parried; but my hands were loath and cold.
Let us sleep now. . . ."   1920

Robert Graves

THE PIER-GLASS

Lost manor where I walk continually
A ghost, though yet in woman's flesh and blood.
Up your broad stairs mounting with outspread fingers
And gliding steadfast down your corridors
I come by nightly custom to this room,
And even on sultry afternoons I come
Drawn by a thread of time-sunk memory.

Empty, unless for a huge bed of state
Shrouded with rusty curtains drooped awry
(A puppet theatre where malignant fancy
Peoples the wings with fear). At my right hand
A ravelled bell-pull hangs in readiness
To summon me from attic glooms above
Service of elder ghosts; here, at my left,
A sullen pier-glass, cracked from side to side,
Scorns to present the face (as do new mirrors)
With a lying flush, but shows it melancholy
And pale, as faces grow that look in mirrors.

Is there no life, nothing but the thin shadow
And blank foreboding, never a wainscot rat
Rasping a crust? Or at the window-pane
No fly, no bluebottle, no starveling spider?
The windows frame a prospect of cold skies
Half-merged with sea, as at the first creation—
Abstract, confusing welter. Face about,
Peer rather in the glass once more, take note
Of self, the grey lips and long hair dishevelled,
Sleep-staring eyes. Ah, mirror, for Christ's love
Give me one token that there still abides
Remote—beyond this island mystery,
So be it only this side Hope, somewhere,

In streams, on sun-warm mountain pasturage—
True life, natural breath; not this phantasma.   *1921*

RICHARD ROE AND JOHN DOE

Richard Roe wished himself Solomon,
Made cuckold, you should know, by one John Doe:
Solomon's neck was firm enough to bear
Some score of antlers more than Roe could wear,

Richard Roe wished himself Alexander,
Being robbed of house and land by the same hand:
Ten thousand acres or a principal town
Would have cost Alexander scarce a frown.

Richard Roe wished himself Job the prophet,
Sunk past reclaim in stinking rags and shame—
However ill Job's plight, his own was worse:
He knew no God to call on or to curse.

He wished himself Job, Solomon, Alexander,
For patience, wisdom, power to overthrow
Misfortune; but with spirit so unmanned
That most of all he wished himself John Doe.   *1923*

TRAVELLER'S CURSE AFTER MISDIRECTION

(from the Welsh)

May they stumble, stage by stage
On an endless pilgrimage,
Dawn and dusk, mile after mile,
At each and every step, a stile;
At each and every step withal
May they catch their feet and fall;
At each and every fall they take
May a bone within them break;
And may the bone that breaks within
Not be, for variation's sake,
Now rib, now thigh, now arm, now shin,
But always, without fail THE NECK.

     1925

WELSH INCIDENT

"But that was nothing to what things came out
From the sea-caves of Criccieth yonder."
"What were they? Mermaids? dragons? ghosts?"
"Nothing at all of any things like that."
"What were they, then?"
                         "All sorts of queer things,
Things never seen or heard or written about,
Very strange, un-Welsh, utterly peculiar
Things. Oh, solid enough they seemed to touch,
Had anyone dared it. Marvellous creation,
All various shapes and sizes and no sizes,
All new, each perfectly unlike his neighbour,
Though all came moving slowly out together."
"Describe just one of them."
                             "I am unable."
"What were their colours?"
                          "Mostly nameless colours,
Colours you'd like to see; but one was puce
Or perhaps more like crimson, but not purplish.
Some had no colour."
                     "Tell me, had they legs?"
"Not a leg or foot among them that I saw."
"But did these things come out in any order?
What o'clock was it? What was the day of the week?
Who else was present? What was the weather?"
"I was coming to that. It was half-past three
On Easter Tuesday last. The sun was shining.
The Harlech Silver Band played *Marchog Jesu*
On thirty-seven shimmering instruments,
Collecting for Carnarvon's (Fever) Hospital Fund.
The populations of Pwlheli, Criccieth,
Portmadoc, Borth, Tremadoc, Penrhyndeudraeth,
Were all assembled. Criccieth's mayor addressed them
First in good Welsh and then in fluent English,
Twisting his fingers in his chain of office,
Welcoming the things. They came out on the sand,
Not keeping time to the band, moving seaward
Silently at a snail's pace. But at last
The most odd, indescribable thing of all
Which hardly one man there could see for wonder
Did something recognizably a something."

"Well, what?"
              "It made a noise."
                            "A frightening noise?"
"No, no."
              "A musical noise? A noise of scuffling?"
"No, but a very loud, respectable noise—
Like groaning to oneself on Sunday morning
In Chapel, close before the second psalm."
"What did the mayor do?"
                            "I was coming to that."   *1929*

SICK LOVE

O Love, be fed with apples while you may,
And feel the sun and go in royal array,
A smiling innocent on the heavenly causeway,

Though in what listening horror for the cry
That soars in outer blackness dismally,
The dumb blind beast, the paranoiac fury:

Be warm, enjoy the season, lift your head,
Exquisite in the pulse of tainted blood,
That shivering glory not to be despised.

Take your delight in momentariness,
Walk between dark and dark—a shining space
With the grave's narrowness, though not its peace.
                            1931

SAINT

This Blatant Beast was finally overcome
And in no secret tourney: wit and fashion
Flocked out and for compassion
Wept as the Red Cross Knight pushed the blade home.

The people danced and sang the paeans due,
Roasting whole oxen on the public spit;
Twelve mountain peaks were lit
With bonfires; yet their hearts were doubt and rue.

Therefore no grave was deep enough to hold
The Beast, who after days came thrusting out,

Wormy from rump to snout,
His yellow cere-cloth patched with the grave's mould.

Nor could sea hold him: anchored with huge rocks,
He swelled and buoyed them up, paddling ashore
As evident as before
With deep-sea ooze and salty creaking bones.

Lime could not burn him, nor the sulphur fire:
So often as the good Knight bound him there,
With stink of singeing hair
And scorching flesh the corpse rolled from the pyre.

In the city-gutter would the Beast lie
Praising the Knight for all his valorous deeds:
"Ay, on those water-meads
He slew even me. These death-wounds testify."

The Knight governed that city, a man shamed
And shrunken: for the Beast was over-dead,
With wounds no longer red
But gangrenous and loathsome and inflamed.

Not all the righteous judgments he could utter,
Nor mild laws frame, nor public works repair,
Nor wars wage, in despair,
Could bury that same Beast, crouched in the gutter.

A fresh remembrance-banquet to forestall,
The Knight turned hermit, went without farewell
To a far mountain-cell;
But the Beast followed as his seneschal,

And there drew water for him and hewed wood
With vacant howling laughter; else all day
Noisome with long decay
Sunning himself at the cave's entry stood.

Would bawl to pilgrims for a dole of bread
To feed the sick saint who once vanquished him
With spear so stark and grim;
Would set a pillow of grass beneath his head,
Would fetch him fever-wort from the pool's brim—
And crept into his grave when he was dead.   *1931*

ULYSSES

To the much-tossed Ulysses, never done
　With woman whether gowned as wife or whore,
Penelope and Circe seemed as one:
She like a whore made his lewd fancies run,
　And wifely she a hero to him bore.

Their counter-changings terrified his way:
　They were the clashing rocks, Symplegades,
Scylla and Charybdis too were they;
Now they were storms frosting the sea with spray
　And now the lotus island's drunken ease.

They multiplied into the Sirens' throng,
　Forewarned by fear of whom he stood bound fast
Hand and foot helpless to the vessel's mast,
Yet would not stop his ears: daring their song
　He groaned and sweated till that shore was past.

One, two and many: flesh had made him blind,
　Flesh had one pleasure only in the act,
Flesh set one purpose only in the mind—
Triumph of flesh and afterwards to find
　Still those same terrors wherewith flesh was racked.

His wiles were witty and his fame far known,
Every king's daughter sought him for her own,
　Yet he was nothing to be won or lost.
　All hands to him with Ithaca: love-tossed
He loathed the fraud, yet would not bed alone.　*1933*

DOWN, WANTON, DOWN!

Down, wanton, down! Have you no shame
That at the whisper of Love's name,
Or Beauty's, presto! up you raise
Your angry head and stand at gaze?

Poor bombard-captain, sworn to reach
The ravelin and effect a breach—
Indifferent what you storm or why,
So be that in the breach you die!

Love may be blind, but Love at least
Knows what is man and what mere beast;
Or Beauty wayward, but requires
More delicacy from her squires.

Tell me, my witless, whose one boast
Could be your staunchness at the post,
When were you made a man of parts
To think fine and profess the arts?

Will many-gifted Beauty come
Bowing to your bald rule of thumb,
Or Love swear loyalty to your crown?
Be gone, have done! Down, wanton, down!

1933

ON DWELLING

Courtesies of good-morning and good-evening
From rustic lips fail as the town encroaches:
Soon nothing passes but the cold quick stare
Of eyes that see ghosts, yet too many for fear.

Here I too walk, silent myself, in wonder
At a town not mine though plainly coextensive
With mine, even in days coincident:
In mine I dwell, in theirs like them I haunt.

And the green country, should I turn again there?
My bumpkin neighbours loom even ghostlier:
Like trees they murmur or like blackbirds sing
Courtesies of good-morning and good-evening.

1933

OGRES AND PYGMIES

Those famous men of old, the Ogres—
They had long beards and stinking arm-pits,
They were wide-mouthed, long-yarded and great-bellied
Yet of no taller stature, Sirs, than you.
They lived on Ogre-Strand, which was no place
But the churl's terror of their vast extent,
Where every foot was three-and-thirty inches

And every penny bought a whole hog.
Now of their company none survive, not one,
The times being, thank God, unfavourable
To all but nightmare shadows of their fame;
Their images stand howling on the hill
(The winds enforced against those wide mouths),
Whose granite haunches country-folk salute
With May Day kisses, and whose knobbed knees.

So many feats they did to admiration:
With their enormous throats they sang louder
Than ten cathedral choirs, with their grand yards
Stormed the most rare and obstinate maidenheads,
With their strong-gutted and capacious bellies
Digested stones and glass like ostriches.
They dug great pits and heaped huge mounds,
Deflected rivers, wrestled with the bear
And hammered judgements for posterity—
For the sweet-cupid-lipped and tassel-yarded
Delicate-stomached dwellers
In Pygmy Alley, where with brooding on them
A foot is shrunk to seven inches
And twelve-pence will not buy a spare rib.
And who would judge between Ogres and Pygmies—
The thundering text, the snivelling commentary—
Reading between such covers he will marvel
How his own members bloat and shrink again.   *1933*

RECALLING WAR

Entrance and exit wounds are silvered clean,
The track aches only when the rain reminds.
The one-legged man forgets his leg of wood,
The one-armed man his jointed wooden arm.
The blinded man sees with his ears and hands
As much or more than once with both his eyes.
Their war was fought these twenty years ago
And now assumes the nature-look of time,
As when the morning traveller turns and views
His wild night-stumbling carved into a hill.

What, then, was war? No mere discord of flags
But an infection of the common sky

That sagged ominously upon the earth
Even when the season was the airiest May.
Down pressed the sky, and we, oppressed, thrust out
Boastful tongue, clenched fist and valiant yard.
Natural infirmities were out of mode,
For Death was young again: patron alone
Of healthy dying, premature fate-spasm.

Fear made fine bed-fellows. Sick with delight
At life's discovered transitoriness,
Our youth became all-flesh and waived the mind.
Never was such antiqueness of romance,
Such tasty honey oozing from the heart.
And old importances came swimming back—
Wine, meat, log-fires, a roof over the head,
A weapon at the thigh, surgeons at call.
Even there was a use again for God—
A word of rage in lack of meat, wine, fire,
In ache of wounds beyond all surgeoning.

War was return of earth to ugly earth,
War was foundering of sublimities,
Extinction of each happy art and faith
By which the world had still kept head in air.
Protesting logic or protesting love,
Until the unendurable moment struck—
The inward scream, the duty to run mad.

And we recall the merry ways of guns—
Nibbling the walls of factory and church
Like a child, piecrust; felling groves of trees
Like a child, dandelions with a switch!
Machine-guns rattle toy-like from a hill,
Down in a row the brave tin-soldiers fall:
A sight to be recalled in elder days
When learnedly the future we devote
To yet more boastful visions of despair.   *1938*

A JEALOUS MAN

To be homeless is a pride
To the jealous man prowling
Hungry down the night lanes,

Who has no steel at his side,
No drink hot in his mouth,
But a mind dream-enlarged,

Who witnesses warfare,
Man with woman, hugely
Raging from hedge to hedge:

The raw knotted oak-club
Clenched in the raw fist,
The ivy-noose well flung,

The thronged din of battle,
Gaspings of the throat-snared,
Snores of the battered dying,

Tall corpses, braced together,
Fallen in clammy furrows,
Male and female,

Or, among haulms of nettle
Humped, in noisome heaps,
Male and female.

He glowers in the choked roadway
Between twin churchyards,
Like a turnip ghost.

(Here, the rain-worn headstone,
There, the Celtic cross
In rank white marble.)

This jealous man is smitten,
His fear-jerked forehead
Sweats a fine musk;

A score of bats bewitched
By the ruttish odour
Swoop singing at his head;

Nuns bricked up alive
Within the neighbouring wall
Wail in cat-like longing.

Crow, cocks, crow loud!
Reprieve the doomed devil,
Has he not died enough?

Now, out of careless sleep,
She wakes and greets him coldly,
The woman at home,

She, with a private wonder
At shoes bemired and bloody—
His war was not hers.   *1938*

A LOVE STORY

The full moon easterly rising, furious,
Against a winter sky ragged with red;
The hedges high in snow, and owls raving—
Solemnities not easy to withstand:
A shiver wakes the spine.

In boyhood, having encountered the scene,
I suffered horror: I fetched the moon home,
With owls and snow, to nurse in my head
Throughout the trials of a new spring,
Famine unassuaged.

But fell in love, and made a lodgement
Of love on those chill ramparts.
Her image was my ensign: snows melted,
Hedges sprouted, the moon tenderly shone,
The owls trilled with tongues of nightingale.

These were all lies, though they matched the time,
And brought me less than luck: her image
Warped in the weather, turned beldamish.
Then back came winter on me at a bound,
The pallid sky heaved with a moon-quake.

Dangerous it had been with love-notes
To serenade Queen Famine.
In tears I recomposed the former scene,
Let the snow lie, watched the moon rise, suffered the owls,
Paid homage to them of unevent.   *1946*

THE GLUTTON

Beyond the Atlas roams a glutton
Lusty and sleek, a shameless robber,
Sacred to Aethiopian Aphrodite;
The aborigines harry it with darts.
And its flesh is esteemed, though of a fishy tang
Tainting the eater's mouth and lips.

Ourselves once, wandering in mid-wilderness
And by despair drawn to this diet,
Before the meal was over sat apart
Loathing each other's carrion company.   *1946*

THE THIEVES

Lovers in the act dispense
With such meum-teum sense
As might warningly reveal
What they must not pick or steal,
And their nostrum is to say:
"I and you are both away."

After, when they disentwine
You from me and yours from mine,
Neither can be certain who
Was that I whose mine was you.
To the act again they go
More completely not to know.

Theft is theft and raid is raid
Though reciprocally made.
Lovers, the conclusion is
Doubled sighs and jealousies
In a single heart that grieves
For lost honour among thieves.   *1946*

TO JUAN AT THE WINTER SOLSTICE

There is one story and one story only
That will prove worth your telling,
Whether as learned bard or gifted child;
To it all lines or lesser gauds belong

That startle with their shining
Such common stories as they stray into.

Is it of trees you tell, their months and virtues,
Or strange beasts that beset you,
Of birds that croak at you the Triple will?
Or of the Zodiac and how slow it turns
Below the Boreal Crown,
Prison of all true kings that ever reigned?

Water to water, ark again to ark,
From woman back to woman:
So each new victim treads unfalteringly
The never altered circuit of his fate,
Bringing twelve peers as witness
Both to his starry rise and starry fall.

Or is it of the Virgin's silver beauty,
All fish below the thighs?
She in her left hand bears a leafy quince;
When, with her right she crooks a finger smiling,
How may the King hold back?
Royally then he barters life for love.

Or of the undying snake from chaos hatched,
Whose coils contain the ocean,
Into whose chops with naked sword he springs,
Then in black water, tangled by the reeds,
Battles three days and nights,
To be spewed up beside her scalloped shore?

Much snow is falling, winds roar hollowly,
The owl hoots from the elder,
Fear in your heart cries to the loving-cup:
Sorrow to sorrow as the sparks fly upward.
The log groans and confesses
There is one story and one story only.
Dwell on her graciousness, dwell on her smiling,
Do not forget what flowers
The great boar trampled down in ivy time.
Her brow was creamy as the crested wave,
Her sea-blue eyes were wild
But nothing promised that is not performed. *1946*

THE PERSIAN VERSION

Truth-loving Persians do not dwell upon
The trivial skirmish fought near Marathon.
As for the Greek theatrical tradition
Which represents that summer's expedition
Not as a mere reconnaissance in force
By three brigades of foot and one of horse
(Their left flank covered by some obsolete
Light craft detached from the main Persian fleet)
But as a grandiose, ill-starred attempt
To conquer Greece—they treat it with contempt;
And only incidentally refute
Major Greek claims, by stressing what repute
The Persian monarch and the Persian nation
Won by this salutary demonstration:
Despite a strong defence and adverse weather
All arms combined magnificently together.   *1946*

GROTESQUES

I

My Chinese uncle, gouty, deaf, half-blinded,
And more than a trifle absent-minded,
Astonished all St. James's Square one day
By giving long and unexceptionably exact directions
To a little coolie girl, who'd lost her way.

II

The Lion-faced Boy at the Fair
And the Heir Apparent
Were equally slow at remembering people's faces.
But whenever they met, incognito, in the Brazilian
Pavilion, the Row and such-like places,
They exchanged, it is said, their sternest nods—
Like gods of dissimilar races.

III

Dr. Newman with the crooked pince-nez
Had studied in Vienna and Chicago.

Chess was his only relaxation.
And Dr. Newman remained unperturbed
By every nastier manifestation
Of plutodemocratic civilization:
All that was cranky, corny, ill-behaved,
Unnecessary, askew or orgiastic
Would creep unbidden to his side-door (hidden
Behind a poster in the Tube Station,
Nearly half-way up the moving-stairs),
Push its way in, to squat there undisturbed

Among box-files and tubular steel-chairs.
He was once seen at the Philharmonic Hall
Noting the reactions of two patients,
With pronounced paranoiac tendencies,
To old Dutch music. He appeared to recall
A tin of lozenges in his breast-pocket,
Put his hand confidently in—
And drew out a black imp, or sooterkin,
Six inches long, with one ear upside-down,
Licking at a vanilla ice-cream cornet—
Then put it back again with a slight frown.

IV

A Royal Duke, with no campaigning medals
To dignify his Orders, he would speak
Nostalgically at times of Mozambique
Where once the ship he cruised in ran aground:
How he drank cocoa, from a sailor's mug,
Poured from the common jug,
While loyal toasts went round.

V

Sir John addressed the Snake God in his temple,
Which was full of bats, not as a votary
But with the somewhat cynical courtesy,
Just short of condescension,
He might have paid the Governor-General
Of a small, hot, backward colony.
He was well versed in primitive religion,
But found this an embarrassing occasion:
The God was immense, noisy and affable,
Began to tickle him with a nervous chuckle,

Unfobbed a great gold clock for him to listen,
Hissed like a snake, and swallowed him at one mouthful.

VI

All horses on the racecourse of Tralee
  Have four more legs in gallop than in trot—
  Two pairs fully extended, two pairs not;
And yet no thoroughbred with either three
  Or five legs but is mercilessly shot.
I watched a filly gnaw her fifth leg free,
Warned by a speaking mare since turned silentiary. *1946*

THE SURVIVOR

To die with a forlorn hope, but soon to be raised
By hags, the spoilers of the field; to elude their claws
And stand once more on a well-swept parade-ground,
Scarred and bemedalled, sword upright in fist
At head of a new undaunted company:

Is this joy? to be doubtless alive again,
And the others dead? Will your nostrils gladly savour
The fragrance, always new, of a first hedge-rose?
Will your ears be charmed by the thrush's melody
Sung as though he had himself devised it?

And is this joy: after the double suicide
(Heart against heart) to be restored entire,
To smooth your hair and wash away the life-blood,
And presently seek a young and innocent bride,
Whispering in the dark: "for ever and ever"? *1951*

THE PORTRAIT

She speaks always in her own voice
Even to strangers; but those other women
Exercise their borrowed, or false, voices
Even on sons and daughters.

She can walk invisibly at noon
Along the high road; but those other women
Gleam phosphorescent—broad hips and gross fingers—
Down every lampless alley.

She is wild and innocent, pledged to love
Through all disaster; but those other women
Decry her for a witch or a common drab
And glare back when she greets them.

Here is her portrait, gazing sidelong at me,
The hair in disarray, the young eyes pleading:
"And you, love? As unlike those other men
As I those other women?"   *1951*

THE BLUE-FLY

Five summer days, five summer nights,
The ignorant, loutish, giddy blue-fly
Hung without motion on the cling peach,
Humming occasionally: "O my love, my fair one!"
          As in the *Canticles*.

Magnified one thousand times, the insect
Looks farcically human; laugh if you will!
Bald head, stage-fairy wings, blear eyes,
A caved-in chest, hairy black mandibles,
          Long spindly thighs.

The crime was detected on the sixth day.
What then could be said or done? By anyone?
It would have been vindictive, mean and what-not
To swat that fly for being a blue-fly,
          For debauch of a peach.

Is it fair, either, to bring a microscope
To bear on the case, even in search of truth?
Nature, doubtless, has some compelling cause
To glut the carriers of her epidemics—
          Nor did the peach complain.   *1953*

TO CALLIOPE

Permit me here a simple brief aside,
          Calliope,
You who have shown such patience with my pride
          And obstinacy:

Am I not loyal to you? I say no less
    Than is to say;
If more, only from angry-heartedness,
    Not for display.

But you know, I know, and you know I know
    My principal curse:
Shame at the mounting dues I have come to owe
    A devil of verse

Who caught me young, ingenuous and uncouth,
    Prompting me how
To evade the patent clumsiness of truth—
    Which I do now.

No: nothing reads so fresh as I first thought,
    Or as you could wish—
Yet must I, when far worse is eagerly bought,
    Cry stinking fish?   1953

C. Day Lewis

[IN HEAVEN, I SUPPOSE, LIE DOWN]

In heaven, I suppose, lie down together
Agonized Pilate and the boa-constrictor
That swallows anything: but we must seize
One horn or the other of our antitheses.
When I consider each independent star
Wearing its world of darkness like a fur
And rubbing shoulders with infinity,
I am content experience should be
More discontinuous than the points pricked
Out by the mazy course of a derelict,
Iceberg, or Flying Dutchman, and the heart
Stationary and passive as a chart.
In such star-frenzy I could boast, betwixt
My yester and my morrow self are fixed
All the birds carolling and all the seas
Groaning from Greenwich to the Antipodes.

But an eccentric hour may come, when systems
Not stars divide the dark; and then life's pistons
Pounding into their secret cylinder
Begin to tickle the most anchorite ear
With hints of mechanisms that include
The man. And once that rhythm arrests the blood,
Who would be satisfied his mind is no
Continent but an archipelago?
They are preposterous paladins and prance
From myth to myth, who take an Agag stance
Upon the needle points of here and now,
Where only angels ought to tread. Allow
One jointure feasible to man, one state
Squared with another—then he can integrate
A million selves and where disorder ruled
Straddle a chaos and beget a world.

Peals of the New Year once for me came tumbling
Out of the narrow night like clusters of humming-
Birds loosed from a black bag, and rose again
Irresponsibly to silence: but now I strain
To follow them and see for miles around
Men square or shrug their shoulders at the sound.
Then I remember the pure and granite hills
Where first I caught an ideal tone that stills,
Like the beloved's breath asleep, all din
Of earth at traffic: silence's first-born,
Carrying over each sensual ravine
To inform the seer and uniform the seen.
So from this ark, this closet of the brain,
The dove emerges and flies back again
With a Messiah sprig of certitude—
Promise of ground below the sprawling flood.   1929

[NOW I HAVE COME TO REASON]

Now I have to come to reason
And cast my schoolboy clout,
Disorder I see is without,
And the mind must sweat a poison
Keener than Thessaly's brew;
A pus that, discharged not thence,
Gangrenes the vital sense
And makes disorder true.
It is certain we shall attain
No life till we stamp on all
Life the tetragonal
Pure symmetry of brain.

I felt, in my scorning
Of common poet's talk,
As arrogant as the hawk
When he mounts above the morning.
"Behold man's droll appearance,
Faith wriggling upon his hooks,
Chin-deep in Eternal Flux
Angling for reassurance!"
I care not if he retorts—
"Of all that labor and wive
And worship, who would give

A fiddlestick for these thoughts
That sluggishly yaw and bend,
Fat strings of barges drawn
By a tug they have never seen
And never will comprehend?"

I sit in a wood and stare
Up at untroubled branches
Locked together and staunch as
Though girders of the air:
And think, the first wind rising
Will crack that intricate crown
And let the daylight down.
But there is naught surprising
Can explode the single mind:—
Let figs from thistles fall
Or stars from their pedestal,
This architecture will stand.   *1929*

[DESIRE IS A WITCH]

Desire is a witch
And runs against the clock.
It can unstitch
The decent hem
Where space tacks on to time:
It can unlock
Pandora's privacies.

It puffs in these
Top-gallants of the mind,
And away I stand
On the elemental gale
Into an ocean
That the liar Lucian
Had never dared retail.

When my love leans with all
Her shining breast and shoulder,
I know she is older
Than Ararat the hill,
And yet more young
Than the first daffodil
That ever shews a spring.

When her eyes delay
On me, so deep are they
Tunnelled by love, although
You poured Atlantic
In this one and Pacific
In the other, I know
They would not overflow.

Desire clicks back
Like cuckoo into clock;
Leaves me to explain
Eyes that a tear will drown
And a body where youth
Nor age will long remain
To implicate the truth.

It seems that we must call
Anything truth whose well
Is deep enough;
For the essential
Philosopher-stone, desire,
Needs no other proof
Than its own fire.   1929

[IN THE CHAOTIC AGE]

In the chaotic age
    This was enough for me—
Her beauty walked the page
    And it was poetry.

Now that the crust has cooled,
    The floods are kept in pen,
Mountains have got their mould
    And air its regimen.

Nothing of heat remains
    But where the sacred hill
Conserves within her veins
    The fiery principle.

Fire can no longer shake
    Stars from their sockets down;

It burns now but to make
Vain motions above the town.

This glum canal has lain
Opaque night after night,
One hour will entertain
A jubilee of light,

And show that beauty is
A motion of the mind
By its own dark caprice
Directed or confined.   *1929*

[NOW SHE IS LIKE THE WHITE TREE-ROSE]

Now she is like the white tree-rose
That takes a blessing from the sun:
Summer has filled her veins with light,
And her warm heart is washed with noon.

Or as a poplar, ceaselessly
Gives a soft answer to the wind:
Cool on the light her leaves lie sleeping,
Folding a column of sweet sound.

Powder the stars. Forbid the night
To wear those brilliants for a brooch
So soon, dark death, you may close down
The mines that made this beauty rich.

Her thoughts are pleiads, stooping low
O'er glades where nightingale has flown:
And like the luminous night around her
She has at heart a certain dawn.   *1931*

[DO NOT EXPECT AGAIN A PHOENIX HOUR]

Do not expect again a phoenix hour,
The triple-towered sky, the dove complaining,
Sudden the rain of gold and heart's first ease
Tranced under trees by the eldritch light of sundown.

By a blazed trail our joy will be returning:
One burning hour throws light a thousand ways,

And hot blood stays into familiar gestures.
The best years wait, the body's plenitude.

Consider then, my lover, this is the end
Of the lark's ascending, the hawk's unearthly hover:
Spring season is over soon and first heatwave;
Grave-browed with cloud ponders the huge horizon.

Draw up the dew. Swell with Pacific violence.
Take shape in silence. Grow as the clouds grew.
Beautiful brood the cornlands, and you are heavy;
Leafy the boughs—they also hide big fruit.   1931

[LET US NOW PRAISE FAMOUS MEN]

Let us now praise famous men,
Not your earth-shakers, not the dynamiters,
But who in the Home Counties or the Khyber,
Trimming their nails to meet an ill wind,
Facing the Adversary with a clean collar,
Justified the system.
Admire the venerable pile that bred them,
Bones are its foundations,
The pinnacles are stone abstractions,
Whose halls are whispering-galleries designed
To echo voices of the past, dead tongues.
White hopes of England here
Are taught to rule by learning to obey,
Bend over before vested interests,
Kiss the rod, salute the quarter-deck;
Here is no savage discipline
Of peregrine swooping, of fire destroying,
But a civil code; no capital offender
But the cool cad, the man who goes too far.
Ours the curriculum
Neither of building birds nor wasteful waters,
Bound in book not violent in vein:
Here we inoculate with dead ideas
Against blood-epidemics, against
The infection of faith and the excess of life.
Our methods are up to date; we teach
Through head and not by heart,
Language with gramophones and sex with charts,

Prophecy by deduction, prayer by numbers.
For honors see prospectus: those who leave us
Will get a post and pity the poor;
Their eyes glaze at strangeness;
They are never embarrassed, have a word for everything,
Living on credit, dying when the heart stops;
Will wear black armlets and stand a moment in silence
For the passing of an era, at their own funeral.   *1933*

FLIGHT TO AUSTRALIA

Sing we the two lieutenants, Parer and M'Intosh,
After the War wishing to hie them home to Australia,
Planned they would take a high way, a hazardous crazy air-way:
Death their foregone conclusion, a flight headlong to failure,
We said. For no silver posh
Plane was their pigeon, no dandy dancer quick-stepping through heaven,
But a craft of obsolete design, a condemned D.H. nine;
Sold for a song it was, patched up though to write an heroic
Line across the world as it reeled on its obstinate stoic
Course to that southern haven.

On January 8, 1920, their curveting wheels kissed
England goodbye. Over Hounslow huddled in morning mist
They rose and circled like buzzards while we rubbed our sleepy eyes:
Like a bird scarce-fledged they flew, whose flying hours are few—
Still dear is the nest but deeper its desire unto the skies—
And they left us to our sleeping.
They felt earth's warning tug on their wings: vain to advance
Asking a thoroughfare through the angers of the air
On so flimsy a frame: but they pulled up her nose and the earth went
     sloping
Away, and they aimed for France.

Fog first, a wet blanket, a kill-joy, the primrose-of-morning's blight,
Blotting out the dimpled sea, the ample welcome of land,
The gay glance from the bright
Cliff-face behind, snaring the sky with treachery, sneering
At hope's loss of height. But they charged it, flying blind;
They took a compass-bearing against that dealer of doubt,
As a saint when the field of vision is fogged gloriously steels
His spirit against the tainter of air, the elusive taunter:
They climbed to win a way out,
Then downward dared till the moody waves snarled at their wheels.

Landing at last near Conteville, who had skimmed the crest of oblivion,
They could not rest, but rose and flew on to Paris, and there
Trivially were delayed—a defective petrol feed—
Three days: a time hung heavy on
Hand and heart, till they leapt again to the upper air,
Their element, their lover, their angel antagonist.
Would have taken a fall without fame, but the sinewy framework the
        wrist
Of steel the panting engine wrestled well: and they went
South while the going was good, as a swallow that guide nor goad
Needs on his sunny scent.

At Lyons the petrol pump failed again, and forty-eight hours
They chafed to be off, the haughty champions whose breathing-space
Was an horizon span and the four winds their fan.
Over Italy's shores
A reverse, the oil ran out and cursing they turned about
Losing a hundred miles to find a landing-place.
Not a coast for a castaway this, no even chance of alighting
On sward or wind-smooth sand:
A hundred miles without pressure they flew, the engine fighting
For breath, and its heart nearly burst before they dropped to land.

And now the earth they had spurned rose up against them in anger,
Tier upon tier it towered, the terrible Apennines:
No sanctuary there for wings, not flares nor landing-lines,
No hope of floor and hangar.
Yet those ice-tipped spears that disputed the passage set spurs
To their two hundred and forty horse power; grimly they gained
Altitude, though the hand of heaven was heavy upon them,
The downdraught from the mountains: though desperate eddies spun
        them
Like a coin, yet unkindly tossed their luck came uppermost
And mastery remained.

Air was all ambushes round them, was avalanche earthquake
Quicksand, a funnel deep as doom, till climbing steep
They crawled like a fly up the face of perpendicular night
And levelled, finding a break
At fourteen thousand feet. Here earth is shorn from sight:
Deadweight a darkness hangs on their eyelids, and they bruise
Their eyes against a void: vindictive the cold airs close
Down like a trap of steel and numb them from head to heel;

Yet they kept an even keel,
For their spirit reached forward and took the controls while their fingers
    froze.

They had not heard the last of death. When the mountains were passed,
He raised another crest, the long crescendo of pain
Kindled to climax, the plane.
Took fire. Alone in the sky with the breath of their enemy
Hot in their face they fought: from three thousand feet they tilted
Over, side-slipped away—a trick for an ace, a race
And running duel with death: flame streamed out behind,
A crimson scarf of, as life-blood out of a wound, but the wind
Of their downfall staunched it; death wilted,
Lagged and died out in smoke—he could not stay their pace.

A lull for a while. The powers of hell rallied their legions.
On Parer now fell the stress of the flight; for the plane had been
    bumped,
Buffeted, thrashed by the air almost beyond repair:
But he tinkered and coaxed, and they limped
Over the Adriatic on into warmer regions.
Erratic their course to Athens, to Crete: coolly they rode her
Like a tired horse at the water-jumps, they jockeyed her over seas,
Till they came at last to a land whose dynasties of sand
Had seen Alexander, Napoleon, many a straddling invader,
But never none like these.

England to Cairo, a joy-ride, a forty-hour journey at most,
Had cost them forty-four days. What centuried strata of life
Fuelled the fire that haled them to heaven, the power that held them
Aloft? For their plane was a laugh,
A patch, brittle as matchstick, a bubble, a lift for a ghost:
Bolts always working loose of propeller, cylinder, bearer;
Instruments faulty; filter, magneto, each strut unsound.
Yet after four days, though we swore she never could leave the ground,
We saw her in headstrong haste diminish towards the east—
That makeshift, mad sky-farer.

Aimed they now for Baghdad, unwritten in air's annals
A voyage. But theirs the fate all flights of logic to refute,
Who obeyed no average law, who buoyed the viewless channels
Of sky with a courage steadfast, luminous. Safe they crossed
Sinai's desert, and daring

The Nejd, the unneighbourly waste of Arabia, yet higher soaring
(Final a fall there for birds of passage, limed and lost
In shifty the sand's embrace) all day they strove to climb
Through stormy rain: but they felt her shorten her stride and falter,
And they fell at evening time.

Slept that night beside their machine, and the next morning
Raider Arabs appeared reckoning this stranded bird
A gift: like cobras they struck, and their gliding shadows athwart
The sand were all their warning.
But the aeronauts, knowing iron the coinage here, had brought
Mills bombs and revolvers, and M'Intosh held them off
While Parer fought for life—
A spark, the mechanic's right answer, and finally wrought
A miracle, for the dumb engine spoke and they rose
Convulsively out of the clutch of the desert, the clench of their foes.

Orchestrate this theme, artificer-poet. Imagine
The roll, crackling percussion, quickening tempo of engine
For a start: the sound as they soar, an octave-upward slur
Scale of sky ascending:
Hours-held note of level flight, a beat unhurried,
Sustaining undertone of movement never-ending:
Wind shrill on the ailerons, flutes and fifes in a flurry
Devilish when they dive, plucking of tense stays.
These hardly heard it, who were the voice, the heavenly air
That sings above always.

We have seen the extremes, the burning, the freezing, the outward face
Of their exploit; heroic peaks, tumbling-to-zero depressions:
Little our graph can show, the line they traced through space,
Of the heart's passionate patience.
How soft drifts of sleep piled on their senses deep
And they dug themselves out often: how the plane was a weight that
    hung
And swung on their aching nerve; how din drilled through the skull
And sight sickened—so slow earth filtered past below.
Yet nerve failed never, heart clung
To height, and the brain kept its course and the hand its skill.

Baghdad renewed a propeller damaged in desert. Arid
Baluchistan spared them that brought down and spoilt with thirst
Armies of Alexander. To Karachi they were carried

On cloud-back: fragile as tinder their plane, but the winds were tender
Now to their need, and nursed
Them along till teeming India made room for them to alight.
Wilting her wings, the sweltering suns had moulted her bright
Plumage, rotten with rain
The fabric: but they packed her with iron washers and tacked her
Together, good for an hour, and took the air again.

Feats for a hundred flights, they were prodigal of: a fairest
Now to tell—how they foiled death when the engine failed
Above the Irrawaddy, over close-woven forest.
What shoals for a pilot there, what a snarled passage and dark
Shelves down to doom and grip
Of green! But look, balanced superbly, quick off the mark
Swooping like centre three-quarter whose impetus storms a gap—
Defenders routed, rooted their feet, and their arms are mown
Aside, that high or low aim at his overthrow—
M'Intosh touched her down.

And they picked her up out of it somehow and put her at the air, a
Sorry hack for such steeplechasing, to leap the sky.
"We'll fly this bloody crate till it falls to bits at our feet,"
Said the mechanic Parer.
And at Moulmein soon they crashed; and the plane by their spirit's high
Tension long pinned, girded and guarded from dissolution,
Fell to bits at their feet. Wrecked was the undercarriage,
Radiator cracked, in pieces, compasses crocked;
Fallen all to confusion.
Their winged hope was a heap of scrap, but unsplintered their courage.

Six weeks they worked in sun-glare and jungle damps, assembling
Fragments to make airworthy what was worth not its weight in air.
As a surgeon, grafter of skin, as a setter of bones tumbling
Apart, they had power to repair
This good for naught but the grave: they livened her engine and gave
Fuselage faith to rise rejuvenated from ruin.
Went with them stowaways, not knowing what hazard they flew in—
Bear-cubs, a baby alligator, lizards and snakes galore;
Mascots maybe, for the plane though twice she was floored again
Always came up for more.

Till they came to the pitiless mountains of Timor. Yet these, untamed,
Not timorous, against the gradient and Niagara of air they climbed

Scarce-skimming the summits; and over the shark-toothed Timor sea
Lost their bearings, but shirked not the odds, the deaths that lurked
A million to one on their trail:
They reached out to the horizon and plucked their destiny.
On for eight hours they flew blindfold against the unknown,
And the oil began to fail
And their flying spirit waned—one pint of petrol remained
When the land stood up to meet them and they came into their own.

Southward still to Melbourne, the bourn of their flight, they pressed
Till at last near Culcairn, like a last fretted leaf
Falling from brave autumn into earth's breast,
D.H. nine, their friend that had seen them to the end,
Gave up her airy life.
The Southern Cross was splendid above the spot where she fell,
The end of her rainbow curve over our weeping day:
And the flyers, glad to be home, unharmed by that dizzy fall,
Dazed as the dead awoken from death, stepped out of the broken
Body and went away.   1935

BOMBERS

Through the vague morning, the heart preoccupied,
A deep in air buried grain of sound
Starts and grows, as yet unwarning—
The tremor of baited deepsea line.

Swells the seed, and now tight sound-buds
Vibrate, upholding their paean flowers
To the sun. There are bees in sky-bells droning,
Flares of crimson at the heart unfold.

Children look up, and the elms spring-garlanded
Tossing their heads and marked for the axe.
Gallant or woebegone, alike unlucky—
Earth shakes beneath us: we imagine loss.

Black as vermin, crawling in echelon
Beneath the cloud-floor, the bombers come:
The heavy angels, carrying harm in
Their wombs that ache to be rid of death.

This is the seed that grows for ruin,
The iron embryo conceived in fear.

Soon or late its need must be answered
In feár delivered and screeching fire.

Choose between your child and this fatal embryo.
Shall your guilt bear arms, and the children you want
Be condemned to die by the powers you paid for
And haunt the houses you never built? *1938*

A HAPPY VIEW

. . . So take a happy view—
This lawn graced with the candle-flames of crocus,
Frail-handed girls under the flowering chestnut,
Or anything will do
That time takes back before it seems untrue:

And, if the truth were told,
You'd count it luck, perceiving in what shallow
Crevices and few crumbling grains of comfort
Man's joy will seed, his cold
And hardy fingers find an eagle's hold. *1938*

OVERTURES TO DEATH

I

For us, born into a world
Of fledged, instinctive trees,
Of lengthening days, snowfall at Christmas
And sentried palaces,

You were the one our parents
Could not forget or forgive—
A remittance man, a very very
Distant relative.

We read your name in the family
Bible. It was tabu
At meals and lessons, but in church sometimes
They seemed to be praying for you.

You lived overseas, we gathered:
And often lying safe

In bed we thought of you, hearing the indrawn
Breath of the outcast surf.

Later we heard them saying
You had done well in the War.
And, though you never came home to us,
We saw your name everywhere.

When home grew unsympathetic,
You were all the rage for a while—
The favorite uncle with the blank-cheque-book
And the understanding smile.

Some of us went to look for you
In aeroplanes and fast cars:
Some tried the hospitals, some took to vice,
Others consulted the stars.

But now, sir, that you may be going
To visit us any night,
We watch the french windows, picturing you
In rather a different light.

The house, we perceive, is shabby,
There's dry-rot in the wood:
It's a poor welcome and it won't keep you out
And we wish we had been good.

But there's no time now for spring-cleaning
Or mending the broken lock.
We are here in the shrouded drawing-room till
Your first, your final knock.

2

When all the sky is skimming
And lovers frisk in the hay,
When it's easy forgiving the dead or the living,
He is not so far away.

When love's hands are too hot, too cold,
And justice turns a deaf ear,
When springs congeal and the skies are sealed,
We know that he is near.

Now here was a property, on all sides
Considered quite imposing:
Take a good look round at house and grounds—
The mortgage is foreclosing.

Now Death he is the bailiff
And he sits in our best room
Appraising chintz and ornaments
And the child in the womb.

We were not shysters or loonies,
Our spirit was up to proof:
Simpler far is the reason for our
Notice to quit this roof.

We paid for our lease and rule of life
In hard cash; and one day
The news got through to you-know-who
That we'd ceased to pay our way.

Oh what will happen to our dear sons,
Our dreams of pensioned ease?
They are downed and shredded, for the wind we dreaded
Worries the blossom trees.

Oh Death he is the bailiff
And his men wait outside:
We shall sleep well in our handsome shell
While he auctions away our pride.

3

Sir, I'd not make so bold as to lack all
Respect for one whose prowess in the bed and the battlefield
Have excited (and justly) universal comment.
Nor could I, if I wished—
Who, in the small hours and the talkative
Reception, have felt you ticking within my belly—
Pretend there's any worse ordeal to come.
You and I, my friend, are antagonists
And the fight's framed: for this I blame not you
But the absentee promoter. If I seem to treat
Your titles, stamina, skill with levity,
Call it the rat's bad-loser snarl, the madman

Humouring the two doctors, the point declaring
War on the calm circumference. . . .
   You have appeared to us in many guises—
Pale priest, black camel, the bemedalled sergeant
Of general conscription, a bugbear to affright
Second childhood, or the curtain drawn so deftly
To show that diamond-tiered tree
Evergreen with bliss for all good boys and girls.
You have been called the Leveller: but little
That meant to the aristos you transferred
Straight from one rotten borough to another;
Nor can our state, hollow and cold as theirs,
Much envy the drab democrats of the grave.
Happiest, in our nervous time, who name you
Peace. You are the peace that millions die for.
   If there's a moment's solace, laid like the bloom
Of dew upon our meadows; if honeysuckle
Clings to its sweetened hour, and the appealing
Beauty of flesh makes time falter in his stride;
If anywhere love-lips, flower-flaunt, crimson of cloud-crest
With flames impassioned hold off the pacing shadows—
You can rest indulgent: soon enough
They shall be all, all of your complexion.
   I grant you the last word. But what of these—
The criminal agents of a dying will
Who, frantic with defeat, conspire to force your
Earlier intervention?
It is they, your damned auxiliaries, must answer
For the self-slain in the foodless, fireless room,
For stunted hearts that droop by our olive-green
Canals, the blossom of children untimely shattered
By their crazed, random fire, and the fear like a black frost
Foreshortening our prospect, metallic on our tongues.
If I am too familiar with you, sir,
It is that these have brought you into contempt.
You are in nature. These are most unnatural.
We shall desire your peace in our own time:
But with those, your free-lance and officious gunmen,
Our war is life itself and shall not fail.

4

    Forgive us, that we ever thought
    You could with innocence be bought,

Or, puffed with queasy power, have tried
Your register to override.

Such diamond-faced and equal laws
Allow no chink or saving clause:
Besotted may-fly, bobbish wren
Count in your books as much as men.

No North-West Passage can be found
To sail those freezing capes around,
Nor no smooth by-pass ever laid
Shall that metropolis evade.

The tampering hand, the jealous eye
That overlooked our infancy—
Forgiven soon, they sank their trust
And our reproach into the dust.

We also, whom a bawdy spring
Tempted to order everything,
Shall shrink beneath your first caress
Into a modest nothingness.

The meshes of the imperious blood,
The wind-flown tower, the poet's word
Can catch no more than a weak sigh
And ghost of immortality.

O lord of leisure, since we know
Your image we shall ne'er outgrow,
Teach us the value of our stay
Lest we insult the living clay.

This clay that binds the roots of man
And firmly foots his flying span—
Only this clay can voice, invest,
Measure and frame our mortal best.

O lord of night, bid us beware
The wistful ghost that speaks us fair:
Once let him in—he clots the veins
And makes a still-birth of our pains.

Now we at last have crossed the line
Where earth's exuberant fields begin,
That green illusion in the sky
Born of our desert years can die.

No longer let predestined need
Cramp our design, or hunger breed
Its windy dreams, or life distil
Rare personal good from common ill.

Lord of us all, now it is true
That we are lords of all but you,
Teach us the order of our day
Lest we deface the honored clay.

5

The sun came out in April,
The hawthorn in May:
We thought the year, like other years,
Would go the Christmas way.

In June we picked the clover,
And sea-shells in July:
There was no silence at the door,
No word from the sky.

A hand came out of August
And flicked his life away:
We had not time to bargain, mope,
Moralize, or pray.

Where he had been, was only
An effigy on a bed
To ask us searching questions or
Hear what we'd left unsaid.

Only that stained parchment
Set out what he had been—
A face we might have learned better,
But now must read unseen.

Thus he resigned his interest
And claims, all in a breath,

Leaving us the long office work
And winding-up of death:

The ordinary anguish,
The stairs, the awkward turn.
The bearers' hats like black mushrooms
Placed upon the lawn.

As a migrant remembers
The sting and warmth of home,
As the fruit bears out the blossom's word,
We remember him.

He loved the sun in April,
The hawthorn in May:
Our tree will not light up for him
Another Christmas Day.

6

It is not you I fear, but the humiliations
You mercifully use to deaden grief—
The downward graph of natural joys,
Imagination's slump, the blunted ear.

I hate this cold and politic self-defence
Of hardening arteries and nerves
Grown dull with time-serving. I see that the heart lives
By self-betrayal, by circumspection is killed.

That boy, whose glance makes heaven open and edges
Each dawning pain with gold, must learn to disbelieve:
The wildfire lust of the eyes will gutter down
To age's dim recalcitrance.

Have we not seen how quick this young girl's thoughts,
Wayward and burning as a charm of goldfinches
Alarmed from thistle-tops, turn into
Spite or a cupboard love or clipped routine?

Nearing the watershed and the difficult passes,
Man wraps up closer against the chill
In his familiar habits; and at the top
Pauses, seeing your kingdom like a net beneath him spread.

Some climbed to this momentous peak of the world
And facing the horizon—that notorious pure woman
Who lures to cheat the last embrace,
Hurled themselves down upon an easier doom.

One the rare air made dizzy renounced
Earth, and the avalanche took him at his word:
One wooed perfection—he's bedded deep in the glacier, perfect
And null, the prince and image of despair.

The best, neither hoarding nor squandering
The radiant flesh and the receptive
Spirit, stepped on together in the rhythm of comrades who
Have found a route on earth's true reckoning based.

They have not known the false humility,
The shamming-dead of the senses beneath your hunter's hand;
But life's green standards they've advanced
To the limit of your salt unyielding zone.

7

For us, born into a still
Unsweetened world, of sparse
Breathing-room, alleys brackish as hell's pit
And heaven-accusing spires,

You were never far nor fable,
Judgement nor happy end:
We have come to think of you, mister, as
Almost the family friend.

Our kiddies play tag with you often
Among the tornado wheels;
Through fevered nights you sit up with them,
You serve their little meals.

You lean with us at street-corners,
We have met you in the mine;
Your eyes are the foundry's glare, you beckon
From the snake-tooth, sly machine.

Low in the flooded engineroom,
High on the yawing steeple—

Wherever we are, we begin to fancy
That we're your chosen people.

They came to us with charity,
They came to us with whips,
They came with chains behind their back
And freedom on their lips:

Castle and field and city—
Ours is a noble land,
Let us work for its fame together, they said;
But we don't quite understand.

For they took the land and the credit,
Took virtue and double-crossed her;
They left us the scrag-end of the luck
And the brunt of their disaster.

And now like horses they fidget
Smelling death in the air:
But we are your chosen people, and
We've little to lose or fear.

When the time comes for a clearance,
When light brims over the hill,
Mister, you can rely on us
To execute your will.   *1938*

THE COMMITTEE

So the committee met again, and again
Nailed themselves to the never-much-altered agenda,
Making their points as to the manner born,
Hammering them home with the skill of long practice.

These men and women are certainly representative
Of every interest concerned. For example, A. wears
Integrity like a sheriff's badge, while B.
Can grind an axe on either side of a question:
C. happens to have the facts, D. a vocation
For interpreting facts to the greater glory of Dogma:
E. is pompously charming, diffidently earnest,
F. is the acid-drop, the self-patented catalyst.

Our chairman's a prince of procedure, in temporizing
Power a Proteus, and adept in seeming to follow
Where actually he leads—as indeed he must be,
Or the rest would have torn him to pieces a long time ago.
Yet all, in a curious way, are public-spirited,
Groping with their *ad hoc* decisions to find
The missing, presumed omnipotent, directive.

Idly the sun tracing upon their papers
Doodles of plane-leaf shadows and rubbing them out:
The buzz of flies, the gen of the breeze, the river
Endlessly stropping its tides against the embankment:
Seasons revolving with colors like stage armies,
Years going west along the one-way street—
All these they ignore, whose session or obsession
Must do with means, not ends. But who called this meeting
Of irreconcileables? Will they work out some positive
Policy, something more than a *modus vivendi?*
Or be adjourned, *sine die,* their task half done?

So the committee, as usual, reached a compromise—
If reach is the word, denoting, as it ought to,
A destination (though why should destiny not
Favor a compromise, which is only the marriage
For better or worse between two or more incompatibles,
Like any marriage of minds?) and left the table,
There being no further business for today.
And the silent secretary wrote up the minutes,
Putting the leaves in order. For what? the eye
Of higher authority? or the seal of the dust?
Or again, to be dispersed irreparably
When the hinge turns and a brusque new life blows in?
And I regret another afternoon wasted,
And wearily think there is something to be said
For the methods of the dictatorships—I who shall waste
Even the last drops of twilight in self-pity
That I should have to be chairman, secretary,
And all the committee, all the one-man committee.   *1957*

ALMOST HUMAN

The man you know, assured and kind,
Wearing fame like an old tweed suit—
You would not think he has an incurable
Sickness upon his mind.

Finely that tongue, for the listening people,
Articulates love, enlivens clay;
While under his valued skin there crawls
An outlaw and a cripple.

Unenviable the renown he bears
When all's awry within? But a soul
Divinely sick may be immunized
From the scourge of common cares.

A woman weeps, a friend's betrayed,
Civilization plays with fire—
His grief or guilt is easily purged
In a rush of words to the head.

The newly dead, and their waxwork faces
With the look of things that could never have lived,
He'll use to prime his cold, strange heart
And prompt the immortal phrases.

Before you condemn this eminent freak
As an outrage upon mankind,
Reflect: something there is in him
That must for ever seek

To share the condition it glorifies,
To shed the skin that keeps it apart,
To bury its grace in a human bed—
And it walks on knives, on knives.   *1957*

William Empson

INVITATION TO JUNO

Lucretius could not credit centaurs;
Such bicycle he deemed asynchronous.
"Man superannuates the horse;
Horse pulses will not gear with ours."

Johnson could see no bicycle would go;
"You bear yourself, and the machine as well."
Gennets for germans sprang not from Othello,
And Ixion rides upon a single wheel.

Courage. Weren't strips of heart culture seen
Of late mating two periodicities?
Could not Professor Charles Darwin
Graft annual upon perennial trees?   *1935*

DISSATISFACTION WITH METAPHYSICS

High over Mecca Allah's prophet's corpse
(The empty focus opposite the sun)
Receives homage, centre of the universe.
How smooth his epicycles round him run,
Whose hearth is cold, and all his wives undone.

Two mirrors with Infinity to dine
Drink him below the table when they please.
Adam and Eve breed still their dotted line,
Repeated incest, a plain series.
Their trick is all philosophers' disease.

New safe straight lines are finite though unbounded,
Old epicycles numberless in vain.
Then deeper than e'er plummet, plummet sounded,
Then corpses flew, when God flooded the plain.
He promised Noah not to flood again.   *1935*

SEA VOYAGE

Re-plyed, extorted, oft transposed, and fleeting,
Tune from plucked cotton, the cat's-cradle pattern
Dances round fingers that would scratch in meeting
And dures and fosters their abandoned kitten.
Drawn taut, this flickering of wit would freeze,
And grave, knot-diamond, its filigrees.

Pillowed on gulfs between exiguous bobbins
The Son of Spiders, crucified to lace,
Suspends a red rag to a thousand dobbins
And sails so powered to a better place.
All his gained ports, thought's inter-reached trapeze,
Map-sail, transport him towards Hercules,

Earth-bound. Blue-sea-bound, the crisp silver foam,
Forbad be crystal, a lace eringo,
Flaps from the haunch seven petticoats at home,
Wards, silk, in ocean overskirt, her rainbow.
Sand-rope, the sodden goblet of the seas
Holds, concentrate, her liquid pedigrees.
We sum in port her banquet of degrees.   *1935*

CAMPING OUT

And now she cleans her teeth into the lake:
Gives it (God's grace) for her own bounty's sake
What morning's pale and the crisp mist debars:
Its glass of the divine (that Will could break)
Restores, beyond Nature: or lets Heaven take
(Itself being dimmed) her pattern, who half awake
Milks between rocks a straddled sky of stars.

Soap tension the star pattern magnifies.
Smoothly Madonna through-assumes the skies
Whose vaults are opened to achieve the Lord.
No, it is we soaring explore galaxies,
Our bullet boat light's speed by thousands flies.
Who moves so among stars their frame unties;
See where they blur, and die, and are outsoared.   *1935*

VILLANELLE

It is the pain, it is the pain, endures.
Your chemic beauty burned my muscles through.
Poise of my hands reminded me of yours.

What later purge from this deep toxin cures?
What kindness now could the old salve renew?
It is the pain, it is the pain, endures.

The infection slept (custom or change inures)
And when pain's secondary phase was due
Poise of my hands reminded me of yours.

How safe I felt, whom memory assures,
Rich that your grace safely by heart I knew.
It is the pain, it is the pain, endures.

My stare drank deep beauty that still allures.
My heart pumps yet the poison draught of you.
Poise of my hands reminded me of yours.

You are still kind whom the same shape immures.
Kind and beyond adieu. We miss our cue.
It is the pain, it is the pain, endures.
Poise of my hands reminded me of yours.   *1935*

THE SCALES

The proper scale would pat you on the head
But Alice showed her pup Ulysses' bough
Well from behind a thistle, wise with dread;

And though your gulf-sprung mountains I allow
(Snow-puppy curves, rose-solemn dado band)
Charming for nurse, I am not nurse just now.

Why pat or stride them, when the train will land
Me high, through climbing tunnels, at your side,
And careful fingers meet through castle sand.

Claim slyly rather that the tunnels hide
Solomon's gems, white vistas, preserved kings,
By jackal sandhole to your air flung wide.

Say (she suspects) to sea Nile only brings
Delta and indecision, who instead
Far back up country does enormous things.

1935

LEGAL FICTION

Law makes long spokes of the short stakes of men.
Your well fenced out real estate of mind
No high flat of the nomad citizen
Looks over, or train leaves behind.

Your rights extend under and above your claim
Without bound; you own land in Heaven and Hell;
Your part of earth's surface and mass the same,
Of all cosmos' volume, and all stars as well.

Your rights reach down where all owners meet, in Hell's
Pointed exclusive conclave, at earth's centre
(Your spun farm's root still on that axis dwells);
And up, through galaxies, a growing sector.

You are nomad yet; the lighthouse beam you own
Flashes, like Lucifer, through the firmament.
Earth's axis varies; your dark central cone
Wavers, a candle's shadow, at the end.   *1935*

EARTH HAS SHRUNK IN THE WASH

They pass too fast. Ships, and there's time for sighing;
Express and motor, Doug can jump between.
Only dry earth now asteroid her flying
Mates, if they miss her, must flick past unseen;

Or striking breasts that once the air defended
(Bubble of rainbow straddling between twilights,
Mother-of-pearl that with earth's oyster ended)
They crash and burrow and spill all through skylights.

There, airless now, from the bare sun take cancer,
Curve spines as earth and gravitation wane,
Starve on the mirror images of plants, or
Miss diabeatic down odd carbon chain.

One daily tortures the poor Christ anew
(On every planet moderately true)
But has much more to do,
And can so much entail here,
Daily brings rabbits to a new Australia,
New unforeseen, new cataclysmic failure,

And cannot tell. He who all answers brings
May (ever in the great taskmaster's eye)
Dowser be of his candle as of springs,
And pump the valley with the tunnel dry.   *1935*

THIS LAST PAIN

This last pain for the damned the Fathers found:
"They knew the bliss with which they were not crowned."
    Such, but on earth, let me foretell,
    Is all, of heaven or of hell.

Man, as the prying housemaid of the soul,
May know her happiness by eye to hole:
    He's safe; the key is lost; he knows
    Door will not open, nor hole close.

"What is conceivable can happen too,"
Said Wittgenstein, who had not dreamt of you;
    But wisely; if we worked it long
    We should forget where it was wrong.

Those thorns are crowns which, woven into knots,
Crackle under and soon boil fool's pots;
    And no man's watching, wise and long,
    Would ever stare them into song.

Thorns burn to a consistent ash, like man;
A splendid cleanser for the frying-pan:

And those who leap from pan to fire
Should this brave opposite admire.

All those large dreams by which men long live well
Are magic-lanterned on the smoke of hell;
    This then is real, I have implied,
    A painted, small, transparent slide.

These the inventive can hand-paint at leisure,
Or most emporia would stock our measure;
    And feasting in their dappled shade
    We should forget how they were made.

Feign then what's by a decent tact believed
And act that state is only so conceived,
    And build an edifice of form
    For house where phantoms may keep warm.

Imagine, then, by miracle, with me,
(Ambiguous gifts, as what gods give must be)
    What could not possibly be there,
    And learn a style from a despair.   *1935*

HOMAGE TO THE BRITISH MUSEUM

There is a supreme God in the ethnological section;
A hollow toad shape, faced with a blank shield.
He needs his belly to include the Pantheon,
Which is inserted through a hole behind.
At the navel, at the points formally stressed, at the organs of sense,
Lice glue themselves, dolls, local deities,
His smooth wood creeps with all the creeds of the world.

Attending there let us absorb the cultures of nations
And dissolve into our judgement all their codes.
Then, being clogged with a natural hesitation
(People are continually asking one the way out),
Let us stand here and admit that we have no road.
Being everything, let us admit that is to be something
Or give ourselves the benefit of the doubt;
Let us offer our pinch of dust all to this God,
And grant his reign over the entire building.   *1935*

IGNORANCE OF DEATH

Then there is this civilizing love of death, by which
Even music and painting tell you what else to love.
Buddhists and Christians contrive to agree about death

Making death their ideal basis for different ideals.
The Communists however disapprove of death
Except when practical. The people who dig up

Corpses and rape them are I understand not reported.
The Freudians regard the death-wish as fundamental,
Though "the clamour of life" proceeds from its rival "Eros."

Whether you are to admire a given case for making less clamour
Is not their story. Liberal hopefulness
Regards death as a mere border to an improving picture.

Because we have neither hereditary nor direct knowledge of death
It is the trigger of the literary man's biggest gun
And we are happy to equate it to any conceived calm.

Heaven me, when a man is ready to die about something
Other than himself, and is in fact ready because of that,
Not because of himself, that is something clear about himself.

Otherwise I feel very blank upon this topic,
And think that though important, and proper for anyone to bring up,
It is one that most people should be prepared to be blank upon.   *1940*

MISSING DATES

Slowly the poison the whole blood stream fills.
It is not the effort nor the failure tires.
The waste remains, the waste remains and kills.

It is not your system or clear sight that mills
Down small to the consequence a life requires;
Slowly the poison the whole blood stream fills.

They bled an old dog dry yet the exchange rills
Of young dog blood gave but a month's desires;
The waste remains, the waste remains and kills.

It is the Chinese tombs and the slag hills
Usurp the soil, and not the soil retires.
Slowly the poison the whole blood stream fills.

Not to have fire is to be a skin that shrills.
The complete fire is death. From partial fires
The waste remains, the waste remains and kills.

It is the poems you have lost, the ills
From missing dates, at which the heart expires.
Slowly the poison the whole blood stream fills.
The waste remains, the waste remains and kills.

1940

W. H. Auden

THE WALKING TOUR

To throw away the key and walk away,
Not abrupt exile, the neighbors asking why,
But following a line with left and right
An altered gradient at another rate
Learns more than maps upon the whitewashed wall
The hand put up to ask; and makes us well
Without confession of the ill. All pasts
Are single old past now, although some posts
Are forwarded, held looking on a new view;
The future shall fulfill a surer vow
Not smiling at queen over the glass rim
Nor making gunpowder in the top room,
Not swooping at the surface still like gulls
But with prolonged drowning shall develop gills.
But there are still to tempt; areas not seen
Because of blizzards or an erring sign
Who guessed-at wonders would be worth alleging,
And lies about the cost of a night's lodging.
Travellers may sleep at inns but not attach,
They sleep one night together, not asked to touch;
Receive no normal welcome, not the pressed lip,
Children to lift, not the assuaging lap.
Crossing the pass descend the growing stream
Too tired to hear except the pulses' strum,
Reach villages to ask for a bed in
Rock shutting out the sky, the old life done.   *1930*

WE ALL MAKE MISTAKES

Watch any day his nonchalant pauses, see
His dextrous handling of a wrap as he
Steps after into cars, the beggar's envy.

"There is a free one," many say, but err.
He is not that returning conqueror,
Nor ever the poles' circumnavigator.

But poised between shocking falls on razor-edge
Has taught himself this balancing subterfuge
Of the accosting profile, the erect carriage.

The song, the varied action of the blood
Would drown the warning from the iron wood
Would cancel the inertia of the buried:

Travelling by daylight on from house to house
The longest way to the intrinsic peace,
With love's fidelity and with love's weakness.

1930

AS WELL AS CAN BE EXPECTED

Taller today, we remember similar evenings,
Walking together in the windless orchard
Where the brook runs over the gravel, far from the glacier.

Again in the room with the sofa hiding the grate,
Look down to the river when the rain is over,
See him turn to the window, hearing our last
Of Captain Ferguson.

It is seen how excellent hands have turned to commonness.
One staring too long, went blind in a tower,
One sold all his manors to fight, broke through, and faltered.

Nights come bringing the snow, and the dead howl
Under the headlands in their windy dwelling
Because the Adversary put too easy questions
On lonely roads.

But happy now, though no nearer each other,
We see the farms lighted all along the valley;
Down at the mill-shed the hammering stops
And men go home.

Noises at dawn will bring
Freedom for some, but not this peace

No bird can contradict: passing, but is sufficient now
For something fulfilled this hour, loved or endured.   *1930*

PETITION

Sir, no man's enemy, forgiving all
But will its negative inversion, be prodigal:
Send to us power and light, a sovereign touch
Curing the intolerable neural itch,
The exhaustion of weaning, the liar's quinsy,
And the distortions of ingrown virginity.
Prohibit sharply the rehearsed response
And gradually correct the coward's stance;
Cover in time with beams those in retreat
That, spotted, they turn though the reverse were great;
Publish each healer that in city lives
Or country houses at the end of drives;
Harrow the house of the dead; look shining at
New styles of architecture, a change of heart.   *1930*

THE DECOYS

There are some birds in these valleys
Who flutter round the careless
With intimate appeal,
By seeming kindness trained to snaring,
They feel no falseness.

Under the spell completely
They circle can serenely,
And in the tricky light
The masked hill has a purer greenness.
Their flight looks fleeter.

But fowlers, O, like foxes,
Lie ambushed in the rushes.
Along the harmless tracks
The madman keeper crawls through brushwood,
Axe under oxter.

Alas, the signal given,
Fingers on trigger tighten.
The real unlucky dove

Must smarting fall away from brightness
Its love from living.   1932

"O WHERE ARE YOU GOING?"

"O where are you going?" said reader to rider,
"That valley is fatal when furnaces burn,
Yonder's the midden whose odours will madden,
That gap is the grave where the tall return."

"O do you imagine," said fearer to farer,
"That dusk will delay on your path to the pass,
Your diligent looking discover the lacking
Your footsteps feel from granite to grass?"

"O what was that bird," said horror to hearer,
"Did you see that shape in the twisted trees?
Behind you swiftly the figure comes softly,
The spot on your skin is a shocking disease?"

"Out of this house"—said rider to reader
"Yours never will"—said farer to fearer
"They're looking for you"—said hearer to horror
As he left them there, as he left them there.

1932

SOMETHING IS BOUND TO HAPPEN

Doom is dark and deeper than any sea-dingle.
Upon what man it fall
In spring, day-wishing flowers appearing,
Avalanche sliding, white snow from rock-face,
That he should leave his house,
No cloud-soft hand can hold him, restraint by women;
But ever that man goes
Through place-keepers, through forest trees,
A stranger to strangers over undried sea,
Houses for fishes, suffocating water,
Or lonely on fell as chat,
By pot-holed becks
A bird stone-haunting, an unquiet bird.

There head falls forward, fatigued at evening,
And dreams of home,

Waving from window, spread of welcome,
Kissing of wife under single sheet;
But waking sees
Bird-flocks nameless to him, through doorway voices
Of new men making another love.

Save him from hostile capture,
From sudden tiger's spring at corner;
Protect his house,
His anxious house where days are counted
From thunderbolt protect,
From gradual ruin spreading like a stain;
Converting number from vague to certain,
Bring joy, bring day of his returning,
Lucky with day approaching, with leaning dawn.

1934

[NOW THE LEAVES ARE FALLING FAST]

Now the leaves are falling fast,
Nurse's flowers will not last;
Nurses to the graves are gone,
And the prams go rolling on.

Whispering neighbours, left and right,
Pluck us from the real delight;
And the active hands must freeze
Lonely on the separate knees.

Dead in hundreds at the back
Follow wooden in our track,
Arms raised stiffly to reprove
In false attitudes of love.

Starving through the leafless wood
Trolls run scolding for their food;
And the nightingale is dumb,
And the angel will not come.

Cold, impossible, ahead
Lifts the mountain's lovely head
Whose white waterfall could bless
Travellers in their last distress.   *1936*

[FISH IN THE UNRUFFLED LAKES]

Fish in the unruffled lakes
The swarming colours wear,
Swans in the winter air
A white perfection have,
And the great lion walks
Through his innocent grove;
Lion, fish, and swan
Act, and are gone
Upon Time's toppling wave.

We till shadowed days are done,
We must weep and sing
Duty's conscious wrong,
The Devil in the clock,
The Goodness carefully worn
For atonement or for luck;
We must lose our loves,
On each beast and bird that moves
Turn an envious look.

Sighs for folly said and done
Twist our narrow days;
But I must bless, I must praise
That you, my swan, who have
All gifts that to the swan
Impulsive Nature gave,
The majesty and pride,
Last night should add
Your voluntary love.   1936

THE QUARRY

O what is that sound which so thrills the ear
    Down in the valley drumming, drumming?
Only the scarlet soldiers, dear,
    The soldiers coming.

O what is that light I see flashing so clear
    Over the distance brightly, brightly?
Only the sun on their weapons, dear,
    As they step lightly.

O what are they doing with all that gear,
  What are they doing this morning, this morning?
Only their usual manoeuvres, dear,
  Or perhaps a warning.

O why have they left the road down there,
  Why are they suddenly wheeling, wheeling?
Perhaps a change in their orders, dear.
  Why are you kneeling?

O haven't they stopped for the doctor's care,
  Haven't they reined their horses, their horses?
Why, they are none of them wounded, dear,
  None of these forces.

O is it the parson they want, with white hair,
  Is it the parson, is it, is it?
No, they are passing his gateway, dear,
  Without a visit.

O it must be the farmer who lives so near.
  It must be the farmer so cunning, so cunning?
They have passed the farmyard already, dear,
  And now they are running.

O where are you going? Stay with me here!
  Were the vows you swore deceiving, deceiving?
No, I promised to love you, dear,
  But I must be leaving.

O it's broken the lock and splintered the door,
  O it's the gate where they're turning, turning;
Their boots are heavy on the floor
  And their eyes are burning.   *1936*

From IN TIME OF WAR

I

So from the years the gifts were showered; each
Ran off with his at once into his life:
Bee took the politics that make a hive,
Fish swam as fish, peach settled into peach.

And were successful at the first endeavour;
The hour of birth their only time at college,
They were content with their precocious knowledge,
And knew their station and were good for ever.

Till finally there came a childish creature
On whom the years could model any feature,
And fake with ease a leopard or a dove;

Who by the lightest wind was changed and shaken,
And looked for truth and was continually mistaken,
And envied his few friends and chose his love.

II

They wondered why the fruit had been forbidden;
It taught them nothing new. They hid their pride,
But did not listen much when they were chidden;
They knew exactly what to do outside.

They left: immediately the memory faded
Of all they'd learnt; they could not understand
The dogs now who, before, had always aided;
The stream was dumb with whom they'd always planned.

They wept and quarrelled: freedom was so wild.
In front, maturity, as he ascended,
Retired like a horizon from the child;

The dangers and the punishments grew greater:
And the way back by angels was defended
Against the poet and the legislator.

IV

He stayed: and was imprisoned in possession.
The seasons stood like guards about his ways,
The mountains chose the mother of his children,
And like a conscience the sun ruled his days.

Beyond him his young cousins in the city
Pursued their rapid and unnatural course,
Believed in nothing but were easy-going,
And treated strangers like a favourite horse.

And he changed little,
But took his colour from the earth,
And grew in likeness to his sheep and cattle.

The townsman thought him miserly and simple,
The poet wept and saw in him the truth,
And the oppressor held him up as an example.

V

His generous bearing was a new invention:
For life was slow; earth needed to be careless:
With horse and sword he drew the girls' attention;
He was the Rich, the Bountiful, the Fearless.

And to the young he came as a salvation;
They needed him to free them from their mothers,
And grew sharp-witted in the long migration,
And round his camp fires learnt all men are brothers.

But suddenly the earth was full: he was not wanted.
And he became the shabby and demented,
And took to drink to screw his nerves to murder;

Or sat in offices and stole,
And spoke approvingly of Law and Order,
And hated life with all his soul.

VI

He watched the stars and noted birds in flight;
The rivers flooded or the Empire fell:
He made predictions and was sometimes right;
His lucky guesses were rewarded well.

And fell in love with Truth before he knew her,
And rode into imaginary lands,
With solitude and fasting hoped to woo her,
And mocked at those who served her with their hands.

But her he never wanted to despise,
But listened always for her voice; and when
She beckoned to him, he obeyed in meekness,

And followed her and looked into her eyes;
Saw there reflected every human weakness,
And saw himself as one of many men.

VII

He was their servant—some say he was blind—
And moved among their faces and their things;
Their feeling gathered in him like a wind
And sang: they cried—"It is a God that sings"—

And worshipped him and set him up apart,
And made him vain, till he mistook for song
The little tremors of his mind and heart
At each domestic wrong.

Songs came no more: he had to make them.
With what precision was each strophe planned,
He hugged his sorrow like a plot of land,

And walked like an assassin through the town,
And looked at men and did not like them,
But trembled if one passed him with a frown.

X

As a young child the wisest could adore him;
He felt familiar to them like their wives:
The very poor saved up their pennies for him,
And martyrs brought him presents of their lives.

But who could sit and play with him all day?
Their other needs were pressing, work, and bed:
The beautiful stone courts were built where they
Could leave him to be worshipped and well fed.

But he escaped. They were too blind to tell
That it was he who came with them to labour,
And talked and grew up with them like a neighbour:

To fear and greed those courts became a centre,
The poor saw there the tyrant's citadel,
And martyrs the lost face of the tormentor.

XII

And the age ended, and the last deliverer died
In bed, grown idle and unhappy; they were safe:
The sudden shadow of the giant's enormous calf
Would fall no more at dusk across the lawn outside.

They slept in peace: in marshes here and there no doubt
A sterile dragon lingered to a natural death,
But in a year the spoor had vanished from the heath;
The kobold's knocking in the mountain petered out.

Only the sculptors and the poets were half sad,
And the pert retinue from the magician's house
Grumbled and went elsewhere. The vanquished powers were glad

To be invisible and free: without remorse
Struck down the sons who strayed into their course,
And ravished the daughters, and drove the fathers mad.

XVIII

Far from the heart of culture he was used:
Abandoned by his general and his lice,
Under a padded quilt he closed his eyes
And vanished. He will not be introduced

When this campaign is tidied into books:
No vital knowledge perished in his skull;
His jokes were stale; like wartime, he was dull;
His name is lost forever like his looks.

He neither knew nor chose the Good, but taught us,
And added meaning like a comma, when
He turned to dust in China that our daughters

Be fit to love the earth, and not again
Disgraced before the dogs; that, where are waters,
Mountains and houses, may be also men.

XXVII

Wandering lost upon the mountains of our choice,
Again and again we sigh for an ancient South,

For the warm nude ages of instinctive poise,
For the taste of joy in the innocent mouth.

Asleep in our huts, how we dream of a part
In the glorious balls of the future; each intricate maze
Has a plan, and the disciplined movements of the heart
Can follow for ever and ever its harmless ways.

We envy streams and houses that are sure:
But we are articled to error; we
Were never nude and calm like a great door,

And never will be perfect like the fountains;
We live in freedom by necessity,
A mountain people dwelling among mountains. *1939*

LAW LIKE LOVE

Law, say the gardeners, is the sun,
Law is the one
All gardeners obey
To-morrow, yesterday, to-day.

Law is the wisdom of the old,
The impotent grandfathers shrilly scold;
The grandchildren put out a treble tongue,
Law is the senses of the young.

Law, says the priest with a priestly look,
Expounding to an unpriestly people,
Law is the words in my priestly book,
Law is my pulpit and my steeple.

Law, says the judge as he looks down his nose,
Speaking clearly and most severely,
Law is as I've told you before,
Law is as you know I suppose,
Law is but let me explain it once more,
Law is The Law.

Yet law-abiding scholars write:
Law is neither wrong nor right,
Law is only crimes

Punished by places and by times,
Law is the clothes men wear
Anytime, anywhere,
Law is Good morning and Good night.

Others say, Law is our Fate;
Others say, Law is our State;
Others say, others say
Law is no more
Law has gone away.

And always the loud angry crowd
Very angry and very loud
Law is We,
And always the soft idiot softly Me.

If we, dear, know we know no more
Than they about the law,
If I no more than you
Know what we should and should not do
Except that all agree
Gladly or miserably
That the law is
And that all know this,
If therefore thinking it absurd
To identify Law with some other word,
Unlike so many men
I cannot say Law is again,
No more than they can we suppress
The universal wish to guess
Or slip out of our own position
Into an unconcerned condition.
Although I can at least confine
Your vanity and mine
To stating timidly
A timid similarity,
We shall boast anyway:
Like love I say.

Like love we don't know where or why
Like love we can't compel or fly
Like love we often weep
Like love we seldom keep.   1940

SEPTEMBER 1, 1939

I sit in one of the dives
On Fifty-second Street
Uncertain and afraid
As the clever hopes expire
Of a low dishonest decade:
Waves of anger and fear
Circulate over the bright
And darkened lands of the earth,
Obsessing our private lives;
The unmentionable odour of death
Offends the September night.

Accurate scholarship can
Unearth the whole offence
From Luther until now
That has driven a culture mad,
Find what occurred at Linz,
What huge imago made
A psychopathic god:
I and the public know
What all schoolchildren learn,
Those to whom evil is done
Do evil in return.

Exiled Thucydides knew
All that a speech can say
About Democracy,
And what dictators do,
The elderly rubbish they talk
To an apathetic grave;
Analysed all in his book,
The enlightenment driven away,
The habit-forming pain,
Mismanagement and grief:
We must suffer them all again.

Into this neutral air
Where blind skyscrapers use
Their full height to proclaim
The strength of Collective Man,

Each language pours its vain
Competitive excuse:
But who can live for long
In an euphoric dream;
Out of the mirror they stare,
Imperialism's face
And the international wrong.

Faces along the bar
Cling to their average day:
The lights must never go out,
The music must always play,
All the conventions conspire
To make this fort assume
The furniture of home;
Lest we should see where we are,
Lost in a haunted wood,
Children afraid of the night
Who have never been happy or good.

The windiest militant trash
Important Persons shout
Is not so crude as our wish:
What mad Nijinsky wrote
About Diaghilev
Is true of the normal heart;
For the error bred in the bone
Of each woman and each man
Craves what it cannot have,
Not universal love
But to be loved alone.

From the conservative dark
Into the ethical life
The dense commuters come,
Repeating their morning vow;
"I *will* be true to the wife,
I'll concentrate more on my work,"
And helpless governors wake
To resume their compulsory game:
Who can release them now,
Who can reach the deaf,
Who can speak for the dumb?

All I have is a voice
To undo the folded lie,
The romantic lie in the brain
Of the sensual man-in-the-street
And the lie of Authority
Whose buildings grope the sky:
There is no such thing as the State
And no one exists alone;
Hunger allows no choice
To the citizen or the police;
We must love one another or die.

Defenceless under the night
Our world in stupor lies;
Yet, dotted everywhere,
Ironic points of light
Flash out wherever the Just
Exchange their messages:
May I, composed like them
Of Eros and of dust,
Beleaguered by the same
Negation and despair,
Show an affirming flame.   *1940*

THE CAPITAL

Quarter of pleasures where the rich are always waiting,
Waiting expensively for miracles to happen,
O little restaurant where the lovers eat each other,
Café where exiles have established a malicious village;

You with your charm and your apparatus have abolished
The strictness of winter and the spring's compulsion;
Far from your lights the outraged punitive father,
The dullness of mere obedience here is apparent.

Yet with orchestras and glances, O, you betray us
To belief in our infinite powers; and the innocent
Unobservant offender falls in a moment
Victim to the heart's invisible furies.

In unlighted streets you hide away the appalling;
Factories where lives are made for a temporary use

Like collars or chairs, rooms where the lonely are battered
Slowly like pebbles into fortuitous shapes.

But the sky you illumine, your glow is visible far
Into the dark countryside, the enormous, the frozen,
Where, hinting at the forbidden like a wicked uncle,
Night after night to the farmer's children you beckon.

1940

OUR BIAS

The hour-glass whispers to the lion's paw,
The clock-towers tell the gardens day and night,
How many errors Time has patience for,
How wrong they are in being always right.

Yet Time, however loud its chimes or deep,
However fast its falling torrent flows,
Has never put the lion off his leap
Nor shaken the assurance of the rose.

For they, it seems, care only for success:
While we choose words according to their sound
And judge a problem by its awkwardness;

And Time with us was always popular.
When have we not preferred some going round
To going straight to where we are?   *1940*

MUSÉE DES BEAUX ARTS

About suffering they were never wrong,
The Old Masters: how well they understood
Its human position; how it takes place
While someone else is eating or opening a window or just walking dully
    along;
How, when the aged are reverently, passionately waiting
For the miraculous birth, there always must be
Children who did not specially want it to happen, skating
On a pond at the edge of the wood:
They never forgot
That even the dreadful martyrdom must run its course
Anyhow in a corner, some untidy spot

Where the dogs go on with their doggy life and the torturer's horse
Scratches its innocent behind on a tree.

In Breughel's *Icarus*, for instance: how everything turns away
Quite leisurely from the disaster; the ploughman may
Have heard the splash, the forsaken cry,
But for him it was not an important failure; the sun shone
As it had to on the white legs disappearing into the green
Water; and the expensive delicate ship that must have seen
Something amazing, a boy falling out of the sky,
Had somewhere to get to and sailed calmly on.   1940

IN MEMORY OF W. B. YEATS

I

He disappeared in the dead of winter:
The brooks were frozen, the airports almost deserted,
And snow disfigured the public statues;
The mercury sank in the mouth of the dying day.
O all the instruments agree
The day of his death was a dark cold day.

Far from his illness
The wolves ran on through the evergreen forests,
The peasant river was untempted by the fashionable quays;
By mourning tongues
The death of the poet was kept from his poems.

But for him it was his last afternoon as himself,
An afternoon of nurses and rumours;
The provinces of his body revolted,
The current of his feeling failed: he became his admirers.

Now he is scattered among a hundred cities
And wholly given over to unfamiliar affections;
To find his happiness in another kind of wood
And be punished under a foreign code of conscience.
The words of a dead man
Are modified in the guts of the living.

But in the importance and noise of to-morrow
When the brokers are roaring like beasts on the floor of the Bourse,
And the poor have the sufferings to which they are fairly accustomed,

And each in the cell of himself is almost convinced of his freedom;
A few thousand will think of this day
As one thinks of a day when one did something slightly unusual.

O all the instruments agree
The day of his death was a dark cold day.

II

You were silly like us: your gift survived it all;
The parish of rich women, physical decay,
Yourself; mad Ireland hurt you into poetry.
Now Ireland has her madness and her weather still,
For poetry makes nothing happen: it survives
In the valley of its saying where executives
Would never want to tamper; it flows south
From ranches of isolation and the busy griefs,
Raw towns that we believe and die in; it survives,
A way of happening, a mouth.

III

Earth, receive an honored guest;
William Yeats is laid to rest:
Let the Irish vessel lie
Emptied of its poetry.

Time that is intolerant
Of the brave and innocent,
And indifferent in a week
To a beautiful physique,

Worships language and forgives
Everyone by whom it lives;
Pardons cowardice, conceit,
Lays its honors at their feet.

Time that with this strange excuse
Pardoned Kipling and his views,
And will pardon Paul Claudel,
Pardons him for writing well.

In the nightmare of the dark
All the dogs of Europe bark,

And the living nations wait,
Each sequestered in its hate;

Intellectual disgrace
Stares from every human face,
And the seas of pity lie
Locked and frozen in each eye.

Follow, poet, follow right
To the bottom of the night,
With your unconstraining voice
Still persuade us to rejoice;

With the farming of a verse
Make a vineyard of the curse,
Sing of human unsuccess
In a rapture of distress;

In the deserts of the heart
Let the healing fountain start,
In the prison of his days
Teach the free man how to praise.
                                    1940

THE PRESUMPTUOUS

They noticed that virginity was needed
To trap the unicorn in every case,
But not that, of those virgins who succeeded,
A high percentage had an ugly face.

The hero was as daring as they thought him,
But his peculiar boyhood missed them all;
The angel of a broken leg had taught him
The right precautions to avoid a fall.

So in presumption they set forth alone
On what, for them, was not compulsory:
And stuck halfway to settle in some cave
With desert lions to domesticity;

Or turned aside to be absurdly brave,
And met the ogre and were turned to stone.
                                    1941

VOCATION

Incredulous, he stared at the amused
Official writing down his name among
Those whose request to suffer was refused.

The pen ceased scratching: though he came too late
To join the martyrs, there was still a place
Among the tempters for a caustic tongue

To test the resolution of the young
With tales of the small failings of the great,
And shame the eager with ironic praise.

Though mirrors might be hateful for a while,
Women and books should teach his middle age
The fencing wit of an informal style
To keep the silences at bay and cage
His pacing manias in a worldly smile.   *1941*

THE USEFUL

The over-logical fell for the witch
Whose argument converted him to stone;
Thieves rapidly absorbed the over-rich;
The over-popular went mad alone,
And kisses brutalised the over-male.

As agents their effectiveness soon ceased;
Yet, in proportion as they seemed to fail,
Their instrumental value was increased
To those still able to obey their wish.

By standing stones the blind can feel their way,
Wild dogs compel the cowardly to fight,
Beggars assist the slow to travel light,
And even madmen manage to convey
Unwelcome truths in lonely gibberish.   *1941*

PRIME

Simultaneously, as soundlessly,
Spontaneously, suddenly

As, at the vaunt of the dawn, the kind
   Gates of the body fly open
To its world beyond, the gates of the mind,
   The horn gate and the ivory gate
Swing to, swing shut, instantaneously
   Quell the nocturnal rummage
Of its rebellious fronde, ill-favored,
   Ill-natured and second-rate,
Disenfranchised, widowed and orphaned
   By an historical mistake:
Recalled from the shades to be a seeing being,
   From absence to be on display,
Without a name or history I wake
   Between my body and the day.

Holy this moment, wholly in the right,
   As, in complete obedience
To the light's laconic outcry, next
   As a sheet, near as a wall,
Out there as a mountain's poise of stone,
   The world is present, about,
And I know that I am, here, not alone
   But with a world, and rejoice
Unvexed, for the will has still to claim
   This adjacent arm as my own.
The memory to name me, resume
   Its routine of praise and blame,
And smiling to me is this instant while
   Still the day is intact and I
The Adam sinless in our beginning,
   Adam still previous to any act.

I draw breath; that is of course to wish
   No matter what to be wise
To be different to die and the cost
   No matter how is Paradise
Lost of course and myself owing a death:
   The eager ridge, the steady sea,
The flat roofs of the fishing village
   Still asleep in its bunny,
Though as fresh and sunny still are not friends
   But things to hand, this ready flesh
No honest equal but my accomplice now

My assassin to be and my name
Stands for my historical share of care
For a lying self-made city,
Afraid of our living task, the dying
Which the coming day will ask.   *1951*

IN PRAISE OF LIMESTONE

If it form the one landscape that we the inconstant ones
    Are consistently homesick for, this is chiefly
Because it dissolves in water. Mark these rounded slopes
    With their surface fragrance of thyme and beneath
A secret system of caves and conduits; hear these springs
    That spurt out everywhere with a chuckle
Each filling a private pool for its fish and carving
    Its own little ravine whose cliffs entertain
The butterfly and the lizard; examine this region
    Of short distances and definite places:
What could be more like Mother or a fitter background
    For her son, the flirtatious male who lounges
Against a rock in the sunlight, never doubting
    That for all his faults he is loved, whose works are but
Extensions of his power to charm? From weathered outcrop
    To hill-top temple, from appearing waters to
Conspicuous fountains, from a wild to a formal vineyard,
    Are ingenious but short steps that a child's wish
To receive more attention than his brothers, whether
    By pleasing or teasing, can easily take.

Watch, then, the band of rivals as they climb up and down
    Their steep stone gennels in twos and threes, sometimes
Arm in arm, but never, thank God, in step; or engaged
    On the shady side of a square at midday in
Voluble discourse, knowing each other too well to think
    There are any important secrets, unable
To conceive a god whose temper-tantrums are moral
    And not to be pacified by a clever line
Or a good lay: for, accustomed to a stone that responds,
    They have never had to veil their faces in awe
Of a crater whose blazing fury could not be fixed;
    Adjusted to the local needs of valleys
Where everything can be touched or reached by walking,
    Their eyes have never looked into infinite space

Through the lattice-work of a nomad's comb; born lucky,
    Their legs have never encountered the fungi
And insects of the jungle, the montrous forms and lives
    With which we have nothing, we like to hope, in common.
So, when one of them goes to the bad, the way his mind works
    Remains comprehensible: to become a pimp
Or deal in fake jewellery or ruin a fine tenor voice
    For effects that bring down the house could happen to all
But the best and the worst of us . . .
                                        That is why, I suppose,
    The best and worst never stayed here long but sought
Immoderate soils where the beauty was not so external,
    The light less public and the meaning of life
Something more than a mad camp. "Come!" cried the granite wastes,
    "How evasive is your humour, how accidental
Your kindest kiss, how permanent is death." (Saints-to-be
    Slipped away sighing.) "Come!" purred the clays and gravels.
"On our plains there is room for armies to drill; rivers
    Wait to be tamed and slaves to construct you a tomb
In the grand manner: soft as the earth is mankind and both
    Need to be altered." (Intendent Caesars rose and
Left, slamming the door.) But the really reckless were fetched
    By an older colder voice, the oceanic whisper:
"I am the solitude that asks and promises nothing;
    That is how I shall set you free. There is no love;
There are only the various envies, all of them sad."

    They were right, my dear, all those voices were right
And still are; this land is not the sweet home that it looks,
    Nor its peace the historical calm of a site
Where something was settled once and for all: A backward
    And delapidated province, connected
To the big busy world by a tunnel, with a certain
    Seedy appeal, is that all it is now? Not quite:
It has a worldly duty which in spite of itself
    It does not neglect, but calls into question
All the Great Powers assume; it disturbs our rights. The poet,
    Admired for his earnest habit of calling
The sun the sun, his mind Puzzle, is made uneasy
    By these solid statues which so obviously doubt
His antimythological myth; and these gamins,
    Pursuing the scientist down the tiled colonnade
With such lively offers, rebuke his concern for Nature's

Remotest aspects: I, too, am reproached, for what
And how much you know. Not to lose time, not to get caught,
  Not to be left behind, not, please! to resemble
The beasts who repeat themselves, or a thing like water
  Or stone whose conduct can be predicted, these
Are our Common Prayer, whose greatest comfort is music
  Which can be made anywhere, is invisible,
And does not smell. In so far as we have to look forward
  To death as a fact, no doubt we are right: but if
Sins can be forgiven, if bodies rise from the dead,
  These modifications of matter into
Innocent athletes and gesticulating fountains,
  Made solely for pleasure, make a further point:
The blessed will not care what angle they are regarded from,
  Having nothing to hide. Dear, I know nothing of
Either, but when I try to imagine a faultless love
  Or the life to come, what I hear is the murmur
Of underground streams, what I see is a limestone landscape.   *1951*

Louis MacNeice

BIRMINGHAM

Smoke from the train-gulf hid by hoardings blunders upward, the
    brakes of cars
Pipe as the policeman pivoting round raises his flat hand, bars
With his figure of a monolith Pharaoh the queue of fidgety machines
(Chromium dogs on the bonnet, faces behind the triplex screens).
Behind him the streets run away between the proud glass of shops,
Cubical scent-bottles artificial legs arctic foxes and electric mops,
But beyond this centre the slumward vista thins like a diagram:
There, unvisited, are Vulcan's forges who doesn't care a tinker's damn.
Splayed outwards through the suburbs houses, houses for rest
Seducingly rigged by the builder, half-timbered houses with lips pressed
So tightly and eyes staring at the traffic through bleary haws
And only a six-inch grip of the racing earth in their concrete claws;
In these houses men as in a dream pursue the Platonic Forms
With wireless and cairn terriers and gadgets approximating to the fickle
    norms
And endeavour to find God and score one over the neighbour
By climbing tentatively upward on jerry-built beauty and sweated
    labour.
The lunch hour: the shops empty, shopgirls' faces relax
Diaphanous as green glass, empty as old almanacs
As incoherent with ticketed gewgaws tiered behind their heads
As the Burne-Jones windows in St. Philip's broken by crawling leads;
Insipid color, patches of emotion, Saturday thrills
(This theatre is sprayed with "June")—the gutter take our old playbills,
Next week-end it is likely in the heart's funfair we shall pull
Strong enough on the handle to get back our money; or at any rate it is
    possible.
On shining lines the trams like vast sarcophagi move
Into the sky, plum after sunset, merging to duck's egg, barred with
    mauve
Zeppelin clouds, and Pentecost-like the cars' headlights bud
Out from sideroads and the traffic signals, crème-de-menthe or bull's
    blood,

Tell one to stop, the engine gently breathing, or to go on
To where like black pipes of organs in the frayed and fading zone
Of the West the factory chimneys on sullen sentry will all night wait
To call, in the harsh morning, sleep-stupid faces through the daily gate.

1933, 1935

MUSEUMS

Museums offer us, running from among the buses,
A centrally heated refuge, parquet floors and sarcophaguses,
Into whose tall fake porches we hurry without a sound
Like a beetle under a brick that lies, useless, on the ground.
Warmed and cajoled by the silence the cowed cypher revives,
Mirrors himself in the cases of pots, paces himself by marble lives,
Makes believe it was he that was the glory that was Rome,
Soft on his cheek the nimbus of other people's martyrdom,
And then returns to the street, his mind an arena where sprawls
Any number of consumptive Keatses and dying Gauls.

1933, 1935

NATURE MORTE

(Even so it is not so easy to be dead)

As tnose who are not athletic at breakfast day by day
Employ and enjoy the sinews of others vicariously,
Shielded by the upheld journal from their dream-puncturing wives
And finding in the printed word a multiplication of their lives,
So we whose senses give us things misfelt and misheard
Turn also, for our adjustment, to the pretentious word
Which stabilizes the light on the sun-fondled trees
And, by photographing our ghosts, claims to put us at our ease;
Yet even so, no matter how solid and staid we contrive
Our reconstructions, even a still life is alive
And in your Chardin the appalling unrest of the soul
Exudes from the dried fish and the brown jug and the bowl.

1933, 1935

AUGUST

The shutter of time darkening ceaselessly
Has whisked away the foam of may and elder
And I realize how now, as every year before,
Once again the gay months have eluded me.

For the mind, by nature stagey, welds its frame
Tomb-like around each little world of a day;
We jump from picture to picture and cannot follow
The living curve that is breathlessly the same.

While the lawn-mower sings moving up and down
Spirting its little fountain of vivid green,
I, like Poussin, make a still-bound fete of us
Suspending every noise, of insect or machine.

Garlands at a set angle that do not slip,
Theatrically (and as if for ever) grace
You and me and the stone god in the garden
And Time who also is shown with a stone face.

But all this is a dilettante's lie,
Time's face is not stone nor still his wings,
Our mind, being dead, wishes to have time die
For we being ghosts cannot catch hold of things.

1933, 1935

ODE

Tonight is so coarse with chocolate
        The wind blowing from Bournville
That I hanker after the Atlantic
        With a frivolous nostalgia
Like that which film-fans feel
        For their celluloid abstractions
The nifty hero and the deathless blonde
        And find escape by proxy
From the eight-hour day or the wheel
        Of work and bearing children.

If God is boundless as the sea or sky
The eye bounds both of them and Him,
We always have the horizon
Not to swim to but to see:
God is seen with shape and limit
More purple towards the rim,
This segment of His infinite extension
Is all the God of Him for me.

And you too, my love, my limit,
So palpable and your hair shot with red—
I do not want a hundred wives or lives
Any more than I want to be too well-read
Or have money like the sand or ability like the hydra's heads
To flicker the tongues of self-engendering power,
I want a sufficient sample, the exact and framed
Balance of definite masses, the islanded hour.

I would pray for that island; mob mania in the air,
I cannot assume their easy bravery
Drugged with a slogan, chewing the old lie
That parallel lines will meet at infinity;
As I walk on the shore of the regular and rounded sea
I would pray off from my son the love of that infinite
Which is too greedy and too obvious; let his Absolute
Like any four-walled house be put up decently.

Let us turn to homeliness,
Born in the middle of May
Let him accumulate, corroborate while he may
The blessedness of fact
Which lives in the dancing atom and the breathing trees
And everywhere except in the fancy of man
Who daubs his slush on the hawthorn and the may.

Let him have five good senses
The feeling for symmetry
And the sense of the magnet,
His mind deft and unflustered
To change gear easily
And let not the blasphemy
Of dusty words deceive him.

May he hit the golden mean
Which contains the seasonal extreme,
May he riot in the diving sun
And die in the crystal dream,
May his good deeds flung forth
Like boomerangs return
To wear around his neck
As beads of definite worth.

May he pick up daintily
The ambiguous joys,
As a bee in May the blossom of fruit
Cross-fertilise his data and distil
From the drum balalaika fiddle and organ
From sun's gunnery splintering glass
More than the twanging dazzle or the dazzling noise.

To get permanence, to hear the personance
Of all the water-gullies and blackbirds' songs
Drained off or died twenty years back
To make his flesh of them and so renounce the mask
Of the sham soul, the cask bobbing empty
On leaden waves, the veneer the years crack.

To ride two horses at once, a foot on each
Tilting outward on space abstract and packed
With the audience of the dead and the unborn,
To pay his debts to each
To beach his boat so that others can use it
To throw his bread on the waters, the best deposit.

That people are lovable is a strange discovery
And there are many conflicting allegiances;
The pedals of a chance bicycle
Make a gold shower turning in the sun,
Trains leave in all directions on wild rails
And for every act determined on and won
There is a possible world denied and lost.

Do not then turn maudlin or weathercock,
We must cut the throat of the hour
That it may not haunt us because our sentiments
Continued its existence to pollute
Its essence; bottled time turns sour upon the sill.
The children play in the park; the ducklings
Rise and scurry on the water, a car
Changes down, the sandwichmen
Move up and down with the never-changing news.
Do not brood too much on the forking paths.

The leaves dark green on top, light green under, seas of green
Had brought him on full flood, the colour laid on in slices

As by a mason's trowel or ice cream in sliders
Bought in dusty streets under the yellow-green beeches,
A little while ago the green was only peppered
But now we gape at a wealthy wave and a tidal tower of green.

Coral azalea and scarlet rhododendron
Syringa and pink horse-chestnut and laburnum
Solid as temples, niched with the song of birds,
Widen the eyes and nostrils, demand homage of words.
And we have to turn from them,
Compose ourselves, fit out an ethic:
Have I anything to hand my son,
Scarab or compass for his journey?

Only so far, so far as I can find, symbols;
No decalogue, no chemical formula;
Unanalysed scent and noise, the fly on the pane,
The tulips banked on the glass-and-black hearse
A memory of a cock crowing in the dark like a curse
The remembered hypnotism of an aeroplane in June—

Watching the cricket from between
Slabs of green and slabs of blue and slowly ladled clouds
We looked at the sky through straw hats,
The sky was turned into black and white small stars.
Then came, southward as always, the angel
His song like the heat dancing on the gravel
High above the bat-chock and the white umpires
Moving south while the clapping of a run turns chill in echo
And his own drone is whittled to the point of a pin
So that dozing boys fumble the ghost of sound.

But this identical sound the then epitome
Of summer's athletic ease and the smell of cut grass
Will sometime be our augury of war
When these tiny flies like nibs will calmly draw our death
A dipping gradient on the graph of Europe
And over the hairy flatnesses of Russia
This sound when we have died will linger to a wisp
And the endless corn wave tiredly.

Humming and buzzing, the bomber and the fly on the pane
And the telephone wires hung on dead pines,

In Ireland once a string of bright-red haws
Hung, thrown up by children, on those wires:
Not to hang so, O God, between your iron spires!
The town-dweller like a rabbit in a greengrocer's
Who was innocent and integral once
Now, red with slit guts, hangs by the heels
Hangs by the heels gut-open against the fog
Between two spires that are not conscious of him.

Therefore let not my son, halving the truth
Be caught between jagged edges;
And let him not falsify the world
By taking it to pieces;
The marriage of Cause and Effect, Form and Content
Let him not part asunder.
Wisdom for him in the time of tulips
Monastic repose, martial élan,
Then the opening mouth a dragon or a voluptuary—
These moments let him retain like limbs
His time not crippled by flaws of faith or memory.

In the Birmingham Market Hall at this time
There are horseshoe wreaths of mauve stock
Fixed with wire and nailed with pale pink roses
The tribute to a life that ran on standard wheels—
May his life be more than this matter of wheels and wire.

I remember all the houses where parents
Have reared their children to be parents
(Cut box and privet and the parrot's voice)
To be clerks to total the flow of alien money
To be florists to design these wreaths and wedding bouquets.

I cannot draw up any code
    There are too many qualifications
Too many asterisk asides
    Too many crosses in the margin
But as others, forgetting the others,
    Run after the nostrums
Of science art and religion
    So would I mystic and maudlin
Dream of the both real and ideal
    Breakers of ocean.
I must put away this drug.

Must become the migrating bird following felt routes
The comet's superficially casual orbit kept
Not self-abandoning to sky-blind chutes
To climb miles and kiss the miles of foam
For nothing is more proud than humbly to accept
And without soaring or swerving win by ignoring
The endlessly curving sea and so come to one's home.

And so come to one's peace while the yellow waves are roaring.

1934, 1935

VENUS' SPEECH

So you think it is all a matter of love?
And what do you think love is a matter of?
Matter is the word for it.
Atoms—permutations, combinations of atoms.
It's not just a fancy ballet, a *fête champêtre*.
The cycle of life demands to be repeated.
You were made by your parents, you must make in return,
You must make children for Death.
Death is a sculptor, you must quarry him marble,
His chisel will find the shape in the blind block.
What you call love is merely an incident;
Wait till you see the end of it.
There is a city beyond this life, no flesh or blood there,
No food in the shops, no fire in the grates, no smoke from the chimneys;
All the people that have ever lived walk there
Renouncing their living,
All the people that have ever loved walk there
Renouncing their loving,
But they do not even think this renunciation
For their brains are solid, of stone,
Their heads and their eyes are of stone,
Being no longer organisms of nature
But final versions of an artist's vision.
For the art of man is supererogation;
Man himself will be a work of art in the end.
Man should not emulate the artist, Death.
Let not man be contriving a frozen beauty;
While he is here and now let him deal in here and now,
Work and fight for meat and love,
Gallant approximation, bravado of defeat.

I am the principle of Unity and Division,
Multiplication by pain,
Spawning of worlds from a discord
Always recurring,
I am the attempt to cover the abyss with grass
And to spangle the grass with flowers
And to put there cattle grazing the grass
And young men picking the flowers,
And to make believe through elaboration of pattern
That life goes on for ever.
Which, thanks to me, is true in a sense.
Which, thanks to me, is true in the world of sense
Though it is not true in the world of precise death,
The world of pure idea, mating statues.
Go to your work, children, the tide is coming in,
The strip of sand is narrow,
You have not much time if you wish to get married,
You have not much time if you wish to build castles.
Blessed are the reckless spendthrifts of vitality
But blessed also are all who last the course,
Blessed are those who endure as a point of etiquette
And blessed are the cynics who carry their cross as a gesture.
Do you remember when you were six years old
The text in the parish church at Christmas,
"Peace on Earth, Goodwill to Men,"
And Christ's lips moving in the stained glass window?
There were no lipreaders present
But I can tell you what he said.
"I come bringing not peace," he said. "I come
Bringing not peace but a sword."
All to their posts. The drum is beating.
Diver, descend. Ploughman, drive your team.
Grapple the bulk of the sea, challenge the flinty soil;
The furrows are there in advance as music is there in the air
Waiting to be realized upon the fiddler's bow.

Chorus

Sleep and wake, sleep and wake,
Sleep to wake but wake to sleep,
And body calling body make
A further body, the insistent task
Of rolling a stone up the steep

Hill of hell, of rolling a stone
Away from the tomb and do not ask
Who comes forth in the dawn alone.   *1937*

THE SUNLIGHT ON THE GARDEN

The sunlight on the garden
Hardens and grows cold,
We cannot cage the minute
Within its nets of gold;
When all is told
We cannot beg for pardon.

Our freedom as free lances
Advances towards its end;
The earth compels, upon it
Sonnets and birds descend;
And soon, my friend,
We shall have no time for dances.

The sky was good for flying
Defying the church bells
And every evil iron
Siren and what it tells:
The earth compels,
We are dying, Egypt, dying

And not expecting pardon,
Hardened in heart anew,
But glad to have sat under
Thunder and rain with you,
And grateful too
For sunlight on the garden.
                          1937, 1938

JUNE THUNDER

The Junes were free and full, driving through tiny
Roads, the mudguards brushing the cowparsley,
Through fields of mustard and under boldly embattled
    Mays and chestnuts

Or between beeches verdurous and voluptuous
Or where broom and gorse beflagged the chalkland—

All the flare and gusto of the unenduring
   Joys of a season

Now returned but I note as more appropriate
To the maturer moods impending thunder
With an indigo sky and the garden hushed except for
   The treetops moving.

Then the curtains in my room blow suddenly inward,
The shrubbery rustles, birds fly heavily homeward,
The white flowers fade to nothing on the trees and rain comes
   Down like a dropscene.

Now there comes the catharsis, the cleansing downpour
Breaking the blossoms of our overdated fancies
Our old sentimentality and whimsicality
   Loves of the morning.

Blackness at half-past eight, the night's precursor,
Clouds like falling masonry and lightning's lavish
Annunciation, the sword of the mad archangel
   Flashed from the scabbard.

If only you would come and dare the crystal
Rampart of rain and the bottomless moat of thunder,
If only now you would come I should be happy
   Now if now only.

                                     1937, 1938

LEAVING BARRA

The dazzle on the sea, my darling,
Leads from the western channel
A carpet of brilliance taking
My leave for ever of the island.

I never shall visit that island
Again with its easy tempo—
The seal sunbathing, the circuit
Of gulls on the wing for garbage.

I go to a different garbage
And scuffle for scraps of notice,

Pretend to ignore the stigma
That stains my life and my leisure.

For fretful even in leisure
I fidget for different values,
Restless as a gull and haunted
By a hankering after Atlantis.

I do not know that Atlantis
Unseen and uncomprehended,
Dimly divined but keenly
Felt with a phantom hunger.

If only I could crush the hunger
If only I could lay the phantom
Then I should no doubt be happy
Like a fool or a dog or a buddha.

O the self-abnegation of Buddha
The belief that is disbelieving
The denial of chiaroscuro
Not giving a damn for existence!

But I would cherish existence
Loving the beast and the bubble
Loving the rain and the rainbow,
Considering philosophy alien.

For all the religions are alien
That allege that life is a fiction,
And when we agree in denial
The cock crows in the morning.

If only I could wake in the morning
And find I had learned the solution,
Wake with the knack of knowledge
Who as yet have only an inkling.

Though some facts foster the inkling—
The beauty of the moon and music,
The routine courage of the worker,
The gay endurance of women,

And you who to me among women
Stand for so much that I wish for,
I thank you, my dear, for the example
Of living in tune and moving.

For few are able to keep moving,
They drag and flag in the traffic;
While you are alive beyond question
Like the dazzle on the sea, my darling.

1937, 1938

From AUTUMN JOURNAL

III

August is nearly over, the people
    Back from holiday are tanned
With blistered thumbs and a wallet of snaps and a little
    Joie de vivre which is contraband;
Whose stamina is enough to face the annual
    Wait for the annual spree,
Whose memories are stamped with specks of sunshine
    Like faded *fleurs de lys*.
Now the till and the typewriter call the fingers,
    The workman gathers his tools
For the eight-hour day but after that the solace
    Of films or football pools
Or of the gossip or cuddle, the moments of self-glory
    Or self-indulgence, blinkers on the eyes of doubt,
The blue smoke rising and the brown lace sinking
    In the empty glass of stout.
Most are accepters, born and bred to harness,
    And take things as they come,
But some refusing harness and more who are refused it
    Would pray that another and a better Kingdom come,
Which now is sketched in the air or travestied in slogans
    Written in chalk or tar on stucco or plaster-board
But in time may find its body in men's bodies,
    Its law and order in their hearts' accord,
Where skill will no longer languish nor energy be trammelled
    To competition and graft,
Exploited in subservience but not allegiance
    To an utterly lost and daft

System that gives a few at fancy prices
  Their fancy lives
While ninety-nine in the hundred who never attend the banquet
  Must wash the grease of ages off the knives.
And now the tempter whispers "But you also
  Have the slave-owner's mind,
Would like to sleep on a mattress of easy profits,
  To snap your fingers or a whip and find
Servants or houris ready to wince and flatter
  And build with their degradation your self-esteem;
What you want is not a world of the free in function
  But a niche at the top, the skimmings of the cream."
And I answer that that is largely so for habit makes me
  Think victory for one implies another's defeat,
That freedom means the power to order, and that in order
  To preserve the values dear to the élite
The élite must remain a few. It is so hard to imagine
  A world where the many would have their chance without
A fall in the standard of intellectual living
  And nothing left that the highbrow cared about.
Which fears must be suppressed. There is no reason for thinking
  That, if you give a chance to people to think or live,
The arts of thought or life will suffer and become rougher
  And not return more than you could ever give.
And now I relapse to sleep, to dreams perhaps and reaction
  Where I shall play the gangster or the sheikh,
Kill for the love of killing, make the world my sofa,
  Unzip the women and insult the meek.
Which fantasies no doubt are due to my private history,
  Matter for the analyst,
But the final cure is not in his past-dissecting fingers
  But in a future of action, the will and fist
Of those who abjure the luxury of self-pity,
  And prefer to risk a movement without being sure
If movement would be better or worse in a hundred
  Years or a thousand when their heart is pure.
None of our hearts are pure, we always have mixed motives,
  Are self deceivers, but the worst of all
Deceits is to murmur "Lord, I am not worthy"
  And, lying easy, turn your face to the wall.
But may I cure that habit, look up and outwards
  And may my feet follow my wider glance
First no doubt to stumble, then to walk with the others
  And in the end—with time and luck—to dance.

IX

Now we are back to normal, now the mind is
  Back to the even tenor of the usual day
Skidding no longer across the uneasy camber
  Of the nightmare way.
We are safe though others have crashed the railings
  Over the river ravine; their wheel-tracks carve the bank
But after the event all we can do is argue
  And count the widening ripples where they sank.
October comes with rain whipping around the ankles
  In waves of white at night
And filling the raw clay trenches (the parks of London
  Are a nasty sight).
In a week I return to work, lecturing, coaching,
  As impresario of the Ancient Greeks
Who wore the chiton and lived on fish and olives
  And talked philosophy or smut in cliques;
Who believed in youth and did not gloze the unpleasant
  Consequences of age;
What is life, one said, or what is pleasant
  Once you have turned the page
Of love? The days grow worse, the dice are loaded
  Against the living man who pays in tears for breath;
Never to be born was the best, call no man happy
  This side death.
Conscious—long before Engels—of necessity
  And therein free
They plotted out their life with truism and humour
  Between the jealous heaven and the callous sea.
And Pindar sang the garland of wild olive
  And Alcibiades lived from hand to mouth
Double-crossing Athens, Persia, Sparta,
  And many died in the city of plague, and many of drouth
In Sicilian quarries, and many by the spear and arrow
  And many more who told their lies too late
Caught in the eternal factions and reactions
  Of the city-state.
And free speech shivered on the pikes of Macedonia
  And later on the swords of Rome
And Athens became a mere university city
  And the goddess born of the foam
Became the kept hetaera, heroine of Menander,

And the philosopher narrowed his focus, confined
His efforts to putting his own soul in order
    And keeping a quiet mind.
And for a thousand years they went on talking,
    Making such apt remarks,
A race no longer of heroes but of professors
    And crooked business men and secretaries and clerks;
Who turned out dapper little elegiac verses
    On the ironies of fate, the transience of all
Affections, carefully shunning an over-statement
    But working the dying fall.
The Glory that was Greece: put it in a syllabus, grade it
    Page by page
To train the mind or even to point a moral
    For the present age:
Models of logic and lucidity, dignity, sanity,
    The golden mean between opposing ills
Though there were exceptions of course but only exceptions—
    The bloody Bacchanals on the Thracian hills.
So the humanist in his room with Jacobean panels
    Chewing his pipe and looking on a lazy quad
Chops the Ancient World to turn a sermon
    To the greater glory of God.
But I can do nothing so useful or so simple;
    These dead are dead.
And when I should remember the paragons of Hellas
    I think instead
Of the crooks, the adventurers, the opportunists,
    The careless athletes and the fancy boys,
The hair-splitters, the pedants, the hard-boiled sceptics
    And the Agora and the noise
Of the demagogues and the quacks; and the women pouring
    Libations over graves
And the trimmers at Delphi and the dummies at Sparta and lastly
    I think of the slaves.
And how one can imagine oneself among them
    I do not know;
It was all so unimaginably different
    And all so long ago.

XII

These days are misty, insulated, mute
    Like a faded tapestry and the soft pedal

Is down and the yellow leaves are falling down
    And we hardly have the heart to meddle
Any more with personal ethics or public calls;
    People have not recovered from the crisis,
Their faces are far away, the tone of the words
    Belies their thesis.
For they say that now it is time unequivocally to act,
    To let the pawns be taken,
That criticism, a virtue previously,
    Now can only weaken
And that when we go to Rome
    We must do as the Romans do, cry out together
For bread and circuses; put on your togas now
    For this is Roman weather.
Circuses of death and from the topmost tiers
    A cataract of goggling, roaring faces;
On the arena sand
    Those who are about to die try out their paces.
Now it is night, a cold mist creeps, the night
    Is still and damp and lonely;
Sitting by the fire it is hard to realise
    That the legions wait at the gates and that there is only
A little time for rest though not by rights for rest,
    Rather for whetting the will, for calculating
A compromise between necessity and wish,
    Apprenticed late to learn the trade of hating.
Remember the sergeant barking at bayonet practice
    When you were small;
To kill a dummy you must act a dummy
    Or you cut no ice at all.
Now it is morning again, the 25th of October,
    In a white fog the cars have yellow lights;
The chill creeps up the wrists, the sun is sallow,
    The silent hours grow down like stalactites.
And reading Plato talking about his Forms
    To damn the artist touting round his mirror,
I am glad that I have been left the third best bed
    And live in a world of error.
His world of capital initials, of transcendent
    Ideas is too bleak;
For me there remain to all intents and purposes
    Seven days in the week
And no one Tuesday is another and you destroy it
    If you subtract the difference and relate

It merely to the Form of Tuesday. This is Tuesday
    The 25th of October, 1938.
Aristotle was better who watched the insect breed,
    The natural world develop,
Stressing the function, scrapping the Form in Itself,
    Taking the horse from the shelf and letting it gallop.
Education gives us too many labels
    And clichés, cuts too many Gordian knots;
Trains us to keep the roads nor reconnoitre
    Any of the beauty-spots or danger-spots.
Not that I would rather be a peasant; the Happy Peasant
    Like the Noble Savage is a myth;
I do not envy the self-possession of an elm-tree
    Nor the aplomb of a granite monolith.
All that I would like to be is human, having a share
    In a civilised, articulate and well-adjusted
Community where the mind is given its due
    But the body is not distrusted.
As it is, the so-called humane studies
    May lead to cushy jobs
But leave the men who land them spiritually bankrupt
    Intellectual snobs.
Not but what I am glad to have my comforts,
    Better authentic mammon than a bogus god;
If it were not for Lit. Hum. I might be climbing
    A ladder with a hod.
And seven hundred a year
    Will pay the rent and the gas and the 'phone and the grocer;
(The Emperor takes his seat beneath the awning,
    Those who are about to die . . .) Come, pull the curtains closer.

From XXIV

    Sleep serene, avoid the backward
        Glance; go forward, dreams, and do not halt
    (Behind you in the desert stands a token
        Of doubt—a pillar of salt).
    Sleep, the past, and wake, the future,
        And walk out promptly through the open door;
    But you, my coward doubts, may go on sleeping,
        You need not wake again—not any more.
    The New Year comes with bombs, it is too late
        To dose the dead with honourable intentions:
    If you have honour to spare, employ it on the living;
        The dead are dead as 1938.

Sleep to the noise of running water
    To-morrow to be crossed, however deep;
This is no river of the dead or Lethe,
    To-night we sleep
On the banks of Rubicon—the die is cast;
    There will be time to audit
The accounts later, there will be sunlight later
    And the equation will come out at last.

1938, 1939

PROGNOSIS

Goodbye, Winter,
The days are getting longer,
The tea-leaf in the teacup
Is herald of a stranger.

Will he bring me business
Or will he bring me gladness
Or will he come for cure
Of his own sickness?

With a pedlar's burden
Walking up the garden
Will he come to beg
Or will he come to bargain?

Will he come to pester,
To cringe or to bluster,
A promise in his palm
Or a gun in his holster?

Will his name be John
Or will his name be Jonah
Crying to repent
On the Island of Iona?

Will his name be Jason
Looking for a seaman
Or a mad crusader
Without rhyme or reason?

What will be his message—
War or work or marriage?

News as new as dawn
Or an old adage?

Will he give a champion
Answer to my question
Or will his words be dark
And his ways evasion?

Will his name be Love
And all his talk be crazy?
Or will his name be Death
And his message easy?
                    Spring 1939, 1940

A TOAST

The slurred and drawled and crooning sounds,
The blurred and suave and sidling smells,
The webs of dew, the bells of buds,
The sun going down in crimson suds—
    This is on me and these are yours.

The bland and sculped and urgent beasts,
The here and there and nowhere birds,
The tongues of fire, the words of foam,
The curdling stars in the night's dome—
    This is on me and these are yours.

The face and grace and muscle of man,
The balance of his body and mind,
Who keeps a trump behind his brain
Till instinct flicks it out again—
    This is on me and these are yours.

The courage of eyes, the craft of hands,
The gay feet, the pulse of hope,
The will that flings a rope—though hard—
To catch the future off its guard—
    This is on me and these are yours.

The luck and pluck and plunge of blood,
The wealth and spilth and sport of breath,
And sleep come down like death above

The fever and the peace of love—
This is on me and these are yours.

May 1939, 1940

ENTIRELY

If we could get the hang of it entirely
    It would take too long;
All we know is the splash of words in passing
    And falling twigs of song,
And when we try to eavesdrop on the great
    Presences it is rarely
That by a stroke of luck we can appropriate
    Even a phrase entirely.

If we could find our happiness entirely
    In somebody else's arms
We should not fear the spears of the spring nor the city's
    Yammering fire alarms
But, as it is, the spears each year go through
    Our flesh and almost hourly
Bell or siren banishes the blue
    Eyes of Love entirely.

And if the world were black or white entirely
    And all the charts were plain
Instead of a mad weir of tigerish waters,
    A prism of delight and pain,
We might be surer where we wished to go
    Or again we might be merely
Bored but in brute reality there is no
    Road that is right entirely.   *1940, 1940*

Kathleen Raine

LYRIC

A bird sings on a matin tree
"Once such a bird was I."

The sky's gaze says
"Remember your mother."

Seas, trees and voices cry
"Nature is your nature."

I reply
"I am what is not what I was.
Seas, trees, and bird, alas!
Sea, tree, and bird was I."

1943

INVOCATION

There is a poem on the way,
there is a poem all round me,
the poem is in the near future,
the poem is in the upper air
above the foggy atmosphere
it hovers, a spirit
that I would make incarnate.
Let my body sweat
let snakes torment my breast
my eyes be blind, ears deaf, hands distraught
mouth parched, uterus cut out,
belly slashed, back lashed,
tongue slivered into thongs of leather
rain stones inserted in my breasts,
head severed,

if only the lips may speak,
if only the god will come.   *1943*

THE CRYSTAL SKULL

At the focus of thought there is no face,
the focus of the sun is in crystal with no shadow.
Death of the victim is the power of the god.

Out of the eyes is the focus of love,
the face of love is the sun, that all see,
the skull of the victim is the temple of sight.

The eyes of the victim are the crystal of divination.
Sun clears the colours of life.
The crystal of the skull is the work of the sun.

The stone of my destruction casts no shadow.
The sun kills perfectly with the stroke of noon.
The clarity of the crystal is the atonement of the god.

The perfection of man is the pride of death,
the crystal skull is the perpetuity of life.
The power of the god is the taking of love.

The perfection of light is the destruction of the world,
death and love turn the faces of day and night.
The illumination of the skull is the joy of the god.   *1943*

IN TIME

The beautiful rain falls, the unheeded angel
lies in the street, spreadeagled under the footfall
that from the divine face wears away the smile

whose tears run in the gutter, melting where
the stationary cars wait for departure;
the letter that says Ave is passed over

for at the ever-present place the angel waits,
passes through walls and hoardings, in dark porches
his face, wounded by us, for us and over us watches.
   1943

IN THE BECK

(For Anna Madge)

There is a fish, that quivers in the pool,
itself a shadow, but its shadow, clear.
Catch it again and again, it still is there.

Against the flowing stream, its life keeps pace
with death—the impulse and the flash of grace
hiding in its stillness, moves, to be motionless.

No net will hold it—always it will return
when the ripples settle, and the sand—
It lives unmoved, equated with the stream,
as flowers are fit for air, man for his dream.

1943

THE HUMAN FORM DIVINE

The human contours are so easily lost,
Only close your eyes and you seem a forest
Of dense vegetation, and the lurking beast

That in the night springs from the cover
Tears with tiger's mouth your living creatures,
A thousand innocent victims without name that suffer.

Science applies its insect-lenses to the form divine
As up the red river (all life comes from the sea)
Swim strange monsters, amoeboid erythrean spawn.

Rock-face of bone, alluvium of cartilage
Remote from man as the surface of the moon
Are vast and unexplored interior desert ranges,

And autonomous cells
Grow like unreaped fields of waving corn.
Air filters through the lungs' fine branches as through trees.

Chemistry dissolves the goddess in the alembic,
Venus the white queen, the universal matrix,
Down to molecular hexagons and carbon-chains,

And the male nerve-impulse, monition of reality,
Conveys the charge, dynamic of non-entity
That sparks across the void *ex nihilo.*

At the extreme of consciousness, prayer
Fixes hands and feet immobile to a chair,
Transmutes all heaven and earth into a globe of air,

And soul streams away out of the top of the head
Like flame in a lamp-glass carried in the draught
Of the celestial fire kindled in the solar plexus.

Oh man, oh Garden of Eden, there is nothing
But the will of love to uphold your seeming world,
To trace in chaos the contours of your beloved form!   1949

THE MOMENT

Never, never again
This moment, never
These slow ripples
Across smooth water,
Never again these
Clouds white and grey
In sky sharp crystalline
Blue as the tern's cry
Shrill in light air
Salt from the ocean,
Sweet from flowers.

Here coincide
The long histories
Of forms recurrent
That meet at a point
And part in a moment,
The rapid waves
Of wind and water
And slower rhythm
Of rock weathering
And land sinking.

In teeming pools
The life cycle
Of brown weed
Is intersecting

The frequencies
Of diverse shells
Each with its variant
Arc or spiral
Spun from a point
In tone and semitone
Of formal octave.

Here come soaring
White gulls
Leisurely wheeling
In air over islands
Sea pinks and salt grass,
Gannet and eider,
Curlew and cormorant
Each a differing
Pattern of ecstasy
Recurring at nodes
In an on-flowing current,
The perpetual species,
Repeated, renewed
By the will of joy
In eggs lodged safe
On perilous ledges.

The sun that rises
Upon one earth
Sets on another.
Swiftly the flowers
Are waxing and waning,
The tall yellow iris
Unfolds its corolla
As primroses wither,
Scrolls of fern
Unroll and midges
Dance for an hour
In the evening air,
The brown moth
From its pupa emerges
And the lark's bones
Fall apart in the grass.

The sun that rose
From the sea this morning
Will never return,
For the broadcast light
That brightens the leaves
And glances on water
Will travel tonight
On its long journey
Out of the universe,
Never this sun,
This world, and never
Again this watcher.   1952

From NORTHUMBRIAN SEQUENCE

So seems the life of man, O King, as a sparrow's flight through the hall when you are sitting at meat in winter-tide, the fire on the hearth, the icy rainstorm without.

The sparrow flies in at one door and tarries for a moment in the light and heat of the hearth-fire, then flies forth into the darkness whence it came.— *Words attributed to an ealdorman, in Bede's account of the conversion of Eadwine, King of Northumberland.*

I

Pure I was before the world began,
I was the violence of wind and wave,
I was the bird before bird ever sang.

I was never still,
I turned upon the axis of my joy,
I was the lonely dancer on the hill,

The rain upon the mountainside,
The rising mist,
I was the sea's unrest.

I wove the web of colour
Before the rainbow,
The intricacy of the flower
Before the leaf grew.

I was the buried ore,
The fossil forest,
I knew the roots of things:

Before death's kingdom
I passed through the grave.

Times out of mind my journey
Circles the universe
And I remain
Before the first day.

IV

Let in the wind
Let in the rain
Let in the moors tonight,

The storm beats on my window-pane,
Night stands at my bed-foot,
Let in the fear,
Let in the pain,
Let in the trees that toss and groan,
Let in the north tonight.

Let in the nameless formless power
That beats upon my door,
Let in the ice, let in the snow,
The banshee howling on the moor,
The bracken-bush on the bleak hillside,
Let in the dead tonight.

The whistling ghost behind the dyke,
The dead that rot in mire,
Let in the thronging ancestors
The unfulfilled desire,
Let in the wraith of the dead earl,
Let in the unborn tonight.

Let in the cold,
Let in the wet,
Let in the loneliness,
Let in the quick,
Let in the dead,
Let in the unpeopled skies.

Oh how can virgin fingers weave
A covering for the void,
How can my fearful heart conceive

Gigantic solitude?
How can a house so small contain
A company so great?
Let in the dark,
Let in the dead,
Let in your love tonight.

Let in the snow that numbs the grave,
Let in the acorn-tree,
The mountain stream and mountain stone,
Let in the bitter sea.

Fearful is my virgin heart
And frail my virgin form,
And must I then take pity on
The raging of the storm
That rose up from the great abyss
Before the earth was made,
That pours the stars in cataracts
And shakes this violent world?

Let in the fire,
Let in the power,
Let in the invading might.

Gentle must my fingers be
And pitiful my heart
Since I must bind in human form
A living power so great,
A living impulse great and wild
That cries about my house
With all the violence of desire
Desiring this my peace.

Pitiful my heart must hold
The lonely stars at rest,
Have pity on the raven's cry
The torrent and the eagle's wing,
The icy water of the tarn
And on the biting blast.

Let in the wound,
Let in the pain,
Let in your child tonight.   *1952*

Stephen Spender

[HE WILL WATCH THE HAWK]

He will watch the hawk with an indifferent eye
      Or pitifully;
Nor on those eagles that so feared him, now
      Will strain his brow;
Weapons men use, stone, sling and strong-thewed bow
      He will not know.
This aristocrat, superb of all instinct,
      With death close linked
Had paced the enormous cloud, almost had won
      War on the sun;
Till now, like Icarus mid-ocean-drowned,
      Hands, wings are found.   *1933*

[ROLLED OVER ON EUROPE]

Rolled over on Europe: the sharp dew frozen to stars
Below us; above our heads, the night
Frozen again to stars; the stars
In pools between our coats; and that charmed moon.
Ah, what supports? What cross draws out our arms,
Heaves up our bodies towards the wind
And hammers us between the mirrored lights?

Only my body is real; which wolves
Are free to oppress and gnaw. Only this rose
My friend laid on my breast, and these few lines
Written from home, are real.   *1933*

[NEVER BEING, BUT ALWAYS AT THE EDGE]

Never being, but always at the edge of Being,
My head,—Death-mask—is brought into the sun.
With shadow pointing finger across cheek,

I move lips for tasting, I move hands for touching,
But never come nearer than touching
Though Spirit lean outward for seeing.
Observing rose, gold, eyes, an admired landscape,
My senses record the act of wishing,
Wishing to be
Rose, gold, landscape or another.
I claim fulfilment in the fact of loving.   *1933*

[YOUR BODY IS STARS]

Your body is stars whose million glitter here:
I am lost among the branches of this sky
Here near my breast, here in my nostrils, here
Where our vast arms like streams of fire lie.

How can this end? My healing fills the night
And hangs its flags in worlds I cannot near.
Our movements range through miles, and when we kiss
The moment widens to enclose the years.

*   *   *

Beholders of the promised dawn of truth,
The explorers of immense and simple lines,
Here is our goal, men cried, but it was lost
Amongst the mountain mists and mountain pines.

So with this face of love, whose breathings are
A mystery shadowed on the desert floor:
The promise hangs, this swarm of stars and flowers,
And then there comes the shutting of a door.   *1933*

[WITHOUT THAT ONCE CLEAR AIM]

Without that once clear aim, the path of flight
To follow for a lifetime through white air,
This century chokes me under roots of night.
I suffer like history in Dark Ages, where
Truth lies in dungeons, too deep for whisper.
We hear of towers long broken off from sight
And tortures and wars, smoky and dark with rumour,
But on Mind's buried thought there falls no light.
Watch me who walk through coiling streets where rain

And fog choke every sigh; round corners of day,
Road-drills explore new areas of pain,
Nor trees reach leaf-lit branches down to play.
The city climbs in horror to my brain,
The writings are my only wings away.   *1933*

[I THINK CONTINUALLY OF THOSE]

I think continually of those who were truly great.
Who, from the womb, remembered the soul's history
Through corridors of light where the hours are suns,
Endless and singing. Whose lovely ambition
Was that their lips, still touched with fire,
Should tell of the Spirit, clothed from head to foot in song.
And who hoarded from the Spring branches
The desires falling across their bodies like blossoms.

What is precious is never to forget
The essential delight of the blood drawn from ageless springs
Breaking through rocks in worlds before our earth.
Never to deny its pleasure in the morning simple light
Nor its grave evening demand for love.
Never to allow gradually the traffic to smother
With noise and fog the flowering of the Spirit.

Near the snow, near the sun, in the highest fields,
See how these names are fêted by the waving grass
And by the streamers of white cloud
And whispers of wind in the listening sky.
The names of those who in their lives fought for life,
Who wore at their hearts the fire's centre.
Born of the sun, they travelled a short while toward the sun
And left the vivid air signed with their honour.   *1933*

THE FUNERAL

Death is another milestone on their way.
With laughter on their lips and with winds blowing round them
They record simply
How this one excelled all others in making driving belts.

This is festivity, it is the time of statistics,
When they record what one unit contributed:

They are glad as they lay him back in the earth
And thank him for what he gave them.

They walk home remembering the straining red flags,
And with pennons of song still fluttering through their blood
They speak of the World State
With its towns like brain centres and its pulsing arteries.

They think how one life hums, revolves and toils,
One cog in a golden singing hive:
Like spark from fire, its task happily achieved,
It falls away quietly.

No more are they haunted by the individual grief
Nor the crocodile tears of European genius,
The decline of a culture
Mourned by scholars who dream of the ghosts of Greek boys.

1933

THE PYLONS

The secret of these hills was stone, and cottages
Of that stone made,
And crumbling roads
That turned on sudden hidden villages.

Now over these small hills they have built the concrete
That trails black wire;
Pylons, those pillars
Bare like nude giant girls that have no secret.

The valley with its gilt and evening look
And the green chestnut
Of customary root
Are mocked dry like the parched bed of a brook.

But far above and far as sight endures
Like whips of anger
With lightning's danger
There runs the quick perspective of the future.

This dwarfs our emerald country by its trek
So tall with prophecy:

Dreaming of cities
Where often clouds shall lean their swan-white neck.

1933

[IN RAILWAY HALLS, ON PAVEMENTS]

In railway halls, on pavements near the traffic,
They beg, their eyes made big by empty staring
And only measuring Time, like the blank clock.

No, I shall wave no tracery of pen-ornament
To make them birds upon my singing-tree:
Time merely drives these lives which do not live
As tides push rotten stuff along the shore.

—There is no consolation, no, none
In the curving beauty of that line
Traced on our graphs through history, where the oppressor
Starves and deprives the poor.

Paint here no draped despairs, no saddening clouds
Where the soul rests, proclaims eternity.
But let the wrong cry out as raw as wounds
This time forgets and never heals, far less transcends.

1933

[NOT PALACES, AN ERA'S CROWN]

Not palaces, an era's crown
Where the mind dwells, intrigues, rests;
Architectural gold-leaved flower
From people ordered like a single mind,
I build. This only what I tell:
It is too late for rare accumulation,
For family pride, for beauty's filtered dusts;
I say, stamping the words with emphasis,
Drink from here energy and only energy,
As from the electric charge of a battery,
To will this Time's change.
Eye, gazelle, delicate wanderer,
Drinker of horizon's fluid line;
Ear that suspends on a chord
The spirit drinking timelessness;
Touch, love, all senses;

Leave your gardens, your singing feasts,
Your dreams of suns circling before our sun,
Of heaven after our world.
Instead, watch images of flashing brass
That strike the outward sense, the polished will
Flag of our purpose which the wind engraves.
No spirit seek here rest. But this: No one
Shall hunger: Man shall spend equally.
Our goal which we compel: Man shall be man.
　　　　That programme of the antique Satan
Bristling with guns on the indented page,
With battleship towering from hilly waves:
For what? Drive of a ruining purpose
Destroying all but its age-long exploiters.
Our programme like this, but opposite,
Death to the killers, bringing light to life.   *1933*

THE EXPRESS

After the first powerful plain manifesto
The black statement of pistons, without more fuss
But gliding like a queen, she leaves the station.
Without bowing and with restrained unconcern
She passes the houses which humbly crowd outside,
The gasworks and at last the heavy page
Of death, printed by gravestones in the cemetery.
Beyond the town there lies the open country
Where, gathering speed, she acquires mystery,
The luminous self-possession of ships on ocean.
It is now she begins to sing—at first quite low
Then loud, and at last with a jazzy madness—
The song of her whistle screaming at curves,
Of deafening tunnels, brakes, innumerable bolts.
And always light, aerial, underneath
Goes the elate meter of her wheels.
Steaming through metal landscape on her lines
She plunges new eras of wild happiness
Where speed throws up strange shapes, broad curves
And parallels clean like the steel of guns.
At last, further than Edinburgh or Rome,
Beyond the crest of the world, she reaches night
Where only a low streamline brightness
Of phosphorus on the tossing hills is white.

Ah, like a comet through flames she moves entranced
Wrapt in her music no bird song, no, nor bough
Breaking with honey buds, shall ever equal. *1933*

THE ROOM ABOVE THE SQUARE

The light in the window seemed perpetual
When you stayed in the high room for me;
It glowed above the trees through leaves
Like my certainty.

The light is fallen and you are hidden
In sunbright peninsulas of the sword:
Torn like leaves through Europe is the peace
That through us flowed.

Now I climb alone to the high room
Above the darkened square
Where among stones and roots the other
Unshattered lovers are. *1939*

THE BOMBED HAPPINESS

Children, who extend their smile of crystal,
And their leaping gold embrace,
And wear their happiness as a frank jewel,
Are forced in the mould of the groaning bull
And engraved with lines on the face.

Their harlequin-striped flesh,
Their blood twisted in rivers of song,
Their flashing, trustful emptiness,
Are trampled by an outer heart that pressed
From the sky right through the coral breast
And kissed the heart and burst.

This timed, exploding heart that breaks
The loved and little hearts, is also one
Splintered through the lungs and wombs
And fragments of squares in the sun,
And crushing the floating, sleeping babe
Into a deeper sleep.

Its victoried drumming enters
Above the limbs of bombed laughter
The body of an expanding State
And throbs there and makes it great,
But nothing nothing can recall
Gaiety buried under these dead years,
Sweet jester and young playing fool
Whose toy was human happiness.   *1939*

TWO KISSES

I wear your kiss like a feather
Laid upon my cheek
While I walk the path where the river
Suggests suggests

Dirt off all the streets
Rotting feet of factories.

Swans and boats and corks ride
Elastic waters
And the eye is carried by the choppy tide
To a shore opposite of opal-green spaces
The ear is belied
By dreams inside the roar outside.
And then the heart in its white sailing pride

Between two sailing swans a light
Stretches on waves, as on your cheek
That other kiss—my life
Waiting for your life to speak.   *1939*

TO A SPANISH POET

(for Manuel Altolaguirre)

You stared out of the window on the emptiness
Of a world exploding:
Stones and rubble thrown upwards in a fountain
Blown to one side by the wind.
Every sensation except being alone
Drained out of your mind.
There was no fixed object for the eye to fix on.

You became a child again
Who sees for the first time how the worst things happen.

Then, stupidly, the stucco pigeon
On the gable roof that was your ceiling,
Parabolized before your window
Uttering (you told me later!) a loud coo.
Alone to your listening self, you told the joke.
Everything in the room broke.
But you remained whole,
Your own image unbroken in your glass soul.

Having heard this all from you, I see you now
—White astonishment haloing irises
Which still retain in their centres
Black laughter of black eyes.
Laughter reverberant through stories
Of an aristocrat lost in the hills near Malaga
Where he had got out of his carriage
And, for a whole week, followed, on foot, a partridge.
Stories of that general, broken-hearted
Because he'd failed to breed a green-eyed bull.

But reading the news, my imagination breeds
The penny-dreadful fear that you are dead.

Well, what of this journalistic dread?

Perhaps it is we—the living—who are dead
We of a world that revolves and dissolves
While we set the steadfast corpse under the earth's lid.
The eyes push irises above the grave
Reaching to the stars, which draw down nearer,
Staring through a rectangle of night like black glass,
Beyond these daylight comedies of falling plaster.

Your heart looks through the breaking ribs—
Oiled axle through revolving spokes.
Unbroken blood of the swift wheel,
You stare through centrifugal bones
Of the revolving and dissolving world.   *1939*

Dylan Thomas

THE FORCE THAT THROUGH THE GREEN FUSE DRIVES THE FLOWER

The force that through the green fuse drives the flower
Drives my green age; that blasts the roots of trees
Is my destroyer.
And I am dumb to tell the crooked rose
My youth is bent by the same wintry fever.

The force that drives the water through the rocks
Drives my red blood; that dries the mouthing streams
Turns mine to wax.
And I am dumb to mouth unto my veins
How at the mountain spring the same mouth sucks.

The hand that whirls the water in the pool
Stirs the quicksand; that ropes the blowing wind
Hauls my shroud sail.
And I am dumb to tell the hanging man
How of my clay is made the hangman's lime.

The lips of time leech to the fountain head;
Love drips and gathers, but the fallen blood
Shall calm her sores.
And I am dumb to tell a weather's wind
How time has ticked a heaven round the stars.

And I am dumb to tell the lover's tomb
How at my sheet goes the same crooked worm.   *1934*

LIGHT BREAKS WHERE NO SUN SHINES

Light breaks where no sun shines;
Where no sea runs, the waters of the heart
Push in their tides;

And, broken ghosts with glow-worms in their heads,
The things of light
File through the flesh where no flesh decks the bones.

A candle in the thighs
Warms youth and seed and burns the seeds of age;
Where no seed stirs,
The fruit of man unwrinkles in the stars,
Bright as a fig;
Where no wax is, the candle shows its hairs.

Dawn breaks behind the eyes;
From poles of skull and toe the windy blood
Slides like a sea;
Nor fenced, nor staked, the gushers of the sky
Spout to the rod
Divining in a smile the oil of tears.

Night in the sockets rounds,
Like some pitch moon, the limit of the globes;
Day lights the bone;
Where no cold is, the skinning gales unpin
The winter's robes;
The film of spring is hanging from the lids.

Light breaks on secret lots,
On tips of thought where thoughts smell in the rain;
When logics die,
The secret of the soil grows through the eye,
And blood jumps in the sun;
Above the waste allotments the dawn halts.   *1934*

AND DEATH SHALL HAVE NO DOMINION

And death shall have no dominion.
Dead men naked they shall be one
With the man in the wind and the west moon;
When their bones are picked clean and the clean bones gone,
They shall have stars at elbow and foot;
Though they go mad they shall be sane,
Though they sink through the sea they shall rise again;
Though lovers be lost love shall not;
And death shall have no dominion.

And death shall have no dominion.
Under the windings of the sea
They lying long shall not die windily;
Twisting on racks when sinews give way,
Strapped to a wheel, yet they shall not break;
Faith in their hands shall snap in two,
And the unicorn evils run them through;
Split all ends up they shan't crack;
And death shall have no dominion.

And death shall have no dominion.
No more may gulls cry at their ears
Or waves break loud on the seashores;
Where blew a flower may a flower no more
Lift its head to the blows of the rain;
Though they be mad and dead as nails,
Heads of the characters hammer through daisies;
Break in the sun till the sun breaks down,
And death shall have no dominion.   *1936*

From *ALTARWISE BY OWL-LIGHT*

I

Altarwise by owl-light in the half-way house
The gentleman lay graveward with his furies;
Abaddon in the hangnail cracked from Adam,
And, from his fork, a dog among the fairies,
The atlas-eater with a jaw for news,
Bit out the mandrake with tomorrow's scream.
Then, penny-eyed, that gentleman of wounds,
Old cock from nowheres and the heaven's egg,
With bones unbuttoned to the half-way winds,
Hatched from the windy salvage on one leg,
Scraped at my cradle in a walking word
That night of time under the Christward shelter,
I am the long world's gentleman, he said,
And share my bed with Capricorn and Cancer.

II

Death is all metaphors, shape in one history;
The child that sucketh long is shooting up,
The planet-ducted pelican of circles
Weans on an artery the gender's strip;

Child of the short spark in a shapeless country
Soon sets alight a long stick from the cradle;
The horizontal cross-bones of Abaddon,
You by the cavern over the black stairs,
Rung bone and blade, the verticals of Adam,
And, manned by midnight, Jacob to the stars.
Hairs of your head, then said the hollow agent,
Are but the roots of nettles and of feathers
Over these groundworks thrusting through a pavement
And hemlock-headed in the wood of weathers.

III

First there was the lamb on knocking knees
And three dead seasons on a climbing grave
That Adam's wether in the flock of horns,
Butt of the tree-tailed worm that mounted Eve,
Horned down with skullfoot and the skull of toes
On thunderous pavements in the garden time;
Rip of the vaults, I took my marrow-ladle
Out of the wrinkled undertaker's van,
And, Rip Van Winkle from a timeless cradle,
Dipped me breast-deep in the descended bone;
The black ram, shuffling of the year, old winter,
Alone alive among his mutton fold,
We rung our weathering changes on the ladder,
Said the antipodes, and twice spring chimed.

IV

What is the metre of the dictionary?
The size of genesis? the short spark's gender?
Shade without shape? the shape of Pharaoh's echo?
(My shape of age nagging the wounded whisper).
Which sixth of wind blew out the burning gentry?
(Questions are hunchbacks to the poker marrow).
What of a bamboo man among your acres?
Corset the boneyards for a crooked boy?
Button your bodice on a hump of splinters,
My camel's eyes will needle through the shroud.
Love's reflection of the mushroom features,
Stills snapped by night in the bread-sided field,
Once close-up smiling in the wall of pictures,
Arc-lamped thrown back upon the cutting flood.

VIII

This was the crucifixion on the mountain,
Time's nerve in vinegar, the gallow grave
As tarred with blood as the bright thorns I wept;
The world's my wound, God's Mary in her grief,
Bent like three trees and bird-papped through her shift,
With pins for teardrops is the long wound's woman.
This was the sky, Jack Christ, each minstrel angle
Drove in the heaven-driven of the nails
Till the three-coloured rainbow from my nipples
From pole to pole leapt round the snail-waked world.
I by the tree of thieves, all glory's sawbones
Unsex the skeleton this mountain minute,
And by this blowclock witness of the sun
Suffer the heaven's children through my heartbeat.

IX

From the oracular archives and the parchment,
Prophets and fibre kings in oil and letter,
The lamped calligrapher, the queen in splints,
Buckle to lint and cloth their natron footsteps,
Draw on the glove of prints, dead Cairo's henna
Pour like a halo on the caps and serpents.
This was the resurrection in the desert,
Death from a bandage, rants the mask of scholars
Gold on such features, and the linen spirit
Weds my long gentleman to dusts and furies;
With priest and pharaoh bed my gentle wound,
World in the sand, on the triangle landscape,
With stones of odyssey for ash and garland
And rivers of the dead around my neck.

X

Let the tale's sailor from a Christian voyage
Atlaswise hold half-way off the dummy bay
Time's ship-racked gospel on the globe I balance:
So shall winged harbours through the rockbirds' eyes
Spot the blown word, and on the seas I imagine
December's thorn screwed in a brow of holly.
Let the first Peter from a rainbow's quayrail
Ask the tall fish swept from the bible east,
What rhubarb man peeled in her foam-blue channel

Has sown a flying garden round that sea-ghost?
Green as beginning, let the garden diving
Soar, with its two bark towers, to that Day
When the worm builds with the gold straws of venom
My nest of mercies in the rude, red tree.   *1936*

AFTER THE FUNERAL

(*In memory of Ann Jones*)

After the funeral, mule praises, brays,
Windshake of sailshaped ears, muffle-toed tap
Tap happily of one peg in the thick
Grave's foot, blinds down the lids, the teeth in black,
The spittled eyes, the salt ponds in the sleeves,
Morning smack of the spade that wakes up sleep,
Shakes a desolate boy who slits his throat
In the dark of the coffin and sheds dry leaves,
That breaks one bone to light with a judgment clout,
After the feast of tear-stuffed time and thistles
In a room with a stuffed fox and a stale fern,
I stand, for this memorial's sake, alone
In the snivelling hours with dead, humped Ann
Whose hooded, fountain heart once fell in puddles
Round the parched worlds of Wales and drowned each sun
(Though this for her is a monstrous image blindly
Magnified out of praise; her death was a still drop;
She would not have me sinking in the holy
Flood of her heart's fame; she would lie dumb and deep
And need no druid of her broken body).
But I, Ann's bard on a raised hearth, call all
The seas to service that her wood-tongued virtue
Babble like a bellbuoy over the hymning heads,
Bow down the walls of the ferned and foxy woods
That her love sing and swing through a brown chapel,
Bless her bent spirit with four, crossing birds.
Her flesh was meek as milk, but this skyward statue
With the wild breast and blessed and giant skull
Is carved from her in a room with a wet window
In a fiercely mourning house in a crooked year.
I know her scrubbed and sour humble hands
Lie with religion in their cramp, her threadbare
Whisper in a damp word, her wits drilled hollow,

Her fist of a face died clenched on a round pain;
And sculptured Ann is seventy years of stone.
These cloud-sopped, marble hands, this monumental
Argument of the hewn voice, gesture and psalm,
Storm me forever over her grave until
The stuffed lung of the fox twitch and cry Love
And the strutting fern lay seeds on the black sill.   *1938*

TWENTY-FOUR YEARS

Twenty-four years remind the tears of my eyes.
(Bury the dead for fear that they walk to the grave in labour.)
In the groin of the natural doorway I crouched like a tailor
Sewing a shroud for a journey
By the light of the meat-eating sun.
Dressed to die, the sensual strut begun,
With my red veins full of money,
In the final direction of the elementary town
I advance for as long as forever is.   *1939*

A REFUSAL TO MOURN THE DEATH, BY FIRE,
OF A CHILD IN LONDON

Never until the mankind making
Bird beast and flower
Fathering and all humbling darkness
Tells with silence the last light breaking
And the still hour
Is come of the sea tumbling in harness

And I must enter again the round
Zion of the water bead
And the synagogue of the ear of corn
Shall I let pray the shadow of a sound
Or sow my salt seed
In the least valley of sackcloth to mourn

The majesty and burning of the child's death.
I shall not murder
The mankind of her going with a grave truth
Nor blaspheme down the stations of the breath
With any further
Elegy of innocence and youth.

Deep with the first dead lies London's daughter,
Robed in the long friends,
The grains beyond age, the dark veins of her mother,
Secret by the unmourning water
Of the riding Thames.
After the first death, there is no other.   *1946*

A WINTER'S TALE

It is a winter's tale
That the snow blind twilight ferries over the lakes
And floating fields from the farm in the cup of the vales,
Gliding windless through the hand folded flakes,
The pale breath of cattle at the stealthy sail,

And the stars falling cold,
And the smell of hay in the snow, and the far owl
Warning among the folds, and the frozen hold
Flocked with the sheep white smoke of the farm house cowl
In the river wended vales where the tale was told.

Once when the world turned old
On a star of faith pure as the drifting bread,
As the food and flames of the snow, a man unrolled
The scrolls of fire that burned in his heart and head,
Torn and alone in a farm house in a fold

Of fields. And burning then
In his firelit island ringed by the winged snow
And the dung hills white as wool and the hen
Roosts sleeping chill till the flame of the cock crow
Combs through the mantled yards and the morning men

Stumble out with their spades,
The cattle stirring, the mousing cat stepping shy,
The puffed birds hopping and hunting, the milkmaids
Gentle in their clogs over the fallen sky,
And all the woken farm at its white trades,

He knelt, he wept, he prayed,
By the spit and the black pot in the log bright light
And the cup and the cut bread in the dancing shade,
In the muffled house, in the quick of night,
At the point of love, forsaken and afraid.

He knelt on the cold stones,
He wept from the crest of grief, he prayed to the veiled sky
May his hunger go howling on bare white bones
Past the statues of the stables and the sky roofed sties
And the duck pond glass and the blinding byres alone

Into the home of prayers
And fires where he should prowl down the cloud
Of his snow blind love and rush in the white lairs.
His naked need struck him howling and bowed
Though no sound flowed down the hand folded air

But only the wind strung
Hunger of birds in the fields of the bread of water, tossed
In high corn and the harvest melting on their tongues.
And his nameless need bound him burning and lost
When cold as snow he should run the wended vales among

The rivers mouthed in night,
And drown in the drifts of his need, and lie curled caught
In the always desiring centre of the white
Inhuman cradle and the bride bed forever sought
By the believer lost and the hurled outcast of light.

Deliver him, he cried,
By losing him all in love, and cast his need
Alone and naked in the engulfing bride,
Never to flourish in the fields of the white seed
Or flower under the time dying flesh astride.

Listen. The minstrels sing
In the departed villages. The nightingale,
Dust in the buried wood, flies on the grains of her wings
And spells on the winds of the dead his winter's tale.
The voice of the dust of water from the withered spring

Is telling. The wizened
Stream with bells and baying water bounds. The dew rings
On the gristed leaves and the long gone glistening
Parish of snow. The carved mouths in the rock are wind swept strings.
Time sings through the intricately dead snow drop. Listen.

It was a hand or sound
In the long ago land that glided the dark door wide

And there outside on the bread of the ground
A she bird rose and rayed like a burning bride.
A she bird dawned, and her breast with snow and scarlet downed.

Look. And the dancers move
On the departed, snow bushed green, wanton in moon light
As a dust of pigeons. Exulting, the grave hooved
Horses, centaur dead, turn and tread the drenched white
Paddocks in the farms of birds. The dead oak walks for love.

The carved limbs in the rock
Leap, as to trumpets. Calligraphy of the old
Leaves is dancing. Lines of age on the stones weave in a flock.
And the harp shaped voice of the water's dust plucks in a fold
Of fields. For love, the long ago she bird rises. Look.

And the wild wings were raised
Above her folded head, and the soft feathered voice
Was flying through the house as though the she bird praised
And all the elements of the slow fall rejoiced
That a man knelt alone in the cup of the vales,

In the mantle and calm,
By the spit and the black pot in the log bright light.
And the sky of birds in the plumed voice charmed
Him up and he ran like a wind after the kindling flight
Past the blind barns and byres of the windless farm.

In the poles of the year
When black birds died like priests in the cloaked hedge row
And over the cloth of counties the far hills rode near,
Under the one leaved trees ran a scarecrow of snow
And fast through the drifts of the thickets antlered like deer,

Rags and prayers down the knee-
Deep hillocks and loud on the numbed lakes,
All night lost and long wading in the wake of the she-
Bird through the times and lands and tribes of the slow flakes.
Listen and look where she sails the goose plucked sea,

The sky, the bird, the bride,
The cloud, the need, the planted stars, the joy beyond
The fields of seed and the time dying flesh astride,

The heavens, the heaven, the grave, the burning font,
In the far ago land the door of his death glided wide,

And the bird descended.
On a bread white hill over the cupped farm
And the lakes and floating fields and the river wended
Vales where he prayed to come to the last harm
And the home of prayers and fires, the tale ended.

The dancing perishes
On the white, no longer growing green, and, minstrel dead,
The singing breaks in the snow shoed villages of wishes
That once cut the figures of birds on the deep bread
And over the glazed lakes skated the shapes of fishes

Flying. The rite is shorn
Of nightingale and centaur dead horse. The springs wither
Back. Lines of age sleep on the stones till trumpeting dawn.
Exultation lies down. Time buries the spring weather
That belled and bounded with the fossil and the dew reborn.

For the bird lay bedded
In a choir of wings, as though she slept or died,
And the wings glided wide and he was hymned and wedded,
And through the thighs of the engulfing bride,
The woman breasted and the heaven headed

Bird, he was brought low,
Burning in the bride bed of love, in the whirl-
Pool at the wanting centre, in the folds
Of Paradise, in the spun bud of the world.
And she rose with him flowering in her melting snow.   1946

IN MY CRAFT OR SULLEN ART

In my craft or sullen art
Exercised in the still night
When only the moon rages
And the lovers lie abed
With all their griefs in their arms,
I labour by singing light
Not for ambition or bread
Or the strut and trade of charms

On the ivory stages
But for the common wages
Of their most secret heart.

Not for the proud man apart
From the raging moon I write
On these spindrift pages
Nor for the towering dead
With their nightingales and psalms
But for the lovers, their arms
Round the griefs of the ages,
Who pay no praise or wages
Nor heed my craft or art.   *1946*

CEREMONY AFTER A FIRE RAID

I

Myselves
The grievers
Grieve
Among the street burned to tireless death
A child of a few hours
With its kneading mouth
Charred on the black breast of the grave
The mother dug, and its arms full of fires.

Begin
With singing
Sing
Darkness kindled back into beginning
When the caught tongue nodded blind,
A star was broken
Into the centuries of the child
Myselves grieve now, and miracles cannot atone.

Forgive
Us forgive
Us your death that myselves the believers
May hold it in a great flood
Till the blood shall spurt,
And the dust shall sing like a bird
As the grains blow, as your death grows, through our heart.

Crying
Your dying
Cry,
Child beyond cockcrow, by the fire-dwarfed
Street we chant the flying sea
In the body bereft.
Love is the last light spoken. Oh
Seed of sons in the loin of the black husk left.

II

I know not whether
Adam or Eve, the adorned holy bullock
Or the white ewe lamb
Or the chosen virgin
Laid in her snow
On the altar of London,
Was the first to die
In the cinder of the little skull,
O bride and bride groom
O Adam and Eve together
Lying in the lull
Under the sad breast of the head stone
White as the skeleton
Of the garden of Eden.

I know the legend
Of Adam and Eve is never for a second
Silent in my service
Over the dead infants
Over the one
Child who was priest and servants,
Word, singers, and tongue
In the cinder of the little skull,
Who was the serpent's
Nightfall and the fruit like a sun,
Man and woman undone,
Beginning crumbled back to darkness
Bare as the nurseries
Of the garden of wilderness.

III

Into the organpipes and steeples
Of the luminous cathedrals,

Into the weathercocks' molten mouths
Rippling in twelve-winded circles,
Into the dead clock burning the hour
Over the urn of sabbaths
Over the whirling ditch of daybreak
Over the sun's hovel and the slum of fire
And the golden pavements laid in requiems,
Into the bread in a wheatfield of flames,
Into the wine burning like brandy,
The masses of the sea
The masses of the sea under
The masses of the infant-bearing sea
Erupt, fountain, and enter to utter for ever
Glory glory glory
The sundering ultimate kingdom of genesis' thunder.   *1946*

FERN HILL

Now as I was young and easy under the apple boughs
About the lilting house and happy as the grass was green,
    The night above the dingle starry,
       Time let me hail and climb
    Golden in the heydays of his eyes,
And honored among wagons I was prince of the apple towns
And once below a time I lordly had the trees and leaves
       Trail with daisies and barley
    Down the rivers of the windfall light.

And as I was green and carefree, famous among the barns
About the happy yard and singing as the farm was home,
    In the sun that is young once only,
       Time let me play and be
    Golden in the mercy of his means,
And green and golden I was huntsman and herdsman, the calves
Sang to my horn, the foxes on the hills barked clear and cold,
       And the sabbath rang slowly
    In the pebbles of the holy streams.

All the sun long it was running, it was lovely, the hay
Fields high as the house, the tunes from the chimneys, it was air
    And playing, lovely and watery
       And fire green as grass.
    And nightly under the simple stars

As I rode to sleep the owls were bearing the farm away,
All the moon long I heard, blessed among stables, the nightjars
    Flying with the ricks, and the horses
        Flashing into the dark.

And then to awake, and the farm, like a wanderer white
With the dew, come back, the cock on his shoulder: it was all
    Shining, it was Adam and maiden,
        The sky gathered again
    And the sun grew round that very day.
So it must have been after the birth of the simple light
In the first, spinning place, the spellbound horses walking warm
    Out of the whinnying green stable
        On to the fields of praise.

And honoured among foxes and pheasants by the gay house
Under the new made clouds and happy as the heart was long,
    In the sun born over and over,
        I ran my heedless ways,
    My wishes raced through the house-high hay
And nothing I cared, at my sky blue trades, that time allows
In all his tuneful turning so few and such morning songs
    Before the children green and golden
        Follow him out of grace.

Nothing I cared, in the lamb white days, that time would take me
Up to the swallow thronged loft by the shadow of my hand,
    In the moon that is always rising,
        Nor that riding to sleep
    I should hear him fly with the high fields
And wake to the farm forever fled from the childless land.
Oh as I was young and easy in the mercy of his means,
    Time held me green and dying
        Though I sang in my chains like the sea.   *1946*

John Betjeman

THE ARREST OF OSCAR WILDE AT THE CADOGAN HOTEL

He sipped at a weak hock and seltzer
  As he gazed at the London skies
Through the Nottingham lace of the curtains
  Or was it his bees-winged eyes?

To the right and before him Pont Street
  Did tower in her new built red,
As hard as the morning gaslight
  That shone on his unmade bed.

"I want some more hock in my seltzer,
  And Robbie, please give me your hand—
Is this the end or beginning?
  How can I understand?

"So you've brought me the latest *Yellow Book*:
  And Buchan has got in it now:
Approval of what is approved of
  Is as false as a well-kept vow.

"More hock, Robbie—where is the seltzer?
  Dear boy, pull again at the bell!
They are all little better than *cretins*,
  Though this *is* the Cadogan Hotel.

"One astrakhan coat is at Willis's—
  Another one's at the Savoy:
Do fetch my morocco portmanteau,
  And bring them on later, dear boy."

A thump, and a murmur of voices—
  ("Oh why must they make such a din?")

As the door of the bedroom swung open
    And TWO PLAIN CLOTHES POLICEMEN came in:

"Mr. Woilde, we 'ave come for tew take yew
    Where felons and criminals dwell:
We must ask yew tew leave with us quoietly
    For this *is* the Cadogan Hotel."

He rose, and he put down *The Yellow Book.*
    He staggered—and, terrible-eyed,
He brushed past the palms on the staircase
    And was helped to a hansom outside.   *1937*

AN INCIDENT IN THE EARLY LIFE OF EBENEZER JONES, POET, 1828

"We were together at a well-known boarding-school of that day (1828), situated at the foot of Highgate Hill, and presided over by a dissenting minister, the Rev. John Bickerdike. . . .

We were together, though not on the same form; and on a hot summer afternoon, with about fifty other boys, were listlessly conning our tasks in a large schoolroom built out from the house, which made a cover for us to play under when it was wet. Up the ladder-like stairs from the playground a lurcher dog had strayed into the schoolroom, panting with the heat, his tongue lolling out with thirst. The choleric usher who presided, and was detested by us for his tyranny, seeing this, advanced down the room. Enraged at our attention being distracted from our tasks, he dragged the dog to the top of the stairs, and there lifted him bodily up with the evident intention—and we had known him do similar things—of hurling the poor creature to the bottom.

'YOU SHALL NOT!' ran through the room, as little Ebby, so exclaiming at the top of his voice, rushed with kindling face to the spot from among all the boys—some of them twice his age.

But even while the words passed his lips, the heavy fall was heard, and the sound seemed to travel through his listening form and face, as, with a strange look of anguish in one so young, he stood still, threw up his arms, and burst into an uncontrollable passion of tears.

With a coarse laugh at this, the usher led him back by his ear to the form; and there he sat, long after his sobbing had subsided, like one dazed and stunned." (*From an account of his brother by Sumner Jones in the 1879 re-issue of Ebenezer Jones's "Studies of Sensation and Event."*)

The lumber of a London-going dray,
The still-new stucco on the London clay,
Hot summer silence over Holloway.

Dissenting chapels, tea-bowers, lovers' lairs,
Neat new-built villas, ample Grecian squares,
Remaining orchards ripening Windsor pears.

Hot silence where the older mansions hide
On Highgate Hill's thick elm-encrusted side,
And Pancras, Hornsey, Islington divide.

June's hottest silence where the hard rays strike
Yon hill-foot house, window and wall alike,
School of the Reverend Mr. Bickerdike,

For sons of Saints, blest with this world's possessions
(Seceders from the Protestant Secessions),
Good grounding in the more genteel professions.

A lurcher dog, which draymen kick and pass,
Tongue lolling, thirsty over shadeless grass,
Leapt up the playground ladder to the class.

The godly usher left his godly seat,
His skin was prickly in the ungodly heat,
The dog lay panting at his godly feet.

The milkman on the road stood staring in.
The playground nettles nodded "Now begin"—
And Evil waited, quivering, for sin.

He lifted it and not a word he spoke,
His big hand tightened. Could he make it choke?
He trembled, sweated, and his temper broke.

"You SHALL NOT!" clear across to Highgate Hill
A boy's voice sounded. Creaking forms were still.
The cat jumped slowly from the window sill.

"You SHALL NOT!" flat against the summer sun,
Hard as the hard sky frowning over one,
Gloat, little boys! enjoy the coming fun!

"GOD DAMNS A CUR. I AM, I AM HIS WORD!"
He flung it, flung it and it never stirred,
"You shall not!—shall not!" ringing on unheard.

Blind desolation! bleeding, burning rod!
Big, bull-necked Minister of Calvin's God!
Exulting milkman, redfaced, shameless clod,

Look on and jeer! Not Satan's thunder-quake
Can cause the mighty walls of Heaven to shake
As now they do, to hear a boy's heart break.   *1940*

TREBETHERICK

We used to picnic where the thrift
    Grew deep and tufted to the edge;
We saw the yellow foam-flakes drift
    In trembling sponges on the ledge
Below us, till the wind would lift
    Them up the cliff and o'er the hedge.
Sand in the sandwiches, wasps in the tea,
Sun on our bathing-dresses heavy with the wet,
Squelch of the bladder-wrack waiting for the sea,
Fleas round the tamarisk, an early cigarette.

From where the coastguard houses stood
    One used to see, below the hill,
The lichened branches of a wood
    In summer silver-cool and still;
And there the Shade of Evil could
    Stretch out at us from Shilla Mill.
Thick with sloe and blackberry, uneven in the light,
Lonely ran the hedge, the heavy meadow was remote,
The oldest part of Cornwall was the wood as black as night,
And the pheasant and the rabbit lay torn open at the throat.

But when a storm was at its height,
    And feathery slate was black in rain,
And tamarisks were hung with light
    And golden sand was brown again,
Spring tide and blizzard would unite
    And sea came flooding up the lane.
Waves full of treasure then were roaring up the beach,
Ropes round our mackintoshes, waders warm and dry,
We waited for the wreckage to come swirling into reach,
Ralph, Vasey, Alastair, Biddy, John and I.

Then roller into roller curled
And thundered down the rocky bay,
And we were in a water-world
Of rain and blizzard, sea and spray,
And one against the other hurled
We struggled round to Greenaway.
Blesséd be St. Enodoc, blesséd be the wave,
Blesséd be the springy turf, we pray, pray to thee,
Ask for our children all the happy days you gave
To Ralph, Vasey, Alastair, Biddy, John and me.   *1940*

BRISTOL AND CLIFTON

"Yes, I was only sidesman here when last
You came to Evening Communion.
But now I have retired from the bank
I have more leisure time for church finance.
We moved into a somewhat larger house
Than when you knew us in Manilla Road.
This is the window to my lady wife.
You cannot see it now, but in the day
The greens and golds are truly wonderful."

"How very sad. I do not mean about
The window, but I mean about the death
Of Mrs. Battlecock. When did she die?"

"Two years ago when we had just moved in
To Pembroke Road. I rather fear the stairs
And basement kitchen were too much for her—
Not that, of course, she did the servants' work—
But supervising servants all the day
Meant quite a lot of climbing up and down."

"How very sad. Poor Mrs. Battlecock."
" 'The glory that men do lives after them,' [1]
And so I gave this window in her name.
It's executed by a Bristol firm;
The lady artist who designed it, made
The figure of the lady on the left
Something like Mrs. Battlecock."
"How nice."

[1] Shakespeare, of course—*Author's note.*

"Yes, was it not? We had
A stained glass window on the stairs at home,
In Pembroke Road. But not so good as this.
This window is the glory of the church
At least I think so—and the unstained oak
Looks very chaste beneath it. When I gave
The oak, that brass inscription on your right
Commemorates the fact, the Dorcas Club
Made these blue kneelers, though we do not kneel:
We leave that to the Roman Catholics."
"How very nice, indeed. How very nice."

"Seeing I have some knowledge of finance
Our kind Parochial Church Council made
Me People's Warden, and I'm glad to say
That our collections are still keeping up.
The chancel has been flood-lit, and the stove
Which used to heat the church was obsolete.
So now we've had some radiators fixed
Along the walls and eastward of the aisles;
This last I thought of lest at any time
A Ritualist should be inducted here
And want to put up altars. He would find
The radiators inconvenient.
Our only ritual here is with the Plate;
I think we make it dignified enough.
I take it up myself, and afterwards,
Count the Collection on the vestry safe."

"Forgive me, aren't we talking rather loud?
I think I see a woman praying there."
"Praying? The service is all over now
And here's the verger waiting to turn out
The lights and lock the church up. She cannot
Be Loyal Church of England. Well, good-bye.
Time flies. I must be going. Come again.
There are some pleasant people living here
I know the Inskips very well indeed."   *1940*

IN WESTMINSTER ABBEY

Let me take this other glove off
As the *vox humana* swells,

And the beauteous fields of Eden
   Bask beneath the Abbey bells.
Here, where England's statesmen lie,
Listen to a lady's cry.

Gracious Lord, oh bomb the Germans.
   Spare their women for Thy Sake,
And if that is not too easy
   We will pardon Thy Mistake.
But, gracious Lord, whate'er shall be,
Don't let anyone bomb me.

Keep our Empire undismembered
   Guide our Forces by Thy Hand,
Gallant blacks from far Jamaica,
   Honduras and Togoland;
Protect them Lord in all their fights,
And, even more, protect the whites.

Think of what our Nation stands for,
   Books from Boots' and country lanes,
Free speech, free passes, class distinction,
   Democracy and proper drains.
Lord, put beneath Thy special care
One-eighty-nine Cadogan Square.

Although dear Lord I am a sinner,
   I have done no major crime;
Now I'll come to Evening Service
   Whensoever I have the time.
So, Lord, reserve for me a crown,
And do not let my shares go down.

I will labour for Thy Kingdom,
   Help our lads to win the war,
Send white feathers to the cowards
   Join the Women's Army Corps,
Then wash the Steps around Thy Throne
In the Eternal Safety Zone.

Now I feel a little better,
   What a treat to hear Thy Word,
Where the bones of leading statesmen,

Have so often been interr'd.
And now, dear Lord, I cannot wait
Because I have a luncheon date.   *1940*

NORTH COAST RECOLLECTIONS

No people on the golf-links, not a crack
Of well-swung driver from the fourteenth tee,
No sailing bounding ball across the turf
And lady's slipper of the fairway. Black
Rises Bray Hill and, Stepper-wards, the sun
Sends Bray Hill's phantom stretching to the church.
The lane, the links, the beach, the cliffs are bare
The neighbourhood is dressing for a dance
And lamps are being lit in bungalows.
      O! thymy time of evening: clover scent
And feathery tamarisk round the churchyard wall
And shrivelled sea-pinks and this foreshore pale
With silver sand and sharpened quartz and slate
And brittle twigs, bleached, salted and prepared
For kindling blue-flamed fires on winter nights.
      Here Petroc landed, here I stand to-day;
The same Atlantic surges roll for me
As rolled for Parson Hawker and for him,
And spent their gathering thunder on the rocks
Crashing with pebbly backwash, burst again
And strewed the nibbled fields along the cliffs.

When low tides drain the estuary gold
Small intersecting breakers far away
Ripple about a bar of shifting sand
Where centuries ago were waving woods
Where centuries hence, there will be woods again.

Within the bungalow of Mrs. Hanks
Her daughter Phoebe now French-chalks the floor.
Norman and Gordon in their dancing pumps
Slide up and down, but can't make concrete smooth.
"My Sweet Hortense . . ."
Sings louder down the garden than the sea.
"A practice record, Phoebe. Mummykins,
Gordon and I will do the washing-up."
"We picnic here; we scrounge and help ourselves,"

Says Mrs. Hanks, and visitors will smile
To see them all turn to it. Boys and girls
Weed in the sterile garden, mostly sand
And dead tomato-plants and chicken-runs.
To-day they cleaned the dulled Benares ware
(Dulled by the sea-mist), early made the beds,
And Phoebe twirled the icing round the cake
And Gordon tinkered with the gramophone
While into an immense enamel jug
Norman poured "Eiffel Tower" for lemonade.

O! healthy bodies, bursting into 'teens
And bursting out of last year's summer clothes,
Fluff barking and French windows banging to
Till the asbestos walling of the place
Shakes with the life it shelters, and with all
The preparations for this evening's dance.

Now drains the colour from the convolvulus,
The windows of Trenain are flashing fire,
Black sways the tamarisk against the West,
And bathing things are taken in from sills.
One child still zig-zags homewards up the lane,
Cold on bare feet he feels the dew-wet sand.
Behind him, from a walk along the cliff,
Come pater and the mater and the dogs.

Four macrocarpa hide the tennis club.
Two children of a chartered actuary
(Beaworthy, Trouncer, Heppelwhite and Co.),
Harold and Bonzo Trouncer are engaged
In semi-finals for the tournament.
"Love thirty!" Pang! across the evening air
Twangs Harold's racquet. Plung! the ball returns.
Experience at Budleigh Salterton
Keeps Bonzo steady at the net. "Well done!"
"Love forty!" Captain Mycroft, midst appplause,
Pronounces for the Trouncers, to be sure
He can't be certain Bonzo didn't reach
A shade across the net, but Demon Sex,
That tulip figure in white cotton dress,
Bare legs, wide eyes and so tip-tilted nose
Quite overset him. Harold serves again
And Mrs Pardon says it's getting cold,

Miss Myatt shivers, Lady Lambourn thinks
These English evenings are a little damp
And dreams herself again in fair Shanghai.
"Game . . . AND! and thank you!"; so the pair from Rock
(A neighbouring and less exclusive place)
Defeated, climb into their Morris Ten.
"The final is to-morrow! Well, good night!"
   He lay in wait, he lay in wait, he did,
John Lambourn, curly-headed; dewy grass
Dampened his flannels, but he still remained.
The sunset drained the colours black and gold,
From his all-glorious First Eleven scarf.
But still he waited by the twilit hedge.
Only his eyes blazed blue with early love,
Blue blazing in the darkness of the lane,
Blue blazer, less incalculably blue,
Dark scarf, white flannels, supple body still,
First love, first light, first life. A heartbeat noise!
His heart or little feet? A snap of twigs
Dry, dead and brown the under branches part
And Bonzo scrambles by their secret way.
First love so deep, John Lambourn cannot speak,
So deep, he feels a tightening in his throat,
So tender, he could brush away the sand
Dried up in patches on her freckled legs,
Could hold her gently till the stars went down,
And if she cut herself would staunch the wound,
Yes, even with his First Eleven scarf,
And hold it there for hours.
So happy, and so deep he loves the world,
Could worship God and rocks and stones and trees,
Be nicer to his mother, kill himself
If that would make him pure enough for her.
And so at last he manages to say
"You going to the Hanks's hop to-night?"
"Well, I'm not sure. Are you?" "I think I may—
It's pretty dud though,—only lemonade."

   Sir Gawaint was a right and goodly knight
   Nor ever wist he to uncurtis be.
So old, so lovely, and so very true!
Then Mrs. Wilder shut the Walter Crane
And tied the tapes and tucked her youngest in

What time without amidst the lavender
At late last 'He' played Primula and Prue
With new-found liveliness, for bed was soon.
And in the garage, serious seventeen
Harvey, the eldest, hammered on, content,
Fixing a mizzen to his model boat.
"Coo-ee! Coo-ee!" across the lavender,
Across the mist of pale gypsophila
And lolling purple poppies, Mumsie called,
A splendid sunset lit the rocking-horse
And Morris pattern of the nursery walls.
"Coo-ee!" the slate-hung, goodly-builded house
And sunset-sodden garden fell to quiet.
"Prue! Primsie! Mumsie wants you. Sleepi-byes!"
Prue jumped the marigolds and hid herself,
Her sister scampered to the Wendy Hut
And Harvey, glancing at his Ingersoll,
Thought "Damn! I must get ready for the dance."

   So on this after-storm-lit evening
To Jim the raindrops in the tamarisk,
The fuchsia bells, the sodden matchbox lid
That checked a tiny torrent in the lane
Were magnified and shining clear with life.
Then pealing out across the estuary
The Padstow bells rang up for practice-night
An undersong to birds and dripping shrubs.
The full Atlantic at September spring
Flooded a final tide-mark up the sand,
And ocean sank to silence under bells,
And the next breaker was a lesser one
Then lesser still. Atlantic, bells and birds
Were layer on interchanging layer of sound.

1948

THE TOWN CLERK'S VIEWS

"Yes, the Town Clerk will see you." In I went.
He was, like all Town Clerks, from north of Trent;
A man with bye-laws busy in his head
Whose Mayor and Council followed where he led.
His most capacious brain will make us cower,
His only weakness is a lust for power—
And that is not a weakness, people think,

When unaccompanied by bribes or drink.
So let us hear this cool careerist tell
His plans to turn our country into hell.
"I cannot say how shock'd I am to see
The *variations* in our scenery.
Just take for instance, at a casual glance,
Our muddled coastline opposite to France:
Dickensian houses by the Channel tides
With old hipp'd roofs and weather-boarded sides.
I blush to think one corner of our isle
Lacks concrete villas in the modern style.
Straight lines of hops in pale brown earth of Kent,
Yeomen's square houses once, no doubt, content
With willow-bordered horse-pond, oast-house, shed,
Wide orchard, garden walls of browny-red—
All useless now, but what fine sites they'ld be
For workers' flats and some light industry.
Those lumpy church towers, unadorned with spires,
And wavy roofs that burn like smouldering fires
In sharp spring sunlight over ashen flint
Are out of date as some old aquatint.
Then glance below the line of Sussex downs
To stucco terraces of seaside towns
Turn'd into flats and residential clubs
Above the wind-slashed Corporation shrubs.
Such Georgian relics should by now, I feel,
Be all rebuilt in glass and polished steel.
Bournemouth is looking up. I'm glad to say
That modernistic there has come to stay.
I walk the asphalt paths of Branksome Chine
In resin-scented air like strong Greek wine
And dream of cliffs of flats along those heights,
Floodlit at night with green electric lights.
But as for Dorset's flint and Purbeck stone,
Its old thatched farms in dips of down alone—
It should be merged with Hants and made to be
A self-contained and plann'd community.
Like Flint and Rutland, it is much too small
And has no reason to exist at all.
Of Devon one can hardly say the same,
But "South-West Area One" 's a better name
For those red sandstone cliffs that stain the sea
By mid-Victoria's Italy—Torquay.

And "South-West Area Two" could well include
The whole of Cornwall from Land's End to Bude.
Need I retrace my steps through other shires?
Pinnacled Somerset? Northampton's spires?
Burford's broad High Street is descending still
Stone-roofed and golden-walled her elmy hill
To meet the river Windrush. What a shame
Her houses are not brick and all the same.
Oxford is growing up to date at last.
Cambridge, I fear, is living in the past.
She needs more factories, not useless things
Like that great chapel which they keep at King's.
As for remote East Anglia, he who searches
Finds only thatch and vast, redundant churches.
But that's the dark side. I can safely say
A beauteous England's really on the way.
Already our hotels are pretty good
For those who're fond of *very simple food*—
Cod and two veg., free pepper, salt and mustard,
Followed by nice hard plums and lumpy custard,
A pint of bitter beer for one-and-four,
Then coffee in the lounge a shilling more.
In a few years this country will be looking
As uniform and tasty as its cooking.
Hamlets which fail to pass the planners' test
Will be demolished. We'll rebuild the rest
To look like Welwyn mixed with Middle West.
All fields we'll turn to sports grounds, lit at night
From concrete standards by fluorescent light:
And over all the land, instead of trees,
Clean poles and wire will whisper in the breeze.
We'll keep one ancient village just to show
What England once was when the times were slow—
Broadway for me. But here I know I must
Ask the opinion of our National Trust.
And ev'ry old cathedral that you enter
By then will be an Area Culture Centre.
Instead of nonsense about Death and Heaven
Lectures on civic duty will be given;
Eurhythmic classes dancing round the spire,
And economics courses in the choir.
So don't encourage tourists. Stay your hand
Until we've really got the country plann'd."   *1948*

THE LICORICE FIELDS AT PONTEFRACT

In the licorice fields at Pontefract
   My love and I did meet
And many a burdened licorice bush
   Was blooming round our feet;
Red hair she had and golden skin,
Her sulky lips were shaped for sin,
Her sturdy legs were flannel-slack'd,
The strongest legs in Pontefract.

The light and dangling licorice flowers
   Gave off the sweetest smells;
From various black Victorian towers
   The Sunday evening bells
Came pealing over dales and hills
And tanneries and silent mills
And lowly streets where country stops
And little shuttered corner shops.

She cast her blazing eyes on me
   And plucked a licorice leaf;
I was her captive slave and she
   My red-haired robber chief.
Oh love! for love I could not speak,
It left me winded, wilting, weak
And held in brown arms strong and bare
And wound with flaming ropes of hair.

1954

LATE-FLOWERING LUST

My head is bald, my breath is bad,
   Unshaven is my chin,
I have not now the joys I had
   When I was young in sin.

I run my fingers down your dress
   With brandy-certain aim
And you respond to my caress
   And maybe feel the same.

But I've a picture of my own
   On this reunion night,
Wherein two skeletons are shown
   To hold each other tight;

Dark sockets look on emptiness
   Which once was loving-eyed,
The mouth that opens for a kiss
   Has got no tongue inside.

I cling to you inflamed with fear
   As now you cling to me,
I feel how frail you are my dear
   And wonder what will be—

A week? or twenty years remain?
   And then—what kind of death?
A losing fight with frightful pain
   Or a gasping fight for breath?

Too long we let our bodies cling,
   We cannot hide disgust
At all the thoughts that in us spring
   From this late-flowering lust.

            1954

THE DEAR OLD VILLAGE

  The dear old village! *Lin-lan-lone* the bells
(Which should be six) ring over hills and dells,
But since the row about the ringers' tea
It's *lin-lan-lone*. They're only ringing three.
The elm leaves patter like a summer shower
As *lin-lan-lone* pours through them from the tower.
From that embattled, lichen-crusted fane
Which scoops the sun into each western pane,
The bells ring over hills and dells in vain.
For we are free to-day. No need to praise
The Unseen Author of our nights and days;
No need to hymn the rich uncurling spring
For DYKES is nowhere half so good as BING.
Nature is out of date and GOD is too;
Think what atomic energy can do!

Farmers have wired the public rights-of-way
Should any wish to walk to church to pray.
Along the village street the sunset strikes
On young men tuning up their motor-bikes,
And country girls with lips and nails vermilion
Wait, nylon-legged, to straddle on the pillion.
Off to the roadhouse and the Tudor Bar
And then the Sunday-opened cinema.
While to the church's iron-studded door
Go two old ladies and a child of four.

   This is the age of progress. Let us meet
The new progressives of the village street.
Hear not the water lapsing down the rills,
Lift not your eyes to the surrounding hills,
While spring recalls the miracle of birth
Let us, for heaven's sake, keep down to earth.

   See that square house, late Georgian and smart,
Two fields away it proudly stands apart,
Dutch barn and concrete cow-sheds have replaced
The old thatched roofs which once the yard disgraced.
Here wallows Farmer WHISTLE in his riches,
His ample stomach heaved above his breeches.
You'd never think that in such honest beef
Lurk'd an adulterous braggart, liar and thief.
His wife brought with her thirty-thousand down:
He keeps his doxy in the nearest town.
No man more anxious on the R.D.C.
For better rural cottages than he,
Especially when he had some land to sell
Which, as a site, would suit the Council well.
So three times what he gave for it he got,
For one undrainable and useless plot
Where now the hideous Council houses stand.
Unworked on and unworkable their land,
The wind blows under each unseason'd door,
The floods pour over every kitchen floor,
And country wit, which likes to laugh at sin,
Christens the Council houses "Whistle's Win."
Woe to some lesser farmer who may try
To call his bluff or to expose his lie.
Remorseless as a shark in London's City,
He gets at them through the War Ag. Committee.
   He takes no part in village life beyond

Throwing his refuse in a neighbour's pond
And closing footpaths, not repairing walls,
Leaving a cottage till at last it falls.
People protest. A law-suit then begins,
But as he's on the Bench, he always wins.
  Behind rank elders, shadowing a pool,
And near the Church, behold the Village School,
Its gable rising out of ivy thick
Shows "Eighteen-Sixty" worked in coloured brick.
By nineteen-forty-seven, hurrah! hooray!
This institution has outlived its day.
In the bad times of old feudality
The villagers were ruled by masters three—
Squire, parson, schoolmaster. Of these, the last
Knew best the village present and its past.
Now, I am glad to say, the man is dead,
The children have a motor-bus instead,
And in a town eleven miles away
We train them to be "Citizens of To-day."
And many a cultivated hour they pass
In a fine school with walls of vita-glass.
Civics, eurhythmics, economics, Marx,
How-to-respect-wild-life-in-National-Parks;
Plastics, gymnastics—thus they learn to scorn
The old thatch'd cottages where they were born.
The girls, ambitious to begin their lives
Serving in WOOLWORTH's, rather than as wives;
The boys, who cannot yet escape the land,
At driving tractors lend a clumsy hand.
An eight-hour day for all, and more than three
Of these are occupied in making tea
And talking over what we all agree—
Though "Music while you work" is now our wont,
It's not so nice as "Music while you don't."
Squire, parson, schoolmaster turn in their graves.
And *let* them turn. We are no longer slaves.
  So much for youth. I fear we older folk
Must be dash'd off with a more hurried stroke.
Old Mrs. SPEAK has cut, for fifteen years,
Her husband's widowed sister Mrs. SHEARS,
Though how she's managed it, I cannot say,
Sharing a cottage with her night and day.
What caused the quarrel fifteen years ago

And how BERT SPEAK gets on, I do not know,
There the three live in that old dwelling quaint
Which water-colourists delight to paint.
Of the large brood round Mrs. COKER's door,
Coker has definitely fathered four
And two are Farmer Whistle's: two they say
Have coloured fathers in the U.S.A.
I learn'd all this and more from Mrs. FREE,
Pride of the Women's Institute is she,
Says "Sir" or "Madam" to you, knows her station
And how to make a quiet insinuation.
The unrespectable must well know why
They fear her lantern jaw and leaden eye.
    There is no space to tell about the chaps—
Which pinch, which don't, which beat their wives with straps.
Go to the Inn on any Friday night
And listen to them while they're getting tight
At the expense of him who stands them drinks,
The Mass-Observer with the Hillman Minx.
(Unwitting he of all the knowing winks)
The more he circulates the bitter ales
The longer and the taller grow the tales.
"Ah! this is England," thinks he, "rich and pure
As tilth and loam and wains and horse-manure,
Slow—yes. But sociologically sound."
"Landlord!" he cries, "the same again all round!"   1954

FALSE SECURITY

I remember the dread with which I at a quarter past four
Let go with a bang behind me our house front door
And, clutching a present for my dear little hostess tight,
Sailed out for the children's party into the night
Or rather the gathering night. For still some boys
In the near municipal acres were making a noise
Shuffling in fallen leaves and shouting and whistling
And running past hedges of hawthorn, spikey and bristling.
And black in the oncoming darkness stood out the trees
And pink shone the ponds in the sunset ready to freeze
And all was still and ominous waiting for dark
And the keeper was ringing his closing bell in the park
And the arc lights started to fizzle and burst into mauve
As I climbed West Hill to the great big house in The Grove,

Where the children's party was and the dear little hostess.
But halfway up stood the empty house where the ghost is
I crossed to the other side and under the arc
Made a rush for the next kind lamp-post out of the dark
And so to the next and the next till I reached the top
Where the Grove branched off to the left. Then ready to drop
I ran to the ironwork gateway of number seven
Secure at last on the lamplit fringe of Heaven.
Oh who can say how subtle and safe one feels
Shod in one's children's sandals from Daniel Neal's,
Clad in one's party clothes made of stuff from Heal's?
And who can still one's thrill at the candle shine
On cakes and ices and jelly and blackcurrant wine,
And the warm little feel of my hostess's hand in mine?
Can I forget my delight at the conjuring show?
And wasn't I proud that I was the last to go?
Too overexcited and pleased with myself to know
That the words I heard my hostess's mother employ
To a guest departing, would ever diminish my joy,
I WONDER WHERE JULIA FOUND THAT STRANGE, RATHER COMMON
    LITTLE BOY?   *1958*

EUNICE

With her latest roses happily encumbered
    Tunbridge Wells Central takes her from the night
Sweet second bloomings frost has faintly umbered
    And some double dahlias waxy red and white.

Shut again till April stands her little hutment
    Peeping over daisies Michaelmas and mauve,
Lock'd is the Elsan in its brick abutment
    Lock'd the little pantry, dead the little stove.

Keys with Mr. Groombridge, but nobody will take them
    To her lonely cottage by the lonely oak
Potatoes in the garden but nobody to bake them
    Fungus in the living room and water in the coke.

I can see her waiting on this chilly Sunday
    For the five forty (twenty minutes late)
One of many hundreds to dread the coming Monday
    To fight with influenza and battle with her weight.

Tweed coat and skirt that with such anticipation
  On a merry spring time a friend had trimm'd with fur,
Now the friend is married and, oh desolation,
  Married to the man who might have married *her*.

High in Onslow Gardens where the soot flakes settle
  An empty flat is waiting her struggle up the stair
And when she puts the wireless on, the heater and the kettle
  It's cream and green and cosy, but home is never there.

Home's here in Kent and how many morning coffees
  And hurried little lunch hours of planning will be spent
Through the busy months of typing in the office
  Until the days are warm enough to take her back to Kent.

                                                    1958

Philip Larkin

PLACES, LOVED ONES

No, I have never found
The place where I could say
This is my proper ground,
Here I shall stay;
Nor met that special one
Who has an instant claim
On everything I own
Down to my name;

To find such seems to prove
You want no choice in where
To build, or whom to love;
You ask them to bear
You off irrevocably,
So that it's not your fault
Should the town turn dreary,
The girl a dolt.

Yet, having missed them, you're
Bound, none the less, to act
As if what you settled for
Mashed you, in fact;
And wiser to keep away
From thinking you still might trace
Uncalled-for to this day
Your person, your place.   *1955*

DRY-POINT

Endlessly, time-honoured irritant,
A bubble is restively forming at your tip.
Burst it as fast as we can—
It will grow again, until we begin dying.

Silently it inflates, till we're enclosed
And forced to start the struggle to get out:
Bestial, intent, real.
The wet spark comes, the bright blown walls collapse,

But what sad scapes we cannot turn from then:
What ashen hills! what salted, shrunken lakes!
How leaden the ring looks,
Birmingham magic all discredited,

And how remote that bare and sunscrubbed room,
Intensely far, that padlocked cube of light
We neither define nor prove,
Where you, we dream, obtain no right of entry.   *1955*

GOING

There is an evening coming in
Across the fields, one never seen before,
That lights no lamps.

Silken it seems at a distance, yet
When it is drawn up over the knees and breast
It brings no comfort.

Where has the tree gone, that locked
Earth to the sky? What is under my hands,
That I cannot feel?

What loads my hands down?   *1955*

CHURCH GOING

Once I am sure there's nothing going on
I step inside, letting the door thud shut.
Another church: matting, seats, and stone,
And little books; sprawlings of flowers, cut
For Sunday, brownish now; some brass and stuff
Up at the holy end; the small neat organ;
And a tense, musty, unignorable silence,
Brewed God knows how long. Hatless, I take off
My cycle-clips in awkward reverence,

Move forward, run my hand around the font.
From where I stand, the roof looks almost new—
Cleaned or restored? Someone would know: I don't.
Mounting the lectern, I peruse a few
Hectoring large-scale verses, and pronounce
"Here endeth" much more loudly than I'd meant.
The echoes snigger briefly. Back at the door
I sign the book, donate an Irish sixpence,
Reflect the place was not worth stopping for.

Yet stop I did: in fact I often do,
And always end much at a loss like this,
Wondering what to look for; wondering, too,
When churches fall completely out of use
What we shall turn them into, if we shall keep
A few cathedrals chronically on show,
Their parchment, plate and pyx in locked cases,
And let the rest rent-free to rain and sheep.
Shall we avoid them as unlucky places?

Or, after dark, will dubious women come
To make their children touch a particular stone;
Pick simples for a cancer; or on some
Advised night see walking a dead one?
Power of some sort or other will go on
In games, in riddles, seemingly at random;
But superstition, like belief, must die,
And what remains when disbelief has gone?
Grass, weedy pavement, brambles, buttress, sky,

A shape less recognisable each week,
A purpose more obscure. I wonder who
Will be the last, the very last, to seek
This place for what it was, one of the crew
That tap and jot and know what rood-lofts were?
Some ruin-bibber, randy for antique,
Or Christmas-addict, counting on a whiff
Of gown-and-bands and organ-pipes and myrrh?
Or will he be my representative,

Bored, uninformed, knowing the ghostly silt
Dispersed, yet tending to this cross of ground
Through suburb scrub because it held unspilt

So long and equably what since is found
Only in separation—marriage, and birth,
And death, and thoughts of these—for whom was built
This special shell? For, though I've no idea
What this accoutred frowsty barn is worth,
It pleases me to stand in silence here;

A serious house on serious earth it is,
In whose blent air all our compulsions meet,
Are recognized, and robed as destinies.
And that much never can be obsolete,
Since someone will forever be surprising
A hunger in himself to be more serious,
And gravitating with it to this ground,
Which, he once heard, was proper to grow wise in,
If only that so many dead lie round.   *1955*

AGE

My age fallen away like white swaddling
Floats in the middle distance, becomes
An inhabited cloud. I bend closer, discern
A lighted tenement scuttling with voices.
O you tall game I tired myself with joining!
Now I wade through you like knee-level weeds,

And they attend me, dear translucent bergs:
Silence and space. By now so much has flown
From the nest here of my head that I needs must turn
To know what prints I leave, whether of feet,
Or spoor of pads, or a bird's adept splay.   *1955*

MYXOMATOSIS

Caught in the centre of a soundless field
While hot inexplicable hours go by
What trap is this? Where were its teeth concealed?
You seem to ask.
                        I make a sharp reply,
Then clean my stick. I'm glad I can't explain
Just in what jaws you were to suppurate:
You may have thought things would come right again
If you could only keep quite still and wait.   *1955*

TOADS

Why should I let the toad *work*
    Squat on my life?
Can't I use my wit as a pitchfork
    And drive the brute off?

Six days of the week it soils
    With its sickening poison—
Just for paying a few bills!
    That's out of proportion.

Lots of folk live on their wits:
    Lecturers, lispers,
Losels, loblolly-men, louts—
    They don't end as paupers;

Lots of folk live up lanes
    With fires in a bucket,
Eat windfalls and tinned sardines—
    They seem to like it.

Their nippers have got bare feet,
    Their unspeakable wives
Are skinny as whippets—and yet
    No one actually *starves*.

Ah, were I courageous enough
    To shout *Stuff your pension!*
But I know, all too well, that's the stuff
    That dreams are made on:

For something sufficiently toad-like
    Squats in me, too;
Its hunkers are heavy as hard luck,
    And cold as snow,

And will never allow me to blarney
    My way to getting
The fame and the girl and the money
    All at one sitting.

I don't say, one bodies the other
  One's spiritual truth;
But I do say it's hard to lose either,
  When you have both.   *1955*

POETRY OF DEPARTURES

Sometimes you hear, fifth-hand,
As epitaph:
*He chucked up everything
And just cleared off,*
And always the voice will sound
Certain you approve
This audacious, purifying,
Elemental move.

And they are right, I think.
We all hate home
And having to be there:
I detest my room,
Its specially-chosen junk,
The good books, the good bed,
And my life, in perfect order:
So to hear it said

He walked out on the whole crowd
Leaves me flushed and stirred,
Like *Then she undid her dress*
Or *Take that you bastard;*
Surely I can, if he did?
And that helps me stay
Sober and industrious.
But I'd go today,

Yes, swagger the nut-strewn roads,
Crouch in the fo'c'sle
Stubbly with goodness, if
It weren't so artificial,
Such a deliberate step backwards
To create an object:
Books; china; a life
Reprehensibly perfect.   *1955*

DECEPTIONS

"Of course I was drugged, and so heavily I did not regain my consciousness till the next morning. I was horrified to discover that I had been ruined, and for some days I was inconsolable, and cried like a child to be killed or sent back to my aunt."—Mayhew, *London Labour and the London Poor.*

Even so distant, I can taste the grief,
Bitter and sharp with stalks, he made you gulp.
The sun's occasional print, the brisk brief
Worry of wheels along the street outside
Where bridal London bows the other way,
And light, unanswerable and tall and wide,
Forbids the scar to heal, and drives
Shame out of hiding. All the unhurried day
Your mind lay open like a drawer of knives.

Slums, years, have buried you. I would not dare
Console you if I could. What can be said,
Except that suffering is exact, but where
Desire takes charge, readings will grow erratic?
For you would hardly care
That you were less deceived, out on that bed,
Than he was, stumbling up the breathless stair
To burst into fulfilment's desolate attic.   *1955*

Charles Tomlinson

DISTINCTIONS

The seascape shifts

Between the minutest interstices of time
Blue is blue.

A pine-branch
Tugs at the eye: the eye
Returns to gray-blue, blue-black or indigo
Or it returns, simply,
To blue-after-the-pine-branch.

Here, there is no question of aberrations
Into pinks, golds, or mauves:
This is the variation Pater indicated
But failed to prove.

Art exists at a remove.
Evocation, at two,
Discusses a blue that someone
Heard someone talking about.   *1958*

PARING THE APPLE

There are portraits and still-lifes.

And there is paring the apple.

And then? Paring it slowly,
From under cool-yellow
Cold-white emerging. And . . . ?

The spring of concentric peel
Unwinding off white,
The blade hidden, dividing.

There are portraits and still-lifes
And the first, because "human"
Does not excel the second, and
Neither is less weighted
With a human gesture, than paring the apple
With a human stillness.

The cool blade
Severs between coolness, apple-rind
Compelling a recognition.   *1958*

POEM

Upended, it crouches on broken limbs
About to run forward. No longer threatened
But surprised into this vigilance
It gapes enmity from its hollowed core.

Moist woodflesh, softened to a paste
Of marl and white splinter, dangles
Where overhead the torn root
Casts up its wounds in a ragged orchis.

The seasons strip, but do not tame you.
I grant you become more smooth
As you are emptied and where the heart shreds
The gap mouths a more practiced silence.

You would impress, but merely startle. Your accomplice
Twilight is dragging its shadows here
Deliberate and unsocial: I leave you
To your own meaning, yourself alone.   *1958*

FAREWELL TO VAN GOGH

The quiet deepens. You will not persuade
    One leaf of the accomplished, steady, darkening
Chestnut-tower to displace itself
    With more of violence than the air supplies
When, gathering dusk, the pond brims evenly
    And we must be content with stillness.

Unhastening, daylight withdraws from us its shapes
    Into their central calm. Stone by stone

Your rhetoric is dispersed until the earth
  Becomes once more the earth, the leaves
A sharp partition against cooling blue.

Farewell, and for your instructive frenzy
  Gratitude. The world does not end tonight
And the fruit that we shall pick tomorrow
  Await us, weighing the unstripped bough.   *1958*

ON THE HALL AT STOWEY

Walking by map, I chose unwonted ground,
  A crooked, questionable path which led
Beyond the margin, then delivered me
  At a turn. Red marl
Had rutted the aimless track
  That firmly withheld the recompense it hid
Till now, close by its end, the day's discoveries
  Began with the dimming night:

A house. The wall-stones, brown.
  The doubtful light, more of a mist than light
Floating at hedge-height through the sodden fields
  Had yielded, or a final glare
Burst there, rather, to concentrate
  Sharp saffron, as the ebbing year—
Or so it seemed, for the dye deepened—poured
  All of its yellow strength through the way I went:

Over grass, garden-space, over the grange
  That jutted beyond, lengthening-down
The house line, tall as it was,
  By tying it to the earth, trying its pride
(Which submitted) under a nest of barns,
  A walled weight of lesser encumbrances—
Few of which worsened it, and none
  As the iron sheds, sealing my own approach.

All stone. I had passed these last, unwarrantable
  Symbols of—no; let me define, rather
The thing they were not, all that we cannot be,
  By the description, simply of that which merits it:

Stone. Why must (as it does at each turn)
    Each day, the mean rob us of patience, distract us
Before even its opposite?—before stone, which
    Cut, piled, mortared, is patience's presence.

The land farmed, the house was neglected: but
    Gashed panes (and there were many) still showed
Into the pride of that presence. I had reached
    Unchallenged, within feet of the door
Ill-painted, but at no distant date—the least
    Our prodigal time could grudge it; paused
To measure the love, to assess its object,
    That trusts for continuance to the mason's hand.

Five centuries—here were (at the least) five—
    In linked love, eager excrescence
Where the door, arched, crowned with acanthus,
    Aimed at a civil elegance, but hit
This sturdier compromise, neither Greek, Gothic
    Nor Strawberry, clumped from the arching-point
And swathing down, like a fist of wheat,
    The unconscious emblem for the house's worth.

Conclusion surrounded it, and the accumulation
    After Lammas growth. Still coming on
Hart's-tongue by maiden-hair
    Thickened beneath the hedges, the corn leveled
And carried, long-since; but the earth
    (Its tint glowed in the house wall)
Out of the reddish dark still thrust up foison
    Through the browning-back of the exhausted year:

Thrust through the unweeded yard, where earth and house
    Debated the terrain. My eye
Caught in those flags a gravestone's fragment
    Set by a careful century. The washed inscription
Still keen, showed only a fragile stem
    A stave, a broken circlet, as
(Unintelligibly clear, craft in the sharp decrepitude)
    A pothook grooved its firm memorial.

Within, wet from the failing roof,
    Walls greened. Each hearth refitted

For a suburban whim, each room
  Denied what it was, diminished thus
To a barbarous mean, had comforted (but for a time)
  Its latest tenant. Angered, I turned to my path
Through the inhuman light, light that a fish might swim
  Stained by the grayness of the smoking fields.

Five centuries. And we? What we had not
  Made ugly, we had laid waste—
Left (I should say) the office to nature
  Whose blind battery, best fitted to perform it
Outdoes us, completes by persistence
  All that our negligence fails in. Saddened,
Yet angered beyond sadness, where the road
  Doubled upon itself I halted, for a moment
Facing the empty house and its laden barns.   *1958*

ANTECEDENTS

A HOMAGE AND VALEDICTION

"Oh! que ses yeux ne parlent plus d'Idéal
Mais simplement d'humains échanges!"

"After such knowledge, what foregiveness?"

THE SCENE: chiefly the Paris of Jules Laforgue and
Stéphane Mallarmé.

I. NOTHING: A DIVAGATION

Not the calm—the clarity
After the storm. There are
In lucidity itself
Its crystal abysses
Perspective within perspective:
The white mind holds
An insufficiency, a style
To contain a solitude
And nothing more. Thus,
The infirm alchemy
Of platonic fantasy—
Word, the idea,
Spacing the vacuum: snow-prints

Wanting a direction; perhaps
At the most, as a constellation
The cut stone
Reassembled on dark.

II. PRAELUDIUM

"Je ne puis quitter ce ton: que d'échos. . . ."—Derniers Vers

The horn has sounded.

Sunsets! They are interminable. Too late, however
For his exclamations. Sunsets. . . . A point,
Of interrogation, perhaps? How long
Can a sun go on setting? The thin refrain
Dies in a dying light as
"The splendor falls." And it continues
Falling flaking into the leaf-drift. First,
It was Byron; the laureate
Next remarked on the inveterate music
Microscopically, reserving his
Tintinnabulations (caught in the half-stopped ear)
For elegiacs between occasions, the slow sun
Maintaining its progress (downwards)
Chromatically lamented. "He is a master
Of miniature," said Nietzsche
Speaking from solitude—he was describing
The bayreuthian minotaur, lamenting the hecatombs,
Yet forced to concede
An undionysiac, unappollonian distinction
In that gamut of melancholias. "Art is a keyboard
For transitions," said Mallarmé: "between something and nothing."
The music persisted
"And when I heard it" (Charles Baudelaire, the
Slow horn pouring through dusk an orange twilight)
"I grew insatiate." We had our laureates, they
Their full orchestra and its various music. To that
        Enter
On an ice-drift
A white bear, the grand Chancellor
From Analyse, uncertain
Of whom he should bow to, or whether
No one is present. It started with Byron, and

Liszt, says Heine, bowed to the ladies. But Jules. . . .
Outside,

De la musique avant toute chose
The thin horns gone glacial
And behind blinds, partitioning Paris
Into the rose-stained mist,
He bows to the looking-glass. Sunsets.

III. LACUNAE

Autumn! Leaves in symphonic tumult,
Fall of Antigones and Philomelas
That my grave-digger (alas, poor Yorick!)
Must shift with his spade; and from the window
In the wet, all my chimneys
On the factories . . .

Chaplin, as Hamlet. A role we have yet to see
For the most part. As also
That spoiled Lutheran, masked
As his Zarathustra. Our innate
Perspicacity for the moderate
Is a national armory. "I have not
Read him; I have read about him":
In usum delphini—for the use
Of the common man. After Nietzsche
(Downwards) Sartre, after whom
Anouilh, dauphin's delight. And thus
Rimbaud the incendiary,
Gamin contemporary
With Gosse, the gentleman
Arrived late. He was dressed
In the skin of a Welsh lion, or the lion
Wore his—for the light
Was dubious, the marsh softening
And the company, willing to be led
Back to the forsaken garden by a route
Unfamiliar—yet as it wound
Dimly among the fetishes, a bewilderment
Of reminiscence. The force
That through the green dark, drove them
Muffled dissatisfactions. Last light, low among tempests
Of restless brass. Last music

For the sable throne (She comes, she comes!)
As the horns, one by one
Extinguish under the wave
Rising into the level darkness.
                    And Chaplin,
As Hamlet? That would have been
A more instructive frenzy. Eye-level light
Disclosing the field's wrinkles
Closes.

IV. MILIEUX

            We lack nothing
But the milieu.
            De la fumée avant toute chose
Weaving the smoke, subjective
Faun with a cigarette, Stéphane assembled one:
The page (the horns gone glacial)
Discovered its landscapes
As arctic gardens,
A luminous aura, hinting the penetration
Of green skeins, a snow-light
Bruising the mind.
            There were divagations (platonic)
There were departures (actual)
And the predilection
For a confirmed madness
Confused them, one with another. Thus Missolonghi
Was re-enacted at Harrar
At Papeete, Atouana—"alone
And surrounded by verdure":
Preludes to Taos.
            We lack nothing
But a significant sun.

V. THE BELLS: A PERIOD PIECE

"What a world of solemn thought. . . ."—POE.

Hygienic bells, pale
Galilean bells (O what a wealth
Of melody!)—the lingering
Aftertone of all that sullen, moneyed harmony
Drove, and will drive, before its tidal choir
The great departures and the soft refusals.

Expostulation with the deaf—impossible
"To modify this situation":
Rustle of lavender and thyme, clean collars
As the wind is gagged
Full of this crystalline confusion:

The sky, dressed in the sound of Sunday colors
The season (fall of Antigones and Philomelas!)
The trains (pictureque destinations!) missed
The girls (white as their prayer-books) are released,
Rustle in lavender and thyme
From incense back to houses where
Their white pianos cool each thirsty square.

Chimeric bells, provincial bells—
And from the rust within their throats (O what a world
Of solemn thought!) now silence breaks:
Secure no longer in their theme
Or violence of its repetitions,
The generations abdicate
To us the means to vacillate.

VI. SOMETHING: A DIRECTION

Out of the shut cell of that solitude there is
    One egress, past point of interrogation.
Sun is, because it is not you; you are
    Since you are self, and self delimited
Regarding sun. It downs? I claim? Cannot
    Beyond such speech as this, gather conviction?
Judge, as you will, not what I say
    But what is, being said. It downs
Recovered, coverless, in a shriven light
    And you, returning, may to a shriven self
As from the scene, your self withdraws. You are downing
    Back from that autumn music of the light, which
Split by your need, to know the textures of your pain,
    Refuses them in your acceptance. You accept
An evening, washed of its overtones
    By strict seclusion, yet are not secluded
Withheld at your proper bounds. From there
    Your returns may enter, welcome strangers
Into a civil country (you were not the first
    To see it), but a country, natural and profuse

Unbroken by past incursions, as the theme
    Strung over stave, is rediscovered
After dismemberment in the canon, and over stave
    Can still proceed, unwound, unwinding
To its established presence, its territory
    Staked and sung; and the phrase descends
As a phase concluded. Released
    From knowing to acknowledgment, from prison
To powers, you are new-found
    Neighbored, having earned relation
With all that is other. Still you must wait,
    For evening's ashen, like the slow fire
Withdrawn through the whitened log
    Glinting through grain marks where the wood splits:
Let be its being: the scene extends
    Not hope, but the urgency that hopes for means.

                                                    1958

Author's Notes

III. LACUNAE

"The force/That through the green dark . . ."
                        (Cf. DYLAN THOMAS, Eighteen Poems.)

IV. MILIEUX

*Rimbaud departed to Harrar; Gaugin to Papeete and Atouana. From Atouana
the latter wrote: "You have no idea of the peace in which I live here, entirely
alone, surrounded by verdure." (Quoted by* R. H. WILENSKI, *p. 177* Modern
French Painters, *Faber 1944.)*

V. THE BELLS

"Impossible de modifier cette situation." In rendering this from Derniers
Vers, *one cannot avoid the tone of (early) Eliot because Eliot himself has
not avoided the tone of Laforgue.*

BIOGRAPHICAL AND BIBLIOGRAPHICAL NOTES

The following notes are intended only to provide the most basic identification of the poets represented in this anthology and a highly selective list of their books. Occasionally commentaries on their lives and work are noted, but only when such commentaries may be particularly useful to the student.

THE BRITISH POETS

Wystan Hugh Auden (b. 1907). Educated Oxford University. Schoolteacher 1930–1935. Leader of Left poetry movement, with Spender, Day Lewis, MacNeice, in 1930's. Emigrated to U. S. in 1939 and became American citizen. After teaching in American colleges and universities, elected Professor of Poetry at Oxford 1956–1961. BOOKS: *Poems*, 1930, 1933, 1934–1935 (three distinct editions); *On This Island*, 1937; *Selected Poems*, 1938; *The Collected Poetry*, 1945; *The Age of Anxiety*, 1947; *Nones*, 1951; *Homage to Clio*, 1960. COMMENTARY: Joseph Warren Beach, *The Making of the Auden Canon*, 1957.

John Betjeman (b. 1916). Educated Oxford University. Schoolteacher, journalist, authority on English architecture. BOOKS: *Mount Zion*, 1932; *Continual Dew*, 1937; *Old Lights from New Chancels*, 1940; *New Bats in Old Belfries*, 1945; *Selected Poems*, 1948; *A Few Late Chrysanthemums*, 1954; *Collected Poems*, 1958; *Summoned* by Bells, 1960.

Robert Bridges (1844–1930). Educated Oxford University. Medical studies St. Bartholomew's Hospital. London physician until 1882, thereafter devoting himself to literature. Appointed Poet Laureate 1913. His devotion to church-music related to special interest in questions of prosody. BOOKS: *Poetical Works*, 1912; *The Testament of Beauty*, 1929; *The Shorter Poems*, 1931 (enlarged edition).

Walter de la Mare (1873–1956). Educated St. Paul's Cathedral Choir School, London. Clerk, Anglo-American branch of Standard Oil Company 1890–1908, after which government grant and pension allowed him to devote himself to poetry and fiction. BOOKS: *Songs of Childhood*, 1902 (pseudonym: Walter Ramal); *Poems*, 1906;

Poems 1901–1918, 1920 (published in U. S. as *Collected Poems: 1901–1918*, 1920); *Collected Poems*, 1941; *Collected Rhymes and Verses*, 1944; *The Traveller*, 1946; *Inward Companion*, 1950; *Winged Chariot*, 1951; *O Lovely England*, 1952. COMMENTARY: *Tribute to Walter de la Mare on His 75th Birthday*, 1948.

William Empson (b. 1906). Educated Cambridge University. Has taught English literature at Chinese and Japanese universities, and since 1953 at Sheffield University in England. One of the leading "New Critics." BOOKS: *Poems*, 1935; *The Gathering Storm*, 1940; *Collected Poems*, 1955. Criticism: *Seven Types of Ambiguity*, 1930; *Some Versions of Pastoral*, 1935; *The Structure of Complex Words*, 1951.

Robert Graves (b. 1895). Son of Irish poet Alfred Perceval Graves. Educated Oxford University. First recognition as poet of World War I. Prolific writer of fiction, criticism, literary polemic, mythological studies. Now perhaps best known for *The White Goddess*, 1948, a study of the continuing inspiration of poetry by certain motifs of ancient myth. Elected Professor of Poetry, Oxford, in 1961. BOOKS: *Collected Poems*, 1955; *Five Pens in Hand*, 1958; *The Poems*, 1958. Autobiography: *Good-Bye to All That*, 1929. Fiction: *I, Claudius*, 1934. Criticism: *A Survey of Modernist Poetry*, 1927 (with Laura Riding); *The Crowning Privilege*, 1955.

Thomas Hardy (1840–1928). Turned from architecture to poetry, then to the novels which earned him his great reputation. Returned to poetry after the indignant reception of his novel *Jude the Obscure*, 1896. BOOKS: *Wessex Poems*, 1898; *Time's Laughingstocks*, 1909; *Satires of Circumstance*, 1914; *The Poetical Works*, 1920–1924. Fiction: *Far from the Madding Crowd*, 1874; *The Return of the Native*, 1878; *The Mayor of Casterbridge*, 1886; *Tess of the D'Urbervilles*, 1891. COMMENTARY: Essays in *The Southern Review*, Volume VI (Summer, 1940); Edmund Blunden, *Thomas Hardy*, 1942.

Gerard Manley Hopkins (1844–1889). Educated Oxford University. Converted to Catholicism, entered Jesuit priesthood. His correspondence with Robert Bridges and other poets a notable contribution to poetic theory. Professor of Greek, Dublin University 1884. BOOKS: *Poems* (edited 1918 by Robert Bridges, 1930 by Charles Williams, 1948 by W. H. Gardner). See also *The Letters of Gerard Manley Hopkins to Robert Bridges*, ed. C. C. Abbott, 1935; *The*

Notebooks and Papers of Gerard Manley Hopkins, ed. Humphrey House and Graham Storey, 1959. COMMENTARY: W. H. Gardner, *Gerard Manley Hopkins,* Vol. I, 1944 (revised 1948) and Vol. II, 1949; *Gerard Manley Hopkins,* by the Kenyon Critics, 1945; Norman Weyand, ed., *Immortal Diamond,* 1949.

A. E. Housman (1859–1936). Educated Oxford University. Employed Patent Office 1882–1892. Professor of Latin, University College, London, 1892–1911; Cambridge University thereafter. An outstanding classical scholar. BOOKS: *A Shropshire Lad,* 1896; *Last Poems,* 1922; *More Poems,* 1936; *Collected Poems,* 1953.

Philip Larkin (b. 1922). Educated Oxford University. Librarian University of Hull. A spokesman for England's postwar literary generation of "Angry Young Men." Poetry: *The North Ship,* 1945; *The Less Deceived,* 1955. Novels: *Jill,* 1946; *A Girl in Winter,* 1947.

D. H. Lawrence (1885–1930). Son of Nottinghamshire miner. (See autobiographical novel *Sons and Lovers,* 1913, for a picture of Lawrence's early years.) Educated Nottingham Day Training College. Schoolteacher for occasional periods. Noted for fiction and poetry especially, but also for critical and social theory and painting. Traveled Australia, Mexico, Sicily, Sardinia, Italy, United States, Mexico after leaving England in 1919. Portrayed as Mark Rampion in Aldous Huxley's *Point Counter Point.* BOOKS: *Look! We Have Come Through!,* 1917; *Birds, Beasts and Flowers,* 1923; *The Collected Poems,* 1928 (American edition 1929); *Pansies,* 1929; *Last Poems,* 1932; *The Ship of Death,* 1933; *Selected Poems,* 1947; *Complete Poems,* 1957. Novels: *The Rainbow,* 1915; *Women in Love,* 1920; *Aaron's Rod,* 1922; *The Plumed Serpent,* 1926; *Lady Chatterley's Lover,* 1928. Other fiction: *The Prussian Officer,* 1914; *The Ladybird, The Fox, The Captain's Doll,* 1923; *The Man Who Died,* 1931. Criticism: *Studies in Classic American Literature,* 1923. Travel: *Twilight in Italy,* 1916; *Sea and Sardinia,* 1921. See also *The Letters,* 1932, ed. Aldous Huxley. COMMENTARY: Horace Gregory, *Pilgrim of the Apocalypse,* 1933; W. Y. Tindall, *D. H. Lawrence and Susan His Cow,* 1939.

Cecil Day Lewis (b. 1904). Born Ireland, son of Anglican clergyman. Educated Oxford University. Schoolteacher 1927–1935. Professor of Poetry, Oxford University, 1951–1956. *A Hope for Poetry,* 1934, was outstanding manifesto of Left poetry movement of 1930's. Translator from the classics. Under pseudonym Nicholas Blake author of detective fiction. BOOKS: *Transitional Poem,* 1929; *From Feathers to Iron,* 1931; *Magnetic Mountain,* 1933; *Collected Poems,* 1954; *Pegasus and Other Poems,* 1957.

Louis MacNeice (b. 1907). Born in Belfast, Ireland, son of an Anglican clergyman. Educated Oxford University. Lecturer in Classics University of Birmingham and other English and American colleges and universities. Translator from the classics. BOOKS: *Blind Fireworks,* 1929; *Poems,* 1935; *Autumn Journal,* 1939; *Selected Poems,* 1940; *Poems 1925–1940,* 1940; *Collected Poems,* 1949; *Ten Burnt Offerings,* 1952; *Autumn Sequel,* 1954; *Visitations,* 1957; *Solstices,* 1961.

John Masefield (b. 1878). Trained at first for the merchant marine, he left the service at fifteen and worked at odd jobs before entering the literary world as poet, free-lance writer, and journalist. Appointed Poet Laureate in 1930, at the death of Robert Bridges. BOOKS: *Salt-Water Ballads,* 1902; *The Everlasting Mercy,* 1911; *The Widow in the Bye Street,* 1912; *Dauber,* 1913 *Reynard the Fox,* 1919; *The Collected Poems of John Masefield,* 1923 (new and enlarged revised ed., 1932); *Poems. Complete Edition, with Recent Poems,* 1935.

Edwin Muir (1887–1958). Born Orkney Islands. Little formal education, poverty-filled youth in Glasgow which opened him to Socialist thought. Later turned to more mystical and religious views. Editor, translator, critic, he became Director of the British Institute in Prague and in Rome after World War II, and in 1950 Warden of Newbattle Abbey College. BOOKS: *First Poems,* 1925; *Chorus of the Newly Dead,* 1926; *Variations on a Time Theme,* 1934; *The Labyrinth,* 1949; *Collected Poems 1921–1951,* 1952; *One Foot in Eden,* 1957. Autobiography: *The Story and The Fable,* 1940.

Wilfred Owen (1893–1918). Educated London University. Killed in action World War I. The most famous of the English war poets, together with Siegfried Sassoon, who first collected his poems in 1920. BOOKS: *Poems,* 1920; *The Poems of Wilfred Owen,* "a new edition including many pieces now first published, and notices of his life and work," 1931 (ed. Edmund Blunden).

Kathleen Raine (b. 1908). Educated Girton College, Cambridge University (with which she is still associated), specializing in botany and zoölogy. Married, and later separated from, the poet and professor Charles Madge. Has long been engaged in a study of the symbolism of William Blake. BOOKS: *Stone and Flower, Poems 1935–1943,* 1943; *Living in Time,* 1946; *The Pythoness,* 1949; *The Year One,* 1952; *Collected Poems,* 1956.

Siegfried Sassoon (b. 1886). Educated Cambridge University. Together with Wilfred Owen, the outstanding English war poet, continuing his pacifist writing after the War. BOOKS: *The War Poems of Siegfried Sassoon,* 1919; *Selected Poems,* 1925; *Collected Poems,* 1947; *Sequences,* 1956. Autobiographical novel: *The Complete Memoirs of George Sherston.*

Edith Sitwell (b. 1887). Member of a famous literary family, sister of Osbert and Sacheverell Sitwell. Privately educated. Editor *Wheels,* 1916–1918, 1921, which attacked the formal limitations of the popular Georgian school. Made a Dame in 1954. BOOKS: *Façade,* 1922; *The Sleeping Beauty,* 1924; *The Collected Poems,* 1930, 1957; *Street Songs,* 1942; *The Song of the Cold,* 1945; *The Canticle of the Rose: Poems 1917–1949,* 1949; *Gardeners and Astronomers,* 1953.

Stephen Spender (b. 1909). Educated at Oxford University. A member of the "Auden group" in the thirties. A distinguished critic and literary journalist as well as poet. BOOKS: *Poems,* 1933; *Vienna,* 1934; *Trial of a Judge,* 1938; *The Still Centre,* 1939; *Selected Poems,* 1940; *Ruins and Visions,* 1942; *Collected Poems,* 1955. Criticism: *The Destructive Element,* 1935. Autobiography: *World Within World,* 1951.

James Stephens (1882–1950). Born Dublin. Childhood in poverty, no formal education. Intense Irish nationalist, reflected in Celtic themes and stylistic mannerisms. BOOKS: *Collected Poems,* 1926. Fiction: *The Crock of Gold,* 1912; *The Demi-Gods,* 1914; *Deirdre,* 1923.

Dylan Thomas (1914–1953). Born Swansea, Wales. Educated Swansea Grammar School. Distinguished career as broadcaster on B. B. C. His rich speaking voice made his reading-tours the most successful of any poet's in this century. (The hectic character of these tours and the self-destructive alcoholism they intensified in Thomas are vividly described in John Malcolm Brinnin, *Dylan Thomas in America: An Intimate Journal,* 1955.) BOOKS: *Eighteen Poems,* 1934; *Twenty-Five Poems,* 1936; *Map of Love: Verse and Prose,* 1939; *New Poems,* 1943; *Selected Writings,* 1946; *Deaths and Entrances,* 1946; *In Country Sleep,* 1952; *The Collected Poems,* 1952. Prose: *Portrait of the Artist as a Young Dog*, 1940. Drama: *Under Milk Wood*, 1954. COMMENTARY: Henry Treece, *Dylan Thomas*, 1949; Elder Olson, *The Poetry of Dylan Thomas*, 1954.

Charles Tomlinson (b. 1927). Educated Cambridge University. Teaches at Bristol University. Exemplar of the influence of American poetry on younger British writers. BOOKS: *Relations and Contraries*, 1951; *The Necklace*, 1955; *Seeing Is Believing*, 1958.

William Butler Yeats (1865–1939). Born Ireland, son of the painter John Butler Yeats. See his *Autobiography*, 1927, for descriptions of the influences of his childhood. No university education, but studied at Erasmus Smith School and the Metropolitan School of Art in Dublin, and private studies in occultism and poetry. His collections of Irish folklore and his early coediting of Blake's works are two instances among many of his capacity to direct his own studies. In the late eighties and the nineties, a leading poet both of England and Ireland. Also, a leader of the Irish Renaissance; he helped found the Abbey Theatre. Senator, Irish Free State, 1922–1928. Nobel Prize for Literature, 1923. Dramatist, critic, mystical thinker (see *A Vision*, 1925; enlarged, revised edition 1937, 1956; the ideas of this work are extremely important in Yeats's later writings). BOOKS: *The Wanderings of Oisin*, 1889; *The Wind among the Reeds*, 1899; *In the Seven Woods*, 1903; *The Green Helmet*, 1910; *Responsibilities*, 1914; *The Wild Swans at Coole*, 1917; *Michael Robartes and the Dancer*, 1920; *The Tower*, 1928; *The Winding Stair*, 1933; *The Collected Poems*, 1933, 1951 (enlarged edition), 1956 ("Definitive Edition"); *Last Poems and Plays*, 1940; *The Variorum Edition of the Poems*, 1957, ed. Peter Allt and Russell K. Alspach; *Selected Poems and Two Plays*, 1962, ed. M. L. Rosenthal. Drama: *The Collected Plays*, 1953 ("New edition, with five additional plays"). Other prose: *Essays*, 1924; *The Letters*, 1955, ed. Allan Wade; *The Autobiography of William Butler Yeats*, 1927 (as *Autobiographies*), 1958; *Mythologies*, 1959; *Essays and Introductions*, 1961. COMMENTARY: Joseph M. Hone, *Life of William Butler Yeats*, 1942; T. R. Henn, *The Lonely Tower*, 1950; Allan Wade, *A Bibliography of the Writings of W. B. Yeats*, 1951; A. Norman Jeffares, *W. B. Yeats, Man and Poet*, 1949; Richard Ellmann, *Yeats: The Man and the Masks*, 1948; Richard Ellmann, *The Identity of Yeats*, 1954; F. A. C. Wilson, *W. B. Yeats and Tradition*, 1958, and *Yeats's Iconography*, 1961.

Modern American Poetry

Modern American poetry began to emerge in the last century whenever the idiom became familiar and the tone was derived from an immediate state of mind rather than from English literary models. The beginning of Emerson's "Hamatreya" is as modern as anything in Robert Frost:

> Bulkeley, Hunt, Willard, Hosmer, Meriam, Flint,
> Possessed the land which rendered to their toil
> Hay, corn, roots, hemp, flax, apples, wool and wood.

Emerson does not sustain this tone throughout the poem. Nor does any poet born before the Civil War, except Whitman and Emily Dickinson, approach its special kind of immediacy in the whole body of his work. Whitman does so very often—

> Where are you off to, lady? For I see you,
> You splash in the water there, yet stay stock still in your room.
> (Song of Myself)

But Whitman, with his stylistic eccentricities and his expansive rhetoric, is not yet of this century, though certainly he is its greatest poetic forerunner. Emily Dickinson is far more naturally a spokesman for the existential moment—that is, for the sense that the true matter of a poem is the feel and body of the awareness it presents. That sense, even more than a free approach to meter, stanza, and theme, is the heart of what we call "modern." Therefore, we may think of her as our first twentieth-century American poet, especially as she did not really come into her own until long after her death in 1886. Look at simple poems like "A Bird Came Down the Walk" and "A Narrow Fellow in the Grass," perfect examples of the way in which she keeps concrete pictures or figures of speech in the foreground throughout a poem yet makes the subjective awareness around the hard image her true concern. The wit, the concentration, and the subordination of syntax, rhyme, and sound to the developing tone all have a contemporary edge for us also.

> I more than once, at morn,
>
> Have passed, I thought, a whip-lash
> Unbraiding in the sun,—
> When, stooping to secure it,
> It wrinkled and was gone. . . .

Look, too, at a poem like " 'Twas like a maelstrom, with a notch," in which we have a series of similes for the unstated "It"—an experience whose crucial moral character we can only surmise by way of its mounting imagery of terror, guilt, and then an infinitely regretted "reprieve." Ezra Pound's famous definition of an image as "an intellectual and emotional complex in an instant of time" has never been more piercingly illustrated than by this poem.

To speak so surely to the essence of an emotion is the purest of poetic tasks. The pressures of her life upon her natural gifts seem to have produced a miraculous, spontaneous outpouring of hundreds of brief, moving poems from Miss Dickinson. Later, when the new American poetry became a recognizable movement, cultivation of a style paced by the rhythms and turns of folk-speech became more deliberate. The best work of Masters, Lindsay, Sandburg, Robinson, Frost, and Williams presents an infinite variety of effects and voices within this general movement. Poetic achievement is not, of course, just a matter of talking well, or even talking well in dialect; yet the good poet has an ear for what he hears in the world around him, and the way he uses it can be deeply involved in the values of his poetry. The poet has to know how to use it, and where to begin and where to end. Sandburg's love affair with American speech and folk-wisdom, for instance, is at once one of the glories and one of the scandals of our poetry: a glory because he records them so faithfully and spiritedly; a scandal because he came gradually to love them for their own sake rather than as elements only incidental, however important, to the making of poems that stand up in their own right. He triumphs when the voice is native and the poem is the main thing, in sardonic pieces like "Balloon Faces" and "The Lawyers Know Too Much," in the occasional lyrical heights of *The People, Yes* (always interesting, but not always interesting as *poetry*), in that colloquially elegiac mood that so many American poets have expressed so well—see his "Cool Tombs," for instance, or Masters's "The Hill," or Fearing's "Memo"—and sometimes in the work that exalts the people's struggles and heroes, such as "Ossawatomie."

Sandburg's populist and Socialist background strongly colors his use of the vernacular. The work of Masters and Lindsay, especially the latter, has its political and social motivations also. The former poet made his great reputation with his *Spoon River Anthology*, at least superficially an "exposé" of provincial American morals and manners closely akin to the fiction of Sherwood Anderson and Sinclair Lewis. A series of monologues by various inhabitants of Spoon River, the book has its muckraking side in such pieces as "Daisy Fraser" and "Editor Whedon." But many of the monologues are much less tough-minded, even sentimental—"Lucinda Matlock," with its praise of the antique virtues needed to make people love life; "Anne Rutledge," with its idealization (like Sandburg's) of the meaning of Lincoln; the rather sententious "Petit, the Poet." Lindsay, on the other hand, made a singing music of religious and political passions deep in the American blood:

In a nation of one hundred fine, mob-hearted, lynching, relenting, repenting millions,
There are plenty of sweeping, singing, stinging, gorgeous things to shout about,
And knock you old blue devils out.

("Bryan, Bryan, Bryan, Bryan")

In "The Congo," his best-known work, Lindsay sinks himself deep into a chant which he calls "a study of the Negro race." It is easy to see now that it leans too heavily on obnoxious racial stereotypes; the opening section is even named "Their Basic Savagery." But Lindsay did not mean it this way. He had a Rousseauan conception, not quite of the noble savage, but of the vital savage in touch with the demonic and, ultimately, the divine forces of life. In this poem, particularly at first, he catches the syncopation of Afro-American music, and his language is appropriately racy and exuberant. He could write more formally and conventionally, and do it rather well—witness "Abraham Lincoln Walks at Midnight" and "The Eagle That Is Forgotten," both poems that derive their passion from the *mystique* of the democratic political tradition. But he realized himself with the fever and ecstasy of transported vision. His best work is invested with the evangelical fervor to which America has been recurrently subject.

The voice in E. A. Robinson's poetry is far subtler, usually, than that of any of the other poets so far mentioned, except, on occasion, that of Emily Dickinson. Her perceptions were every bit as subtle, but her statements were arrows that went heartbreakingly to the mark. Robinson gives us something else—statements that are imbued with the opacity, the deceptiveness of things. He is often most interested in the irony and pity of individual lives, generally lives that are somehow marked by failure. "Richard Cory" and "Flammonde" are bold enough in outline to escape ambiguity, yet both are, characteristically, *about* ambiguous lives whose meaning never will be altogether clear. When we turn to something like "Eros Turannos," we see Robinson when he was nearest to greatness, his mind playing over and over the treacherous surfaces of human lives, in this case a marriage that has fallen into the abyss. He resembles Henry James here in his curiosity about what lies behind the social mask of character, and in his dark hints about sexuality, loyalty, and man's terrible will to defeat himself. Robinson belonged to a group of Americans obsessed with nostalgia for a simpler nobility to cope with the demands of life.

Robinson thus takes us deep into the "psychology" of a changing America and of the conflicts between certain lingering chivalric ideals and the rise of a more ruthless, impersonal structure of values than the past knew. Robert Frost, too, is engaged by these themes, but his more local, New England emphasis and his ability to present the physical presence of people and scenes rather conceal the fact. No one has evoked the pastoral side of a region with such authority as Frost; no one has better pictured country life in all its reality. Nor has anyone better pictured the barrenness and the terror such life can hold. "The Hill Wife," "Home-Burial," "An Old Man's Winter Night," "A Servant to Servants," "The Witch of Coös" embody a dread of the ultimate brutality of existence that belies the idyllic surface impressions of Frost's happier poetry. Within the limits of a quite conventional verse technique, Frost has grown a body of poetry remarkably powerful in its sensuous repossession of one kind of American experience that throws all the rest of American life into complex, critical perspective.

Perhaps the most striking difference between Frost and William Carlos Williams as "localist" poets lies in the amazing liberation of Williams's poetic form. His verse never drowses, never goes off into ponderosities as do Robinson's and Frost's, at times, under the hypnosis of the iambic pentameter line. In "Spring and All," "To Elsie," or "The Crowd at the Ball Game" we see poetic form handled most cleanly and functionally. In the first of these we have an irregular series of longer (but not very long) stanzas and two-line stanzas; the second is made up of three-line stanzas; the third of two-line units. The line-length varies according to the sequence of thought and feeling, the poet maintaining just enough pattern to keep a general over-all sense of structure and of the discipline of compressed form, while he relies on his extraordinary ear and sense of timing to establish a deeper underlying rhythm. In these as in most of his other poems, there is a stronger urban feeling, and a more cosmopolitan viewpoint, than in Frost. Williams's characteristic locale is the area around Rutherford and Paterson, New Jersey, a region intimately linked with New York City, on the one hand, and with the great factory- and railroad-dominated as well as the farming areas of what he calls "the ribbed end of North Jersey." At the same time, Williams is often just as much a "nature-poet" as Frost. Trees, flowers, landscapes are the subjects of a great many of his poems—he displays an intense, mysterious, often violent empathy for them that is doubtless connected with his primitivist love of vitality for its own sake. Like many another modern writer, he has looked to the undereducated and the deprived classes for their latent, unrealized power. His theme again and again, particularly in the long *Paterson* sequence, has been the need for America to discover a voice of her own so that she can create a civilization both indigenous and related to the great European tradition.

Here Williams is very close to Pound and Eliot. All three are explicitly critics of a civilization they believe has gone radically wrong, and, though Williams has insisted on finding a poetic line and diction that are intrinsically American, he shares with the other two their revulsion against what has happened to our manners and values and their castigation of the whole tendency of

Western society to discard traditions without wishing to create new values worthy of civilization. Williams has even gone a certain way with Pound's criticism of the money and banking systems as the root of our disorders, though never with Pound's more extreme advocacy of Italian Fascism and certain kindred ideas. Both writers are among the great lyrical and rhetorical poets of this century. Both have whatever it is in poetry that corresponds to "absolute pitch" in music. And both make of their commitment to aesthetic values ("pure beauty") a standard by which the age can be judged. Pound's *Hugh Selwyn Mauberley* finds that modern Anglo-American society has stripped the artist of his status and substituted commercialism for every kind of integrity and faith. The "he" of the first poem is presented as a modern Odysseus who has tried to restore the sense of the sublime to England and failed, and the succeeding poems of the sequence describe what has happened to the great traditions in detail. The *Cantos* elaborate on this conception of the true poet as a modern Odysseus with an epic mission who, in the course of his wanderings, passes through the desolation of the modern world and rediscovers certain moments and figures of the past that are touchstones of meaning for the present: the wise Confucius and his disciples, the *caveat* of the medieval Church against usury, the great names of heroic myth and literature, the ancient vision of an earthly paradise. Brilliant incantatory poems like "The Return" and "The Alchemist," and the equally brilliant translations from the Chinese and the Latin and other languages mean for Pound not only the making of beautiful poems but also the rediscovery of continuities with other cultures.

Pound's strong sense of the social relevance of what most people consider unworldly, and his messianic demand for a "hard" poetry, organic in form, without "emotional slither" or verbosity or enslavement to the "beat of the metronome," was an enormously important factor in the rise of the poetry of this century. This poetry has emphasized the image and the necessity of making a poem thoroughly alive in every respect, moment by moment and line by line, free of the patness of "magazine-verse." Modern poetry had been tending in these directions by the end of the first decade of this century, a fact which helps account for Yeats's responsiveness to Pound's criticism of his poems when they first met, and for Eliot's experimentation along similar lines before he was "discovered" by

Pound. What Emily Dickinson had done almost instinctively now became conscious method. Eliot's "The Love Song of J. Alfred Prufrock," "Gerontion," and "The Waste Land" are perhaps our most extraordinary examples outside the work of the French Symbolists of the application of the "new" principles.

The poet's own voice is almost never directly heard in these poems. "Prufrock" is a figure in a dramatic monologue of a new sort, a purposeful reverie in which the speaker takes a hypothetical listener through a journey among images, psychological impressions, remembered moments, literary echoes, in search of the meaning of his own failure to meet the adult challenge of life. The old man of "Gerontion" is a more symbolic figure—he too has failed to meet the challenge, but he embodies the defeat of a whole culture, its loss of creative integrity and, especially, of religious faith. Both "Gerontion" and "The Waste Land" are close to the spirit of Pound's "Mauberley." "The Waste Land" even takes us through a similar review of contemporary society. But Eliot's poem is completely "presentative"; that is, instead of stating an abstract "message" it projects a host of effects and voices to evoke and suggest what it has to say, so that—as with "Prufrock" and "Gerontion"— our first impression is of an unrelated *mélange* of momentarily spectacular, moving, and comic passages. Gradually, however, the order of the poem emerges: the broad canvas of "The Burial of the Dead," introducing the general theme of cultural sterility, the major symbolic figures of the poem in the Tarot pack of the fortune-teller (herself a representative of the meaningless, commercial manipulation of what were once sacred meanings), the Inferno-like vision of modern city-life as a living death; the two closeups of "A Game of Chess," showing that the upper and lower classes alike suffer from the failure to love and communicate concern; the many instances of the triumph of uncontrolled lust in a world without moral or aesthetic perspective in "The Fire Sermon"; the implied call for a devout and heroic commitment, rather than submission to the pointlessness of a life without such commitment, in the elegy for Phlebas the Phoenician called "Death by Water"; and the imagery of promised redemption through following the Hindu message in "What the Thunder Said." Eliot's virtuosity is dazzling throughout this sequence. He combines precise and evocative imagery, exquisite lyricism, high and low comic effects, startlingly dramatic moments, parody both serious and witty, in a display of mastery of his art all the more impressive because so many varied tones and styles are bent to the service of the driving spirit behind the whole work. Eliot's ultimate stress is a religious one—this is his sharpest distinction from Williams and Pound, with whom he shares so many root-attitudes otherwise. Very likely this fact is intimately related to the struggle his poems seem constantly to carry on against a profound, depressed disgust with life.

We generally think of Wallace Stevens, Marianne Moore, H. D. (Hilda Doolittle), and E. E. Cummings as very much a part, in their several ways, of the modern movement of American poetry "led" by Pound and Eliot. As with the latter two poets, all four have cultivated a perfectionism of style that is a proliferation of the special speaking voice of each. Cummings is the most experimental, exploding words and sentences, working out typographical patterns so that at times his poems are visual jokes or pictures of a mood much more than they are the design of *sounds* we expect a poem to be. Yet he is often the most conventional of poets in what he has to say (romantic love poems, poems on mutability or in praise of youth and feminine beauty, satires against philistinism) and even in the basic forms he employs. Many of his poems, for instance, are sonnets open or disguised by the rearrangement of lines. Bohemian, pacifist, and political conservative at the same time, Cummings presents the same curious fusion of pure poetry and tendentiousness as do Pound and Eliot. He veers easily into sentimentality and often repeats himself, but his work contains some of the freshest, most concentrated lyricism of our century, and his forays into the American idiom are triumphs of humor as well as of poetic power.

Marianne Moore and Wallace Stevens are less obviously experimental than Cummings, whose methods have been compared (though the resemblance is only superficial) with those of European Dadaism and Futurism. Miss Moore is, poetically, an elegant conversationalist who constructs out of detailed observation a set of principles at once hardheaded and ladylike. Small animals and plants that survive not by aggressiveness but by special devices for resistance and endurance—the armadillo, the porcupine, the chambered nautilus, the "wood-weasel" or skunk—are among the subjects dearest to her. They suit her advocacy of the unsensationally functional in all aspects of life. (See her "Poetry" for a striking application of this view to the art of poetry, which she defends because it has, "after all, a place for the genuine," and because it reveals the realities at the heart of imagination.) Yeats once described as an aristocratic ideal the uniting of "passion and precision"; Miss Moore makes them pragmatic and democratic ideals as well. But the pleasures her methods of advocacy afford, that delightful fastidiousness and pungency, which never lapse into either mere gentility or mere "charm," should no more conceal her darker strands of thought and feeling than Frost's pastoralism should conceal his.

Wallace Stevens, too, contains these depths within a high-spirited style that sometimes appears pure dandyism, sometimes an exquisite spoofing of all ideology and all art. Like Williams, he believes in the healing and revealing power of art—paradoxically, the purer the art the more meaningful its expression of the truly human. The viewpoint is fundamental to his secular humanism and to his constant speculations on the relation between imagination and reality. It underlies his tricky arguments in "Sunday Morning" and "Peter Quince at the Clavier," to the effect that the intensities of experience and the repetitions of nature—the return of the birds each spring, the renewal of gardens each year, the constant replacement of youthful beauty by the "maidens" of newer generations—are the closest we shall ever come to eternity. Out of our own experience, deprivations, and observation of cyclical nature we project the "truths" of myth and faith, and in art we learn to play with these motifs and search out our ideal visions of the self. How bitterly deceptive all this may be Stevens confesses in a poem like "The Emperor of Ice-Cream"; how impossible for the human spirit to avoid such projections he shows in a poem like "The Idea of Order at Key West." But always in his work there is the richest overlay of sound, an exuberance of language and a wit alert to all its possibilities. Among younger American poets, Richard Wilbur has best learned from Stevens and Miss Moore to cultivate these gifts.

H. D. has given a body of poems which, taken together, represent precisely the Imagist ideal put forward by Pound and others of a poetry centered on a single sensuous effect or a single emotion, concrete, unredundant, an effect in action. Like Pound and the other early Imagists, she did not, of course, allow herself to be bound in all her work within the confines of this narrow if necessary discipline. (That is, the Imagist movement seemed a necessary stage in the liberation of modern verse from sentimentality, mere self-indulgence, and post-Tennysonian rhetoric.) She has also given us a small body of erotic and mystical poetry that is lovely, if not quite as immediate, in its own way. In this latter phase of her work she seems as independent of the general drift of our modern poetry as Conrad Aiken, who has always reserved to himself the right to resist the special tendencies of the Pound-Eliot movement and to cultivate a more "old-fashioned" sort of lyricism and impressionism. His modernity consists more in the kind of awareness he reveals and in the general resilience of fibre in his versification than in his particular poetic methods, although he is a skilful craftsman who knows how to depart from conventional rhythms and line-patterns without getting out of touch with his overall design. In certain ways Aiken and Edna St. Vincent Millay resemble one another, particularly in their shorter, more simple poems. Rarely, it is true, does he have the popular touch that her feminine voice possessed, ardent, often anguished, often very much of the brittle 'twenties,' like the novels of Fitzgerald or the early poetry of Cummings, and a little careless of the sustaining of effects. But Aiken's "Music I heard with you was more than music" and Millay's "Song of a Second April" or "Love is not all; it is not meat or drink" are remarkably alike in their essentials, and both writers are "natural" poets in love with language. Their easy skill may be compared, again, with that of the versatile Archibald MacLeish. And it may be compared and contrasted with that of John Crowe Ransom, whose elegiac, highly disciplined verse, with its aristocratic-Southern allusions and ironies, strikes the ear with a finely intellectualized grace and sweetness.

An interesting feature of the whole movement of modern poetry has been that, while from its beginnings it has appeared to struggle toward the kind of "purity" we associate with, say, Imagism—that is, a freedom from sentimentality and rhetoric and an assertion of intensity itself, whether of emotion or sensation, as a value independent of political, religious, or moral considerations—it has nevertheless been steeped in the dominant issues of the period. As a result, our poetry, despite its high aesthetic standards, has been profoundly, even violently, involved in the intellectual and social struggles of the age. The most successful poetry has been that which could transcend those struggles not so much by ignoring them as by remaining art even while wrestling with them. One reason for the authority of Pound, Williams, and Eliot has been their triumph in certain poems over the problems this has entailed. The political poetry of figures like Millay and MacLeish, on the other hand, has often seemed to go against the grain of their natural talents, and the overinsistence of so much of Robinson Jeffers' work on pointing certain anti-machine-age morals for the times has greatly marred his reputation as one of our finest narrative and descriptive poets. The late 1920's and the 1930's, of course, were in the United States and England a time for the exploration of revolutionary perspectives on our society, and it is striking to see the uses to which the delicately perceptive sensibility of Horace Gregory, whose best writing is either elegiac or psychologically interpretative, and the equally elegiac and also mordantly sardonic voice of Kenneth Fearing, were bent during this period.

Hart Crane, who died in 1932 at the age of thirty-three, and therefore still seems one of our "younger poets," was close to the same impulse when he wrote "The Bridge," which attempts to find a guiding spiritual symbolism for an industrial society in one of its great engineering artifacts. Nevertheless, it is a sequence whose speaking sensibility, like that in *The Waste Land* and in the *Cantos,* is seeking to define the poet's self, both in purely personal terms and in relation to the world he knows. As in those works, the pressures upon the protagonist are psychological as well as social. The speaker measures himself against the ideal of wholeness and radiant meaning apotheosized in the Brooklyn Bridge. As he does so, the play of contrasts between his rather depressed view of himself and the possibilities he envisions gives the sequence a perhaps unintended poignancy. In other poems Crane's "social" perspectives enter only obliquely—for instance, in his identification in "Chaplinesque" with Charlie Chaplin's comically gallant little tramp, or in his passing reference to the harm done by city-life to the psyche, in "Repose of Rivers." It is the wound of sentient life that is his main subject, and at the same time his will—a characteristically Romantic motif—to triumph over that wound (though in a poem like "Passage" he recognizes the impossibility of doing so).

Many of our poets have shared these perspectives of Crane's, in as many different fashions as their differences of personality and experience would suggest. Thus, Richard Eberhart has constantly set against each other an acute sense of the pity of death, an ecstatic mysticism, and a rather abstract, "Metaphysical" cast of mind. The second World War gave him ample scope for the interplay of these characteristics, but even in a poem as elementary in its theme as his famous "The Groundhog" or as private as "The Soul Longs to Return Whence It Came" they make for a powerful personal art built around the need for realization against all the odds. Randall Jarrell's emphasis is more on the vulnerability of each person, whether soldier, adult civilian, or child—especially child. Karl Shapiro throws a bright, sardonic light over our machine-made culture and its betrayals of the individual lost within it. Howard Nemerov, though a prolific poet who writes in many moods including that of a caustically satirical Liberal wit, confronts in his most serious work the absolute, inhuman terror of things very much in the spirit of Crane at his bleakest and most tragic. It is Robert Lowell, however, who seems closest to the spirit of Crane among our youngest established poets. The speaking voice of Lowell's poems is that of a man whose private guilt and anxiety are also the guilt and anxiety of his culture and of its history. He associates these with his Puritan, New England background and with the evils of our economic order. Lowell's savage power at first found characteristic expression in the portrayal of figures somehow involved with moral and religious burdens, particularly of a sexual nature. His *Life Studies* is a largely autobiographical sequence in which the poet uses himself frankly as the central symbol of modern life and of the prevailing neurotic condition we must all face if we are to survive and make a saner world. He is like Dylan Thomas in the stormy energy with which he makes himself his own greatest metaphor.

Emily Dickinson

[SUCCESS IS COUNTED SWEETEST]

Success is counted sweetest
By those who ne'er succeed.
To comprehend a nectar
Requires sorest need.

Not one of all the purple host
Who took the flag today
Can tell the definition,
So clear of victory

As he, defeated—dying—
On whose forbidden ear
The distant strains of triumph
Burst agonized and clear!

1859, 1878

[I NEVER HEAR THE WORD]

I never hear the word "escape"
Without a quicker blood,
A sudden expectation,
A flying attitude!

I never hear of prisons broad
By soldiers battered down,
But I tug childish at my bars
Only to fail again!

c. 1859, 1891

[I'M WIFE; I'VE FINISHED THAT]

I'm "wife"; I've finished that—
That other state;

II-13

I'm Czar—I'm "woman" now—
It's safer so.

How odd the girl's life looks
Behind this soft eclipse—
I think that earth feels so
To folks in heaven now.

This being comfort, then
That other kind was pain;
But why compare?
I'm "wife"! stop there!

                    c. 1860, 1890

[COME SLOWLY, EDEN]

Come slowly, Eden!
Lips unused to thee—
Bashful—sip thy jessamines
As the fainting bee,

Reaching late his flower,
Round her chamber hums,
Counts his nectars—
Enters and is lost in balms.

                    c. 1860, 1890

[I TASTE A LIQUOR NEVER BREWED]

I taste a liquor never brewed,
From tankards scooped in pearl;
Not all the vats upon the Rhine
Yield such an alcohol!

Inebriate of air am I,
And debauchee of dew,
Reeling, through endless summer days,
From inns of molten blue.

When landlords turn the drunken bee
Out of the foxglove's door,
When butterflies renounce their drams,
I shall but drink the more!

Till seraphs swing their snowy hats,
And saints to windows run,
To see the little tippler
Leaning against the sun!

                c. 1860, 1861

[WHAT IS PARADISE]

What is "Paradise"—
Who live there—
Are they "Farmers"—
Do they "hoe"—
Do they know that this is "Amherst"—
And that I am coming too—

Do they wear "new shoes" in "Eden"—
Is it always pleasant there—
Won't they scold us when we're hungry—
Or tell God how cross we are?

You are sure there's such a person
As "a Father" in the sky—
So if I get lost—there—ever—
Or do what the nurse calls "die"—
I shan't walk the "Jasper" barefoot—
Ransomed folks won't laugh at me?
Maybe "Eden" a'n't so lonesome
As New England used to be!

                c. 1860, 1945

[THERE'S A CERTAIN SLANT OF LIGHT]

There's a certain slant of light
Winter afternoons,
That oppresses like the heft
Of cathedral tunes.

Heavenly hurt it gives us;
We can find no scar,
But internal difference
Where the meanings are.

None may teach it—any—
'Tis the seal, despair—

An imperial affliction
Sent us of the air.

When it comes, the landscape listens,
Shadows hold their breath;
When it goes, 'tis like the distance
On the look of death.   *c. 1861, 1890*

[I FELT A FUNERAL IN MY BRAIN]

I felt a funeral in my brain,
And mourners to and fro
Kept treading—treading—till it seemed
That sense was breaking through.

And when they all were seated,
A service like a drum
Kept beating—beating—till I thought
My mind was going numb.

And then I heard them lift a box,
And creak across my soul
With those same boots of lead, again.
Then space began to toll

As all the heavens were a bell,
And Being but an ear,
And I, and silence, some strange race,
Wrecked, solitary, here.

And then a plank in reason broke,
And I dropped down, and down—
And hit a world, at every plunge,
And finished knowing—then—
                    c. 1861, 1896

[I GOT SO I COULD HEAR HIS NAME]

I got so I could hear his name
Without—tremendous gain—
That stop-sensation on my soul
And thunder in the room.

I got so I could walk across
That angle in the floor.

Where he turned so, and I turned—how—
And all our sinew tore.

I got so I could stir the box
In which his letters grew
Without that forcing, in my breath—
As staples driven through;

Could dimly recollect a Grace—
I think, they call it "God"—
Renowned to ease extremity
When formula had failed.

And shape my hands
Petition's way,
Tho' ignorant of a word
That ordination utters.

My business, with the Cloud,
If any Power behind it, be,
Not subject to despair—
It care, in some remoter way,
For so minute affair
As misery—
Itself, too great—for interrupting—more—
                              c. 1861, 1929

[THE SOUL SELECTS HER OWN SOCIETY]

The soul selects her own society,
Then shuts the door;
To her divine majority
Present no more.

Unmoved, she notes the chariot's pausing
At her low gate;
Unmoved, an emperor be kneeling
Upon her mat.

I've known her from an ample nation
Choose one;
Then close the valves of her attention
Like stone.   *c. 1862, 1890*

[A BIRD CAME DOWN THE WALK]

A bird came down the walk:
He did not know I saw;
He bit an angleworm in halves
And ate the fellow, raw.

And then he drank a dew
From a convenient grass,
And then hopped sidewise to the wall
To let a beetle pass.

He glanced with rapid eyes
That hurried all around—
They looked like frightened beads, I thought—
He stirred his velvet head

Like one in danger; cautious,
I offered him a crumb,
And he unrolled his feathers
And rowed him softer home

Than oars divide the ocean,
Too silver for a seam,
Or butterflies, off banks of noon,
Leap, plashless, as they swim.   *1862, 1891*

['TWAS LIKE A MAELSTROM]

'Twas like a maelstrom, with a notch,
That nearer every day
Kept narrowing its boiling wheel
Until the agony

Toyed coolly with the final inch
Of your delirious hem,
And you dropped, lost,
When something broke
And let you from a dream—

As if a goblin with a gauge
Kept measuring the hours,

Until you felt your second
Weight helpless in his paws,

And not a sinew, stirred, could help,
And sense was setting numb,
When God remembered, and the fiend
Let go then, overcome;

As if your sentence stood pronounced,
And you were frozen led
From dungeon's luxury of doubt
To gibbets and the dead;

And when the film had stitched your eyes,
A creature gasped "Reprieve!"
Which anguish was the utterest, then,
To perish, or to live?   *c. 1862, 1945*

[MUCH MADNESS IS DIVINEST SENSE]

Much madness is divinest sense
To a discerning eye;
Much sense the starkest madness.
'Tis the majority
In this, as all, prevail.
Assent, and you are sane;
Demur,—you're straightway dangerous,
And handled with a chain.
                    c. 1862, 1890

[I HEARD A FLY BUZZ]

I heard a fly buzz when I died—
The stillness in the room
Was like the stillness in the air
Between the heaves of storm.

The eyes around had wrung them dry,
And breaths were gathering firm
For that last onset, when the King
Be witnessed in the room.

I willed my keepsakes, signed away
What portion of me be

Assignable,—and then it was
There interposed a fly,

With blue, uncertain, stumbling buzz,
Between the light and me;
And then the windows failed, and then
I could not see to see.   *c. 1862, 1896*

['TWAS WARM—AT FIRST—LIKE US]

'Twas warm—at first—like us
Until there crept upon
A chill—like frost upon a glass—
Till all the scene be gone.

The forehead copied stone—
The fingers grew too cold
To ache—and like a skater's brook
The busy eyes congealed.

It straightened—that was all—
It crowded cold to cold—
It multiplied indifference
As pride were all it could—

And even when with cords
'Twas lowered, like a weight,
It made no signal, nor demurred,
But dropped like adamant.
                    c. 1862, 1929

[THE HEART ASKS PLEASURE FIRST]

The heart asks pleasure first,
And then, excuse from pain;
And then, those little anodynes
That deaden suffering;

And then, to go to sleep;
And then, if it should be
The will of its Inquisitor,
The privilege to die.
                c. 1862, 1890

[BECAUSE I COULD NOT STOP FOR DEATH]

Because I could not stop for Death,
He kindly stopped for me;
The carriage held but just ourselves
And Immortality.

We slowly drove, he knew no haste,
And I had put away
My labor, and my leisure too,
For his civility.

We passed the school where children strove
At recess, in the ring;
We passed the fields of gazing grain,
We passed the setting sun—

Or rather, he passed us;
The dews grew quivering and chill,
For only gossamer my gown,
My tippet only tulle.

We paused before a house that seemed
A swelling of the ground;
The roof was scarcely visible,
The cornice in the ground.

Since then 'tis centuries, and yet
Feels shorter than the day
I first surmised the horses' heads
Were toward eternity.   *c. 1863, 1890*

[IT DROPPED SO LOW IN MY REGARD]

It dropped so low in my regard
I heard it hit the ground,
And go to pieces on the stones
At bottom of my mind;

Yet blamed the fate that fractured, less
Then I reviled myself
For entertaining plated wares
Upon my silver shelf.
               c. 1863, 1896

[THIS QUIET DUST]

This quiet dust was gentlemen and ladies,
And lads and girls;
Was laughter and ability and sighing,
And frocks and curls.

This passive place a summer's nimble mansion,
Where bloom and bees
Exist an oriental circuit,
Then cease, like these.   *c. 1864, 1914*

[I STEPPED FROM PLANK TO PLANK]

I stepped from plank to plank
    A slow and cautious way;
The stars about my head I felt,
    About my feet the sea.

I knew not but the next
    Would be my final inch,—
This gave me that precarious gait
    Some call experience.
                c. 1864, 1896

[A NARROW FELLOW IN THE GRASS]

A narrow fellow in the grass
Occasionally rides;
You may have met him—did you not
His notice sudden is.

The grass divides as with a comb,
A spotted shaft is seen;
And then it closes at your feet
And opens further on.

He likes a boggy acre,
A floor too cool for corn.
Yet when a boy, and barefoot,
I more than once, at noon,

Have passed, I thought, a whip-lash
Unbraiding in the sun,
When, stooping to secure it,
It wrinkled, and was gone.

Several of nature's people
I know, and they know me;
I feel for them a transport
Of cordiality;

But never met this fellow,
Attended or alone,
Without a tighter breathing,
And zero at the bone.   *1865, 1866*

[AS IMPERCEPTIBLY AS GRIEF]

As imperceptibly as grief
The summer lapsed away,—
Too imperceptible at last
To seem like perfidy.

A quietness distilled,
As twilight long begun,
Or Nature, spending with herself
Sequestered afternoon.

The dusk drew earlier in,
The morning foreign shone,—
A courteous, yet harrowing grace,
As guest that would be gone.

And thus, without a wing,
Or service of a keel,
Our summer made her light escape
Into the beautiful.   *1865, 1891*

[THE LAST NIGHT THAT SHE LIVED]

The last night that she lived,
It was a common night
Except the dying; this to us
Made nature different.

We noticed smallest things,—
Things overlooked before,
By this great light upon our minds
Italicized, as 'twere.

As we went out and in
Between her final room
And rooms where those to be alive
Tomorrow were, a blame

That others could exist
While she must finish quite,
A jealousy for her arose
So nearly infinite—

We waited while she passed—
It was a narrow time—
Too jostled were our souls to speak;
At length the notice came.

She mentioned, and forgot;
Then lightly as a reed
Bent to the water, struggled scarce,
Consented, and was dead.

And we—we placed the hair,
And drew the head erect;
And then an awful leisure was,
Belief to regulate.   *c. 1866, 1890*

[THERE CAME A WIND LIKE A BUGLE]

There came a wind like a bugle—
It quivered through the grass,
And a green chill upon the heat
So ominous did pass
We barred the windows and the doors
As from an emerald ghost;
The doom's electric moccasin
That very instant passed.
On a strange mob of panting trees,
And fences fled away,
And rivers where the houses ran

Those looked that lived that day.
The bell within the steeple wild
The flying tidings told,
How much can come
And much can go,
And yet abide the world!

c. *1883, 1891*

[DROWNING IS NOT SO PITIFUL]

Drowning is not so pitiful
As the attempt to rise.
Three times, 'tis said, a sinking man
Comes up to face the skies,
And then declines forever
To that abhorred abode
Where hope and he part company,—
For he is grasped of God.
The Maker's cordial visage,
However good to see,
Is shunned, we must admit it,
Like an adversity.   *1896*

Edgar Lee Masters

THE HILL

Where are Elmer, Herman, Bert, Tom and Charley,
The weak of will, the strong of arm, the clown, the boozer, the fighter?
All, all, are sleeping on the hill.

One passed in a fever,
One was burned in a mine,
One was killed in a brawl,
One died in a jail,
One fell from a bridge toiling for children and wife—
All, all are sleeping, sleeping, sleeping on the hill.

Where are Ella, Kate, Mag, Lizzie and Edith,
The tender heart, the simple soul, the loud, the proud, the happy
    one?—
All, all, are sleeping on the hill.

One died in shameful child-birth,
One of a thwarted love,
One at the hands of a brute in a brothel,
One of a broken pride, in the search for heart's desire,
One after life in far-away London and Paris
Was brought to her little space by Ella and Kate and Mag—
All, all are sleeping, sleeping, sleeping on the hill.

Where are Uncle Isaac and Aunt Emily,
And old Towny Kincaid and Sevigne Houghton,
And Major Walker who had talked
With venerable men of the revolution?—
All, all, are sleeping, on the hill.

They brought them dead sons from the war,
And daughters whom life had crushed,
And their children fatherless, crying—
All, all, are sleeping, sleeping, sleeping on the hill.

Where is Old Fiddler Jones
Who played with life all his ninety years,
Braving the sleet with bared breast,
Drinking, rioting, thinking neither of wife nor kin,
Nor gold, nor love, nor heaven?
Lo! he babbles of the fish-frys of long ago,
Of the horse-races of long ago at Clary's Grove,
Of what Abe Lincoln said
One time at Springfield.   *1915*

PETIT, THE POET

Seeds in a dry pod, tick, tick, tick,
Tick, tick, tick, like mites in a quarrel—
Faint iambics that the full breeze wakens—
But the pine tree makes a symphony thereof.
Triolets, villanelles, rondels, rondeaus,
Ballades by the score with the same old thought:
The snows and the roses of yesterday are vanished;
And what is love but a rose that fades?
Life all around me here in the village:
Tragedy, comedy, valor, and truth,
Courage, constancy, heroism, failure—
All in the loom, and oh what patterns!
Woodlands, meadows, streams, and rivers—
Blind to all of it all my life long.
Triolets, villanelles, rondels, rondeaus,
Seeds in a dry pod, tick, tick, tick,
Tick, tick, tick, what little iambics,
While Homer and Whitman roared in the pines?
                                                  1915

CARL HAMBLIN

The press of the Spoon River *Clarion* was wrecked,
And I was tarred and feathered,
For publishing this on the day the Anarchists were hanged in Chicago:
"I saw a beautiful woman with bandaged eyes
Standing on the steps of a marble temple.
Great multitudes passed in front of her,
Lifting their faces to her imploringly.
In her left hand she held a sword.
She was brandishing the sword,

Sometimes striking a child, again a laborer,
Again a slinking woman, again a lunatic.
In her right hand she held a scale;
Into the scale pieces of gold were tossed
By those who dodged the strokes of the sword.
A man in a black gown read from a manuscript:
'She is no respecter of persons.'
Then a youth wearing a red cap
Leaped to her side and snatched away the bandage.
And lo, the lashes had been eaten away
From the oozy eye-lids;
The eye-balls were seared with a milky mucus;
The madness of a dying soul
Was written on her face—
But the multitude saw why she wore the bandage."

1915

EDITOR WHEDON

To be able to see every side of every question;
To be on every side, to be everything, to be nothing long;
To pervert truth, to ride it for a purpose,
To use great feelings and passions of the human family
For base designs, for cunning ends,
To wear a mask like the Greek actors—
Your eight-page paper—behind which you huddle,
Bawling through the megaphone of big type:
"This is I, the giant."
Thereby also living the life of a sneak-thief,
Poisoned with the anonymous words
Of your clandestine soul.
To scratch dirt over scandal for money,
And exhume it to the winds for revenge,
Or to sell papers,
Crushing reputations, or bodies, if need be,
To win at any cost, save your own life.
To glory in demoniac power, ditching civilization,
As a paranoiac boy puts a log on the track
And derails the express train.
To be an editor, as I was.
Then to lie here close by the river over the place
Where the sewage flows from the village,
And the empty cans and garbage are dumped,
And abortions are hidden.

1915

DAISY FRASER

Did you ever hear of Editor Whedon
Giving to the public treasury any of the money he received
For supporting candidates for office?
Or for writing up the canning factory
To get people to invest?
Or for suppressing the facts about the bank,
When it was rotten and ready to break?
Did you ever hear of the Circuit Judge
Helping anyone except the "Q" railroad,
Or the bankers? Or did Rev. Peet or Rev. Sibley
Give any part of their salary, earned by keeping still,
Or speaking out as the leaders wished them to do,
To the building of the water works?
But I—Daisy Fraser who always passed
Along the streets through rows of nods and smiles,
And coughs and words such as "there she goes,"
Never was taken before Justice Arnett
Without contributing ten dollars and costs
To the school fund of Spoon River!   *1915*

FIDDLER JONES

The earth keeps some vibration going
There in your heart, and that is you.
And if the people find you can fiddle,
Why, fiddle you must, for all your life.
What do you see, a harvest of clover?
Or a meadow to walk through to the river?
The wind's in the corn; you rub your hands
For beeves hereafter ready for market;
Or else you hear the rustle of skirts
Like the girls when dancing at Little Grove.
To Cooney Potter a pillar of dust
Or whirling leaves meant ruinous drouth;
They looked to me like Red-Head Sammy
Stepping it off, to "Toor-a-Loor."
How could I till my forty acres
Not to speak of getting more,
With a medley of horns, bassoons and piccolos
Stirred in my brain by crows and robins

And the creak of a wind-mill—only these?
And I never started to plow in my life
That some one did not stop in the road
And take me away to a dance or picnic.
I ended up with forty acres;
I ended up with a broken fiddle—
And a broken laugh, and a thousand memories,
And not a single regret.   *1915*

ANNE RUTLEDGE

Out of me unworthy and unknown
The vibrations of deathless music;
"With malice toward none, with charity for all."
Out of me the forgiveness of millions toward millions,
And the beneficent face of a nation
Shining with justice and truth.
I am Anne Rutledge who sleep beneath these weeds,
Beloved in life of Abraham Lincoln,
Wedded to him, not through union,
But through separation.
Bloom forever, O Republic,
From the dust of my bosom!   *1915*

LUCINDA MATLOCK

I went to the dances at Chandlerville,
And played snap-out at Winchester.
One time we changed partners,
Driving home in the moonlight of middle June,
And then I found Davis.
We were married and lived together for seventy years,
Enjoying, working, raising the twelve children,
Eight of whom we lost
Ere I had reached the age of sixty.
I spun, I wove, I kept the house, I nursed the sick,
I made the garden, and for holiday
Rambled over the fields where sang the larks,
And by Spoon River gathering many a shell,
And many a flower and medicinal weed—
Shouting to the wooded hills, singing to the green valleys.
At ninety-six I had lived enough, that is all,
And passed to a sweet repose.

What is this I hear of sorrow and weariness,
Anger, discontent, and drooping hopes?
Degenerate sons and daughters,
Life is too strong for you—
It takes life to love Life.   *1915*

THE MOURNER'S BENCH

They're holding a revival at New Hope Meeting house,
I can't keep from going, I ought to stay away.
For I come home and toss in bed till day,
For thinking of my sin, and the trouble I am in.
I dream I hear the dancers
In the steps and swings,
The quadrilles and the lancers
They danced at Revis Springs.
I lie and think of Charley, Charley, Charley
The Bobtown dandy
Who had his way with me.
And no one is so handy
A dancer as Charley
To *Little Drops of Brandy,*
Or *The Wind that Shakes the Barley,*
Or *Good Mornin', Uncle Johnny, I've Fetched Your Wagon Home*

And Greenberry Atterberry, who toed it like a pigeon
Has gone and got religion;
He's deserted the dancers, the fiddlers, merry-makers,
And I should do it too.
For Charley, Charley has left me for to roam.
But a woman at the mourner's bench must tell her story true—
What shall I do? What shall I do?

My grandmother told me of Old Peter Cartwright
Who preached hell-fire
And the worm that never dies.
And here's a young preacher at the New Hope Meeting house,
And every one allows, he has old Peter's brows,
And flaming of the eyes,
And the very same way, they say.
Last night he stuck his finger right down in my direction,
And said: "God doesn't care
For your woman's hair.

Jesus wants to know if your soul is fair
As your woman's complexion."
And then I thought he knew—
O what shall I do?

Greenberry Atterberry, weeping and unsteady
Had left his seat already.
He stood at the mourner's bench in great tribulation
And told the congregation:
That fiddling and dancing and tobacco chewin'
Led up to whisky and to woman's ruin—
And I thought he looked at me.
Well, you can stop dancing, and you can stop drinking
And you can leave the quarter-horses at the crooked races.
But a woman, a woman, the people will be thinking
Forever of a woman who confesses her behavior.
And then I couldn't look in the people's faces,
All weeping and singing, *O Gentle Saviour!*

Then the devil said: You wench
You'd cut a pretty figure at the mourner's bench,
Go out and look for Charley,
Go out and look for Charley,
He's down at Leese's Grove.
He has found a fresh love
Go win him back again.
He is dancing on the platform to *The Speckled Hen.*

O Saviour, Saviour, how can I join the mourners,
Face all the scorners?
But how can I hunt Charley at Leese's Grove?
How can I stand the staring, the whispering of things
Down at Revis Springs?
How can I stand the mocking of the fiddle strings?
Charley! Charley!
So it's knowing what's best to do,
Saviour! Saviour!
It's knowing what's best to do!   *1916*

JAY HAWKINS

Jay walking! Reading the headlines! Struck down
By a flivver and killed while reading

About the man-girl slayer!
For years haunting the news stands,
Waiting for the latest paper from Chicago,
Cursed with the newspaper habit:
Snuffing the powder of monstrous news
Heralding shame and hate and murder:
What dive was raided, what rum was seized;
Who was indicted, and who was lynched;
Who got the rope at the end of the trial;
What governor, officer was accused
Of bribery, graft, or peculation.
Whose picture appeared divorced or caught—
(Were they never noble, did they never achieve,
And so have their pictures printed?)
All about hating, hunting, fighting,
Lying, stealing, lusting, wasting,
Who had been killed, and who had been hanged.
And I ask if life is full of beauty,
And full of nobility and creating,
Why don't they write about it?   *1924*

EURIPIDES ALEXOPOULOS

I had a vision at last:
A divine youth was playing a harp near Trainor's Drug Store.
They listened, passed, conferred on the matter.
They returned and told him to work or get out of town.
He began then to carry coal and sell newspapers,
Playing his harp in the evenings.
The neighbors complained:
He was leading people to idleness, dreams.
He went on playing, emerged to the streets again.
Some tore at him, others hooted him, some praised him;
But he was in need of money, always money.
He put his harp by to work for money . . . no money for harping!
He took forth his harp again.
The strings were loose, it had to be tuned.
He tuned it and played better than ever.
In the midst of this his money was taken from him.
Shadows had come over him, he was no longer young.
His children were half grown, making voracious demands.
Should he play the harp or work for the children?
Every one said, work for the children.

They must feed and be educated,
And what is this harping after all?
They caught him then and put him to work.
His beard grew long and gray, his eyes were haggard,
He was bent, his hands were thick and dull.
He could neither work now nor play the harp.
Suddenly as he was sitting on a bench in the park
He shed his rags, as the sun sheds clouds.
He rose to the spire of the church,
Stood on one foot,
And spit on the town—
It was Apollo!   1924

NATHAN SUFFRIN

Jail would have killed me
Except for my cell mate, Henry Luthinger,
Who had been there often before,
And knew how to soften the walls and bars,
And how to be a friend in jail.
So when they let me out,
I knew at last that life is a prison.
And the best that a man can hope for it
Is a cell mate wise and good!   1924

THE LOST ORCHARD

Loves and sorrows of those who lose an orchard
Are less seen than the shadow shells
Of butterflies whose wings are tortured
In the perilous escape of rainy dells,
In the ecstatic flight of blinding Junes.
Save for the breath dirge of the wind-rung harebells
They have no words that ever shall be known,
Neither have they speech or tone,
Save the tones when the sun with gold galloons
Trims the blue edges of the air;
And save the quiet which quells
The music of the water drop in the well's
Water far down, where vision swoons.

These are the voices and these alone
Of the lost orchard, and its vague despair.
Branches may gnarl with scale and lift their bare

Paralysis, or the withered crone
Of loneliness breed water sprouts; or frost
Heap the dull turf over the strawberry vines;
Or rust unhinge the gates; or the fallen pear
Waste like the Cretan gold of ruined shrines
In tangled grasses; or the broken share
Be sunk in leaf mould—these are noonday signs
Of the deserted, but not of the orchard that is lost.
Silver secrets speak of the lost orchard, as the shells
Of butterflies escaped whisper the vanished wings;
Or as light shaken from the field of clover tells
Of the zephyr's irised wanderings.

A lost orchard is the memory of a friend
Wronged by life to death, who lies
Lifelike, but with unseeing eyes.
It is music made a ghost, because the end
Of life has come which made the music mean
Eyes that look and lips that thrill.
Music is no breast where wounded souls may lean,
If played when hands it signified are still.
A lost orchard is the road on which we passed
Where a house was with a candle in the night;
And we must go that way still, but at last
The house is by the roadside, but no light.

Over a lost orchard I have strayed
In March when down the wooded ravine
The behemoth wind bellowed to the glade
By the sky-blue water before the rushes were green.
While yet the acorn cups crushed under feet
Against the moss mould, yellow as smoke;
And the lanterns of wild cucumbers quenched by sleet,
And gusts of winter hung by the leafless oak;
When the crow's nest was a splotch of sticks on the sky,
And burnt out torches of feasts the sumach cone.
And I have climbed till the wind was naught but a sigh
Over the stairs of stone and the seat of stone.
And there I have seen the orchard, the apple trees
Patient in loneliness, and forgotten care;
And the grass as heavy as the Sargasso Sea's
Around the trunks, grown like a dead man's hair.
And I have returned in Spring when the nebulae

Of early blossoms whitened before it was June;
And I have seen them merge in their leafy sky
Till they became the light of the full moon.
Warm is the orchard as the stalls of the sun
At midnight, when each budded stem is dewed
With a firefly and the whispering zephyrs run
From leaf to leaf, awaking the dreams that brood
Before the gray woolens of the shadows fall
From the sleeping earth, and the lights of the orchard are wooed
From sea gray to sea green in a carnival
Change of flame, in a dawning many hued.
Till the long winds come, blowing from woodlands over
The glistening water, and meadows beyond the citrine
Sand of the hill that walls the field of clover
Nod their blossoms amid a tide of green.

Angels are never in caverns, nor presences
That speak the will to leave it lingering
About the orchard lost. Nor does the chrysalis
Lie thick in paths of the arisen wing;
Nor butterflies haunt the grasses like innocent
Desires defeated; nor the coverts mourn
With doves; nor are the wild bees rent
From habitations in old trees; nor the forlorn
Grass grow rich bespeaking humble hopes;
Nor corners of giant heliotropes
Droop so memorially; nor the stair of stone
Hold the silence that follows a footfall; nor the sky
Above the stone seat by its emptiness alone
Tell of a face and of a wondering eye;
Nor are flowers without the fruit so richly grown.

The house of the lost orchard is loneliness to the uttermost:
The chimney in the top of the elm tree,
Like the open mouth of a musing ghost
Has nothing but the void of the sky,
And the sequestered flight of the passing cloud,
Though the expectant breeze goes by
To gather smoke from the hearth long disavowed.
And under a brick of the porch the key to the fastened door
Glints out of rust and waits
For those who won the orchard to explore
The rooms and find the unveiled Fates.

Out of the lost orchard is life that needs the orchard no more,
The fence has broken places, and the gates
Swing to the passing wind. But butterflies soar
Over the tree tops to predestined mates.   *1935*

ALDHELM

This is a tale that true gold from dross tells,
Tale of Aldhelm standing on the bridge,
Singing ballads, singing happy gospels
To the people thick as midge on midge,
Bankers, merchants, lawyers in a hurry
On the walk below the bridge to town.
Only Aldhelm free from all the worry
Sang and watched the fear, the money-frown.

That was ages past. Gone with the gopher,
The water-rats and fish are scribe and clerk,
Only Aldhelm stays, the happy loafer
Singing as the city went to work.
Who preserved this Aldhelm, also the many
Stories of his life who lived for song?
We the people do and did, nor are there any
Merchants now remembered of that throng.
That's to say delight lives on forever,
Song that floats like a feather on the stream;
Man will waste and ruin, man will never
Leave behind the singer and his dream.
                              April 10, 1937

E. A. Robinson

RICHARD CORY

Whenever Richard Cory went down town,
We people on the pavement looked at him:
He was a gentleman from sole to crown,
Clean favored, and imperially slim.

And he was always quietly arrayed,
And he was always human when he talked;
But still he fluttered pulses when he said,
"Good-morning," and he glittered when he walked.

And he was rich—yes, richer than a king—
And admirably schooled in every grace:
In fine, we thought that he was everything
To make us wish that we were in his place.

So on we worked, and waited for the light,
And went without the meat, and cursed the bread;
And Richard Cory, one calm summer night,
Went home and put a bullet through his head   *1897*

CREDO

I cannot find my way: there is no star
In all the shrouded heavens anywhere;
And there is not a whisper in the air
Of any living voice but one so far
That I can hear it only as a bar
Of lost, imperial music, played when fair
And angel fingers wove, and unaware,
Dead leaves to garlands where no roses are.

No, there is not a glimmer, nor a call,
For one that welcomes, welcomes when he fears,

The black and awful chaos of the night;
For through it all—above, beyond it all—
I know the far-sent message of the years,
I feel the coming glory of the Light.   1897

THE FIELD OF GLORY

War shook the land where Levi dwelt,
And fired the dismal wrath he felt,
That such a doom was ever wrought
As his, to toil while others fought;
To toil, to dream—and still to dream,
With one day barren as another;
To consummate, as it would seem,
The dry despair of his old mother.

Far off one afternoon began
The sound of man destroying man;
And Levi, sick with nameless rage,
Condemned again his heritage,
And sighed for scars that might have come,
And would, if once he could have sundered
Those harsh, inhering claims of home
That held him while he cursed and wondered.

Another day, and then there came,
Rough, bloody, ribald, hungry, lame,
But yet themselves, to Levi's door,
Two remnants of the day before.
They laughed at him and what he sought;
They jeered him, and his painful acre;
But Levi knew that they had fought,
And left their manners to their Maker.

That night, for the grim widow's ears,
With hopes that hid themselves in fears,
He told of arms, and fiery deeds,
Whereat one leaps the while he reads,
And said he'd be no more a clown,
While others drew the breath of battle.—
The mother looked him up and down,
And laughed—a scant laugh with a rattle.

She told him what she found to tell,
And Levi listened, and heard well
Some admonitions of a voice
That left him no cause to rejoice.—
He sought a friend, and found the stars,
And prayed aloud that they should aid him;
But they said not a word of wars,
Or of a reason why God made him.

And who's of this or that estate
We do not wholly calculate,
When baffling shades that shift and cling
Are not without their glimmering;
When even Levi, tired of faith,
Beloved of none, forgot by many,
Dismissed as an inferior wraith,
Reborn may be as great as any.   *1902*

MINIVER CHEEVY

Miniver Cheevy, child of scorn,
  Grew lean while he assailed the seasons;
He wept that he was ever born,
  And he had reasons.

Miniver loved the days of old
  When swords were bright and steeds were prancing;
The vision of a warrior bold
  Would set him dancing.

Miniver sighed for what was not,
  And dreamed, and rested from his labors;
He dreamed of Thebes and Camelot,
  And Priam's neighbors.

Miniver mourned the ripe renown
  That made so many a name so fragrant;
He mourned Romance, now on the town,
  And Art, a vagrant.

Miniver loved the Medici,
  Albeit he had never seen one;

He would have sinned incessantly
  Could he have been one.

Miniver cursed the commonplace
  And eyed a khaki suit with loathing;
He missed the mediæval grace
  Of iron clothing.

Miniver scorned the gold he sought,
  But sore annoyed was he without it;
Miniver thought, and thought, and thought,
  And thought about it.

Miniver Cheevy, born too late,
  Scratched his head and kept on thinking;
Miniver coughed, and called it fate,
  And kept on drinking.   *1910*

FOR A DEAD LADY

No more with overflowing light
  Shall fill the eyes that now are faded,
Nor shall another's fringe with night
  Their woman-hidden world as they did.
No more shall quiver down the days
The flowing wonder of her ways,
Whereof no language may requite
The shifting and the many-shaded.

The grace, divine, definitive,
Clings only as a faint forestalling;
The laugh that love could not forgive
Is hushed, and answers to no calling;
The forehead and the little ears
Have gone where Saturn keeps the years;
The breast where roses could not live
Has done with rising and with falling.

The beauty, shattered by the laws
That have creation in their keeping,
No longer trembles at applause,
Or over children that are sleeping;

And we who delve in beauty's lore
Know all that we have known before
Of what inexorable cause
Makes Time so vicious in his reaping.

1910

FLAMMONDE

The man Flammonde, from God knows where,
With firm address and foreign air,
With news of nations in his talk
And something royal in his walk,
With glint of iron in his eyes,
But never doubt, nor yet surprise,
Appeared, and stayed, and held his head
As one by kings accredited.

Erect, with his alert repose
About him, and about his clothes,
He pictured all tradition hears
Of what we owe to fifty years.
His cleansing heritage of taste
Paraded neither want nor waste;
And what he needed for his fee
To live, he borrowed graciously.

He never told us what he was,
Or what mischance, or other cause,
Had banished him from better days
To play the Prince of Castaways.
Meanwhile he played surpassing well
A part, for most, unplayable;
In fine, one pauses, half afraid
To say for certain that he played.

For that, one may as well forego
Conviction as to yes or no;
Nor can I say just how intense
Would then have been the difference
To several, who, having striven
In vain to get what he was given,
Would see the stranger taken on
By friends not easy to be won.

Moreover, many a malcontent
He soothed and found munificent;
His courtesy beguiled and foiled
Suspicion that his years were soiled;
His mien distinguished any crowd,
His credit strengthened when he bowed;
And women, young and old, were fond
Of looking at the man Flammonde.

There was a woman in our town
On whom the fashion was to frown;
But while our talk renewed the tinge
Of a long-faded scarlet fringe,
The man Flammonde saw none of that,
And what he saw we wondered at—
That none of us, in her distress,
Could hide or find our littleness.

There was a boy that all agreed
Had shut within him the rare seed
Of learning. We could understand,
But none of us could lift a hand.
The man Flammonde appraised the youth,
And told a few of us the truth;
And thereby, for a little gold,
A flowered future was unrolled.

There were two citizens who fought
For years and years, and over nought;
They made life awkward for their friends,
And shortened their own dividends.
The man Flammonde said what was wrong
Should be made right; nor was it long
Before they were again in line,
And had each other in to dine.

And these I mention are but four
Of many out of many more.
So much for them. But what of him—
So firm in every look and limb?
What small satanic sort of kink
Was in his brain? What broken link
Withheld him from the destinies
That came so near to being his?

What was he, when we came to sift
His meaning, and to note the drift
Of incommunicable ways
That make us ponder while we praise?
Why was it that his charm revealed
Somehow the surface of a shield?
What was it that we never caught?
What was he, and what was he not?

How much it was of him we met
We cannot ever know; nor yet
Shall all he gave us quite atone
For what was his, and his alone;
Nor need we now, since he knew best,
Nourish an ethical unrest:
Rarely at once will nature give
The power to be Flammonde and live.

We cannot know how much we learn
From those who never will return,
Until a flash of unforeseen
Remembrance falls on what has been.
We've each a darkening hill to climb;
And this is why, from time to time
In Tilbury Town, we look beyond
Horizons for the man Flammonde.   1916

CASSANDRA

I heard one who said: "Verily,
    What word have I for children here?
Your Dollar is your only Word,
    The wrath of it your only fear.

"You build it altars tall enough
    To make you see, but you are blind;
You cannot leave it long enough
    To look before you or behind.

"When Reason beckons you to pause,
    You laugh and say that you know best;
But what it is you know, you keep
    As dark as ingots in a chest.

"You laugh and answer, 'We are young;
　O leave us now, and let us grow.'—
Not asking how much more of this
　Will Time endure or Fate bestow.

"Because a few complacent years
　Have made your peril of your pride,
Think you that you are to go on
　Forever pampered and untried?

"What lost eclipse of history,
　What bivouac of the marching stars,
Has given the sign for you to see
　Millenniums and last great wars?

"What unrecorded overthrow
　Of all the world has ever known,
Or ever been, has made itself
　So plain to you, and you alone!

"Your Dollar, Dove and Eagle make
　A Trinity that even you
Rate higher than you rate yourselves;
　It pays, it flatters, and it's new.

"And though your very flesh and blood
　Be what your Eagle eats and drinks,
You'll praise him for the best of birds,
　Not knowing what the Eagle thinks.

"The power is yours, but not the sight;
　You see not upon what you tread;
You have the ages for your guide,
　But not the wisdom to be led.

"Think you to tread forever down
　The merciless old verities?
And are you never to have eyes
　To see the world for what it is?

"Are you to pay for what you have
　With all you are?"—no other word
We caught, but with a laughing crowd
　Moved on. None heeded, and few heard.
　　　　　　　　　　　1916

EROS TURANNOS

She fears him, and will always ask
    What fated her to choose him;
She meets in his engaging mask
    All reasons to refuse him;
But what she meets and what she fears
Are less than are the downward years,
Drawn slowly to the foamless weirs
    Of age, were she to lose him.

Between a blurred sagacity
    That once had power to sound him,
And Love, that will not let him be
    The Judas that she found him,
Her pride assuages her almost,
As if it were alone the cost.—
He sees that he will not be lost,
    And waits and looks around him.

A sense of ocean and old trees
    Envelops and allures him;
Tradition, touching all he sees,
    Beguiles and reassures him;
And all her doubts of what he says
Are dimmed with what she knows of days—
Till even prejudice delays
    And fades, and she secures him.

The falling leaf inaugurates
    The reign of her confusion;
The pounding wave reverberates
    The dirge of her illusion;
And home, where passion lived and died,
Becomes a place where she can hide,
While all the town and harbor side
    Vibrate with her seclusion.

We tell you, tapping on our brows,
    The story as it should be,—
As if the story of a house
    Were told, or ever could be;

We'll have no kindly veil between
Her visions and those we have seen,—
As if we guessed what hers have been,
    Or what they are or would be.

Meanwhile we do no harm; for they
    That with a god have striven,
Not hearing much of what we say,
    Take what the god has given;
Though like waves breaking it may be
Or like a changed familiar tree,
Or like a stairway to the sea
    Where down the blind are driven.

1916

THE UNFORGIVEN

When he, who is the unforgiven,
Beheld her first, he found her fair:
No promise ever dreamt in heaven
Could then have lured him anywhere
That would have been away from there;
And all his wits had lightly striven,
Foiled with her voice, and eyes, and hair.

There's nothing in the saints and sages
To meet the shafts her glances had,
Or such as hers have had for ages
To blind a man till he be glad,
And humble him till he be mad.
The story would have many pages,
And would be neither good nor bad.

And, having followed, you would find him
Where properly the play begins;
But look for no red light behind him—
No fumes of many-colored sins,
Fanned high by screaming violins.
God knows what good it was to blind him,
Or whether man or woman wins.

And by the same eternal token,
Who knows just how it will all end?—

This drama of hard words unspoken,
This fireside farce, without a friend
Or enemy to comprehend
What augurs when two lives are broken,
And fear finds nothing left to mend.

He stares in vain for what awaits him,
And sees in Love a coin to toss;
He smiles, and her cold hush berates him
Beneath his hard half of the cross;
They wonder why it ever was;
And she, the unforgiving, hates him
More for her lack than for her loss.

He feeds with pride his indecision,
And shrinks from what will not occur,
Bequeathing with infirm derision
His ashes to the days that were,
Before she made him prisoner;
And labors to retrieve the vision
That he must once have had of her.

He waits, and there awaits an ending,
And he knows neither what nor when;
But no magicians are attending
To make him see as he saw then,
And he will never find again
The face that once had been the rending
Of all his purpose among men.

He blames her not, nor does he chide her,
And she has nothing new to say;
If he were Bluebeard he could hide her,
But that's not written in the play,
And there will be no change to-day;
Although, to the serene outsider,
There still would seem to be a way. *1916*

BEWICK FINZER

Time was when his half million drew
  The breath of six per cent;
But soon the worm of what-was-not

Fed hard on his content;
And something crumbled in his brain
    When his half million went.

Time passed, and filled along with his
    The place of many more;
Time came, and hardly one of us
    Had credence to restore,
From what appeared one day, the man
    Whom we had known before.

The broken voice, the withered neck,
    The coat worn out with care,
The cleanliness of indigence,
    The brilliance of despair,
The fond imponderable dreams
    Of affluence,—all were there.

Poor Finzer, with his dreams and schemes,
    Fares hard now in the race,
With heart and eye that have a task
    When he looks in the face
Of one who might so easily
    Have been in Finzer's place.

He comes unfailing for the loan
    We give and then forget;
He comes, and probably for years
    Will he be coming yet,—
Familiar as an old mistake,
    And futile as regret.   *1916*

THE MAN AGAINST THE SKY

Between me and the sunset, like a dome
Against the glory of a world on fire,
Now burned a sudden hill,
Bleak, round, and high, by flame-lit height made higher,
With nothing on it for the flame to kill
Save one who moved and was alone up there
To loom before the chaos and the glare
As if he were the last god going home
Unto his last desire.

Dark, marvelous, and inscrutable he moved on
Till down the fiery distance he was gone,
Like one of those eternal, remote things
That range across a man's imaginings
When a sure music fills him and he knows
What he may say thereafter to few men,—
The touch of ages having wrought
An echo and a glimpse of what he thought
A phantom or a legend until then;
For whether lighted over ways that save,
Or lured from all repose,
If he go on too far to find a grave,
Mostly alone he goes.

Even he, who stood where I had found him,
On high with fire all round him,
Who moved along the molten west,
And over the round hill's crest
That seemed half ready with him to go down,
Flame-bitten and flame-cleft,
As if there were to be no last thing left
Of a nameless unimaginable town,—
Even he who climbed and vanished may have taken
Down to the perils of a depth not known,
From death defended though by men forsaken,
The bread that every man must eat alone;
He may have walked while others hardly dared
Look on to see him stand where many fell;
And upward out of that, as out of hell,
He may have sung and striven
To mount where more of him shall yet be given,
Bereft of all retreat,
To sevenfold heat,—
As on a day when three in Dura shared
The furnace, and were spared
For glory by that king of Babylon
Who made himself so great that God, who heard,
Covered him with long feathers, like a bird.

Again, he may have gone down easily,
By comfortable altitudes, and found,
As always, underneath him solid ground
Whereon to be sufficient and to stand

Possessed already of the promised land,
Far stretched and fair to see:
A good sight, verily,
And one to make the eyes of her who bore him
Shine glad with hidden tears.
Why question of his ease of who before him,
In one place or another where they left
Their names as far behind them as their bones,
And yet by dint of slaughter, toil and theft,
And shrewdly sharpened stones,
Carved hard the way for his ascendency
Through deserts of lost years?
Why trouble him now who sees and hears
No more than what his innocence requires,
And therefore to no other height aspires
Than one at which he neither quails nor tires?
He may do more by seeing what he sees
Than others eager for iniquities;
He may, by seeing all things for the best,
Incite futurity to do the rest.

Or with an even likelihood,
He may have met with atrabilious eyes
The fires of time on equal terms and passed
Indifferently down, until at last
His only kind of grandeur would have been,
Apparently, in being seen.
He may have had for evil or for good
No argument; he may have had no care
For what without himself went anywhere
To failure or to glory, and least of all
For such a stale, flamboyant miracle;
He may have been the prophet of an art
Immovable to old idolatries;
He may have been a player without a part,
Annoyed that even the sun should have the skies
For such a flaming way to advertise;
He may have been a painter sick at heart
With Nature's toiling for a new surprise;
He may have been a cynic, who now, for all
Of anything divine that his effete
Negation may have tasted,
Saw truth in his own image, rather small.

Forbore to fever the ephemeral,
Found any barren height a good retreat
From any swarming street,
And in the sun saw power superbly wasted;
And when the primitive old-fashioned stars
Came out again to shine on joys and wars
More primitive, and all arrayed for doom,
He may have proved a world a sorry thing
In his imagining,
And life a lighted highway to the tomb.

Or, mounting with infirm unsearching tread,
His hopes to chaos led,
He may have stumbled up there from the past,
And with an aching strangeness viewed the last
Abysmal conflagration of his dreams,—
A flame where nothing seems
To burn but flame itself, by nothing fed;
And while it all went out,
Not even the faint anodyne of doubt
May then have eased a painful going down
From pictured heights of power and lost renown,
Revealed at length to his outlived endeavor
Remote and unapproachable forever;
And at his heart there may have gnawed
Sick memories of a dead faith foiled and flawed
And long dishonored by the living death
Assigned alike by chance
To brutes and hierophants;
And anguish fallen on those he loved around him
May once have dealt the last blow to confound him,
And so have left him as death leaves a child,
Who sees it all too near;
And he who knows no young way to forget
May struggle to the tomb unreconciled.
Whatever suns may rise or set
There may be nothing kinder for him here
Than shafts and agonies;
And under these
He may cry out and stay on horribly;
Or, seeing in death too small a thing to fear,
He may go forward like a stoic Roman
Where pangs and terrors in his pathway lie,—

Or, seizing the swift logic of a woman,
Curse God and die.

Or maybe there, like many another one
Who might have stood aloft and looked ahead,
Black-drawn against wild red,
He may have built, unawed by fiery gules
That in him no commotion stirred,
A living reason out of molecules
Why molecules occurred,
And one for smiling when he might have sighed
Had he seen far enough,
And in the same inevitable stuff
Discovered an odd reason too for pride
In being what he must have been by laws
Infrangible and for no kind of cause.
Deterred by no confusion or surprise
He may have seen with his mechanic eyes
A world without a meaning, and had room,
Alone amid magnificence and doom,
To build himself an airy monument
That should, or fail him in his vague intent,
Outlast an accidental universe—
To call it nothing worse—
Or, by the burrowing guile
Of Time disintegrated and effaced,
Like once-remembered mighty trees go down
To ruin, of which by man may now be traced
No part sufficient even to be rotten,
And in the book of things that are forgotten
Is entered as a thing not quite worth while.
He may have been so great
That satraps would have shivered at his frown,
And all he prized alive may rule a state
No larger than a grave that holds a clown;
He may have been a master of his fate,
And of his atoms,—ready as another
In his emergence to exonerate
His father and his mother;
He may have been a captain of a host,
Self-eloquent and ripe for prodigies,
Doomed here to swell by dangerous degrees,
And then give up the ghost.

Nahum's great grasshoppers were such as these,
Sun-scattered and soon lost.

Whatever the dark road he may have taken,
This man who stood on high
And faced alone the sky,
Whatever drove or lured or guided him,—
A vision answering a faith unshaken,
An easy trust assumed of easy trials,
A sick negation born of weak denials,
A crazed abhorrence of an old condition,
A blind attendance on a brief ambition,—
Whatever stayed him or derided him,
His way was even as ours;
And we, with all our wounds and all our powers,
Must each await alone at his own height
Another darkness or another light;
And there, of our poor self dominion reft,
If inference and reason shun
Hell, Heaven, and Oblivion,
May thwarted will (perforce precarious,
But for our conservation better thus)
Have no misgiving left
Of doing yet what here we leave undone?
Or if unto the last of these we cleave,
Believing or protesting we believe
In such an idle and ephemeral
Florescence of the diabolical,—
If, robbed of two fond old enormities,
Our being had no onward auguries,
What then were this great love of ours to say
For launching other lives to voyage again
A little farther into time and pain,
A little faster in a futile chase
For a kingdom and a power and a Race
That would have still in sight
A manifest end of ashes and eternal night?
Is this the music of the toys we shake
So loud,—as if there might be no mistake
Somewhere in our indomitable will?
Are we no greater than the noise we make
Along one blind atomic pilgrimage
Whereon by crass chance billeted we go

Because our brains and bones and cartilage
Will have it so?
If this we say, then let us all be still
About our share in it, and live and die
More quietly thereby.

Where was he going, this man against the sky?
You know not, nor do I.
But this we know, if we know anything:
That we may laugh and fight and sing
And of our transience here make offering
To an orient Word that will not be erased,
Or, save in incommunicable gleams
Too permanent for dreams,
Be found or known.
No tonic and ambitious irritant
Of increase or of want
Has made an otherwise insensate waste
Of ages overthrown
A ruthless, veiled, implacable foretaste
Of other ages that are still to be
Depleted and rewarded variously
Because a few, by fate's economy,
Shall seem to move the world the way it goes;
No soft evangel of equality,
Safe-cradled in a communal repose
That huddles into death and may at last
Be covered well with equatorial snows—
And all for what, the devil only knows—
Will aggregate an inkling to confirm
The credit of a sage or of a worm,
Or tell us why one man in five
Should have a care to stay alive
While in his heart he feels no violence
Laid on his humor and intelligence
When infant Science makes a pleasant face
And waves again that hollow toy, the Race;
No planetary trap where souls are wrought
For nothing but the sake of being caught
And sent again to nothing will attune
Itself to any key of any reason
Why man should hunger through another season
To find out why 'twere better late than soon

To go away and let the sun and moon
And all the silly stars illuminate
A place for creeping things,
And those that root and trumpet and have wings,
And herd and ruminate,
Or dive and flash and poise in rivers and seas,
Or by their loyal tails in lofty trees
Hang screeching lewd victorious derision
Of man's immortal vision.

Shall we, because Eternity records
Too vast an answer for the time-born words
We spell, whereof so many are dead that once
In our capricious lexicons
Were so alive and final, hear no more
The Word itself, the living word
That none alive has ever heard
Or ever spelt,
And few have ever felt
Without the fears and old surrenderings
And terrors that began
When Death let fall a feather from his wings
And humbled the first man?
Because the weight of our humility,
Wherefrom we gain
A little wisdom and much pain,
Falls here too sore and there too tedious,
Are we in anguish or complacency,
Not looking far enough ahead
To see by what mad couriers we are led
Along the roads of the ridiculous,
To pity ourselves and laugh at faith
And while we curse life bear it?
And if we see the soul's dead end in death,
Are we to fear it?
What folly is here that has not yet a name
Unless we say outright that we are liars?
What have we seen beyond our sunset fires
That lights again the way by which we came?
Why pay we such a price, and one we give
So clamoringly, for each racked empty day
That leads one more last human hope away,
As quiet fiends would lead past our crazed eyes

Our children to an unseen sacrifice?
If after all that we have lived and thought,
All comes to Nought,—
If there be nothing after Now,
And we be nothing anyhow,
And we know that,—why live?
'Twere sure but weaklings' vain distress
To suffer dungeons where so many doors
Will open on the cold eternal shores
That look sheer down
To the dark tideless floods of Nothingness
Where all who know may drown.   *1916*

THE MILL

The miller's wife had waited long,
  The tea was cold, the fire was dead;
And there might yet be nothing wrong
  In how he went and what he said:
"There are no millers any more,"
  Was all that she had heard him say;
And he had lingered at the door
  So long that it seemed yesterday.

Sick with a fear that had no form
  She knew that she was there at last;
And in the mill there was a warm
  And mealy fragrance of the past.
What else there was would only seem
  To say again what he had meant;
And what was hanging from a beam
  Would not have heeded where she went.

And if she thought it followed her,
  She may have reasoned in the dark
That one way of the few there were
  Would hide her and would leave no mark:
Black water, smooth above the weir
  Like starry velvet in the night,
Though ruffled once, would soon appear
  The same as ever to the sight.   *1920*

TASKER NORCROSS

"Whether all towns and all who live in them—
So long as they be somewhere in this world
That we in our complacency call ours—
Are more or less the same, I leave to you.
I should say less. Whether or not, meanwhile,
We've all two legs—and as for that, we haven't—
There were three kinds of men where I was born:
The good, the not so good, and Tasker Norcross.
Now there are two kinds."

                      "Meaning, as I divine,
Your friend is dead," I ventured.

                          Ferguson,
Who talked himself at last out of the world
He censured, and is therefore silent now,
Agreed indifferently: "My friends are dead—
Or most of them."

                  "Remember one that isn't,"
I said, protesting. "Honor him for his ears;
Treasure him also for his understanding."
Ferguson sighed, and then talked on again:
"You have an overgrown alacrity
For saying nothing much and hearing less;
And I've a thankless wonder, at the start,
How much it is to you that I shall tell
What I have now to say of Tasker Norcross,
And how much to the air that is around you.
But given a patience that is not averse
To the slow tragedies of haunted men—
Horrors, in fact, if you've a skillful eye
To know them at their firesides, or out walking,—"

"Horrors," I said, "are my necessity;
And I would have them, for their best effect,
Always out walking."

                 Ferguson frowned at me:
"The wisest of us are not those who laugh
Before they know. Most of us never know—

Or the long toil of our mortality
Would not be done. Most of us never know—
And there you have a reason to believe
In God, if you may have no other. Norcross,
Or so I gather of his infirmity,
Was given to know more than he should have known,
And only God knows why. See for yourself
An old house full of ghosts of ancestors,
Who did their best, or worst, and having done it,
Died honorably; and each with a distinction
That hardly would have been for him that had it,
Had honor failed him wholly as a friend.
Honor that is a friend begets a friend.
Whether or not we love him, still we have him;
And we must live somehow by what we have,
Or then we die. If you say chemistry,
Then you must have your molecules in motion,
And in their right abundance. Failing either,
You have not long to dance. Failing a friend,
A genius, or a madness, or a faith
Larger than desperation, you are here
For as much longer than you like as may be.
Imagining now, by way of an example,
Myself a more or less remembered phantom—
Again, I should say less—how many times
A day should I come back to you? No answer.
Forgive me when I seem a little careless,
But we must have examples, or be lucid
Without them; and I question your adherence
To such an undramatic narrative
As this of mine, without the personal hook."

"A time is given in Ecclesiastes
For divers works," I told him. "Is there one
For saying nothing in return for nothing?
If not, there should be." I could feel his eyes,
And they were like two cold inquiring points
Of a sharp metal. When I looked again,
To see them shine, the cold that I had felt
Was gone to make way for a smouldering
Of lonely fire that I, as I knew then,
Could never quench with kindness or with lies.
I should have done whatever there was to do

For Ferguson, yet I could not have mourned
In honesty for once around the clock
The loss of him, for my sake or for his,
Try as I might; nor would his ghost approve,
Had I the power and the unthinking will
To make him tread again without an aim
The road that was behind him—and without
The faith, or friend, or genius, or the madness
That he contended was imperative.

After a silence that had been too long,
"It may be quite as well we don't," he said;
"As well, I mean, that we don't always say it.
You know best what I mean, and I suppose
You might have said it better. What was that?
Incorrigible? Am I incorrigible?
Well, it's a word; and a word has its use,
Or, like a man, it will soon have a grave.
It's a good word enough. Incorrigible,
May be, for all I know, the word for Norcross.
See for yourself that house of his again
That he called home: An old house, painted white,
Square as a box, and chillier than a tomb
To look at or to live in. There were trees—
Too many of them, if such a thing may be—
Before it and around it. Down in front
There was a road, a railroad, and a river;
Then there were hills behind it, and more trees.
The thing would fairly stare at you through trees,
Like a pale inmate out of a barred window
With a green shade half down; and I dare say
People who passed have said: 'There's where he lives.
We know him, but we do not seem to know
That we remember any good of him,
Or any evil that is interesting.
There you have all we know and all we care.'
They might have said it in all sorts of ways;
And then, if they perceived a cat, they might
Or might not have remembered what they said.
The cat might have a personality—
And maybe the same one the Lord left out
Of Tasker Norcross, who, for lack of it,
Saw the same sun go down year after year;

All which at last was my discovery.
And only mine, so far as evidence
Enlightens one more darkness. You have known
All round you, all your days, men who are nothing—
Nothing, I mean, so far as time tells yet
Of any other need it has of them
Than to make sextons hardy—but no less
Are to themselves incalculably something,
And therefore to be cherished. God, you see,
Being sorry for them in their fashioning,
Indemnified them with a quaint esteem
Of self, and with illusions long as life.
You know them well, and you have smiled at them;
And they, in their serenity, may have had
Their time to smile at you. Blessed are they
That see themselves for what they never were
Or were to be, and are, for their defect,
At ease with mirrors and the dim remarks
That pass their tranquil ears."

                  "Come, come," said I;
"There may be names in your compendium
That we are not yet all on fire for shouting.
Skin most of us of our mediocrity,
We should have nothing then that we could scratch.
The picture smarts. Cover it, if you please,
And do so rather gently. Now for Norcross."

Ferguson closed his eyes in resignation,
While a dead sigh came out of him. "Good God!"
He said, and said it only half aloud,
As if he knew no longer now, nor cared,
If one were there to listen: "Have I said nothing—
Nothing at all—of Norcross? Do you mean
To patronize him till his name becomes
A toy made out of letters? If a name
Is all you need, arrange an honest column
Of all the people you have ever known
That you have never liked. You'll have enough;
And you'll have mine, moreover. No, not yet.
If I assume too many privileges,
I pay, and I alone, for their assumption;
By which, if I assume a darker knowledge

Of Norcross than another, let the weight
Of my injustice aggravate the load
That is not on your shoulders. When I came
To know this fellow Norcross in his house,
I found him as I found him in the street—
No more, no less; indifferent, but no better.
'Worse' were not quite the word: he was not bad;
He was not . . . well, he was not anything.
Has your invention ever entertained
The picture of a dusty worm so dry
That even the early bird would shake his head
And fly on farther for another breakfast?"

"But why forget the fortune of the worm,"
I said, "if in the dryness you deplore
Salvation centered and endured? Your Norcross
May have been one for many to have envied."

"Salvation? Fortune? Would the worm say that?
He might; and therefore I dismiss the worm
With all dry things but one. Figures away,
Do you begin to see this man a little?
Do you begin to see him in the air,
With all the vacant horrors of his outline
For you to fill with more than it will hold?
If so, you needn't crown yourself at once
With epic laurel if you seem to fill it.
Horrors, I say, for in the fires and forks
Of a new hell—if one were not enough—
I doubt if a new horror would have held him
With a malignant ingenuity
More to be feared than his before he died.
You smile, as if in doubt. Well, smile again.
Now come into his house, along with me:
The four square sombre things that you see first
Around you are four walls that go as high
As to the ceiling. Norcross knew them well,
And he knew others like them. Fasten to that
With all the claws of your intelligence;
And hold the man before you in his house
As if he were a white rat in a box,
And one that knew himself to be no other.
I tell you twice that he knew all about it,

That you may not forget the worst of all
Our tragedies begin with what we know.
Could Norcross only not have known, I wonder
How many would have blessed and envied him!
Could he have had the usual eye for spots
On others, and for none upon himself,
I smile to ponder on the carriages
That might as well as not have clogged the town
In honor of his end. For there was gold,
You see, though all he needed was a little,
And what he gave said nothing of who gave it.
He would have given it all if in return
There might have been a more sufficient face
To greet him when he shaved. Though you insist
It is the dower, and always, of our degree
Not to be cursed with such invidious insight,
Remember that you stand, you and your fancy,
Now in his house; and since we are together,
See for yourself and tell me what you see.
Tell me the best you see. Make a slight noise
Of recognition when you find a book
That you would not as lief read upside down
As otherwise, for example. If there you fail,
Observe the walls and lead me to the place,
Where you are led. If there you meet a picture
That holds you near it for a longer time
Than you are sorry, you may call it yours,
And hang it in the dark of your remembrance,
Where Norcross never sees. How can he see
That has no eyes to see? And as for music,
He paid with empty wonder for the pangs
Of his infrequent forced endurance of it;
And having had no pleasure, paid no more
For needless immolation, or for the sight
Of those who heard what he was never to hear.
To see them listening was itself enough
To make him suffer; and to watch worn eyes,
On other days, of strangers who forgot
Their sorrows and their failures and themselves
Before a few mysterious odds and ends
Of marble carted from the Parthenon—
And all for seeing what he was never to see,
Because it was alive and he was dead,—

Here was a wonder that was more profound
Than any that was in fiddles and brass horns.

"He knew, and in his knowledge there was death.
He knew there was a region all around him
That lay outside man's havoc and affairs,
And yet was not all hostile to their tumult,
Where poets would have served and honored him,
And saved him, had there been anything to save.
But there was nothing, and his tethered range
Was only a small desert. Kings of song
Are not for thrones in deserts. Towers of sound
And flowers of sense are but a waste of heaven
Where there is none to know them from the rocks
And sand-grass of his own monotony
That makes earth less than earth. He could see that,
And he could see no more. The captured light
That may have been or not, for all he cared,
The song that is in sculpture was not his,
But only, to his God-forgotten eyes,
One more immortal nonsense in a world
Where all was mortal, or had best be so,
And so be done with. 'Art,' he would have said,
'Is not life, and must therefore be a lie';
And with a few profundities like that
He would have controverted and dismissed
The benefit of the Greeks. He had heard of them,
As he had heard of his aspiring soul—
Never to the perceptible advantage,
In his esteem, of either. 'Faith,' he said,
Or would have said if he had thought of it,
'Lives in the same house with Philosophy,
Where the two feed on scraps and are forlorn
As orphans after war.' He could see stars,
On a clear night, but he had not an eye
To see beyond them. He could hear spoken words,
But had no ear for silence when alone.
He could eat food of which he knew the savor,
But had no palate for the Bread of Life,
That human desperation, to his thinking,
Made famous long ago, having no other.
Now do you see? Do you begin to see?"
I told him that I did begin to see;

And I was nearer than I should have been
To laughing at his malign inclusiveness,
When I considered that, with all our speed,
We are not laughing yet at funerals.
I see him now as I could see him then,
And I see now that it was good for me,
As it was good for him, that I was quiet;
For Time's eye was on Ferguson, and the shaft
Of its inquiring hesitancy had touched him,
Or so I chose to fancy more than once
Before he told of Norcross. When the word
Of his release (he would have called it so)
Made half an inch of news, there were no tears
That are recorded. Women there may have been
To wish him back, though I should say, not knowing,
The few there were to mourn were not for love,
And were not lovely. Nothing of them, at least,
Was in the meagre legend that I gathered
Years after, when a chance of travel took me
So near the region of his nativity
That a few miles of leisure brought me there;
For there I found a friendly citizen
Who led me to his house among the trees
That were above a railroad and a river.
Square as a box and chillier than a tomb
It was indeed, to look at or to live in—
All which had I been told. "Ferguson died,"
The stranger said, "and then there was an auction.
I live here, but I've never yet been warm.
Remember him? Yes, I remember him.
I knew him—as a man may know a tree—
For twenty years. He may have held himself
A little high when he was here, but now . . .
Yes, I remember Ferguson. Oh, yes."

Others, I found, remembered Ferguson,
But none of them had heard of Tasker Norcross.

1920

DISCOVERY

We told of him as one who should have soared
And seen for us the devastating light

Whereof there is not either day or night,
And shared with us the glamour of the Word
That fell once upon Amos to record
For men at ease in Zion, when the sight
Of ills obscured aggrieved him and the might
Of Hamath was a warning of the Lord.

Assured somehow that he would make us wise,
Our pleasure was to wait; and our surprise
Was hard when we confessed the dry return
Of his regret. For we were still to learn
That earth has not a school where we may go
For wisdom, or for more than we may know.

1920

FIRELIGHT

Ten years together without yet a cloud,
They seek each other's eyes at intervals
Of gratefulness to firelight and four walls
For love's obliteration of the crowd.
Serenely and perennially endowed
And bowered as few may be, their joy recalls
No snake, no sword; and over them there falls
The blessing of what neither says aloud.

Wiser for silence, they were not so glad
Were she to read the graven tale of lines
On the wan face of one somewhere alone;
Nor were they more content could he have had
Her thoughts a moment since of one who shines
Apart, and would be hers if he had known.

1920

MR. FLOOD'S PARTY

Old Eben Flood, climbing alone one night
Over the hill between the town below
And the forsaken upland hermitage
That held as much as he should ever know
On earth again of home, paused warily.
The road was his with not a native near;

And Eben, having leisure, said aloud,
For no man else in Tilbury Town to hear:

"Well, Mr. Flood, we have the harvest moon
Again, and we may not have many more;
The bird is on the wing, the poet says,
And you and I have said it here before.
Drink to the bird." He raised up to the light
The jug that he had gone so far to fill,
And answered huskily: "Well, Mr. Flood,
Since you propose it, I believe I will."

Alone, as if enduring to the end
A valiant armor of scarred hopes outworn,
He stood there in the middle of the road
Like Roland's ghost winding a silent horn.
Below him, in the town among the trees,
Where friends of other days had honored him,
A phantom salutation of the dead
Rang thinly till old Eben's eyes were dim.

Then, as a mother lays her sleeping child
Down tenderly, fearing it may awake,
He set the jug down slowly at his feet
With trembling care, knowing that most things break;
And only when assured that on firm earth
It stood, as the uncertain lives of men
Assuredly did not, he paced away,
And with his hand extended paused again:

"Well, Mr. Flood, we have not met like this
In a long time; and many a change has come
To both of us, I fear, since last it was
We had a drop together. Welcome home!"
Convivially returning with himself,
Again he raised the jug up to the light;
And with an acquiescent quaver said:
"Well, Mr. Flood, if you insist, I might.

"Only a very little, Mr. Flood—
For auld lang syne. No more, sir; that will do."
So, for the time, apparently it did,
And Eben evidently thought so too;

For soon amid the silver loneliness
Of night he lifted up his voice and sang,
Secure, with only two moons listening,
Until the whole harmonious landscape rang—

"For auld lang syne." The weary throat gave out,
The last word wavered; and the song being done,
He raised again the jug regretfully
And shook his head, and was again alone.
There was not much that was ahead of him,
And there was nothing in the town below—
Where strangers would have shut the many doors
That many friends had opened long ago.   *1921*

LOST ANCHORS

Like a dry fish flung inland far from shore,
There lived a sailor, warped and ocean-browned,
Who told of an old vessel, harbor-drowned
And out of mind a century before,
Where divers, on descending to explore
A legend that had lived its way around
The world of ships, in the dark hulk had found
Anchors, which had been seized and seen no more.

Improving a dry leisure to invest
Their misadventure with a manifest
Analogy that he may read who runs,
The sailor made it old as ocean grass—
Telling of much that once had come to pass
With him, whose mother should have had no sons.   *1921*

THE SHEAVES

Where long the shadows of the wind had rolled,
Green wheat was yielding to the change assigned;
And as by some vast magic undivined
The world was turning slowly into gold.
Like nothing that was ever bought or sold
It waited there, the body and the mind;
And with a mighty meaning of a kind
That tells the more the more it is not told.

So in a land where all days are not fair,
Fair days went on till on another day
A thousand golden sheaves were lying there,
Shining and still, but not for long to stay—
As if a thousand girls with golden hair
Might rise from where they slept and go away.

1925

AS IT LOOKED THEN

In a sick shade of spruce, moss-webbed, rock-fed,
Where, long unfollowed by sagacious man,
A scrub that once had been a pathway ran
Blindly from nowhere and to nowhere led,
One might as well have been among the dead
As half way there alive; so I began
Like a malingering pioneer to plan
A vain return—with one last look ahead.

And it was then that like a spoken word
Where there was none to speak, insensibly
A flash of blue that might have been a bird
Grew soon to the calm wonder of the sea—
Calm as a quiet sky that looked to be
Arching a world where nothing had occurred.

1925

KARMA

Christmas was in the air and all was well
With him, but for a few confusing flaws
In divers of God's images. Because
A friend of his would neither buy nor sell,
Was he to answer for the axe that fell?
He pondered; and the reason for it was,
Partly, a slowly freezing Santa Claus
Upon the corner, with his beard and bell.

Acknowledging an improvident surprise,
He magnified a fancy that he wished
The friend whom he had wrecked were here again.
Not sure of that, he found a compromise;
And from the fulness of his heart he fished
A dime for Jesus who had died for men.   *1925*

WHY HE WAS THERE

Much as he left it when he went from us
Here was the room again where he had been
So long that something of him should be seen,
Or felt—and so it was. Incredulous,
I turned about, loath to be greeted thus,
And there he was in his old chair, serene
As ever, and as laconic and as lean
As when he lived, and as cadaverous.

Calm as he was of old when we were young,
He sat there gazing at the pallid flame
Before him. "And how far will this go on?"
I thought. He felt the failure of my tongue,
And smiled: "I was not here until you came;
And I shall not be here when you are gone."

1925

Robert Frost

STORM FEAR

When the wind works against us in the dark,
And pelts with snow
The lower chamber window on the east,
And whispers with a sort of stifled bark,
The beast,
"Come out! Come out!"—
It costs no inward struggle not to go,
Ah, no!
I count our strength,
Two and a child,
Those of us not asleep subdued to mark
How the cold creeps as the fire dies at length,—
How drifts are piled,
Dooryard and road ungraded,
Till even the comforting barn grows far away,
And my heart owns a doubt
Whether 'tis in us to arise with day
And save ourselves unaided.   *1913*

MOWING

There was never a sound beside the wood but one,
And that was my long scythe whispering to the ground.
What was it it whispered? I knew not well myself;
Perhaps it was something about the heat of the sun,
Something, perhaps, about the lack of sound—
And that was why it whispered and did not speak.
It was no dream of the gift of idle hours,
Or easy gold at the hand of fay or elf:
Anything more than the truth would have seemed too weak
To the earnest love that laid the swale in rows,
Not without feeble-pointed spikes of flowers
(Pale orchises), and scared a bright green snake.

The fact is the sweetest dream that labor knows.
My long scythe whispered and left the hay to make. *1913*

RELUCTANCE

Out through the fields and the woods
    And over the walls I have wended;
I have climbed the hills of view
    And looked at the world, and descended;
I have come by the highway home,
    And lo, it is ended.

The leaves are all dead on the ground,
    Save those that the oak is keeping
To ravel them one by one
    And let them go scraping and creeping
Out over the crusted snow,
    When others are sleeping.

And the dead leaves lie huddled and still,
    No longer blown hither and thither;
The last lone aster is gone;
    The flowers of the witch-hazel wither;
The heart is still aching to seek,
    But the feet question "Whither?"

Ah, when to the heart of man
    Was it ever less than a treason
To go with the drift of things,
    To yield with a grace to reason,
And bow and accept the end
    Of a love or a season? *1913*

THE PASTURE

I'm going out to clean the pasture spring;
I'll only stop to rake the leaves away
(And wait to watch the water clear, I may):
I sha'n't be gone long.—You come too.

I'm going out to fetch the little calf
That's standing by the mother. It's so young,
It totters when she licks it with her tongue.
I sha'n't be gone long.—You come too. *1914*

MENDING WALL

Something there is that doesn't love a wall,
That sends the frozen-ground-swell under it,
And spills the upper boulders in the sun;
And makes gaps even two can pass abreast.
The work of hunters is another thing:
I have come after them and made repair
Where they have left not one stone on a stone,
But they would have the rabbit out of hiding,
To please the yelping dogs. The gaps I mean,
No one has seen them made or heard them made,
But at spring mending-time we find them there.
I let my neighbor know beyond the hill;
And on a day we meet to walk the line
And set the wall between us once again.
We keep the wall between us as we go.
To each the boulders that have fallen to each.
And some are loaves and some so nearly balls
We have to use a spell to make them balance:
"Stay where you are until our backs are turned!"
We wear our fingers rough with handling them.
Oh, just another kind of outdoor game,
One on a side. It comes to little more:
There where it is we do not need the wall:
He is all pine and I am apple orchard.
My apple trees will never get across
And eat the cones under his pines, I tell him.
He only says, "Good fences make good neighbors."
Spring is the mischief in me, and I wonder
If I could put a notion in his head:
"Why do they make good neighbors? Isn't it
Where there are cows? But here there are no cows.
Before I built a wall I'd ask to know
What I was walling in or walling out,
And to whom I was like to give offence.
Something there is that doesn't love a wall,
That wants it down." I could say "Elves" to him,
But it's not elves exactly, and I'd rather
He said it for himself. I see him there
Bringing a stone grasped firmly by the top
In each hand, like an old-stone savage armed.

He moves in darkness as it seems to me,
Not of woods only and the shade of trees.
He will not go behind his father's saying,
And he likes having thought of it so well
He says again, "Good fences make good neighbors."

1914

A SERVANT TO SERVANTS

I didn't make you know how glad I was
To have you come and camp here on our land.
I promised myself to get down some day
And see the way you lived, but I don't know!
With a houseful of hungry men to feed
I guess you'd find. . . . It seems to me
I can't express my feelings any more
Than I can raise my voice or want to lift
My hand (oh, I can lift it when I have to).
Did ever you feel so? I hope you never.
It's got so I don't even know for sure
Whether I *am* glad, sorry, or anything.
There's nothing but a voice-like left inside
That seems to tell me how I ought to feel,
And would feel if I wasn't all gone wrong.
You take the lake. I look and look at it.
I see it's a fair, pretty sheet of water.
I stand and make myself repeat out loud
The advantages it has, so long and narrow,
Like a deep piece of some old running river
Cut short off at both ends. It lies five miles
Straight away through the mountain notch
From the sink window where I wash the plates,
And all our storms come up toward the house,
Drawing the slow waves whiter and whiter and whiter.
It took my mind off doughnuts and soda biscuit
To step outdoors and take the water dazzle
A sunny morning, or take the rising wind
About my face and body and through my wrapper,
When a storm threatened from the Dragon's Den,
And a cold chill shivered across the lake.
I see it's a fair, pretty sheet of water,
Our Willoughby! How did you hear of it?
I expect, though, everyone's heard of it.

In a book about ferns? Listen to that!
You let things more like feathers regulate
Your going and coming. And you like it here?
I can see how you might. But I don't know!
It would be different if more people came,
For then there would be business. As it is,
The cottages Len built, sometimes we rent them,
Sometimes we don't. We've a good piece of shore
That ought to be worth something, and may yet.
But I don't count on it as much as Len.
He looks on the bright side of everything,
Including me. He thinks I'll be all right
With doctoring. But it's not medicine—
Lowe is the only doctor's dared to say so—
It's rest I want—there, I have said it out—
From cooking meals for hungry hired men
And washing dishes after them—from doing
Things over and over that just won't stay done.
By good rights I ought not to have so much
Put on me, but there seems no other way.
Len says one steady pull more ought to do it.
He says the best way out is always through.
And I agree to that, or in so far
As that I can see no way out but through—
Leastways for me—and then they'll be convinced.
It's not that Len don't want the best for me.
It was his plan our moving over in
Beside the lake from where that day I showed you
We used to live—ten miles from anywhere.
We didn't change without some sacrifice,
But Len went at it to make up the loss.
His work's a man's, of course, from sun to sun,
But he works when he works as hard as I do—
Though there's small profit in comparisons.
(Women and men will make them all the same.)
But work ain't all. Len undertakes too much.
He's into everything in town. This year
It's highways, and he's got too many men
Around him to look after that make waste.
They take advantage of him shamefully,
And proud, too, of themselves for doing so.
We have four here to board, great good-for-nothings,
Sprawling about the kitchen with their talk

While I fry their bacon. Much they care!
No more put out in what they do or say
Than if I wasn't in the room at all.
Coming and going all the time, they are:
I don't learn what their names are, let alone
Their characters, or whether they are safe
To have inside the house with doors unlocked.
I'm not afraid of them, though, if they're not
Afraid of me. There's two can play at that.
I have my fancies: it runs in the family.
My father's brother wasn't right. They kept him
Locked up for years back there at the old farm.
I've been away once—yes, I've been away.
The State Asylum. I was prejudiced;
I wouldn't have sent anyone of mine there;
You know the old idea—the only asylum
Was the poorhouse, and those who could afford,
Rather than send their folks to such a place,
Kept them at home; and it does seem more human.
But it's not so: the place is the asylum.
There they have every means proper to do with,
And you aren't darkening other people's lives—
Worse than no good to them, and they no good
To you in your condition; you can't know
Affection or the want of it in that state.
I've heard too much of the old-fashioned way.
My father's brother, he went mad quite young.
Some thought he had been bitten by a dog,
Because his violence took on the form
Of carrying his pillow in his teeth;
But it's more likely he was crossed in love,
Or so the story goes. It was some girl.
Anyway all he talked about was love.
They soon saw he would do someone a mischief
If he wa'n't kept strict watch of, and it ended
In father's building him a sort of cage,
Or room within a room, of hickory poles,
Like stanchions in the barn, from floor to ceiling,—
A narrow passage all the way around.
Anything they put in for furniture
He'd tear to pieces, even a bed to lie on.
So they made the place comfortable with straw,
Like a beast's stall, to ease their consciences.

Of course they had to feed him without dishes.
They tried to keep him clothed, but he paraded
With his clothes on his arm—all of his clothes.
Cruel—it sounds. I 'spose they did the best
They knew. And just when he was at the height,
Father and mother married, and mother came,
A bride, to help take care of such a creature,
And accommodate her young life to his.
That was what marrying father meant to her.
She had to lie and hear love things made dreadful
By his shouts in the night. He'd shout and shout
Until the strength was shouted out of him,
And his voice died down slowly from exhaustion.
He'd pull his bars apart like bow and bowstring,
And let them go and make them twang until
His hands had worn them smooth as any oxbow.
And then he'd crow as if he thought that child's play
The only fun he had. I've heard them say, though,
They found a way to put a stop to it.
He was before my time—I never saw him;
But the pen stayed exactly as it was
There in the upper chamber in the ell,
A sort of catch-all full of attic clutter.
I often think of the smooth hickory bars.
It got so I would say—you know, half fooling—
"It's time I took my turn upstairs in jail"—
Just as you will till it becomes a habit.
No wonder I was glad to get away.
Mind you, I waited till Len said the word.
I didn't want the blame if things went wrong.
I was glad though, no end, when we moved out,
And I looked to be happy, and I was,
As I said, for a while—but I don't know!
Somehow the change wore out like a prescription.
And there's more to it than just window-views
And living by a lake. I'm past such help—
Unless Len took the notion, which he won't,
And I won't ask him—it's not sure enough.
I 'spose I've got to go the road I'm going:
Other folks have to, and why shouldn't I?
I almost think if I could do like you,
Drop everything and live out on the ground—
But it might be, come night, I shouldn't like it,

Or a long rain. I should soon get enough,
And be glad of a good roof overhead.
I've lain awake thinking of you, I'll warrant,
More than you have yourself, some of these nights.
The wonder was the tents weren't snatched away
From over you as you lay in your beds.
I haven't courage for a risk like that.
Bless you, of course, you're keeping me from work,
But the thing of it is, I need to *be* kept.
There's work enough to do—there's always that;
But behind's behind. The worst that you can do
Is set me back a little more behind.
I sha'n't catch up in this world, anyway.
I'd *rather* you'd not go unless you must.   1914

THE DEATH OF THE HIRED MAN

Mary sat musing on the lamp-flame at the table
Waiting for Warren. When she heard his step,
She ran on tip-toe down the darkened passage
To meet him in the doorway with the news
And put him on his guard. "Silas is back."
She pushed him outward with her through the door
And shut it after her. "Be kind," she said.
She took the market things from Warren's arms
And set them on the porch, then drew him down
To sit beside her on the wooden steps.

"When was I ever anything but kind to him?
But I'll not have the fellow back," he said.
"I told him so last haying, didn't I?
If he left then, I said, that ended it.
What good is he? Who else will harbor him
At his age for the little he can do?
What help he is there's no depending on.
Off he goes always when I need him most.
He thinks he ought to earn a little pay,
Enough at least to buy tobacco with,
So he won't have to beg and be beholden.
'All right,' I say, 'I can't afford to pay
Any fixed wages, though I wish I could.'
'Someone else can.' 'Then someone else will have to.'
I shouldn't mind his bettering himself

If that was what it was. You can be certain,
When he begins like that, there's someone at him
Trying to coax him off with pocket-money,—
In haying time, when any help is scarce.
In winter he comes back to us. I'm done."

"Sh! not so loud: he'll hear you," Mary said.

"I want him to: he'll have to soon or late."

"He's worn out. He's asleep beside the stove.
When I came up from Rowe's I found him here,
Huddled against the barn-door fast asleep,
A miserable sight, and frightening, too—
You needn't smile—I didn't recognize him—
I wasn't looking for him—and he's changed.
Wait till you see."

                    "Where did you say he'd been?"

"He didn't say. I dragged him to the house,
And gave him tea and tried to make him smoke.
I tried to make him talk about his travels.
Nothing would do: he just kept nodding off."

"What did he say? Did he say anything?"

"But little."

          "Anything? Mary, confess
He said he'd come to ditch the meadow for me."

"Warren!"

          "But did he? I just want to know."

"Of course he did. What would you have him say?
Surely you wouldn't grudge the poor old man
Some humble way to save his self-respect.
He added, if you really care to know,
He meant to clear the upper pasture, too.
That sounds like something you have heard before?

Warren, I wish you could have heard the way
He jumbled everything. I stopped to look
Two or three times—he made me feel so queer—
To see if he was talking in his sleep.
He ran on Harold Wilson—you remember—
The boy you had in haying four years since.
He's finished school, and teaching in his college.
Silas declares you'll have to get him back.
He says they two will make a team for work:
Between them they will lay this farm as smooth!
The way he mixed that in with other things.
He thinks young Wilson a likely lad, though daft
On education—you know how they fought
All through July under the blazing sun,
Silas up on the cart to build the load,
Harold along beside to pitch it on."

"Yes, I took care to keep well out of earshot."

"Well, those days trouble Silas like a dream.
You wouldn't think they would. How some things linger!
Harold's young college boy's assurance piqued him.
After so many years he still keeps finding
Good arguments he sees he might have used.
I sympathize. I know just how it feels
To think of the right thing to say too late.
Harold's associated in his mind with Latin.
He asked me what I thought of Harold's saying
He studied Latin like the violin
Because he liked it—that an argument!
He said he couldn't make the boy believe
He could find water with a hazel prong—
Which showed how much good school had ever done him.
He wanted to go over that. But most of all
He thinks if he could have another chance
To teach him how to build a load of hay—"

"I know, that's Silas' one accomplishment.
He bundles every forkful in its place,
And tags and numbers it for future reference,
So he can find and easily dislodge it
In the unloading. Silas does that well.
He takes it out in bunches like big birds' nests.

You never see him standing on the hay
He's trying to lift, straining to lift himself."

"He thinks if he could teach him that, he'd be
Some good perhaps to someone in the world.
He hates to see a boy the fool of books.
Poor Silas, so concerned for other folk,
And nothing to look backward to with pride,
And nothing to look forward to with hope,
So now and never any different."

Part of a moon was falling down the west,
Dragging the whole sky with it to the hills.
Its light poured softly in her lap. She saw
And spread her apron to it. She put out her hand
Among the harp-like morning-glory strings,
Taut with the dew from garden bed to eaves,
As if she played unheard the tenderness
That wrought on him beside her in the night.
"Warren," she said, "he has come home to die:
You needn't be afraid he'll leave you this time."

"Home," he mocked gently.

                              "Yes, what else but home?
It all depends on what you mean by home.
Of course he's nothing to us, any more
Than was the hound that came a stranger to us
Out of the woods, worn out upon the trail."

"Home is the place where, when you have to go there,
They have to take you in."

                              "I should have called it
Something you somehow haven't to deserve."

Warren leaned out and took a step or two,
Picked up a little stick, and brought it back
And broke it in his hand and tossed it by.
"Silas has better claim on us you think
Than on his brother? Thirteen little miles
As the road winds would bring him to his door.
Silas has walked that far no doubt today.

Why didn't he go there? His brother's rich,
A somebody—director in the bank."

"He never told us that."

                              "We know it though."

"I think his brother ought to help, of course.
I'll see to that if there is need. He ought of right
To take him in, and might be willing to—
He may be better than appearances.
But have some pity on Silas. Do you think
If he'd had any pride in claiming kin
Or anything he looked for from his brother,
He'd keep so still about him all this time?"

"I wonder what's between them."

                              "I can tell you.
Silas is what he is—we wouldn't mind him—
But just the kind that kinsfolk can't abide.
He never did a thing so very bad.
He don't know why he isn't quite as good
As anybody. Worthless though he is,
He won't be made ashamed to please his brother."

"I can't think Si ever hurt anyone."

"No, but he hurt my heart the way he lay
And rolled his old head on that sharp-edged chair-back.
He wouldn't let me put him on the lounge.
You must go in and see what you can do.
I made the bed up for him there tonight.
You'll be surprised at him—how much he's broken.
His working days are done; I'm sure of it."

"I'd not be in a hurry to say that."

"I haven't been. Go, look, see for yourself,
But, Warren, please remember how it is:
He's come to help you ditch the meadow.
He has a plan. You mustn't laugh at him.

He may not speak of it, and then he may.
I'll sit and see if that small sailing cloud
Will hit or miss the moon."

It hit the moon.
Then there were three there, making a dim row,
The moon, the little silver cloud, and she.
Warren returned—too soon, it seemed to her,
Slipped to her side, caught up her hand and waited.
"Warren?" she questioned.

"Dead," was all he answered.

1914

AFTER APPLE-PICKING

My long two-pointed ladder's sticking through a tree
Toward heaven still,
And there's a barrel that I didn't fill
Beside it, and there may be two or three
Apples I didn't pick upon some bough.
But I am done with apple-picking now.
Essence of winter sleep is on the night,
The scent of apples: I am drowsing off.
I cannot rub the strangeness from my sight
I got from looking through a pane of glass
I skimmed this morning from the drinking trough
And held against the world of hoary grass.
It melted, and I let it fall and break.
But I was well
Upon my way to sleep before it fell,
And I could tell
What form my dreaming was about to take.
Magnified apples appear and disappear,
Stem end and blossom end,
And every fleck of russet showing clear.
My instep arch not only keeps the ache,
It keeps the pressure of a ladder-round.
I feel the ladder sway as the boughs bend.
And I keep hearing from the cellar bin
The rumbling sound
Of load on load of apples coming in.
For I have had too much

Of apple-picking: I am overtired
Of the great harvest I myself desired.
There were ten thousand thousand fruit to touch,
Cherish in hand, lift down, and not let fall.
For all
That struck the earth,
No matter if not bruised or spiked with stubble,
Went surely to the cider-apple heap
As of no worth.
One can see what will trouble
This sleep of mine, whatever sleep it is.
Were he not gone,
The woodchuck could say whether it's like his
Long sleep, as I describe its coming on,
Or just some human sleep.   *1914*

THE ROAD NOT TAKEN

Two roads diverged in a yellow wood,
And sorry I could not travel both
And be one traveler, long I stood
And looked down one as far as I could
To where it bent in the undergrowth;

Then took the other, as just as fair,
And having perhaps the better claim,
Because it was grassy and wanted wear;
Though as for that the passing there
Had worn them really about the same,

And both that morning equally lay
In leaves no step had trodden black.
Oh, I kept the first for another day!
Yet knowing how way leads on to way,
I doubted if I should ever come back.

I shall be telling this with a sigh
Somewhere ages and ages hence:
Two roads diverged in a wood, and I—
I took the one less traveled by,
And that has made all the difference.
                    1916

A PATCH OF OLD SNOW

There's a patch of old snow in a corner
  That I should have guessed
Was a blow-away paper the rain
  Had brought to rest.

It is speckled with grime as if
  Small print overspread it,
The news of a day I've forgotten—
  If I ever read it.   *1916*

BIRCHES

When I see birches bend to left and right
Across the lines of straighter darker trees,
I like to think some boy's been swinging them.
But swinging doesn't bend them down to stay
As ice-storms do. Often you must have seen them
Loaded with ice a sunny winter morning
After a rain. They click upon themselves
As the breeze rises, and turn many-colored
As the stir cracks and crazes their enamel.
Soon the sun's warmth makes them shed crystal shells
Shattering and avalanching on the snow-crust—
Such heaps of broken glass to sweep away
You'd think the inner dome of heaven had fallen.
They are dragged to the withered bracken by the load,
And they seem not to break; though once they are bowed
So low for long, they never right themselves:
You may see their trunks arching in the woods
Years afterwards, trailing their leaves on the ground
Like girls on hands and knees that throw their hair
Before them over their heads to dry in the sun.
But I was going to say when Truth broke in
With all her matter-of-fact about the ice-storm
I should prefer to have some boy bend them
As he went out and in to fetch the cows—
Some boy too far from town to learn baseball,
Whose only play was what he found himself,
Summer or winter, and could play alone.
One by one he subdued his father's trees

By riding them down over and over again
Until he took the stiffness out of them,
And not one but hung limp, not one was left
For him to conquer. He learned all there was
To learn about not launching out too soon
And so not carrying the tree away
Clear to the ground. He always kept his poise
To the top branches, climbing carefully
With the same pains you use to fill a cup
Up to the brim, and even above the brim.
Then he flung outward, feet first, with a swish,
Kicking his way down through the air to the ground.
So was I once myself a swinger of birches.
And so I dream of going back to be.
It's when I'm weary of considerations,
And life is too much like a pathless wood
Where your face burns and tickles with the cobwebs
Broken across it, and one eye is weeping
From a twig's having lashed across it open.
I'd like to get away from earth awhile
And then come back to it and begin over.
May no fate willfully misunderstand me
And half grant what I wish and snatch me away
Not to return. Earth's the right place for love:
I don't know where it's likely to go better.
I'd like to go by climbing a birch tree,
And climb black branches up a snow-white trunk
Toward heaven, till the tree could bear no more,
But dipped its top and set me down again.
That would be good both going and coming back.
One could do worse than be a swinger of birches.   *1916*

THE HILL WIFE

LONELINESS

Her Word

One ought not to have to care
    So much as you and I
Care when the birds come round the house
    To seem to say good-by;

Or care so much when they come back
 With whatever it is they sing;
The truth being we are as much
 Too glad for the one thing

As we are too sad for the other here—
 With birds that fill their breasts
But with each other and themselves
 And their built or driven nests.

HOUSE FEAR

Always—I tell you this they learned—
Always at night when they returned
To the lonely house from far away
To lamps unlighted and fire gone gray,
They learned to rattle the lock and key
To give whatever might chance to be
Warning and time to be off in flight:
And preferring the out- to the in-door night,
They learned to leave the house-door wide
Until they had lit the lamp inside.

THE SMILE

Her Word

I didn't like the way he went away.
That smile! It never came of being gay.
Still he smiled—did you see him?—I was sure!
Perhaps because we gave him only bread
And the wretch knew from that that we were poor.
Perhaps because he let us give instead
Of seizing from us as he might have seized.
Perhaps he mocked at us for being wed,
Or being very young (and he was pleased
To have a vision of us old and dead).
I wonder how far down the road he's got.
He's watching from the woods as like as not.

THE OFT-REPEATED DREAM

She had no saying dark enough
 For the dark pine that kept

Forever trying the window-latch
    Of the room where they slept.

The tireless but ineffectual hands
    That with every futile pass
Made the great tree seem as a little bird
    Before the mystery of glass!

It never had been inside the room,
    And only one of the two
Was afraid in an oft-repeated dream
    Of what the tree might do.

THE IMPULSE

It was too lonely for her there,
    And too wild,
And since there were but two of them,
    And no child,

And work was little in the house,
    She was free,
And followed where he furrowed field,
    Or felled tree.

She rested on a log and tossed
    The fresh chips,
With a song only to herself
    On her lips.

And once she went to break a bough
    Of black alder.
She strayed so far she scarcely heard
    When he called her—

And didn't answer—didn't speak—
    Or return.
She stood, and then she ran and hid
    In the fern.

He never found her, though he looked
    Everywhere,

And he asked at her mother's house
   Was she there.

Sudden and swift and light as that
   The ties gave,
And he learned of finalities
   Besides the grave.   *1916*

TWO WITCHES

I

THE WITCH OF COÖS

I staid the night for shelter at a farm
Behind the mountain, with a mother and son,
Two old-believers. They did all the talking.

MOTHER. Folks think a witch who has familiar spirits
She could call up to pass a winter evening,
But won't, should be burned at the stake or something.
Summoning spirits isn't "Button, button,
Who's got the button," I would have them know.

SON. Mother can make a common table rear
And kick with two legs like an army mule.

MOTHER. And when I've done it, what good have I done?
Rather than tip a table for you, let me
Tell you what Ralle the Sioux Control once told me.
He said the dead had souls, but when I asked him
How could that be—I thought the dead were souls,
He broke my trance. Don't that make you suspicious
That there's something the dead are keeping back?
Yes, there's something the dead are keeping back.

SON. You wouldn't want to tell him what we have
Up attic, mother?

MOTHER. Bones—a skeleton.

SON. But the headboard of mother's bed is pushed
Against the attic door: the door is nailed.

It's harmless. Mother hears it in the night
Halting perplexed behind the barrier
Of door and headboard. Where it wants to get
Is back into the cellar where it came from.

MOTHER. We'll never let them, will we, son! We'll never!

SON. It left the cellar forty years ago
And carried itself like a pile of dishes
Up one flight from the cellar to the kitchen,
Another from the kitchen to the bedroom,
Another from the bedroom to the attic,
Right past both father and mother, and neither stopped it.
Father had gone upstairs; mother was downstairs.
I was a baby: I don't know where I was.

MOTHER. The only fault my husband found with me—
I went to sleep before I went to bed,
Especially in winter when the bed
Might just as well be ice and the clothes snow.
The night the bones came up the cellar-stairs
Toffile had gone to bed alone and left me,
But left an open door to cool the room off
So as to sort of turn me out of it.
I was just coming to myself enough
To wonder where the cold was coming from,
When I heard Toffile upstairs in the bedroom
And thought I heard him downstairs in the cellar.
The board we had laid down to walk dry-shod on
When there was water in the cellar in spring
Struck the hard cellar bottom. And then someone
Began the stairs, two footsteps for each step,
The way a man with one leg and a crutch,
Or a little child, comes up. It wasn't Toffile:
It wasn't anyone who could be there.
The bulkhead double-doors were double-locked
And swollen tight and buried under snow.
The cellar windows were banked up with sawdust
And swollen tight and buried under snow.
It was the bones. I knew them—and good reason.
My first impulse was to get to the knob
And hold the door. But the bones didn't try
The door; they halted helpless on the landing,

Waiting for things to happen in their favor.
The faintest restless rustling ran all through them.
I never could have done the thing I did
If the wish hadn't been too strong in me
To see how they were mounted for this walk.
I had a vision of them put together
Not like a man, but like a chandelier.
So suddenly I flung the door wide on him.
A moment he stood balancing with emotion,
And all but lost himself. (A tongue of fire
Flashed out and licked along his upper teeth.
Smoke rolled inside the sockets of his eyes.)
Then he came at me with one hand outstretched,
The way he did in life once; but this time
I struck the hand off brittle on the floor,
And fell back from him on the floor myself.
The finger-pieces slid in all directions.
(Where did I see one of those pieces lately?
Hand me my button-box—it must be there.)
I sat up on the floor and shouted, "Toffile,
It's coming up to you." It had its choice
Of the door to the cellar or the hall.
It took the hall door for the novelty,
And set off briskly for so slow a thing,
Still going every which way in the joints, though,
So that it looked like lightning or a scribble,
From the slap I had just now given its hand.
I listened till it almost climbed the stairs
From the hall to the only finished bedroom,
Before I got up to do anything;
Then ran and shouted, "Shut the bedroom door,
Toffile, for my sake!" "Company?" he said,
"Don't make me get up; I'm too warm in bed."
So lying forward weakly on the handrail
I pushed myself upstairs, and in the light
(The kitchen had been dark) I had to own
I could see nothing. "Toffile, I don't see it.
It's with us in the room though. It's the bones."
"What bones?" "The cellar bones—out of the grave."
That made him throw his bare legs out of bed
And sit up by me and take hold of me.
I wanted to put out the light and see
If I could see it, or else mow the room,

With our arms at the level of our knees,
And bring the chalk-pile down. "I'll tell you what–
It's looking for another door to try.
The uncommonly deep snow has made him think
Of his old song, *The Wild Colonial Boy,*
He always used to sing along the tote road.
He's after an open door to get outdoors.
Let's trap him with an open door up attic."
Toffile agreed to that, and sure enough,
Almost the moment he was given an opening,
The steps began to climb the attic stairs.
I heard them. Toffile didn't seem to hear them.
"Quick!" I slammed to the door and held the knob.
"Toffile, get nails." I made him nail the door shut,
And push the headboard of the bed against it.
Then we asked was there anything
Up attic that we'd ever want again.
The attic was less to us than the cellar.
If the bones liked the attic, let them have it.
Let them stay in the attic. When they sometimes
Come down the stairs at night and stand perplexed
Behind the door and headboard of the bed,
Brushing their chalky skull with chalky fingers,
With sounds like the dry rattling of a shutter,
That's what I sit up in the dark to say—
To no one any more since Toffile died.
Let them stay in the attic since they went there.
I promised Toffile to be cruel to them
For helping them be cruel once to him.

SON. We think they had a grave down in the cellar.

MOTHER. We know they had a grave down in the cellar.

SON. We never could find out whose bones they were.

MOTHER. Yes, we could too, son. Tell the truth for once.
They were a man's his father killed for me.
I mean a man he killed instead of me.
The least I could do was to help dig their grave.
We were about it one night in the cellar.
Son knows the story: but 'twas not for him
To tell the truth, suppose the time had come.

Son looks surprised to see me end a lie
We'd kept all these years between ourselves
So as to have it ready for outsiders.
But tonight I don't care enough to lie—
I don't remember why I ever cared.
Toffile, if he were here, I don't believe
Could tell you why he ever cared himself. . . .

She hadn't found the finger-bone she wanted
Among the buttons poured out in her lap.
I verified the name next morning: Toffile.
The rural letter box said Toffile Lajway.

II

THE PAUPER WITCH OF GRAFTON

Now that they've got it settled whose I be,
I'm going to tell them something they won't like:
They've got it settled wrong, and I can prove it.
Flattered I must be to have two towns fighting
To make a present of me to each other.
They don't dispose me, either one of them,
To spare them any trouble. Double trouble's
Always the witch's motto anyway.
I'll double theirs for both of them—you watch me.
They'll find they've got the whole thing to do over,
That is, if facts is what they want to go by.
They set a lot (now don't they?) by a record
Of Arthur Amy's having once been up
For Hog Reeve in March Meeting here in Warren.
I could have told them any time this twelvemonth
The Arthur Amy I was married to
Couldn't have been the one they say was up
In Warren at March Meeting for the reason
He wa'n't but fifteen at the time they say.
The Arthur Amy I was married to
Voted the only times he ever voted,
Which wasn't many, in the town of Wentworth.
One of the times was when 'twas in the warrant
To see if the town wanted to take over
The tote road to our clearing where we lived.
I'll tell you who'd remember—Heman Lapish.
Their Arthur Amy was the father of mine.

So now they've dragged it through the law courts once
I guess they'd better drag it through again.
Wentworth and Warren's both good towns to live in,
Only I happen to prefer to live
In Wentworth from now on; and when all's said,
Right's right, and the temptation to do right
When I can hurt someone by doing it
Has always been too much for me, it has.
I know of some folks that'd be set up
At having in their town a noted witch:
But most would have to think of the expense
That even I would be. They ought to know
That as a witch I'd often milk a bat
And that'd be enough to last for days.
It'd make my position stronger, think,
If I was to consent to give some sign
To make it surer that I was a witch?
It wa'n't no sign, I s'pose, when Mallice Huse
Said that I took him out in his old age
And rode all over everything on him
Until I'd had him worn to skin and bones,
And if I'd left him hitched unblanketed
In front of one Town Hall, I'd left him hitched
In front of every one in Grafton County.
Some cried shame on me not to blanket him,
The poor old man. It would have been all right
If someone hadn't said to gnaw the posts
He stood beside and leave his trade mark on them,
So they could recognize them. Not a post
That they could hear tell of was scarified.
They made him keep on gnawing till he whined.
Then that same smarty someone said to look—
He'd bet Huse was a cribber and had gnawed
The crib he slept in—and as sure's you're born
They found he'd gnawed the four posts of his bed,
All four of them to splinters. What did that prove?
Not that he hadn't gnawed the hitching posts
He said he had besides. Because a horse
Gnaws in the stable ain't no proof to me
He don't gnaw trees and posts and fences too.
But everybody took it for a proof.
I was a strapping girl of twenty then.
The smarty someone who spoiled everything

Was Arthur Amy. You know who he was.
That was the way he started courting me.
He never said much after we were married,
But I mistrusted he was none too proud
Of having interfered in the Huse business.
I guess he found he got more out of me
By having me a witch. Or something happened
To turn him round. He got to saying things
To undo what he'd done and make it right,
Like, "No, she ain't come back from kiting yet.
Last night was one of her nights out. She's kiting.
She thinks when the wind makes a night of it
She might as well herself." But he liked best
To let on he was plagued to death with me:
If anyone had seen me coming home
Over the ridgepole, 'stride of a broomstick,
As often as he had in the tail of the night,
He guessed they'd know what he had to put up with.
Well, I showed Arthur Amy signs enough
Off from the house as far as we could keep
And from barn smells you can't wash out of plowed ground
With all the rain and snow of seven years;
And I don't mean just skulls of Rogers' Rangers
On Moosilauke, but woman signs to man,
Only bewitched so I would last him longer.
Up where the trees grow short, the mosses tall,
I made him gather me wet snow berries
On slippery rocks beside a waterfall.
I made him do it for me in the dark.
And he liked everything I made him do.
I hope if he is where he sees me now
He's so far off he can't see what I've come to.
You *can* come down from everything to nothing.
All is, if I'd a-known when I was young
And full of it, that this would be the end,
It doesn't seem as if I'd had the courage
To make so free and kick up in folks' faces.
I might have, but it doesn't seem as if.   *1923*

FIRE AND ICE

Some say the world will end in fire,
Some say in ice.

From what I've tasted of desire
I hold with those who favor fire.
But if it had to perish twice,
I think I know enough of hate
To say that for destruction ice
Is also great
And would suffice.   *1923*

DUST OF SNOW

The way a crow
Shook down on me
The dust of snow
From a hemlock tree

Has given my heart
A change of mood
And saved some part
Of a day I had rued.
                    1923

STOPPING BY WOODS ON A SNOWY EVENING

Whose woods these are I think I know.
His house is in the village though;
He will not see me stopping here
To watch his woods fill up with snow.

My little horse must think it queer
To stop without a farmhouse near
Between the woods and frozen lake
The darkest evening of the year.

He gives his harness bells a shake
To ask if there is some mistake.
The only other sound's the sweep
Of easy wind and downy flake.

The woods are lovely, dark and deep,
But I have promises to keep,
And miles to go before I sleep,
And miles to go before I sleep.   *1923*

THE ONSET

Always the same, when on a fated night
At last the gathered snow lets down as white
As may be in dark woods, and with a song
It shall not make again all winter long
Of hissing on the yet uncovered ground,
I almost stumble looking up and round,
As one who overtaken by the end
Gives up his errand, and lets death descend
Upon him where he is, with nothing done
To evil, no important triumph won,
More than if life had never been begun.

Yet all the precedent is on my side:
I know that winter death has never tried
The earth but it has failed: the snow may heap
In long storms an undrifted four feet deep
As measured against maple, birch, and oak,
It cannot check the peeper's silver croak;
And I shall see the snow all go down hill
In water of a slender April rill
That flashes tail through last year's withered brake
And dead weeds, like a disappearing snake.
Nothing will be left white but here a birch,
And there a clump of houses with a church.   1923

GOOD-BY AND KEEP COLD

This saying good-by on the edge of the dark
And cold to an orchard so young in the bark
Reminds me of all that can happen to harm
An orchard away at the end of the farm
All winter, cut off by a hill from the house.
I don't want it girdled by rabbit and mouse,
I don't want it dreamily nibbled for browse
By deer, and I don't want it budded by grouse.
(If certain it wouldn't be idle to call
I'd summon grouse, rabbit, and deer to the wall
And warn them away with a stick for a gun.)
I don't want it stirred by the heat of the sun.
(We made it secure against being, I hope,

By setting it out on a northerly slope.)
No orchard's the worse for the wintriest storm;
But one thing about it, it mustn't get warm.
"How often already you've had to be told,
Keep cold, young orchard. Good-by and keep cold.
Dread fifty above more than fifty below."
I have to be gone for a season or so.
My business awhile is with different trees,
Less carefully nourished, less fruitful than these,
And such as is done to their wood with an ax—
Maples and birches and tamaracks.
I wish I could promise to lie in the night
And think of an orchard's arboreal plight
When slowly (and nobody comes with a light)
Its heart sinks lower under the sod.
But something has to be left to God.   1923

NOT TO KEEP

They sent him back to her. The letter came
Saying . . . And she could have him. And before
She could be sure there was no hidden ill
Under the formal writing, he was there,
Living. They gave him back to her alive—
How else? They are not known to send the dead—
And not disfigured visibly. His face?
His hands? She had to look, to look and ask,
"What is it, dear?" And she had given all
And still she had all—*they* had—they the lucky!
Wasn't she glad now? Everything seemed won,
And all the rest for them permissible ease.
She had to ask, "What was it, dear?"

                                  "Enough,
Yet not enough. A bullet through and through,
High in the breast. Nothing but what good care
And medicine and rest, and you a week,
Can cure me of to go again." The same
Grim giving to do over for them both.
She dared no more than ask him with her eyes
How was it with him for a second trial.
And with his eyes he asked her not to ask.
They had given him back to her, but not to keep.

                                          1923

A HILLSIDE THAW

To think to know the country and not know
The hillside on the day the sun lets go
Ten million silver lizards out of snow!
As often as I've seen it done before
I can't pretend to tell the way it's done.
It looks as if some magic of the sun
Lifted the rug that bred them on the floor
And the light breaking on them made them run.
But if I thought to stop the wet stampede,
And caught one silver lizard by the tail,
And put my foot on one without avail,
And threw myself wet-elbowed and wet-kneed
In front of twenty others' wriggling speed,—
In the confusion of them all aglitter,
And birds that joined in the excited fun
By doubling and redoubling song and twitter,
I have no doubt I'd end by holding none.

It takes the moon for this. The sun's a wizard
By all I tell; but so's the moon a witch.
From the high west she makes a gentle cast
And suddenly, without a jerk or twitch,
She has her spell on every single lizard.
I fancied when I looked at six o'clock
The swarm still ran and scuttled just as fast.
The moon was waiting for her chill effect.
I looked at nine: the swarm was turned to rock
In every lifelike posture of the swarm,
Transfixed on mountain slopes almost erect.
Across each other and side by side they lay.
The spell that so could hold them as they were
Was wrought through trees without a breath of storm
To make a leaf, if there had been one, stir.
It was the moon's: she held them until day,
One lizard at the end of every ray.
The thought of my attempting such a stay!   1923

ACCEPTANCE

When the spent sun throws up its rays on cloud
And goes down burning into the gulf below,

No voice in nature is heard to cry aloud
At what has happened. Birds, at least, must know
It is the change to darkness in the sky.
Murmuring something quiet in its breast,
One bird begins to close a faded eye;
Or overtaken too far from its nest,
Hurrying low above the grove, some waif
Swoops just in time to his remembered tree.
At most he thinks or twitters softly, "Safe!
Now let the night be dark for all of me.
Let the night be too dark for me to see
Into the future. Let what will be, be."   *1928*

A MINOR BIRD

I have wished a bird would fly away,
And not sing by my house all day;

Have clapped my hands at him from the door
When it seemed as if I could bear no more.

The fault must partly have been in me.
The bird was not to blame for his key.

And of course there must be something wrong
In wanting to silence any song.   *1928*

ONCE BY THE PACIFIC

The shattered water made a misty din.
Great waves looked over others coming in,
And thought of doing something to the shore
That water never did to land before.
The clouds were low and hairy in the skies,
Like locks blown forward in the gleam of eyes.
You could not tell, and yet it looked as if
The shore was lucky in being backed by cliff,
The cliff in being backed by continent;
It looked as if a night of dark intent
Was coming, and not only a night, an age.
Someone had better be prepared for rage.
There would be more than ocean-water broken
Before God's last *Put out the Light* was spoken.

1928

ACQUAINTED WITH THE NIGHT

I have been one acquainted with the night.
I have walked out in rain—and back in rain.
I have outwalked the furthest city light.

I have looked down the saddest city lane.
I have passed by the watchman on his beat
And dropped my eyes, unwilling to explain.

I have stood still and stopped the sound of feet
When far away an interrupted cry
Came over houses from another street,

But not to call me back or say good-by;
And further still at an unearthly height,
One luminary clock against the sky

Proclaimed the time was neither wrong nor right.
I have been one acquainted with the night.   *1928*

THE INVESTMENT

Over back where they speak of life as staying
("You couldn't call it living, for it ain't"),
There was an old, old house renewed with paint,
And in it a piano loudly playing.

Out in the ploughed ground in the cold a digger,
Among unearthed potatoes standing still,
Was counting winter dinners, one a hill,
With half an ear to the piano's vigor.

All that piano and new paint back there,
Was it some money suddenly come into?
Or some extravagance young love had been to?
Or old love on an impulse not to care—

Not to sink under being man and wife,
But get some color and music out of life?   *1928*

THE ARMFUL

For every parcel I stoop down to seize,
I lose some other off my arms and knees,
And the whole pile is slipping, bottles, buns,
Extremes too hard to comprehend at once,
Yet nothing I should care to leave behind.
With all I have to hold with, hand and mind
And heart, if need be, I will do my best
To keep their building balanced at my breast.
I crouch down to prevent them as they fall;
Then sit down in the middle of them all.
I had to drop the armful in the road
And try to stack them in a better load.   *1928*

ON LOOKING UP BY CHANCE
AT THE CONSTELLATIONS

You'll wait a long, long time for anything much
To happen in heaven beyond the floats of cloud
And the Northern Lights that run like tingling nerves.
The sun and moon get crossed, but they never touch,
Nor strike out fire from each other, nor crash out loud.
The planets seem to interfere in their curves,
But nothing ever happens, no harm is done.
We may as well go patiently on with our life,
And look elsewhere than to stars and moon and sun
For the shocks and changes we need to keep us sane.
It is true the longest drouth will end in rain,
The longest peace in China will end in strife.
Still it wouldn't reward the watcher to stay awake
In hopes of seeing the calm of heaven break
On his particular time and personal sight.
That calm seems certainly safe to last tonight.   *1928*

TWO TRAMPS IN MUD TIME

Out of the mud two strangers came
And caught me splitting wood in the yard.
And one of them put me off my aim
By hailing cheerily "Hit them hard!"
I knew pretty well why he dropped behind

And let the other go on a way.
I knew pretty well what he had in mind:
He wanted to take my job for pay.

Good blocks of beech it was I split,
As large around as the chopping block;
And every piece I squarely hit
Fell splinterless as a cloven rock.
The blows that a life of self-control
Spares to strike for the common good
That day, giving a loose to my soul,
I spent on the unimportant wood.

The sun was warm but the wind was chill.
You know how it is with an April day
When the sun is out and the wind is still,
You're one month on in the middle of May.
But if you so much as dare to speak,
A cloud comes over the sunlit arch,
A wind comes off a frozen peak,
And you're two months back in the middle of March.

A bluebird comes tenderly up to alight
And fronts the wind to unruffle a plume,
His song so pitched as not to excite
A single flower as yet to bloom.
It is snowing a flake: and he half knew
Winter was only playing possum.
Except in color he isn't blue,
But he wouldn't advise a thing to blossom.

The water for which we may have to look
In summertime with a witching-wand,
In every wheelrut's now a brook,
In every print of a hoof a pond.
Be glad of water, but don't forget
The lurking frost in the earth beneath
That will steal forth after the sun is set
And show on the water its crystal teeth.

The time when most I loved my task
These two must make me love it more
By coming with what they came to ask.

You'd think I never had felt before
The weight of an ax-head poised aloft,
The grip on earth of outspread feet,
The life of muscles rocking soft
And smooth and moist in vernal heat.

Out of the woods two hulking tramps
(From sleeping God knows where last night,
But not long since in the lumber camps).
They thought all chopping was theirs of right.
Men of the woods and lumberjacks,
They judged me by their appropriate tool.
Except as a fellow handled an ax,
They had no way of knowing a fool.

Nothing on either side was said.
They knew they had but to stay their stay
And all their logic would fill my head:
As that I had no right to play
With what was another man's work for gain.
My right might be love but theirs was need.
And where the two exist in twain
Theirs was the better right—agreed.

But yield who will to their separation,
My object in living is to unite
My avocation and my vocation
As my two eyes make one in sight.
Only where love and need are one,
And the work is play for mortal stakes,
Is the deed ever really done
For Heaven and the future's sakes.   *1936*

ON THE HEART'S BEGINNING TO CLOUD THE MIND

Something I saw or thought I saw
In the desert at midnight in Utah,
Looking out of my lower berth
At moonlit sky and moonlit earth.
The sky had here and there a star;
The earth had a single light afar,
A flickering, human pathetic light,
That was maintained against the night,

It seemed to me, by the people there,
With a God-forsaken brute despair.
It would flutter and fall in half an hour
Like the last petal off a flower.
But my heart was beginning to cloud my mind.
I knew a tale of a better kind.
That far light flickers because of trees.
The people can burn it as long as they please:
And when their interests in it end,
They can leave it to someone else to tend.
Come back that way a summer hence,
I should find it no more no less intense.
I pass, but scarcely pass no doubt,
When one will say, "Let us put it out."
The other without demur agrees.
They can keep it burning as long as they please;
They can put it out whenever they please.
One looks out last from the darkened room
At the shiny desert with spots of gloom
That might be people and are but cedar,
Have no purpose, have no leader,
Have never made the first move to assemble,
And so are nothing to make her tremble.
She can think of places that are not thus
Without indulging a "Not for us!"
Life is not so sinister-grave.
Matter of fact has made them brave.
He is husband, she is wife.
She fears not him, they fear not life.
They know where another light has been
And more than one to theirs akin,
But earlier out for bed tonight,
So lost on me in my surface flight.

This I saw when waking late,
Going by at a railroad rate,
Looking through wreaths of engine smoke
Far into the lives of other folk.   *1936*

DESERT PLACES

Snow falling and night falling fast, oh, fast
In a field I looked into going past,

And the ground almost covered smooth in snow,
But a few weeds and stubble showing last.

The woods around it have it—it is theirs.
All animals are smothered in their lairs.
I am too absent-spirited to count;
The loneliness includes me unawares.

And lonely as it is that loneliness
Will be more lonely ere it will be less—
A blanker whiteness of benighted snow
With no expression, nothing to express.

They cannot scare me with their empty spaces
Between stars—on stars where no human race is.
I have it in me so much nearer home
To scare myself with my own desert places.

1936

THE STRONG ARE SAYING NOTHING

The soil now gets a rumpling soft and damp,
And small regard to the future of any weed.
The final flat of the hoe's approval stamp
Is reserved for the bed of a few selected seed.

There is seldom more than a man to a harrowed piece.
Men work alone, their lots plowed far apart,
One stringing a chain of seed in an open crease,
And another stumbling after a halting cart.

To the fresh and black of the squares of early mould
The leafless bloom of a plum is fresh and white;
Though there's more than a doubt if the weather is not too cold
For the bees to come and serve its beauty aright.

Wind goes from farm to farm in wave on wave,
But carries no cry of what is hoped to be.
There may be little or much beyond the grave,
But the strong are saying nothing until they see.   1936

DESIGN

I found a dimpled spider, fat and white,
On a white heal-all, holding up a moth

Like a white piece of rigid satin cloth—
Assorted characters of death and blight
Mixed ready to begin the morning right,
Like the ingredients of a witches' broth—
A snow-drop spider, a flower like froth,
And dead wings carried like a paper kite.

What had that flower to do with being white,
The wayside blue and innocent heal-all?
What brought the kindred spider to that height,
Then steered the white moth thither in the night?
What but design of darkness to appall?—
If design govern in a thing so small.   *1936*

THERE ARE ROUGHLY ZONES

We sit indoors and talk of the cold outside.
And every gust that gathers strength and heaves
Is a threat to the house. But the house has long been tried.
We think of the tree. If it never again has leaves,
We'll know, we say, that this was the night it died.
It is very far north, we admit, to have brought the peach.
What comes over a man, is it soul or mind—
That to no limits and bounds he can stay confined?
You would say his ambition was to extend the reach
Clear to the Arctic of every living kind.
Why is his nature forever so hard to teach
That though there is no fixed line between wrong and right,
There are roughly zones whose laws must be obeyed.
There is nothing much we can do for the tree tonight,
But we can't help feeling more than a little betrayed
That the northwest wind should rise to such a height
Just when the cold went down so many below.
The tree has no leaves and may never have them again.
We must wait till some months hence in the spring to know.
But if it is destined never again to grow,
It can blame this limitless trait in the hearts of men.   *1936*

PROVIDE, PROVIDE

The witch that came (the withered hag)
To wash the steps with pail and rag,
Was once the beauty Abishag,

The picture pride of Hollywood.
Too many fall from great and good
For you to doubt the likelihood.

Die early and avoid the fate.
Or if predestined to die late,
Make up your mind to die in state.

Make the whole stock exchange your own!
If need be occupy a throne,
Where nobody can call *you* crone.

Some have relied on what they knew;
Others on simply being true.
What worked for them might work for you.

No memory of having starred
Atones for later disregard,
Or keeps the end from being hard.

Better to go down dignified
With boughten friendship at your side
Than none at all. Provide, provide!   *1936*

THE GIFT OUTRIGHT

The land was ours before we were the land's.
She was our land more than a hundred years
Before we were her people. She was ours
In Massachusetts, in Virginia;
But we were England's, still colonials,
Possessing what we still were unpossessed by,
Possessed by what we now no more possessed.
Something we were withholding made us weak
Until we found out that it was ourselves
We were withholding from our land of living,
And forthwith found salvation in surrender.
Such as we were we gave ourselves outright
(The deed of gift was many deeds of war)
To the land vaguely realizing westward,
But still unstoried, artless, unenhanced,
Such as she was, such as she would become.

1942

THE SUBVERTED FLOWER

She drew back; he was calm:
"It is this that had the power."
And he lashed his open palm
With the tender-headed flower.
He smiled for her to smile,
But she was either blind
Or willfully unkind.
He eyed her for a while
For a woman and a puzzle.
He flicked and flung the flower,
And another sort of smile
Caught up like finger tips
The corners of his lips
And cracked his ragged muzzle.
She was standing to the waist
In goldenrod and brake,
Her shining hair displaced.
He stretched her either arm
As if she made it ache
To clasp her—not to harm;
As if he could not spare
To touch her neck and hair.
"If this has come to us
And not to me alone—"
So she thought she heard him say;
Though with every word he spoke
His lips were sucked and blown
And the effort made him choke
Like a tiger at a bone.
She had to lean away.
She dared not stir a foot,
Lest movement should provoke
The demon of pursuit
That slumbers in a brute.
It was then her mother's call
From inside the garden wall
Made her steal a look of fear
To see if he could hear
And would pounce to end it all
Before her mother came.

She looked and saw the shame:
A hand hung like a paw,
An arm worked like a saw
As if to be persuasive,
An ingratiating laugh
That cut the snout in half,
An eye become evasive.
A girl could only see
That a flower had marred a man,
But what she could not see
Was that the flower might be
Other than base and fetid:
That the flower had done but part,
And what the flower began
Her own too meager heart
Had terribly completed.
She looked and saw the worst.
And the dog or what it was,
Obeying bestial laws,
A coward save at night,
Turned from the place and ran.
She heard him stumble first
And use his hands in flight.
She heard him bark outright.
And oh, for one so young
The bitter words she spit
Like some tenacious bit
That will not leave the tongue.
She plucked her lips for it,
And still the horror clung.
Her mother wiped the foam
From her chin, picked up her comb
And drew her backward home.

1942

DIRECTIVE

Back out of all this now too much for us,
Back in a time made simple by the loss
Of detail, burned, dissolved, and broken off
Like graveyard marble sculpture in the weather,
There is a house that is no more a house
Upon a farm that is no more a farm

And in a town that is no more a town.
The road there, if you'll let a guide direct you
Who only has at heart your getting lost,
May seem as if it should have been a quarry—
Great monolithic knees the former town
Long since gave up pretence of keeping covered.
And there's a story in a book about it:
Besides the wear of iron wagon wheels
The ledges show lines ruled southeast northwest,
The chisel work of an enormous Glacier
That braced his feet against the Arctic Pole.
You must not mind a certain coolness from him
Still said to haunt this side of Panther Mountain.
Nor need you mind the serial ordeal
Of being watched from forty cellar holes
As if by eye pairs out of forty firkins.
As for the woods' excitement over you
That sends light rustle rushes to their leaves,
Charge that to upstart inexperience.
Where were they all not twenty years ago?
They think too much of having shaded out
A few old pecker-fretted apple trees.
Make yourself up a cheering song of how
Someone's road home from work this once was,
Who may be just ahead of you on foot
Or creaking with a buggy load of grain.
The height of the adventure is the height
Of country where two village cultures faded
Into each other. Both of them are lost.
And if you're lost enough to find yourself
By now, pull in your ladder road behind you
And put a sign up CLOSED to all but me.
Then make yourself at home. The only field
Now left's no bigger than a harness gall.
First there's the children's house of make believe,
Some shattered dishes underneath a pine,
The playthings in the playhouse of the children.
Weep for what little things could make them glad.
Then for the house that is no more a house,
But only a belilaced cellar hole,
Now slowly closing like a dent in dough.
This was no playhouse but a house in earnest.
Your destination and your destiny's

A brook that was the water of the house,
Cold as a spring as yet so near its source,
Too lofty and original to rage.
(We know the valley streams that when aroused
Will leave their tatters hung on barb and thorn.)
I have kept hidden in the instep arch
Of an old cedar at the waterside
A broken drinking goblet like the Grail
Under a spell so the wrong ones can't find it,
So can't get saved, as Saint Mark says they mustn't.
(I stole the goblet from the children's playhouse.)
Here are your waters and your watering place.
Drink and be whole again beyond confusion.

                                                    1947

Carl Sandburg

CHICAGO

Hog Butcher for the World,
Tool Maker, Stacker of Wheat,
Player with Railroads and the Nation's Freight Handler;
Stormy, husky, brawling,
City of the Big Shoulders:

They tell me you are wicked and I believe them, for I have seen your
    painted women under the gas lamps luring the farm boys.
And they tell me you are crooked and I answer: Yes, it is true I have
    seen the gunman kill and go free to kill again.
And they tell me you are brutal and my reply is: On the faces of
    women and children I have seen the marks of wanton hunger.
And having answered so I turn once more to those who sneer at this
    my city, and I give them back the sneer and say to them:
Come and show me another city with lifted head singing so proud to
    be alive and coarse and strong and cunning.
Flinging magnetic curses amid the toil of piling job on job, here is a
    tall bold slugger set vivid against the little soft cities;
Fierce as a dog with tongue lapping for action, cunning as a savage
    pitted against the wilderness,
        Bareheaded,
        Shoveling,
        Wrecking,
        Planning,
        Building, breaking, rebuilding,
Under the smoke, dust all over his mouth, laughing with white teeth,
Under the terrible burden of destiny laughing as a young man laughs,
Laughing even as an ignorant fighter laughs who has never lost a battle,
Bragging and laughing that under his wrist is the pulse, and under his
    ribs the heart of the people,
        Laughing!
Laughing the stormy, husky, brawling laughter of Youth, half-naked,

sweating, proud to be Hog Butcher, Tool Maker, Stacker of
Wheat, Player with Railroads and Freight Handler to the Nation.

1916

LOST

Desolate and lone
All night long on the lake
Where fog trails and mist creeps,
The whistle of a boat
Calls and cries unendingly,
Like some lost child
In tears and trouble
Hunting the harbor's breast
And the harbor's eyes.   *1916*

CABOOSE THOUGHTS

It's going to come out all right—do you know?
The sun, the birds, the grass—they know.
They get along—and we'll get along.

Some days will be rainy and you will sit waiting
And the letter you wait for won't come,
And I will sit watching the sky tear off gray and gray
And the letter I wait for won't come.

There will be ac-ci-dents.
I know ac-ci-dents are coming.
Smash-ups, signals wrong, washouts, trestles rotten,
Red and yellow ac-ci-dents.
But somehow and somewhere the end of the run
The train gets put together again
And the caboose and the green tail lights
Fade down the right of way like a new white hope.

I never heard a mockingbird in Kentucky
Spilling its heart in the morning.

I never saw the snow on Chimborazo.
It's a high white Mexican hat, I hear.

I never had supper with Abe Lincoln,
Nor a dish of soup with Jim Hill.

But I've been around.
I know some of the boys here who can go a little.
I know girls good for a burst of speed any time.

I heard Williams and Walker
Before Walker died in the bughouse.

I knew a mandolin player
Working in a barber shop in an Indiana town,
And he thought he had a million dollars.

I knew a hotel girl in Des Moines.
She had eyes; I saw her and said to myself
The sun rises and the sun sets in her eyes.
I was her steady and her heart went pit-a-pat.
We took away the money for a prize waltz at a Brotherhood dance.
She had eyes; she was safe as the bridge over the Mississippi at Burling-
    ton; I married her.

Last summer we took the cushions going west.
Pike's Peak is a big old stone, believe me.
It's fastened down; something you can count on.

It's going to come out all right—do you know?
The sun, the birds, the grass—they know.
They get along—and we'll get along.

LOAM

In the loam we sleep,
In the cool moist loam,
To the lull of years that pass
And the break of stars,

From the loam, then,
The soft warm loam,
    We rise:
To shape of rose leaf,
Of face and shoulder.

    We stand, then,
    To a whiff of life,
Lifted to the silver of the sun
Over and out of the loam
    A day.   *1918*

PRAYERS OF STEEL

Lay me on an anvil, O God.
Beat me and hammer me into a crowbar.
Let me pry loose old walls.
Let me lift and loosen old foundations.

Lay me on an anvil, O God.
Beat me and hammer me into a steel spike.
Drive me into the girders that hold a skyscraper together.
Take red-hot rivets and fasten me into the central girders.
Let me be the great nail holding a skyscraper through blue nights into
    white stars.   *1918*

COOL TOMBS

When Abraham Lincoln was shoveled into the tombs, he forgot the
    copperheads and the assassin . . . in the dust, in the cool tombs.
And Ulysses Grant lost all thought of con men and Wall Street, cash
    and collateral turned ashes . . . in the dust, in the cool tombs.
Pocahontas' body, lovely as a poplar, sweet as a red haw in November
    or a pawpaw in May, did she wonder? does she remember? . . .
    in the dust, in the cool tombs?
Take any streetful of people buying clothes and groceries, cheering a
    hero or throwing confetti and blowing tin horns . . . tell me if
    the lovers are losers . . . tell me if any get more than the lovers
    . . . in the dust . . . in the cool tombs.   *1918*

HOUSE

Two Swede families live downstairs and an Irish policeman upstairs,
    and an old soldier, Uncle Joe.
Two Swede boys go upstairs and see Joe. His wife is dead, his only son
    is dead, and his two daughters in Missouri and Texas don't want
    him around.
The boys and Uncle Joe crack walnuts with a hammer on the bottom
    of a flatiron while the January wind howls and the zero air weaves
    laces on the window glass.
Joe tells the Swede boys all about Chickamauga and Chattanooga, how
    the Union soldiers crept in rain somewhere a dark night and ran
    forward and killed many Rebels, took flags, held a hill, and won a
    victory told about in the histories in school.

Joe takes a piece of carpenter's chalk, draws lines on the floor and piles
    stove wood to show where six regiments were slaughtered climbing
    a slope.
"Here they went" and "Here they went," says Joe, and the January
    wind howls and the zero air weaves laces on the window glass.
The two Swede boys go downstairs with a big blur of guns, men, and
    hills in their heads. They eat herring and potatoes and tell the
    family war is a wonder and soldiers are a wonder.
One breaks out with a cry at supper: I wish we had a war now and I
    could be a soldier.

1918

RED-HEADED RESTAURANT CASHIER

Shake back your hair, O red-headed girl.
Let go your laughter and keep your two proud freckles on your chin.
Somewhere is a man looking for a red-headed girl and some day maybe
    he will look into your eyes for a restaurant cashier and find a
    lover, maybe.
Around and around go ten thousand men hunting a red-headed girl
    with two freckles on her chin.
I have seen them hunting, hunting.
        Shake back your hair; let go your laughter.

1920

THE HANGMAN AT HOME

    What does the hangman think about
    When he goes home at night from work?
    When he sits down with his wife and
    Children for a cup of coffee and a
    Plate of ham and eggs, do they ask
    Him if it was a good day's work
    And everything went well, or do they
    Stay off some topics and talk about
    The weather, baseball, politics
    And the comic strips in the papers
    And the movies? Do they look at his
    Hands when he reaches for the coffee
    Or the ham and eggs? If the little
    Ones say, Daddy, play horse, here's
    A rope—does he answer like a joke:
    I seen enough rope for today?
    Or does his face light up like a

Bonfire of joy and does he say:
It's a good and dandy world we live
In. And if a white face moon looks
In through a window where a baby girl
Sleeps and the moon-gleams mix with
Baby ears and baby hair—the hangman—
How does he act then? It must be easy
For him. Anything is easy for a hangman,
I guess.

                                        1920

DEATH SNIPS PROUD MEN

Death is stronger than all the governments because the governments
are men and men die and then death laughs: Now you see 'em,
now you don't.

Death is stronger than all proud men and so death snips proud men on
the nose, throws a pair of dice and says: Read 'em and weep.

Death sends a radiogram every day: When I want you I'll drop in—
and then one day he comes with a master-key and lets himself in
and says: We'll go now.

Death is a nurse mother with big arms: 'Twon't hurt you at all; it's
your time now; you just need a long sleep, child; what have you
had anyhow better than sleep?

                                        1920

LOSERS

If I should pass the tomb of Jonah
I would stop there and sit for awhile;
Because I was swallowed one time deep in the dark
And came out alive after all.

If I pass the burial spot of Nero
I shall say to the wind, "Well, well!"—
I who have fiddled in a world on fire,
I who have done so many stunts not worth doing.

I am looking for the grave of Sinbad too.
I want to shake his ghost-hand and say,
"Neither of us died very early, did we?"

And the last sleeping-place of Nebuchadnezzar—
When I arrive there I shall tell the wind:
"You ate grass; I have eaten crow—
Who is better off now or next year?"

Jack Cade, John Brown, Jesse James,
There too I could sit down and stop for awhile.
I think I could tell their headstones:
"God, let me remember all good losers."

I could ask people to throw ashes on their heads
In the name of that sergeant at Belleau Woods,
Walking into the drumfires, calling his men,
    "Come on, you . . . Do you want to live forever?"

                                        1920

SANDHILL PEOPLE

I took away three pictures.
One was a white gull forming a half-mile arch from the pines toward
    Waukegan.
One was a whistle in the little sandhills, a bird crying either to the
    sunset gone or the dusk come.
One was three spotted waterbirds, zigzagging, cutting scrolls and jags,
    writing a bird Sanscrit of wing points, half over the sand, half over
    the water, a half-love for the sea, a half-love for the land.

I took away three thoughts.
One was a thing my people call "love," a shut-in river hunting the sea,
    breaking white falls between tall clefts of hill country.
One was a thing my people call "silence," the wind running over the
    butter faced sand-flowers, running over the sea, and never heard
    of again.
One was a thing my people call "death," neither a whistle in the little
    sandhills, nor a bird Sanscrit of wing points, yet a coat all the stars
    and seas have worn, yet a face the beach wears between sunset
    and dusk.

                                        1920

MIST FORMS

The sheets of night mist travel a long valley.
I know why you came at sundown in a scarf mist.

What was it we touched asking nothing and asking all?
How many times can death come and pay back what we saw?

In the oath of the sod, the lips that swore,
In the oath of night mist, nothing and all,
A riddle is here no man tells, no woman.   *1920*

FOUR PRELUDES ON PLAYTHINGS OF THE WIND

"The Past Is a Bucket of Ashes."

1

The woman named Tomorrow
sits with a hairpin in her teeth
and takes her time
and does her hair the way she wants it
and fastens at last the last braid and coil
and puts the hairpin where it belongs
and turns and drawls: Well, what of it?
My grandmother, Yesterday, is gone.
What of it? Let the dead be dead.

2

The doors were cedar
and the panel strips of gold
and the girls were golden girls
and the panels read and the girls chanted:
    We are the greatest city,
    the greatest nation:
    nothing like us ever was.
The doors are twisted on broken hinges.
Sheets of rain swish through on the wind
    where the golden girls ran and the panels read:
    We are the greatest city,
    the greatest nation,
    nothing like us ever was.

3

It has happened before.
Strong men put up a city and got
    a nation together,

And paid singers to sing and women
    to warble: We are the greatest city,
        the greatest nation,
        nothing like us ever was.

And while the singers sang
and the strong men listened
and paid the singers well
and felt good about it all,
    there were rats and lizards who listened
    . . . and the only listeners left now
    . . . are . . . the rats . . . and the lizards.

And there are black crows
crying, "Caw, caw,"
bringing mud and sticks
building a nest
over the words carved
on the doors where the panels were cedar
and the strips on the panels were gold
and the golden girls came singing:
    We are the greatest city,
    the greatest nation:
    nothing like us ever was.

The only singers now are crows crying, "Caw, caw,"
And the sheets of rain whine in the wind and doorways.
And the only listeners now are . . . the rats . . . and the lizards.

4

The feet of the rats
scribble on the doorsills;
the hieroglyphs of the rat footprints
chatter the pedigrees of the rats
and babble of the blood
and gabble of the breed
of the grandfathers and the great-grandfathers
of the rats.

And the wind shifts
and the dust on a doorsill shifts
and even the writing of the rat footprints
tells us nothing, nothing at all

about the greatest city, the greatest nation
where the strong men listened
and the women warbled: Nothing like us ever was.

1920

THE LAWYERS KNOW TOO MUCH

The lawyers, Bob, know too much.
They are chums of the books of old John Marshall.
They know it all, what a dead hand wrote,
A stiff dead hand and its knuckles crumbling,
The bones of the fingers a thin white ash.
    The lawyers know
    a dead man's thoughts too well.

In the heels of the higgling lawyers, Bob,
Too many slippery ifs and buts and howevers,
Too much hereinbefore provided whereas,
Too many doors to go in and out of.

    When the lawyers are through
    What is there left, Bob?
    Can a mouse nibble at it
    And find enough to fasten a tooth in?

    Why is there always a secret singing
    When a lawyer cashes in?
    Why does a hearse horse snicker
    Hauling a lawyer away?

The work of a bricklayer goes to the blue.
The knack of a mason outlasts a moon.
The hands of a plasterer hold a room together.
The land of a farmer wishes him back again.
    Singers of songs and dreamers of plays
    Build a house no wind blows over.
The lawyers—tell me why a hearse horse snickers
    hauling a lawyer's bones.   1920

OSSAWATOMIE

I don't know how he came,
shambling, dark, and strong.

He stood in the city and told men:
My people are fools, my people are young and strong, my people must
    learn, my people are terrible workers and fighters.
Always he kept on asking: Where did that blood come from?

They said: You for the fool killer,
          you for the booby hatch
          and a necktie party.

    They hauled him into jail.
    They sneered at him and spit on him,
    And he wrecked their jails,
    Singing, "God damn your jails,"
    And when he was most in jail
    Crummy among the crazy in the dark
    Then he was most of all out of jail
    Shambling, dark, and strong,
Always asking: Where did that blood come from?

    They laid hands on him
    And the fool killers had a laugh
    And the necktie party was a go, by God.
They laid hands on him and he was a goner.
    They hammered him to pieces and he stood up.
They buried him and he walked out of the grave, by God,
    Asking again: Where did that blood come from?   *1920*

THREES

    I was a boy when I heard three red words
    a thousand Frenchmen died in the streets
    for: Liberty, Equality, Fraternity—I asked
    why men die for words.

    I was older; men with mustaches, sideburns,
    lilacs, told me the high golden words are:
    Mother, Home, and Heaven—other older men with
    face decorations said: God, Duty, Immortality
    —they sang these threes slow from deep lungs.

    Years ticked off their say-so on the great clocks
    of doom and damnation, soup and nuts: meteors flashed

their say-so: and out of great Russia came three
dusky syllables workmen took guns and went out to die
for: Bread, Peace, Land.

And I met a marine of the U.S.A., a leatherneck with
a girl on his knee for a memory in ports circling the
earth and he said: Tell me how to say three things
and I always get by—gimme a plate of ham and eggs—
how much?—and, do you love me, kid?   1920

A. E. F.

There will be a rusty gun on the wall, sweetheart,
The rifle grooves curling with flakes of rust.
A spider will make a silver string nest in the darkest, warmest corner
     of it.
The trigger and the range-finder, they too will be rusty.
And no hands will polish the gun, and it will hang on the wall.
Forefingers and thumbs will point absently and casually toward it.
It will be spoken among half-forgotten, wished-to-be-forgotten things.
They will tell the spider: Go on, you're doing good work.   1920

BALLOON FACES

The balloons hang on wires in the Marigold Gardens.
They spot their yellow and gold, they juggle their blue and red, they
     float their faces on the face of the sky.
Balloon face eaters sit by hundreds reading the eat cards, asking, "What
     shall we eat?"—and the waiters, "Have you ordered?" they are sixty
     balloon faces sifting white over the tuxedos.
Poets, lawyers, ad men, mason contractors, smart-alecks discussing
     "educated jackasses," here they put crabs into their balloon faces.
Here sit the heavy balloon face women lifting crimson lobsters into
     their crimson faces, lobsters out of Sargossa sea bottoms.
Here sits a man cross-examining a woman, "Where were you last night?
     What do you do with all your money? Who's buying your shoes
     now, anyhow?"
So they sit eating whitefish, two balloon faces swept on God's night
     wind.
And all the time the balloon spots on the wires, a little mile of festoons,
     they play their own silence play of film yellow and film gold,
     bubble blue and bubble red.

The wind crosses the town, the wind from the west side comes to the
    banks of marigolds boxed in the Marigold Gardens.
Night moths fly and fix their feet in the leaves and eat and are seen
    by the eaters.
The jazz outfit sweats and the drums and the saxophones reach for the
    ears of the eaters.
The chorus brought from Broadway works at the fun and the slouch
    of their shoulders, the kick of their ankles, reach for the eyes of
    the eaters.
These girls from Kokomo and Peoria, these hungry girls, since they are
    paid-for, let us look on and listen, let us get their number.

Why do I go again to the balloons on the wires, something for nothing,
    kin women of the half-moon, dream women?
And the half-moon swinging on the wind crossing the town—these two,
    the half-moon and the wind—this will be about all, this will be
    about all.

Eaters, go to it: your mazuma pays for it all; it's a knockout, a classy
    knockout—and payday always comes.
The moths in the marigolds will do for me, the half-moon, the wishing
    wind and the little mile of balloon spots on wires—this will be
    about all, this will be about all.   *1920*

WASHINGTON MONUMENT BY NIGHT

I

The stone goes straight.
A lean swimmer dives into night sky,
Into half-moon mist.

II

Two trees are coal black.
This is a great white ghost between.
It is cool to look at.
Strong men, strong women, come here.

III

Eight years is a long time
To be fighting all the time.

IV

The republic is a dream.
Nothing happens unless first a dream.

V

The wind bit hard at Valley Forge one Christmas.
Soldiers tied rags on their feet.
Red footprints wrote on the snow . . .
. . . and stone shoots into stars here
. . . into half-moon mist tonight.

VI

Tongues wrangled dark at a man.
He buttoned his overcoat and stood alone.
In a snowstorm, red hollyberries, thoughts, he stood alone.

VII

Women said: He is lonely
. . . fighting . . . fighting . . . eight years . . .

VIII

The name of an iron man goes over the world.
It takes a long time to forget an iron man.

IX

. . . .
. . . .   1922

From THE PEOPLE, YES : I

From the four corners of the earth,
from corners lashed in wind
and bitten with rain and fire,
from places where the winds begin
and fogs are born with mist children,
tall men from tall rocky slopes came
and sleepy men from sleepy valleys,
their women tall, their women sleepy,
with bundles and belongings,
with little ones babbling, "Where to now?
what next?"

The people of the earth, the family of man,
wanted to put up something proud to look at,
a tower from the flat land of earth
on up through the ceiling into the top of the sky.

And the big job got going,
the caissons and pilings sunk,
floors, walls and winding staircases
aimed at the stars high over,
aimed to go beyond the ladders of the moon.

And God Almighty could have struck them dead
or smitten them deaf and dumb.

And God was a whimsical fixer.
God was an understanding Boss
with another plan in mind,
And suddenly shuffled all the languages,
        changed the tongues of men
        so they all talked different
And the masons couldn't get what the hodcarriers said,
The helpers handed the carpenters the wrong tools,
Five hundred ways to say, "W h o a r e y o u?"
Changed ways of asking, "Where do we go from here?"
Or of saying, "Being born is only the beginning,"
Or, "Would you just as soon sing as make that noise?"
Or, "What you don't know won't hurt you."
And the material-and-supply men started disputes
With the hauling gangs and the building trades
And the architects tore their hair over the blueprints
And the brickmakers and the mule skinners talked back
To the straw bosses who talked back to the superintendents
And the signals got mixed; the men who shovelled the bucket
Hooted the hoisting men—and the job was wrecked.

Some called it the Tower of Babel job
And the people gave it many other names.
The wreck of it stood as a skull and a ghost,
a memorandum hardly begun,
swaying and sagging in tall hostile winds,
held up by slow friendly winds.   *1936*

Vachel Lindsay

GENERAL WILLIAM BOOTH ENTERS INTO HEAVEN

(To be sung to the tune of "The Blood of the Lamb"
with indicated instrument.)

I

(*Bass drum beaten loudly.*)
Booth led boldly with his big bass drum—
(Are you washed in the blood of the Lamb?)
The Saints smiled gravely and they said: "He's come."
(Are you washed in the blood of the Lamb?)
Walking lepers followed, rank on rank,
Lurching bravos from the ditches dank,
Drabs from the alleyways and drug fiends pale—
Minds still passion-ridden, soul-powers frail:—
Vermin-eaten saints with moldy breath,
Unwashed legions with the ways of Death—
(Are you washed in the blood of the Lamb?)

(*Banjos.*)
Every slum had sent its half-a-score
The round world over. (Booth had groaned for more.)
Every banner that the wide world flies
Bloomed with glory and transcendent dyes.
Big-voiced lasses made their banjos bang;
Tranced, fanatical they shrieked and sang:—
"Are you washed in the blood of the Lamb?"
Hallelujah! It was queer to see
Bull-necked convicts with that land make free.
Loons with trumpets blowed a blare, blare, blare
On, on upward thro' the golden air!
(Are you washed in the blood of the Lamb?)

II

(Bass drum slower and softer.)
Booth died blind and still by faith he trod,
Eyes still dazzled by the ways of God.
Booth led boldly, and he looked the chief,
Eagle countenance in sharp relief,
Beard a-flying, air of high command
Unabated in that holy land.

(Sweet flute music.)
Jesus came from out the court-house door,
Stretched his hands above the passing poor.
Booth saw not, but led his queer ones there
Round and round the mighty court-house square.
Then, in an instant all that blear review
Marched on spotless, clad in raiment new.
The lame were straightened, withered limbs uncurled
And blind eyes opened on a new, sweet world.

(Bass drum louder.)
Drabs and vixens in a flash made whole!
Gone was the weasel-head, the snout, the jowl!
Sages and sibyls now, and athletes clean,
Rulers of empires, and of forests green!

(Grand chorus of all instruments. Tambourines to the foreground.)
The hosts were sandalled, and their wings were fire!
(Are you washed in the blood of the Lamb?)
But their noise played havoc with the angel-choir.
(Are you washed in the blood of the Lamb?)
Oh, shout Salvation! It was good to see
Kings and Princes by the Lamb set free.
The banjos rattled and the tambourines
Jing-jing-jingled in the hands of Queens.

(Reverently sung, no instruments.)
And when Booth halted by the curb for prayer
He saw his Master thro' the flag-filled air.
Christ came gently with a robe and crown
For Booth the soldier, while the throng knelt down.
He saw King Jesus. They were face to face,

And he knelt a-weeping in that holy place.
Are you washed in the blood of the Lamb? *1913*

THE EAGLE THAT IS FORGOTTEN

(JOHN P. ALTGELD. BORN DECEMBER 30, 1847; DIED MARCH 12, 1902)

Sleep softly . . . eagle forgotten . . . under the stone.
Time has its way with you there, and the clay has its own.

"We have buried him now," thought your foes, and in secret rejoiced.
They made a brave show of their mourning, their hatred unvoiced.
They had snarled at you, barked at you, foamed at you day after day.
Now you were ended. They praised you, . . . and laid you away.

The others that mourned you in silence and terror and truth,
The widow bereft of her crust, and the boy without youth,
The mocked and the scorned and the wounded, the lame and the poor
That should have remembered forever, . . . remember no more.

Where are those lovers of yours, on what name do they call,
The lost, that in armies wept over your funeral pall?
They call on the names of a hundred high-valiant ones;
A hundred white eagles have risen the sons of your sons;
The zeal in their wings is a zeal that your dreaming began,
The valor that wore out your soul in the service of man.

Sleep softly, . . . eagle forgotten, . . . under the stone,
Time has its way with you there, and the clay has its own.
Sleep on, O brave-hearted, O wise man, that kindled the flame—
To live in mankind is far more than to live in a name,
To live in mankind, far, far more . . . than to live in a name. *1913*

A NET TO SNARE THE MOONLIGHT

(WHAT THE MAN OF FAITH SAID)

The dew, the rain and moonlight
All prove our Father's mind.
The dew, the rain and moonlight
Descend to bless mankind.

Come, let us see that all men
Have land to catch the rain,

Have grass to snare the spheres of dew,
And fields spread for the grain.

Yea, we would give to each poor man
Ripe wheat and poppies red,—
A peaceful place at evening
With the stars just overhead:

A net to snare the moonlight,
A sod spread to the sun,
A place of toil by daytime,
Of dreams when toil is done.   *1913*

THE CONGO

A STUDY OF THE NEGRO RACE

I. THEIR BASIC SAVAGERY

Fat black bucks in a wine-barrel room,
Barrel-house kings, with feet unstable,
Sagged and reeled and pounded on the table,   *A deep roll-*
Pounded on the table,   *ing bass.*
Beat an empty barrel with the handle of a broom,
Hard as they were able,
Boom, boom, Boom,
With a silk umbrella and the handle of a broom,
Boomlay, boomlay, boomlay, Boom.
Then I had religion, Then I had a vision.
I could not turn from their revel in derision.
Then i saw the Congo, creeping through the black,   *More*
Cutting through the forest with a golden track.   *deliberate.*
Then along that riverbank   *Solemnly*
A thousand miles   *chanted.*
Tattooed cannibals danced in files;
Then I heard the boom of the blood-lust song
And a thigh-bone beating on a tin-pan gong.   *A rapidly*
And "Blood" screamed the whistles and the fifes of the   *piling cli-*
    warriors,   *max of*
"Blood" screamed the skull-faced, lean witch-doctors,   *speed and*
"Whirl ye the deadly voo-doo rattle,   *racket.*
Harry the uplands,
Steal all the cattle,
Rattle-rattle, rattle-rattle,
Bing.

Boomlay, boomlay, boomlay, BOOM,"
A roaring, epic, rag-time tune
From the mouth of the Congo
To the Mountains of the Moon.

With a
philosophic
pause.

Death is an Elephant,
Torch-eyed and horrible,
Foam-flanked and terrible.
BOOM, steal the pygmies,
BOOM, kill the Arabs,
BOOM, kill the white men,
Hoo, Hoo, Hoo.

Shrilly and
with a
heavily ac-
cented
metre.

Listen to the yell of Leopold's ghost
Burning in Hell for his hand-maimed host.
Hear how the demons chuckle and yell
Cutting his hands off, down in Hell.

Like the
wind in the
chimney.

Listen to the creepy proclamation,
Blown through the lairs of the forest-nation,
Blown past the white-ants' hill of clay,
Blown past the marsh where the butterflies play:
"Be careful what you do,
Or Mumbo-Jumbo, God of the Congo,
And all the other
Gods of the Congo,
Mumbo-Jumbo will hoo-doo you,
Mumbo-Jumbo will hoo-doo you,
Mumbo-Jumbo will hoo-doo you."

All the "o" sounds
very golden.
Heavy accents very
heavy. Light accents
very light. Last line
whispered.

II. THEIR IRREPRESSIBLE HIGH SPIRITS

Wild crap-shooters with a whoop and a call
Danced the juba in their gambling hall

Rather shrill
and high.

And laughed fit to kill, and shook the town,
And guyed the policemen and laughed them down
With a boomlay, boomlay, boomlay, BOOM.
THEN I SAW THE CONGO, CREEPING THROUGH THE BLACK,
CUTTING THROUGH THE FOREST WITH A GOLDEN TRACK.

Read ex-
actly as in
first section.

A negro fairyland swung into view,
A minstrel river
Where dreams come true.
The ebony palace soared on high
Through the blossoming trees to the evening sky.
The inlaid porches and casements shone
With gold and ivory and elephant-bone.

Lay em-
phasis on
the deli-
cate ideas.
Keep as
light-footed
as possible.

And the black crowd laughed till their sides were sore
At the baboon butler in the agate door,
And the well-known tunes of the parrot band
That trilled on the bushes of that magic land.

A troupe of skull-faced witch-men came   *With*
Through the agate doorway in suits of flame,   *pomposity.*
Yea, long-tailed coats with a gold-leaf crust
And hats that were covered with diamond-dust.
And the crowd in the court gave a whoop and a call
And danced the juba from wall to wall.
But the witch-men suddenly stilled the throng   *With a great delibera-*
With a stern cold glare, and a stern old song:—   *tion and ghostliness.*
"Mumbo-Jumbo will hoo-doo you." . . .
Just then from the doorway, as fat as shotes,   *With overwhelming assur-*
Came the cake-walk princes in their long   *ance, good cheer, and pomp.*
      red coats,
Canes with a brilliant lacquer shine,
And tall silk hats that were red as wine.
And they pranced with their butterfly partners there,   *With grow-*
Coal-black maidens with pearls in their hair,   *ing speed*
Knee-skirts trimmed with the jassamine sweet,   *and sharply*
And bells on their ankles and little black feet.   *marked*
And the couples railed at the chant and the frown   *dance-*
Of the witch-men lean, and laughed them down.   *rhythm.*
(Oh, rare was the revel, and well worth while
That made those glowering witch-men smile.)

The cake-walk royalty then began
To walk for a cake that was tall as a man
To the tune of "Boomlay, boomlay, BOOM,"
While the witch-men laughed, with a sinister air,.   *With a*
And sang with the scalawags prancing there:—   *touch of*
"Walk with care, walk with care,   *negro*
Or Mumbo-Jumbo, God of the Congo,   *dialect, and*
And all of the other Gods of the Congo,   *as rapidly*
Mumbo-Jumbo will hoo-doo you.   *as possible*
Beware, beware, walk with care,   *toward*
Boomlay, boomlay, boomlay, boom.   *the end.*
Boomlay, boomlay, boomlay, boom.
Boomlay, boomlay, boomlay, boom.
Boomlay, boomlay, boomlay,
BOOM."

(Oh, rare was the revel, and well worth while
That made those glowering witch-men smile.)

Slow philo-
sophic calm.

III. THE HOPE OF THEIR RELIGION

A good old negro in the slums of the town
Preached at a sister for her velvet gown.
Howled at a brother for his low-down ways,
His prowling, guzzling, sneak-thief days.
Beat on the Bible till he wore it out
Starting the jubilee revival shout.
And some had visions, as they stood on chairs,
And sang of Jacob, and the golden stairs,
And they all repented, a thousand strong,
From their stupor and savagery and sin and wrong,
And slammed with their hymn books till they shook
      the room
With "Glory, glory, glory,"
And "Boom, boom, BOOM."
THEN I SAW THE CONGO, CREEPING THROUGH THE BLACK,
CUTTING THROUGH THE JUNGLE WITH A GOLDEN TRACK.
And the gray sky opened like a new-rent veil
And showed the Apostles with their coats of mail.
In bright white steel they were seated round
And their fire-eyes watched where the Congo wound
And the twelve Apostles, from their thrones on high,
Thrilled all the forest with their heavenly cry:—
"Mumbo-Jumbo will die in the jungle;
Never again will he hoo-doo you,
Never again will he hoo-doo you."

Heavy bass.
With a
literal imi-
tation of
camp-meet-
ing racket,
and trance.

Exactly as
in the first
section.
Begin with
terror and
power, end
with joy.

Sung to the tune of
"Hark, ten thousand
harps and voices."

Then along that river, a thousand miles,
The vine-snared trees fell down in files.
Pioneer angels cleared the way
For a Congo paradise, for babes at play,
For sacred capitals, for temples clean.
Gone were the skull-faced witch-men lean.
There, where the wild ghost-gods had wailed
A million boats of the angels sailed
With oars of silver, and prows of blue
And silken pennants that the sun shone through.
'Twas a land transfigured, 'twas a new creation.
Oh, a singing wind swept the negro nation

With
growing de-
liberation
and joy.

In a rather
high key—
as delicately
as possible.

And on through the backwoods clearing flew:—
"Mumbo-Jumbo is dead in the jungle. *To the tune of*
Never again will he hoo-doo you. *"Hark, ten thousand*
Never again will he hoo-doo you." *harps and voices."*

Redeemed were the forests, the beasts and the men,
And only the vulture dared again
By the far, lone mountains of the moon
To cry, in the silence, the Congo tune:—
"Mumbo-Jumbo will hoo-doo you, *Dying down into a*
Mumbo-Jumbo will hoo-doo you, *penetrating, terrified*
Mumbo . . . Jumbo . . . will . . . hoo-doo *whisper.*
. . . you."

1914

THE LEADEN-EYED

Let not young souls be smothered out before
They do quaint deeds and fully flaunt their pride.
It is the world's one crime its babes grow dull,
Its poor are ox-like, limp and leaden-eyed.

Not that they starve, but starve so dreamlessly,
Not that they sow, but that they seldom reap,
Not that they serve, but have no gods to serve,
Not that they die, but that they die like sheep.

1914

ABRAHAM LINCOLN WALKS AT MIDNIGHT

(In Springfield, Illinois)

It is portentous, and a thing of state
That here at midnight, in our little town
A mourning figure walks, and will not rest,
Near the old court-house pacing up and down,

Or by his homestead, or in shadowed yards
He lingers where his children used to play,
Or through the market, on the well-worn stones
He stalks until the dawn-stars burn away.

A bronzed, lank man! His suit of ancient black,
A famous high top-hat and plain worn shawl

Make him the quaint great figure that men love,
The prairie-lawyer, master of us all.

He cannot sleep upon his hillside now.
He is among us:—as in times before!
And we who toss and lie awake for long
Breathe deep, and start, to see him pass the door.

His head is bowed. He thinks on men and kings.
Yea, when the sick world cries, how can he sleep?
Too many peasants fight, they know not why,
Too many homesteads in black terror weep.

The sins of all the war-lords burn his heart.
He sees the dreadnaughts scouring every main.
He carries on his shawl-wrapped shoulders now
The bitterness, the folly and the pain.

He cannot rest until a spirit-dawn
Shall come;—the shining hope of Europe free:
The league of sober folk, the Workers' Earth,
Bringing long peace to Cornland, Alp and Sea.

It breaks his heart that kings must murder still,
That all his hours of travail here for men
Seem yet in vain. And who will bring white peace
That he may sleep upon his hill again?   *1914*

THE UNPARDONABLE SIN

This is the sin against the Holy Ghost:—
To speak of bloody power as right divine,
And call on God to guard each vile chief's house,
And for such chiefs, turn men to wolves and swine:—

To go forth killing in White Mercy's name,
Making the trenches stink with spattered brains,
Tearing the nerves and arteries apart,
Sowing with flesh the unreaped golden plains.

In any Church's name, to sack fair towns,
And turn each home into a screaming sty,

To make the little children fugitive,
And have their mothers for a quick death cry,—

This is the sin against the Holy Ghost:
This is the sin no purging can atone:—
To send forth rapine in the name of Christ:—
To set the face, and make the heart a stone.   *1914*

BRYAN, BRYAN, BRYAN, BRYAN

THE CAMPAIGN OF EIGHTEEN NINETY-SIX, AS VIEWED AT THE TIME BY A SIXTEEN-YEAR-OLD, ETC.

I

In a nation of one hundred fine, mob-hearted, lynching, relenting,
    repenting millions,
There are plenty of sweeping, swinging, stinging, gorgeous things to
    shout about,
And knock your old blue devils out.

I brag and chant of Bryan, Bryan, Bryan,
Candidate for president who sketched a silver Zion,
The one American Poet who could sing outdoors,
He brought in tides of wonder, of unprecedented splendor,
Wild roses from the plains, that made hearts tender,
All the funny circus silks
Of politics unfurled,
Bartlett pears of romance that were honey at the cores,
And torchlights down the street, to the end of the world.

There were truths eternal in the gab and tittle-tattle.
There were real heads broken in the fustian and the rattle.
There were real lines drawn:
Not the silver and the gold,
But Nebraska's cry went eastward against the dour and old,
The mean and cold.

It was eighteen ninety-six, and I was just sixteen
And Altgeld ruled in Springfield, Illinois,
When there came from the sunset Nebraska's shout of joy:
In a coat like a deacon, in a black Stetson hat

He scourged the elephant plutocrats
With barbed wire from the Platte.
The scales dropped from their mighty eyes.
They saw that summer's noon
A tribe of wonders coming
To a marching tune.

Oh, the longhorns from Texas,
The jay hawks from Kansas,
The plop-eyed bungaroo and giant giassicus,
The varmint, chipmunk, bugaboo,
The horned-toad, prairie-dog and ballyhoo,
From all the newborn states arow,
Bidding the eagles of the west fly on,
Bidding the eagles of the west fly on.
The fawn, prodactyl and thing-a-ma-jig,
The rakaboor, the hellangone,
The whangdoodle, batfowl and pig,
The coyote, wild-cat and grizzly in a glow,
In a miracle of health and speed, the whole breed abreast,
They leaped the Mississippi, blue border of the West,
From the Gulf to Canada, two thousand miles long:—
Against the towns of Tubal Cain,
Ah,—sharp was their song.
Against the ways of Tubal Cain, too cunning for the young,
The longhorn calf, the buffalo and wampus gave tongue.

These creatures were defending things Mark Hanna never dreamed:
The moods of airy childhood that in desert dews gleamed,
The gossamers and whimsies,
The monkeyshines and didoes
Rank and strange
Of the canyons and the range,
The ultimate fantastics
Of the far western slope,
And of prairie schooner children
Born beneath the stars,
Beneath falling snows,
Of the babies born at midnight
In the sod huts of lost hope,
With no physician there,
Except a Kansas prayer,
With the Indian raid a howling through the air.

And all these in their helpless days
By the dour East oppressed,
Mean paternalism
Making their mistakes for them,
Crucifying half the West,
Till the whole Atlantic coast
Seemed a giant spiders' nest.

And these children and their sons
At last rode through the cactus,
A cliff of mighty cowboys
On the lope,
With gun and rope.
And all the way to frightened Maine the old East heard them call,
And saw our Bryan by a mile lead the wall
Of men and whirling flowers and beasts,
The bard and the prophet of them all.
Prairie avenger, mountain lion,
Bryan, Bryan, Bryan, Bryan,
Gigantic troubadour, speaking like a siege gun,
Smashing Plymouth Rock with his boulders from the West,
And just a hundred miles behind, tornadoes piled across the sky,
Blotting out sun and moon,
A sign on high.

Headlong, dazed and blinking in the weird green light,
The scalawags made moan,
Afraid to fight.

II

When Bryan came to Springfield, and Altgeld gave him greeting,
Rochester was deserted, Divernon was deserted,
Mechanicsburg, Riverton, Chickenbristle, Cotton Hill,
Empty: for all Sangamon drove to the meeting—
In silver-decked racing cart,
Buggy, buckboard, carryall,
Carriage, phaeton, whatever would haul,
And silver-decked farm-wagons gritted, banged and rolled,
With the new tale of Bryan by the iron tires told.

The State House loomed afar,
A speck, a hive, a football,

A captive balloon!
And the town was all one spreading wing of bunting, plumes, and
 sunshine,
Every rag and flag, and Bryan picture sold,
When the rigs in many a dusty line
Jammed our streets at noon,
And joined the wild parade against the power of gold.

We roamed, we boys from High School,
With mankind,
While Springfield gleamed,
Silk-lined.
Oh, Tom Dines, and Art Fitzgerald,
And the gangs that they could get!
I can hear them yelling yet.
Helping the incantation,
Defying aristocracy,
With every bridle gone,
Ridding the world of the low down mean,
Bidding the eagles of the West fly on,
Bidding the eagles of the West fly on,
We were bully, wild and woolly,
Never yet curried below the knees.
We saw flowers in the air,
Fair as the Pleiades, bright as Orion,
—Hopes of all mankind,
Made rare, resistless, thrice refined.
Oh, we bucks from every Springfield ward!
Colts of democracy—
Yet time-winds out of Chaos from the star-fields of the Lord.

The long parade rolled on. I stood by my best girl.
She was a cool young citizen, with wise and laughing eyes.
With my necktie by my ear, I was stepping on my dear,
But she kept like a pattern, without a shaken curl.

She wore in her hair a brave prairie rose.
Her gold chums cut her, for that was not the pose.
No Gibson Girl would wear it in that fresh way.
But we were fairy Democrats, and this was our day.

The earth rocked like the ocean, the sidewalk was a deck.
The houses for the moment were lost in the wide wreck.

And the bands played strange and stranger music as they trailed along.
Against the ways of Tubal Cain,
Ah, sharp was their song!
The demons in the bricks, the demons in the grass,
The demons in the bank-vaults peered out to see us pass,
And the angels in the trees, the angels in the grass,
The angels in the flags, peered out to see us pass.
And the sidewalk was our chariot, and the flowers bloomed higher,
And the street turned to silver and the grass turned to fire,
And then it was but grass, and the town was there again,
A place for women and men.

III

Then we stood where we could see
Every band,
And the speaker's stand.
And Bryan took the platform.
And he was introduced.
And he lifted his hand
And cast a new spell.
Progressive silence fell
In Springfield,
In Illinois,
Around the world.
Then we heard these glacial boulders across the prairie rolled:
"The people have a right to make their own mistakes. . . .
You shall not crucify mankind
Upon a cross of gold."

And everybody heard him—
In the streets and State House yard.
And everybody heard him
In Springfield,
In Illinois,
Around and around and around the world,
That danced upon its axis
And like a darling broncho whirled.

IV

July, August, suspense.
Wall Street lost to sense.

August, September, October,
More suspense,
And the whole East down like a wind-smashed fence.

Then Hanna to the rescue,
Hanna of Ohio,
Rallying the roller-tops,
Rallying the bucket-shops.
Threatening drouth and death,
Promising manna,
Rallying the trusts against the bawling flannelmouth;
Invading misers' cellars,
Tin-cans, socks,
Melting down the rocks,
Pouring out the long green to a million workers,
Spondulix by the mountain-load, to stop each new tornado
And beat the cheapskate, blatherskite,
Populistic, anarchistic,
Deacon—desperado.

V

Election night at midnight:
Boy Bryan's defeat.
Defeat of western silver.
Defeat of the wheat.
Victory of letterfiles
And plutocrats in miles
With dollar signs upon their coats,
Diamond watchchains on their vests
And spats on their feet.
Victory of custodians,
Plymouth Rock,
And all that inbred landlord stock.
Victory of the neat.
Defeat of the aspen groves of Colorado valleys,
The blue bells of the Rockies,
And blue bonnets of old Texas,
By the Pittsburgh alleys.
Defeat of alfalfa and the Mariposa lily.
Defeat of the Pacific and the long Mississippi.
Defeat of the young by the old and silly.
Defeat of tornadoes by the poison vats supreme.
Defeat of my boyhood, defeat of my dream.

VI

Where is McKinley, that respectable McKinley,
The man without an angle or a tangle,
Who soothed down the city man and soothed down the farmer,
The German, the Irish, the Southerner, the Northerner,
Who climbed every greasy pole, and slipped through every crack;
Who soothed down the gambling hall, the bar-room, the church,
The devil vote, the angel vote, the neutral vote,
The desperately wicked, and their victims on the rack,
The gold vote, the silver vote, the brass vote, the lead vote,
Every vote? . . .

Where is McKinley, Mark Hanna's McKinley,
His slave, his echo, his suit of clothes?
Gone to join the shadows, with the pomps of that time,
And the flame of that summer's prairie rose.

Where is Cleveland whom the Democratic platform
Read from the party in a glorious hour,
Gone to join the shadows with pitchfork Tillman,
And sledge-hammer Altgeld who wrecked his power.

Where is Hanna, bulldog Hanna,
Low-browed Hanna, who said: "Stand pat"?
Gone to his place with old Pierpont Morgan.
Gone somewhere . . . with lean rat Platt.

Where is Roosevelt, the young dude cowboy,
Who hated Bryan, then aped his way?
Gone to join the shadows with mighty Cromwell
And tall King Saul, till the Judgment day.

Where is Altgeld, brave as the truth,
Whose name the few still say with tears?
Gone to join the ironies with Old John Brown,
Whose fame rings loud for a thousand years.

Where is that boy, that Heaven-born Bryan,
That Homer Bryan, who sang from the West?
Gone to join the shadows with Altgeld the Eagle,
Where the kings and the slaves and the troubadours rest.

August, 1919,1920

WHEN THE MISSISSIPPI FLOWED IN INDIANA

INSCRIBED TO BRUCE CAMPBELL, WHO READ "TOM SAWYER"
WITH ME IN THE OLD HOUSE

Beneath Time's roaring cannon
Many walls fall down.
But though the guns break every stone,
Level every town: —
Within our Grandma's old front hall
Some wonders flourish yet: —
The Pavement of Verona,
Where stands young Juliet;
The roof of Blue-beard's palace,
And Kubla Khan's wild ground;
The cave of young Aladdin,
Where the jewel-flowers were found;
And the garden of old Sparta
Where little Helen played;
The grotto of Miranda
That Prospero arrayed;
And the cave, by the Mississippi,
Where Becky Thatcher strayed.

On that Indiana stairway
Gleams Cinderella's shoe.
Upon that mighty mountainside
Walks Snow-white in the dew.
Upon that grassy hillside
Trips shining Nicolette: —
That stairway of remembrance
Time's cannon will not get—
That chattering slope of glory
Our little cousins made,
That hill by the Mississippi
Where Becky Thatcher strayed.

Spring beauties on that cliffside,
Love in the air,
While the soul's deep Mississippi
Sweeps on, forever fair.

And he who enters in the cave,
Nothing shall make afraid,
The cave by the Mississippi
Where Tom and Becky strayed. *1920*

THE COMET OF GOING-TO-THE-SUN

On the mountain peak, called "Going-to-the-Sun,"
A comet stopped to drink from a cool spring
And like a spirit-harp began to sing
To us, then hurried on to reach the sun.
We called him "Homer's soul," and "Milton's wing."
The harp-sound stayed, though he went up and on.
It turned to thunder, when he had quite gone—
And yet was like a soft voice of the sea,
And every whispering root and every blade of grass
And every tree
In the whole world, and brought thoughts of old songs
That blind men sang ten thousand years ago,
And all the springtime hearts of every nation know.
                                    1923

THE APPLE-BARREL OF JOHNNY APPLESEED

On the mountain peak called "Going-to-the-Sun,"
I saw gray Johnny Appleseed at prayer
Just as the sunset made the old earth fair.
Then darkness came; in an instant, like great smoke,
The sun fell down as though its great hoops broke
And dark rich apples, poured from the dim flame
Where the sun set, came rolling toward the peak,
A storm of fruit, a mighty cider-reek,
The perfume of the orchards of the world,
From apple-shadows: red and russet domes
That turned to clouds of glory and strange homes
Above the mountain tops for cloud-born souls:
Reproofs for men who build the world like moles,
Models for men, if they would build the world
As Johnny Appleseed would have it done—
Praying, and reading the books of Swedenborg
On the mountain top called "Going-to-the-Sun."
                                    1923

THE FLOWER-FED BUFFALOES

The flower-fed buffaloes of the spring
In the days of long ago,
Ranged where the locomotives sing
And the prairie flowers lie low:
The tossing, blooming, perfumed grass
Is swept away by the wheat,
Wheels and wheels and wheels spin by
In the spring that still is sweet.
But the flower-fed buffaloes of the spring
Left us, long ago.
They gore no more, they bellow no more,
They trundle around the hills no more:
With the Blackfeet, lying low.
With the Pawnees, lying low,
Lying low.   1926

RAIN

Each storm-soaked flower has a beautiful eye.
And this is the voice of the stone-cold sky:
"Only boys keep their cheeks dry.
Only boys are afraid to cry.
Men thank God for tears,
Alone with the memory of their dead,
Alone with lost years."   1926

NANCY HANKS, MOTHER OF ABRAHAM LINCOLN

Out of the eater came forth meat; and out of the strong came forth sweetness.—Judges XIV, 14.

A sweet girl graduate, lean as a fawn,
The very whimsy of time,
Read her class poem Commencement Day—
A trembling filigree rhyme.

The pansy that blooms on the window sill,
Blooms in exactly the proper place;
And she nodded just like a pansy there,
And her poem was all about bowers and showers,

Sugary streamlet and mossy rill,
All about daisies on dale and hill—
And she was the mother of Buffalo Bill.

Another girl, a cloud-drift sort,
Dreamlit, moonlit, marble-white,
Light-footed saint on the pilgrim shore,
The best since New England fairies began,
Was the mother of Barnum, the circus man.

A girl from Missouri, snippy and vain,
As frothy a miss as any you know,
A wren, a toy, a pink silk bow,
The belle of the choir, she drove insane
Missouri deacons and all the sleek,
Her utter tomfoolery made men weak,
Till they could not stand and they could not speak.
Oh, queen of fifteen and sixteen,
Missouri sweetened beneath her reign—
And she was the mother of bad Mark Twain.

Not always are lions born of lions,
Roosevelt sprang from a palace of lace;
On the other hand is the dizzy truth:
Not always is beauty born of beauty.
Some treasures wait in a hidden place.
All over the world were thousands of belles
In far-off eighteen hundred and nine,
Girls of fifteen, girls of twenty,
Their mammas dressed them up a-plenty—
Each garter was bright, each stocking fine,
But for all their innocent devices,
Their cheeks of fruit and their eyes of wine,
And each voluptuous design,
And all soft glories that we trace
In Europe's palaces of lace,
A girl who slept in dust and sorrow,
Nancy Hanks, in a lost log cabin,
Nancy Hanks had the loveliest face!   1926

Wallace Stevens

PETER QUINCE AT THE CLAVIER

I

Just as my fingers on these keys
Make music, so the selfsame sounds
On my spirit make a music, too.

Music is feeling, then, not sound;
And thus it is that what I feel,
Here in this room, desiring you,

Thinking of your blue-shadowed silk,
Is music. It is like the strain
Waked in the elders by Susanna.

Of a green evening, clear and warm,
She bathed in her still garden, while
The red-eyed elders watching, felt

The basses of their beings throb
In witching chords, and their thin blood
Pulse pizzicati of Hosanna.

II

In the green water, clear and warm,
Susanna lay.
She searched
The touch of springs,
And found
Concealed imaginings.
She sighed,
For so much melody.

Upon the bank, she stood
In the cool
Of spent emotions.
She felt, among the leaves,
The dew
Of old devotions.

She walked upon the grass,
Still quavering.
The winds were like her maids,
On timid feet,
Fetching her woven scarves,
Yet wavering.

A breath upon her hand
Muted the night.
She turned—
A cymbal crashed,
And roaring horns.

III

Soon, with a noise like tambourines,
Came her attendant Byzantines.

They wondered why Susanna cried
Against the elders by her side;

And as they whispered, the refrain
Was like a willow swept by rain.

Anon, their lamps' uplifted flame
Revealed Susanna and her shame.

And then, the simpering Byzantines
Fled, with a noise like tambourines.

IV

Beauty is momentary in the mind—
The fitful tracing of a portal;
But in the flesh it is immortal.

The body dies; the body's beauty lives.
So evenings die, in their green going,

A wave, interminably flowing.
So gardens die, their meek breath scenting
The cowl of winter, done repenting.
So maidens die, to the auroral
Celebration of a maiden's choral.

Susanna's music touched the bawdy strings
Of those white elders; but, escaping,
Left only Death's ironic scraping.
Now, in its immortality, it plays
On the clear viol of her memory,
And makes a constant sacrament of praise.

1915

DISILLUSIONMENT OF TEN O'CLOCK

The houses are haunted
By white night-gowns.
None are green,
Or purple with green rings,
Or green with yellow rings,
Or yellow with blue rings.
None of them are strange,
With socks of lace
And beaded ceintures.
People are not going
To dream of baboons and periwinkles.
Only, here and there, an old sailor,
Drunk and asleep in his boots,
Catches tigers
In red weather.

1915

SUNDAY MORNING

I

Complacencies of the peignoir, and late
Coffee and oranges in a sunny chair,
And the green freedom of a cockatoo
Upon a rug mingle to dissipate
The holy hush of ancient sacrifice.
She dreams a little, and she feels the dark
Encroachment of that old catastrophe,

As a calm darkens among water-lights.
The pungent oranges and bright, green wings
Seem things in some procession of the dead,
Winding across wide water, without sound.
The day is like wide water, without sound,
Stilled for the passing of her dreaming feet
Over the seas, to silent Palestine,
Dominion of the blood and sepulchre.

II

Why should she give her bounty to the dead?
What is divinity if it can come
Only in silent shadows and in dreams?
Shall she not find in comforts of the sun,
In pungent fruit and bright, green wings, or else
In any balm or beauty of the earth,
Things to be cherished like the thought of heaven?
Divinity must live within herself:
Passions of rain, or moods in falling snow;
Grievings in loneliness, or unsubdued
Elations when the forest blooms; gusty
Emotions on wet roads on autumn nights;
All pleasures and all pains, remembering
The bough of summer and the winter branch.
These are the measures destined for her soul.

III

Jove in the clouds had his inhuman birth.
No mother suckled him, no sweet land gave
Large-mannered motions to his mythy mind.
He moved among us, as a muttering king,
Magnificent, would move among his hinds,
Until our blood, commingling, virginal,
With heaven, brought such requital to desire
The very hinds discerned it, in a star.
Shall our blood fail? Or shall it come to be
The blood of paradise? And shall the earth
Seem all of paradise that we shall know?
The sky will be much friendlier then than now,
A part of labor and a part of pain,
And next in glory to enduring love,
Not this dividing and indifferent blue.

IV

She says, "I am content when wakened birds,
Before they fly, test the reality
Of misty fields, by their sweet questionings;
But when the birds are gone, and their warm fields
Return no more, where, then, is paradise?"
There is not any haunt of prophecy,
Nor any old chimera of the grave,
Neither the golden underground, nor isle
Melodious, where spirits gat them home,
Nor visionary south, nor cloudy palm
Remote on heaven's hill, that has endured
As April's green endures; or will endure
Like her remembrance of awakened birds,
Or her desire for June and evening, tipped
By the consummation of the swallow's wings.

V

She says, "But in contentment I still feel
The need of some imperishable bliss."
Death is the mother of beauty; hence from her,
Alone, shall come fulfilment to our dreams
And our desires. Although she strews the leaves
Of sure obliteration on our paths,
The path sick sorrow took, the many paths
Where triumph rang its brassy phrase, or love
Whispered a little out of tenderness,
She makes the willow shiver in the sun
For maidens who were wont to sit and gaze
Upon the grass, relinquished to their feet.
She causes boys to pile new plums and pears
On disregarded plate. The maidens taste
And stray impassioned in the littering leaves.

VI

Is there no change of death in paradise?
Does ripe fruit never fall? Or do the boughs
Hang always heavy in that perfect sky,
Unchanging, yet so like our perishing earth,
With rivers like our own that seek for seas
They never find, the same receding shores

That never touch with inarticulate pang?
Why set the pear upon those river-banks
Or spice the shores with odors of the plum?
Alas, that they should wear our colors there,
The silken weavings of our afternoons,
And pick the strings of our insipid lutes!
Death is the mother of beauty, mystical,
Within whose burning bosom we devise
Our earthly mothers waiting, sleeplessly.

VII

Supple and turbulent, a ring of men
Shall chant in orgy on a summer morn
Their boisterous devotion to the sun,
Not as a god, but as a god might be,
Naked among them, like a savage source.
Their chant shall be a chant of paradise,
Out of their blood, returning to the sky;
And in their chant shall enter, voice by voice,
The windy lake wherein their lord delights,
The trees, like serafin, and echoing hills,
That choir among themselves long afterward.
They shall know well the heavenly fellowship
Of men that perish and of summer morn.
And whence they came and whither they shall go
The dew upon their feet shall manifest.

VIII

She hears, upon that water without sound,
A voice that cries, "The tomb in Palestine
Is not the porch of spirits lingering.
It is the grave of Jesus, where he lay."
We live in an old chaos of the sun,
Or old dependency of day and night,
Or island solitude, unsponsored, free,
Of that wide water, inescapable.
Deer walk upon our mountains, and the quail
Whistle about us their spontaneous cries;
Sweet berries ripen in the wilderness;
And, in the isolation of the sky,
At evening, casual flocks of pigeons make
Ambiguous undulations as they sink,
Downward to darkness, on extended wings. *1915*

THIRTEEN WAYS OF LOOKING AT A BLACKBIRD

I

Among twenty snowy mountains,
The only moving thing
Was the eye of the blackbird.

II

I was of three minds,
Like a tree
In which there are three blackbirds.

III

The blackbird whirled in the autumn winds.
It was a small part of the pantomime.

IV

A man and a woman
Are one.
A man and a woman and a blackbird
Are one.

V

I do not know which to prefer,
The beauty of inflections
Or the beauty of innuendoes,
The blackbird whistling
Or just after.

VI

Icicles filled the long window
With barbaric glass.
The shadow of the blackbird
Crossed it, to and fro.
The mood
Traced in the shadow
An indecipherable cause.

VII

O thin men of Haddam,
Why do you imagine golden birds?

Do you not see how the blackbird
Walks around the feet
Of the women about you?

VIII

I know noble accents
And lucid, inescapable rhythms;
But I know, too,
That the blackbird is involved
In what I know.

IX

When the blackbird flew out of sight,
It marked the edge
Of one of many circles.

X

At the sight of blackbirds
Flying in a green light,
Even the bawds of euphony
Would cry out sharply.

XI

He rode over Connecticut
In a glass coach.
Once, a fear pierced him,
In that he mistook
The shadow of his equipage
For blackbirds.

XII

The river is moving.
The blackbird must be flying.

XIII

It was evening all afternoon.
It was snowing
And it was going to snow.
The blackbird sat
In the cedar-limbs.   *1917*

ANECDOTE OF THE JAR

I placed a jar in Tennessee,
And round it was, upon a hill.
It made the slovenly wilderness
Surround that hill.

The wilderness rose up to it,
And sprawled around, no longer wild.
The jar was round upon the ground
And tall and of a port in air.

It took dominion everywhere.
The jar was gray and bare.
It did not give of bird or bush,
Like nothing else in Tennessee.   *1919*

BANTAMS IN PINE-WOODS

Chieftain Iffucan of Azcan in caftan
Of tan with henna hackles, halt!

Damned universal cock, as if the sun
Was blackamoor to bear your blazing tail.

Fat! Fat! Fat! Fat! I am the personal.
Your world is you. I am my world.

You ten-foot poet among inchlings. Fat!
Begone! An inchling bristles in these pines,

Bristles, and points their Appalachian tangs,
And fears not portly Azcan nor his hoos.
                                    1922

A HIGH-TONED OLD CHRISTIAN WOMAN

Poetry is the supreme fiction, madame.
Take the moral law and make a nave of it
And from the nave build haunted heaven. Thus,
The conscience is converted into palms,
Like windy citherns hankering for hymns.
We agree in principle. That's clear. But take

The opposing law and make a peristyle,
And from the peristyle project a masque
Beyond the planets. Thus, our bawdiness,
Unpurged by epitaph, indulged at last,
Is equally converted into palms,
Squiggling like saxophones. And palm for palm,
Madame, we are where we began. Allow,
Therefore, that in the planetary scene
Your disaffected flagellants, well-stuffed,
Smacking their muzzy bellies in parade,
Proud of such novelties of the sublime,
Such tink and tank and tunk-a-tunk-tunk,
May, merely may, madame, whip from themselves
A jovial hullabaloo among the spheres.
This will make widows wince. But fictive things
Wink as they will. Wink most when widows wince.

                                              1922

THE EMPEROR OF ICE-CREAM

Call the roller of big cigars,
The muscular one, and bid him whip
In kitchen cups concupiscent curds.
Let the wenches dawdle in such dress
As they are used to wear, and let the boys
Bring flowers in last month's newspapers.
Let be be finale of seem.
The only emperor is the emperor of ice-cream.

Take from the dresser of deal,
Lacking the three glass knobs, that sheet
On which she embroidered fantails once
And spread it so as to cover her face.
If her horny feet protrude, they come
To show how cold she is, and dumb.
Let the lamp affix its beam.
The only emperor is the emperor of ice-cream.

                                              1922

EARTHY ANECDOTE

Every time the bucks went clattering
Over Oklahoma
A firecat bristled in the way.

Wherever they went,
They went clattering,
Until they swerved
In a swift, circular line
To the right,
Because of the firecat.

Or until they swerved
In a swift, circular line
To the left,
Because of the firecat.

The bucks clattered.
The firecat went leaping,
To the right, to the left,
And
Bristled in the way.

Later, the firecat closed his bright eyes
And slept.   1923

THE PLOT AGAINST THE GIANT

First Girl

When this yokel comes maundering,
Whetting his hacker,
I shall run before him,
Diffusing the civilest odors
Out of geraniums and unsmelled flowers.
It will check him.

Second Girl

I shall run before him,
Arching cloths besprinkled with colors
As small as fish-eggs.
The threads
Will abash him.

Third Girl

Oh, la . . . le pauvre!
I shall run before him,

With a curious puffing.
He will bend his ear then.
I shall whisper
Heavenly labials in a world of gutturals.
It will undo him.   *1923*

NUANCES OF A THEME BY WILLIAMS

It's a strange courage
you give me, ancient star:

Shine alone in the sunrise
toward which you lend no part!

I

Shine alone, shine nakedly, shine like bronze,
that reflects neither my face nor any inner part
of my being, shine like fire, that mirrors nothing.

II

Lend no part to any humanity that suffuses
you in its own light.
Be not chimera of morning,
Half-man, half-star.
Be not an intelligence,
Like a widow's bird
Or an old horse.   *1923*

SEA SURFACE FULL OF CLOUDS

I

In that November off Tehuantepec,
The slopping of the sea grew still one night
And in the morning summer hued the deck

And made one think of rosy chocolate
And gilt umbrellas. Paradisal green
Gave suavity to the perplexed machine

Of ocean, which like limpid water lay.
Who, then, in that ambrosial latitude
Out of the light evolved the moving blooms,

Who, then, evolved the sea-blooms from the clouds
Diffusing balm in that Pacific calm?
C'était mon enfant, mon bijou, mon âme.

The sea-clouds whitened far below the calm
And moved, as blooms move, in the swimming green
And in its watery radiance, while the hue

Of heaven in an antique reflection rolled
Round those flotillas. And sometimes the sea
Poured brilliant iris on the glistening blue.

II

In that November off Tehuantepec
The slopping of the sea grew still one night.
At breakfast jelly yellow streaked the deck

And made one think of chop-house chocolate
And sham umbrellas. And a sham-like green
Capped summer-seeming on the tense machine

Of ocean, which in sinister flatness lay.
Who, then, beheld the rising of the clouds
That strode submerged in that malevolent sheen,

Who saw the mortal massives of the blooms
Of water moving on the water-floor?
C'était mon frère du ciel, ma vie, mon or.

The gongs rang loudly as the windy booms
Hoo-hooed it in the darkened ocean-blooms.
The gongs grew still. And then blue heaven spread

Its crystalline pendentives on the sea
And the macabre of the water-glooms
In an enormous undulation fled.

III

In that November off Tehuantepec,
The slopping of the sea grew still one night
And a pale silver patterned on the deck

And made one think of porcelain chocolate
And pied umbrellas. An uncertain green,
Piano-polished, held the tranced machine

Of ocean, as a prelude holds and holds.
Who, seeing silver petals of white blooms
Unfolding in the water, feeling sure

Of the milk within the saltiest spurge, heard, then,
The sea unfolding in the sunken clouds?
Oh! C'était mon extase et mon amour.

So deeply sunken were they that the shrouds,
The shrouding shadows, made the petals black
Until the rolling heaven made them blue,

A blue beyond the rainy hyacinth,
And smiting the crevasses of the leaves
Deluged the ocean with a sapphire blue.

IV

In that November off Tehuantepec
The night-long slopping of the sea grew still.
A mallow morning dozed upon the deck

And made one think of musky chocolate
And frail umbrellas. A too-fluent green
Suggested malice in the dry machine

Of ocean, pondering dank stratagem.
Who then beheld the figures of the clouds
Like blooms secluded in the thick marine?

Like blooms? Like damasks that were shaken off
From the loosed girdles in the spangling must.
C'était ma foi, la nonchalance divine.

The nakedness would rise and suddenly turn
Salt masks of beard and mouths of bellowing,
Would—But more suddenly the heaven rolled

Its bluest sea-clouds in the thinking green,
And the nakedness became the broadest blooms,
Mile-mallows that a mallow sun cajoled.

V

In that November off Tehuantepec
Night stilled the slopping of the sea. The day
Came, bowing and voluble, upon the deck,

Good clown. . . . One thought of Chinese chocolate
And large umbrellas. And a motley green
Followed the drift of the obese machine

Of ocean, perfected in indolence.
What pistache one, ingenious and droll,
Beheld the sovereign clouds as jugglery

And the sea as turquoise-turbaned Sambo, neat
At tossing saucers—cloudy-conjuring sea?
C'était mon esprit bâtard, l'ignominie.

The sovereign clouds came clustering. The conch
Of loyal conjuration trumped. The wind
Of green blooms turning crisped the motley hue

To clearing opalescence. Then the sea
And heaven rolled as one and from the two
Came fresh transfigurings of freshest blue.   *1924*

THE IDEA OF ORDER AT KEY WEST

She sang beyond the genius of the sea.
The water never formed to mind or voice,
Like a body wholly body, fluttering
Its empty sleeves; and yet its mimic motion
Made constant cry, caused constantly a cry,
That was not ours although we understood,
Inhuman, of the veritable ocean.

The sea was not a mask. No more was she.
The song and water were not medleyed sound
Even if what she sang was what she heard,
Since what she sang was uttered word by word.
It may be that in all her phrases stirred
The grinding water and the gasping wind;
But it was she and not the sea we heard.

For she was the maker of the song she sang.
The ever-hooded, tragic-gestured sea
Was merely a place by which she walked to sing.
Whose spirit is this? we said, because we knew
It was the spirit that we sought and knew
That we should ask this often as she sang.

If it was only the dark voice of the sea
That rose, or even colored by many waves;
If it was only the outer voice of sky
And cloud, of the sunken coral water-walled,
However clear, it would have been deep air,
The heaving speech of air, a summer sound
Repeated in a summer without end
And sound alone. But it was more than that,
More even than her voice, and ours, among
The meaningless plungings of water and the wind,
Theatrical distances, bronze shadows heaped
On high horizons, mountainous atmospheres
Of sky and sea.
                    It was her voice that made
The sky acutest at its vanishing.
She measured to the hour its solitude.
She was the single artificer of the world
In which she sang. And when she sang, the sea,
Whatever self it had, became the self
That was her song, for she was the maker. Then we,
As we beheld her striding there alone,
Knew that there never was a world for her
Except the one she sang and, singing, made.

Ramon Fernandez, tell me, if you know,
Why, when the singing ended and we turned
Toward the town, tell why the glassy lights,
The lights in the fishing boats at anchor there,
As the night descended, tilting in the air,
Mastered the night and portioned out the sea,
Fixing emblazoned zones and fiery poles,
Arranging, deepening, enchanting night.

Oh! Blessed rage for order, pale Ramon,
The maker's rage to order words of the sea,
Words of the fragrant portals, dimly-starred,

And of ourselves and of our origins,
In ghostlier demarcations, keener sounds.   *1934*

DANCE OF THE MACABRE MICE

In the land of turkeys in turkey weather
At the base of the statue, we go round and round.
What a beautiful history, beautiful surprise!
Monsieur is on horseback. The horse is covered with mice.

This dance has no name. It is a hungry dance.
We dance it out to the tip of Monsieur's sword,
Reading the lordly language of the inscription,
Which is like zithers and tambourines combined:

The Founder of the State. Whoever founded
A state that was free, in the dead of winter, from mice?
What a beautiful tableau tinted and towering,
The arm of bronze outstretched against all evil!   *1935*

From THE MAN WITH THE BLUE GUITAR

I

The man bent over his guitar,
A shearsman of sorts. The day was green.

They said, "You have a blue guitar,
You do not play things as they are."

The man replied, "Things as they are
Are changed upon the blue guitar."

And they said then, "But play, you must,
A tune beyond us, yet ourselves,
A tune upon the blue guitar
Of things exactly as they are."

II

I cannot bring a world quite round,
Although I patch it as I can.

I sing a hero's head, large eye
And bearded bronze, but not a man,

Although I patch him as I can
And reach through him almost to man.

If to serenade almost to man
Is to miss, by that, things as they are,

Say that it is the serenade
Of a man that plays a blue guitar.

VI

A tune beyond us as we are,
Yet nothing changed by the blue guitar;

Ourselves in the tune as if in space,
Yet nothing changed, except the place

Of things as they are and only the place
As you play them, on the blue guitar,

Placed, so, beyond the compass of change,
Perceived in a final atmosphere;

For a moment final, in the way
The thinking of art seems final when

The thinking of god is smoky dew.
The tune is space. The blue guitar

Becomes the place of things as they are,
A composing of senses of the guitar.

XII

Tom-tom, c'est moi. The blue guitar
And I are one. The orchestra

Fills the high hall with shuffling men
High as the hall. The whirling noise

Of a multitude dwindles, all said,
To his breath that lies awake at night.

I know that timid breathing. Where
Do I begin and end? And where,

As I strum the thing, do I pick up
That which momentously declares

Itself not to be I and yet
Must be. It could be nothing else.   *1937*

From *ESTHÉTIQUE DU MAL*

I

He was at Naples writing letters home
And, between his letters, reading paragraphs
On the sublime. Vesuvius had groaned
For a month. It was pleasant to be sitting there,
While the sultriest fulgurations, flickering,
Cast corners in the glass. He could describe
The terror of the sound because the sound
Was ancient. He tried to remember the phrases: pain
Audible at noon, pain torturing itself,
Pain killing pain on the very point of pain.
The volcano trembled in another ether,
As the body trembles at the end of life.

It was almost time for lunch. Pain is human.
There were roses in the cool café. His book
Made sure of the most correct catastrophe.
Except for us, Vesuvius might consume
In solid fire the utmost earth and know
No pain (ignoring the cocks that crow us up
To die). This is a part of the sublime
From which we shrink. And yet, except for us,
The total past felt nothing when destroyed.

VII

How red the rose that is the soldier's wound,
The wounds of many soldiers, the wounds of all
The soldiers that have fallen, red in blood,
The soldier of time grown deathless in great size.

A mountain in which no ease is ever found,
Unless indifference to deeper death

Is ease, stands in the dark, a shadows' hill,
And there the soldier of time has deathless rest.

Concentric circles of shadows, motionless
Of their own part, yet moving on the wind,
Form mystical convolutions in the sleep
Of time's red soldier deathless on his bed.

The shadows of his fellows ring him round
In the high night, the summer breathes for them
Its fragrance, a heavy somnolence, and for him,
For the soldier of time, it breathes a summer sleep,

In which his wound is good because life was.
No part of him was ever part of death.
A woman smoothes her forehead with her hand
And the soldier of time lies calm beneath that stroke.

XI

Life is a bitter aspic. We are not
At the centre of a diamond. At dawn,
The paratroopers fall and as they fall
They mow the lawn. A vessel sinks in waves
Of people, as big bell-billows from its bell
Bell-bellow in the village steeple. Violets,
Great tufts, spring up from buried houses
Of poor, dishonest people, for whom the steeple,
Long since, rang out farewell, farewell, farewell.

Natives of poverty, children of malheur,
The gaiety of language is our seigneur.

A man of bitter appetite despises
A well-made scene in which paratroopers
Select adieux; and he despises this:
A ship that rolls on a confected ocean,
The weather pink, the wind in motion; and this:
A steeple that tip-tops the classic sun's
Arrangements; and the violets' exhumo.
The tongue caresses these exacerbations.
They press it as epicure, distinguishing
Themselves from its essential savor,
Like hunger that feeds on its own hungriness.   *1944*

From THE AURORAS OF AUTUMN

I

This is where the serpent lives, the bodiless.
His head is air. Beneath his tip at night
Eyes open and fix on us in every sky.

Or is this another wriggling out of the egg,
Another image at the end of the cave,
Another bodiless for the body's slough?

This is where the serpent lives. This is his nest,
These fields, these hills, these tinted distances,
And the pines above and along and beside the sea.

This is form gulping after formlessness,
Skin flashing to wished-for disappearances
And the serpent body flashing without the skin.

This is the height emerging and its base
These lights may finally attain a pole
In the midmost midnight and find the serpent there,

In another nest, the master of the maze
Of body and air and forms and images,
Relentlessly in possession of happiness.

This is his poison: that we should disbelieve
Even that. His meditations in the ferns,
When he moved so slightly to make sure of sun,

Made us no less as sure. We saw in his head,
Black beaded on the rock, the flecked animal,
The moving grass, the Indian in his glade.

II

Farewell to an idea . . . A cabin stands,
Deserted, on a beach. It is white,
As by a custom or according to

An ancestral theme or as a consequence
Of an infinite course. The flowers against the wall
Are white, a little dried, a kind of mark

Reminding, trying to remind, of a white
That was different, something else, last year
Or before, not the white of an aging afternoon,

Whether fresher or duller, whether of winter cloud
Or of winter sky, from horizon to horizon.
The wind is blowing the sand across the floor.

Here, being visible is being white,
Is being of the solid of white, the accomplishment
Of an extremist in an exercise . . .

The season changes. A cold wind chills the beach.
The long lines of it grow longer, emptier,
A darkness gathers though it does not fall

And the whiteness grows less vivid on the wall.
The man who is walking turns blankly on the sand.
He observes how the north is always enlarging the change,

With its frigid brilliances, its blue-red sweeps
And gusts of great enkindlings, its polar green,
The color of ice and fire and solitude.

<h1 style="text-align:center">X</h1>

An unhappy people in a happy world—
Read, rabbi, the phases of this difference.
An unhappy people in an unhappy world—

Here are too many mirrors for misery.
A happy people in an unhappy world—
It cannot be. There's nothing there to roll

On the expressive tongue, the finding fang.
A happy people in a happy world—
Buffo! A ball, an opera, a bar.

Turn back to where we were when we began:
An unhappy people in a happy world.
Now, solemnize the secretive syllables.

Read to the congregation, for today
And for tomorrow, this extremity,
This contrivance of the spectre of the spheres,

Contriving balance to contrive a whole,
The vital, the never-failing genius,
Fulfilling his meditations, great and small.

In these unhappy he meditates a whole,
The full of fortune and the full of fate,
As if he lived all lives, that he might know,

In hall harridan, not hushful paradise,
To a haggling of wind and weather, by these lights
Like a blaze of summer straw, in winter's nick.   *1950*

William Carlos Williams

PORTRAIT OF A LADY

Your thighs are appletrees
whose blossoms touch the sky.
Which sky? The sky
where Watteau hung a lady's
slipper. Your knees
are a southern breeze—or
a gust of snow. Agh! what
sort of man was Fragonard?
—as if that answered
anything. Ah, yes—below
the knees, since the tune
drops that way, it is
one of those white summer days,
the tall grass of your ankles
flickers upon the shore—
Which shore?—
the sand clings to my lips—
Which shore?
Agh, petals maybe. How
should I know?
Which shore? Which shore?
I said petals from an appletree.

1913

EL HOMBRE

It's a strange courage
you give me ancient star:

Shine alone in the sunrise
toward which you lend no part!

1917

II-171

DANSE RUSSE

If I when my wife is sleeping
and the baby and Kathleen
are sleeping
and the sun is a flame-white disc
in silken mists
above shining trees,—
if I in my north room
dance naked, grotesquely
before my mirror
waving my shirt round my head
and singing softly to myself:
"I am lonely, lonely.
I was born to be lonely,
I am best so!"
If I admire my arms, my face
my shoulders, flanks, buttocks
against the yellow drawn shades,—

Who shall say I am not
the happy genius of my household?

1917

THE WIDOW'S LAMENT IN SPRINGTIME

Sorrow is my own yard
where the new grass
flames as it has flamed
often before but not
with the cold fire
that closes round me this year.
Thirtyfive years
I lived with my husband.
The plumtree is white today
with masses of flowers.
Masses of flowers
load the cherry branches
and color some bushes
yellow and some red
but the grief in my heart
is stronger than they

for though they were my joy
formerly, today I notice them
and turned away forgetting.
Today my son told me
that in the meadows,
at the edge of the heavy woods
in the distance, he saw
trees of white flowers.
I feel that I would like
to go there
and fall into those flowers
and sink into the marsh near them.

1921

SPRING AND ALL

By the road to the contagious hospital
under the surge of the blue
mottled clouds driven from the
northeast—a cold wind. Beyond, the
waste of broad, muddy fields
brown with dried weeds, standing and fallen

patches of standing water
the scattering of tall trees

All along the road the reddish
purplish, forked, upstanding, twiggy
stuff of bushes and small trees
with dead, brown leaves under them
leafless vines—

Lifeless in appearance, sluggish
dazed spring approaches—

They enter the new world naked,
cold, uncertain of all
save that they enter. All about them
the cold, familiar wind—

Now the grass, tomorrow
the stiff curl of wildcarrot leaf

One by one objects are defined—
It quickens: clarity, outline of leaf

But now the stark dignity of
entrance—Still, the profound change
has come upon them: rooted they
grip down and begin to awaken   *1923*

TO ELSIE

The pure products of America
go crazy—
mountain folk from Kentucky

or the ribbed north end of
Jersey
with its isolate lakes and

valleys, its deaf-mutes, thieves
old names
and promiscuity between

devil-may-care men who have taken
to railroading
out of sheer lust of adventure—

and young slatterns, bathed
in filth
from Monday to Saturday

to be tricked out that night
with gauds
from imaginations which have no

peasant traditions to give them
character
but flutter and flaunt

sheer rags—succumbing without
emotion
save numbed terror

under some hedge of choke-cherry
or viburnum—
which they cannot express—

Unless it be that marriage
perhaps
with a dash of Indian blood

will throw up a girl so desolate
so hemmed round
with disease or murder

that she'll be rescued by an
agent—
reared by the state and

sent out at fifteen to work in
some hard pressed
house in the suburbs—

some doctor's family, some Elsie—
voluptuous water
expressing with broken

brain the truth about us—
her great
ungainly hips and flopping breasts

addressed to cheap
jewelry
and rich young men with fine eyes

as if the earth under our feet
were
an excrement of some sky

and we degraded prisoners
destined
to hunger until we eat filth

while the imagination strains
after deer
going by fields of goldenrod in

the stifling heat of September
Somehow
it seems to destroy us

It is only in isolate flecks that
something
is given off

No one
to witness
and adjust, no one to drive the car   1923

THE RED WHEELBARROW

so much depends
upon

a red wheel
barrow

glazed with rain
water

beside the white
chickens.   1923

AT THE BALL GAME

The crowd at the ball game
is moved uniformly

by a spirit of uselessness
which delights them—

all the exciting detail
of the chase

and the escape, the error
the flash of genius—

all to no end save beauty
the eternal—

So in detail they, the crowd,
are beautiful

for this
to be warned against

saluted and defied—
It is alive, venomous

it smiles grimly
its words cut—

The flashy female with her
mother, gets it—

The Jew gets it straight—it
is deadly, terrifying—

It is the Inquisition, the
Revolution

It is beauty itself
that lives

day by day in them
idly—

This is
the power of their faces

It is summer, it is the solstice
the crowd is

cheering, the crowd is laughing
in detail

permanently, seriously
without thought   1923

THE YACHTS

contend in a sea which the land partly encloses
shielding them from the too heavy blows
of an ungoverned ocean which when it chooses

tortures the biggest hulls, the best man knows
to pit against its beatings, and sinks them pitilessly.
Mothlike in mists, scintillant in the minute

brilliance of cloudless days, with broad bellying sails
they glide to the wind tossing green water
from their sharp prows while over them the crew crawls

ant-like, solicitously grooming them, releasing,
making fast as they turn, lean far over and having
caught the wind again, side by side, head for the mark.

In a well guarded arena of open water surrounded by
lesser and greater craft which, sycophant, lumbering
and flittering follow them, they appear youthful, rare

as the light of a happy eye, live with the grace
of all that in the mind is feckless, free and
naturally to be desired. Now the sea which holds them

is moody, lapping their glossy sides, as if feeling
for some slightest flaw but fails completely.
Today no race. Then the wind comes again. The yachts

move, jockeying for a start, the signal is set and they
are off. Now the waves strike at them but they are too
well made, they slip through, though they take in canvas.

Arms with hands grasping seek to clutch at the prows.
Bodies thrown recklessly in the way are cut aside.
It is a sea of faces about them in agony, in despair

until the horror of the race dawns staggering the mind,
the whole sea become an entanglement of watery bodies
lost to the world bearing what they cannot hold. Broken,

beaten, desolate, reaching from the dead to be taken up
they cry out, failing, failing! their cries rising
in waves still as the skillful yachts pass over.   *1935*

FLOWERS BY THE SEA

When over the flowery, sharp pasture's
edge, unseen, the salt ocean

lifts its form—chickory and daisies
tied, released, seem hardly flowers alone

but color and the movement—or the shape
perhaps—of restlessness, whereas

the sea is circled and sways
peacefully upon its plantlike stem   *1935*

THE CATHOLIC BELLS

Tho' I'm no Catholic
I listen hard when the bells
in the yellow-brick tower
of their new church

ring down the leaves
ring in the frost upon them
and the death of the flowers
ring out the grackle

toward the south, the sky
darkened by them, ring in
the new baby of Mr. and Mrs.
Krantz which cannot

for the fat of its cheeks
open well its eyes, ring out
the parrot under its hood
jealous of the child

ring in Sunday morning
and old age which adds as it
takes away. Let them ring
only ring! over the oil

painting of a young priest
on the church wall advertising
last week's Novena to St.
Anthony, ring for the lame

young man in black with
gaunt cheeks and wearing a

Derby hat, who is hurrying
to 11 o'clock Mass (the

grapes still hanging to
the vines along the nearby
Concordia Halle like broken
teeth in the head of an

old man) Let them ring
for the eyes and ring for
the hands and ring for
the children of my friend

who no longer hears
them ring but with a smile
and in a low voice speaks
of the decisions of her

daughter and the proposals
and betrayals of her
husband's friends. O bells
ring for the ringing!

the beginning and the end
of the ringing! Ring ring
ring ring ring ring ring!
Catholic bells—!   *1935*

THE DANCE

In Breughel's great picture, The Kermess,
the dancers go round, they go round and
around, the squeal and the blare and the
tweedle of bagpipes, a bugle and fiddles
tipping their bellies (round as the thick-
sided glasses whose wash they impound)
their hips and their bellies off balance
to turn them. Kicking and rolling about
the Fair Grounds, swinging their butts, those
shanks must be sound to bear up under such
rollicking measures, prance as they dance
in Breughel's great picture, The Kermess.

                                    1944

From *PATERSON: BOOK I*

Preface

"Rigor of beauty is the quest. But how will you find beauty when it is locked in the mind past all remonstrance?"

To make a start,
out of particulars
and make them general, rolling
up the sum, by defective means—
Sniffing the trees,
just another dog
among a lot of dogs. What
else is there? And to do?
The rest have run out—
after the rabbits.
Only the lame stands—on
three legs. Scratch front and back.
Deceive and eat. Dig
a musty bone

For the beginning is assuredly
the end—since we know nothing, pure
and simple, beyond
our own complexities.

        Yet there is
no return: rolling up out of chaos,
a nine months' wonder, the city
the man, an identity—it can't be
otherwise—an
interpenetration, both ways. Rolling
up! obverse, reverse;
the drunk the sober; the illustrious
the gross; one. In ignorance
a certain knowledge and knowledge,
undispersed, its own undoing.

        (The multiple seed,
packed tight with detail, soured,
is lost in the flux and the mind,

distracted, floats off in the same
scum)

Rolling up, rolling up heavy with
numbers.

          It is the ignorant sun
rising in the slot of
hollow suns risen, so that never in this
world will a man live well in his body
save dying—and not know himself
dying; that is
the design. Renews himself
thereby, in addition and subtraction,
walking up and down.

          and the craft,
subverted by thought, rolling up, let
him beware lest he turn to no more than
the writing of stale poems . . .
Minds like beds always made up,
                    (more stony than a shore)
unwilling or unable.

                    Rolling in, top up,
under, thrust and recoil, a great clatter:
lifted as air, boated, multicolored, a
wash of seas—
from mathematics to particulars—

                    divided as the dew,
floating mists, to be rained down and
regathered into a river that flows
and encircles:

                    shells and animalcules
generally and so to man,

                    to Paterson.   *1946*

THE HORSE SHOW

Constantly near you, I never in my entire
sixty four years knew you so well as yesterday
or half so well. We talked. You were never

so lucid, so disengaged from all exigencies
of place and time. We talked of ourselves,
intimately, a thing never heard of between us.
How long have we waited? almost a hundred years.

You said, Unless there is some spark, some
spirit we keep within ourselves, life, a
continuing life's impossible—and it is all
we have. There is no other life, only the one.
The world of the spirits that comes afterward
is the same as our own, just like you sitting
there they come and talk to me, just the same.

They come to bother us. Why? I said. I don't
know. Perhaps to find out what we are doing.
Jealous, do you think? I don't know. I
don't know why they should want to come back.
I was reading about some men who had been
buried under a mountain, I said to her, and
one of them came back after two months,

digging himself out. It was in Switzerland,
you remember? Of course I remember. The
villagers tho't it was a ghost coming down
to complain. They were frightened. They
do come, she said, what you call
my "visions." I talk to them just as I
am talking to you. I see them plainly.

Oh if I could only read! You don't know
what adjustments I have made. All
I can do is to try to live over again
what I knew when your brother and you
were children—but I can't always succeed.
Tell me about the horse show. I have
been waiting all week to hear about it.

Mother darling, I wasn't able to get away.
Oh that's too bad. It was just a show;
they make the horses walk up and down
to judge them by their form. Oh is that
all? I tho't it was something else. Oh
they jump and run too. I wish you had been
there, I was so interested to hear about it.   *1949*

Ezra Pound

THE TREE

I stood still and was a tree amid the wood,
Knowing the truth of things unseen before;
Of Daphne and the laurel bow
And that god-feasting couple old
That grew elm-oak amid the wold.
'Twas not until the gods had been
Kindly entreated, and been brought within
Unto the hearth of their heart's home
That they might do this wonder thing;
Nathless I have been a tree amid the wood
And many a new thing understood
That was rank folly to my head before.

1908

SESTINA: ALTAFORTE

LOQUITUR: *En* Bertrans de Born. Dante Alighieri put this man in hell for
that he was a stirrer up of strife. Eccovi! Judge ye! Have I dug him up
again? The scene is at his castle, Altaforte. "Papiols" is his jongleur. "The
Leopard," the *device* of Richard Cœur de Lion.

I

Damn it all! all this our South stinks peace.
You whoreson dog, Papiols, come! Let's to music!
I have no life save when the swords clash.
But ah! when I see the standards gold, vair, purple, opposing
And the broad fields beneath them turn crimson,
Then howl I my heart nigh mad with rejoicing.

II

In hot summer have I great rejoicing
When the tempests kill the earth's foul peace,
And the lightnings from black heav'n flash crimson,

II-184

And the fierce thunders roar me their music
And the winds shriek through the clouds mad, opposing,
And through all the riven skies God's swords clash.

III

Hell grant soon we hear again the swords clash!
And the shrill neighs of destriers in battle rejoicing,
Spiked breast to spiked breast opposing!
Better one hour's stour than a year's peace
With fat boards, bawds, wine and frail music!
Bah! there's no wine like the blood's crimson!

IV

And I love to see the sun rise blood-crimson.
And I watch his spears through the dark clash
And it fills all my heart with rejoicing
And pries wide my mouth with fast music
When I see him so scorn and defy peace,
His lone might 'gainst all darkness opposing.

V

The man who fears war and squats opposing
My words for stour, hath no blood of crimson
But is fit only to rot in womanish peace
Far from where worth's won and the swords clash
For the death of such sluts I go rejoicing;
Yea, I fill all the air with my music.

VI

Papiols, Papiols, to the music!
There's no sound like to swords swords opposing,
No cry like the battle's rejoicing
When our elbows and swords drip the crimson
And our charges 'gainst "The Leopard's" rush clash.
May God damn for ever all who cry "Peace!"

VII

And let the music of the swords make them crimson!
Hell grant soon we hear again the swords clash!
Hell blot black for alway the thought "Peace!"   *1909*

BALLAD OF THE GOODLY FERE

Simon Zelotes speaketh it somewhile after the Crucifixion.

Ha' we lost the goodliest fere o' all
For the priests and the gallows tree?
Aye lover he was of brawny men,
O' ships and the open sea.

When they came wi' a host to take Our Man
His smile was good to see;
"First let these go!" quo' our Goodly Fere,
"Or I'll see ye damned," says he.

Aye, he sent us out through the crossed high spears,
And the scorn of his laugh rang free;
"Why took ye not me when I walked about
Alone in the town?" says he.

Oh, we drunk his "Hale" in the good red wine
When we last made company;
No capon priest was the Goodly Fere
But a man o' men was he.

I ha' seen him drive a hundred men
Wi' a bundle o' cords swung free,
That they took the high and holy house
For their pawn and treasury.

They'll no' get him a' in a book I think,
Though they write it cunningly;
No mouse of the scrolls was the Goodly Fere
But aye loved the open sea.

If they think they ha' snared our Goodly Fere
They are fools to the last degree.
"I'll go to the feast," quo' our Goodly Fere,
"Though I go to the gallows tree."

"Ye ha' seen me heal the lame and blind,
And wake the dead," says he;
"Ye shall see one thing to master all:
'Tis how a brave man dies on the tree."

A son of God was the Goodly Fere
That bade us his brothers be.
I ha' seen him cow a thousand men.
I have seen him upon the tree.

He cried no cry when they drave the nails
And the blood gushed hot and free;
The hounds of the crimson sky gave tongue
But never a cry cried he.

I ha' seen him cow a thousand men
On the hills o' Galilee;
They whined as he walked out calm between,
Wi' his eyes like the grey o' the sea,

Like the sea that brooks no voyaging
With the winds unleashed and free,
Like the sea that he cowed at Genseret
Wi' twey words spoke' suddenly.

A master of men was the Goodly Fere,
A mate of the wind and sea;
If they think they ha' slain our Goodly Fere
They are fools eternally.

I ha' seen him eat o' the honey-comb
Sin' they nailed him to the tree.   *1909*

AN IMMORALITY

Sing we for love and idleness,
Naught else is worth the having.

Though I have been in many a land,
There is naught else in living.

And I would rather have my sweet,
Though rose-leaves die of grieving,

Than do high deeds in Hungary
To pass all men's believing.   *1912*

A VIRGINAL

No, no! Go from me. I have left her lately.
I will not spoil my sheath with lesser brightness,
For my surrounding air hath a new lightness;
Slight are her arms, yet they have bound me straitly
And left me cloaked as with a gauze of æther;
As with sweet leaves; as with a subtle clearness.
Oh, I have picked up magic in her nearness
To sheathe me half in half the things that sheathe her.

No, no! Go from me. I have still the flavour,
Soft as spring wind that's come from birchen bowers.
Green come the shoots, aye April in the branches,
As winter's wound with her sleight hand she staunches,
Hath of the trees a likeness of the savour:
As white their bark, so white this lady's hours.   *1912*

THE ALCHEMIST

Chant for the Transmutation of Metals

Saîl of Claustra, Aelis, Azalais,
As you move among the bright trees;
As your voices, under the larches of Paradise
Make a clear sound,
Saîl of Claustra, Aelis, Azalais,
Raimona, Tibors, Berangère,
'Neath the dark gleam of the sky;
Under night, the peacock-throated,
Bring the saffron-coloured shell,
Bring the red gold of the maple,
Bring the light of the birch tree in autumn
Mirals, Cembelins, Audiarda,
                    Remember this fire.
Elain, Tireis, Alcmena
'Mid the silver rustling of wheat,
Agradiva, Anhes, Ardenca,
From the plum-coloured lake, in stillness,
From the molten dyes of the water
Bring the burnished nature of fire;

Briseis, Lianor, Loica,
From the wide earth and the olive,
From the poplars weeping their amber,
By the bright flame of the fishing torch
                              Remember this fire.
Midonz, with the gold of the sun, the leaf of the poplar, by the light of
      the amber,
Midonz, daughter of the sun, shaft of the tree, silver of the leaf, light
      of the yellow of the amber,
Midonz, gift of the God, gift of the light, gift of the amber of the sun,
                  Give light to the metal.
Anhes of Rocacoart, Ardenca, Aemelis,
From the power of grass,
From the white, alive in the seed,
From the heat of the bud,
From the copper of the leaf in autumn,
From the bronze of the maple, from the sap in the bough;
Lianor, Ioanna, Loica,
By the stir of the fin,
By the trout asleep in the gray-green of water;
Vanna, Mandetta, Viera, Alodetta, Picarda, Manuela
From the red gleam of copper,
Ysaut, Ydone, slight rustling of leaves,
Vierna, Jocelynn, daring of spirits,
By the mirror of burnished copper,
                        O Queen of Cypress,
Out of Erebus, the flat-lying breadth,
Breath that is stretched out beneath the world:
Out of Erebus, out of the flat waste of air, lying beneath the world;
Out of the brown leaf-brown colourless
                        Bring the imperceptible cool.
Elain, Tireis, Alcmena,
                        Quiet this metal!
Let the manes put off their terror, let them put off their aqueous bodies
      with fire.
Let them assume the milk-white bodies of agate.
Let them draw together the bones of the metal.

Selvaggia, Guiscarda, Mandetta,
                        Rain flakes of gold on the water
Azure and flaking silver of water,
Alcyon, Phætona, Alcmena,
Pallor of silver, pale lustre of Latona,

By these, from the malevolence of the dew
                    Guard this alembic.
Elain, Tireis, Allodetta
                    Quiet this metal.   *1913*

PORTRAIT D'UNE FEMME

Your mind and you are our Sargasso Sea,
London has swept about you this score years
And bright ships left you this or that in fee:
Ideas, old gossip, oddments of all things,
Strange spars of knowledge and dimmed wares of price.
Great minds have sought you—lacking someone else.
You have been second always. Tragical?
No. You preferred it to the usual thing:
One dull man, dulling and uxorious,
One average mind—with one thought less, each year.
Oh, you are patient, I have seen you sit
Hours, where something might have floated up.
And now you pay one. Yes, you richly pay.
You are a person of some interest, one comes to you
And takes strange gain away:
Trophies fished up; some curious suggestion;
Fact that leads nowhere; and a tale or two,
Pregnant with mandrakes, or with something else
That might prove useful and yet never proves,
That never fits a corner or shows use,
Or finds its hour upon the loom of days:
The tarnished, gaudy, wonderful old work;
Idols and ambergris and rare inlays,
These are your riches, your great store; and yet
For all this sea-hoard of deciduous things,
Strange woods half sodden, and new brighter stuff:
In the slow float of differing light and deep,
No! there is nothing! In the whole and all,
Nothing that's quite your own.
                    Yet this is you.   *1913*

THE RETURN

See, they return; ah, see the tentative
Movements, and the slow feet,

The trouble in the pace and the uncertain
Wavering!

See, they return, one, and by one,
With fear, as half-awakened;
As if the snow should hesitate
And murmur in the wind,
          and half turn back;
These were the "Wing'd-with-Awe,"
        Inviolable,

Gods of the wingèd shoe!
With them the silver hounds,
          sniffing the trace of air!

Haie! Haie!
    These were the swift to harry;
These the keen-scented;
These were the souls of blood.

Slow on the leash,
         pallid the leash-men! *1913*

THE STUDY IN ÆSTHETICS

The very small children in patched clothing,
Being smitten with an unusual wisdom,
Stopped in their play as she passed them
And cried up from their cobbles:

    Guarda! Ahi, guarda! ch' è be'a!

But three years after this
I heard the young Dante, whose last name I do not know—
For there are, in Sirmione, twenty-eight young Dantes and thirty-four
    Catulli;
And there had been a great catch of sardines,
And his elders
Were packing them in the great wooden boxes
For the market in Brescia, and he
Leapt about, snatching at the bright fish
And getting in both of their ways;
And in vain they commanded him to *sta fermo!*

And when they would not let him arrange
The fish in the boxes
He stroked those which were already arranged,
Murmuring for his own satisfaction
This identical phrase:

    Ch' è be'a.

And at this I was mildly abashed.   *1916*

APRIL

Nympharum membra disjecta

Three spirits came to me
And drew me apart
To where the olive boughs
Lay stripped upon the ground:
Pale carnage beneath bright mist.

    1917

THE COMING OF WAR: ACTAEON

An image of Lethe,
    and the fields
Full of faint light
    but golden,
Gray cliffs,
    and beneath them
A sea
Harsher than granite,
    unstill, never ceasing;
High forms
    with the movement of gods,
Perilous aspect;
    And one said:
"This is Actaeon."
    Actaeon of golden greaves!
Over fair meadows,
Over the cool face of that field,
Unstill, ever moving
Hosts of an ancient people,
The silent cortège.   *1917*

From HOMAGE TO SEXTUS PROPERTIUS

I

Shades of Callimachus, Coan ghosts of Philetas
It is in your grove I would walk,
I who come first from the clear font
Bringing the Grecian orgies into Italy,
                and the dance into Italy.
Who hath taught you so subtle a measure,
          in what hall have you heard it;
What foot beat out your time-bar,
         what water has mellowed your whistles?

Out-weariers of Apollo will, as we know, continue their Martian gen-
    eralities,
    We have kept our erasers in order.
A new-fangled chariot follows the flower-hung horses;
A young Muse with young loves clustered about her
            ascends with me into the æther, . . .
And there is no high-road to the Muses.

Annalists will continue to record Roman reputations,
Celebrities from the Trans-Caucasus will belaud Roman celebrities
And expound the distentions of Empire,
But for something to read in normal circumstances?
For a few pages brought down from the forked hill unsullied?
I ask a wreath which will not crush my head.
          And there is no hurry about it;
I shall have, doubtless, a boom after my funeral,
Seeing that long standing increases all things
              regardless of quality.

And who would have known the towers
         pulled down by a deal-wood horse;
Or of Achilles withstaying waters by Simois
Or of Hector spattering wheel-rims,
Or of Polydmantus, by Scamander, or Helenus and Deiphoibos?
Their door-yards would scarcely know them, or Paris.
Small talk O Ilion, and O Troad
         twice taken by Oetian gods,
If Homer had not stated your case!

And I also among the later nephews of this city
                    shall have my dog's day,
With no stone upon my contemptible sepulchre;
My vote coming from the temple of Phoebus in Lycia, at Patara,
And in the mean time my songs will travel,
And the devirginated young ladies will enjoy them
              when they have got over the strangeness,
For Orpheus tamed the wild beasts—
                  and held up the Threician river;
And Citharaon shook up the rocks by Thebes
       and danced them into a bulwark at his pleasure,
And you, O Polyphemus? Did harsh Galatea almost
Turn to your dripping horses, because of a tune, under Aetna?
We must look into the matter.
Bacchus and Apollo in favour of it,
There will be a crowd of young women doing homage to my palaver,
Though my house is not propped up by Taenarian columns from
      Laconia (associated with Neptune and Cerberus),
Though it is not stretched upon gilded beams;
My orchards do not lie level and wide
              as the forests of Phaecia,
              the luxurious and Ionian,
Nor are my caverns stuffed stiff with a Marcian vintage,
My cellar does not date from Numa Pompilius,
Nor bristle with wine jars,
Nor is it equipped with a frigidaire patent;
Yet the companions of the Muses
           will keep their collective nose in my books,
And weary with historical data, they will turn to my dance tune.

Happy who are mentioned in my pamphlets,
      the songs shall be a fine tomb-stone over their beauty.
              But against this?
Neither expensive pyramids scraping the stars in their route,
Nor houses modelled upon that of Jove in East Elis,
Nor the monumental effigies of Mausolus,
             are a complete elucidation of death.

Flame burns, rain sinks into the cracks
And they all go to rack ruin beneath the thud of the years.
Stands genius a deathless adornment,
           a name not to be worn out with the years.   *1919*

From HUGH SELWYN MAUBERLEY

I

E. P. ODE POUR L'ELECTION DE SON SEPULCHRE

For three years, out of key with his time,
He strove to resuscitate the dead art
Of poetry; to maintain "the sublime"
In the old sense. Wrong from the start—

No, hardly, but seeing he had been born
In a half savage country, out of date;
Bent resolutely on wringing lilies from the acorn;
Capaneus; trout for factitious bait;

Ἴδμεν γάρ τοι πάνθ’, ὅσ’ ἐνὶ Τροίῃ
Caught in the unstopped ear;
Giving the rocks small lee-way
The chopped seas held him, therefore, that year.

His true Penelope was Flaubert,
He fished by obstinate isles;
Observed the elegance of Circe's hair
Rather than the mottoes on sun-dials.

Unaffected by "the march of events,"
He passed from men's memory in *l'an trentiesme*
De son eage; the case presents
No adjunct to the Muses' diadem.

II

The age demanded an image
Of its accelerated grimace,
Something for the modern stage,
Not, at any rate, an Attic grace;

Not, not certainly, the obscure reveries
Of the inward gaze;
Better mendacities
Than the classics in paraphrase!

The "age demanded" chiefly a mould in plaster,
Made with no loss of time,

A prose kinema, not, not assuredly, alabaster
Or the "sculpture" of rhyme.

III

The tea-rose tea-gown, etc.
Supplants the mousseline of Cos,
The pianola "replaces"
Sappho's barbitos.

Christ follows Dionysus,
Phallic and ambrosial
Made way for macerations;
Caliban casts out Ariel.

All things are a flowing,
Sage Heracleitus says;
But a tawdry cheapness
Shall outlast our days.

Even the Christian beauty
Defects—after Samothrace;
We see τὸ καλὸν
Decreed in the market place.

Faun's flesh is not to us,
Nor the saint's vision.
We have the press for wafer;
Franchise for circumcision.

All men, in law, are equals.
Free of Pisistratus,
We choose a knave or an eunuch
To rule over us.

O bright Apollo,
τίν᾽ ἄνδρα, τίν᾽ ἥρωα, τίνα θεὸν
What god, man, or hero
Shall I place a tin wreath upon!

IV

These fought in any case,
and some believing,
                  pro domo, in any case . . .

Some quick to arm,
some for adventure,
some from fear of weakness,
some from fear of censure,
some for love of slaughter, in imagination,
learning later . . .
some in fear, learning love of slaughter;

Died some, pro patria,
        non "dulce" non "et decor" . . .
walked eye-deep in hell
believing in old men's lies, then unbelieving
came home, home to a lie,
home to many deceits,
home to old lies and new infamy;
usury age-old and age-thick
and liars in public places.

Daring as never before, wastage as never before.
Young blood and high blood,
fair cheeks, and fine bodies;

fortitude as never before

frankness as never before,
disillusions as never told in the old days,
hysterias, trench confessions,
laughter out of dead bellies.

V

There died a myriad,
And of the best, among them,

For an old bitch gone in the teeth,
For a botched civilization,

Charm, smiling at the good mouth,
Quick eyes gone under earth's lid,
For two gross of broken statues,
For a few thousand battered books.

YEUX GLAUQUES

Gladstone was still respected,
When John Ruskin produced

"King's Treasuries"; Swinburne
And Rossetti still abused.

Fœtid Buchanan lifted up his voice
When that faun's head of hers
Became a pastime for
Painters and adulterers.

The Burne-Jones cartons
Have preserved her eyes;
Still, at the Tate, they teach
Cophetua to rhapsodize;

Thin like brook-water,
With a vacant gaze.
The English Rubaiyat was still-born
In those days.

The thin, clear gaze, the same
Still darts out faunlike from the half-ruin'd face,
Questing and passive. . . .
"Ah, poor Jenny's case" . . .

Bewildered that a world
Shows no surprise
At her last maquero's
Adulteries.

"SIENA MI FE'; DISFECEMI MAREMMA"

Among the pickled fœtuses and bottled bones,
Engaged in perfecting the catalogue,
I found the last scion of the
Senatorial families of Strasbourg, Monsieur Verog.

For two hours he talked of Gallifet;
Of Dowson; of the Rhymers' Club;
Told me how Johnson (Lionel) died
By falling from a high stool in a pub . . .

But showed no trace of alcohol
At the autopsy, privately performed—
Tissue preserved—the pure mind
Arose toward Newman as the whiskey warmed.

Dowson found harlots cheaper than hotels;
Headlam for uplift; Image impartially imbued
With raptures for Bacchus, Terpsichore and the Church.
So spoke the author of "The Dorian Mood,"

M. Verog, out of step with the decade,
Detached from his contemporaries,
Neglected by the young,
Because of these reveries.

MR. NIXON

In the cream gilded cabin of his steam yacht
Mr. Nixon advised me kindly, to advance with fewer
Dangers of delay. "Consider
        "Carefully the reviewer.

"I was as poor as you are;
"When I began I got, of course,
"Advance on royalties, fifty at first," said Mr. Nixon,
"Follow me, and take a column,
"Even if you have to work free.

"Butter reviewers. From fifty to three hundred
"I rose in eighteen months;
"The hardest nut I had to crack
"Was Dr. Dundas.

"I never mentioned a man but with the view
"Of selling my own works.
"The tip's a good one, as for literature
"It gives no man a sinecure.

"And no one knows, at sight, a masterpiece.
"And give up verse, my boy,
"There's nothing in it."

         *   *   *   *

Likewise a friend of Bloughram's once advised me:
Don't kick against the pricks,
Accept opinion. The "Nineties" tried your game
And died, there's nothing in it.

XI

"Conservatrix of Milésien"
Habits of mind and feeling,
Possibly. But in Ealing
With the most bank-clerkly of Englishmen?

No, "Milesian" is an exaggeration.
No instinct has survived in her
Older than those her grandmother
Told her would fit her station.

XII

"Daphne with her thighs in bark
"Stretches toward me her leafy hands,"—
Subjectively. In the stuffed-satin drawing-room
I await The Lady Valentine's commands,

Knowing my coat has never been
Of precisely the fashion
To stimulate, in her,
A durable passion;

Doubtful, somewhat, of the value
Of well-gowned approbation
Of literary effort,
But never of The Lady Valentine's vocation:

Poetry, her border of ideas,
The edge, uncertain, but a means of blending
With other strata
Where the lower and higher have ending;

A hook to catch the Lady Jane's attention,
A modulation toward the theatre,
Also, in the case of revolution,
A possible friend and comforter.

* * * *

Conduct, on the other hand, the soul
"Which the highest cultures have nourished"

To Fleet St. where
Dr. Johnson flourished;

Beside this thoroughfare
The sale of half-hose has
Long since superseded the cultivation
Of Pierian roses.

ENVOI (1919)

Go, dumb-born book,
Tell her that sang me once that song of Lawes:
Hadst thou but song
As thou hast subjects known,
Then were there cause in thee that should condone
Even my faults that heavy upon me lie,
And build her glories their longevity.

Tell her that sheds
Such treasure in the air,
Recking naught else but that her graces give
Life to the moment,
I would bid them live
As roses might, in magic amber laid,
Red overwrought with orange and all made
One substance and one colour
Braving time.

Tell her that goes
With song upon her lips
But sings not out the song, nor knows
The maker of it, some other mouth
May be as fair as hers,
Might, in new ages, gain her worshippers
When our two dusts with Waller's shall be laid,
Siftings on siftings in oblivion,
Till change hath broken down
All things save Beauty alone.   1920

From CANTO I

And then went down to the ship,
Set keel to breakers, forth on the godly sea, and
We set up mast and sail on that swart ship,

Bore sheep aboard her, and our bodies also
Heavy with weeping, and winds from sternward
Bore us out onward with bellying canvas,
Circe's this craft, the trim-coifed goddess.
Then sat we amidships, wind jamming the tiller,
Thus with stretched sail, we went over sea till day's end.
Sun to his slumber, shadows o'er all the ocean,
Came we then to the bounds of deepest water,
To the Kimmerian lands, and peopled cities
Covered with close-webbed mist, unpierced ever
With glitter of sun-rays
Nor with stars stretched, nor looking back from heaven
Swartest night stretched over wretched men there.
The ocean flowing backward, came we then to the place
Aforesaid by Circe.
Here did they rites, Perimedes and Eurylochus,
And drawing sword from my hip
I dug the ell-square pitkin;
Poured we libations unto each the dead,
First mead and then sweet wine, water mixed with white flour.
Then prayed I many a prayer to the sickly death's-heads;
As set in Ithaca, sterile bulls of the best
For sacrifice, heaping the pyre with goods,
A sheep to Tiresias only, black and a bell-sheep.
Dark blood flowed in the fosse,
Souls out of Erebus, cadaverous dead, of brides
Of youths and of the old who had borne much;
Souls stained with recent tears, girls tender,
Men many, mauled with bronze lance heads,
Battle spoil, bearing yet dreary arms,
These many crowded about me; with shouting,
Pallor upon me, cried to my men for more beasts;
Slaughtered the herds, sheep slain of bronze;
Poured ointment, cried to the gods,
To Pluto the strong, and praised Proserpine;
Unsheathed the narrow sword,
I sat to keep off the impetuous impotent dead,
Till I should hear Tiresias.
But first Elpenor came, our friend Elpenor,
Unburied, cast on the wide earth,
Limbs that we left in the house of Circe,
Unwept, unwrapped in sepulchre, since toils urged other.
Pitiful spirit. And I cried in hurried speech:
"Elpenor, how art thou come to this dark coast?

"Cam'st thou afoot, outstripping seamen?"
                    And he in heavy speech:
"Ill fate and abundant wine. I slept in Circe's ingle.
"Going down the long ladder unguarded,
"I fell against the buttress,
"Shattered the nape-nerve, the soul sought Avernus.
"But thou, O King, I bid remember me, unwept, unburied,
"Heap up mine arms, be tomb by sea-bord, and inscribed:
"*A man of no fortune, and with a name to come.*
"And set my oar up, that I swung mid fellows."
And Anticlea came, whom I beat off, and then Tiresias Theban,
Holding his golden wand, knew me, and spoke first:
"A second time? why? man of ill star,
"Facing the sunless dead and this joyless region?
"Stand from the fosse, leave me my bloody bever
"For soothsay."
                    And I stepped back,
And he strong with the blood, said then: "Odysseus
"Shalt return through spiteful Neptune, over dark seas,
"Lose all companions." And then Anticlea came. . . .   *1917*

CANTO XIII

Kung walked
            by the dynastic temple
and into the cedar grove,
            and then out by the lower river,
And with him Khieu Tchi
            and Tian the low speaking
And "we are unknown," said Kung,
"You will take up charioteering?
            Then you will become known,
"Or perhaps I should take up charioteering, or archery?
"Or the practice of public speaking?"
And Tseu-lou said, "I would put the defences in order,"
And Khieu said, "If I were lord of a province
I would put it in better order than this is."
And Tchi said, "I would prefer a small mountain temple,
"With order in the observances,
            with a suitable performance of the ritual,"
And Tian said, with his hand on the strings of his lute
The low sounds continuing
            after his hand left the strings,

And the sound went up like smoke, under the leaves,
And he looked after the sound:
   "The old swimming hole,
"And the boys flopping off the planks,
"Or sitting in the underbrush playing mandolins."
   And Kung smiled upon all of them equally.
And Thseng-sie desired to know:
   "Which had answered correctly?"
And Kung said, "They have all answered correctly,
"That is to say, each in his nature."
And Kung raised his cane against Yuan Jang,
   Yuan Jang being his elder,
For Yuan Jang sat by the roadside pretending to
   be receiving wisdom.
And Kung said
   "You old fool, come out of it,
"Get up and do something useful."
   And Kung said
"Respect a child's faculties
"From the moment it inhales the clear air,
"But a man of fifty who knows nothing
   Is worthy of no respect."
And "When the prince has gathered about him
"All the savants and artists, his riches will be fully employed."
And Kung said, and wrote on the bo leaves:
   If a man have not order within him
He can not spread order about him;
And if a man have not order within him
His family will not act with due order;
   And if the prince have not order within him
He can not put order in his dominions.
And Kung gave the words "order"
and "brotherly deference"
And said nothing of the "life after death."
And he said
   "Anyone can run to excesses,
"It is easy to shoot past the mark,
"It is hard to stand firm in the middle."

And they said: If a man commit murder
   Should his father protect him, and hide him?
And Kung said:
   He should hide him.

And Kung gave his daughter to Kong-Tchang
    Although Kong-Tchang was in prison.
And he gave his niece to Nan-Young
    although Nan-Young was out of office.
And Kung said "Wang ruled with moderation,
    "In his day the State was well kept,
"And even I can remember
"A day when the historians left blanks in their writings,
"I mean for things they didn't know,
"But that time seems to be passing.
A day when the historians left blanks in their writings,
But that time seems to be passing."
And Kung said, "Without character you will
    be unable to play on that instrument
"Or to execute the music fit for the Odes.
"The blossoms of the apricot
    blow from the east to the west,
"And I have tried to keep them from falling."   *1925*

CANTO XLV

With *Usura*

With usura hath no man a house of good stone
each block cut smooth and well fitting
that design might cover their face,
with usura
hath no man a painted paradise on his church wall
harpes et luthes
or where virgin receiveth message
and halo projects from incision,
with usura
seeth no man Gonzaga his heirs and his concubines
no picture is made to endure nor to live with
but it is made to sell and sell quickly
with usura, sin against nature,
is thy bread ever more of stale rags
is thy bread dry as paper,
with no mountain wheat, no strong flour
with usura the line grows thick
with usura is no clear demarcation
and no man can find site for his dwelling.
Stone cutter is kept from his stone

weaver is kept from his loom
WITH USURA
wool comes not to market
sheep bringeth no gain with usura
Usura is a murrain, usura
blunteth the needle in the maid's hand
and stoppeth the spinner's cunning. Pietro Lombardo
came not by usura
Duccio came not by usura
nor Pier della Francesca; Zuan Bellin' not by usura
nor was 'La Calunnia' painted.
Came not by usura Angelico; came not Ambrogio Praedis,
Came no church of cut stone signed: *Adamo me fecit*.
Not by usura St Trophime
Not by usura Saint Hilaire,
Usura rusteth the chisel
It rusteth the craft and the craftsman
It gnaweth the thread in the loom
None learneth to weave gold in her pattern;
Azure hath a canker by usura; cramoisi is unbroidered
Emerald findeth no Memling
Usura slayeth the child in the womb
It stayeth the young man's courting
It hath brought palsey to bed, lyeth
between the young bride and her bridegroom
                         CONTRA NATURAM
They have brought whores for Eleusis
Corpses are set to banquet
at behest of usura.   *1937*

Hilda Doolittle (H. D.)

EVENING

The light passes
from ridge to ridge,
from flower to flower—
the hypaticas, wide-spread
under the light
grow faint—
the petals reach inward,
the blue tips bend
toward the bluer heart
and the flowers are lost.

The cornel-buds are still white,
but shadows dart
from the cornel-roots—
black creeps from root to root,
each leaf
cuts another leaf on the grass,
shadow seeks shadow,
then both leaf
and leaf-shadow are lost.   *1916*

HEAT

O wind, rend open the heat,
cut apart the heat,
rend it to tatters.

Fruit cannot drop
through this thick air—
fruit cannot fall into heat
that presses up and blunts
the points of pears
and rounds the grapes.

Cut the heat—
plough through it,
turning it on either side
of your path.   *1916*

ORCHARD

I saw the first pear
as it fell—
the honey-seeking, golden-banded,
the yellow swarm
was not more fleet than I,
(spare us from loveliness)
and I fell prostrate,
crying:
you have flayed us
with your blossoms,
spare us the beauty
of fruit-trees.

The honey-seeking
paused not,
the air thundered their song,
and I alone was prostrate.

O rough-hewn
god of the orchard,
I bring an offering—
do you, alone unbeautiful,
son of the god,
spare us from loveliness:

these fallen hazel-nuts,
stripped late of their green sheaths,
grapes, red-purple,
their berries
dripping with wine,
pomegranates already broken,
and shrunken figs
and quinces untouched,
I bring you as offering.   *1916*

PEAR TREE

Silver dust,
lifted from the earth,

higher than my arms reach,
you have mounted,
O, silver,
higher than my arms reach,
you front us with great mass;

no flower ever opened
so staunch a white leaf,
no flower ever parted silver
from such rare silver;

O, white pear,
your flower-tufts
thick on the branch
bring summer and ripe fruits
in their purple hearts.

1916

THE HELMSMAN

O be swift—
we have always known you wanted us.

We fled inland with our flocks,
we pastured them in hollows,
cut off from the wind
and the salt track of the marsh.

We worshipped inland—
we stepped past wood-flowers,
we forgot your tang,
we brushed wood-grass.

We wandered from pine-hills
through oak and scrub-oak tangles,
we broke hyssop and bramble,
we caught flower and new bramble-fruit
in our hair: we laughed
as each branch whipped back,
we tore our feet in half-buried rocks
and knotted roots and acorn-cups.

We forgot—we worshipped,
we parted green from green,

we sought further thickets,
we dipped our ankles
through leaf-mold and earth,
and wood and wood-bank enchanted us—
and the feel of the clefts in the bark,
and the slope between tree and tree—
and a slender path strung field to field
and wood to wood
and hill to hill
and the forest after it.

We forgot for a moment;
tree-resin, tree-bark,
sweat of a torn branch
were sweet to the taste.

We were enchanted with the fields,
the tufts of coarse grass—
in the shorter grass—
we loved all this.

But now, our boat climbs—hesitates—drops—
climbs—hesitates—crawls back—
climbs—hesitates—
O be swift—
we have always known you wanted us.   *1916*

OREAD

Whirl up, sea—
whirl your pointed pines,
splash your great pines
on our rocks,
hurl your green over us,
cover us with your pools of fir.
1924

THE POOL

Are you alive?
I touch you.
You quiver like a sea-fish.
I cover you with my net.
What are you—banded one?
1924

FRAGMENT THIRTY-SIX

I know not what to do: my mind is divided.—Sappho.

I know not what to do,
my mind is reft:
is song's gift best?
is love's gift loveliest?
I know not what to do,
now sleep has pressed
weight on your eyelids.

Shall I break your rest,
devouring, eager?
is love's gift best?
nay, song's the loveliest:
yet were you lost,
what rapture
could I take from song?
what song were left?

I know not what to do:
to turn and slake
the rage that burns,
with my breath burn
and trouble your cool breath?
so shall I turn and take
snow in my arms?
(is love's gift best?)
yet flake on flake
of snow were comfortless,
did you lie wondering,
wakened yet unawake.

Shall I turn and take
comfortless snow within my arms?
press lips to lips
that answer not,
press lips to flesh
that shudders not nor breaks?

Is love's gift best?

shall I turn and slake
all the wild longing?
O I am eager for you!
as the Pleiads shake
white light in whiter water
so shall I take you?

My mind is quite divided,
my minds hesitate,
so perfect matched,
I know not what to do:
each strives with each
as two white wrestlers
standing for a match,
ready to turn and clutch
yet never shake muscle nor nerve nor tendon;
so my mind waits
to grapple with my mind,
yet I lie quiet,
I would seem at rest.

I know not what to do:
strain upon strain,
sound surging upon sound
makes my brain blind;
as a wave-line may wait to fall
yet (waiting for its falling)
still the wind may take
from off its crest,
white flake on flake of foam,
that rises,
seeming to dart and pulse
and rend the light,
so my mind hesitates
above the passion
quivering yet to break,
so my mind hesitates
above my mind,
listening to song's delight.

I know not what to do:
will the sound break,
rending the night

with rift on rift of rose
and scattered light?
will the sound break at last
as the wave hesitant,
or will the whole night pass
and I lie listening awake?   1924

LETHE

Nor skin nor hide nor fleece
   Shall cover you,
Nor curtain of crimson nor fine
Shelter of cedar-wood be over you,
   Nor the fir-tree
   Nor the pine.

Nor sight of whin nor gorse
   Nor river-yew,
Nor fragrance of flowering bush,
Nor wailing of reed-bird to waken you,
   Nor of linnet,
   Nor of thrush.

Nor word nor touch nor sight
   Of lover; you
Shall long through the night but for this:
The roll of the full tide to cover you
   Without question,
   Without kiss.   1924

ERIGE COR TUUM AD ME IN CAELUM

(September 1940)

I

Lift up your eyes on high,
under the sky—
indeed?
watch planets swerve and lend
lustre to partner-planet,
as they serve
magnetic stress, and turn
subservient to your hands,

your will that guides
majestic cycle of obedient tides?

lift up our eyes to you?
no, God, we stare and stare,
upon a nearer thing
that greets us here,
Death, violent and near.

2

The alchemy and mystery is this,
no cross to kiss,
but a cross pointing on a compass-face,
east, west, south, north;

the secret of the ages is revealed,
the book un-sealed,
the fisherman entangled in his nets
felled where he waded
for the evening catch,
the house-door
swinging on the broken latch,
the woman with her basket on the quay,
shading her eyes to see
if the last boat
really is the last,
the house-dog lost,
the little hen escaped,
the precious hay-rick scattered,
and the empty cage,
the book of life is open,
turn and read:

the linnet picking at the wasted seed
is holy ghost,
the weed,
broken by iron axle,
is the flower
magicians bartered for.   *1957*

Robinson Jeffers

SHINE, PERISHING REPUBLIC

While this America settles in the mould of its vulgarity, heavily thickening to empire,
And protest, only a bubble in the molten mass, pops and sighs out, and
the mass hardens,

I sadly smiling remember that the flower fades to make fruit, the fruit
rots to make earth.
Out of the mother; and through the spring exultances, ripeness and
decadence; and home to the mother.

You making haste haste on decay: not blameworthy; life is good, be it
stubbornly long or suddenly
A mortal splendor: meteors are not needed less than mountains: shine,
perishing republic.

But for my children, I would have them keep their distance from the
thickening center; corruption
Never has been compulsory, when the cities lie at the monster's feet
there are left the mountains.

And boys, be in nothing so moderate as in love of man, a clever servant,
insufferable master.
There is the trap that catches noblest spirits, that caught—they say—
God, when he walked on earth.   *1925*

JOY

Though joy is better than sorrow, joy is not great;
Peace is great, strength is great.
Not for joy the stars burn, not for joy the vulture
Spreads her gray sails on the air
Over the mountain; not for joy the worn mountain
Stands, while years like water

Trench his long sides. "I am neither mountain nor bird
Nor star; and I seek joy."
The weakness of your breed: yet at length quietness
Will cover those wistful eyes.   *1925*

GALE IN APRIL

Intense and terrible beauty, how has our race with the frail naked
    nerves,
So little a craft swum down from its far launching?
Why now, only because the northwest blows and the headed grass
    billows,
Great seas jagging the west and on the granite
Blanching, the vessel is brimmed, this dancing play of the world is too
    much passion.
A gale in April so overfilling the spirit,
Though his ribs were thick as the earth's, arches of mountain, how shall
    one dare to live,
Though his blood were like the earth's rivers and his flesh iron,
How shall one dare to live? One is born strong, how do the weak
    endure it?
The strong lean upon death as on a rock,
After eighty years there is shelter and the naked nerves shall be covered
    with deep quietness,
O beauty of things go on, go on, O torture
Of intense joy I have lasted out my time, I have thanked God and
    finished,
Roots of millennial trees fold me in the darkness,
Northwest wind shake their tops, not to the root, not to the root, I have
    passed
From beauty to the other beauty, peace, the night splendor.   *1925*

HURT HAWKS

I

The broken pillar of the wing jags from the clotted shoulder,
The wing trails like a banner in defeat,
No more to use the sky forever but live with famine
And pain a few days: cat nor coyote
Will shorten the week of waiting for death, there is game without talons.
He stands under the oak-bush and waits
The lame feet of salvation; at night he remembers freedom

And flies in a dream, the dawns ruin it.
He is strong and pain is worse to the strong, incapacity is worse.
The curs of the day come and torment him
At distance, no one but death the redeemer will humble that head,
The intrepid readiness, the terrible eyes.
The wild God of the world is sometimes merciful to those
That ask mercy, not often to the arrogant.
You do not know him, you communal people, or you have forgotten him;
Intemperate and savage, the hawk remembers him;
Beautiful and wild, the hawks, and men that are dying, remember him.

II

I'd sooner, except the penalties, kill a man than a hawk; but the great redtail
Had nothing left but unable misery
From the bone too shattered for mending, the wing that trailed under his talons when he moved.
We had fed him six weeks, I gave him freedom,
He wandered over the foreland hill and returned in the evening, asking for death,
Not like a beggar, still eyed with the old
Implacable arrogance. I gave him the lead gift in the twilight. What fell was relaxed,
Owl-downy, soft feminine feathers; but what
Soared: the fierce rush: the night-herons by the flooded river cried fear at its rising
Before it was quite unsheathed from reality.   1928

MEDITATION ON SAVIOURS

I

When I considered it too closely, when I wore it like an element and smelt it like water,
Life is become less lovely, the net nearer than the skin, a little troublesome, a little terrible.

I pledged myself awhile ago not to seek refuge, neither in death nor in a walled garden,
In lies nor gated loyalties, nor in the gates of contempt, that easily lock the world out of doors.

Here on the rock it is great and beautiful, here on the foam-wet granite
    sea-fang it is easy to praise
Life and water and the shining stones: but whose cattle are the herds
    of the people that one should love them?

If they were yours, then you might take a cattle-breeder's delight in the
    herds of the future. Not yours.
Where the power ends let love, before it sours to jealousy. Leave the
    joys of government to Caesar.

Who is born when the world wanes, when the brave soul of the world
    falls on decay in the flesh increasing
Comes one with a great level mind, sufficient vision, sufficient blindness,
    and clemency for love.

This is the breath of rottenness I smelt; from the world waiting, stalled
    between storms, decaying a little,
Bitterly afraid to be hurt, but knowing it cannot draw the saviour
    Caesar but out of the blood-bath.

The apes of Christ lift up their hands to praise love: but wisdom
    without love is the present saviour,
Power without hatred, mind like a many-bladed machine subduing the
    world with deep indifference.

The apes of Christ itch for a sickness they have never known; words
    and the little envies will hardly
Measure against that blinding fire behind the tragic eyes they have
    never dared to confront.

II

Point Lobos lies over the hollowed water like a humped whale swimming
    to shoal; Point Lobos
Was wounded with that fire; the hills at Point Sur endured it; the
    palace at Thebes; the hill Calvary.

Out of incestuous love power and then ruin. A man forcing the
    imaginations of men,
Possessing with love and power the people: a man defiling his own
    household with impious desire.

King Oedipus reeling blinded from the palace doorway, red tears
    pouring from the torn pits

Under the forehead; and the young Jew writhing on the domed hill in
the earthquake, against the eclipse

Frightfully uplifted for having turned inward to love the people:—that
root was so sweet Oh, dreadful agonist?—
I saw the same pierced feet, that walked in the same crime to its
expiation; I heard the same cry.

A bad mountain to build your world on. Am I another keeper of the
people, that on my own shore,
On the gray rock, by the grooved mass of the ocean, the sicknesses
I left behind me concern me?

Here where the surf has come incredible ways out of the splendid west,
over the deeps
Light nor life sounds forever; here where enormous sundowns flower
and burn through color to quietness;

Then the ecstasy of the stars is present? As for the people, I have found
my rock, let them find theirs.
Let them lie down at Caesar's feet and be saved; and he in his time
reap their daggers of gratitude.

III

Yet I am the one made pledges against the refuge contempt, that easily
locks the world out of doors.
This people as much as the sea-granite is part of the God from whom
I desire not to be fugitive.

I see them: they are always crying. The shored Pacific makes perpetual
music, and the stone mountains
Their music of silence, the stars blow long pipings of light: the people
are always crying in their hearts.

One need not pity; certainly one must not love. But who has seen
peace, if he should tell them where peace
Lives in the world . . . they would be powerless to understand; and
he is not willing to be reinvolved.

IV

How should one caught in the stone of his own person dare tell the
people anything but relative to that?

But if a man could hold in his mind all the conditions at once, of man
and woman, of civilized

And barbarous, of sick and well, of happy and under torture, of living
and dead, of human and not
Human, and dimly all the human future:—what should persuade him
to speak? And what could his words change?

The mountain ahead of the world is not forming but fixed. But the
man's words would be fixed also,
Part of that mountain, under equal compulsion; under the same present
compulsion in the iron consistency.

And nobody sees good or evil but out of a brain a hundred centuries
quieted, some desert
Prophet's, a man humped like a camel, gone mad between the mud-
walled village and the mountain sepulchres.

V

Broad wagons before sunrise bring food into the city from the open
farms, and the people are fed.
They import and they consume reality. Before sunrise a hawk in the
desert made them their thoughts.

VI

Here is an anxious people, rank with suppressed bloodthirstiness.
Among the mild and unwarlike
Gautama needed but live greatly and be heard, Confucius needed but
live greatly and be heard.

This people has not outgrown blood-sacrifice, one must writhe on the
high cross to catch at their memories;
The price is known. I have quieted love; for love of the people I would
not do it. For power I would do it.

—But that stands against reason: what is power to a dead man, dead
under torture?—What is power to a man
Living, after the flesh is content? Reason is never a root, neither of act
nor desire.

For power living I would never do it; they are not delightful to touch,
one wants to be separate. For power

After the nerves are put away underground, to lighten the abstract
    unborn children toward peace . . .

A man might have paid anguish indeed. Except he had found the
    standing sea-rock that even this last
Temptation breaks on; quieter than death but lovelier; peace that quiets
    the desire even of praising it.

VII

Yet look: are they not pitiable? No: if they lived forever they would
    be pitiable:
But a huge gift reserved quite overwhelms them at the end; they are
    able then to be still and not cry.

And having touched a little of the beauty and seen a little of the beauty
    of things, magically grow
Across the funeral fire or the hidden stench of burial themselves into
    the beauty they admired,

Themselves into the God, themselves into the sacred steep unconscious-
    ness they used to mimic
Asleep between lamp's death and dawn, while the last drunkard
    stumbled homeward down the dark street.

They are not to be pitied but very fortunate; they need no saviour,
    salvation comes and takes them by force,
It gathers them into the great kingdoms of dust and stone, the blown
    storms, the stream's-end ocean.

With this advantage over their granite grave-marks, of having realized
    the petulant human consciousness
Before, and then the greatness, the peace: drunk from both pitchers:
    these to be pitied? These not fortunate?

But while he lives let each man make his health in his mind, to love
    the coast opposite humanity
And so be freed of love, laying it like bread on the waters; it is worst
    turned inward, it is best shot farthest.

Love, the mad wine of good and evil, the saint's and murderer's, the
    mote in the eye that makes its object
Shine the sun black; the trap in which it is better to catch the inhuman
    God than the hunter's own image.   *1928*

FIRE ON THE HILLS

The deer were bounding like blown leaves
Under the smoke in front of the roaring wave of the brushfire;
I thought of the smaller lives that were caught.
Beauty is not always lovely; the fire was beautiful, the terror
Of the deer was beautiful; and when I returned
Down the black slopes after the fire had gone by, an eagle
Was perched on the jag of a burnt pine,
Insolent and gorged, cloaked in the folded storms of his shoulders.
He had come from far off for the good hunting
With fire for his beater to drive the game; the sky was merciless
Blue, and the hills merciless black,
The sombre-feathered great bird sleepily merciless between them.
I thought, painfully, but the whole mind,
The destruction that brings an eagle from heaven is better than mercy.

1932

MARGRAVE

On the small marble-paved platform
On the turret on the head of the tower,
Watching the night deepen.
I feel the rock-edge of the continent
Reel eastward with me below the broad stars,
I lean on the broad worn stones of the parapet top
And the stones and my hands that touch them reel eastward.
The inland mountains go down and new lights
Glow over the sinking east rim of the earth.
The dark ocean comes up,
And reddens the western stars with its fog-breath
And hides them with its mounded darkness.

The earth was the world and man was its measure, but our minds have
    looked
Through the little mock-dome of heaven the telescope-slotted observa-
    tory eye-ball, there space and multitude came in
And the earth is a particle of dust by a sand-grain sun, lost in a name-
    less cove of the shores of a continent.
Galaxy on galaxy, innumerable swirls of innumerable stars, endured
    as it were forever and humanity
Came into being, its two or three million years are a moment, in a
    moment it will certainly cease out from being.

And galaxy on galaxy endure after that as it were forever . . . But man
  is conscious,
He brings the world to focus in a feeling brain,
In a net of nerves catches the splendor of things,
Breaks the somnambulism of nature . . . His distinction perhaps.
Hardly his advantage. To slaver for contemptible pleasures
And scream with pain are hardly an advantage.
Consciousness? The learned astronomer
Analyzing the light of most remote star-swirls
Has found them—or a trick of distance deludes his prism—
All at incredible speeds fleeing outward from ours.
I thought, no doubt they are fleeing the contagion
Of consciousness that infects this corner of space.

For often I have heard the hard rocks I handled
Groan, because lichen and time and water dissolve them,
And they have to travel down the strange falling scale
Of soil and plants and the flesh of beasts to become
The bodies of men; they murmur at their fate
In the hollows of windless nights, they'd rather be anything
Than human flesh played on by pain and joy,
They pray for annihilation sooner, but annihilation's
Not in the book yet.

        So, I thought, the rumor
Of human consciousness has gone abroad in the world,
The sane uninfected far-outer universes
Flee it in a panic of escape, as men flee the plague
Taking a city: for look at the fruits of consciousness:
As in young Walter Margrave when he'd been sentenced for murder:
  he was thinking when they brought him back
To the cell in jail, "I've only a moment to arrange my thoughts, I must
  think quickly, I must think clearly,
And settle the world in my mind before I kick off," but to feel the
  curious eyes of his fellow-prisoners
And the wry-mouthed guard's and so forth torment him through the
  steel bars put his mind in a stupor, he could only
Sit frowning, ostentatiously unafraid. "But I can control my mind, their
  eyes can't touch my will.
One against all. What use is will at this end of everything? A kind of
  nausea is the chief feeling . . .
In my stomach and throat . . . but in my head pride: I fought a good
  fight and they can't break me; alone, unbroken,

Against a hundred and twenty-three million people. They are going to
    kill the best brain perhaps in the world,
That might have made such discoveries in science
As would set the world centuries ahead, for I had the mind and the
    power. Boo, it's their loss. Blind fools,
Killing their best." When his mind forgot the eyes it made rapid capri-
    cious pictures instead of words,
But not of the medical school and the laboratories, its late intense
    interest; not at all of his crime; glimpses
Of the coast-range at home; the V of a westward canyon with the
    vibrating
Blue line of the ocean strung sharp across it; that domed hill up the
    valley, two cows like specks on the summit
And a beautiful-colored jungle of poison-oak at the foot; his sister half
    naked washing her hair,
"My dirty sister," whose example and her lovers had kept him chaste
    by revulsion; the reed-grown mouth of the river
And the sand-bar against the stinging splendor of the sea . . . and
    anguish behind all the pictures
(He began to consider his own mind again) "like a wall they hang on."
    Hang. The anguish came forward, an actual
Knife between two heart-beats, the organ stopped and then raced. He
    experimented awhile with his heart,
Making in his mind a picture of a man hanged, pretending to himself
    it was to happen next moment,
Trying to observe whether the beat suspended—"suspended," he thought
    —in systole or in diastole.
The effect soon failed; the anguish remained. "Ah my slack lawyer,
    damn him, let slip chance after chance.
Scared traitor." Then broken pictures of the scenes in court, the jury,
    the judge, the idlers, and not one face
But bleak with hatred. "But I met their eyes, one against all." Suddenly
    his mind became incapable
Of making pictures or words, but still wildly active, striking in all
    directions like a snake in a fire,
Finding nothing but the fiery element of its own anguish. He got up
    and felt the guard's eyes and sat down,
Turned side-face, resting his chin on his fist, frowning and trembling.
    He saw clearly in his mind the little
Adrenal glands perched on the red-brown kidneys, as if all his doomed
    tissues became transparent,
Pouring in these passions their violent secretion
Into his blood-stream, raising the tension unbearably. And the thyroids;
    tension, tension. A long course of that

Should work grave changes. "If they tortured a man like a laboratory
    dog for discovery: there'd be value gained: but by process
Of law for vengeance, because his glands and his brain have made him
    act in another than common manner:
You incredible breed of asses!" He smiled self-consciously in open scorn
    of the people, the guard at the door
To observe that smile—"my God, do I care about the turnkey's opinion?"
    —suddenly his mind again
Was lashing like a burnt snake. Then it was torpid for a while. This
    continued for months.

His father had come to visit him, he saw the ruinous white-haired head
Through two steel wickets under the bluish electric light that seemed
    to peel the skin from the face.
Walter said cheerfully too loudly, "Hullo. You look like a skull." The
    shaven sunk jaws in answer chewed
Inaudible words. Walter with an edge of pleasure thought "Once he
    was stronger than I! I used to admire
This poor old man's strength when I was a child," and said "Buck up,
    old fellow, it will soon be over. Here's nothing
To cry for. Do you think I'm afraid to die? It's good people that fear
    death, people with the soft streak
Of goodness in them fear death: but I, you know, am a monster, don't
    you read the papers? Caught at last:
I fought a hundred and twenty-three million people. How's Hazel?
    How's the farm? I could get out of this scrape
By playing dementia, but I refuse to, there's not an alienist living
Could catch me out. I'm the king of Spain dying for the world. I've
    been persecuted since I was born
By a secret sect, they stuck pins into me
And fed me regular doses of poison for a certain reason. Why do you
    pretend that you're my father?
God is. . . . Believe me, I could get by with it.
But I refuse."
                    Old Margrave looked timidly at the two guards
    listening, and drew his brown tremulous hand
Across his eyes below the white hair. "I thought of going to try to see
    the governor, Walter."
"That's it!" "Don't hope for anything, Walter, they tell me that there's
    no hope. They say that I shan't even
Be allowed to see him." "By God," the young man said trembling, "you
    can if you want to. Never believe that lawyer.
If I'd had Dorking: but you couldn't afford him. Poor men have no
    right to breed sons. I'd not be here

If you'd had money to put me through college. Tell the governor
I know he won't pardon, but he can commute the sentence to life
    imprisonment. Then I can read and study,
I can help the penitentiary doctor, I can do something to help humanity.
    Tell him it's madness
To throw such a brain as mine into the garbage. Don't deny my guilt
    but tell him my reasons.
I kidnapped the little girl to get money to finish my medical education.
    What's one child's life
Against a career like mine that might have saved
Thousands of children? Say I'd isolated the organism of infantile
    paralysis: I'd have done more:
But that alone would save thousands of children. I was merciful; she
    died quietly; tell him that.
It was only pithing a little white frog.
Don't you think you can make him understand? I'm not a criminal: I
    judge differently from others. I wasn't
Afraid to think for myself. All I did
Was for money for my education, to help humanity. And tell him if
    I've done wrong—what's wrong?—I've paid for it
With frightful suffering: the more developed the brain the greater the
    agony. He won't admit that. Oh God,
These brains the size of a pea! To be juried
And strangled by a hundred and twenty-three million peas. Go down
    on your knees to him. You owe me that: you'd no right
To breed, you're poor.
But you itched for a woman, you had to fetch me out of the happy hill
    of not-being. Pfah, to hug a woman
And make this I. That's the evil in the world, that letter. I—I—Tell the
    governor
That I'm not afraid of dying, that I laugh at death. No, no, we'll laugh
    in private. Tell him I'm crazy.
I've come to that: after being the only sane mind among a hundred and
    twenty-three million peas.
Anything, anything . . ."

                                        He had let his nerves go wild on
    purpose, to edge on the old man to action, now at last
Escaping utterly out of control they stumbled into a bog of thick sobs.
    The guards pulled him up
And walked him away as if he were half insensible. He was not
    insensible, but more acutely aware
Than ever in his life before of all that touched him, and of shame and
    anguish.

You would be wise, you far stars,
To flee with the speed of light this infection.
For here the good sane invulnerable material
And nature of things more and more grows alive and cries.
The rock and water grow human, the bitter weed
Of consciousness catches the sun, it clings to the near stars,
Even the nearer portion of the universal God
Seems to become conscious, yearns and rejoices
And suffers: I believe this hurt will be healed
Some age of time after mankind has died,
Then the sun will say "What ailed me a moment?" and resume
The old soulless triumph, and the iron and stone earth
With confident inorganic glory obliterate
Her ruins and fossils, like that incredible unfading red rose
Of desert in Arizona glowing life to scorn,
And grind the chalky emptied seed-shells of consciousness
The bare skulls of the dead to powder; after some million
Courses around the sun her sadness may pass:
But why should you worlds of the virgin distance
Endure to survive what it were better to escape.

I also am not innocent
Of contagion, but have spread my spirit on the deep world.
I have gotten sons and sent the fire wider.
I have planted trees, they also feel while they live.
I have humanized the ancient sea-sculptured cliff
And the ocean's wreckage of rock
Into a house and a tower,
Hastening the sure decay of granite with my hammer,
Its hard dust will make soft flesh;
And have widened in my idleness
The disastrous personality of life with poems,
That are pleasant enough in the breeding but go bitterly at last
To envy oblivion and the early deaths of nobler
Verse, and much nobler flesh;
And I have projected my spirit
Behind the superb sufficient forehead of nature
To gift the inhuman God with this rankling consciousness.

But who is our judge? It is likely the enormous
Beauty of the world requires for completion our ghostly increment,
It has to dream, and dream badly, a moment of its night.

On the little stone-belted platform
On the turret on the head of the tower,

Between the stars and the earth,
And the ocean and the continent.
One ship's light shines and eclipses
Very far out, behind the high waves on the hill of water.
In the east under the Hyades and rising Orion
Are many cities and multitudes of people,
But westward a long way they are few enough.
It is fortunate to look westward as to look upward.
In the south the dark river-mouth pool mirrors a star
That stands over Margrave's farmhouse. The old man has lost it, he
    isn't there any more. He went down to the river-mouth
Last December, when recent rains had opened the stream and the
    salmon were running. Fishermen very solemnly
Stood all along the low sand like herons, and sea-lions offshore in the
    rolling waves with deep wet voices
Coughed at each other; the sea air is hoarse with their voices that time
    of year. Margrave had rambled since noon
Among the little folds of the seaward field that he had forgotten to plow
    and was trying to sell
Though he used to love it, but everything was lost now. He lay awhile
    on his face in the rotting stubble and random
Unsown green blades, then he got up and drifted over the ridge to the
    river-mouth sands, unaimed,
Pale and gap-eyed, as the day moon a clear morning, opposite the sun.
    He noticed with surprise the many
Fishermen like herons in the shallows and along the sands; and then
    that his girl Hazel was with him: who'd feared
What he might do to himself and had come to watch him when he lay
    face down in the field. "I know what they're doing,"
He said slyly, "Hazel, they're fishing! I guess they don't know,"
He whispered, "about our trouble. Oh no, don't tell them." She said,
    "Don't go down, father, your face would tell them.
Sit here on the edge of grass, watch the brown river meet the blue sea.
    Do look: that boy's caught something.
How the line cuts the water and the small wheel sings." "If I'd been
    rich,"
Old Margrave answered, "they'd have fixed the hook for . . . Walter
    . . . with some other bait. It sticks in my mind that . . . Wal-
    ter
Blames me too much." "Look," Hazel said, "he's landing it now. Oh,
    it's a big one." "I dreamed about fishing,
Some time ago," he answered, "but we were the fish. I saw the people
    all running reaching for prizes

That dangled on long lines from the sky. A lovely girl or a sack of
   money or a case of whiskey,
Or fake things like reputation, hackle-feathers and a hook. A man would
   reach up and grab and the line
Jerked, then you knew by his face that the hook was in him, wherever
   he went. Often they're played for half
A lifetime before they're landed: others, like . . . my son . . . pulled
   up short. Oh, Oh,
It's not a dream." He said gently, "He wanted money for his education,
   but you poor girl
Wanted boy friends, now you've got a round belly. That's the hook.
   I wanted children and got
Walter and you. Hm? Hooked twice is too much. Let's walk." "Not that
   way: let's go up home, daddy.
It makes you unhappy to see them fishing." "No," he answered, "nothing
   can. I have it in my pocket." She walked behind him,
Hiding herself, ashamed of her visible pregnancy and her brother's fate;
   but when the old man stumbled
And wavered on the slope she went beside him to support him, her
   right hand under his elbow, and wreathed his body
With the other arm.

                                   The clear brown river ran eagerly
         through the sand-hill, undercutting its banks,
That slid in masses; tall waves walked very slowly up stream from the
   sea, and stood
Stationary in the throat of the channel before they dissolved. The rock
   the children call Red-cap stood
High and naked among the fishermen, the orange lichen on its head.
   At the sea-end of the sand
Two boys and a man had rifles instead of rods, they meant to punish
   the salmon-devouring sea-lions
Because the fish were fewer than last year; whenever a sleek brown
   head with the big questioning eyes
Broke sea they fired. Margrave had heard the shots but taken no notice,
   but when he walked by the stream
He saw a swimmer look up from the water and its round dark eye
Suddenly burst red blood before it went down. He cried out and twisted
   himself from Hazel's hand
And ran like a squirrel along the stream-bank. "I'll not allow it!" He
   snatched at a rifle. "Why should my lad
Be hanged for killing and all you others go free?" He wrestled feebly
   to gain the rifle, the sand-bank

Slid under his feet, he slipped and lay face down in the running stream
    and was hauled astrand. Then Hazel
Came running heavily, and when he was able to walk she led him
    away. The sea-beast, blinded but a painful
Vain gleam, starved long before it could die; old Margrave still lives.
    Death's like a little gay child that runs
The world around with the keys of salvation in his foolish fingers,
    lends them at random where they're not wanted,
But often withholds them where most required.

                                       Margrave's
    son at this time
Had only four days to wait, but death now appeared so dreadful to him
    that to speak of his thoughts and the abject
Horror, would be to insult humanity more than it deserves. At last the
    jerked hemp snapped the neck sideways
And bruised the cable of nerves that threads the bone rings; the
    intolerably strained consciousness in a moment changed.
It was strangely cut in two parts at the noose, the head's
Consciousness from the body's; both were set free and flamed; the head's
    with flashing paradisal light
Like the wild birth of a star, but crying in bewilderment and suddenly
    extinguished; the body's with a sharp emotion
Of satisfied love, a wave of hard warmth and joy, that ebbed cold on
    darkness. After a time of darkness
The dreams that follow upon death came and subsided, like fibrillar
    twitchings
Of the nerves unorganizing themselves; and some of the small dreams
    were delightful and some, slight miseries,
But nothing intense; then consciousness wandered home from the cell
    to the molecule, was utterly dissolved and changed;
Peace was the end of the play, so far as concerns humanity. Oh beautiful
    capricious little saviour,
Death, the gay child with the gipsy eyes, to avoid you for a time I think
    is virtuous, to fear you is insane.

On the little stone-girdled platform
Over the earth and the ocean
I seem to have stood a long time and watched the stars pass.
They also shall perish I believe.
Here to-day, gone to-morrow, desperate wee galaxies
Scattering themselves and shining their substance away
Like a passionate thought. It is very well ordered.

                                             1932

STILL THE MIND SMILES

Still the mind smiles at its own rebellions,
Knowing all the while that civilization and the other evils
That make humanity ridiculous, remain
Beautiful in the whole fabric, excesses that balance each other
Like the paired wings of a flying bird.
Misery and riches, civilization and squalid savagery,
Mass war and the odor of unmanly peace:
Tragic flourishes above and below the normal of life.
In order to value this fretful time
It is necessary to remember our norm, the unaltered passions,
The same-colored wings of imagination,
That the crowd clips, in lonely places new-grown; the unchanged
Lives of herdsmen and mountain farms,
Where men are few, and few tools, a few weapons, and their dawns
  are beautiful.
From here for normal one sees both ways,
And listens to the splendor of God, the exact poet, the sonorous
Antistrophe of desolation to the strophe multitude.   *1933*

CRUMBS OR THE LOAF

If one should tell them what's clearly seen
They'd not understand; if they understood they would not believe;
If they understood and believed they'd say,
"Hater of men, annihilating with a sterile enormous
Splendor our lives: where are our lives?"
A little chilled perhaps, but not hurt. But it's quite true
The invulnerable love is not bought for nothing.
It is better no doubt to give crumbs than the loaf; make fables again,
Tell people not to fear death, toughen
Their bones if possible with bitter fables not to fear life.
—And one's own, not to have pity too much;
For it seems compassion sticks longer than the other colors, in this
  bleaching cloth.   *1933*

LIFE FROM THE LIFELESS

Spirits and illusions have died,
The naked mind lives
In the beauty of inanimate things.

Flowers wither, grass fades, trees wilt,
The forest is burnt;
The rock is not burnt.

The deer starve, the winter birds
Die on their twigs and lie
In the blue dawns in the snow.

Men suffer want and become
Curiously ignoble; as prosperity
Made them curiously vile.

But look how noble the world is,
The lonely-flowing waters, the secret-
Keeping stones, the flowing sky.

1935

GRAY WEATHER

It is true that, older than man and ages to outlast him, the Pacific surf
Still cheerfully pounds the worn granite drum;
But there's no storm; and the birds are still, no song; no kind of excess;
Nothing that shines, nothing is dark;
There is neither joy nor grief nor a person, the sun's tooth sheathed in
cloud,
And life has no more desires than a stone.
The stormy conditions of time and change are all abrogated, the essential
Violences of survival, pleasure,
Love, wrath and pain, and the curious desire of knowing, all perfectly
suspended.
In the cloudy light, in the timeless quietness,
One explores deeper than the nerves or heart of nature, the womb
or soul,
To the bone, the careless white bone, the excellence.   *1935*

THE PURSE-SEINE

Our sardine fishermen work at night in the dark of the moon; daylight
or moonlight
They could not tell where to spread the net, unable to see the phos-
phorescence of the shoals of fish.
They work northward from Monterey, coasting Santa Cruz; off New
Year's Point or off Pigeon Point

The look-out man will see some lakes of milk-color light on the sea's
    night-purple; he points, and the helmsman
Turns the dark prow, the motorboat circles the gleaming shoal and
    drifts out her seine-net. They close the circle
And purse the bottom of the net, then with great labor haul it in.

                              I cannot tell you
How beautiful the scene is, and a little terrible, then, when the crowded
    fish
Know they are caught, and wildly beat from one wall to the other of
    their closing destiny the phosphorescent
Water to a pool of flame, each beautiful slender body sheeted with
    flame, like a live rocket
A comet's tail wake of clear yellow flame; while outside the narrowing
Floats and cordage of the net great sea-lions come up to watch, sighing
    in the dark; the vast walls of night
Stand erect to the stars.
                    Lately I was looking from a night mountain-top
On a wide city, the colored splendor, galaxies of light: how could I help
    but recall the seine-net
Gathering the luminous fish? I cannot tell you how beautiful the city
    appeared, and a little terrible.
I thought, We have geared the machines and locked all together into
    interdependence; we have built the great cities; now
There is no escape. We have gathered vast populations incapable of free
    survival, insulated
From the strong earth, each person in himself helpless, on all dependent.
    The circle is closed, and the net
Is being hauled in. They hardly feel the cords drawing, yet they shine
    already. The inevitable mass-disasters
Will not come in our time nor in our children's, but we and our
    children
Must watch the net draw narrower, government take all powers—or
    revolution, and the new government
Take more than all, add to kept bodies kept souls—or anarchy, the
    mass-disasters.
                      These things are Progress;
Do you marvel our verse is troubled or frowning, while it keeps its
    reason? Or it lets go, lets the mood flow
In the manner of the recent young men into mere hysteria, splintered
    gleams, crackled laughter. But they are quite wrong.
There is no reason for amazement: surely one always knew that cultures
    decay, and life's end is death.   *1937*

THE ANSWER

Then what is the answer?—Not to be deluded by dreams.
To know that great civilizations have broken down into violence, and
    their tyrants come, many times before.
When open violence appears, to avoid it with honor or choose the least
    ugly faction; these evils are essential.
To keep one's own integrity, be merciful and uncorrupted and not wish
    for evil; and not be duped
By dreams of universal justice or happiness. These dreams will not be
    fulfilled.
To know this, and to know that however ugly the parts appear the
    whole remains beautiful. A severed hand
Is an ugly thing, and man dissevered from the earth and stars and his
    history . . . for contemplation or in fact . . .
Often appears atrociously ugly. Integrity is wholeness, the greatest
    beauty is
Organic wholeness, the wholeness of life and things, the divine beauty
    of the universe. Love that, not man
Apart from that, or else you will share man's pitiful confusions, or
    drown in despair when his days darken.   1937

NOVA

That Nova was a moderate star like our good sun; it stored no doubt a
    little more than it spent
Of heat and energy until the increasing tension came to the trigger-
    point
Of a new chemistry; then what was already flaming found a new
    manner of flaming ten-thousandfold
More brightly for a brief time; what was a pin-point fleck on a sensitive
    plate at the great telescope's
Eye-piece now shouts down the steep night to the naked eye, a nine-day
    super-star.
                                        It is likely our moderate
Father the sun will sometime put off his nature for a similar glory. The
    earth would share it; these tall
Green trees would become a moment's torches and vanish, the oceans
    would explode into invisible steam,
The ships and the great whales fall through them like flaming meteors
    into the emptied abysm, the six mile
Hollows of the Pacific sea-bed might smoke for a moment. Then the
    earth would be like the pale proud moon,

Nothing but vitrified sand and rock would be left on earth. This is a
    probable death-passion
For the sun's planets; we have no knowledge to assure us it may not
    happen at any moment of time.

Meanwhile the sun shines wisely and warm, trees flutter green in the
    wind, girls take their clothes off
To bathe in the cold ocean or to hunt love; they stand laughing in the
    white foam, they have beautful
Shoulders and thighs, they are beautiful animals, all life is beautiful.
    We cannot be sure of life for one moment;
We can, by force and self-discipline, by many refusals and a few
    assertions, in the teeth of fortune assure ourselves
Freedom and integrity in life or integrity in death. And we know that
    the enormous invulnerable beauty of things
Is the face of God, to live gladly in its presence, and die without grief
    or fear knowing it survives us.   1937

WATCH THE LIGHTS FADE

    Gray steel, cloud-shadow-stained,
    The ocean takes the last lights of evening.
    Loud is the voice and the foam lead-color,
    And flood-tide devours the sands.

    Here stand, like an old stone,
    And watch the lights fade and hear the sea's voice.
    Hate and despair take Europe and Asia,
    And the sea-wind blows cold.

    Night comes: night will claim all.
    The world is not changed, only more naked:
    The strong struggle for power, and the weak
    Warm their poor hearts with hate.

    Night comes: come into the house,
    Try around the dial for a late news-cast.
    These others are America's voices: naïve and
    Powerful, spurious, doom-touched.

    How soon? Four years or forty?
    Why should an old stone pick at the future?
    Stand on your shore, old stone, be still while the
    Sea-wind salts your head white.   1941

THE BLOODY SIRE

It is not bad. Let them play.
Let the guns bark and the bombing-plane
Speak his prodigious blasphemies.
It is not bad, it is high time,
Stark violence is still the sire of all the world's values.

What but the wolf's tooth whittled so fine
The fleet limbs of the antelope?
What but fear winged the birds, and hunger
Jeweled with such eyes the great goshawk's head?
Violence has been the sire of all the world's values.

Who would remember Helen's face
Lacking the terrible halo of spears?
Who formed Christ but Herod and Casear,
The cruel and bloody victories of Caesar?
Violence, the bloody sire of all the world's values.

Never weep, let them play,
Old violence is not too old to beget new values.

_1941_

Marianne Moore

POETRY

I, too, dislike it: there are things that are important beyond all this fiddle.
  Reading it, however, with a perfect contempt for it, one discovers in
  it after all, a place for the genuine.
      Hands that can grasp, eyes
      that can dilate, hair that can rise
        if it must, these things are important not because a

high-sounding interpretation can be put upon them but because they are
  useful. When they become so derivative as to become unintelligible,
  the same thing may be said for all of us, that we
      do not admire what
      we cannot understand: the bat
        holding on upside down or in quest of something to

eat, elephants pushing, a wild horse taking a roll, a tireless wolf under
  a tree, the immovable critic twitching his skin like a horse that feels
      a flea, the base-
  ball fan, the statistician—
      nor is it valid
        to discriminate against "business documents and

school-books"; all these phenomena are important. One must make a
      distinction
    however: when dragged into prominence by half poets, the result is
        not poetry,
  nor till the poets among us can be
      "literalists of
      the imagination"—above
        insolence and triviality and can present

for inspection, "imaginary gardens with real toads in them," shall we
      have

it. In the meantime, if you demand on the one hand,
the raw material of poetry in
all its rawness and
that which is on the other hand
genuine, you are interested in poetry.   *1921*

CRITICS AND CONNOISSEURS

There is a great amount of poetry in unconscious
fastidiousness. Certain Ming
products, imperial floor-coverings of coach-
wheel yellow, are well enough in their way but I have seen something
that I like better—a
mere childish attempt to make an imperfectly ballasted animal
stand up,
similar determination to make a pup
eat his meat from the plate.

I remember a swan under the willows in Oxford,
with flamingo-coloured, maple-
leaflike feet. It reconnoitred like a battleship. Disbelief and conscious fastidiousness were the staple
ingredients in its
disinclination to move. Finally its hardihood was not proof
against its
proclivity to more fully appraise such bits
of food as the stream

bore counter to it; it made away with what I gave it
to eat. I have seen this swan and
I have seen you; I have seen ambition without
understanding in a variety of forms. Happening to stand
by an ant-hill, I have
seen a fastidious ant carrying a stick north, south, east, west, till
it turned on
itself, struck out from the flower-bed into the lawn,
and returned to the point

from which it had started. Then abandoning the stick as
useless and overtaxing its
jaws with a particle of whitewash—pill-like but
heavy, it again went through the same course of procedure.

What is
there in being able
to say that one has dominated the stream in an attitude of self-
defence;
in proving that one has had the experience
of carrying a stick?   *1924*

PETER

Strong and slippery, built for the midnight grass-party confronted by
four cats,
he sleeps his time away—the detached first claw on the foreleg, which
corresponds
to the thumb, retracted to its tip; the small tuft of fronds
or katydid-legs above each eye, still numbering the units in each
group;
the shadbones regularly set about the mouth, to droop or rise

in unison like the porcupine's quills—motionless. He lets himself be flattened out by gravity, as it were a piece of seaweed tamed and weakened by
exposure to the sun; compelled when extended, to lie
stationary. Sleep is the result of his delusion that one must do as
well as one can for oneself; sleep—epitome of what is to

him as to the average person, the end of life. Demonstrate on him how
the lady caught the dangerous southern snake, placing a forked stick
on either
side of its innocuous neck; one need not try to stir
him up; his prune-shaped head and alligator eyes are not a party to
the
joke. Lifted and handled, he may be dangled like an eel or set

up on the forearm like a mouse; his eyes bisected by pupils of a pin's
width, are flickeringly exhibited, then covered up. May be? I should
say
might have been; when he has been got the better of in a
dream—as in a fight with nature or with cats—we all know it.
Profound sleep is
not with him a fixed illusion. Springing about with froglike ac-

curacy, emitting jerky cries when taken in the hand, he is himself
again; to sit caged by the rungs of a domestic chair would be unprofit-

able—human. What is the good of hypocrisy? It
    is permissible to choose one's employment, to abandon the wire
        nail, the
        roly-poly, when it shows signs of being no longer a pleas-

ure, to score the adjacent magazine with a double line of strokes. He can
    talk, but insolently says nothing. What of it? When one is frank,
        one's very
presence is a compliment. It is clear that he can see
    the virtue of naturalness, that he is one of those who do not regard
    the published fact as a surrender. As for the disposition

invariably to affront, an animal with claws wants to have to use
    them; that eel-like extension of trunk into tail is not an accident. To
leap, to lengthen out, divide the air—to purloin, to pursue.
    To tell the hen: fly over the fence, go in the wrong way in your
        perturba-
    tion—this is life; to do less would be nothing but dishonesty.

1924

A GRAVE

Man looking into the sea,
  taking the view from those who have as much right to it as you have
    to it yourself,
it is human nature to stand in the middle of a thing,
but you cannot stand in the middle of this;
the sea has nothing to give but a well excavated grave.
The firs stand in a procession, each with an emerald turkey-foot at
    the top,
reserved as their contours, saying nothing;
repression, however, is not the most obvious characteristic of the sea;
the sea is a collector, quick to return a rapacious look.
There are others besides you who have worn that look—
whose expression is no longer a protest; the fish no longer investigate
    them
for their bones have not lasted:
men lower nets, unconscious of the fact that they are desecrating a
    grave,
and row quickly away—the blades of the oars
moving together like the feet of water-spiders as if there were no such
    thing as death.
The wrinkles progress among themselves in a phalanx—beautiful under
    networks of foam,

and fade breathlessly while the sea rustles in and out of the seaweed;
the birds swim through the air at top speed, emitting catcalls as here-
    tofore—
the tortoise-shell scourges about the feet of the cliffs, in motion beneath
    them;
and the ocean, under the pulsation of lighthouses and noise of bell-
    buoys,
advances as usual, looking as if it were not that ocean in which dropped
    things are bound to sink—
in which if they turn and twist, it is neither with volition nor con-
    sciousness.   1924

SNAKES, MONGOOSES, SNAKE-CHARMERS
AND THE LIKE

I have a friend who would give a price for those long fingers all of
    one length—
those hideous bird's claws, for that exotic asp and the mongoose—
products of the country in which everything is hard work, the country
    of the grass-getter,
the torch-bearer, the dog-servant, the messenger-bearer, the holy-man.
Engrossed in this distinguished worm nearly as wild and as fierce as the
    day it was caught,
he gazes as if incapable of looking at anything with a view to analysis.
"The slight snake rippling quickly through the grass,
the leisurely tortoise with its pied back,
the chameleon passing from twig to stone, from stone to straw,"
lit his imagination at one time; his admiration now converges upon
    this.
Thick, not heavy, it stands up from its travelling-basket,
the essentially Greek, the plastic animal all of a piece from nose to tail;
one is compelled to look at it as at the shadows of the alps
imprisoning in their folds like flies in amber, the rhythms of the skating
    rink.
This animal to which from the earliest times, importance has attached,
fine as its worshippers have said—for what was it invented?
To show that when intelligence in its pure form
has embarked on a train of thought which is unproductive, it will come
    back?
We do not know; the only positive thing about it is its shape; but why
    protest?
The passion for setting people right is in itself an afflictive disease.
Distaste which takes no credit to itself is best.   1924

TO A STEAM ROLLER

The illustration
is nothing to you without the application.
    You lack half wit. You crush all the particles down
        into close conformity, and then walk back and forth on them.

Sparkling chips of rock
are crushed down to the level of the parent block.
    Were not "impersonal judgment in aesthetic
        matters, a metaphysical impossibility," you

might fairly achieve
it. As for butterflies, I can hardly conceive
    of one's attending upon you, but to question
        the congruence of the complement is vain, if it exists.   *1924*

TO A SNAIL

If "compression is the first grace of style,"
you have it. Contractility is a virtue
as modesty is a virtue.
It is not the acquisition of any one thing
that is able to adorn,
or the incidental quality that occurs
as a concomitant of something well said,
that we value in style,
but the principle that is hid:
in the absence of feet, "a method of conclusions";
"a knowledge of principles,"
in the curious phenomenon of your occipital horn.
        1924

SILENCE

My father used to say,
"Superior people never make long visits,
have to be shown Longfellow's grave
or the glass flowers at Harvard.
Self-reliant like the cat—
that takes its prey to privacy,
the mouse's limp tail hanging like a shoelace from its mouth—

they sometimes enjoy solitude,
and can be robbed of speech
by speech which has delighted them.
The deepest feeling always shows itself in silence;
not in silence, but restraint."
Nor was he insincere in saying, "Make my house your inn."
Inns are not residences.   1924

THE MONKEYS

winked too much and were afraid of snakes. The zebras, supreme in
their abnormality; the elephants with their fog-coloured skin
    and strictly practical appendages
        were there, the small cats; and the parrakeet—
            trivial and humdrum on examination, destroying
        bark and portions of the food it could not eat.

I recall their magnificence, now not more magnificent
than it is dim. It is difficult to recall the ornament,
    speech, and precise manner of what one might
        call the minor acquaintances twenty
            years back; but I shall not forget him—that Gilgamesh
                among
        the hairy carnivora—that cat with the

wedge-shaped, slate-grey marks on its forelegs and the resolute tail,
astringently remarking, "They have imposed on us with their pale
    half-fledged protestations, trembling about
        in inarticulate frenzy, saying
            it is not for us to understand art; finding it
        all so difficult, examining the thing

as if it were inconceivably arcanic, as symmet-
rically frigid as if it had been carved out of chrysoprase
    or marble—strict with tension, malignant
        in its power over us and deeper
            than the sea when it proffers flattery in exchange for hemp,
            rye, flax, horses, platinum, timber, and fur."   1935

THE STEEPLE-JACK

Dürer would have seen a reason for living
        in a town like this, with eight stranded whales
    to look at; with the sweet sea air coming into your house

on a fine day, from water etched
        with waves as formal as the scales
on a fish.

One by one, in two's, in three's, the seagulls keep
        flying back and forth over the town clock,
or sailing around the lighthouse without moving their wings—
rising steadily with a slight
        quiver of the body—or flock
mewing where

a sea the purple of the peacock's neck is
        paled to greenish azure as Dürer changed
the pine green of the Tyrol to peacock blue and guinea
grey. You can see a twenty-five-
        pound lobster and fish-nets arranged
to dry. The

whirlwind fife-and-drum of the storm bends the salt
        marsh grass, disturbs stars in the sky and the
star on the steeple; it is a privilege to see so
much confusion.

                A steeple-jack in red, has let
        a rope down as a spider spins a thread;
he might be part of a novel, but on the sidewalk a
sign says C. J. Poole, Steeple-Jack,
        in black and white; and one in red
and white says

Danger. The church portico has four fluted
        columns, each a single piece of stone, made
modester by white-wash. This would be a fit haven for
waifs, children, animals, prisoners,
        and presidents who have repaid
sin-driven

senators by not thinking about them. One
        sees a school-house, a post-office in a
store, fish-houses, hen-houses, a three-masted schooner on
the stocks. The hero, the student,
        the steeple-jack, each in his way,
is at home.

It scarcely could be dangerous to be living
   in a town like this, of simple people
who have a steeple-jack placing danger-signs by the church
when he is gilding the solid-
   pointed star, which on a steeple
stands for hope.   1935

THE HERO

Where there is personal liking we go.
   Where the ground is sour; where there are
   weeds of beanstalk height,
   snakes' hypodermic teeth, or
   the wind brings the "scarebabe voice"
   from the neglected yew set with
   the semi-precious cat's eyes of the owl—
awake, asleep, "raised ears extended to fine points," and so
on—love won't grow.

We do not like some things, and the hero
   doesn't; deviating head-stones
   and uncertainty;
   going where one does not wish
   to go; suffering and not
   saying so; standing and listening where something
   is hiding. The hero shrinks
as what it is flies out on muffled wings, with twin yellow
eyes—to and fro—

with quavering water-whistle note, low,
   high, in basso-falsetto chirps
   until the skin creeps.
   Jacob when a-dying, asked
   Joseph: Who are these? and blessed
   both sons, the younger most, vexing Joseph. And
   Joseph was vexing to some.
Cincinnatus was; Regulus; and some of our fellow
men have been, though

devout, like Pilgrim having to go slow
   to find his roll; tired but hopeful—
   hope not being hope
   until all ground for hope has

vanished; and lenient, looking
upon a fellow creature's error with the
  feelings of a mother—a
woman or a cat. The decorous frock-coated Negro
  by the grotto

answers the fearless sightseeing hobo
  who asks the man she's with, what's this,
  what's that, where's Martha
  buried, "Gen-ral Washington
  there; his lady, here"; speaking
  as if in a play—not seeing her; with a
  sense of human dignity
and reverence for mystery, standing like the shadow
of the willow.

Moses would not be grandson to Pharaoh.
  It is not what I eat that is
  my natural meat,
  the hero says. He's not out
  seeing a sight but the rock
  crystal thing to see—the startling El Greco
  brimming with inner light—that
covets nothing that it has let go. This then you may know
as the hero.   1935

THE JERBOA

TOO MUCH

A Roman had an
artist, a freedman,
  contrive a cone—pine-cone
  or fir-cone—with holes for a fountain. Placed on
    the Prison of St. Angelo, this cone
    of the Pompeys which is known

now as the Popes', passed
for art. A huge cast
  bronze, dwarfing the peacock
  statue in the garden of the Vatican,
    it looks like a work of art made to give
    to a Pompey, or native

of Thebes. Others could
build, and understood
   making colossi and
   how to use slaves, and kept crocodiles and put
      baboons on the necks of giraffes to pick
      fruit, and used serpent magic.

They had their men tie
hippopotami
   and bring out dapple dog-
   cats to course antelopes, dikdik, and ibex;
      or used small eagles. They looked on as theirs,
      impallas and onigers,

the wild ostrich herd
with hard feet and bird
   necks rearing back in the
   dust like a serpent preparing to strike, cranes,
      mongooses, storks, anoas, Nile geese;
      and there were gardens for these—

combining planes, dates,
limes, and pomegranates,
   in avenues—with square
   pools of pink flowers, tame fish, and small frogs. Besides
      yarns dyed with indigo, and red cotton,
      they had a flax which they spun

into fine linen
cordage for yachtsmen.
   These people liked small things;
   they gave to boys little paired playthings such as
      nests of eggs, ichneumon and snake, paddle
      and raft, badger and camel;

and made toys for them-
selves: the royal totem;
   and toilet-boxes marked
   with the contents. Lords and ladies put goose-grease
      paint in round bone boxes with pivoting
      lid incised with the duck-wing

or reverted duck-
head; kept in a buck

or rhinoceros horn,
the ground horn; and locust oil in stone locusts.
It was a picture with a fine distance;
of drought, and of assistance

in time, from the Nile
rising slowly, while
the pig-tailed monkey on
slab-hands, with arched-up slack-slung gait, and the brown
dandy, looked at the jasmine two-leafed twig
and bud, cactus-pads, and fig.

Dwarfs here and there, lent
to an evident
poetry of frog greys,
duck-egg greens, and egg-plant blues, a fantasy
and a verisimilitude that were
right to those with, everywhere,

power over the poor.
The bees' food is your
food. Those who tended flower-
beds and stables were like the king's cane in the
form of a hand, or the folding bedroom
made for his mother of whom

he was fond. Princes
clad in queens' dresses,
calla or petunia
white, that trembled at the edge, and queens in a
king's underskirt of fine-twilled thread like silk-
worm gut, as bee-man and milk-

maid, kept divine cows
and bees; limestone brows,
and gold-foil wings. They made
basalt serpents and portraits of beetles; the
king gave his name to them and he was named
for them. He feared snakes, and tamed

Pharaoh's rat, the rust-
backed mongoose. No bust
of it was made, but there

was pleasure for the rat. Its restlessness was
   its excellence; it was praised for its wit;
   and the jerboa, like it,

a small desert rat,
and not famous, that
   lives without water, has
   happiness. Abroad seeking food, or at home
      in its burrow, the Sahara field-mouse
      has a shining silver house

of sand. O rest and
joy, the boundless sand,
   the stupendous sand-spout,
   no water, no palm-trees, no ivory bed,
      tiny cactus; but one would not be he
      who has nothing but plenty.   *1935*

WHAT ARE YEARS?

   What is our innocence,
   what is our guilt? All are
      naked, none is safe. And whence
   is courage: the unanswered question,
   the resolute doubt,—
      dumbly calling, deafly listening—that
   in misfortune, even death,
         encourages others
         and in its defeat, stirs

   the soul to be strong? He
sees deep and is glad, who
      accedes to mortality
   and in his imprisonment rises
   upon himself as
   the sea in a chasm, struggling to be
   free and unable to be,
         in its surrendering
         finds its continuing.

   So he who strongly feels,
behaves. The very bird,
      grown taller as he sings, steels

his form straight up. Though he is captive,
his mighty singing
says, satisfaction is a lowly
thing, how pure a thing is joy.
    This is mortality.
    this is eternity.   *1941*

HE "DIGESTETH HARDE YRON"

Although the aepyornis
   or roc that lived in Madagascar, and
the moa are extinct,
the camel-sparrow, linked
   with them in size—the large sparrow
Xenophon saw walking by a stream—was and is
a symbol of justice.

   This bird watches his chicks with
     a maternal concentration—and he's
been mothering the eggs
at night six weeks—his legs
     their only weapon of defence.
He is swifter than a horse; he has a foot hard
as a hoof; the leopard

     is not more suspicious. How
     could he, prized for plumes and eggs and young, use**d**
even as a riding-
beast, respect men hiding
     actor-like in ostrich-skins, with
the right hand making the neck move as if alive and
from a bag the left hand

     strewing grain, that ostriches
     might be decoyed and killed! Yes this is he
whose plume was anciently
the plume of justice; he
     whose comic duckling head on its
great neck revolves with compass-needle nervous**s**
when he stands guard, in S-

     like foragings as he is
     preening the down on his leaden-skinned back.

The egg piously shown
as Leda's very own
    from which Castor and Pollux hatched,
was an ostrich-egg. And what could have been more fit
for the Chinese lawn it

    grazed on as a gift to an
    emperor who admired strange birds, than this
one who builds his mud-made
nest in dust yet will wade
    in lake or sea till only the head shows.

        .   .   .   .   .   .

    Six hundred ostrich-brains served
    at one banquet, the ostrich-plume-tipped tent
and desert spear, jewel-
gorgeous ugly egg-shell
    goblets, eight pairs of ostriches
in harness, dramatize a meaning always missed
by the externalist.

    The power of the visible
    is the invisible; as even where
no tree of freedom grows,
so-called brute courage knows.
    Heroism is exhausting, yet
it contradicts a greed that did not wisely spare
the harmless solitaire

    or great auk in its grandeur;
    unsolicitude having swallowed up
all giant birds but an
alert gargantuan
    little-winged, magnificently speedy running-bird. This one
remaining rebel
is the sparrow-camel.   *1941*

BIRD-WITTED

    With innocent wide penguin eyes, three
        large fledgling mocking-birds below
    the pussy-willow tree,
        stand in a row,

wings touching, feebly solemn,
till they see
    their no longer larger
    mother bringing
something which will partially
feed one of them.

Toward the high-keyed intermittent squeak
    of broken carriage-springs, made by
the three similar, meek-
    coated bird's-eye
freckled forms she comes; and when
from the beak
    of one, the still living
    beetle has dropped
out, she picks it up and puts
it in again.

Standing in the shade till they have dressed
    their thickly-filamented, pale
pussy-willow-surfaced
    coats, they spread tail
and wings, showing one by one,
the modest
    white stripe lengthwise on the
    tail and crosswise
underneath the wing, and the
accordion

is closed again. What delightful note
    with rapid unexpected flute-
sounds leaping from the throat
    of the astute
grown bird, comes back to one from
the remote
    unenergetic sun-
    lit air before
the brood was here? How harsh
the bird's voice has become.

A piebald cat observing them,
    is slowly creeping toward the trim

trio on the tree-stem.
    Unused to him
the three make room—uneasy
new problem.
        A dangling foot that missed
        its grasp, is raised
and finds the twig on which it
planned to perch. The

parent darting down, nerved by what chills
    the blood, and by hope rewarded—
of toil—since nothing fills
    squeaking unfed
mouths, wages deadly combat,
and half kills
        with bayonet beak and
        cruel wings, the
intellectual cautious-
ly creeping cat.   *1941*

NEVERTHELESS

you've seen a strawberry
        that's had a struggle; yet
        was, where the fragments met,

a hedgehog or a star-
        fish for the multitude
        of seeds. What better food

than apple-seeds—the fruit
        within the fruit—locked in
        like counter-curved twin

hazel-nuts? Frost that kills
        the little rubber-plant-
        leaves of *kok-saghyz*-stalks, can't

harm the roots; they still grow
        in frozen ground. Once where
        there was a prickly-pear-

    leaf clinging to barbed wire,
       a root shot down to grow
       in earth two feet below;

  as carrots form mandrakes
       or a ram's-horn root some-
       times. Victory won't come

to me unless I go
       to it; a grape-tendril
       ties a knot in knots till

  knotted thirty times,—so
       the bound twig that's under-
       gone and over-gone, can't stir.

The weak overcomes its
       menace, the strong over-
       comes itself. What is there

like fortitude! What sap
       went through that little thread
       to make the cherry red!   *1944*

THE WOOD-WEASEL

emerges daintily, the skunk—
don't laugh—in sylvan black and white chipmunk
regalia. The inky thing
adaptively whited with glistening
goat-fur, is wood-warden. In his
ermined well-cuttlefish-inked wool, he is
determination's totem. Out-
lawed? His sweet face and powerful feet go about
in chieftain's coat of Chilcat cloth.
He is his own protection from the moth,

noble little warrior. That
otter-skin on it, the living pole-cat,
smothers anything that stings. Well,—
this same weasel's playful and his weasel
associates are too. Only
Wood-weasels shall associate with me.   *1944*

THE MIND IS AN ENCHANTING THING

is an enchanted thing
    like the glaze on a
katydid-wing
        subdivided by sun
          till the nettings are legion.
Like Gieseking playing Scarlatti;

like the apteryx-awl
    as a beak, or the
kiwi's rain-shawl
        of haired feathers, the mind
          feeling its way as though blind,
walks along with its eyes on the ground.

It has memory's ear
    that can hear without
having to hear.
        Like the gyroscope's fall,
          truly unequivocal
because trued by regnant certainty,

it is a power of
    strong enchantment. It
is like the dove-
        neck animated by
          sun; it is memory's eye;
it's conscientious inconsistency.

It tears off the veil; tears
    the temptation, the
mist the heart wears,
        from its eyes,—if the heart
          has a face; it takes apart
dejection. It's fire in the dove-neck's

iridescence; in the
    inconsistencies
of Scarlatti.
        Unconfusion submits
          its confusion to proof; it's
not a Herod's oath that cannot change.

            1944

John Crowe Ransom

BELLS FOR JOHN WHITESIDES' DAUGHTER

There was such speed in her little body,
And such lightness in her footfall,
It is no wonder that her brown study
Astonishes us all.

Her wars were bruited in our high window.
We looked among orchard trees and beyond,
Where she took arms against her shadow,
Or harried unto the pond

The lazy geese, like a snow cloud
Dripping their snow on the green grass,
Tricking and stopping, sleepy and proud,
Who cried in goose, Alas,

For the tireless heart within the little
Lady with rod that made them rise
From their noon apple dreams, and scuttle
Goose-fashion under the skies!

But now go the bells, and we are ready;
In one house we are sternly stopped
To say we are vexed at her brown study,
Lying so primly propped.   *1924*

HERE LIES A LADY

Here lies a lady of beauty and high degree.
Of chills and fever she died, of fever and chills,
The delight of her husband, her aunts, an infant of three,
And of medicos marvelling sweetly on her ills.

For either she burned, and her confident eyes would blaze,
And her fingers fly in a manner to puzzle their heads—

What was she making? Why, nothing; she sat in a maze
Of old scraps of laces, snipped into curious shreds—

Or this would pass, and the light of her fire decline
Till she lay discouraged and cold as a thin stalk white and blown,
And would not open her eyes, to kisses, to wine;
The sixth of these states was her last; the cold settled down.

Sweet ladies, long may ye bloom, and toughly I hope ye may thole,
But was she not lucky? In flowers and lace and mourning,
In love and great honor we bade God rest her soul
After six little spaces of chill, and six of burning.

1924

MISS EUPHEMIA

Out of her house she crept,
Which was her winter's gaol,
Hearing the rumor that now
Was the birds' common tale—
Birds for all the ladies,
And husbands at church-door—
In fine, a spring was promised
As fifty years before.

A phase of green and tender
Was on the mortal clay,
But white upon her stick went
Miss Euphemia,
To count up all her tulips
That celebrated March,
Out of the frore escaping
To the blue upper arch.

Into her house she fled,
Buffeted back to prison,
And sought the very great-chair
From which she had arisen;
Down sat in her whiteness—
Bitter how she laughed—
Opening doors to March, yet
Quaking in his draught.

Nor scarcely can she, dwindling,
Throw down a bridge of dream
For a broken lady's traverse,
Neat-footing on the beam;
She had too much of winter,
And all her ways were lost,
And she sits with us only
Till next Pentecost.   *1924*

PHILOMELA

Procne, Philomela, and Itylus,
Your names are liquid, your improbable tale
Is recited in the classic numbers of the nightingale.
Ah, but our numbers are not felicitous,
It goes not liquidly for us.

Perched on a Roman ilex, and duly apostrophized,
The nightingale descanted unto Ovid;
She has even appeared to the Teutons, the swilled and gravid;
At Fontainebleau it may be the bird was gallicized;
Never was she baptized.

To England came Philomela with her pain,
Fleeing the hawk her husband; querulous ghost,
She wanders when he sits heavy on his roost,
Utters herself in the original again,
The untranslatable refrain.

Not to these shores she came! this other Thrace,
Environ barbarous to the royal Attic;
How could her delicate dirge run democratic,
Delivered in a cloudless boundless public place
To an inordinate race?

I pernoctated with the Oxford students once,
And in the quadrangles, in the cloisters, on the Cher,
Precociously knocked at antique doors ajar,
Fatuously touched the hems of the hierophants,
Sick of my dissonance.

I went out to Bagley Wood, I climbed the hill;
Even the moon had slanted off in a twinkling,

I heard the sepulchral owl and a few bells tinkling,
There was no more villainous day to unfulfil,
The diuturnity was still.

Up from the darkest wood where Philomela sat,
Her fairy numbers issued. What then ailed me?
My ears are called capacious but they failed me,
Her classics registered a little flat!
I rose, and venomously spat.

Philomela, Philomela, lover of song,
I am in despair if we may make us worthy,
A bantering breed sophistical and swarthy;
Unto more beautiful, persistently more young,
Thy fabulous provinces belong.   *1924*

EMILY HARDCASTLE, SPINSTER

We shall come to-morrow morning, who were not to have her love;
We shall bring no face of envy, but a gift of praise and lilies
To the stately ceremonial we are not the heroes of.

Let the sisters now attend her, who are red-eyed, who are wroth;
They were younger, she was finer, for they wearied of the waiting
And they married them to merchants, being unbelievers both.

I was dapper when I dangled in my pepper-and-salt;
We were only local beauties, and we beautifully trusted
If the proud one had to tarry we would take her by default.

But right across her threshold has the Grizzled Baron come;
Let them wrap her as a princess, who would patter down a stairway
Where the foreigner may take her for his gloomy halidom.   *1924*

INLAND CITY

She lies far inland, and no stick nor stone of her
Ever has looked on the sounding sea,
And how should she speak of her swift barks and roadways
And white sloops crowding to lift and be free?

"Ye towers and steeples, and belfries and crosses,
Toll for the doomed ships passing to sea.

But ye walls and gateposts, and ye halls and gardens,
Moor in my little boats vigilantly!"   *1924*

BLUE GIRLS

Twirling your blue skirts, travelling the sward
Under the towers of your seminary,
Go listen to your teachers old and contrary
Without believing a word.

Tie the white fillets then about your lustrous hair
And think no more of what will come to pass
Than bluebirds that go walking on the grass
And chattering on the air.

Practise your beauty, blue girls, before it fail;
And I will cry with my loud lips and publish
Beauty which all our power shall never establish,
It is so frail.

For I could tell you a story which is true;
I know a lady with a terrible tongue,
Blear eyes fallen from blue,
All her perfections tarnished—and yet it is not long
Since she was lovelier than any of you.   *1927*

SOMEWHERE IS SUCH A KINGDOM

The famous kingdom of the birds
Has a sweet tongue and liquid words,—
The red-birds polish their notes
In their easy practised throats,—
Smooth as orators are the thrushes
Of the airy city of the bushes,—
And God reward the fierce cock wrens
Who have such suavity with their hens.

To me this has its worth
As I sit upon the earth
Lacking my winter and quiet hearth.
For I go up into a nook
With a mind burdened, or a book,
And hear no strife or quarreling
As the birds and their wives sing.

Or, so it has been today.
Yet I cannot therefore say
If the red-bird, wren, or thrush
Know when to speak and when to hush;
Though their manifest education
Be a right enunciation
And their chief excellence
A verbal elegance,
I cannot say if the wind never blows,
Nor how it sometimes goes.

This I know, that if they wrangle
Their words inevitably will jangle.

If they be hateful as men
They will be harsh as we have been.
When they go to pecking
You will soon hear shrieking,
And they who will have the law,
How those will jaw!
Girls that dream unlawful dreams
Will waken full of their own screams,
And boys that get too arrant
Will have rows with a parent,—
And when friend falls out with friend,
All songs must have quick end.

Have they not claws like knives?
Have not these gentlemen wives?

But when they croak and fleer and swear,
My dull heart I must take elsewhere;
For I will see if God has made
Otherwhere another shade
Where the men or beasts or birds
Exchange few words and pleasant words.
And dare I think it is absurd
If no such beast were, no such bird?   *1927*

THE EQUILIBRISTS

Full of her long white arms and milky skin
He had a thousand times remembered sin.

Alone in the press of people travelled he,
Minding her jacinth and myrrh and ivory.

Mouth he remembered: the quaint orifice
From which came heat that flamed upon the kiss,
Till cold words came down spiral from the head,
Grey doves from the officious tower illsped.

Body: it was a white field ready for love.
On her body's field, with the gaunt tower above,
The lilies grew, beseeching him to take,
If he would pluck and wear them, bruise and break.

Eyes talking: Never mind the cruel words,
Embrace my flowers but not embrace the swords.
But what they said, the doves came straightway flying
And unsaid: Honor, Honor, they came crying.

Importunate her doves. Too pure, too wise,
Clambering on his shoulder, saying, Arise,
Leave me now, and never let us meet,
Eternal distance now command thy feet.

Predicament indeed, which thus discovers
Honor among thieves, Honor between lovers.
O such a little word is Honor, they feel!
But the grey word is between them cold as steel.

At length I saw these lovers fully were come
Into their torture of equilibrium:
Dreadfully had forsworn each other, and yet
They were bound each to each, and they did not forget.

And rigid as two painful stars, and twirled
About the clustered night their prison world,
They burned with fierce love always to come near,
But Honor beat them back and kept them clear.

Ah, the strict lovers, they are ruined now!
I cried in anger. But with puddled brow
Devising for those gibbeted and brave
Came I descanting: Man, what would you have?

For spin your period out, and draw your breath,
A kinder saeculum begins with Death.
Would you ascend to Heaven and bodiless dwell?
Or take your bodies honorless to Hell?

In Heaven you have heard no marriage is,
No white flesh tinder to your lecheries,
Your male and female tissue sweetly shaped
Sublimed away, and furious blood escaped.

Great lovers lie in Hell, the stubborn ones
Infatuate of the flesh upon the bones;
Stuprate, they rend each other when they kiss;
The pieces kiss again—no end to this.

But still I watched them spinning, orbited nice.
Their flames were not more radiant than their ice.
I dug in the quiet earth and wrought the tomb
And made these lines to memorize their doom:—

Equilibrists lie here; stranger, tread light;
Close, but untouching in each other's sight;
Mouldered the lips and ashy the tall skull,
Let them lie perilous and beautiful.   1927

DEAD BOY

The little cousin is dead, by foul subtraction,
A green bough from Virginia's aged tree,
And none of the county kin like the transaction,
Nor some of the world of outer dark, like me.

A boy not beautiful, not good, nor clever,
A black cloud full of storms too hot for keeping,
A sword beneath his mother's heart—yet never
Woman bewept her babe as this is weeping.

A pig with a pasty face, so I had said,
Squealing for cookies, kinned by poor pretense
With a noble house. But the little man quite dead,
I see the forbears' antique lineaments.

The elder men have strode by the box of death
To the wide flag porch, and muttering low send round

The bruit of the day. O friendly waste of breath!
Their hearts are hurt with a deep dynastic wound.

He was pale and little, the foolish neighbors say;
The first-fruits, saith the Preacher, the Lord hath taken;
But this was the old tree's late branch wrenched away,
Grieving the sapless limbs, the shorn and shaken.   *1927*

JANET WAKING

Beautifully Janet slept
Till it was deeply morning. She woke then
And thought about her dainty-feathered hen,
To see how it had kept.

One kiss she gave her mother.
Only a small one gave she to her daddy
Who would have kissed each curl of his shining baby;
No kiss at all for her brother.

"Old Chucky, old Chucky!" she cried,
Running across the world upon the grass
To Chucky's house, and listening. But alas,
Her Chucky had died.

It was a transmogrifying bee
Came droning down on Chucky's old bald head
And sat and put the poison. It scarcely bled,
But how exceedingly

And purply did the knot
Swell with the venom and communicate
Its rigor! Now the poor comb stood up straight
But Chucky did not.

So there was Janet
Kneeling on the wet grass, crying her brown hen
(Translated far beyond the daughters of men)
To rise and walk upon it.

And weeping fast as she had breath
Janet implored us, "Wake her from her sleep!"
And would not be instructed in how deep
Was the forgetful kingdom of death.   *1927*

VISION BY SWEETWATER

Go and ask Robin to bring the girls over
To Sweetwater, said my Aunt; and that was why
It was like a dream of ladies sweeping by
The willows, clouds, deep meadowgrass, and the river.

Robin's sisters and my Aunt's lily daughter
Laughed and talked, and tinkled light as wrens
If there were a little colony all hens
To go walking by the steep turn of Sweetwater.

Let them alone, dear Aunt, just for one minute
Till I go fishing in the dark of my mind:
Where have I seen before, against the wind,
These bright virgins, robed and bare of bonnet,

Flowing with music of their strange quick tongue
And adventuring with delicate paces by the stream,—
Myself a child, old suddenly at the scream
From one of the white throats which it hid among?

1927

T. S. Eliot

THE LOVE SONG OF J. ALFRED PRUFROCK

S'io credesse che mia risposta fosse
A persona che mai tornasse al mondo,
Questa fiamma staria senza piu scosse.
Ma perciocche giammai di questo fondo
Non torno vivo alcun, s'i'odo il vero,
Senza tema d'infamia ti rispondo.

Let us go then, you and I,
When the evening is spread out against the sky
Like a patient etherised upon a table;
Let us go, through certain half-deserted streets,
The muttering retreats
Of restless nights in one-night cheap hotels
And sawdust restaurants with oyster-shells:
Streets that follow like a tedious argument
Of insidious intent
To lead you to an overwhelming question . . .
Oh, do not ask, "What is it?"
Let us go and make our visit.

In the room the women come and go
Talking of Michelangelo.

The yellow fog that rubs its back upon the window-panes,
The yellow smoke that rubs its muzzle on the window-panes
Licked its tongue into the corners of the evening,
Lingered upon the pools that stand in drains,
Let fall upon its back the soot that falls from chimneys,
Slipped by the terrace, made a sudden leap,
And seeing that it was a soft October night,
Curled once about the house, and fell asleep.

And indeed there will be time
For the yellow smoke that slides along the street,
Rubbing its back upon the window-panes;

There will be time, there will be time
To prepare a face to meet the faces that you meet;
There will be time to murder and create,
And time for all the works and days of hands
That lift and drop a question on your plate;
Time for you and time for me,
And time yet for a hundred indecisions,
And for a hundred visions and revisions,
Before the taking of a toast and tea.

In the room the women come and go
Talking of Michelangelo.

And indeed there will be time
To wonder, "Do I dare?" and, "Do I dare?"
Time to turn back and descend the stair,
With a bald spot in the middle of my hair—
(They will say: "How his hair is growing thin!")
My morning coat, my collar mounting firmly to the chin,
My necktie rich and modest, but asserted by a simple pin—
(They will say: "But how his arms and legs are thin!")
Do I dare
Disturb the universe?
In a minute there is time
For decisions and revisions which a minute will reverse.

For I have known them all already, known them all:
Have known the evenings, mornings, afternoons,
I have measured out my life with coffee spoons;
I know the voices dying with a dying fall
Beneath the music from a farther room.
    So how should I presume?

And I have known the eyes already, known them all—
The eyes that fix you in a formulated phrase,
And when I am formulated, sprawling on a pin,
When I am pinned and wriggling on the wall,
Then how should I begin
To spit out all the butt-ends of my days and ways?
    And how should I presume?

And I have known the arms already, known them all—
Arms that are braceleted and white and bare

(But in the lamplight, downed with light brown hair!)
Is it perfume from a dress
That makes me so digress?
Arms that lie along a table, or wrap about a shawl.
   And should I then presume?
   And how should I begin?

               .   .   .   .   .

Shall I say, I have gone at dusk through narrow streets
And watched the smoke that rises from the pipes
Of lonely men in shirt-sleeves, leaning out of windows? . . .

   I should have been a pair of ragged claws
Scuttling across the floors of silent seas.

             .   .   .   .   .

And the afternoon, the evening, sleeps so peacefully!
Smoothed by long fingers,
Asleep . . . tired . . . or it malingers,
Stretched on the floor, here beside you and me.
Should I, after tea and cakes and ices,
Have the strength to force the moment to its crisis?
But though I have wept and fasted, wept and prayed,
Though I have seen my head (grown slightly bald) brought in upon a
    platter,
I am no prophet—and here's no great matter;
I have seen the moment of my greatness flicker,
And I have seen the eternal Footman hold my coat, and snicker,
And in short, I was afraid.

   And would it have been worth it, after all,
After the cups, the marmalade, the tea,
Among the porcelain, among some talk of you and me,
Would it have been worth while,
To have bitten off the matter with a smile,
To have squeezed the universe into a ball
To roll it toward some overwhelming question,
To say: "I am Lazarus, come from the dead,
Come back to tell you all, I shall tell you all"—
If one, settling a pillow by her head,
   Should say: "That is not what I meant at all;
   That is not it, at all."

And would it have been worth it, after all,
Would it have been worth while,
After the sunsets and the dooryards and the sprinkled streets,
After the novels, after the teacups, after the skirts that trail along the
 floor—
And this, and so much more?—
It is impossible to say just what I mean!
But as if a magic lantern threw the nerves in patterns on a
 screen:
Would it have been worth while
If one, settling a pillow or throwing off a shawl,
And turning toward the window, should say:
 "That is not it at all,
 That is not what I meant, at all."

 . . . . .

No! I am not Prince Hamlet, nor was meant to be;
Am an attendant lord, one that will do
To swell a progress, start a scene or two,
Advise the prince; no doubt, an easy tool,
Deferential, glad to be of use,
Politic, cautious, and meticulous;
Full of high sentence, but a bit obtuse;
At times, indeed, almost ridiculous—
Almost, at times, the Fool.

 I grow old . . . I grow old . . .
I shall wear the bottoms of my trousers rolled.

 Shall I part my hair behind? Do I dare to eat a peach?
I shall wear white flannel trousers, and walk upon the beach.
I have heard the mermaids singing, each to each.

 I do not think that they will sing to me.

 I have seen them riding seaward on the waves
Combing the white hair of the waves blown back
When the wind blows the water white and black.

 We have lingered in the chambers of the sea
By sea-girls wreathed with seaweed red and brown
Till human voices wake us, and we drown.   1917

RHAPSODY ON A WINDY NIGHT

Twelve o'clock.
Along the reaches of the street
Held in a lunar synthesis,
Whispering lunar incantations
Dissolve the floors of memory
And all its clear relations
Its divisions and precisions,
Every street lamp that I pass
Beats like a fatalistic drum,
And through the spaces of the dark
Midnight shakes the memory
As a madman shakes a dead geranium.

Half-past one,
The street-lamp sputtered,
The street-lamp muttered,
The street-lamp said, "Regard that woman
Who hesitates toward you in the light of the door
Which opens on her like a grin.
You see the border of her dress
Is torn and stained with sand,
And you see the corner of her eye
Twists like a crooked pin."

The memory throws up high and dry
A crowd of twisted things;
A twisted branch upon the beach
Eaten smooth, and polished
As if the world gave up
The secret of its skeleton,
Stiff and white.
A broken spring in a factory yard,
Rust that clings to the form that the strength has left
Hard and curled and ready to snap.

Half-past two,
The street-lamp said,
"Remark the cat which flattens itself in the gutter,
Slips out its tongue
And devours a morsel of rancid butter."
So the hand of the child, automatic,

Slipped out and pocketed a toy that was running along the quay.
I could see nothing behind that child's eye.
I have seen eyes in the street
Trying to peer through lighted shutters,
And a crab one afternoon in a pool,
An old crab with barnacles on his back,
Gripped the end of a stick which I held him.

Half-past three,
The lamp sputtered,
The lamp muttered in the dark.
The lamp hummed:
"Regard the moon,
La lune ne garde aucune rancune,
She winks a feeble eye,
She smiles into corners.
She smooths the hair of the grass.
The moon has lost her memory.
A washed-out smallpox cracks her face,
Her hand twists a paper rose,
That smells of dust and eau de Cologne,
She is alone
With all the old nocturnal smells
That cross and cross across her brain."
The reminiscence comes
Of sunless dry geraniums
And dust in crevices,
Smells of chestnuts in the streets,
And female smells in shuttered rooms,
And cigarettes in corridors
And cocktail smells in bars.

The lamp said,
"Four o'clock,
Here is the number on the door.
Memory!
You have the key,
The little lamp spreads a ring on the stair.
Mount,
The bed is open; the tooth-brush hangs on the wall,
Put your shoes at the door, sleep, prepare for life."

The last twist of the knife.   *1917*

GERONTION

*Thou hast nor youth nor age
But as it were an after dinner sleep
Dreaming of both.*

Here I am, an old man in a dry month,
Being read to by a boy, waiting for rain.
I was neither at the hot gates
Nor fought in the warm rain
Nor knee deep in the salt marsh, heaving a cutlass,
Bitten by flies, fought.
My house is a decayed house,
And the jew squats on the window sill, the owner,
Spawned in some estaminet of Antwerp,
Blistered in Brussels, patched and peeled in London.
The goat coughs at night in the field overhead;
Rocks, moss, stonecrop, iron, merds.
The woman keeps the kitchen, makes tea,
Sneezes at evening, poking the peevish gutter.
                    I an old man,
A dull head among windy spaces.

   Signs are taken for wonders. "We would see a sign!"
The word within a word, unable to speak a word,
Swaddled with darkness. In the juvescence of the year
Came Christ the tiger

   In depraved May, dogwood and chestnut, flowering judas,
To be eaten, to be divided, to be drunk
Among whispers; by Mr. Silvero
With caressing hands, at Limoges
Who walked all night in the next room:

   By Hakagawa, bowing among the Titians;
By Madame de Tornquist, in the dark room
Shifting the candles; Fräulein von Kulp
Who turned in the hall, one hand on the door.
   Vacant shuttles
Weave the wind. I have no ghosts,
An old man in a draughty house
Under a windy knob.

After such knowledge, what forgiveness? Think now
History has many cunning passages, contrived corridors
And issues, deceives with whispering ambitions,
Guides us by vanities. Think now
She gives when our attention is distracted
And what she gives, gives with such supple confusions
That the giving famishes the craving. Gives too late
What's not believed in, or if still believed,
In memory only, reconsidered passion. Gives too soon
Into weak hands, what's thought can be dispensed with
Till the refusal propagates a fear. Think
Neither fear nor courage saves us. Unnatural vices
Are fathered by our heroism. Virtues
Are forced upon us by our impudent crimes.
These tears are shaken from the wrath-bearing tree.

  The tiger springs in the new year. Us he devours. Think at last
We have not reached conclusion, when I
Stiffen in a rented house. Think at last
I have not made this show purposelessly
And it is not by any concitation
Of the backward devils.
I would meet you upon this honestly.
I that was near your heart was removed therefrom
To lose beauty in terror, terror in inquisition.
I have lost my passion: why should I need to keep it
Since what is kept must be adulterated?
I have lost my sight, smell, hearing, taste, and touch:
How should I use them for your closer contact?

  These with a thousand small deliberations
Protract the profit of their chilled delirium,
Excite the membrane, when the sense has cooled,
With pungent sauces, multiply variety
In a wilderness of mirrors. What will the spider do,
Suspend its operations, will the weevil
Delay? De Bailhache, Fresca, Mrs. Cammel, whirled
Beyond the circuit of the shuddering Bear
In fractured atoms. Gull against the wind, in the windy straits
Of Belle Isle, or running on the Horn,
White feathers in the snow, the Gulf claims,
And an old man driven by the Trades
To a sleepy corner.

Tenants of the house,
Thoughts of a dry brain in a dry season.   1920

WHISPERS OF IMMORTALITY

Webster was much possessed by death
And saw the skull beneath the skin;
And breastless creatures under ground
Leaned backward with a lipless grin.

Daffodil bulbs instead of balls
Stared from the sockets of the eyes!
He knew that thought clings round dead limbs
Tightening its lusts and luxuries.

Donne, I suppose, was such another
Who found no substitute for sense,
To seize and clutch and penetrate;
Expert beyond experience,

He knew the anguish of the marrow
The ague of the skeleton;
No contact possible to flesh
Allayed the fever of the bone.

           *   *   *   *

Grishkin is nice: her Russian eye
Is underlined for emphasis;
Uncorseted, her friendly bust
Gives promise of pneumatic bliss.

The couched Brazilian jaguar
Compels the scampering marmoset
With subtle effluence of cat;
Grishkin has a maisonette;

The sleek Brazilian jaguar
Does not in its arboreal gloom
Distil so rank a feline smell
As Grishkin in a drawing-room.

And even the Abstract Entities
Circumambulate her charm;

But our lot crawls between dry ribs
To keep our metaphysics warm.   1920

SWEENEY AMONG THE NIGHTINGALES

ὤμοι, πέπληγμαι καιρίαν πληγὴν ἔσω.

Apeneck Sweeney spreads his knees
Letting his arms hang down to laugh,
The zebra stripes along his jaw
Swelling to maculate giraffe.

The circles of the stormy moon
Slide westward toward the River Plate,
Death and the Raven drift above
And Sweeney guards the hornèd gate.

Gloomy Orion and the Dog
Are veiled; and hushed the shrunken seas;
The person in the Spanish cape
Tries to sit on Sweeney's knees

Slips and pulls the table cloth
Overturns a coffee-cup,
Reorganized upon the floor
She yawns and draws a stocking up;

The silent man in mocha brown
Sprawls at the window-sill and gapes;
The waiter brings in oranges
Bananas figs and hothouse grapes;

The silent vertebrate in brown
Contracts and concentrates, withdraws;
Rachel *née* Rabinovitch
Tears at the grapes with murderous paws;

She and the lady in the cape
Are suspect, thought to be in league;
Therefore the man with heavy eyes
Declines the gambit, shows fatigue,

Leaves the room and reappears
Outside the window, leaning in,

Branches of wistaria
Circumscribe a golden grin;

The host with someone indistinct
Converses at the door apart,
The nightingales are singing near
The Convent of the Sacred Heart,

And sang within the bloody wood
When Agamemnon cried aloud,
And let their liquid siftings fall
To stain the stiff dishonored shroud.   1920

THE WASTE LAND

"Nam Sibyllam quidem Cumis ego ipse oculis meis vidi in ampulla pendere, et cum illi pueri dicerent: Σίβυλλα τί θέλεις; respondebat illa: ἀποθανεῖν θέλω."

For Ezra Pound *il miglior fabbro.*

I. THE BURIAL OF THE DEAD

April is the cruellest month, breeding
Lilacs out of the dead land, mixing
Memory and desire, stirring
Dull roots with spring rain.
Winter kept us warm, covering
Earth in forgetful snow, feeding
A little life with dried tubers.
Summer surprised us, coming over the Starnbergersee
With a shower of rain; we stopped in the colonnade,
And went on in sunlight, into the Hofgarten,   10
And drank coffee, and talked for an hour.
Bin gar keine Russin, stamm' aus Litauen, echt deutsch.
And when we were children, staying at the archduke's,
My cousin's, he took me out on a sled,
And I was frightened. He said, Marie,
Marie, hold on tight. And down we went.
In the mountains, there you feel free.
I read, much of the night, and go south in the winter.

   What are the roots that clutch, what branches grow
Out of this stony rubbish? Son of man,   20

You cannot say, or guess, for you know only
A heap of broken images, where the sun beats,
And the dead tree gives no shelter, the cricket no relief,
And the dry stone no sound of water. Only
There is shadow under this red rock
(Come in under the shadow of this red rock),
And I will show you something different from either
Your shadow at morning striding behind you
Or your shadow at evening rising to meet you;
I will show you fear in a handful of dust.   30

            Frisch weht der Wind
            Der Heimat zu
            Mein Irisch Kind,
            Wo weilest du?

"You gave me hyacinths first a year ago;
They called me the hyacinth girl."
—Yet when we came back, late, from the Hyacinth garden,
Your arms full, and your hair wet, I could not
Speak, and my eyes failed, I was neither
Living nor dead, and I knew nothing,   40
Looking into the heart of light, the silence.
Oed' und leer das Meer.

   Madame Sosostris, famous clairvoyante,
Had a bad cold, nevertheless
Is known to be the wisest woman in Europe,
With a wicked pack of cards. Here, said she,
Is your card, the drowned Phoenician Sailor,
(Those are pearls that were his eyes. Look!)
Here is Belladonna, the Lady of the Rocks,
The lady of situations.   50
Here is the man with three staves, and here the Wheel,
And here is the one-eyed merchant, and this card,
Which is blank, is something he carries on his back,
Which I am forbidden to see. I do not find
The Hanged Man. Fear death by water.
I see crowds of people, walking round in a ring.
Thank you. If you see dear Mrs. Equitone,
Tell her I bring the horoscope myself:
One must be so careful these days.

Unreal City, 60
Under the brown fog of a winter dawn,
A crowd flowed over London Bridge, so many,
I had not thought death had undone so many.
Sighs, short and infrequent, were exhaled,
And each man fixed his eyes before his feet.
Flowed up the hill and down King William Street,
To where Saint Mary Woolnoth kept the hours
With a dead sound on the final stroke of nine.
There I saw one I knew, and stopped him, crying: "Stetson!
You who were with me in the ships at Mylae! 70
That corpse you planted last year in your garden,
Has it begun to sprout? Will it bloom this year?
Or has the sudden frost disturbed its bed?
Oh keep the Dog far hence, that's friend to men,
Or with his nails he'll dig it up again!
You! hypocrite lecteur!—mon semblable,—mon frère!"

II. A GAME OF CHESS

The Chair she sat in, like a burnished throne,
Glowed on the marble, where the glass
Held up by standards wrought with fruited vines
From which a golden Cupidon peeped out 80
(Another hid his eyes behind his wing)
Doubled the flames of sevenbranched candelabra
Reflecting light upon the table as
The glitter of her jewels rose to meet it,
From satin cases poured in rich profusion;
In vials of ivory and coloured glass
Unstoppered, lurked her strange synthetic perfumes,
Unguent, powdered, or liquid—troubled, confused
And drowned the sense in odours; stirred by the air
That freshened from the window, these ascended 90
In fattening the prolonged candle-flames,
Flung their smoke into the laquearia,
Stirring the pattern on the coffered ceiling.
Huge sea-wood fed with copper
Burned green and orange, framed by the coloured stone,
In which sad light a carvèd dolphin swam.
Above the antique mantel was displayed
As though a window gave upon the sylvan scene

The change of Philomel, by the barbarous king
So rudely forced; yet there the nightingale   100
Filled all the desert with inviolable voice
And still she cried, and still the world pursues,
"Jug Jug" to dirty ears.
And other withered stumps of time
Were told upon the walls; staring forms
Leaned out, leaning, hushing the room enclosed.
Footsteps shuffled on the stair.
Under the firelight, under the brush, her hair
Spread out in fiery points
Glowed into words, then would be savagely still.   110

   "My nerves are bad to-night. Yes, bad. Stay with me.
Speak to me. Why do you never speak. Speak.
   What are you thinking of? What thinking? What?
I never know what you are thinking. Think."

   I think we are in rats' alley
Where the dead men lost their bones.

"What is that noise?"
               The wind under the door.
"What is that noise now? What is the wind doing?"
               Nothing again nothing.   120
                      "Do
You know nothing? Do you see nothing? Do you remember
Nothing?"

   I remember
Those are pearls that were his eyes.
"Are you alive, or not? Is there nothing in your head?"
                          But

O O O O that Shakespeherian Rag—
It's so elegant
So intelligent   130
"What shall I do now? What shall I do?"
"I shall rush out as I am, and walk the street
With my hair down, so. What shall we do to-morrow?
What shall we ever do?"
               The hot water at ten.
And if it rains, a closed car at four.

And we shall play a game of chess,
Pressing lidless eyes and waiting for a knock upon the door.

    When Lil's husband got demobbed, I said—
I didn't mince my words, I said to her myself,   140
HURRY UP PLEASE ITS TIME
Now Albert's coming back, make yourself a bit smart.
He'll want to know what you done with that money he gave you
To get yourself some teeth. He did, I was there.
You have them all out, Lil, and get a nice set,
He said, I swear, I can't bear to look at you.
And no more can't I, I said, and think of poor Albert,
He's been in the army four years, he wants a good time,
And if you don't give it him, there's others will, I said.
Oh is there, she said. Something o' that, I said.   150
Then I'll know who to thank, she said, and give me a straight look.
HURRY UP PLEASE ITS TIME
If you don't like it you can get on with it, I said.
Others can pick and choose if you can't.
But if Albert makes off, it won't be for lack of telling.
You ought to be ashamed, I said, to look so antique.
(And her only thirty-one.)
I can't help it, she said, pulling a long face,
It's them pills I took, to bring it off, she said.
(She's had five already, and nearly died of young George.)   160
The chemist said it would be all right, but I've never been the same.
You *are* a proper fool, I said.
Well, if Albert won't leave you alone, there it is, I said,
What you get married for if you don't want children?
HURRY UP PLEASE ITS TIME
Well, that Sunday Albert was home, they had a hot gammon,
And they asked me in to dinner, to get the beauty of it hot—
HURRY UP PLEASE ITS TIME
HURRY UP PLEASE ITS TIME
Goonight Bill. Goonight Lou. Goonight May. Goonight.   170
Ta ta. Goonight. Goonight.
Good night, ladies, good night, sweet ladies, good night, good night.

III. THE FIRE SERMON

The river's tent is broken: the last fingers of leaf
Clutch and sink into the wet bank. The wind

Crosses the brown land, unheard. The nymphs are departed.
Sweet Thames, run softly, till I end my song.
The river bears no empty bottles, sandwich papers,
Silk handkerchiefs, cardboard boxes, cigarette ends
Or other testimony of summer nights. The nymphs are departed.
And their friends, the loitering heirs of city directors—   180
Departed, have left no addresses.
By the waters of Leman I sat down and wept . . .
Sweet Thames, run softly till I end my song,
Sweet Thames, run softly, for I speak not loud or long.
But at my back in a cold blast I hear
The rattle of the bones, and chuckle spread from ear to ear.
A rat crept softly through the vegetation
Dragging its slimy belly on the bank
While I was fishing in the dull canal
On a winter evening round behind the gashouse   190
Musing upon the king my brother's wreck
And on the king my father's death before him.
White bodies naked on the low damp ground
And bones cast in a little low dry garret,
Rattled by the rat's foot only, year to year.
But at my back from time to time I hear
The sound of horns and motors, which shall bring
Sweeney to Mrs. Porter in the spring.
O the moon shone bright on Mrs. Porter
And on her daughter   200
They wash their feet in soda water
Et O ces voix d'enfants, chantant dans la coupole!

   Twit twit twit
Jug jug jug jug jug jug
So rudely forc'd.
Tereu

   Unreal City
Under the brown fog of a winter noon
Mr. Eugenides, the Smyrna merchant
Unshaven, with a pocket full of currants   210
C.i.f. London: documents at sight,
Asked me in demotic French
To luncheon at the Cannon Street Hotel
Followed by a weekend at the Metropole.

At the violet hour, when the eyes and back
Turn upward from the desk, when the human engine waits
Like a taxi throbbing waiting,
I Tiresias, though blind, throbbing between two lives,
Old man with wrinkled female breasts, can see
At the violet hour, the evening hour that strives   220
Homeward, and brings the sailor home from sea,
The typist home at teatime, clears her breakfast, lights
Her stove, and lays out food in tins.
Out of the window perilously spread
Her drying combinations touched by the sun's last rays,
On the divan are piled (at night her bed)
Stockings, slippers, camisoles, and stays.
I Tiresias, old man with wrinkled dugs
Perceived the scene, and foretold the rest—
I too awaited the expected guest.   230
He, the young man carbuncular, arrives,
A small house agent's clerk, with one bold stare,
One of the low on whom assurance sits
As a silk hat on a Bradford millionaire.
The time is now propitious, as he guesses,
The meal is ended, she is bored and tired,
Endeavours to engage her in caresses
Which still are unreproved, if undesired.
Flushed and decided, he assaults at once;
Exploring hands encounter no defence;   240
His vanity requires no response,
And makes a welcome of indifference.
(And I Tiresias have foresuffered all
Enacted on this same divan or bed;
I who have sat by Thebes below the wall
And walked among the lowest of the dead.)
Bestows one final patronising kiss,
And gropes his way, finding the stairs unlit . . .

She turns and looks a moment in the glass,
Hardly aware of her departed lover;   250
Her brain allows one half-formed thought to pass:
"Well now that's done: and I'm glad it's over."
When lovely woman stoops to folly and
Paces about her room again, alone,
She smoothes her hair with automatic hand,
And puts a record on the gramophone.

"This music crept by me upon the waters"
And along the Strand, up Queen Victoria Street.
O City city, I can sometimes hear
Beside a public bar in Lower Thames Street,   260
The pleasant whining of a mandoline
And a clatter and a chatter from within
Where fishmen lounge at noon: where the walls
Of Magnus Martyr hold
Inexplicable splendour of Ionian white and gold.

      The river sweats
Oil and tar
The barges drift
With the turning tide
Red sails   270
Wide
To leeward, swing on the heavy spar.
The barges wash
Drifting logs
Down Greenwich reach
Past the Isle of Dogs.
      Weialala leia
      Wallala leialala

      Elizabeth and Leicester
Beating oars   280
The stern was formed
A gilded shell
Red and gold
The brisk swell
Rippled both shores
Southwest wind
Carried down stream
The peal of bells
White towers
      Weialala leia   290
      Wallala leialala

"Trams and dusty trees.
Highbury bore me. Richmond and Kew
Undid me. By Richmond I raised my knees
Supine on the floor of a narrow canoe."
"My feet are at Moorgate, and my heart

Under my feet. After the event
He wept. He promised 'a new start.'
I made no comment. What should I resent?"

   "On Margate Sands.   300
I can connect
Nothing with nothing.
The broken fingernails of dirty hands.
My people humble people who expect
Nothing."
     la la

   To Carthage then I came

   Burning burning burning burning
   O Lord Thou pluckest me out
   O Lord Thou pluckest   310

burning

IV. DEATH BY WATER

Phlebas the Phoenician, a fortnight dead,
Forgot the cry of gulls, and the deep sea swell
And the profit and loss.
               A current under sea
Picked his bones in whispers. As he rose and fell
He passed the stages of his age and youth
Entering the whirlpool.
              Gentile or Jew
O you who turn the wheel and look to windward,   320
Consider Phlebas, who was once handsome and tall as you.

V. WHAT THE THUNDER SAID

After the torchlight red on sweaty faces
After the frosty silence in the gardens
After the agony in stony places
The shouting and the crying
Prison and palace and reverberation
Of thunder of spring over distant mountains
He who was living is now dead
We who were living are now dying
With a little patience   330

    Here is no water but only rock
Rock and no water and the sandy road
The road winding above among the mountains
Which are mountains of rock without water
If there were water we should stop and drink
Amongst the rock one cannot stop or think
Sweat is dry and feet are in the sand
If there were only water amongst the rock
Dead mountain mouth of carious teeth that cannot spit
Here one can neither stand nor lie nor sit   340
There is not even silence in the mountains
But dry sterile thunder without rain
There is not even solitude in the mountains
But red sullen faces sneer and snarl
From doors of mudcracked houses
                                            If there were water
    And no rock
    If there were rock
    And also water
    And water   350
    A spring
    A pool among the rock
    If there were the sound of water only
    Not the cicada
    And dry grass singing
    But sound of water over a rock
    Where the hermit-thrush sings in the pine trees
    Drip drop drip drop drop drop drop
    But there is no water

    Who is the third who walks always beside you?   360
When I count, there are only you and I together
But when I look ahead up the white road
There is always another one walking beside you
Gliding wrapt in a brown mantle, hooded
I do not know whether a man or a woman
—But who is that on the other side of you?

    What is that sound high in the air
Murmur of maternal lamentation
Who are those hooded hordes swarming
Over endless plains, stumbling in cracked earth   370

Ringed by the flat horizon only
What is the city over the mountains
Cracks and reforms and bursts in the violet air
Falling towers
Jerusalem Athens Alexandria
Vienna London
Unreal

 A woman drew her long black hair out tight
And fiddled whisper music on those strings
And bats with baby faces in the violet light   380
Whistled, and beat their wings
And crawled head downward down a blackened wall
And upside down in air were towers
Tolling reminiscent bells, that kept the hours
And voices singing out of empty cisterns and exhausted wells.

 In this decayed hole among the mountains
In the faint moonlight, the grass is singing
Over the tumbled graves, about the chapel
There is the empty chapel, only the wind's home.
It has no windows, and the door swings,   390
Dry bones can harm no one.
Only a cock stood on the rooftree
Co co rico co co rico
In a flash of lightning. Then a damp gust
Bringing rain

 Ganga was sunken, and the limp leaves
Waited for rain, while the black clouds
Gathered far distant, over Himavant.
The jungle crouched, humped in silence.
Then spoke the thunder   400
DA
Datta: what have we given?
My friend, blood shaking my heart
The awful daring of a moment's surrender
Which an age of prudence can never retract
By this, and this only, we have existed
Which is not to be found in our obituaries
Or in memories draped by the beneficent spider
Or under seals broken by the lean solicitor

In our empty rooms   410
Da
Dayadhvam: I have heard the key
Turn in the door once and turn once only
We think of the key, each in his prison
Thinking of the key, each confirms a prison
Only at nightfall, aethereal rumours
Revive for a moment a broken Coriolanus
Da
Damyata: The boat responded
Gaily, to the hand expert with sail and oar   420
The sea was calm, your heart would have responded
Gaily, when invited, beating obedient
To controlling hands
                            I sat upon the shore
Fishing, with the arid plain behind me
Shall I at least set my lands in order?
London Bridge is falling down falling down falling down
Poi s'ascose nel foco che gli affina
Quando fiam uti chelidon—O swallow swallow
Le Prince d'Aquitaine à la tour abolie   430
These fragments I have shored against my ruins
Why then Ile fit you. Hieronymo's mad againe.
Datta. Dayadhvam. Damyata.
          Shantih   shantih   shantih   1922

AUTHOR'S NOTES ON THE WASTE LAND

Not only the title, but the plan and a good deal of the incidental symbolism
of the poem were suggested by Miss Jessie L. Weston's book on the Grail
legend: *From Ritual to Romance* (Cambridge). Indeed, so deeply am I
indebted, Miss Weston's book will elucidate the difficulties of the poem
much better than my notes can do; and I recommend it (apart from the
great interest of the book itself) to any who think such elucidation of the
poem worth the trouble. To another work of anthropology I am indebted
in general, one which has influenced our generation profoundly; I mean
The Golden Bough; I have used especially the two volumes *Adonis, Attis,
Osiris.* Anyone who is acquainted with these works will immediately recognize in the poem certain references to vegetation ceremonies.

I. THE BURIAL OF THE DEAD

Line 20. Cf. *Ezekiel* II, i.
23. Cf. *Ecclesiastes* XII, v.
31. V. *Tristan und Isolde,* I, verses 5–8.

42. Id. III, verse 24.

46. I am not familiar with the exact constitution of the Tarot pack of cards, from which I have obviously departed to suit my own convenience. The Hanged Man, a member of the traditional pack, fits my purpose in two ways: because he is associated in my mind with the Hanged God of Frazer, and because I associate him with the hooded figure in the passage of the disciples to Emmaus in Part V. The Phoenician Sailor and the Merchant appear later; also the "crowds of people," and Death by Water is executed in Part IV. The Man with Three Staves (an authentic member of the Tarot pack) I associate, quite arbitrarily, with the Fisher King himself.

60. Cf. Baudelaire:
"Fourmillante cité, cité pleine de rêves,
Où le spectre en plein jour raccroche le passant."

63. Cf. *Inferno*, III, 55–7:
"si lunga tratta
di gente, ch'io non avrei mai creduto
che morte tanta n'avesse disfatta."

64. Cf. *Inferno*, IV, 25–7:
"Quivi, secondo che per ascoltare,
"non avea pianto, ma' che di sospiri,
"che l'aura eterna facevan tremare."

68. A phenomenon which I have often noticed.

74. Cf. the Dirge in Webster's *White Devil*.

76. V. Baudelaire, Preface to *Fleurs du Mal*.

II. A GAME OF CHESS

77. Cf. *Antony and Cleopatra*, II, ii, l. 190.

92. Laquearia. V. *Aeneid*, I, 726:
dependent lychni laquearibus aureis incensi, et noctem flammis funalia vincunt.

98. Sylvan scene. V. Milton, *Paradise Lost*, IV, 140.

99. V. Ovid, *Metamorphoses*, VI, Philomela.

100. Cf. Part III, l. 204.

115. Cf. Part III, l. 195.

118. Cf. Webster: "Is the wind in that door still?"

126. Cf. Part I, l. 37, 48.

138. Cf. the game of chess in Middleton's *Women beware Women*.

III. THE FIRE SERMON

176. V. Spenser, *Prothalamion*.

192. Cf. *The Tempest*, I, ii.

196. Cf. Marvell, *To His Coy Mistress*.

197. Cf. Day, *Parliament of Bees*:
"When of the sudden, listening, you shall hear,
"A noise of horns and hunting, which shall bring

"Actaeon to Diana in the spring,
"Where all shall see her naked skin . . ."

199. I do not know the origin of the ballad from which these lines are taken: it was reported to me from Sydney, Australia.

202. V. Verlaine, *Parsifal*.

210. The currants were quoted at a price "carriage and insurance free to London"; and the Bill of Lading, etc., were to be handed to the buyer upon payment of the sight draft.

218. Tiresias, although a mere spectator and not indeed a "character," is yet the most important personage in the poem, uniting all the rest. Just as the one-eyed merchant, seller of currants, melts into the Phoenician Sailor, and the latter is not wholly distinct from Ferdinand Prince of Naples, so all the women are one woman, and the two sexes meet in Tiresias. What Tiresias *sees*, in fact, is the substance of the poem. The whole passage from Ovid is of great anthropological interest:

". . . Cum Iunone iocos et maior vestra profecto est
    Quam, quae contingit maribus," dixisse, "voluptas."
Illa negat; placuit quae sit sententia docti
Quaerere Tiresiae: venus huic erat utraque nota.
Nam duo magnorum viridi coeuntia silva
Corpora serpentum baculi violaverat ictu
Deque viro factus, mirabile, femina septem
Egerat autumnos; octavo rursus eosdem
Vidit et "est vestrae si tanta potentia plagae,"
Dixit "ut auctoris sortem in contraria mutet,
Nunc quoque vos feriam!" percussis anguibus isdem
Forma prior rediit genetivaque venit imago.
Arbiter hic igitur sumptus de lite iocosa
Dicta Iovis firmat; gravius Saturnia iusto
Nec pro materia fertur doluisse suique
Iudicis aeterna damnavit lumina nocte,
At pater omnipotens (neque enim licet inrita cuiquam
Facta dei fecisse deo) pro lumine adempto
Scire futura dedit poenamque levavit honore.

221. This may not appear as exact as Sappho's lines, but I had in mind the "longshore" or "dory" fisherman, who returns at nightfall.

253. V. Goldsmith, the song in *The Vicar of Wakefield*.

257. V. *The Tempest*, as above.

264. The interior of St. Magnus Martyr is to my mind one of the finest among Wren's interiors. See *The Proposed Demolition of Nineteen City Churches* (P. S. King & Son, Ltd.).

266. The Song of the (three) Thames-daughters begins here. From line 292 to 306 inclusive they speak in turn. V. *Götterdämmerung*, III, i: the Rhine-daughters.

279. V. Froude, *Elizabeth*, Vol. I, ch. iv, letter of De Quadra to Philip of Spain:
"In the afternoon we were in a barge, watching the games on the river.

(The queen) was alone with Lord Robert and myself on the poop, when they began to talk nonsense, and went so far that Lord Robert at last said, as I was on the spot there was no reason why they should not be married if the queen pleased."

293. Cf. *Purgatorio*, V., 133:

> "Ricorditi di me, che son la Pia;
> "Siena mi fe', disfecemi Maremma."

307. V. St. Augustine's *Confessions*: "to Carthage then I came, where a cauldron of unholy loves sang all about mine ears."

308. The complete text of the Buddha's Fire Sermon (which corresponds in importance to the Sermon on the Mount) from which these words are taken, will be found translated in the late Henry Clarke Warren's *Buddhism in Translation* (Harvard Oriental Series). Mr. Warren was one of the great pioneers of Buddhist studies in the Occident.

309. From St. Augustine's *Confessions* again. The collocation of these two representatives of eastern and western asceticism, as the culmination of this part of the poem, is not an accident.

V. WHAT THE THUNDER SAID

In the first part of Part V three themes are employed: the journey to Emmaus, the approach to the Chapel Perilous (see Miss Weston's book) and the present decay of eastern Europe.

357. This is *Turdus aonalaschkae pallasii*, the hermit-thrush which I have heard in Quebec County. Chapman says (*Handbook of Birds of Eastern North America*) "it is most at home in secluded woodland and thickety retreats. . . . Its notes are not remarkable for variety or volume, but in purity and sweetness of tone and exquisite modulation they are unequalled." Its "water-dripping song" is justly celebrated.

360. The following lines were stimulated by the account of one of the Antarctic expeditions (I forget which, but I think one of Shackleton's): it was related that the party of explorers, at the extremity of their strength, had the constant delusion that there was *one more member* than could actually be counted.

367–77. Cf. Hermann Hesse, *Blick ins Chaos*: "Schon ist halb Europa, schon ist zumindest der halbe Osten Europas auf dem Wege zum Chaos, fährt betrunken im heiligen Wahn am Abgrund entlang und singt dazu, singt betrunken und hymnisch wie Dmitri Karamasoff sang. Ueber diese Lieder lacht der Bürger beleidigt, der Heilige und Seher hört sie mit Tränen."

402. "Datta, dayadhvam, damyata" (Give, sympathize, control). The fable of the meaning of the Thunder is found in the *Brihadaranyaka—Upanishad*, 5, 1. A translation is found in Deussen's *Sechzig Upanishads des Veda*, p. 489.

408. Cf. Webster, *The White Devil*, V, vi:

> ". . . they'll remarry
> Ere the worm pierce your winding-sheet, ere the spider
> Make a thin curtain for your epitaphs."

412. Cf. *Inferno*, XXXIII, 46:
> "ed io sentii chiavar l'uscio di sotto
> all'orribile torre."

Also F. H. Bradley, *Appearance and Reality*, p. 346. "My external sensations are no less private to myself than are my thoughts or my feelings. In either case my experience falls within my own circle, a circle closed on the outside; and, with all its elements alike, every sphere is opaque to the others which surround it. . . . In brief, regarded as an existence which appears in a soul, the whole world for each is peculiar and private to that soul."

425. V. Weston: *From Ritual to Romance;* chapter on the Fisher King.

428. V. *Purgatorio*, XXVI, 148:
> " 'Ara vos prec, per aquella valor
> que vos guida al som de l'escalina,
> sovegna vos a temps de ma dolor.'
> Poi s'ascose nel foco che gli affina."

429. V. *Pervigilium Veneris*. Cf. Philomela in Parts II and III.

430. V. Gerard de Nerval, Sonnet *El Desdichado*.

432. V. Kyd's *Spanish Tragedy*.

434. Shantih. Repeated as here, a formal ending to an Upanishad. "The Peace which passeth understanding" is our equivalent to this word.

MARINA

Quis hic locus, quae regio, quae mundi plaga?

What seas what shores what grey rocks and what islands
What water lapping the bow
And scent of pine and the woodthrush singing through the fog
What images return
O my daughter.

   Those who sharpen the tooth of the dog, meaning
Death
Those who glitter with the glory of the humming-bird, meaning
Death
Those who sit in the stye of contentment, meaning
Death
Those who suffer the ecstasy of the animals, meaning
Death

   Are become unsubstantial, reduced by a wind,
A breath of pine, and the woodsong fog
By this grace dissolved in place

What is this face, less clear and clearer
The pulse in the arm, less strong and stronger—
Given or lent? more distant than stars and nearer than the eye

Whispers and small laughter between leaves and hurrying feet
Under sleep, where all the waters meet.

Bowsprit cracked with ice and paint cracked with heat.
I made this, I have forgotten
And remember.
The rigging weak and the canvas rotten
Between one June and another September.
Made this unknowing, half conscious, unknown, my own.
The garboard strake leaks, the seams need caulking.
This form, this face, this life
Living to live in a world of time beyond me; let me
Resign my life for this life, my speech for that unspoken,
The awakened, lips parted, the hope, the new ships.

What seas what shores what granite islands towards my timbers
And woodthrush calling through the fog
My daughter.   1930

BURNT NORTON

τοῦ λόγου δ'ἐόντος ξυνοῦ ζώουσιν οἱ πολλοὶ
ὡς ἰδίαν ἔχοντες φρόνησιν.—I. p. 77. Fr. 2.
ὁδὸς ἄνω κάτω μία καὶ ὡυτή.—I, p. 89. Fr. 60.
Diels: Die Fragmente der Vorsokratiker (Herakleitos).

I

Time present and time past
Are both perhaps present in time future,
And time future contained in time past.
If all time is eternally present
All time is unredeemable.
What might have been is an abstraction
Remaining a perpetual possibility
Only in a world of speculation.
What might have been and what has been
Point to one end, which is always present.
Footfalls echo in the memory

Down the passage which we did not take
Towards the door we never opened
Into the rose-garden. My words echo
Thus, in your mind.
                    But to what purpose
Disturbing the dust on a bowl of rose-leaves
I do not know.
                    Other echoes
Inhabit the garden. Shall we follow?
Quick, said the bird, find them, find them,
Round the corner. Through the first gate,
Into our first world, shall we follow
The deception of the thrush? Into our first world.
There they were, dignified, invisible,
Moving without pressure, over the dead leaves,
In the autumn heat, through the vibrant air,
And the bird called, in response to
The unheard music hidden in the shrubbery,
And the unseen eyebeam crossed, for the roses
Had the look of flowers that are looked at.
There they were as our guests, accepted and accepting.
So we moved, and they, in a formal pattern,
Along the empty alley, into the box circle,
To look down into the drained pool.
Dry the pool, dry concrete, brown edged,
And the pool was filled with water out of sunlight,
And the lotos rose, quietly, quietly,
The surface glittered out of heart of light,
And they were behind us, reflected in the pool.
Then a cloud passed, and the pool was empty.
Go, said the bird, for the leaves were full of children,
Hidden excitedly, containing laughter.
Go, go, go, said the bird: human kind
Cannot bear very much reality.
Time past and time future
What might have been and what has been
Point to one end, which is always present.

II

Garlic and sapphires in the mud
Clot the bedded axle-tree.
The trilling wire in the blood

Sings below inveterate scars
And reconciles forgotten wars.
The dance along the artery
The circulation of the lymph
Are figured in the drift of stars
Ascend to summer in the tree
We move above the moving tree
In light upon the figured leaf
And hear upon the sodden floor
Below, the boarhound and the boar
Pursue their pattern as before
But reconciled among the stars.

　　At the still point of the turning world. Neither flesh nor fleshless;
Neither from nor towards; at the still point, there the dance is,
But neither arrest nor movement. And do not call it fixity,
Where past and future are gathered. Neither movement from nor to-
　　　　wards,
Neither ascent nor decline. Except for the point, the still point,
There would be no dance, and there is only the dance.
I can only say, *there* we have been: but I cannot say where.
And I cannot say, how long, for that is to place it in time.

　　The inner freedom from the practical desire,
The release from action and suffering, release from the inner
And the outer compulsion, yet surrounded
By a grace of sense, a white light still and moving,
Erhebung without motion, concentration
Without elimination, both a new world
And the old made explicit, understood
In the completion of its partial ecstasy,
The resolution of its partial horror.
Yet the enchainment of past and future
Woven in the weakness of the changing body,
Protects mankind from heaven and damnation
Which flesh cannot endure.
　　　　　　　　　　　Time past and time future
Allow but a little consciousness.
To be conscious is not to be in time
But only in time can the moment in the rose-garden,
The moment in the arbour where the rain beat,
The moment in the draughty church at smokefall

Be remembered; involved with past and future.
Only through time time is conquered.

III

Here is a place of disaffection
Time before and time after
In a dim light: neither daylight
Investing form with lucid stillness
Turning shadow into transient beauty
With slow rotation suggesting permanence
Nor darkness to purify the soul
Emptying the sensual with deprivation
Cleansing affection from the temporal.
Neither plenitude nor vacancy. Only a flicker
Over the strained time-ridden faces
Distracted from distraction by distraction
Filled with fancies and empty of meaning
Tumid apathy with no concentration
Men and bits of paper, whirled by the cold wind
That blows before and after time,
Wind in and out of unwholesome lungs
Time before and time after.
Eructation of unhealthy souls
Into the faded air, the torpid
Driven on the wind that sweeps the gloomy hills of London,
Hampstead and Clerkenwell, Campden and Putney,
Highgate, Primrose and Ludgate. Not here
Not here the darkness, in this twittering world.

Descend lower, descend only
Into the world of perpetual solitude,
World not world, but that which is not world,
Internal darkness, deprivation
And destitution of all property,
Desiccation of the world of sense,
Evacuation of the world of fancy,
Inoperancy of the world of spirit;
This is the one way, and the other
Is the same, not in movement
But abstention from movement; while the world moves
In appetency, on its metalled ways
Of time past and time future.

IV

Time and the bell have buried the day,
The black cloud carries the sun away.
Will the sunflower turn to us, will the clematis
Stray down, bend to us; tendril and spray
Clutch and cling?
Chill
Fingers of yew be curled
Down on us? After the kingfisher's wing
Has answered light to light, and is silent, the light is still
At the still point of the turning world.

V

Words move, music moves
Only in time; but that which is only living
Can only die. Words, after speech, reach
Into the silence. Only by the form, the pattern,
Can words or music reach
The stillness, as a Chinese jar still
Moves perpetually in its stillness.
Not the stillness of the violin, while the note lasts,
Not that only, but the co-existence,
Or say that the end precedes the beginning,
And the end and the beginning were always there
Before the beginning and after the end.
And all is always now. Words strain,
Crack and sometimes break, under the burden,
Under the tension, slip, slide, perish,
Decay with imprecision, will not stay in place,
Will not stay still. Shrieking voices
Scolding, mocking, or merely chattering,
Always assail them. The Word in the desert
Is most attacked by voices of temptation,
The crying shadow in the funeral dance,
The loud lament of the disconsolate chimera.

The detail of the pattern is movement,
As in the figure of the ten stairs.
Desire itself is movement
Not in itself desirable;
Love is itself unmoving,

Only the cause and end of movement,
Timeless, and undesiring
Except in the aspect of time
Caught in the form of limitation
Between un-being and being.
Sudden in a shaft of sunlight
Even while the dust moves
There rises the hidden laughter
Of children in the foliage
Quick now, here, now, always—
Ridiculous the waste sad time
Stretching before and after.   1936

Conrad Aiken

[MUSIC I HEARD WITH YOU]

Music I heard with you was more than music,
And bread I broke with you was more than bread;
Now that I am without you, all is desolate;
All that was once so beautiful is dead.

Your hands once touched this table and this silver,
And I have seen your fingers hold this glass.
These things do not remember you, belovèd,—
And yet your touch upon them will not pass.

For it was in my heart you moved among them,
And blessed them with your hands and with your eyes;
And in my heart they will remember always,—
They knew you once, O beautiful and wise.   *1916*

[DEAD CLEOPATRA LIES IN A CRYSTAL CASKET]

Dead Cleopatra lies in a crystal casket,
Wrapped and spiced by the cunningest of hands.
Around her neck they have put a golden necklace,
Her tatbebs, it is said, are worn with sands.

Dead Cleopatra was once revered in Egypt,
Warm-eyed she was, this princess of the South.
Now she is very old and dry and faded,
With black bitumen they have sealed up her mouth.

Grave-robbers pulled the gold rings from her fingers,
Despite the holy symbols across her breast;
They scared the bats that quietly whirled above her,
Poor lady! she would have been long since at rest,

If she had not been wrapped and spiced so shrewdly,
Preserved, obscene, to mock black flights of years. . . .
What would her lover have said,—had he foreseen it?
Had he been moved to ecstasy,—or tears?

O sweet clean earth, from whom the green blade cometh!
When we are dead, my best belovèd and I,
Close well above us, that we may rest forever,
Sending up grass and blossoms to the sky.   *1916*

[MORNING SONG OF SENLIN]

It is morning, Senlin says, and in the morning
When the light drips through the shutters like the dew,
I arise, I face the sunrise,
And do the things my fathers learned to do.
Stars in the purple dusk above the rooftops
Pale in a saffron mist and seem to die,
And I myself on a swiftly tilting planet
Stand before a glass and tie my tie.

Vine leaves tap my window,
Dew-drops sing to the garden stones,
The robin chirps in the chinaberry tree
Repeating three clear tones.

It is morning. I stand by the mirror
And tie my tie once more,
While waves far off in a pale rose twilight
Crash on a white sand shore.
I stand by a mirror and comb my hair:
How small and white my face!—
The green earth tilts through a sphere of air
And bathes in a flame of space.

There are houses hanging above the stars
And stars hung under a sea . . .
And a sun far off in a shell of silence
Dapples my walls for me . . .

It is morning, Senlin says, and in the morning
Should I not pause in the light to remember god?
Upright and firm I stand on a star unstable,

He is immense and lonely as a cloud.
I will dedicate this moment before my mirror
To him alone; for him I will comb my hair.
Accept these humble offerings, cloud of silence!
I will think of you as I descend the stair.

Vine leaves tap my window,
The snail-track shines on the stones,
Dew-drops flash from the chinaberry tree
Repeating two clear tones.

It is morning, I awake from a bed of silence,
Shining I rise from the starless waters of sleep.
The walls are about me still as in the evening,
I am the same, and the same name still I keep.

The earth revolves with me, yet makes no motion,
The stars pale silently in a coral sky.
In a whistling void I stand before my mirror,
Unconcerned, and tie my tie.

There are horses neighing on far-off hills
Tossing their long white manes,
And mountains flash in the rose-white dusk,
Their shoulders black with rains . . .
It is morning. I stand by the mirror
And surprise my soul once more;
The blue air rushes above my ceiling,
There are suns beneath my floor . . .

. . . It is morning, Senlin says, I ascend from darkness
And depart on the winds of space for I know not where,
My watch is wound, a key is in my pocket,
And the sky is darkened as I descend the stair.
There are shadows across the windows, clouds in heaven,
And a god among the stars; and I will go
Thinking of him as I might think of daybreak
And humming a tune I know . . .

Vine leaves tap at the window,
Dew-drops sing to the garden stones,
The robin chirps in the chinaberry tree
Repeating three clear tones.   *1918*

TETÉLESTAI

I

How shall we praise the magnificence of the dead,
The great man humbled, the haughty brought to dust?
Is there a horn we should not blow as proudly
For the meanest of us all, who creeps his days,
Guarding his heart from blows, to die obscurely?
I am no king, have laid no kingdoms waste,
Taken no princes captive, led no triumphs
Of weeping women through long walls of trumpets;
Say rather, I am no one, or an atom;
Say rather, two great gods, in a vault of starlight,
Play ponderingly at chess, and at the game's end
One of the pieces, shaken, falls to the floor
And runs to the darkest corner; and that piece
Forgotten there, left motionless, is I. . . .
Say that I have no name, no gifts, no power,
Am only one of millions, mostly silent;
One who came with eyes and hands and a heart,
Looked on beauty, and loved it, and then left it.
Say that the fates of time and space obscured me,
Led me a thousand ways to pain, bemused me,
Wrapped me in ugliness; and like great spiders
Dispatched me at their leisure. . . . Well, what then?
Should I not hear, as I lie down in dust,
The horns of glory blowing above my burial?

II

Morning and evening opened and closed above me:
Houses were built above me; trees let fall
Yellowing leaves upon me, hands of ghosts;
Rain has showered its arrows of silver upon me
Seeking my heart; winds have roared and tossed me;
Music in long blue waves of sound has borne me
A helpless weed to shores of unthought silence;
Time, above me, within me, crashed its gongs
Of terrible warning, sifting the dust of death;
And here I lie. Blow now your horns of glory
Harshly over my flesh, you trees, you waters!
You stars and suns, Canopus, Deneb, Rigel,
Let me, as ⊥ lie down, here in this dust,

Hear, far off, your whispered salutation!
Roar now above my decaying flesh, you winds,
Whirl out your earth-scents over this body, tell me
Of ferns and stagnant pools, wild roses, hillsides!
Anoint me, rain, let crash your silver arrows
On this hard flesh! I am the one who named you,
I lived in you, and now I die in you.
I your son, your daughter, treader of music,
Lie broken, conquered . . . Let me not fall in silence.

III

I, the restless one; the circler of circles;
Herdsman and roper of stars, who could not capture
The secret of self; I who was tyrant to weaklings,
Striker of children; destroyer of women; corrupter
Of innocent dreamers, and laugher at beauty; I,
Too easily brought to tears and weakness by music,
Baffled and broken by love, the helpless beholder
Of the war in my heart of desire with desire, the struggle
Of hatred with love, terror with hunger; I
Who laughed without knowing the cause of my laughter, who grew
Without wishing to grow, a servant to my own body;
Loved without reason the laughter and flesh of a woman,
Enduring such torments to find her! I who at last
Grow weaker, struggle more feebly, relent in my purpose,
Choose for my triumph an easier end, look backward
At earlier conquests; or, caught in the web, cry out
In a sudden and empty despair, "Tetélestai!"
Pity me, now! I, who was arrogant, beg you!
Tell me, as I lie down, that I was courageous.
Blow horns of victory now, as I reel and am vanquished.
Shatter the sky with trumpets above my grave.

IV

. . . Look! this flesh how it crumbles to dust and is blown!
These bones, how they grind in the granite of frost and are nothing!
This skull, how it yawns for a flicker of time in the darkness,
Yet laughs not and sees not! It is crushed by a hammer of sunlight,
And the hands are destroyed. . . . Press down through the leaves of
    the jasmine,
Dig through the interlaced roots—nevermore will you find me;
I was no better than dust, yet you cannot replace me. . . .
Take the soft dust in your hand—does it stir: does it sing?

Has it lips and a heart? Does it open its eyes to the sun?
Does it run, does it dream, does it burn with a secret, or tremble
In terror of death? Or ache with tremendous decisions? . . .
Listen! . . . It says: "I lean by the river. The willows
Are yellowed with bud. White clouds roar up from the south
And darken the ripples; but they cannot darken my heart,
Nor the face like a star in my heart! . . . Rain falls on the water
And pelts it, and rings it with silver. The willow trees glisten,
The sparrows chirp under the eaves; but the face in my heart
Is a secret of music. . . . I wait in the rain and am silent."
Listen again! . . . It says: "I have worked, I am tired,
The pencil dulls in my hand: I see through the window
Walls upon walls of windows with faces behind them,
Smoke floating up to the sky, an ascension of sea-gulls.
I am tired. I have struggled in vain, my decision was fruitless,
Why then do I wait? with darkness, so easy, at hand! . . .
But to-morrow, perhaps . . . I will wait and endure till to-morrow!" . . .
Or again: "It is dark. The decision is made. I am vanquished
By terror of life. The walls mount slowly about me
In coldness. I had not the courage. I was forsaken.
I cried out, was answered by silence . . . Tetélestai! . . ."

V

Hear how it babbles!—Blow the dust out of your hand,
With its voices and visions, tread on it, forget it, turn homeward
With dreams in your brain. . . . This, then, is the humble, the name-
    less,—
The lover, the husband and father, the struggler with shadows,
The one who went down under shoutings of chaos, the weakling
Who cried his "forsaken!" like Christ on the darkening hilltop! . . .
This, then, is the one who implores, as he dwindles to silence,
A fanfare of glory . . . And which of us dares to deny him?

1918, 1925

From PRIAPUS AND THE POOL
IV

This is the shape of the leaf, and this of the flower,
    And this the pale bole of the tree
Which watches its bough in a pool of unwavering water
    In a land we never shall see.

The thrush on the bough is silent, the dew falls softly,
    In the evening is hardly a sound.

And the three beautiful pilgrims who come here together
Touch lightly the dust of the ground,

Touch it with feet that trouble the dust but as wings do,
Come shyly together, are still,
Like dancers who wait, in a pause of the music, for music
The exquisite silence to fill.

This is the thought of the first, and this of the second,
And this the grave thought of the third:
"Linger we thus for a moment, palely expectant,
And silence will end, and the bird

"Sing the pure phrase, sweet phrase, clear phrase in the twilight
To fill the blue bell of the world;
And we, who on music so leaflike have drifted together,
Leaflike apart shall be whirled

"Into what but the beauty of silence, silence forever?" . . .
. . . This is the shape of the tree,
And the flower, and the leaf, and the three pale beautiful pilgrims
This is what you are to me.

IX

There is nothing moving there, in that desert of silence,
Nothing living there, not even a blade of grass.
The morning there is as silent as the evening;
The nights and days with an equal horror pass.

Nothing moving except the cold, slow shadow
Thrown on sand by a boulder, or by the cliff
Whose rock not even a lichen comes to cover,
To hide—from what?—time's ancient hieroglyph.

The sun, at noon, sings like a flaming cymbal
Above that waste: but the waste makes no reply.
In all that desolation of rock and gravel
There is no water, no answer to the sky.

Sometimes, perhaps, from other lands more happy,
A faint wind, slow, exhausted, ventures there,
And loses itself in silence, like a music.
And then—who knows?—beneath that alien air,

Which moves mysteriously as memory over
Forlorn abysms and peaks of stone and sand,
Ghosts of delight awake for a shining moment,
And all is troubled, and that desolate land

Remembers grass and flowers, and birds that sang there
Their miracles of song in lovely trees,
And waters that poured, or stood, in dreaming azure,
Praising the sky. Perhaps once more it sees

The rose, the moon, the pool, in the blue evening,
And knows that silence in which one bird will sing
Slowly and sleepily his praise of gardens.
Perhaps once more, for a moment, it remembers spring.

XV

There was an island in the sea
That out of immortal chaos reared
Towers of topaz, trees of pearl,
For maidens adored and warriors feared.

Long ago it sank in the sea;
And now, a thousand fathoms deep,
Sea-worms above it whirl their lamps,
Crabs on the pale mosaic creep.

Voyagers over that haunted sea
Hear from the waters under the keel
A sound that is not wave or foam;
Nor do they only hear, but feel

The timbers quiver, as eerily comes
Up from the dark an elfin singing
Of voices happy as none can be,
And bells an ethereal anthem ringing.

Thereafter, where they go or come,
They will be silent; they have heard
Out of the infinite of the soul
An incommunicable word;

Thereafter, they are as lovers who
Over an infinite brightness lean:

"It is Atlantis!" all their speech;
"To lost Atlantis have we been."

1920–21, 1925

THE WEDDING

At noon, Tithonus, withered by his singing,
Climbing the oatstalk with his hairy legs,
Met grey Arachne, poisoned and shrunk down
By her own beauty; pride had shrivelled both.
In the white web—where seven flies hung wrapped—
She heard his footstep; hurried to him; bound him;
Enshrouded him in silk; then poisoned him.
Twice shrieked Tithonus, feebly; then was still.
Arachne loved him. Did he love Arachne?
She watched him with red eyes, venomous sparks,
And the furred claws outspread . . . "O sweet Tithonus!
Darling! Be kind, and sing that song again!
Shake the bright web again with that deep fiddling!
Are you much poisoned? sleeping? do you dream?
Darling Tithonus!"

         And Tithonus, weakly
Moving one hairy shin against the other
Within the silken sack, contrived to fiddle
A little tune, half-hearted: "Shrewd Arachne!
Whom pride in beauty withered to this shape
As pride in singing shrivelled me to mine—
Unwrap me, let me go—and let me limp,
With what poor strength your venom leaves me, down
This oatstalk, and away."

         Arachne, angry,
Stung him again, twirling him with rough paws,
The red eyes keen. "What! you would dare to leave me?
Unkind Tithonus! Sooner I'll kill and eat you
Than let you go. But sing that tune again—
So plaintive was it!"

         And Tithonus faintly
Moved the poor fiddles, which were growing cold,
And sang: "Arachne, goddess envied of gods,
Beauty's eclipse eclipsed by angry beauty,

Have pity, do not ask the withered heart
To sing too long for you! My strength goes out,
Too late we meet for love. O be content
With friendship, which the noon sun once may kindle
To give one flash of passion, like a dewdrop,
Before it goes! . . . Be reasonable, Arachne!"

Arachne heard the song grow weaker, dwindle
To first a rustle, and then half a rustle,
And last a tick, so small no ear could hear it
Save hers, a spider's ear. And her small heart,
(Rusted away, like his, to a pinch of dust,)
Gleamed once, like his, and died. She clasped him tightly
And sunk her fangs in him. Tithonus dead,
She slept awhile, her last sensation gone;
Woke from the nap, forgetting him; and ate him.   *1925*

AT A CONCERT OF MUSIC

Be still, while the music rises about us; the deep enchantment
Towers, like a forest of singing leaves and birds,
Built, for an instant, by the heart's troubled beating,
Beyond all power of words.

And while you are listening, silent, I escape you;
And I run by a secret path through that dark wood
To another time, long past, and another woman,
And another mood.

Then, too, the music's cold algebra of enchantment
Wrought all about us a bird-voice-haunted grove;
Then, too, I escaped, as now, to an earlier moment,
And a brighter love.

Alas! Can I never have peace in the shining instant?
The hard bright crystal of being, in time and space?
Must I always touch, in the moment, an earlier moment,
And an earlier face?

Absolve me. I would adore you, had I the secret,
With all this music's power, for yourself alone;
I would try to answer, in the world's chaotic symphony,
Your one clear tone;

But alas, alas, being everything you are nothing—
The history of all my life is in your face;
And all I can know is an earlier, more haunted moment,
And a happier place.   *1930*

[WATCH LONG ENOUGH, AND YOU WILL SEE]

Watch long enough, and you will see the leaf   22
Fall from the bough. Without a sound it falls:
And soundless meets the grass. . . . And so you have
A bare bough, and a dead leaf in dead grass.
Something has come and gone. And that is all.

But what were all the tumults in this action?
What wars of atoms in the twig, what ruins,
Fiery and disastrous, in the leaf?
Timeless the tumult was, but gave no sign.
Only, the leaf fell, and the bough is bare.

This is the world: there is no more than this.
The unseen and disastrous prelude, shaking
The trivial act from the terrific action.
Speak: and the ghosts of change, past and to come,
Throng the brief word. The maelstrom has us all.   *1931*

[KEEP IN THE HEART THE JOURNAL]

Keep in the heart the journal nature keeps;
Mark down the limp nasturtium leaf with frost;
See that the hawthorn bough is ice-embossed,
And that the snail, in season, has his grief;
Design the winter on the window pane;
Admit pale sun through cobwebs left from autumn;
Remember summer when the flies are stilled;
Remember spring, when the cold spider sleeps.

Such diary, too, set down as this: the heart
Beat twice or thrice this day for no good reason;
For friends and sweethearts dead before their season;
For wisdom come too late, and come to naught.
Put down "the hand that shakes," "the eye that glazes";
The "step that falters betwixt thence and hence";
Observe that hips and haws burn brightest red
When the North Pole and sun are most apart.

Note that the moon is here, as cold as ever,
With ages on her face, and ice and snow;
Such as the freezing mind alone can know,
When loves and hates are only twigs that shiver.
Add in a postscript that the rain is over,
The wind from southwest backing to the south,
Disasters all forgotten, hurts forgiven;
And that the North Star, altered, shines forever.

Then say: I was a part of nature's plan;
Knew her cold heart, for I was consciousness;
Came first to hate her, and at last to bless;
Believed in her; doubted; believed again.
My love the lichen had such roots as I,—
The snowflake was my father; I return,
After this interval of faith and question,
To nature's heart, in pain, as I began.   *1931*

[BEND AS THE BOW BENDS]

Bend as the bow bends, and let fly the shaft,
the strong cord loose its word as light as flame;
speak without cunning, love, as without craft,
careless of answer, as of shame or blame.
This to be known, that love is love, despite
knowledge or ignorance, truth, untruth, despair;
careless of all things, if that love be bright,
careless of hate and fate, careless of care.
Spring the word as it must, the leaf or flower,
broken or bruised, yet let it, broken, speak
of time transcending this too transient hour,
and space that finds the beating heart too weak.
Thus, and thus only, will our tempest come
by continents of snow to find a home.   *1940*

[SNOWFLAKE ON ASPHODEL]

Snowflake on asphodel, clear ice on rose,
frost over thistledown, the instant death
that speaks Time's judgment, turning verse to prose,
or withering June to blackness in a breath—
icicle, cheek by jowl with goldenrod,
and on the purple aster silver rime,

a web of death, bright as the web of god,
spun on these simple themes and schemes by time:
snowflake on asphodel—how clear, how bright
the blue burns through the melting star! how brave
the dying flower, and the snow how light
that on the dying flower makes his grave!
Snow's death on dying flower, yet both immortal—
love, these are you and I—enter this portal.   *1940*

SOUTH END

The benches are broken, the grassplots brown and bare,
the laurels dejected, in this neglected square.
Dogs couple undisturbed. The roots of trees
heave up the bricks in the sidewalk as they please.

Nobody collects the papers from the grass,
nor the dead matches, nor the broken glass.
The elms are old and shabby; the houses, around,
stare lazily through paintless shutters at forgotten ground.

Out of the dusty fountain, with the dust,
the leaves fly up like birds on a sudden gust.
The leaves fly up like birds, and the papers flap,
or round the legs of benches wrap and unwrap.

Here, for the benefit of some secret sense,
warm-autumn-afternoon finds permanence.
No one will hurry, or wait too long, or die:
all is serenity, under a serene sky.

Dignity shines in old brick and old dirt,
in elms and houses now hurt beyond all hurt.
A broken square, where little lives or moves;
these are the city's earliest and tenderest loves.   *1942*

THE WINDOW

She looks out in the blue morning
and sees a whole wonderful world
she looks out in the morning
and sees a whole world

she leans out of the window
and this is what she sees
a wet rose singing to the sun
with a chorus of red bees

she leans out of the window
and laughs for the window is high
she is in it like a bird on a perch
and they scoop the blue sky

she and the window scooping
the morning as if it were air
scooping a green wave of leaves
above a stone stair

and an urn hung with leaden garlands
and girls holding hands in a ring
and raindrops on an iron railing
shining like a harp string

an old man draws with his ferrule
in wet sand a map of Spain
the marble soldier on his pedestal
draws a stiff diagram of pain

but the walls around her tremble
with the speed of the earth the floor
curves to the terrestrial center
and behind her the door

opens darkly down to the beginning
far down to the first simple cry
and the animal waking in water
and the opening of the eye

she looks out in the blue morning
and sees a whole wonderful world
she looks out in the morning
and sees a whole world.   *1949*

Edna St. Vincent Millay

GOD'S WORLD

O World, I cannot hold thee close enough!
   Thy winds, thy wide grey skies!
   Thy mists, that roll and rise!
Thy woods, this autumn day, that ache and sag
And all but cry with color! That gaunt crag
To crush! To lift the lean of that black bluff!
World, World, I cannot get thee close enough!

Long have I known a glory in it all,
   But never knew I this;
   Here such a passion is
As stretcheth me apart,—Lord, I do fear
Thou'st made the world too beautiful this year;
My soul is all but out of me,—let fall
No burning leaf; prithee, let no bird call.

1917

[THOU ART NOT LOVELIER THAN LILACS]

Thou art not lovelier than lilacs,—no,
Nor honeysuckle; thou art not more fair
Than small white single poppies,—I can bear
Thy beauty; though I bend before thee, though
From left to right, not knowing where to go,
I turn my troubled eyes, nor here nor there
Find any refuge from thee, yet I swear
So has it been with mist,—with moonlight so.

Like him who day by day unto his draught
Of delicate poison adds him one drop more
Till he may drink unharmed the death of ten,

Even so, inured to beauty, who have quaffed
Each hour more deeply than the hour before,
I drink—and live—what has destroyed some men.

1917

THE PHILOSOPHER

And what are you that, missing you,
    I should be kept awake
As many nights as there are days
    With weeping for your sake?

And what are you that, missing you,
    As many days as crawl
I should be listening to the wind
    And looking at the wall?

I know a man that's a braver man
    And twenty men as kind,
And what are you, that you should be
    The one man in my mind?

Yet women's ways are witless ways,
    As any sage will tell,—
And what am I, that I should love
    So wisely and so well?   1920

[OH, THINK NOT I AM FAITHFUL TO A VOW]

Oh, think not I am faithful to a vow!
Faithless am I save to love's self alone.
Were you not lovely I would leave you now:
After the feet of beauty fly my own.
Were you not still my hunger's rarest food,
And water ever to my wildest thirst,
I would desert you—think not but I would!—
And seek another as I sought you first.
But you are mobile as the veering air,
And all your charms more changeful than the tide,
Wherefore to be inconstant is no care:
I have but to continue at your side.
    So wanton, light and false, my love, are you,
    I am most faithless when I most am true.   1920

ELEGY BEFORE DEATH

There will be rose and rhododendron
   When you are dead and under ground;
Still will be heard from white syringas
   Heavy with bees, a sunny sound;

Still will the tamaracks be raining
   After the rain has ceased, and still
Will there be robins in the stubble,
   Brown sheep upon the warm green hill.

Spring will not ail nor autumn falter;
   Nothing will know that you are gone,
Saving alone some sullen plough-land
   None but yourself sets foot upon;

Saving the may-weed and the pig-weed
   Nothing will know that you are dead,—
These, and perhaps a useless wagon
   Standing beside some tumbled shed.

Oh, there will pass with your great passing
   Little of beauty not your own,—
Only the light from common water,
   Only the grace from simple stone! *1921*

PASSER MORTUUS EST

Death devours all lovely things:
   Lesbia with her sparrow
Shares the darkness,—presently
   Every bed is narrow.

Unremembered as old rain
   Dries the sheer libation;
And the little petulant hand
   Is an annotation.

After all, my erstwhile dear,
   My no longer cherished,
Need we say it was not love,
   Just because it perished?

1921

SONG OF A SECOND APRIL

April this year, not otherwise
    Than April of a year ago,
Is full of whispers, full of sighs,
    Of dazzling mud and dingy snow;
    Hepaticas that pleased you so
Are here again, and butterflies.

There rings a hammering all day,
    And shingles lie about the doors;
In orchards near and far away
    The grey wood-pecker taps and bores;
    And men are merry at their chores,
And children earnest at their play.

The larger streams run still and deep,
    Noisy and swift the small brooks run;
Among the mullein stalks the sheep
    Go up the hillside in the sun,
    Pensively,—only you are gone,
You that alone I cared to keep.   *1921*

ELEGY

Let them bury your big eyes
In the secret earth securely,
Your thin fingers, and your fair,
Soft, indefinite-coloured hair,—
All of these in some way, surely,
From the secret earth shall rise;
Not for these I sit and stare,
Broken and bereft completely:
Your young flesh that sat so neatly
On your little bones will sweetly
Blossom in the air.

But your voice . . . never the rushing
Of a river underground,
Not the rising of the wind
In the trees before the rain,
Not the woodcock's watery call,

Not the note the white-throat utters,
Not the feet of children pushing
Yellow leaves along the gutters
In the blue and bitter fall,
Shall content my musing mind
For the beauty of that sound
That in no new way at all
Ever will be heard again.

Sweetly through the sappy stalk
Of the vigourous weed,
Holding all it held before,
Cherished by the faithful sun,
On and on eternally
Shall your altered fluid run,
Bud and bloom and go to seed:
But your singing days are done;
But the music of your talk
Never shall the chemistry
Of the secret earth restore.
All your lovely words are spoken.
Once the ivory box is broken,
Beats the golden bird no more.   *1921*

WILD SWANS

I looked in my heart while the wild swans went over.
And what did I see I had not seen before?
Only a question less or a question more;
Nothing to match the flight of wild birds flying.
Tiresome heart, forever living and dying,
House without air, I leave you and lock your door.
Wild swans, come over the town, come over
The town again, trailing your legs and crying!   *1921*

[I KNOW I AM BUT SUMMER TO YOUR HEART]

I know I am but summer to your heart,
And not the full four seasons of the year;
And you must welcome from another part
Such noble moods as are not mine, my dear.
No gracious weight of golden fruits to sell
Have I, nor any wise and wintry thing;
And I have loved you all too long and well

To carry still the high sweet breast of Spring.
Wherefore I say: O love, as summer goes,
I must be gone, steal forth with silent drums,
That you may hail anew the bird and rose
When I come back to you, as summer comes.
  Else will you seek, at some not distant time,
  Even your summer in another clime.   *1923*

[PITY ME NOT BECAUSE THE LIGHT OF DAY]

Pity me not because the light of day
At close of day no longer walks the sky;
Pity me not for beauties passed away
From field and thicket as the year goes by;
Pity me not the waning of the moon,
Nor that the ebbing tide goes out to sea,
Nor that a man's desire is hushed so soon,
And you no longer look with love on me.
This have I known always: Love is no more
Than the wide blossom which the wind assails,
Than the great tide that treads the shifting shore,
Strewing fresh wreckage gathered in the gales:
Pity me that the heart is slow to learn
What the swift mind beholds at every turn.

1923

[EUCLID ALONE HAS LOOKED ON BEAUTY]

Euclid alone has looked on Beauty bare.
Let all who prate of Beauty hold their peace,
And lay them prone upon the earth and cease
To ponder on themselves, the while they stare
At nothing, intricately drawn nowhere
In shapes of shifting lineage; let geese
Gabble and hiss, but heroes seek release
From dusty bondage into luminous air.

O blinding hour, O holy, terrible day,
When first the shaft into his vision shone
Of light anatomized! Euclid alone
Has looked on Beauty bare. Fortunate they
Who, though once only and then but far away,
Have heard her massive sandal set on stone.

1923

DIRGE WITHOUT MUSIC

I am not resigned to the shutting away of loving hearts in the hard
 ground.
So it is, and so it will be, for so it has been, time out of mind:
Into the darkness they go, the wise and the lovely.
Crowned with lilies and with laurel they go; but I am not resigned.

Lovers and thinkers, into the earth with you.
Be one with the dull, the indiscriminate dust.
A fragment of what you felt, of what you knew,
A formula, a phrase remains,—but the best is lost.

The answers quick and keen, the honest look, the laughter, the love,—
They are gone. They are gone to feed the roses. Elegant and curled
Is the blossom. Fragrant is the blossom. I know. But I do not approve.
More precious was the light in your eyes than all the roses in the world.

Down, down, down into the darkness of the grave
Gently they go, the beautiful, the tender, the kind;
Quietly they go, the intelligent, the witty, the brave.
I know. But I do not approve. And I am not resigned.   1928

[NOT THAT IT MATTERS]

Not that it matters, not that my heart's cry
Is potent to deflect our common doom,
Or bind to truce in this ambiguous room
The planets of the atom as they ply;
But only to record that you and I,
Like thieves that scratch the jewels from a tomb,
Have gathered delicate love in hardy bloom
Close under Chaos,—I rise to testify.
This is my testament: that we are taken;
Our colours are as clouds before the wind;
Yet for a moment stood the foe forsaken,
Eyeing Love's favour to our helmet pinned;
Death is our master,—but his seat is shaken;
He rides victorious,—but his ranks are thinned.
                                                    1928

SONNET TO GATH

Country of hunchbacks!—where the strong, straight spine,
Jeered at by crooked children, makes his way
Through by-streets at the kindest hour of day,
Till he deplore his stature, and incline
To measure manhood with a gibbous line;
Till out of loneliness, being flawed with clay,
He stoop into his neighbour's house and say,
"Your roof is low for me—the fault is mine."
Dust in an urn long since, dispersed and dead
Is great Apollo; and the happier he;
Since who amongst you all would lift a head
At a god's radiance on the mean door-tree,
Saving to run and hide your dates and bread,
And cluck your children in about your knee?   *1928*

From *FATAL INTERVIEW*

XI

Not in a silver casket cool with pearls
Or rich with red corundum or with blue,
Locked, and the key withheld, as other girls
Have given their loves, I give my love to you;
Not in a lovers'-knot, not in a ring
Worked in such fashion, and the legend plain—
Semper fidelis, where a secret spring
Kennels a drop of mischief for the brain:
Love in the open hand, no thing but that,
Ungemmed, unhidden, wishing not to hurt,
As one should bring you cowslips in a hat
Swung from the hand, or apples in her skirt,
    I bring you, calling out as children do:
    "Look what I have!—And these are all for you."

XXVI

Women have loved before as I love now;
At least, in lively chronicles of the past—
Of Irish waters by a Cornish prow
Or Trojan waters by a Spartan mast
Much to their cost invaded—here and there,

Hunting the amorous line, skimming the rest,
I find some woman bearing as I bear
Love like a burning city in the breast.
I think however that of all alive
I only in such utter, ancient way
Do suffer love; in me alone survive
The unregenerate passions of a day
When treacherous queens, with death upon the tread,
Heedless and wilful, took their knights to bed.

XXX

Love is not all; it is not meat nor drink
Nor slumber nor a roof against the rain,
Nor yet a floating spar to men that sink
And rise and sink and rise and sink again;
Love can not fill the thickened lung with breath,
Nor clean the blood, nor set the fractured bone;
Yet many a man is making friends with death
Even as I speak, for lack of love alone.
It well may be that in a difficult hour,
Pinned down by pain and moaning for release,
Or nagged by want past resolution's power,
I might be driven to sell your love for peace,
    Or trade the memory of this night for food.
    It well may be. I do not think I would.

XXXVI

Hearing your words, and not a word among them
Tuned to my liking, on a salty day
When inland woods were pushed by winds that flung them
Hissing to leeward like a ton of spray,
I thought how off Matinicus the tide
Came pounding in, came running through the Gut,
While from the Rock the warning whistle cried,
And children whimpered, and the doors blew shut;
There in the autumn when the men go forth,
With slapping skirts the island women stand
In gardens stripped and scattered, peering north,
With dahlia tubers dripping from the hand:
The wind of their endurance, driving south,
Flattened your words against your speaking mouth.

XLVIII

Now by the path I climbed, I journey back.
The oaks have grown; I have been long away.
Taking with me your memory and your lack
I now descend into a milder day;
Stripped of your love, unburdened of my hope,
Descend the path I mounted from the plain;
Yet steeper than I fancied seems the slope
And stonier, now that I go down again.
Warm falls the dusk; the clanking of a bell
Faintly ascends upon this heavier air;
I do recall those grassy pastures well:
In early spring they drove the cattle there.
And close at hand should be a shelter, too,
From which the mountain peaks are not in view.

LII

Oh, sleep forever in the Latmian cave,
Mortal Endymion, darling of the Moon!
Her silver garments by the senseless wave
Shouldered and dropped and on the shingle strewn,
Her fluttering hand against her forehead pressed,
Her scattered looks that trouble all the sky,
Her rapid footsteps running down the west—
Of all her altered state, oblivious lie!
Whom earthen you, by deathless lips adored,
Wild-eyed and stammering to the grasses thrust,
And deep into her crystal body poured
The hot and sorrowful sweetness of the dust:
Whereof she wanders mad, being all unfit
For mortal love, that might not die of it.   *1931*

From *EPITAPH FOR THE RACE OF MAN*
VI

See where Capella with her golden kids
Grazes the slope between the east and north:
Thus when the builders of the pyramids
Flung down their tools at nightfall and poured forth
Homeward to supper and a poor man's bed,

Shortening the road with friendly jest and slur,
The risen She-Goat showing blue and red
Climbed the clear dusk, and three stars followed her.
Safe in their linen and their spices lie
The kings of Egypt; even as long ago
Under these constellations, with long eye
And scented limbs they slept, and feared no foe.
Their will was law; their will was not to die:
And so they had their way; or nearly so.

X

The broken dike, the levee washed away,
The good fields flooded and the cattle drowned,
Estranged and treacherous all the faithful ground,
And nothing left but floating disarray
Of tree and home uprooted,—was this the day
Man dropped upon his shadow without a sound
And died, having laboured well and having found
His burden heavier than a quilt of clay?
No, no. I saw him when the sun had set
In water, leaning on his single oar
Above his garden faintly glimmering yet . . .
There bulked the plough, here washed the updrifted weeds . . .
And scull across his roof and make for shore,
With twisted face and pocket full of seeds.   1934

ON THE WIDE HEATH

On the wide heath at evening overtaken,
    When the fast-reddening sun
Drops, and against the sky the looming bracken
    Waves, and the day is done,

Though no unfriendly nostril snuffs his bone,
    Though English wolves be dead,
The fox abroad on errands of his own,
    The adder gone to bed,

The weary traveler from his aching hip
    Lengthens his long stride;
Though Home be but a humming on his lip,
    No happiness, no pride,

He does not drop him under the yellow whin
    To sleep the darkness through;
Home to the yellow light that shines within
    The kitchen of a loud shrew.

Home over stones and sand, through stagnant water
    He goes, mile after mile
Home to a wordless poaching son and a daughter
    With a disdainful smile,

Home to the worn reproach, the disagreeing,
    The shelter, the stale air; content to be
Pecked at, confined, encroached upon,—it being
    Too lonely, to be free.   *1934*

THE STRAWBERRY SHRUB

Strawberry Shrub, old-fashioned, quaint as quinces,
Hard to find in a world where neon and noise
Have flattened the ends of the three more subtle senses;
And blare and magenta are all that a child enjoys.

More brown than red the bloom—it is a dense colour;
Colour of dried blood; colour of the key of F.
Tie it in your handkerchief, Dorcas, take it to school
To smell. But no, as I said, it is browner than red; it is duller
Than history, tinnier than algebra; and you are colour-deaf.

Purple, a little, the bloom, like musty chocolate;
Purpler than the purple avens of the wet fields;
But brown and red and hard and hiding its fragrance;
More like an herb it is: it is not exuberant.
You must bruise it a bit: it does not exude; it yields.

Clinker-built, the bloom, over-lapped its petals
Like clapboards; like a boat I had; like the feathers of a wing;
Not graceful, not at all Grecian, something from the provinces:
A chunky, ruddy, beautiful Boeotian thing.

Take it to school, knotted in your handkerchief, Dorcas,
Corner of your handkerchief, take it to school, and see
What your teacher says; show your pretty teacher the curious
Strawberry Shrub you took to school for me.   *1954*

Archibald MacLeish

THE SILENT SLAIN

We too, we too, descending once again
The hills of our own land, we too have heard
Far off—Ah, *que ce cor a longue haleine*—
The horn of Roland in the passages of Spain,
The first, the second blast, the failing third,
And with the third turned back and climbed once more
The steep road southward, and heard faint the sound
Of swords, of horses, the disastrous war,
And crossed the dark defile at last, and found
At Roncevaux upon the darkening plain
The dead against the dead and on the silent ground
The silent slain—   *1926*

LE SECRET HUMAIN

It was not God that told us. We knew
Before, long before, long, long ago.
We knew that tonight—or tomorrow—. We know
Still—tomorrow. It is true that we know.

The incredulous surprise
In the faces of the dead, in dead eyes:
There was something still to happen—
There was someone that was always going to come.

And the eyes of those that sleep,
The puzzled eyes:
There are promises the silence does not keep—
And the dark has no replies.

Ah, we know
As the wind blows,
Not to the south, the north,
Not to, not ever to, but toward.

We know beyond the doors we press and open,
Beyond the smell of breakfast in the hall,
Beyond the soggy towel and the soap—
Wait! We shall know all.

We that sit and think and talk,
We that lie awake till late,
We that walk beside the river:
We can wait—O we can wait!   1926

EINSTEIN

Standing between the sun and moon preserves
A certain secrecy. Or seems to keep
Something inviolate if only that
His father was an ape.
                    Sweet music makes
All of his walls sound hollow and he hears
Sighs in the paneling and underfoot
Melancholy voices. So there is a door
Behind the seamless arras and within
A living something:—but no door that will
Admit the sunlight nor no windows where
The mirror moon can penetrate his bones
With cold deflection. He is small and tight
And solidly contracted into space
Opaque and perpendicular which blots
Earth with its shadow. And he terminates
In shoes which bearing up against the sphere
Attract his concentration,

*Einstein upon a public
bench Wednesday the
ninth contemplates finity*

                    for he ends
If there why then no farther, as, beyond
Extensively the universe itself,
Or chronologically the two dates
Original and ultimate of time,

Nor could Jehovah and the million stars
Staring within their solitudes of light,
Nor all night's constellations be contained
Between his boundaries,
                    nor could the sun

Receive him nor his groping roots run down
Into the loam and steaming sink of time
Where coils the middle serpent and the ooze
Breeds maggots.
        But it seems assured he ends
Precisely at his shoes in proof whereof
He can revolve in orbits opposite
The orbit of the earth and so refuse
All planetary converse. And he wears
Cloths that distinguish him from what is not
His own circumference, as first a coat
Shaped to his back or modeled in reverse
Of the surrounding cosmos and below
Trousers preserving his detachment from
The revolutions of the stars.

Einstein descends the
Hartmannsweilerstrasse

        His hands
And face go naked and alone converse
With what encloses him, as rough and smooth
And sound and silence and the intervals
Of rippling ether and the swarming motes
Clouding a privy: move to them and make
Shadows that mirror them within his skull
In perpendiculars and curves and planes
And bodiless significances blurred
As figures undersea and images
Patterned from eddies of the air.

        Which are
Perhaps not shadows but the thing itself
And may be understood.

Einstein provisionally before
a mirror accepts the hy-
pothesis of subjective reality

        Decorticate
The petals of the enfolding world and leave
A world in reason which is in himself
And has his own dimensions. Here do trees
Adorn the hillside and hillsides enrich
The hazy marches of the sky and skies
Kindle and char to ashes in the wind,
And winds blow toward him from the verge, and suns
Rise on his dawn and on his dusk go down
And moons prolong his shadow. And he moves
Here as within a garden in a close

And where he moves the bubble of the world
Takes center and there circle round his head
Like golden flies in summer the gold stars.

. . . rejects it

Disintegrates.

For suddenly he feels
The planet plunge beneath him, and a flare
Falls from the upper darkness to the dark
And awful shadows loom across the sky
That have no life from him and suns go out
And livid as a drowned man's face the moon
Floats to the lapsing surface of the night
And sinks discolored under.
So he knows
Less than a world and must communicate
Beyond his knowledge.

Einstein unsuccessfully after
lunch attempts to enter, es-
saying synthesis with what's
not he, the Bernese Oberland

Outstretched on the earth
He plunges both his arms into the swirl
Of what surrounds him but the yielding grass
Excludes his finger tips and the soft soil
Will not endure confusion with his hands
Nor will the air receive him nor the light
Dissolve their difference but recoiling turns
Back from his touch. By which denial he can
Crawl on the earth and sense the opposing sun
But not make answer to them.
Put out leaves
And let the old remembering wind think through
A green intelligence or under sea
Float out long filaments of amber in
The numb and wordless revery of tides.

In autumn the black branches dripping rain
Bruise his uncovered bones and in the spring
His swollen tips are gorged with aching blood
That bursts the laurel.
But although they seize
His sense he has no name for them, no word

To give them meaning and no utterance
For what they say. Feel the new summer's sun
Crawl up the warmed relaxing hide of earth
And weep for his lost youth, his childhood home
And a wide water on an inland shore!
Or to the night's mute asking in the blood
Give back a girl's name and three notes together!
He cannot think the smell of after rain
Nor close his thought around the long smooth lag
And falter of a wind, nor bring to mind
Dusk and the whippoorwill.

Einstein dissolved in violins invades the molecular structure of F. P. Paepke's Sommergarten. Is repulsed.

But violins
Split out of trees and strung to tone can sing
Strange nameless words that image to the ear
What has no waiting image in the brain.

She plays in darkness and the droning wood
Dissolves to reverberations of a world
Beating in waves against him till his sense
Trembles to rhythm and his naked brain
Feels without utterance in form the flesh
Of dumb and incommunicable earth,
And knows at once, and without knowledge how,
The stroke of the blunt rain, and blind receives
The sun.
When he a moment occupies
The hollow of himself and like an air
Pervades all other.
But the violin
Presses its dry insistence through the dream
That swims above it, shivering its speech
Back to a rhythm that becomes again
Music and vaguely ravels into sound.

To Einstein asking at the gate of stone none opens

So then there is no speech that can resolve
Their texture to clear thought and enter them.

The Virgin of Chartres whose bleaching bones still wear
The sapphires of her glory knew a word—
That now is three round letters like tne three

Round empty staring punctures in a skull.
And there were words in Rome once and one time
Words at Eleusis.

                          Now there are no words
Nor names to name them and they will not speak
But grope against his groping touch and throw
The long unmeaning shadows of themselves
Across his shadow and resist his sense.

*Einstein hearing behind
the wall of the Grand
Hôtel du Nord the stars
discovers the Back Stair*

Why then if they resist destroy them. Dumb
Yet speak them in their elements. Whole,
Break them to reason.

                          He lies upon his bed
Exerting on Arcturus and the moon
Forces proportional inversely to
The squares of their remoteness and conceives
The universe.
                  Atomic.
                              He can count
Ocean in atoms and weigh out the air
In multiples of one and subdivide
Light to its numbers.
                          If they will not speak
Let them be silent in their particles.
Let them be dead and he will lie among
Their dust and cipher them—undo the signs
Of their unreal identities and free
The pure and single factor of all sums—
Solve them to unity.
                          Democritus
Scooped handfuls out of stones and like the sea
Let earth run through his fingers. Well, he too,
He can achieve obliquity and learn
The cold distortion of the winter's sun
That breaks the surfaces of summer.

*Einstein on the terrasse of The
Acacias forces the secret door*

                          Stands
Facing the world upon a windy slope
And with his mind relaxes the stiff forms
Of all he sees until the heavy hills
Impend like rushing water and the earth

Hangs on the steep and momentary crest
Of overflowing ruin.
              Overflow!
Sweep over into movement and dissolve
All differences in the indifferent flux!
Crumble to eddyings of dust and drown
In change the thing that changes!
                    There begins
A vague unquiet in the fallow ground,
A seething in the grass, a bubbling swirl
Over the surface of the fields that spreads
Around him gathering until the green
Boils and under frothy loam the rocks
Ferment and simmer and like thinning smoke
The trees melt into nothing.
                    Still he stands
Watching the vortex widen and involve
In swirling dissolution the whole earth
And circle through the skies till swaying time
Collapses crumpling into dark the stars
And motion ceases and the sifting world
Opens beneath.
            When he shall feel infuse
His flesh with the rent body of all else
And spin within his opening brain the motes
Of suns and worlds and spaces.   *Einstein enters*
                Like a foam
His flesh is withered and his shriveling
And ashy bones are scattered on the dark.
But still the dark denies him. Still withstands
The dust his penetration and flings back
Himself to answer him.
              Which seems to keep
Something inviolate. A living something.   *1926*

ELEVEN

And summer mornings the mute child, rebellious,
Stupid, hating the words, the meanings, hating
The Think now, Think, the O but Think! would leave
On tiptoe the three chairs on the verandah
And crossing tree by tree the empty lawn
Push back the shed door and upon the sill

Stand pressing out the sunlight from his eyes
And enter and with outstretched fingers feel
The grindstone and behind it the bare wall
And turn and in the corner on the cool
Hard earth sit listening. And one by one,
Out of the dazzled shadow in the room
The shapes would gather, the brown plowshare, spades,
Mattocks, the polished helves of picks, a scythe
Hung from the rafters, shovels, slender tines
Glinting across the curve of sickles—shapes
Older than men were, the wise tools, the iron
Friendly with earth. And sit there quiet, breathing
The harsh dry smell of withered bulbs, the faint
Odor of dung, the silence. And outside
Beyond the half-shut door the blind leaves
And the corn moving. And at noon would come,
Up from the garden, his hard crooked hands
Gentle with earth, his knees still earth-stained, smelling
Of sun, of summer, the old gardener, like
A priest, like an interpreter, and bend
Over his baskets.
           And they would not speak:
They would say nothing. And the child would sit there
Happy as though he had no name, as though
He had been no one: like a leaf, a stem,
Like a root growing—   1926

MEMORIAL RAIN

Ambassador Puser the ambassador
Reminds himself in French, felicitous tongue,
What these (young men no longer) lie here for
In rows that once, and somewhere else, were young—

      All night in Brussels the wind had tugged at my door:
      I had heard the wind at my door and the trees strung
      Taut, and to me who had never been before
      In that country it was a strange wind blowing
      Steadily, stiffening the walls, the floor,
      The roof of my room. I had not slept for knowing
      He too, dead, was a stranger in that land
      And felt beneath the earth in the wind's flowing

A tightening of roots and would not understand,
Remembering lake winds in Illinois,
That strange wind. I had felt his bones in the sand
Listening.

    —Reflects that these enjoy
Their country's gratitude, that deep repose,
That peace no pain can break, no hurt destroy,
That rest, that sleep—

      At Ghent the wind rose.
There was a smell of rain and a heavy drag
Of wind in the hedges but not as the wind blows
Over fresh water when the waves lag
Foaming and the willows huddle and it will rain:
I felt him waiting.

    —Indicates the flag
Which (may he say) enisles in Flanders' plain
This little field these happy, happy dead
Have made America—

      In the ripe grain
The wind coiled glistening, darted, fled,
Dragging its heavy body: at Waereghem
The wind coiled in the grass above his head:
Waiting—listening—

    —Dedicates to them
This earth their bones have hallowed, this last gift
A grateful country—

      Under the dry grass stem
The words are blurred, are thickened, the words sift
Confused by the rasp of the wind, by the thin grating
Of ants under the grass, the minute shift
And tumble of dusty sand separating
From dusty sand. The roots of the grass strain,
Tighten, the earth is rigid, waits—he is waiting—

And suddenly, and all at once, the rain!

The living scatter, they run into houses, the wind
Is trampled under the rain, shakes free, is again

Trampled. The rain gathers, running in thinned
Spurts of water that ravel in the dry sand
Seeping in the sand under the grass roots, seeping
Between cracked boards to the bones of a clenched hand:
The earth relaxes, loosens; he is sleeping,
He rests, he is quiet, he sleeps in a strange land.   *1926*

THE END OF THE WORLD

Quite unexpectedly as Vasserot
The armless ambidextrian was lighting
A match between his great and second toe
And Ralph the lion was engaged in biting
The neck of Madame Sossman while the drum
Pointed, and Teeny was about to cough
In waltz-time swinging Jocko by the thumb—
Quite unexpectedly the top blew off:

And there, there overhead, there, there, hung over
Those thousands of white faces, those dazed eyes,
There in the starless dark the poise, the hover,
There with vast wings across the canceled skies,
There in the sudden blackness the black pall
Of nothing, nothing, nothing—nothing at all.   *1926*

ARS POETICA

A poem should be palpable and mute
As a globed fruit,

Dumb
As old medallions to the thumb,

Silent as the sleeve-worn stone
Of casement ledges where the moss has grown—

A poem should be wordless
As the flight of birds.

*   *   *

A poem should be motionless in time
As the moon climbs,

Leaving, as the moon releases
Twig by twig the night-entangled trees,

Leaving, as the moon behind the winter leaves,
Memory by memory the mind—

A poem should be motionless in time
As the moon climbs

*   *   *

A poem should be equal to:
Not true

For all the history of grief
An empty doorway and a maple leaf

For love
The leaning grasses and the two lights above the sea—

A poem should not mean
But be   1926

"NOT MARBLE NOR THE GILDED MONUMENTS"

The praisers of women in their proud and beautiful poems
Naming the grave mouth and the hair and the eyes
Boasted those they loved should be forever remembered
These were lies

The words sound but the face in the Istrian sun is forgotten
The poet speaks but to her dead ears no more
The sleek throat is gone—and the breast that was troubled to listen
Shadow from door

Therefore I will not praise your knees nor your fine walking
Telling you men shall remember your name as long
As lips move or breath is spent or the iron of English
Rings from a tongue

I shall say you were young and your arms straight and your mouth
     scarlet
I shall say you will die and none will remember you

Your arms change and none remember the swish of your garments
Nor the click of your shoe

Not with my hand's strength not with difficult labor
Springing the obstinate words to the bones of your breast
And the stubborn line to your young stride and the breath to your
    breathing
And the beat to your haste
Shall I prevail on the hearts of unborn men to remember

(What is a dead girl but a shadowy ghost
Or a dead man's voice but a distant and vain affirmation
Like dream words most)

Therefore I will not speak of the undying glory of women
I will say you were young and straight and your skin fair
And you stood in the door and the sun was a shadow of leaves on your
    shoulders
And a leaf on your hair

I will not speak of the famous beauty of dead women
I will say the shape of a leaf lay once on your hair
Till the world ends and the eyes are out and the mouths broken
Look! It is there!   *1930*

YOU, ANDREW MARVELL

And here face down beneath the sun
And here upon earth's noonward height
To feel the always coming on
The always rising of the night

To feel creep up the curving east
The earthy chill of dusk and slow
Upon those under lands the vast
And ever climbing shadow grow

And strange at Ecbatan the trees
Take leaf by leaf the evening strange
The flooding dark about their knees
The mountains over Persia change

And now at Kermanshah the gate
Dark empty and the withered grass

And through the twilight now the late
Few travelers in the westward pass

And Baghdad darken and the bridge
Across the silent river gone
And through Arabia the edge
Of evening widen and steal on

And deepen on Palmyra's street
The wheel rut in the ruined stone
And Lebanon fade out and Crete
High through the clouds and overblown

And over Sicily the air
Still flashing with the landward gulls
And loom and slowly disappear
The sails above the shadowy hulls

And Spain go under and the shore
Of Africa the gilded sand
And evening vanish and no more
The low pale light across that land

Nor now the long light on the sea

And here face downward in the sun
To feel how swift how secretly
The shadow of the night comes on . . .
                                    1930

SALUTE

O sun! Instigator of cocks!
                Thou . . .

Quickener! Maker of sound in the leaves
                        and of running
Stir over the curve of the earth like the ripple of
Scarlet under the skin of the lizard
                        Hunter!
Starter of westward birds!

Be heard

Sun on our mountains! Oh be now
Loud with us! Wakener let the wings
Descend of dawn on our roof-trees! Bring
Bees now! Let the cicadas sing
In the heat on the gummed trunks of the pine!
Make now the winds! Take thou the orchards!

(We that have heard the beat of our hearts in the silence
And the count of the clock all night at our listening ears)
Be near!
Shake the branches of day on our roofs!
Oh
Be over us!   *1930*

IMMORTAL AUTUMN

I speak this poem now with grave and level voice
In praise of autumn of the far-horn-winding fall
I praise the flower-barren fields the clouds the tall
Unanswering branches where the wind makes sullen noise

I praise the fall it is the human season
now
No more the foreign sun does meddle at our earth
Enforce the green and bring the fallow land to birth
Nor winter yet weigh all with silence the pine bough

But now in autumn with the black and outcast crows
Share we the spacious world the whispering year is gone
There is more room to live now the once secret dawn
Comes late by daylight and the dark unguarded goes

Between the mutinous brave burning of the leaves
And winter's covering of our hearts with his deep snow
We are alone there are no evening birds we know
The naked moon the tame stars circle at our eaves

It is the human season on this sterile air
Do words outcarry breath the sound goes on and on.
I hear a dead man's cry from autumn long since gone.

I cry to you beyond upon this bitter air.   *1930*

REPROACH TO DEAD POETS

You who have spoken words in the earth
You who have broken the silence
                              utterers
Sayers in all lands to all peoples
Writers in candle soot on the skins
Of rams for those who come after you
                              voices
Echoed at night in the arched doors
And at noon in the shadow of fig trees
Hear me
                              Were there not
Words
     Were there not words to tell with
     Were there not leaf sounds in the mouths
Of women from over-sea and a call
Of birds on the lips of the children of strangers
Were there not words in all languages
In many tongues the same thing differently
The name cried out Thalassa the sea
The Sea
The sun and moon character representing
Brightness the night sound of the wind for
Always for ever and ever the verb
Created after the speech of crickets
               Were there not words to tell with
                              to tell
What lands these are
                    What are these
Lights through the night leaves and these voices
Crying among us as winds rise

Or whence of what race we are that dwell with them

Were there not words to tell with
                         you that have told
The kings' names and the hills remembered for battles

1930

EPISTLE TO BE LEFT IN THE EARTH

. . . It is colder now
                        there are many stars
                                                we are drifting
North by the Great Bear
                        the leaves are falling
The water is stone in the scooped rocks
                                        to southward
Red sun grey air
                the crows are
Slow on their crooked wings
                                the jays have left us
Long since we passed the flares of Orion
Each man believes in his heart he will die
Many have written last thoughts and last letters
None know if our deaths are now or forever
None know if this wandering earth will be found

We lie down and the snow covers our garments
I pray you
                you (if any open this writing)
Make in your mouths the words that were our names
I will tell you all we have learned
                                I will tell you everything
The earth is round
                        there are springs under the orchards
The loam cuts with a blunt knife
                                beware of
Elms in thunder
                the lights in the sky are stars
We think they do not see
                        we think also
The trees do not know nor the leaves of the grasses
                                                hear us
The birds too are ignorant
                                Do not listen
Do not stand at dark in the open windows
We before you have heard this
                                they are voices
They are not words at all but the wind rising
Also none among us has seen God

(. . . We have thought often
The flaws of sun in the late and driving weather
Pointed to one tree but it was not so.)
As for the nights I warn you the nights are dangerous
The wind changes at night and the dreams come

It is very cold
                    there are strange stars near Arcturus

Voices are crying an unknown name in the sky   *1930*

LINES FOR AN INTERMENT

Now it is fifteen years you have lain in the meadow:
The boards at your face have gone through: the earth is
Packed down and the sound of the rain is fainter:
The roots of the first grass are dead:

It's a long time to lie in the earth with your honor:
The world, Soldier, the world has been moving on:

The girls wouldn't look at you twice in the cloth cap:
Six years old they were when it happened:

It bores them even in books: "Soissons besieged!"
As for the gents they have joined the American Legion:

Belts and a brass band and the ladies' auxiliaries:
The Californians march in the OD silk:

We are all acting again like civilized beings:
People mention it at tea . . .

The Facts of Life we have learned are Economic:
You were deceived by the detonations of bombs:

You thought of courage and death when you thought of warfare:
Hadn't they taught you the fine words were unfortunate?

Now that we understand we judge without bias:
We feel of course for those who had to die:

Women have written us novels of great passion
Proving the useless death of the dead was a tragedy:

Nevertheless it is foolish to chew gall:
The foremost writers on both sides have apologized:

The Germans are back in the Midi with cropped hair:
The English are drinking the better beer in Bavaria:

You can rest now in the rain in the Belgian meadow—
Now that it's all explained away and forgotten:
Now that the earth is hard and the wood rots:

Now you are dead . . .   1933

PONY ROCK

FOR THE MEMORY OF H. T. C.

One who has loved the hills and died, a man
Intimate with them—how their profiles fade
Large out of evening or through veils of rain
Vanish and reappear or how the sad
Long look of moonlight troubles their blind stones—
One who has loved them does not utterly,
Letting his fingers loosen and the green
Ebb from his eyeballs, close his eyes and go:
But other men long after he is dead
Seeing those hills will catch their breath and stare
As one who reading in a book some word
That calls joy back but can recall not where—
Only the crazy sweetness in the head—
Will stare at the black print till the page is blurred.

                                                  1933

LANDSCAPE AS A NUDE

She lies on her left side her flank golden:
Her hair is burned black with the strong sun:
The scent of her hair is of rain in the dust on her shoulders:
She has brown breasts and the mouth of no other country:

Ah she is beautiful here in the sun where she lies—
Not like the soft girls naked in vineyards
Nor the soft naked girls of the English islands
Where the rain comes in with the surf on an east wind:

Hers is the west wind and the sunlight: the west
Wind is the long clean wind of the continents—
The wind turning with earth: the wind descending
Steadily out of the evening and following on:

The wind here where she lies is west: the trees
Oak ironwood cottonwood hickory: standing in
Great groves they roll on the wind as the sea would:
The grasses of Iowa Illinois Indiana

Run with the plunge of the wind as a wave tumbling:

Under her knees there is no green lawn of the Florentines:
Under her dusty knees is the corn stubble:
Her belly is flecked with the flickering light of the corn:

She lies on her left side her flank golden:
Her hair is burned black with the strong sun:
The scent of her hair is of dust and of smoke on her shoulders:
She has brown breasts and the mouth of no other country.

1933

E. E. Cummings

[ALL IN GREEN WENT MY LOVE RIDING]

All in green went my love riding
on a great horse of gold
into the silver dawn.

four lean hounds crouched low and smiling
the merry deer ran before.

Fleeter be they than dappled dreams
the swift sweet deer
the red rare deer.

Four red roebuck at a white water
the cruel bugle sang before.

Horn at hip went my love riding
riding the echo down
into the silver dawn.

four lean hounds crouched low and smiling
the level meadows ran before.

Softer be they than slippered sleep
the lean lithe deer
the fleet flown deer.

Four fleet does at a gold valley
the famished arrow sang before.

Bow at belt went my love riding
riding the mountain down
into the silver dawn.

four lean hounds crouched low and smiling
the sheer peaks ran before.

Paler be they than daunting death
the sleek slim deer
the tall tense deer.

Four tall stags at a green mountain
the lucky hunter sang before.

All in green went my love riding
on a great horse of gold
into the silver dawn.

four lean hounds crouched low and smiling
my heart fell dead before.   *1923*

[THE HOURS RISE UP PUTTING OFF STARS AND IT IS]

the hours rise up putting off stars and it is
dawn
into the street of the sky light walks scattering poems

on earth a candle is
extinguished   the city
wakes
with a song upon her
mouth having death in her eyes

and it is dawn
the world
goes forth to murder dreams . . . .

i see in the street where strong
men are digging bread
and i see the brutal faces of
people contented hideous hopeless cruel happy

and it is day,

in the mirror
i see a frail
man

dreaming
dreams
dreams in the mirror

and it
is dusk   on earth

a candle is lighted
and it is dark.
the people are in their houses
the frail man is in his bed
the city

sleeps with death upon her mouth having a song in her eyes
the hours descend,
putting on stars . . . .

in the street of the sky night walks scattering poems   *1923*

[WHEN GOD LETS MY BODY BE]

when god lets my body be

From each brave eye shall sprout a tree
fruit that dangles therefrom

the purpled world will dance upon
Between my lips which did sing

a rose shall beget the spring
that maidens whom passion wastes

will lay between their little breasts
My strong fingers beneath the snow

Into strenuous birds shall go
my love walking in the grass

their wings will touch with her face
and all the while shall my heart be

With the bulge and nuzzle of the sea

1923

[WHO'S MOST AFRAID OF DEATH?]

who's most afraid of death? thou

                         art of him
utterly afraid, i love of thee
(beloved) this

               and truly i would be
near when his scythe takes crisply the whim
of thy smoothness. and mark the fainting
murdered petals. with the caving stem.

But of all most would i be one of them

round the hurt heart which do so fraily cling . . . .)
i who am but imperfect in my fear

Or with thy mind against my mind, to hear
nearing our hearts' irrevocable play—
through the mysterious high futile day

and enormous stride
                    (and drawing thy mouth toward

my mouth, steer our lost bodies carefully downward)

                                 1925

[NOBODY LOSES ALL THE TIME]

nobody loses all the time

i had an uncle named
Sol who was a born failure and
nearly everybody said he should have gone
into vaudeville perhaps because my Uncle Sol could
sing McCann He Was A Diver on Xmas Eve like Hell Itself which
may or may not account for the fact that my Uncle

Sol indulged in that possibly most inexcusable
of all to use a highfalootin phrase
luxuries that is or to
wit fa·rning and be

it needlessly
added

my Uncle Sol's farm
failed because the chickens
ate the vegetables so
my Uncle Sol had a
chicken farm till the
skunks ate the chickens when

my Uncle Sol
had a skunk farm but
the skunks caught cold and
died and so
my Uncle Sol imitated the
skunks in a subtle manner

or by drowning himself in the watertank
but somebody who'd given my Uncle Sol a Victor
Victrola and records while he lived presented to
him upon the auspicious occasion of his decease a
scrumptious not to mention splendiferous funeral with
tall boys in black gloves and flowers and everything and

i remember we all cried like the Missouri
when my Uncle Sol's coffin lurched because
somebody pressed a button
(and down went
my Uncle
Sol

and started a worm farm)   1926

[(PONDER,DARLING,THESE BUSTED STATUES]

          (ponder,darling,these busted statues
          of yon motheaten forum be aware
          notice what hath remained
          —the stone cringes
          clinging to the stone, how obsolete

          lips utter their extant smile . . . .
          remark

a few deleted of texture
or meaning monuments and dolls

resist Them Greediest Paws of careful
time all of which is extremely
unimportant) whereas Life

matters if or

when the your- and my-
idle vertical worthless
self unite in a peculiarly
momentary

partnership (to instigate
constructive
                    Horizontal
business . . . . even so, let us make haste
—consider well this ruined aqueduct

lady,
which used to lead something into somewhere)
                                           1926

[IT IS SO LONG SINCE MY HEART HAS BEEN WITH YOURS]

it is so long since my heart has been with yours

shut by our mingling arms through
a darkness where new lights begin and
increase,
since your mind has walked into
my kiss as a stranger
into the streets and colours of a town—

that i have perhaps forgotten
how, always(from
these hurrying crudities
of blood and flesh)Love
coins His most gradual gesture,

and whittles life to eternity

—after which our separating selves become museums
filled with skilfully stuffed memories   1926

[IF I HAVE MADE,MY LADY,INTRICATE]

if i have made,my lady,intricate
imperfect various things chiefly which wrong
your eyes(frailer than most deep dreams are frail)
songs less firm than your body's whitest song
upon my mind—if i have failed to snare
the glance too shy—if through my singing slips
the very skillful strangeness of your smile
the keen primeval silence of your hair

—let the world say "his most wise music stole
nothing from death"—

                          you only will create
(who are so perfectly alive)my shame:
lady through whose profound and fragile lips
the sweet small clumsy feet of April came

into the ragged meadow of my soul.   *1926*

[IF YOU CAN'T EAT YOU GOT TO]

If you can't eat you got to

smoke and we aint got
nothing to smoke:come on kid

let's go to sleep
if you can't smoke you got to

Sing and we aint got

nothing to sing;come on kid
let's go to sleep

if you can't sing you got to
die and we aint got

Nothing to die,come on kid

let's go to sleep
if you can't die you got to

dream and we aint got
nothing to dream(come on kid

Let's go to sleep)   *1940*

[A PRETTY A DAY]

a pretty a day
(and every fades)
is here and away
(but born are maids
to flower an hour
in all,all)

o yes to flower
until so blithe
a doer a wooer
some limber and lithe
some very fine mower
a tall;tall

some jerry so very
(and nellie and fan)
some handsomest harry
(and sally and nan
they tremble and cower
so pale:pale)

for betty was born
to never say nay
but lucy could learn
and lily could pray
and fewer were shyer
than doll.   doll   *1940*

[AS FREEDOM IS A BREAKFASTFOOD]

as freedom is a breakfastfood
or truth can live with right and wrong
or molehills are from mountains made

—long enough and just so long
will being pay the rent of seem
and genius please the talentgang
and water most encourage flame

as hatracks into peachtrees grow
or hopes dance best on bald men's hair
and every finger is a toe
and any courage is a fear
—long enough and just so long
will the impure think all things pure
and hornets wail by children stung

or as the seeing are the blind
and robins never welcome spring
nor flatfolk prove their world is round
nor dingsters die at break of dong
and common's rare and millstones float
—long enough and just so long
tomorrow will not be too late

worms are the words but joy's the voice
down shall go which and up come who
breasts will be breasts thighs will be thighs
deeds cannot dream what dreams can do
—time is a tree(this life one leaf)
but love is the sky and i am for you
just so long and long enough   1940

[ANYONE LIVED IN A PRETTY HOW TOWN]

anyone lived in a pretty how town
(with up so floating many bells down)
spring summer autumn winter
he sang his didn't he danced his did.

Women and men(both little and small)
cared for anyone not at all
they sowed their isn't they reaped their same
sun moon stars rain

children guessed(but only a few
and down they forgot as up they grew

autumn winter spring summer)
that noone loved him more by more

when by now and tree by leaf
she laughed his joy she cried his grief
bird by snow and stir by still
anyone's any was all to her

someones married their everyones
laughed their cryings and did their dance
(sleep wake hope and then)they
said their nevers they slept their dream

stars rain sun moon
(and only the snow can begin to explain
how children are apt to forget to remember
with up so floating many bells down)

one day anyone died i guess
(and noone stooped to kiss his face)
busy folk buried them side by side
little by little and was by was

all by all and deep by deep
and more by more they dream their sleep
noone and anyone earth by april
wish by spirit and if by yes.

Women and men(both dong and ding)
summer autumn winter spring
reaped their sowing and went their came
sun moon stars rain   *1940*

[MY FATHER MOVED THROUGH DOOMS OF LOVE]

my father moved through dooms of love
through sames of am through haves of give,
singing each morning out of each night
my father moved through depths of height

this motionless forgetful where
turned at his glance to shining here;

that if(so timid air is firm)
under his eyes would stir and squirm

newly as from unburied which
floats the first who,his april touch
drove sleeping selves to swarm their fates
woke dreamers to their ghostly roots

and should some why completely weep
my father's fingers brought her sleep:
vainly no smallest voice might cry
for he could feel the mountains grow.

Lifting the valleys of the sea
my father moved through griefs of joy;
praising a forehead called the moon
singing desire into begin

joy was his song and joy so pure
a heart of star by him could steer
and pure so now and now so yes
the wrists of twilight would rejoice

keen as midsummer's keen beyond
conceiving mind of sun will stand,
so strictly(over utmost him
so hugely)stood my father's dream

his flesh was flesh his blood was blood:
no hungry man but wished him food;
no cripple wouldn't creep one mile
uphill to only see him smile.

Scorning the pomp of must and shall
my father moved through dooms of feel;
his anger was as right as rain
his pity was as green as grain

septembering arms of year extend
less humbly wealth to foe and friend
than he to foolish and to wise
offered immeasurable is

proudly and(by octobering flame
beckoned)as earth will downward climb,
so naked for immortal work
his shoulders marched against the dark

his sorrow was as true as bread:
no liar looked him in the head;
if every friend became his foe
he'd laugh and build a world with snow.

My father moved through theys of we,
singing each new leaf out of each tree
(and every child was sure that spring
danced when she heard my father sing)

then let men kill which cannot share,
let blood and flesh be mud and mire,
scheming imagine,passion willed,
freedom a drug that's bought and sold

giving to steal and cruel kind,
a heart to fear,to doubt a mind,
to differ a disease of same,
conform the pinnacle of am

though dull were all we taste as bright,
bitter all utterly things sweet,
maggoty minus and dumb death
all we inherit,all bequeath

and nothing quite so least as truth
—i say though hate were why men breathe—
because my father lived his soul
love is the whole and more than all   1940

[I AM SO GLAD AND VERY]

i am so glad and very
merely my fourth will cure
the laziest self of weary
the hugest sea of shore

so far your nearness reaches
a lucky fifth of you
turns people into eachs
and cowards into grow

our can'ts were born to happen
our mosts have died in more
our twentieth will open
wide a wide open door

we are so both and oneful
night cannot be so sky
sky cannot be so sunful
i am through you so i   *1940*

[LOVE IS THE EVERY ONLY GOD]

love is the every only god

who spoke this earth so glad and big
even a thing all small and sad
man,may his mighty briefness dig

for love beginning means return
seas who could sing so deep and strong

one queerying wave will whitely yearn
from each last shore and home come young

so truly perfectly the skies
by merciful love whispered were,
completes its brightness with your eyes

any illimitable star   *1940*

Horace Gregory

LONGFACE MAHONEY DISCUSSES HEAVEN

If someone said, *Escape.*
Let's get away from here,
you'd see snow mountains thrown
against the sky,
cold, and you'd draw your breath and feel
air like cold water going through your veins,
but you'd be free, up so high,
or you'd see a row of girls dancing on a beach
with tropic trees and a warm moon
and warm air floating under your clothes
and through your hair.
Then you'd think of heaven
where there's peace, away from here
and you'd go someplace unreal
where everybody goes after something happens,
set up in the air, safe, a room in a hotel.
A brass bed, military hair brushes,
a couple of coats, trousers, maybe a dress
on a chair or draped on the floor.
This room is not on earth, feel the air,
warm like heaven and far away.

This is a place
where marriage nights are kept
and sometimes here you say Hello
to a neat girl with you
and sometimes she laughs
because she thinks it's funny to be sitting here
for no reason at all, except, perhaps,
she likes to see how strong you are
and the color of your eyes.
Maybe this isn't heaven but near
to something like it,
more like love coming up in elevators

and nothing to think about, except, O God,
you love her now and it makes no difference
if it isn't spring. All seasons are warm
in the warm air
and the brass bed is always there.

If you've done something
and the cops get you afterwards, you
can't remember the place again,
away from cops and streets—
it's all unreal—
the warm air, a dream
that couldn't save you now.
No one would care
to hear about it,
it would be heaven
far away, dark and no music,
not even a girl there.   *1930*

NO COCK CROWS AT MORNING

There is no cock crowing in our bedroom,
waking good morning startled by his cries:
the great bird has vanished in a fiery dream,
his clamorous wings are shut
and his rolling golden eye
has gone blind
and his radiant comb is a laurel of ashes.

Listen, there is no cock crowing
(Somebody murdered someone else's wife
and left a pool of blood in the subway,
crying his matins out of Gothic type,
shouting the resurrection and the life,
rising in vapors from an invisible flame,
sloughing his shirt and trousers
in an electric chair).

There is no cock crowing,
but there is a phantom bird walking
through prison walls, walking through streets and houses,
silent, invulnerable, walking over the dead—
ever the martyrs and the wrongdoers
there is no cock crowing.   *1930*

O MORS AETERNA

Be for a little while eternal,
singing with all the songs in your body
but making no sound.

The Rose of Sharon singing in an old city
was eternal suddenly
for a little while.

And the mountains fell away
and the city sank into earth again
and the voices of dead men came from the ground
crying, Incest and poverty and murder
(all in the many dead years
that had sent them into the earth)
but now rising, crying against the world
and mortal sun and moon and stars,
against life and the masters
in purple victories, clothed with iron wars.

For a little while
the Rose of Sharon sang eternally
until the city came around her again
and there was no sound.   1930

AND OF COLUMBUS

Columbus is remembered by young men
walking the world at night in street-walled prison:
Where is my country? Why do I return
at midnight to a moonlit, inland ocean
whose waves beat as a heart beats in my side?

Is the return to these receding shores
the end of earth, fallen to deep-sea traffic,
the end of all things?

Even the cities that coil upward
from sumac bush and sand flow into grass:
roofs, towers mingling
with roots and the bodies of men who died in wars
against the masters.

Columbus who believed his own miracles,
conquered his India, oceans, mermaids, golden savages—
where was his country?

It was a small stone room at night
where a man walked over the world and seasons merged
in darkness. And time echoes time saying: Columbus no more,
no more Columbus. He is a vanished cloud in the sky
where stars move toward the sun.

And in Havana under the Southern Cross, all that is his
is where his bones lie.   1933

EMERSON: LAST DAYS AT CONCORD

Enter America at Concord's bridge,
true marriage of the east and west, Brahma
whose lips nurse at my veins.

Where was the green brass cannon
sunken in churchyards after the shots were fired?
Listen, the world is sleeping and the noise
coils in thunder where Dover's beach
shall wake no more
and the Indian ocean
pours its blood into the sun when evening's tide
uncovers bones upon the shore.

Cut me a frock coat, for the oversoul
lies naked: parts, limbs exposed
within a broken coffin. O light that stirs in dust
as eastwind darkens nightfall into rain.

Where are your lips, hands, Brahma?
What was the name, your name or mine?
Come, friend,
we shall walk in the west orchard drinking russet wine,
kiss daisies where the transcendental tree
(look how the death worm feeds upon its roots)
shelters our love and fiery blossoms fall in Plato's vineyard.
I have rolled the world in my brain, have seen its heroes
diminish,
saw oceans, continents dissolve in sunlight
on Concord window sills:

Are you my friend?
Then here's my secret; I have forgotten
all friends and the words that joined my lips to theirs.
Better to keep faith
                         and believe
no one. Better to be a patriot disowning
this land. Give back America to sunlight, wind and rain;
set sail for India from Concord's bridge,
leap to the quarter-deck where our Columbus
once more commands his ships.
                                        Is that a storm in the sky?
And are these apples ripe? I grew this orchard to be a paradise
this side of Eden.   1933

SALVOS FOR RANDOLPH BOURNE

O bitterness never spoken, the death mask etched in silver,
the dark limbs rolled in lead where the shallow grave conceals
despair: the image of a large head, forward, devouring
the collarbone. No general in brass over it and no
conquering angel kneels.

This was the end:
                         there were no firing squads,
no City Hall Nathan Hale with a bronze cord at his throat
speaking of lives and his country where a hundred million lives
rose, wavered, shattered like an invisible sea coiling
against a rock (no longer there) but sunken
into a shore line of weeds and sand.

Only a small room and a million words to be written before midnight
against poverty and idiot death like the gray face of Emerson
fading in New England winter twilight; the hard face vanishing
in snow, the passionately soft words issuing from the mouth.
Listen to the rock, the oracle no longer there!

To be the last American, an embryo coiled in a test tube,
to be a fixed and paralytic smile cocked upward to the clouds,
to see friends and enemies depart (around the corner)
their sticks and smart fedoras bright in sunlight,
to be or not to be Hamlet, the Prince of Wales,
or last week's *New Republic;*

to be death delicately walking between chimney pots on Eighth Street,
possibly this is best to be

or not to be.   1933

From CHORUS FOR SURVIVAL

I

Tell us that love
                    returns,
O Hymen, sing
In every hour that burns
After the midnight hour
In darkness here.
                    Wake with thy song
The antique smiling year,
Always thy axis turning to restore
The Greek dawn breaking
On Aegean seas.
                    Break here
The silent wave upon the shore
In dreams to darkness-driven memories;
Wake with thy song,
Tell us to wake and sing—
Midnight and starlight night are always long
For the impatient young.
Open gray skies and fling
Thy yellow veil, the sun,
                    down city streets
Where tireless seasons run,
Speed here October, our retarded spring,
Daylight and green
Live forests blossoming:
The wave-washed rock in embers glowing red,
Wake even here,
                    till climbing overhead,
Window and cornice on steel branches bear
Fire of morning from another spring.

Wake with thy song
                    time-darkened waters
That have not reached their end
Westward to India, passage through storm,

Bearing the image of a Grecian bride,
Eyes like cornflowers staring at our side,
The blue flame lighting darkness in the shade
Of trees knee-deep in grass
At summer's tide . . . .
Only our lips recall
That she was beautiful:
                                    the pure
Alcestis memory of a kiss:
                                    the violet-
Scented breast, the virginal
Breathing light in sunlit air;
Handclasp remembers hand,
                                    quick limbs enthrall
Entwining limbs, the nervous, flexible,
Growing green grape vine,
                                    until the blood
Flows into sleep and blood is wine.

This is thy memory, America,
The tenuous marriage of disunited blood,
Captain and slave one bed,
                                    in dust until the wind
Stirs dust to life again . . .
                                    and walking here,
Conquered and conqueror
(The apple blossoms white in midnight hair).

Wake with thy song
Even in death (they sleep like death)
Men in the wilderness
(The night is long),
                                    breaking through forests of a foreign land,
Sell and move on, *We have no heritage,*
This place no name;
Westward we follow to an unknown star
And shall not come again the way we came.

Tell us that love
                                    returns
After the midnight hour
In darkness here,
Season of iron cities against the sky,

The cold room where I write my signature
Toward my survival in the waning year:
Winter and frost, each day revolves to night,
The longer night that brings a short tomorrow
Of middle-age in dark, divided faces,
In faces that I know too well, my own
Face staring likeness in the mirror
Beyond the hour of death or hope or doom;
When doors swing wide upon an empty room,
Window and door open to empty air
Echo in darkness of the lost frontier.

Wake with thy song
                    the voices
Of men who cannot sleep:
                         We count our losses
In decimals of time, the ten per cent
Of what we hope: To let:
                        the naked bed, the folding chair,
Space for the body motionless in air,
Permit survival if we stand alone.
Voiceless we smile; we are not violent.

And from these places
On the abyss of loss,
                    the steel-edged towers
Pierce the moon, the sun:
Look where Atlantis leaves forgotten traces,
Empire of empty houses under seas.

This is thy heritage, America,
Scaffold of iron deep in stone.
                        Destroy the ruins,
This is the place; wreck here and build again.

Tell us that love
                returns,
Not soft nor kind,
But like a crystal turning in the mind,
Light where the body is:
                    thy limbs are fire
Walking alive among the ancient trees,
The ruined town, cathedral wall, church spire.

Say love, though always young,
Remembers these . . .
                    place, house we entered
And shall not return . . . .
                         Spirit that outlives time
To join our hands in love,
                    do you remember
Serpent and dove, the wild rose and the thorn,
Blossom and leaf in secret flowering
Read in a book of broken prophecies?

Wake with thy song
                    (I speak a difficult and treacherous tongue
That was not made for wedding song or carol;
Measure my dwindling shadow on the wall,
Wait for the silence when my lips are gone
That say:
          Though night is long, this bitter hour wakes
And is not sterile).

Wake here
          Atlantis under hard blue skies,
Thy Indian Summer bride is like the spring
Roof-tree in light
                    thy blossoming
In fire to love returns.

4

Ask no return for love that's given
embracing mistress, wife or friend,
                         ask no return:
on this deep earth or in pale heaven,
awake and spend
hands, lips, and eyes in love,
in darkness burn,
                    the limbs entwined until the soul ascend.

Ask no return of seasons gone:
the fire of autumn and the first hour of spring,
the short bough blossoming
through city windows when night's done,
when fears adjourn
                    backward in memory where all loves end

in self again, again the inward tree
growing against the heart
and no heart free.
From love that sleeps behind each eye
in double symmetry
                    ask no return,
even in enmity, look! I shall take your hand;
nor can our limbs disjoin in separate ways again,
walking, even at night on foreign land
through houses open to the wind, through cold and rain,
waking alive, meet, kiss and understand.   *1935*

TWO MONOLOGUES FROM THE PASSION OF M'PHAIL

I

Do I have to prove I can sell anything?
You can see it in my eyes, the way I brush my hair,
even when I need a drink and can't stop talking.

Do I have to prove it with my two hands and arms,
lifting five hundred pounds above my head,
until the house cheers and something falls,
the platform broken and the lights gone out,
crowds calling for police,
and a child crying for its mother down the aisles?

If the park is beautiful and the day is warm,
I can sell the power in my eyes that makes life grow
where not even one blade of grass has grown before,
that is like sunlight breaking through
darkness in a small room,
that shines and pours and flows,
that is here forever when it is here
and is gone forever as sunlight drops to darkness
when it goes.

I could even teach millions how to sell,
how to own a car and pay the rent,
how to live as though you were living in the sky,
your children happy before they get too old.
If you do it right, you can sell anything,
even your voice and what you think you hear,

even your face on billboards ten feet high,
your youth, your age and what you hate and love,
and it gets sold.

If you can wake up in the morning early,
if you can teach yourself to catch the train,
if you can hang out everything for sale,
if you can say, "I am a man,
I can sell asphalt off the street,
I can sell snowbright
dead women gleaming through shop windows,
or diamond horseshoe naked dancing girls,
or eight hours on my feet,
or twenty years of talk in telephones,
or fifty years behind a desk"—
you need not fail.

If you are strong as I am, you can hear
yourself talking to yourself at night
until your hair turns gray:
"I am God's white-haired boy,
I almost love the way I sell
my lips, my blood, my heart: and leave them there,
and no one else can sell such pity and such glory,
such light, such hope
                          even down to the last magnificent,
half-forgotten love affair."

Perhaps only I can do it as it should be done,
selling what remains, yet knowing that a last
day will come and a last half-hour,
or five minutes left impossible to sell,
the last more valuable than all the rest.

2

When you are caught breathless in an empty station,
and silence tells you that the train is gone
as though it were something for which
you alone were not prepared,
and yet was here and could not be denied;
when you whisper, "Why was I late, what have I done?"
you know the waiting hour is at your side.

If the time becomes your own, you need not fear it;
if you can tell yourself the hour is not
the thing that takes you when you sit
staring through clinic waiting-room white walls
into the blank blue northern sky
frozen a quarter-mile above the street,
and you are held there by your veins and nerves,
spreading and grasping as a grapevine curves
through the arms and back of
an enameled iron riverside park seat,
you need not think, Why must I wait
until the doctors say:
                    "We have come to lock you up.
It's the psychology of things that has got you down;
if you complain, we shall take care of you
until you know at last you can't escape.
                                    Is your dream
the dream of a child kept after school
made to write a hundred times
what three times seven means,
while in your sleep, before you get the answer,
the blackness fills and swells with pictures
of Technicolor ink-stained butterflies?
                            Is that ink-blot a tiger
in a bonfire? Are these the spines
of ancient caterpillars?
Is this the shadow of a wild-wood, leaping deer?
Is that what you see, or what you think you see?
Then we can tell you what you are,
what you can do, and what you ought to be,
as though your life were written down in court,
your name the last word on a questionnaire.
There is nothing private that we do not know;
you can't deny these figures on a chart
that follow you no matter where you go.
Each zero is an open, sleepless eye
piercing the hidden chambers of the heart,
and if you fail, or if you kill yourself,
we shall know why."

It is when the waiting forces you to stop
in stillness that you wish would not return
that you say, "I am not the same as other men;

I must live to wake beyond the fears of hope
into an hour that does not quite arrive. . . ."

And in that quiet, lost in space, almost remember
the difficult, new-born creature you once were,
in love with all the wonders of the world,
seeing a girl step, white and glittering as a fountain,
into cool evening air,
knowing you could not touch her,
nor dare to still the floating, flawless motion
of that pale dress above its glancing knees,
brief as the sight of sun on Easter morning
dancing its joy of earth and spring and heaven
over the sleeping bodies of men in cities
and between the branches of the tallest trees.

It is then you tell yourself:
"Everything I live for is not quite lost,"
even if you've waited someplace far too long:
if you can't call it peace, you call it rest;
if you can't call it luck, you call it fate,
you then know that when anything goes wrong,
perhaps it also happened in the past.

You light a cigarette, you carefully
blow out the match.
                    You know again you have to wait.
                                                    1941

Hart Crane

MY GRANDMOTHER'S LOVE LETTERS

There are no stars to-night
But those of memory.
Yet how much room for memory there is
In the loose girdle of soft rain.

There is even room enough
For the letters of my mother's mother,
Elizabeth,
That have been pressed so long
Into a corner of the roof
That they are brown and soft,
And liable to melt as snow.

Over the greatness of such space
Steps must be gentle.
It is all hung by an invisible white hair.
It trembles as birch limbs webbing the air.

And I ask myself:

"Are your fingers long enough to play
Old keys that are but echoes:
Is the silence strong enough
To carry back the music to its source
And back to you again
As though to her?"

Yet I would lead my grandmother by the hand
Through much of what she would not understand;
And so I stumble. And the rain continues on the roof
With such a sound of gently pitying laughter.   *1926*

PRAISE FOR AN URN

IN MEMORIAM: ERNEST NELSON

It was a kind and northern face
That mingled in such exile guise
The everlasting eyes of Pierrot
And, of Gargantua, the laughter.

His thoughts, delivered to me
From the white coverlet and pillow,
I see now, were inheritances—
Delicate riders of the storm.

The slant moon on the slanting hill
Once moved us toward presentiments
Of what the dead keep, living still,
And such assessments of the soul

As, perched in the crematory lobby,
The insistent clock commented on,
Touching as well upon our praise
Of glories proper to the time.

Still, having in mind gold hair,
I cannot see that broken brow
And miss the dry sound of bees
Stretching across a lucid space.

Scatter these well-meant idioms
Into the smoky spring that fills
The suburbs, where they will be lost.
They are no trophies of the sun.

1926

CHAPLINESQUE

We make our meek adjustments,
Contented with such random consolations
As the wind deposits
In slithered and too ample pockets.

For we can still love the world, who find
A famished kitten on the step, and know

Recesses for it from the fury of the street,
Or warm torn elbow coverts.

We will sidestep, and to the final smirk
Dally the doom of that inevitable thumb
That slowly chafes its puckered index toward us,
Facing the dull squint with what innocence
And what surprise!

And yet these fine collapses are not lies
More than the pirouettes of any pliant cane;
Our obsequies are, in a way, no enterprise.
We can evade you, and all else but the heart:
What blame to us if the heart live on.

The game enforces smirks; but we have seen
The moon in lonely alleys make
A grail of laughter of an empty ash can,
And through all sound of gaiety and quest
Have heard a kitten in the wilderness.   *1926*

NORTH LABRADOR

A land of leaning ice
Hugged by plaster-grey arches of sky,
Flings itself silently
Into eternity.

"Has no one come here to win you,
Or left you with the faintest blush
Upon your glittering breasts?
Have you no memories, O Darkly Bright?"

Cold-hushed, there is only the shifting of moments
That journey toward no Spring—
No birth, no death, no time nor sun
In answer.   *1926*

VOYAGES

I

Above the fresh ruffles of the surf
Bright striped urchins flay each other with sand.

They have contrived a conquest for shell shucks,
And their fingers crumble fragments of baked weed
Gaily digging and scattering.

And in answer to their treble interjections
The sun beats lightning on the waves,
The waves fold thunder on the sand;
And could they hear me I would tell them:

O brilliant kids, frisk with your dog,
Fondle your shells and sticks, bleached
By time and the elements; but there is a line
You must not cross nor ever trust beyond it
Spry cordage of your bodies to caresses
Too lichen-faithful from too wide a breast.
The bottom of the sea is cruel.

II

And yet this great wink of eternity,
Of rimless floods, unfettered leewardings,
Samite sheeted and processioned where
Her undinal vast belly moonward bends,
Laughing the wrapt inflections of our love;

Take this Sea, whose diapason knells
On scrolls of silver snowy sentences,
The sceptred terror of whose sessions rends
As her demeanors motion well or ill,
All but the pieties of lovers' hands.

And onward, as bells off San Salvador
Salute the crocus lustres of the stars,
In these poinsettia meadows of her tides,—
Adagios of islands, O my Prodigal,
Complete the dark confessions her veins spell.

Mark how her turning shoulders wind the hours,
And hasten while her penniless rich palms
Pass superscription of bent foam and wave —
Hasten, while they are true,—sleep, death, desire,
Close round one instant in one floating flower.

Bind us in time, O Seasons clear, and awe.
O minstrel galleons of Carib fire,
Bequeath us to no earthly shore until
Is answered in the vortex of our grave
The seal's wide spindrift gaze toward paradise.

III

Infinite consanguinity it bears—
This tendered theme of you that light
Retrieves from sea plains where the sky
Resigns a breast that every wave enthrones;
While ribboned water lanes I wind
Are laved and scattered with no stroke
Wide from your side, whereto this hour
The sea lifts, also, reliquary hands.

And so, admitted through black swollen gates
That must arrest all distance otherwise,—
Past whirling pillars and lithe pediments,
Light wrestling there incessantly with light,
Star kissing star through wave on wave unto
Your body rocking!
        and where death, if shed,
Presumes no carnage, but this single change,—
Upon the steep floor flung from dawn to dawn
The silken skilled transmemberment of song;

Permit me voyage, love, into your hands. . .

IV

Whose counted smile of hours and days, suppose
I know as spectrum of the sea and pledge
Vastly now parting gulf on gulf of wings
Whose circles bridge, I know, (from palms to the severe
Chilled albatross's white immutability)
No stream of greater love advancing now
Than, singing, this mortality alone
Through clay aflow immortally to you.

All fragrance irrefragably, and claim
Madly meeting logically in this hour
And region that is ours to wreathe again,

Portending eyes and lips and making told
The chancel port and portion of our June—

Shall they not stem and close in our own steps
Bright staves of flowers and quills to-day as I
Must first be lost in fatal tides to tell?
In signature of the incarnate word
The harbor shoulders to resign in mingling
Mutual blood, transpiring as foreknown
And widening noon within your breast for gathering
All bright insinuations that my years have caught
For islands where must lead inviolably
Blue latitudes and levels of your eyes,—

In this expectant, still exclaim receive
The secret oar and petals of all love.

V

Meticulous, past midnight in clear rime,
Infrangible and lonely, smooth as though cast
Together in one merciless white blade—
The bay estuaries fleck the hard sky limits.

—As if too brittle or too clear to touch!
The cables of our sleep so swiftly filed,
Already hang, shred ends from remembered stars.
One frozen tractless smile . . . What words
Can strangle this deaf moonlight? For we

Are overtaken. Now no cry, no sword
Can fasten or deflect this tidal wedge,
Slow tyranny of moonlight, moonlight loved
And changed . . . "There's

Nothing like this in the world," you say,
Knowing I cannot touch your hand and look
Too, into that godless cleft of sky
Where nothing turns but dead sands flashing.

"—And never to quite understand!" No,
In all the argosy of your bright hair I dreamed
Nothing so flagless as this piracy.

But now
Draw in your head, alone and too tall here.
Your eyes already in the slant of drifting foam;
Your breath sealed by the ghosts I do not know:
Draw in your head and sleep the long way home.

VI

Where icy and bright dungeons lift
Of swimmers their lost morning eyes,
And ocean rivers, churning, shift
Green borders under stranger skies,

Steadily as a shell secretes
Its beating leagues of monotone,
Or as many waters trough the sun's
Red kelson past the cape's wet stone;

O rivers mingling toward the sky
And harbor of the phœnix' breast—
My eyes pressed black against the prow,
—Thy derelict and blinded guest

Waiting, afire, what name, unspoke,
I cannot claim: let thy waves rear
More savage than the death of kings,
Some splintered garland for the seer.

Beyond siroccos harvesting
The solstice thunders, crept away,
Like a cliff swinging or a sail
Flung into April's inmost day—

Creation's blithe and petalled word
To the lounged goddess when she rose
Conceding dialogue with eyes
That smile unsearchable repose—

Still fervid covenant, Belle Isle,
—Unfolded floating dais before
Which rainbows twine continual hair—
Belle Isle, white echo of the oar!

The imaged Word, it is, that holds
Hushed willows anchored in its glow.
It is the unbetrayable reply
Whose accent no farewell can know.   *1926*

PASSAGE

Where the cedar leaf divides the sky
I heard the sea.
In sapphire arenas of the hills
I was promised an improved infancy.

Sulking, sanctioning the sun,
My memory I left in a ravine,—
Casual louse that tissues the buckwheat,
Aprons rocks, congregates pears
In moonlit bushels
And wakens alleys with a hidden cough.

Dangerously the summer burned
(I had joined the entrainments of the wind).
The shadows of boulders lengthened my back:
In the bronze gongs of my cheeks
The rain dried without odour.

"It is not long, it is not long;
See where the red and black
Vine-stanchioned valleys—": but the wind
Died speaking through the ages that you know
And hug, chimney-sooted heart of man!
So was I turned about and back, much as your smoke
Compiles a too well-known biography.

The evening was spear in the ravine
That throve through very oak. And had I walked
The dozen particular decimals of time?
Touching an opening laurel, I found
A thief beneath, my stolen book in hand.

"Why are you back here—smiling an iron coffin?"
"To argue with the laurel," I replied:
"Am justified in transience, fleeing
Under the constant wonder of your eyes—."

He closed the book. And from the Ptolemies
Sand troughed us in a glittering abyss.
A serpent swam a vertex to the sun
—On unpaced beaches leaned its tongue and drummed.
What fountains did I hear? what icy speeches?
Memory, committed to the page, had broke.   *1926*

REPOSE OF RIVERS

The willows carried a slow sound,
A sarabande the wind mowed on the mead.
I could never remember
That seething, steady leveling of the marshes
Till age had brought me to the sea.

Flags, weeds. And remembrance of steep alcoves
Where cypresses shared the noon's
Tyranny; they drew me into hades almost.
And mammoth turtles climbing sulphur dreams
Yielded, while sun-silt rippled them
Asunder. . .

How much I would have bartered! the black gorge
And all the singular nestings in the hills
Where beavers learn stitch and tooth.
The pond I entered once and quickly fled—
I remember now its singing willow rim.

And finally, in that memory all things nurse;
After the city that I finally passed
With scalding unguents spread and smoking darts
The monsoon cut across the delta
At gulf gates . . . There, beyond the dykes

I heard wind flaking sapphire, like this summer,
And willows could not hold more steady sound.
                                             1926

From THE BRIDGE

PROEM: TO BROOKLYN BRIDGE

How many dawns, chill from his rippling rest
The seagull's wings shall dip and pivot him,

Shedding white rings of tumult, building high
Over the chained bay waters Liberty—

Then, with inviolate curve, forsake our eyes
As apparitional as sails that cross
Some page of figures to be filed away;
—Till elevators drop us from our day . . .

I think of cinemas, panoramic sleights
With multitudes bent toward some flashing scene
Never disclosed, but hastened to again,
Foretold to other eyes on the same screen;

And Thee, across the harbor, silver-paced
As though the sun took step of thee, yet left
Some motion ever unspent in thy stride,—
Implicitly thy freedom staying thee!

Out of some subway scuttle, cell or loft
A bedlamite speeds to thy parapets,
Tilting there momently, shrill shirt ballooning,
A jest falls from the speechless caravan.

Down Wall, from girder into street noon leaks,
A rip-tooth of the sky's acetylene;
All afternoon the cloud-flown derricks turn . . .
Thy cables breathe the North Atlantic still.

And obscure as that heaven of the Jews,
Thy guerdon . . . Accolade thou dost bestow
Of anonymity time cannot raise:
Vibrant reprieve and pardon thou dost show.

O harp and altar, of the fury fused,
(How could mere toil align thy choiring strings!)
Terrific threshold of the prophet's pledge,
Prayer of pariah, and the lover's cry,—

Again the traffic lights that skim thy swift
Unfractioned idiom, immaculate sigh of stars,
Beading thy path—condense eternity:
And we have seen night lifted in thine arms.

Under thy shadow by the piers I waited;
Only in darkness is thy shadow clear.
The City's fiery parcels all undone,
Already snow submerges an iron year . . .

O Sleepless as the river under thee,
Vaulting the sea, the prairies' dreaming sod,
Unto us lowliest sometime sweep, descend
And of the curveship lend a myth to God.

From II. POWHATAN'S DAUGHTER

The River

[. . . and past the din and slogans of the year—]

Stick your patent name on a signboard
brother—all over—going west—young man
Tintex—Japalac—Certain-teed Overalls ads
and lands sakes! under the new playbill ripped
in the guaranteed corner—see Bert Williams what?
Minstrels when you steal a chicken just
save me the wing for if it isn't
Erie it ain't for miles around a
Mazda—and the telegraphic night coming on Thomas

a Ediford—and whistling down the tracks
a headlight rushing with the sound—can you
imagine—while an EXPRESS makes time like
SCIENCE—COMMERCE and the HOLYGHOST
RADIO ROARS IN EVERY HOME WE HAVE THE NORTHPOLE
WALLSTREET AND VIRGINBIRTH WITHOUT STONES OR
WIRES OR EVEN RUNNING brooks connecting ears
and no more sermons windows flashing roar
Breathtaking—as you like it . . . eh?

                So the 20th Century—so
whizzed the Limited—roared by and left
three men, still hungry on the tracks, ploddingly
watching the tail lights wizen and converge, slipping gimleted and neatly out of sight.

                              *

[to those whose addresses are never near]
The last bear, shot drinking in the Dakotas

Loped under wires that span the mountain stream.
Keen instruments, strung to a vast precision
Bind town to town and dream to ticking dream.
But some men take their liquor slow—and count
—Though they'll confess no rosary nor clue—
The river's minute by the far brook's year.
Under a world of whistles, wires and steam
Caboose-like they go ruminating through
Ohio, Indiana—blind baggage—
To Cheyenne tagging . . . Maybe Kalamazoo.

Time's rendings, time's blendings they construe
As final reckonings of fire and snow;
Strange bird-wit, like the elemental gist
Of unwalled winds they offer, singing low
My Old Kentucky Home and *Casey Jones,*
Some Sunny Day. I heard a road-gang chanting so.
And afterwards, who had a colt's eyes—one said,
"Jesus! Oh I remember watermelon days!" And sped
High in a cloud of merriment, recalled
"—And when my Aunt Sally Simpson smiled," he drawled—
"It was almost Louisiana, long ago."
"There's no place like Booneville though, Buddy,"
One said, excising a last burr from his vest,
"—For early trouting." Then peering in the can,
"—But I kept on the tracks." Possessed, resigned,
He trod the fire down pensively and grinned,
Spreading dry shingles of a beard. . . .

Behind

My father's cannery works I used to see
Rail-squatters ranged in nomad raillery,
The ancient men—wifeless or runaway
Hobo-trekkers that forever search
An empire wilderness of freight and rails.
Each seemed a child, like me, on a loose perch,
Holding to childhood like some termless play.
John, Jake or Charley, hopping the slow freight
—Memphis to Tallahassee—riding the rods,
Blind fists of nothing, humpty-dumpty clods.

[but who have touched her, knowing her without name]

Yet they touch something like a key perhaps.

From pole to pole across the hills, the states
—They know a body under the wide rain;
Youngsters with eyes like fjords, old reprobates
With racetrack jargon,—dotting immensity
They lurk across her, knowing her yonder breast
Snow-silvered, sumac-stained or smoky blue—
Is past the valley-sleepers, south or west.
—As I have trod the rumorous midnights, too,
And past the circuit of the lamp's thin flame
(O Nights that brought me to her body bare!)
Have dreamed beyond the print that bound her name.
Trains sounding the long blizzards out—I heard
Wail into distances I knew were hers.
Papooses crying on the wind's long mane
Screamed redskin dynasties that fled the brain,
—Dead echoes! But I knew her body there,
Time like a serpent down her shoulder, dark,
And space, an eaglet's wing, laid on her hair.

[nor the myths of her fathers . . .]

Under the Ozarks, domed by Iron Mountain,
The old gods of the rain lie wrapped in pools
Where eyeless fish curvet a sunken fountain
And re-descend with corn from querulous crows.
Such pilferings make up their timeless eatage,
Propitiate them for their timber torn
By iron, iron—always the iron dealt cleavage!
They doze now, below axe and powder horn.

And Pullman breakfasters glide glistening steel
From tunnel into field—iron strides the dew—
Straddles the hill, a dance of wheel on wheel.
You have a half-hour's wait at Siskiyou,
Or stay the night and take the next train through.
Southward, near Cairo passing, you can see
The Ohio merging,—borne down Tennessee;
And if it's summer and the sun's in dusk
Maybe the breeze will lift the River's musk
—As though the waters breathed that you might know
Memphis Johnny, Steamboat Bill, Missouri Joe.
Oh, lean from the window, if the train slows down,
As though you touched hands with some ancient clown,

—A little while gaze absently below
And hum *Deep River* with them while they go.

Yes, turn again and sniff once more—look see,
O Sheriff, Brakeman and Authority—
Hitch up your pants and crunch another quid,
For you, too, feed the River timelessly.
And few evade full measure of their fate;
Always they smile out eerily what they seem.
I could believe he joked at heaven's gate—
Dan Midland—jolted from the cold brake-beam.

Down, down—born pioneers in time's despite,
Grimed tributaries to an ancient flow—
They win no frontier by their wayward plight,
But drift in stillness, as from Jordan's brow.

You will not hear it as the sea; even stone
Is not more hushed by gravity . . . But slow,
As loth to take more tribute—sliding prone
Like one whose eyes were buried long ago

The River, spreading, flows—and spends your dream.
What are you, lost within this tideless spell?
You are your father's father, and the stream—
A liquid theme that floating niggers swell.

Damp tonnage and alluvial march of days—
Nights turbid, vascular with silted shale
And roots surrendered down of moraine clays:
The Mississippi drinks the farthest dale.

O quarrying passion, undertowed sunlight!
The basalt surface drags a jungle grace
Ochreous and lynx-barred in lengthening might;
Patience! and you shall reach the biding place!

Over De Soto's bones the freighted floors
Throb past the City storied of three thrones.
Down two more turns the Mississippi pours
(Anon tall ironsides up from salt lagoons)

And flows within itself, heaps itself free.

All fades but one thin skyline 'round . . . Ahead
No embrace opens but the stinging sea;
The River lifts itself from its long bed,

Poised wholly on its dream, a mustard glow
Tortured with history, its one will—flow!
—The Passion spreads in wide tongues, choked and slow,
Meeting the Gulf, hosannas silently below.

VII. THE TUNNEL

*To Find the Western path
Right thro' the Gates of Wrath.*
BLAKE

Performances, assortments, résumés—
Up Times Square to Columbus Circle lights
Channel the congresses, nightly sessions,
Refractions of the thousand theatres, faces—
Mysterious kitchens. . . . You shall search them all.
Some day by heart you'll learn each famous sight
And watch the curtain lift in hell's despite;
You'll find the garden in the third act dead,
Finger your knees—and wish yourself in bed
With tabloid crime-sheets perched in easy sight.

> Then let you reach your hat
> and go.
> As usual, let you—also
> walking down—exclaim
> to twelve upward leaving
> a subscription praise
> for what time slays.

Or can't you quite make up your mind to ride;
A walk is better underneath the L a brisk
Ten blocks or so before? But you find yourself
Preparing penguin flexions of the arms,—
As usual you will meet the scuttle yawn:
The subway yawns the quickest promise home.

Be minimum, then, to swim the hiving swarms
Out of the Square, the Circle burning bright—

Avoid the glass doors gyring at your right,
Where boxed alone a second, eyes take fright
—Quite unprepared rush naked back to light:
And down beside the turnstile press the coin
Into the slot. The gongs already rattle.

       And so
       of cities you bespeak
       subways, rivered under streets
       and rivers. . . . In the car
       the overtone of motion
       underground, the monotone
       of motion is the sound
       of other faces, also underground—

"Let's have a pencil Jimmy—living now
at Floral Park
Flatbush—on the Fourth of July—
like a pigeon's muddy dream—potatoes
to dig in the field—travlin the town—too—
night after night—the Culver line—the
girls all shaping up—it used to be—"

Our tongues recant like beaten weather vanes.
This answer lives like verdigris, like hair
Beyond extinction, surcease of the bone;
And repetition freezes—"What

"what do you want? getting weak on the links?
fandaddle daddy don't ask for change—IS THIS
FOURTEENTH? it's half past six she said—if
you don't like my gate why did you
swing on it, why *didja*
swing on it
anyhow—"

       And somehow anyhow swing—

The phonographs of hades in the brain
Are tunnels that re-wind themselves, and love
A burnt match skating in a urinal—
Somewhere above Fourteenth TAKE THE EXPRESS
To brush some new presentiment of pain—

"But I want service in this office SERVICE
I said—after
the show she cried a little afterwards but—"
Whose head is swinging from the swollen strap?
Whose body smokes along the bitten rails,
Bursts from a smoldering bundle far behind
In back forks of the chasms of the brain,—
Puffs from a riven stump far out behind
In interborough fissures of the mind . . . ?

And why do I often meet your visage here,
Your eyes like agate lanterns—on and on
Below the toothpaste and the dandruff ads?
—And did their riding eyes right through your side,
And did their eyes like unwashed platters ride?
And Death, aloft,—gigantically down
Probing through you—toward me, O evermore!
And when they dragged your retching flesh,
Your trembling hands that night through Baltimore—
That last night on the ballot rounds, did you
Shaking, did you deny the ticket, Poe?

For Gravesend Manor change at Chambers Street.
The platform hurries along to a dead stop.

The intent escalator lifts a serenade
Stilly
Of shoes, umbrellas, each eye attending its shoe, then
Bolting outright somewhere above where streets
Burst suddenly in rain. . . . The gongs recur:
Elbows and levers, guard and hissing door.
Thunder is galvothermic here below. . . . The car
Wheels off. The train rounds, bending to a scream,
Taking the final level for the dive
Under the river—
And somewhat emptier than before,
Demented, for a hitching second, humps; then
Lets go. . . . Toward corners of the floor
Newspapers wing, revolve and wing.
Blank windows gargle signals through the roar.

And does the Dæmon take you home, also,
Wop washerwoman. with the bandaged hair?

After the corridors are swept, the cuspidors—
The gaunt sky-barracks cleanly now, and bare,
O Genoese, do you bring mother eyes and hands
Back home to children and to golden hair?

Dæmon, demurring and eventful yawn!
Whose hideous laughter is a bellows mirth
—Or the muffled slaughter of a day in birth—
O cruelly to inoculate the brinking dawn
With antennæ toward worlds that glow and sink;—
To spoon us out more liquid than the dim
Locution of the eldest star, and pack
The conscience navelled in the plunging wind,
Umbilical to call—and straightway die!

O caught like pennies beneath soot and steam,
Kiss of our agony thou gatherest;
Condensed, thou takest all—shrill ganglia
Impassioned with some song we fail to keep.
And yet, like Lazarus, to feel the slope,
The sod and billow breaking,—lifting ground,
—A sound of waters bending astride the sky
Unceasing with some Word that will not die . . . !

*

A tugboat, wheezing wreaths of steam,
Lunged past, with one galvanic blare stove up the River.
I counted the echoes assembling, one after one,
Searching, thumbing the midnight on the piers.
Lights, coasting, left the oily tympanum of waters;
The blackness somewhere gouged glass on a sky.
And this thy harbor, O my City, I have driven under,
Tossed from the coil of ticking towers. . . . Tomorrow,
And to be. . . . Here by the River that is East—
Here at the waters' edge the hands drop memory;
Shadowless in that abyss they unaccounting lie.
How far away the star has pooled the sea—
Or shall the hands be drawn away, to die?

Kiss of our agony Thou gatherest,
                    O Hand of Fire
                        gatherest—   1930

KEY WEST

Here has my salient faith annealed me.
Out of the valley, past the ample crib
To skies impartial, that do not disown me
Nor claim me, either, by Adam's spine—nor rib.

The oar plash, and the meteorite's white arch
Concur with wrist and bicep. In the moon
That now has sunk I strike a single march
To heaven or hades—to an equally frugal noon.

Because these millions reap a dead conclusion
Need I presume the same fruit of my bone
As draws them towards a doubly mocked confusion
Of apish nightmares into steel-strung stone?

O, steel and stone! But gold was, scarcity before.
And here is water, and a little wind. . . .
There is no breath of friends and no more shore
Where gold has not been sold and conscience tinned.

1933

ROYAL PALM

FOR GRACE HART CRANE

Green rustlings, more than regal charities
Drift coolly from that tower of whispered light.
Amid the noontide's blazed asperities
I watched the sun's most gracious anchorite

Climb up as by communings, year on year
Uneaten of the earth or aught earth holds,
And the grey trunk, that's elephantine, rear
Its frondings sighing in ætherial folds.

Forever fruitless, and beyond that yield
Of sweat the jungle presses with hot love
And tendril till our deathward breath is sealed—
It grazes the horizons, launched above

Mortality—ascending emerald-bright,
A fountain at salute, a crown in view—
Unshackled, casual of its azured height
As though it soared suchwise through heaven too.

1933

THE HURRICANE

Lo, Lord, Thou ridest!
Lord, Lord, Thy swifting heart

Naught stayeth, naught now bideth
But's smithereened apart!

Ay! Scripture flee'th stone!
Milk-bright, Thy chisel wind

Rescindeth flesh from bone
To quivering whittlings thinned—

Swept—whistling straw! Battered,
Lord, e'en boulders now out-leap

Rock sockets, levin-lathered!
Nor, Lord, may worm out-deep

Thy drum's gambade, its plunge abscond!
Lord God, while summits crashing

Whip sea-kelp screaming on blond
Sky-seethe, high heaven dashing—

Thou ridest to the door, Lord!
Thou bidest wall nor floor, Lord!

1933

TO EMILY DICKINSON

You who desired so much—in vain to ask—
Yet fed your hunger like an endless task,
Dared dignify the labor, bless the quest—
Achieved that stillness ultimately best,

Being, of all, least sought for: Emily, hear!
O sweet, dead Silencer, most suddenly clear
When singing that Eternity possessed
And plundered momently in every breast;

—Truly no flower yet withers in your hand,
The harvest you descried and understand
Needs more than wit to gather, love to bind.
Some reconcilement of remotest mind—

Leaves Ormus rubyless, and Ophir chill.
Else tears heap all within one clay-cold hill.

1933

THE PHANTOM BARK

So dream thy sails, O phantom bark
That I thy drownèd man may speak again
Perhaps as once Will Collins spoke the lark,
And leave me half a-dream upon the main.

For who shall lift head up to funnel smoke,
And who trick back the leisured winds again
As they were fought—and wooed? They now but stoke
Their vanity, and dream no land in vain.

Of old there was a promise, and thy sails
Have kept no faith but wind, the cold stream
—The hot fickle wind, the breath of males
Imprisoned never, no not soot or rain.   1933

THE BROKEN TOWER

The bell-rope that gathers God at dawn
Dispatches me as though I dropped down the knell
Of a spent day—to wander the cathedral lawn
From pit to crucifix, feet chill on steps from hell.

Have you not heard, have you not seen that corps
Of shadows in the tower, whose shoulders sway
Antiphonal carillons launched before
The stars are caught and hived in the sun's ray?

The bells, I say, the bells break down their tower;
And swing I know not where. Their tongues engrave
Membrane through marrow, my long-scattered score
Of broken intervals. . . . And I, their sexton slave!

Oval encyclicals in canyons heaping
The impasse high with choir. Banked voices slain!
Pagodas, campaniles with reveilles outleaping—
O terraced echoes prostrate on the plain! . . .

And so it was I entered the broken world
To trace the visionary company of love, its voice
An instant in the wind (I know not whither hurled)
But not for long to hold each desperate choice.

My word I poured. But was it cognate, scored
Of that tribunal monarch of the air
Whose thigh embronzes earth, strikes crystal Word
In wounds pledged once to hope—cleft to despair?

The steep encroachments of my blood left me
No answer (could blood hold such a lofty tower
As flings the question true?)—or is it she
Whose sweet mortality stirs latent power?—

And through whose pulse I hear, counting the strokes
My veins recall and add, revived and sure
The angelus of wars my chest evokes:
What I hold healed, original now, and pure . . .

And builds, within, a tower that is not stone
(Not stone can jacket heaven)—but slip
Of pebbles—visible wings of silence sown
In azure circles, widening as they dip

The matrix of the heart, lift down the eye
That shrines the quiet lake and swells a tower . . .
The commodious, tall decorum of that sky
Unseals her earth, and lifts love in its shower.   1933

Kenneth Fearing

CULTURAL NOTES

Professor Burke's symphony, "Colorado Vistas,"
In four movements,
I Mountains, II Canyons, III Dusk, IV Dawn,
Was played recently by the Philharmonic.
Snapshots of the localities described in music were passed around and
    the audience checked for accuracy.
All O.K.
After the performance Maurice Epstein, 29, tuberculosis, stoker on the
    S.S. *Tarboy*, rose to his feet and shouted,
"He's crazy, them artists are all crazy,
I can prove it by Max Nordau. They poison the minds of young girls."
Otto Svoboda, 500 Avenue A, butcher, Pole, husband, philosopher,
    argued in rebuttal,
"Shut your trap, you.
The question is, does the symphony fit in with Karl Marx?"

At the Friday evening meeting of the Browning Writing League, Mrs.
    Whittamore Ralston-Beckett,
Traveler, lecturer, novelist, critic, poet, playwright, editor, mother,
    idealist,
Fascinated her audience with a brief talk, whimsical and caustic,
Appealing to the younger generation to take a brighter, happier, more
    sunny and less morbid view of life's eternal fundamentals.
Mrs. Ralston-Beckett quoted Sir Henry Parke-Bennett: "O Beauty,"
    she said,
"Take your fingers off my throat, take your elbow out of my eye,
Take your sorrow off my sorrow,
Take your hat, take your gloves, take your feet down off the table,
Take your beauty off my beauty, and go."

In the open discussion that followed, Maurice Epstein, 29, tuberculosis,
    stoker on the S.S. *Tarboy*, arose and queried the speaker,

"Is it true, as certain scientists assert, that them artists are all of them
    crazy?"
A Mr. Otto Svoboda present spoke in reply,
"Shut your trap, you. The question is, what about Karl Marx?"   *1929*

EVENING SONG

Go to sleep, McKade;
Fold up the day, it was a bright scarf;
Put it away;
Take yourself apart like a house of cards.

It is time to be a gray mouse under a tall building;
Go there; go there now.
Look at the huge nails; run behind the pipes;
Scamper in the walls;
Crawl toward the beckoning girl, her breasts are warm.
But here is a dead man. A lunatic?
Kill him with your pistol. Creep past him to the girl.

Sleep, McKade;
Throw one arm across the bed; wind your watch;
You are a gentleman, and important;
Yawn; go to sleep.

The continent, turning from the sun, is dark and quiet;
Your ticker waits for tomorrow morning,
And you are alive now;
It will be a long time before they put McKade under the sod.
Sometime, but not now.
Sometime, though. Sometime, for certain.

Take apart your brain,
Close the mouths in it that have been hungry, they are fed for a while,
Go to sleep, you are a gentleman, McKade, alive and sane, a gentleman
    of position.
Tip your hat to the lady;
Speak to the mayor;
You are a friend of the mayor's, are you not?
True, a friend of the mayor's.
And you met the Queen of Rumania? True.

Then go to sleep;
Be a dog sleeping in the old sun;
Be an animal dreaming in the old sun, beside a Roman road;
Be a dog lying in the meadow, watching soldiers pass;
Follow the girl who beckons to you;
Run from the man with the dagger; it can split your bones;
Be terrified of strangers, and the sea, and of great height;
Forget it, then; curl up and dream in the old sun that warms Manhattan.
Sleep, McKade.
Yawn. Go to sleep.   *1929*

RESURRECTION

You will remember the kisses, real or imagined;
You will remember the faces that were before you, and the words exchanged;
You will remember the minute crowded with meaning, the moment of pain, the aimless hour;
You will remember the cities, and the plains, and the mountains, and the sea,

And recall the friendly voice of the killer, or the voice of the priest, inhumanly sweet;
Recall the triumphant smile of the duped;
You will not forget compassion that glittered in the eyes of the moneylender, refusing you, not forget the purpose that lay beneath the merchant's warmth;
You will not forget the voice of the bought magistrate quivering in horror through the courtroom above prostitute and pimp,
The majesty of the statesman at the microphone, the sober majesty of the listening clerk,
The face of the fool, radiant on newspaper and screen;

You will remember hope that crawled up the bar-room tap and spoke through the confident speech of the lost,
Happiness clearly displayed on the glaring billboards,
Love casually revealed in the magazines and novels, or stated in the trembling limbs of ancient millionaires;
You will remember the triumph easily defined by the rebel messiah, by the breadloaf in the hand of the ghetto wife, by the inscription on the patriot tomb;

You will remember your laughter that rose with the steam from the
    carcass on the street
In hatred and pity exactly matched.
These are the things that will return to you,
To mingle with the days and nights, with the sound of motors and
    the sun's warmth,
With fatigue and desire,
As you work, and sleep, and talk, and laugh, and die.   *1935*

NO CREDIT

Whether dinner was pleasant, with the windows lit by gunfire, and no
    one disagreed; or whether, later, we argued in the park, and there
    was a touch of vomit-gas in the evening air;
Whether we found a greater, deeper, more perfect love, by courtesy of
    Camels, over NBC; whether the comics amused us, or the news-
    papers carried a hunger death and a White House prayer for
    mother's day;
Whether the bills were paid or not, whether or not we had our doubts,
    whether we spoke our minds at Joe's, and the receipt said "Not
    Returnable," and the cash-register rang up "No Sale,"
Whether the truth was then, or later, or whether the best had already
    gone—

Nevertheless, we know; as every turn is measured; as every unavoidable
    risk is known;
As nevertheless, the flesh grows old, dies, dies in its only life, is gone;
The reflection goes from the mirror, as the shadow, of even a rebel, is
    gone from the wall;
As nevertheless, the current is thrown and the wheels revolve; and
    nevertheless, as the word is spoken and the wheat grows tall and
    the ships sail on—

None but the fool is paid in full; none but the broker, none but the
    scab is certain of profit;
The sheriff alone may attend a third degree in formal attire; alone, the
    academy artists multiply in dignity as trooper's bayonet guards
    the door;
Only Steve, the side-show robot, knows content; only Steve, the
    mechanical man in love with a photo-electric beam, remains aloof;
    only Steve, who sits and smokes or stands in salute, is secure;
Steve, whose shoebutton eyes are blind to terror, whose painted ears
    are deaf to appeal, whose welded breast will never be slashed by
    bullets, whose armature soul can hold no fear.   *1935*

LULLABY

Wide as this night, old as this night is old and young as it is young,
 still as this, strange as this;
Filled as this night is filled with the light of a moon as gray;
Dark as these trees, heavy as this scented air from the fields, warm as
 this hand;
As warm, as strong;

Is the night that wraps all the huts of the south and folds the empty
 barns of the west;
Is the wind that fans the roadside fire;
Are the trees that line the country estates, tall as the lynch trees, as
 straight, as black;
Is the moon that lights the mining towns, dim as the light upon tenement roofs, gray upon the hands of the bars of Moabit, cold as
 the bars of the Tombs.   *1935*

TWENTIETH-CENTURY BLUES

What do you call it, bobsled champion, and you, too, Olympic roller-
 coaster ace,
High-diving queen, what is the word,
Number one man on the Saturday poker squad, motion-picture star
 incognito as a home girl, life of the party or you, the serious type,
 what is it, what is it,

When it's just like a fever shooting up and up and up but there are
 no chills and there is no fever,
Just exactly like a song, like a knockout, like a dream, like a book,

What is the word, when you know that all the lights of all the cities
 of all the world are burning bright as day, and you know that some
 time they all go out for you,
Or your taxi rolls and rolls through streets made of velvet, what is the
 feeling, what is the feeling when the radio never ends, but the
 hour, the swift, the electric, the invisible hour does not stop and
 does not turn,
What does it mean, when the get-away money burns in dollars big as
 moons, but where is there to go that's just exactly right,

What have you won, plunger, when the 20-to-1 comes in; what have
    you won, salesman, when the dotted line is signed; irresistible lover,
    when her eyelids flutter shut at last, what have you really, finally
    won;
And what is gone soldier, soldier, step-and-a-half marine who saw the
    whole world; hot-tip addict, what is always just missed; picker of
    crumbs, how much has been lost, denied, what are all the things
    destroyed,
Question mark, question mark, question mark, question mark,
And you, fantasy Frank, and dreamworld Dora and hallucination
    Harold, and delusion Dick, and nightmare Ned,

What is it, how do you say it, what does it mean, what's the word,
That miracle thing, the thing that can't be so, quote, unquote, but just
    the same it's true,
That third-rail, million-volt exclamation mark, that ditto, ditto, ditto,
That stop, stop, go.   *1935*

MEMO

Is there still any shadow there, on the rainwet window of the coffee pot,
Between the haberdasher's and the pinball arcade,
There, where we stood one night in the warm, fine rain, and smoked
    and laughed and talked.

Is there now any sound at all,
Other than the sound of tires, and motors, and hurrying feet,
Is there on tonight's damp, heelpocked pavement somewhere the mark
    of a certain toe, an especial nail, or the butt of a particular dropped
    cigarette?—

(There must be, there has to be, no heart could beat if this were not so,
That was an hour, a glittering hour, an important hour in a tremendous
    year)

Where we talked for a while of life and love, of logic and the senses, of
    you and of me, character and fate, pain, revolution, victory and
    death,

Is there tonight any shadow, at all,
Other than the shadows that stop for a moment and then hurry past
    the windows blurred by the same warm, slow, still rain?   *1938*

DEVIL'S DREAM

But it could never be true;
How could it ever happen, if it never did before, and it's not so now?

But suppose that the face behind those steel prison bars—
Why do you dream about a face lying cold in the trenches streaked with
    rain and dirt and blood?
Is it the very same face seen so often in the mirror?
Just as though it could be true—

But what if it is, what if it is, what if it is, what if the thing that
    cannot happen really happens just the same.
Suppose the fever goes a hundred, then a hundred and one,
What if Holy Savings Trust goes from 98 to 88 to 78 to 68, then drops
    down to 28 and 8 and out of sight,
And the fever shoots a hundred two, a hundred three, a hundred four,
    then a hundred five and out?

But now there's only the wind and the sky and sunlight and the clouds,
With everyday people walking and talking as they always have before
    along the everyday street,
Doing ordinary things with ordinary faces and ordinary voices in the
    ordinary way,
Just as they always will—

Then why does it feel like a bomb, why does it feel like a target,
Like standing on the gallows with the trap about to drop,
Why does it feel like a thunderbolt the second before it strikes, why
    does it feel like a tight-rope walk high over hell?

Because it is not, will not, never could be true
That the whole wide, bright, green, warm, calm world goes:
CRASH.   1938

TOMORROW

Now that the others are gone, all of them, forever,
And they have your answer, and you have theirs, and the decision is
    made,
And the river of minutes between you widens to a tide of hours, a flood
    of days, a gulf of years and a sea of silence;

If, now, there are any questions you would like to ask of the shapes that
    still move and speak inaudibly in the empty room,
If there are any different arrangements you would like to suggest,

Make them to the river boats, whose echoing whistle will be a clear
    reply,
Speak to the seagulls, their effortless flight will provide any answer you
    may wish to hear,
Ask the corner chestnut vendor, ask the tireless hammer and pulse of
    the subway,
Speak to the family on the illuminated billboard, forever friendly, or
    to the wind, or to the sign that sways and creaks above the sta-
    tioner's door.   1938

REQUIEM

Will they stop,
Will they stand there for a moment, perhaps before some shop where
    you have gone so many times
(Stand with the same blue sky above them and the stones, so often
    walked, beneath)

Will it be a day like this—
As though there could be such a day again—
And will their own concerns still be about the same,
And will the feeling still be this that you have felt so many times,
Will they meet and stop and speak, one perplexed and one aloof,

Saying: Have you heard,
Have you heard,
Have you heard about the death?

Yes, choosing the words, tragic, yes, a shock,
One who had so much of this, they will say, a life so filled with that,
Then will one say that the days are growing crisp again, the other that
    the leaves are turning,
And will they say good-bye, good-bye, you must look me up some time,
    good-bye,
Then turn and go, each of them thinking, and yet, and yet,

Each feeling, if it were I, instead, would that be all,
Each wondering, suddenly alone, if that is all, in fact—

And will that be all?
On a day like this, with motors streaming through the fresh parks, the
    streets alive with casual people,
And everywhere, on all of it, the brightness of the sun.   1938

AD

WANTED: Men;
Millions of men are WANTED AT ONCE in a big new field;
NEW, TREMENDOUS, THRILLING, GREAT.

If you've ever been a figure in the chamber of horrors,
If you've ever escaped from a psychiatric ward,
If you thrill at the thought of throwing poison into wells, have heavenly
    visions of people, by the thousands, dying in flames—

YOU ARE THE VERY MAN WE WANT
We mean business and our business is YOU
WANTED: A race of brand-new men.
Apply: Middle Europe;
No skill needed;
No ambition required; no brains wanted and no character allowed;

TAKE A PERMANENT JOB IN THE COMING PROFESSION
Wages: DEATH.   1938

PACT

It is written in the skyline of the city (you have seen it, that bold and
    accurate inscription), where the gray and gold and soot-black roofs
    project against the rising or the setting sun,
It is written in the ranges of the farthest mountains, and written by the
    lightning bolt,
Written, too, in the winding rivers of the prairies, and in the strangely
    familiar effigies of the clouds,

That there will be other days and remoter times, by far, than these,
    still more prodigious people and still less credible events,
When there will be a haze, as there is today, not quite blue and not
    quite purple, upon the river, a green mist upon the valley below,
    as now,

And we will build, upon that day, another hope (because these cities
    are young and strong),

And we will raise another dream (because these hills and fields are rich
and green),

And we will fight for all of this again, and if need be again,
And on that day, and in that place, we will try again, and this time we
shall win.   *1940*

HOMAGE

They said to him, "It is a very good thing that you have done, yes, both
good and great, proving this other passage to the Indies. Marvelous," they said. "Very. But where, Señor, is the gold?"

They said: "We like it, we admire it very much, don't misunderstand
us, in fact we think it's almost great. But isn't there, well, a little
too much of this Prince of Denmark? After all, there is no one
quite like you in your lighter vein."
"Astonishing," they said. "Who would have thought you had it in you,
Orville?" They said, "Wilbur, this machine of yours is amazing,
if it works, and perhaps some day we can use it to distribute eggs,
or to advertise."

And they were good people, too. Decent people.
They did not beat their wives. They went to church. And they kept
the law.   *1940*

ANY MAN'S ADVICE TO HIS SON

If you have lost the radio beam, then guide yourself by the sun or the
stars.
(By the North Star at night, and in daytime by the compass and the
sun.)
Should the sky be overcast and there are neither stars nor a sun, then
steer by dead reckoning.
If the wind and direction and speed are not known, then trust to your
wits and your luck.

Do you follow me? Do you understand? Or is this too difficult to learn?
But you must and you will, it is important that you do,
Because there may be troubles even greater than these that I have said.

Because, remember this: Trust no man fully.
Remember: If you must shoot at another man squeeze, do not jerk the
trigger. Otherwise you may miss and die, yourself, at the hand of
some other man's son.

And remember: In all this world there is nothing so easily squandered,
or once gone, so completely lost as life.

I tell you this because I remember you when you were small,
And because I remember all your monstrous infant boasts and lies,
And the way you smiled, and how you ran and climbed, as no one else
quite did, and how you fell and were bruised,
And because there is no other person, anywhere on earth, who remem-
bers these things as clearly as I do now.   *1940*

A LA CARTE

Some take to liquor, some turn to prayer,
Many prefer to dance, others to gamble, and a few resort to gas or the
gun.
(Some are lucky, and some are not.)

Name your choice, any selection from one to twenty-five:
Music from Harlem? A Viennese waltz on the slot-machine phono-
graph at Jack's Bar & Grill? Or a Brahms Concerto over WXV?
(Many like it wild, others sweet.)

Champagne for supper, murder for breakfast, romance for lunch and
terror for tea,
This is not the first time, nor will it be the last time the world has
gone to hell.
(Some can take it, and some cannot.)   *1940*

PAY-OFF

Do you, now, as the news becomes known,
And you have the telegram still in your hand, here in the familiar room
where there is no sound but the ticking of the clock,
Or there on the street, where you see the first headlines, and it is true
this time, really true, actual as the green and red of the traffic lights,
as real as the fruit vendor's rhythmic cry,

Do you recall any being other than this, before your world suddenly
shook and settled to this new, strange axis upon which it will turn,
now, always while you live?
Does it seem possible, now, you were ever bored? Or drunk and confident? Or sober and afraid?
Will the sound of the clock ever fade, or the voice of the vendor sometime stop?   *1940*

Richard Eberhart

FOR A LAMB

I saw on the slant hill a putrid lamb,
Propped with daisies. The sleep looked deep,
The face nudged in the green pillow
But the guts were out for crows to eat.

Where's the lamb? whose tender plaint
Said all for the mute breezes.
Say he's in the wind somewhere,
Say, there's a lamb in the daisies.   *1936*

THE GROUNDHOG

In June, amid the golden fields,
I saw a groundhog lying dead.
Dead lay he; my senses shook,
And mind outshot our naked frailty.
There lowly in the vigorous summer
His form began its senseless change,
And made my senses waver dim
Seeing nature ferocious in him.
Inspecting close his maggots' might
And seething cauldron of his being,
Half with loathing, half with a strange love,
I poked him with an angry stick.
The fever arose, became a flame
And Vigour circumscribed the skies,
Immense energy in the sun,
And through my frame a sunless trembling.
My stick had done nor good nor harm.
Then stood I silent in the day
Watching the object, as before;
And kept my reverence for knowledge

Trying for control, to be still,
To quell the passion of the blood;
Until I had bent down on my knees
Praying for joy in the sight of decay.
And so I left; and I returned
In Autumn strict of eye, to see
The sap gone out of the groundhog,
But the bony sodden hulk remained.
But the year had lost its meaning,
And in intellectual chains
I lost both love and loathing,
Mured up in the wall of wisdom.
Another summer took the fields again
Massive and burning, full of life,
But when I chanced upon the spot
There was only a little hair left,
And bones bleaching in the sunlight
Beautiful as architecture;
I watched them like a geometer,
And cut a walking stick from a birch.
It has been three years, now.
There is no sign of the groundhog.
I stood there in the whirling summer,
My hand capped a withered heart,
And thought of China and of Greece,
Of Alexander in his tent;
Of Montaigne in his tower,
Of Saint Theresa in her wild lament.   *1936*

"IN A HARD INTELLECTUAL LIGHT"

In a hard intellectual light
I will kill all delight,
And I will build a citadel
Too beautiful to tell

O too austere to tell
And far too beautiful to see,
Whose evident distance
I will call the best of me.

And this light of intellect
Will shine on all my desires,

It will my flesh protect
And flare my bold constant fires,

For the hard intellectual light
Will lay the flesh with nails.
And it will keep the world bright
And closed the body's soft jails.

And from this fair edifice
I shall see, as my eyes blaze,
The moral grandeur of man
Animating all his days.

And peace will marry purpose,
And purity married to grace
Will make the human absolute
As sweet as the human face.

Until my hard vision blears,
And Poverty and Death return
In organ music like the years,
Making the spirit leap, and burn

For the hard intellectual light
That kills all delight
And brings the solemn, inward pain
Of truth into the heart again.   *1936*

THE SOUL LONGS TO RETURN WHENCE IT CAME

I drove up to the graveyard, which
Used to frighten me as a boy,
When I walked down the river past it,
And even was coming on. I'd make sure
I came home from the woods early enough.
I drove in, I found to the place, I
Left the motor running. My eyes hurried,
To recognize the great oak tree
On the little slope, among the stones.
It was a high day, a crisp day,
The cleanest kind of Autumn day,
With brisk intoxicating air, a
Little wind that frisked, yet there was

Old age in the atmosphere, nostalgia,
The subtle heaviness of the Fall.
I stilled the motor. I walked a few paces;
It was good, the tree; the friendliness of it.
I touched it, I thought of the roots;
They would have pierced her seven years.
O all peoples! O mighty shadows!
My eyes opened along the avenue
Of tombstones, the common land of death.
Humiliation of all loves lost,
That might have had full meaning in any
Plot of ground, come, hear the silence,
See the quivering light. My mind worked
Almost imperceptibly, I
In the command, I the wilful ponderer.
I must have stood silent and thoughtful
There. A host of dry leaves
Danced on the ground in the wind.
They startled, they curved up from the ground,
There was a dry rustling, rattling.
The sun was motionless and brittle.
I felt the blood darken in my cheeks
And burn. Like running. My eyes
Telescoped on decay, I out of command.
Fear, tenderness, they seized me.
My eyes were hot, I dared not look
At the leaves. A pagan urge swept me.
Multitudes, O multitudes in one.
The urge of the earth, the titan
Wild and primitive lust, fused
On the ground of her grave.
I was a being of feeling alone.
I flung myself down on the earth
Full length on the great earth, full length
I wept out the dark load of human love.
In pagan adoration I adored her.
I felt the actual earth of her.
Victor and victim of humility,
I closed in the wordless ecstasy
Of mystery: where there is no thought
But feeling lost in itself forever,
Profound, remote, immediate, and calm.
Frightened, I stood up, I looked about

Suspiciously, hurriedly (a rustling),
As if the sun, the air, the trees
Were human, might not understand.
I drew breath, it made a sound,
I stepped gingerly away. Then
The mind came like a fire, it
Tortured man, I thought of madness.
The mind will not accept the blood.
The sun and sky, the trees and grasses,
And the whispering leaves, took on
Their usual characters. I went away,
Slowly, tingling, elated, saying, saying
Mother, Great Being, O Source of Life
To whom in wisdom we return,
Accept this humble servant evermore.   1940

TWO LOVES

That her serene influence should spread
An afternoon of soft autumnal light
Is to my heart not unaccountable
For she was young, and is not dead.
And still her cheek is red and white.

But that this stealthy still insistent power
Pervades my mind and will not slumber me
Is delicate woe and glory hard to bear;
Her life lives in a ghost-wrought hour,
From whose chill spirit I am not free.

The one was willow to an ardent touch
And she was mood that had a right to die.
But she, the other, the passion of my mind
Long-living still, does overmuch
Come from the dead, and from the sky.

   1940

"WHEN DORIS DANCED"

When Doris danced under the oak tree
The sun himself might wish to see,
Might bend beneath those lovers, leaves,
While her her virgin step she weaves

And envious cast his famous hue
To make her daft, yet win her too.

When Doris danced under the oak tree
Slow John, so stormed in heart, at sea
Gone all his store, a wreck he lay.
But on the ground the sun-beams play.
They lit his face in such degree
Doris lay down, all out of pity.   *1940*

THE FURY OF AERIAL BOMBARDMENT

You would think the fury of aerial bombardment
Would rouse God to relent; the infinite spaces
Are still silent. He looks on shock-pried faces.
History, even, does not know what is meant.

You would feel that after so many centuries
God would give man to repent; yet he can kill
As Cain could, but with multitudinous will,
No farther advanced than in his ancient furies.

Was man made stupid to see his own stupidity?
Is God by definition indifferent, beyond us all?
Is the eternal truth man's fighting soul
Wherein the Beast ravens in its own avidity?

Of Van Wettering I speak, and Averill,
Names on a list, whose faces I do not recall
But they are gone to early death, who late in school
Distinguished the belt feed lever from the belt holding pawl.
                                                    1944

THE HORSE CHESTNUT TREE

Boys in sporadic but tenacious droves
Come with sticks, as certainly as Autumn,
To assault the great horse chestnut tree.

There is a law governs their lawlessness.
Desire is in them for a shining amulet
And the best are those that are highest up.

They will not pick them easily from the ground.
With shrill arms they fling to the higher branches,
To hurry the work of nature for their pleasure.

I have seen them trooping down the street
Their pockets stuffed with chestnuts shucked, unshucked.
It is only evening keeps them from their wish.

Sometimes I run out in a kind of rage
To chase the boys away: I catch an arm,
Maybe, and laugh to think of being the lawgiver.

I was once such a young sprout myself
And fingered in my pocket the prize and trophy.
But still I moralize upon the day

And see that we, outlaws on God's property,
Fling out imagination beyond the skies,
Wishing a tangible good from the unknown.

And likewise death will drive us from the scene
With the great flowering world unbroken yet,
Which we held in idea, a little handful.   1953

THE ROC

The perfervid Roc, sitting on candle light,
The moon's, inaccessible to night,
Thrusting invention, as if he were human,
Thought he could do anything in the world.

Sidereal emblem, come from far away,
This Roc had made amends with flight; and thought,
As men lean upward on the shaft of God,
He'd lean to mankind's aspirations, downward.

Thus is a stance of heavenly approbation,
Sitting in silence where the moonbeams glow,
Fluffing, not taking, the winds of other worlds,
The Roc's imagination grew, a perfect bird

For being beyond his native limitations.
The planets were in order marked, but nebulous;

He sat upon the edges of the world
And sorted the rhythms of the Field stars.

How small they are, down on that sphere,
The good Roc said, becoming a mental power.
I who know all of flight and fight and light
Will tell these creatures what they need to know.

They are afraid. See how each in his heart
Recoils from vistas of revenging evil.
They thrust their chests out cobalt bomb-wise
And bruit the big wars with their minds like boys'.

They are accursed. And what has cursed them is
The forcing gods they have themselves created,
The inability to look at anything
Explicitly, or straight enough to see it straight,

But they look with their old blood-dimmed feelings
And they feel with their old avenging muscles;
They are surprised at all access of wit,
And intellectual laughter they endure but little.

They fear their death because they do not understand it.
They fear insecurity, which lacks philosophy,
Presuming that so timed a creature could be safe.
And they fear injustice, a lack of reality.

The Roc began his acclamation thus.
He preened, and he aspired, and he espied,
And thought that he would move the world,
But the bedrock seemed to give, to fly.

It was the bedrock that buckled and roared.
He, who had defeated flight, a flying bird
Beyond birdhood, an angel of a newer motion,
Felt, in looking down, a crepitation:

The gravid base gave out; tumultuous waters
Crested black upheavals: the groined earth
Rocked spasmodically and lurched in space,
Its mankind clinging to the crust unknowingly.

He could not reach them. His new dimension
Affronted the clear light of the old moon.
The Roc then lifted up his ancient wings
And flew, instinctively, toward the dawn.   *1957*

VAST LIGHT

The fighting nature of the intellect,
The loving nature of the heart,
The head that hits, the blood that lets,
The lift, and the abandonment,

Concern us not fitfully, in no abatement,
Speak to us not evenly, advance
Our good in no equal certainties,
Prevail without finalities,

As when we dare not speak out for justice
Having too fine a sense of discrimination,
Or as we do not know what to do
Speculating upon the imprecision of action,

While time rolls over the richest meadows.
It is now the soul rolls over us.
It is the soul between the head and the heart
Is our air-borne master and our hair-shirt.

It is the soul that cannot be put into words
Is the word of control. Like it or not,
The soul is all that is left of time:
We see through it: we breathe it out.

I have come back to old streets at nightfall
After journeys among volcanoes and icebergs.
I have been up in sidereal glows,
I have eaten of the chill taunt of the spirit.

Whether I apply to the light of reason,
Or feed on insatiable night,
I am aware of light and of vastness,
It is the vague of the soul that I know.

1957

Karl Shapiro

AUTO WRECK

Its quick soft silver bell beating, beating,
And down the dark one ruby flare
Pulsing out red light like an artery,
The ambulance at top speed floating down
Past beacons and illuminated clocks
Wings in a heavy curve, dips down,
And brakes speed, entering the crowd.
The doors leap open, emptying light;
Stretchers are laid out, the mangled lifted
And stowed into the little hospital.
Then the bell, breaking the hush, tolls once,
And the ambulance with its terrible cargo
Rocking, slightly rocking, moves away,
As the doors, an afterthought, are closed.

We are deranged, walking among the cops
Who sweep glass and are large and composed.
One is still making notes under the light.
One with a bucket douches ponds of blood
Into the street and gutter.
One hangs lanterns on the wrecks that cling,
Empty husks of locusts, to iron poles.

Our throats were tight as tourniquets,
Our feet were bound with splints, but now,
Like convalescents intimate and gauche,
We speak through sickly smiles and warn
With the stubborn saw of common sense,
The grim joke and the banal resolution.
The traffic moves around with care,
But we remain, touching a wound
That opens to our richest horror.

Already old, the question Who shall die?
Becomes unspoken Who is innocent?
For death in war is done by hands;
Suicide has cause and stillbirth, logic;
And cancer, simple as a flower, blooms.
But this invites the occult mind,
Cancels our physics with a sneer,
And spatters all we knew of denouement
Across the expedient and wicked stones.

1942

BUICK

As a sloop with a sweep of immaculate wing on her delicate spine
And a keel as steel as a root that holds in the sea as she leans,
Leaning and laughing, my warm-hearted beauty, you ride, you ride,
You tack on the curves with parabola speed and a kiss of goodbye,
Like a thoroughbred sloop, my new high-spirited spirit, my kiss.

As my foot suggests that you leap in the air with your hips of a girl,
My finger that praises your wheel and announces your voices of song,
Flouncing your skirts, you blueness of joy, you flirt of politeness,
You leap, you intelligence, essence of wheelness with silvery nose,
And your platinum clocks of excitement stir like the hairs of a fern.

But how alien you are from the booming belts of your birth and the
    smoke
Where you turned on the stinging lathes of Detroit and Lansing at night
And shrieked at the torch in your secret parts and the amorous tests,
But now with your eyes that enter the future of roads you forget;
You are all instinct with your phosphorous glow and your streaking hair

And now when we stop it is not as the bird from the shell that I leave
Or the leathery pilot who steps from his bird with a sneer of delight,
And not as the ignorant beast do you squat and watch me depart,
But with exquisite breathing you smile, with satisfaction of love,
And I touch you again as you tick in the silence and settle in sleep.

1942

THE DOME OF SUNDAY

With focus sharp as Flemish-painted face
In film of varnish brightly fixed

And through a polished hand-lens deeply seen,
Sunday at noon through hyaline thin air
Sees down the street,
And in the camera of my eye depicts
Row-houses and row-lives:
Glass after glass, door after door the same,
Face after face the same, the same,
The brutal visibility the same;

As if one life emerging from one house
Would pause, a single image caught between
Two facing mirrors where vision multiplies
Beyond perspective,
A silent clatter in the high-speed eye
Spinning out photo-circulars of sight.

I see slip to the curb the long machines
Out of whose warm and windowed rooms pirouette
Shellacked with silk and light
The hard legs of our women.
Our women are one woman, dressed in black.
The carmine printed mouth
And cheeks as soft as muslin-glass belong
Outright to one dark dressy man,
Merely a swagger at her curvy side.
This is their visit to themselves:
All day from porch to porch they weave
A nonsense pattern through the even glare,
Stealing in surfaces
Cold vulgar glances at themselves.

And high up in the heated room all day
I wait behind the plate glass pane for one,
Hot as a voyeur for a glimpse of one,
The vision to blot out this woman's sheen;
All day my sight records expensively
Row-houses and row-lives.

But nothing happens; no diagonal
With melting shadow falls across the curb:
Neither the blinded negress lurching through fatigue,
Nor exiles bleeding from their pores,
Nor that bright bomb slipped lightly from its rack

To splinter every silvered glass and crystal prism,
Witch-bowl and perfume bottle
And billion candle-power dressing-bulb,
No direct hit to smash the shatter-proof
And lodge at last the quivering needle
Clean in the eye of one who stands transfixed
In fascination of her brightness.   *1942*

DRUG STORE

I do remember an apothecary,
And hereabouts 'a dwells

It baffles the foreigner like an idiom,
And he is right to adopt it as a form
Less serious than the living-room or bar;
        For it disestablishes the café,
Is a collective, and on basic country.

Not that it praises hygiene and corrupts
The ice-cream parlor and the tobacconist's
Is it a center; but that the attractive symbols
        Watch over puberty and leer
Like rubber bottles waiting for sick-use.

Youth comes to jingle nickels and crack wise;
The baseball scores are his, the magazines
Devoted to lust, the jazz, the Coca-Cola,
        The lending-library of love's latest.
He is the customer; he is heroized.

And every nook and cranny of the flesh
Is spoken to by packages with wiles.
"Buy me, buy me," they whimper and cajole;
        The hectic range of lipstick pouts,
Revealing the wicked and the simple mouth.

With scarcely any evasion in their eye
They smoke, undress their girls, exact a stance;
But only for a moment. The clock goes round;
        Crude fellowships are made and lost;
They slump in booths like rags, not even drunk.

                                           1942

NOSTALGIA

My soul stands at the window of my room,
  And I ten thousand miles away;
My days are filled with Ocean's sound of doom,
  Salt and cloud and the bitter spray.
Let the wind blow, for many a man shall die.

My selfish youth, my books with gilded edge,
  Knowledge and all gaze down the street;
The potted plants upon the window ledge
  Gaze down with selfish lives and sweet.
Let the wind blow, for many a man shall die.

My night is now her day, my day her night,
  So I lie down, and so I rise;
The sun burns close, the star is losing height,
  The clock is hunted down the skies.
Let the wind blow, for many a man shall die.

Truly a pin can make the memory bleed,
  A world explode the inward mind
And turn the skulls and flowers never freed
  Into the air, no longer blind.
Let the wind blow, for many a man shall die.

Laughter and grief join hands. Always the heart
  Clumps in the breast with heavy stride;
The face grows lined and wrinkled like a chart,
  The eyes bloodshot with tears and tide.
Let the wind blow, for many a man shall die.

1942

POET

Il arrive que l'esprit demande la poésie

Left leg flung out, head cocked to the right,
Tweed coat or army uniform, with book,
Beautiful eyes, who is this walking down?
Who, glancing at the pane of glass looks sharp
And thinks it is not he—as when a poet

Comes swiftly on some half-forgotten poem
And loosely holds the page, steady of mind,
     Thinking it is not his?

And when will *you* exist?—Oh, it is I,
Incredibly skinny, stooped, and neat as pie,
Ignorant as dirt, erotic as an ape,
Dreamy as puberty—with dirty hair!
Into the room like kangaroo he bounds,
Ears flopping like the most expensive hound's;
His chin receives all questions as he bows
     Mouthing a green bon-bon.

Has no more memory than rubber. Stands
Waist-deep in heavy mud of thought and broods
At his own wetness. When he would get out,
To his surprise he lifts in air a phrase
As whole and clean and silvery as a fish
Which jumps and dangles on his damned hooked grin,
But like a name-card on a man's lapel
     Calls him a conscious fool.

And child-like he remembers all his life
And cannily constructs it, fact by fact,
As boys paste postage stamps in careful books,
Denoting pence and legends and profiles,
Nothing more valuable.—And like a thief,
His eyes glassed over and congealed with guilt,
Fondles his secrets like a case of tools,
     And waits in empty doors.

By men despised for knowing what he is,
And by himself. But he exists for women.
As dolls to girls, as perfect wives to men,
So he to women. And to himself a thing,
All ages, epicene, without a trade.
To girls and wives always alive and fated;
To men and scholars always dead like Greek
     And always mistranslated.

Towards exile and towards shame he lures himself,
Tongue winding on his arm, and thinks like Eve
By biting apple will become most wise.

Sentio ergo sum: he feels his way
And words themselves stand up for him like Braille
And punch and perforate his parchment ear.
All language falls like Chinese on his soul,
      Image of song unsounded.

This is the coward's coward that in his dreams
Sees shapes of pain grow tall. Awake at night
He peers at sounds and stumbles at a breeze.
And none holds life less dear. For as a youth
Who by some accident observes his love
Naked and in some natural ugly act,
He turns with loathing and with flaming hands,
      Seared and betrayed by sight.

He is the business man, on beauty trades,
Dealer in arts and thoughts who, like the Jew,
Shall rise from slums and hated dialects
A tower of bitterness. Shall be always strange,
Hunted and then sought after. Shall be sat
Like an ambassador from another race
At tables rich with music. He shall eat flowers,
Chew honey and spit out gall. They shall all smile
      And love and pity him.

His death shall be by drowning. In that hour
When the last bubble of pure heaven's air
Hovers within his throat, safe on his bed,
A small eternal figurehead in terror,
He shall cry out and clutch his days of straw
Before the blackest wave. Lastly, his tomb
Shall list and founder in the troughs of grass
      And none shall speak his name.   *1942*

SIX RELIGIOUS LYRICS: I

I sing the simplest flower,
    The earliest quest of day,
That wears in its white corolla
    The signet of breathing May.

For the envelope of beauty
    Discloses the female part,

The bending and swollen stigma,
The sly tongue of the heart.

And the dusty bee for nectar
Enters and drinks his fill,
And the wind comes freely, freshly
To assist the season's will.

I give you the simplest flower,
The color of air, a dress
Self-woven and frail and holy,
The signet of love's distress.

1942

THE INTELLECTUAL

What should the wars do with these jigging fools?

The man behind the book may not be man,
His own man or the book's or yet the time's,
But still be whole, deciding what he can
In praise of politics or German rimes;

But the intellectual lights a cigarette
And offers it lit to the lady, whose odd smile
Is the merest hyphen—lest he should forget
What he has been resuming all the while.

He talks to overhear, she to withdraw
To some interior feminine fireside
Where the back arches, beauty puts forth a paw
Like a black puma stretching in velvet pride,

Making him think of cats, a stray of which
Some days sets up a howling in his brain,
Pure interference such as this neat bitch
Seems to create from listening disdain.

But talk is all the value, the release,
Talk is the very fillip of an act,
The frame and subject of the masterpiece
Under whose film of age the face is cracked.

His own forehead glows like expensive wood,
But back of it the mind is disengaged,

Self-sealing clock recording bad and good
At constant temperature, intact, unaged.

But strange, his body is an open house
Inviting every passerby to stay;
The city to and fro beneath his brows
Wanders and drinks and chats from night to day.

Think of a private thought, indecent room
Where one might kiss his daughter before bed!
Life is embarrassed; shut the family tomb,
Console your neighbor for his recent dead;

Do something! die in Spain or paint a green
Gouache, go into business (Rimbaud did),
Or start another Little Magazine,
Or move in with a woman, have a kid.

Invulnerable, impossible, immune,
Do what you will, your will will not be done
But dissipate the light of afternoon
Till evening flickers like the midnight sun,

And midnight shouts and dies: I'd rather be
A milkman walking in his sleep at dawn
Bearing fat quarts of cream, and so be free,
Crossing alone and cold from lawn to lawn.

I'd rather be a barber and cut hair
Than walk with you in gilt museum halls,
You and the puma-lady, she so rare
Exhaling her silk soul upon the walls.

Go take yourselves apart, but let me be
The fault you find with everyman. I spit,
I laugh, I fight; and you, *l'homme qui rît,*
Swallow your stale saliva, and still sit.   *1944*

THE PHENOMENON

How lovely it was, after the official fright,
To walk in the shadowy drifts, as if the clouds
Saturated with the obscurity of night
Had died and fallen piecemeal into shrouds.

What crepes there were, what sables heaped on stones,
What soft shakos on posts, tragically gay!
And oil-pool flooded fields that blackly shone
The more black under the liquid eye of day!

It was almost warmer to the touch than sands
And sweeter-tasting than the white, and yet
Walking, the children held their fathers' hands
Like visitors to a mine or parapet.

Then black it snowed again and while it fell
You could see the sun, an irritated rim
Wheeling through smoke; each from his shallow hell
Experienced injured vision growing dim.

But one day all was clear, and one day soon,
Sooner than those who witnessed it had died,
Nature herself forgot the phenomenon,
Her faulty snowfall brilliantly denied.   1953

Randall Jarrell

2nd AIR FORCE

Far off, above the plain the summer dries,
The great loops of the hangars sway like hills.
Buses and weariness and loss, the nodding soldiers
Are wire, the bare frame building, and a pass
To what was hers; her head hides his square patch
And she thinks heavily: My son is grown.
She sees a world: sand roads, tar-paper barracks,
The bubbling asphalt of the runways, sage,
The dunes rising to the interminable ranges,
The dim flights moving over clouds like clouds.
The armorers in their patched faded green,
Sweat-stiffened, banded with brass cartridges,
Walk to the line; their Fortresses, all tail,
Stand wrong and flimsy on their skinny legs,
And the crews climb to them clumsily as bears.
The head withdraws into its hatch (a boy's),
The engines rise to their blind laboring roar,
And the green, made beasts run home to air.
Now in each aspect death is pure.
(At twilight they wink over men like stars
And hour by hour, through the night, some see
The great lights floating in—from Mars, from Mars.)
How emptily the watchers see them gone.

They go, there is silence; the woman and her son
Stand in the forest of the shadows, and the light
Washes them like water. In the long-sunken city
Of evening, the sunlight stills like sleep
The faint wonder of the drowned; in the evening,
In the last dreaming light, so fresh, so old,
The soldiers pass like beasts, unquestioning,
And the watcher for an instant understands

What there is then no need to understand;
But she wakes from her knowledge, and her stare,
A shadow now, moves emptily among
The shadows learning in their shadowy fields
The empty missions.
                Remembering,
She hears the bomber calling, *Little Friend!*
To the fighter hanging in the hostile sky,
And sees the ragged flame eat, rib by rib,
Along the metal of the wing into her heart:
The lives stream out, blossom, and float steadily
To the flames of the earth, the flames
That burn like stars above the lands of men.

She saves from the twilight that takes everything
A squadron shipping, in its last parade—
Its dogs run by it, barking at the band—
A gunner walking to his barracks, half-asleep,
Starting at something, stumbling (above, invisible,
The crews in the steady winter of the sky
Tremble in their wired fur); and feels for them
The love of life for life. The hopeful cells
Heavy with someone else's death, cold carriers
Of someone else's victory, grope past their lives
Into her own bewilderment: The years meant *this?*

But for them the bombers answer everything.

                    1945

THE DEATH OF THE BALL TURRET GUNNER

From my mother's sleep I fell into the State,
And I hunched in its belly till my wet fur froze.
Six miles from earth, loosed from its dream of life,
I woke to black flak and the nightmare fighters.
When I died they washed me out of the turret with a hose.

                    1945

A CAMP IN THE PRUSSIAN FOREST

I walk beside the prisoners to the road.
Load on puffed load,

Their corpses, stacked like sodden wood,
Lie barred or galled with blood

By the charred warehouse. No one comes today
In the old way
To knock the fillings from their teeth;
The dark, coned, common wreath

Is plaited for their grave—a kind of grief.
The living leaf
Clings to the planted profitable
Pine if it is able;

The boughs sigh, mile on green, calm, breathing mile,
From this dead file
The planners ruled for them. . . . One year
They sent a million here:

Here men were drunk like water, burnt like wood.
The fat of good
And evil, the breast's star of hope
Were rendered into soap.

I paint the star I sawed from yellow pine—
And plant the sign
In soil that does not yet refuse
Its usual Jews

Their first asylum. But the white, dwarfed star—
This dead white star—
Hides nothing, pays for nothing; smoke
Fouls it, a yellow joke,

The needles of the wreath are chalked with ash,
A filmy trash
Litters the black woods with the death
Of men; and one last breath

Curls from the monstrous chimney. . . . I laugh aloud
Again and again;
The star laughs from its rotting shroud
Of flesh. O star of men!   *1948*

THE MÄRCHEN

(GRIMM'S TALES)

Listening, listening; it is never still.
This is the forest: long ago the lives
Edged armed into its tides (the axes were its stone
Lashed with the skins of dwellers to its boughs);
We felled our islands there, at last, with iron.
The sunlight fell to them, according to our wish,
And we believed, till nightfall, in that wish;
And we believed, till nightfall, in our lives.

The bird is silent; but its cold breast stirs
Raggedly, and the gloom the moonlight bars
Is blurred with the fluff its long death strewed
In the crumpled fern; and far off something falls.
If the firs forget their breath, if the leaf that perishes
Holds, a bud, to spring; sleeps, fallen, under snow—
It is never still. The darkness quakes with blood;
From its pulse the dark eyes of the hunter glow
Green as their forest, fading images
Of the dream in the firelight: shudder of the coals
In their short Hell, vined skeleton
Of the charcoal-burner dozing in the snow.
Hänsel, to map the hard way, cast his bones
Up clouds to Paradise; His sparrows ate
And he plunged home, past peat and measures, to his kin
Furred in the sooty darkness of the cave
Where the old gods nodded. How the devil's beard
Coiled round the dreaming Hänsel, till his limbs
Grew gnarled as a fakir's on the spindling Cross
The missions rowed from Asia: eternal corpse
Of the Scapegoat, gay with His blood's watered beads,
Red wax in the new snow (strange to His warmed stare);
The wooden mother and the choir of saints, His stars;
And God and His barons, always, iron behind.
Gorged Hänsel felt His blood burn thin as air
In a belly swollen with the airy kine;
How many ages boiled Christ's bark for soup!
Giddy with emptiness, a second wife
Scolding the great-eyed children of a ghost,

He sends them, in his tale, not out to death
(Godfather Death, the reaping messenger),
Nor to the devil cringing in the gloom,
Shifting his barred hooves with a crunch like snow—
But to a king: the blind untroubled Might
Renting a destiny to men on terms—
Come, mend me and wed half of me, my son!
Behind, the headsman fondles his gnawn block.
So men have won a kingdom—there are kings;
Are giants, warlocks, the unburied dead
Invulnerable to any power—the Necessity
Men spring from, die under: the unbroken wood.

Noon, the gold sun of hens and aldermen
Inked black as India, on the green ground,
Our patterns, homely, mercenary, magnified—
Bewitching as the water of Friar Bacon's glass.
(*Our* farmer fooled the devil with a turnip,
Our tailor won a queen with seven flies;
Mouser and mousie and a tub of fat
Kept house together—and a louse, a louse
Brewed small beer in an eggshell with a flea.)
But at evening the poor light, far-off, fantastic—
Sun of misers and of mermen, the last foolish gold
Of soldiers wandering through the country with a crutch—
Scattered its leagues of shadows on the plots
Where life, horned sooty lantern patched with eyes,
Hides more than it illumines, dreams the hordes
Of imps and angels, all of its own hue.
In the great world everything is just the same
Or just the opposite, we found (we never went).
The tinkers, peddlers brought their pinch of salt:
In our mouths the mill of the unresting sea
Ground till their very sores were thirsty.
Quaking below like quicksand, there is fire—
The dowser's twig dips not to water but to Hell;
And the Father, uncomfortable overseer,
Shakes from the rain-clouds Heaven's branding bolt.
Beyond, the Alps ring, avalanche on avalanche,
And the lost palmers freeze to bliss, a smile
Baring their poor teeth, blackened as the skulls
Of sanctuaries—splinters of the Cross, the Ark, the Tree
Jut from a saint's set jawbone, to put out

With one bought vision many a purging fire.
As the circles spread, the stone hopes like a child.
The weak look to the helpless for their aid—
The beasts who, ruled by their god, Death,
Bury the son with their enchanted thanks
For the act outside their possibility:
The victim spared, the labors sweated through, for love
Neither for mate nor litter, but for—anything.
When had it mattered whom we helped? It always paid.
When the dead man's heart broke they found written there
(He could not write): *The wish has made it so.*
Or so he wished. The platter appliquéd
With meals for parents, scraps for children, gristle
For Towser, a poor dog; the walnut jetting wine;
The broom that, fretting for a master, swept a world;
The spear that, weeping for a master, killed a child;
And gold to bury, from the deepest mines—
These neither to wisdom nor to virtue, but to Grace,
The son remembered in the will of God—
These were wishes. The glass in which I saw
Somewhere else, someone else: the field upon which sprawled
Dead, and the ruler of the dead, my twin—
Were wishes? Hänsel, by the eternal sea,
Said to the flounder for his first wish, *Let me wish
And let my wish be granted;* it was granted.
Granted, granted. . . . Poor Hänsel, once too powerless
To shelter your own children from the cold
Or quiet their bellies with the thinnest gruel,
It was not power that you lacked, but wishes.
Had you not learned—have we not learned, from tales
Neither of beasts nor kingdoms nor their Lord,
But of our own hearts, the realm of death—
Neither to rule nor die? to change, to change!   *1948*

THE ORIENT EXPRESS

One looks from the train
Almost as one looked as a child. In the sunlight
What I see still seems to me plain,
I am safe; but at evening
As the lands darken, a questioning
Precariousness comes over everything.

Once after a day of rain
I lay longing to be cold; and after a while
I was cold again, and hunched shivering
Under the quilt's many colors, gray
With the dull ending of the winter day.
Outside me there were a few shapes
Of chairs and tables, things from a primer;
Outside the window
There were the chairs and tables of the world. . . .
I saw that the world
That had seemed to me the plain
Gray mask of all that was strange
Behind it—of all that *was*—was all.

But it is beyond belief.
One thinks, "Behind everything
An unforced joy, an unwilling
Sadness (a willing sadness, a forced joy)
Moves changelessly"; one looks from the train
And there is something, the same thing
Behind everything: all these little villages,
A passing woman, a field of grain,
The man who says good-bye to his wife—
A path through a wood full of lives, and the train
Passing, after all unchangeable
And not now ever to stop, like a heart—

It is like any other work of art.
It is and never can be changed.
Behind everything there is always
The unknown unwanted life.   *1951*

A SOUL

It is evening. One bat dances
Alone, where there were swallows.
The waterlilies are shadowed
With cattails, the cattails with willows.

The moon sets; after a little
The reeds sigh from the shore.
Then silence. There is a whisper,
"Thou art here once more."

In the castle someone is singing.
"Thou art warm and dry as the sun."
You whisper, and laugh with joy.
"Yes, here is one,

"Here is the other . . . *Legs* . . .
And they move so?"
I stroke the scales of your breast, and answer:
"Yes, as you know."

But you murmur, "How many years
Thou hast wandered there above!
Many times I had thought thee lost
Forever, my poor love.

"How many years, how many years
Thou hast wandered in air, thin air!
Many times I had thought thee lost,
My poor soul, forever."   1951

THE BLACK SWAN

When the swans turned my sister into a swan
    I would go to the lake, at night, from milking:
The sun would look out through the reeds like a swan,
    A swan's red beak; and the beak would open
And inside there was darkness, the stars and the moon.

Out on the lake a girl would laugh.
    "Sister, here is your porridge, sister,"
I could call; and the reeds would whisper,
    "Go to sleep, go to sleep, little swan."
My legs were all hard and webbed, and the silky

Hairs of my wings sank away like stars
    In the ripples that ran in and out of the reeds:
I heard through the lap and hiss of water
    Someone's "Sister . . . sister," far away on the shore,
And then as I opened my beak to answer

I heard my harsh laugh go out to the shore
    And saw—saw at last, swimming up from the green
Low mounds of the lake, the white stone swans:

The white, named swans . . . "It is all a dream,"
I whispered, and reached from the down of the pallet

To the lap and hiss of the floor.
   And "Sleep, little sister," the swans all sang
From the moon and stars and frogs of the floor.
   But the swan my sister called, "Sleep at last, little sister,"
And stroked all night, with a black wing, my wings. *1951*

Robert Lowell

CHILDREN OF LIGHT

Our fathers wrung their bread from stocks and stones
And fenced their gardens with the Redman's bones;
Embarking from the Nether Land of Holland,
Pilgrims unhouseled by Geneva's night,
They planted here the Serpent's seeds of light;
And here the pivoting searchlights probe to shock
The riotous glass houses built on rock,
And candles gutter by an empty altar,
And light is where the landless blood of Cain
Is burning, burning the unburied grain.   *1944*

THE DRUNKEN FISHERMAN

Wallowing in this bloody sty,
I cast for fish that pleased my eye
(Truly Jehovah's bow suspends
No pots of gold to weight its ends);
Only the blood-mouthed rainbow trout
Rose to my bait. They flopped about
My canvas creel until the moth
Corrupted its unstable cloth.

A calendar to tell the day;
A handkerchief to wave away
The gnats; a couch unstuffed with storm
Pouching a bottle in one arm;
A whiskey bottle full of worms;
And bedroom slacks: are these fit terms
To mete the worm whose molten rage
Boils in the belly of old age?

Once fishing was a rabbit's foot—
O wind blow cold, O wind blow hot,

II-430

Let suns stay in or suns step out:
Life danced a jig on the sperm-whale's spout—
The fisher's fluent and obscene
Catches kept his conscience clean.
Children, the raging memory drools
Over the glory of past pools.

Now the hot river, ebbing, hauls
Its bloody waters into holes;
A grain of sand inside my shoe
Mimics the moon that might undo
Man and Creation too; remorse,
Stinking, has puddled up its source;
Here tantrums thrash to a whale's rage.
This is the pot-hole of old age.

Is there no way to cast my hook
Out of this dynamited brook?
The Fisher's sons must cast about
When shallow waters peter out.
I will catch Christ with a greased worm,
And when the Prince of Darkness stalks
My bloodstream to its Stygian term . . .
On water the Man-Fisher walks.   *1944*

MR. EDWARDS AND THE SPIDER

I saw the spiders marching through the air,
Swimming from tree to tree that mildewed day
   In latter August when the hay
   Came creaking to the barn. But where
      The wind is westerly,
Where gnarled November makes the spiders fly
Into the apparitions of the sky,
   They purpose nothing but their ease and die
Urgently beating east to sunrise and the sea;

What are we in the hands of the great God?
It was in vain you set up thorn and briar
   In battle array against the fire
   And treason crackling in your blood;
      For the wild thorns grow tame

And will do nothing to oppose the flame;
Your lacerations tell the losing game
You play against a sickness past your cure.
How will the hands be strong? How will the heart endure?

A very little thing, a little worm,
Or hourglass-blazoned spider, it is said,
   Can kill a tiger. Will the dead
   Hold up his mirror and affirm
      To the four winds the smell
And flash of his authority? It's well
If God who holds you to the pit of hell,
Much as one holds a spider, will destroy,
Baffle and dissipate your soul. As a small boy

On Windsor Marsh, I saw the spider die
When thrown into the bowels of fierce fire:
   There's no long struggle, no desire
   To get up on its feet and fly—
      It stretches out its feet
And dies. This is the sinner's last retreat;
Yes, and no strength exerted on the heat
Then sinews the abolished will, when sick
And full of burning, it will whistle on a brick.

But who can plumb the sinking of that soul?
Josiah Hawley, picture yourself cast
   Into a brick-kiln where the blast
   Fans your quick vitals to a coal—
      If measured by a glass,
How long would it seem burning! Let there pass
A minute, ten, ten trillion; but the blaze
Is infinite, eternal: this is death,
To die and know it. This is the Black Widow, death.

1946

AS A PLANE TREE BY THE WATER

Darkness has called to darkness, and disgrace
Elbows about our windows in this planned
Babel of Boston where our money talks
And multiplies the darkness of a land
Of preparation where the Virgin walks

And roses spiral her enamelled face
Or fall to splinters on unwatered streets.
Our Lady of Babylon, go by, go by,
I was once the apple of your eye;
Flies, flies are on the plane tree, on the streets.

The flies, the flies, the flies of Babylon
Buzz in my ear-drums while the devil's long
Dirge of the people detonates the hour
For floating cities where his golden tongue
Enchants the masons of the Babel Tower
To raise tomorrow's city to the sun
That never sets upon these hell-fire streets
Of Boston, where the sunlight is a sword
Striking at the withholder of the Lord:
Flies, flies are on the plane tree, on the streets.

Flies strike the miraculous waters of the iced
Atlantic and the eyes of Bernadette
Who saw Our Lady standing in the cave
At Massabielle, saw her so squarely that
Her vision put out reason's eyes. The grave
Is open-mouthed and swallowed up in Christ.
O walls of Jericho! And all the streets
To our Atlantic wall are singing: "Sing,
Sing for the resurrection of the King."
Flies, flies are on the plane tree, on the streets.

                                    1946

THE DEAD IN EUROPE

After the planes unloaded, we fell down
Buried together, unmarried men and women;
Not crown of thorns, not iron, not Lombard crown,
Not grilled and spindle spires pointing to heaven
Could save us. Raise us, Mother, we fell down
Here hugger-mugger in the jellied fire:
Our sacred earth in our day was our curse.

Our Mother, shall we rise on Mary's day
In Maryland, wherever corpses married
Under the rubble, bundled together? Pray
For us whom the blockbusters marred and buried;

When Satan scatters us on Rising-day,
O Mother, snatch our bodies from the fire:
Our sacred earth in our day was our curse.

Mother, my bones are trembling and I hear
The earth's reverberations and the trumpet
Bleating into my shambles. Shall I bear,
(O Mary!) unmarried man and powder-puppet,
Witness to the Devil? Mary, hear,
O Mary, marry earth, sea, air and fire;
Our sacred earth in our day is our curse.   1946

THE QUAKER GRAVEYARD IN NANTUCKET

(for Warren Winslow, Dead at Sea)

Let man have dominion over the fishes of the sea and the fowls of the air and the beasts and the whole earth, and every creeping creature that moveth upon the earth.

I

A brackish reach of shoal off Madaket,—
The sea was still breaking violently and night
Had steamed into our North Atlantic Fleet,
When the drowned sailor clutched the drag-net. Light
Flashed from his matted head and marble feet,
He grappled at the net
With the coiled, hurdling muscles of his thighs:
The corpse was bloodless, a botch of reds and whites,
Its open, staring eyes
Were lustreless dead-lights
Or cabin-windows on a stranded hulk
Heavy with sand. We weight the body, close
Its eyes and heave it seaward whence it came,
Where the heel-headed dogfish barks its nose
On Ahab's void and forehead; and the name
Is blocked in yellow chalk.
Sailors, who pitch this portent at the sea
Where dreadnaughts shall confess
Its hell-bent deity,
When you are powerless
To sand-bag this Atlantic bulwark, faced
By the earth-shaker, green, unwearied, chaste

In his steel scales: ask for no Orphean lute
To pluck life back. The guns of the steeled fleet
Recoil and then repeat
The hoarse salute.

II

Whenever winds are moving and their breath
Heaves at the roped-in bulwarks of this pier,
The terns and sea-gulls tremble at your death
In these home waters. Sailor, can you hear
The Pequod's sea wings, beating landward, fall
Headlong and break on our Atlantic wall
Off 'Sconset, where the yawing S-boats splash
The bellbuoy, with ballooning spinnakers,
As the entangled, screeching mainsheet clears
The blocks: off Madaket, where lubbers lash
The heavy surf and throw their long lead squids
For blue-fish? Sea-gulls blink their heavy lids
Seaward. The winds' wings beat upon the stones,
Cousin, and scream for you and the claws rush
At the sea's throat and wring it in the slush
Of this old Quaker graveyard where the bones
Cry out in the long night for the hurt beast
Bobbing by Ahab's whaleboats in the East.

III

All you recovered from Poseidon died
With you, my cousin, and the harrowed brine
Is fruitless on the blue beard of the god,
Stretching beyond us to the castles in Spain,
Nantucket's westward haven. To Cape Cod
Guns, cradled on the tide,
Blast the eelgrass about a waterclock
Of bilge and backwash, roil the salt and sand
Lashing earth's scaffold, rock
Our warships in the hand
Of the great God, where time's contrition blues
Whatever it was these Quaker sailors lost
In the mad scramble of their lives. They died
When time was open-eyed,
Wooden and childish; only bones abide
There, in the nowhere, where their boats were tossed

Sky-high, where mariners had fabled news
Of IS, the whited monster. What it cost
Them is their secret. In the sperm-whale's slick
I see the Quakers drown and hear their cry:
"If God himself had not been on our side,
If God himself had not been on our side,
When the Atlantic rose against us, why,
Then it had swallowed us up quick."

IV

This is the end of the whaleroad and the whale
Who spewed Nantucket bones on the thrashed swell
And stirred the troubled waters to whirlpools
To send the Pequod packing off to hell:
This is the end of them, three-quarters fools,
Snatching at straws to sail
Seaward and seaward on the turntail whale,
Spouting out blood and water as it rolls,
Sick as a dog to these Atlantic shoals:
Clamavimus, O depths. Let the sea-gulls wail

For water, for the deep where the high tide
Mutters to its hurt self, mutters and ebbs.
Waves wallow in their wash, go out and out,
Leave only the death-rattle of the crabs,
The beach increasing, its enormous snout
Sucking the ocean's side.
This is the end of running on the waves;
We are poured out like water. Who will dance
The mast-lashed master of Leviathans
Up from this field of Quakers in their unstoned graves?

V

When the whale's viscera go and the roll
Of its corruption overruns this world
Beyond tree-swept Nantucket and Wood's Hole
And Martha's Vineyard, Sailor, will your sword
Whistle and fall and sink into the fat?
In the great ash-pit of Jehoshaphat
The bones cry for the blood of the white whale,
The fat flukes arch and whack about its ears,
The death-lance churns into the sanctuary, tears

The gun-blue swingle, heaving like a flail,
And hacks the coiling life out: it works and drags
And rips the sperm-whale's midriff into rags,
Gobbets of blubber spill to wind and weather,
Sailor, and gulls go round the stoven timbers
Where the morning stars sing out together
And thunder shakes the white surf and dismembers
The red flag hammered in the mast-head. Hide,
Our steel, Jonas Messias, in Thy side.

VI

OUR LADY OF WALSINGHAM

There once the penitents took off their shoes
And then walked barefoot the remaining mile;
And the small trees, a stream and hedgerows file
Slowly along the munching English lane,
Like cows to the old shrine, until you lose
Track of your dragging pain.
The stream flows down under the druid tree,
Shiloah's whirlpools gurgle and make glad
The castle of God. Sailor, you were glad
And whistled Sion by that stream. But see:

Our Lady, too small for her canopy,
Sits near the altar. There's no comeliness
At all or charm in that expressionless
Face with its heavy eyelids. As before,
This face, for centuries a memory,
Non est species, neque decor,
Expressionless, expresses God: it goes
Past castled Sion. She knows what God knows,
Not Calvary's Cross nor crib at Bethlehem
Now, and the world shall come to Walsingham.

VII

The empty winds are creaking and the oak
Splatters and splatters on the cenotaph,
The boughs are trembling and a gaff
Bobs on the untimely stroke
Of the greased wash exploding on a shoal-bell
In the old mouth of the Atlantic. It's well;
Atlantic, you are fouled with the blue sailors,

Sea-monsters, upward angel, downward fish:
Unmarried and corroding, spare of flesh
Mart once of supercilious, wing'd clippers,
Atlantic, where your bell-trap guts its spoil
You could cut the brackish winds with a knife
Here in Nantucket, and cast up the time
When the Lord God formed man from the sea's slime
And breathed into his face the breath of life,
And blue-lung'd combers lumbered to the kill.
The Lord survives the rainbow of His will.   *1946*

WORDS FOR HART CRANE

"When the Pulitzers showered on some dope
or screw who flushed our dry mouths out with soap,
few people would consider why I took
to stalking sailors, and scattered Uncle Sam's
phoney gold-plated laurels to the birds.
Because I knew my Whitman like a book,
stranger in America, tell my country: I,
Catullus redivivus, once the rage
of the Village and Paris, used to play my role
of homosexual, wolfing the stray lambs
who hungered by the Place de la Concorde.
My profit was a pocket with a hole.
Who asks for me, the Shelley of my age,
must lay his heart out for my bed and board."   *1959*

SKUNK HOUR

(For Elizabeth Bishop)

Nautilus Island's hermit
heiress still lives through winter in her Spartan cottage;
her sheep still graze above the sea.
Her son's a bishop. Her farmer
is first selectman in our village;
she's in her dotage.

Thirsting for
the hierarchic privacy
of Queen Victoria's century,
she buys up all

the eyesores facing her shore,
and lets them fall.

The season's ill—
we've lost our summer millionaire,
who seemed to leap from an L. L. Bean
catalogue. His nine-knot yawl
was auctioned off to lobstermen.
A red fox stain covers Blue Hill.

And now our fairy
decorator brightens his shop for fall;
his fishnet's filled with orange cork,
orange, his cobbler's bench and awl;
there is no money in his work,
he'd rather marry.

One dark night,
my Tudor Ford climbed the hill's skull;
I watched for love-cars. Lights turned down,
they lay together, hull to hull,
where the graveyard shelves on the town. . . .
My mind's not right.

A car radio bleats,
"Love, O careless Love. . . ." I hear
my ill-spirit sob in each blood cell,
as if my hand were at its throat. . . .
I myself am hell;
nobody's here—

only skunks, that search
in the moonlight for a bite to eat.
They march on their soles up Main Street:
white stripes, moonstruck eyes' red fire
under the chalk-dry and spar spire
of the Trinitarian Church.

I stand on top
of our back steps and breathe the rich air—
a mother skunk with her column of kittens swills the garbage pail.
She jabs her wedge-head in a cup
of sour cream, drops her ostrich tail,
and will not scare.   *1959*

Howard Nemerov

THE GOOSE FISH

On the long shore, lit by the moon
To show them properly alone,
Two lovers suddenly embraced
So that their shadows were as one.
The ordinary night was graced
For them by the swift tide of blood
That silently they took at flood,
And for a little time they prized
   Themselves emparadised.

Then, as if shaken by stage-fright
Beneath the hard moon's bony light,
They stood together on the sand
Embarrassed in each other's sight
But still conspiring hand in hand,
Until they saw, there underfoot,
As though the world had found them out,
The goose fish turning up, though dead,
   His hugely grinning head.

There in the china light he lay,
Most ancient and corrupt and grey.
They hesitated at his smile,
Wondering what it seemed to say
To lovers who a little while
Before had thought to understand,
By violence upon the sand,
The only way that could be known
   To make a world their own.

It was a wide and moony grin
Together peaceful and obscene;
They knew not what he would express,